405

WELLINGTON
The Years of the Sword

Also by Elizabeth Longford

VICTORIA R.I.

By the same author writing as
Elizabeth Pakenham

JAMESON'S RAID

WELLINGTON
The Years of the Sword

ELIZABETH
LONGFORD

WORLD BOOKS · LONDON

This edition published 1971 by
World Books
By arrangement with Weidenfeld & Nicolson

© Elizabeth Longford, 1969.

Printed in Great Britain
by Richard Clay (The Chaucer Press) Ltd,
Bungay, Suffolk

To the descendants of
the First Duke of Wellington
and
the Second Earl of Longford
Gerry Wellington
and
Frank
and
in memory of my daughter
Catherine Pakenham

CONTENTS

Contents

ILLUSTRATIONS

Illustrations

ACKNOWLEDGEMENTS

The author and publishers are grateful to the following for their permission to reproduce pictures in their possession: His Grace the Duke of Wellington for numbers 1, 2, 3, 4, 5, 8, 9, 10, 14, 18, 21, 24 and 30; the Victoria and Albert Museum for numbers 6, 7, 11, 13, 15, 17, 20, 23, 27, 29 and 35 (all are Crown Copyright material); the Mansell Collection for numbers 12, 19, 22, 25, 32 and 33; the Royal Military Academy, Sandhurst, for number 31; the Trustees of the British Museum for number 26; the Bibliothèque Nationale, Paris, for number 28 and Mr M. C. Farrar Bell for number 16.

MAPS

AUTHOR'S NOTE

At the opening of 1769 two phenomenal characters, Wellington and Napoleon, were awaiting birth, as it happened within three and a half months of each other. A renewed study of Wellington in this bicentenary year is particularly rewarding. The human side of the army he commanded has been brilliantly emphasized by a new generation of military historians. The process had begun with their predecessors, Sir Charles Oman and Sir John Fortescue. But writers like Sir Basil Liddell Hart and Mr Antony Brett-James have set up new signposts for the biographer leading directly to Wellington's men. Private Wheeler and his comrades are among the best interpreters of Field-Marshal Wellington.

It has always been easier to present the out-and-out egotist redeemed by genius than the hero with unfashionable weaknesses such as reserve and rigidity. Wellington, to adapt his own words, has not only been 'much exposed to authors' but much exposed, *tout court*. Unlike Napoleon he made no attempt to rewrite history in his favour. His two major twentieth-century biographers, Sir Herbert Maxwell and Mr Philip Guedalla, have made their distinctive contributions to a balanced judgement.

It is now accepted that the private lives of the great are relevant, and that even the greatest has his human weaknesses. In Wellington's case, many private letters and journals have already appeared throwing light on his marriage and alleged love-affairs. My aim has been to use every available document, military, political and personal, which illuminates Wellington the man.

By gracious permission of Her Majesty the Queen I have been given access to the Royal Archives, Windsor, and by gracious permission of Her Majesty the Queen of the Netherlands, to the Archives in the Royal House, The Hague. I warmly thank the Royal Librarians, Mr Robert Mackworth-Young and Mr Pelinck, for all their help. Through Mr Pelinck I would also like to thank the Dutch military experts for their valuable suggestions. Nor do I forget my great debt to His Excellency the Netherlands Ambassador.

I must try to convey the fullness of my gratitude to the present Duke of Wellington not only for giving me free access to all unpublished family papers but also for an immediate response to requests for information and advice. It has been my privilege to enjoy whatever scholarship, generosity and encouragement could contribute to make an absorbing task even more agreeable. Through his kindness and that of his librarian, Mr Francis Needham, my manuscript has been read chapter by chapter. I am profoundly grateful to them both.

I wish to express my very warm thanks to others who have allowed me to use unpublished papers: Lord Raglan (Fitzroy Somerset MSS), Lady Albemarle (Arthur Shakespear MSS), Sir Anthony Weldon (Arthur Kennedy MSS), Mrs Freda Loch (George Seymour MSS), Comte Sébastien Foy (Général Maximilien Foy MSS), L'Abbé A. Chapeau, Angers University (Records of the Pignerolle family), Mr Edmund de Rothschild (Archives of the House of Rothschild), the Rector of Maynooth College, Dublin (Records of the Irish College, Salamanca), and the Curator of the Archives, Household Cavalry Museum, Windsor.

For my visits to the Portuguese battlefields I am immensely indebted to the Gulbenkian Foundation, and to the kindness of Mr J. C. Thornton, Miss M. H. Knott, Miss M. O'Donovan and Mr F. P. Almeida Langhane. I must thank Colonel Francisco Eduardo Baptista for his untiring energy and thoughtfulness. Without the initial enthusiasm of His Excellency the Portuguese Ambassador none of this could have taken place, and I thank him most deeply. Sir George and Lady Labouchère were the kindest of hosts in Madrid; Mr and Mrs Nicholas Henderson and Mme Peru Urquijo were true 'Empecinados'; my sister-in-law, Lady Mary Clive located half-obliterated sites with an inherited flair; His Excellency the Spanish Ambassador was extremely kind in answering questions, as were Professor Claveria and Miss Thain of the Spanish Institute, London, and Professor Pabón in Madrid. A very special word of thanks is due to His Excellency the Chilean Ambassador for his translations. I am indeed grateful to Sir Roderick and Lady Barclay for their hospitality during the 150th Anniversary of the Battle of Waterloo, and to the Aberdeen family for allowing me to be present at the ceremony at the Gordon Monument.

For giving me the benefit of their expert knowledge I wish to thank especially Mr and Mrs Jac Weller, Field-Marshal Sir Gerald Templer, Colonel Sir Thomas Butler, Mr Anthony Powell, Sir

Arthur Bryant, Mr Tom Goff, Reverend J. C. Bowmer (Librarian at Epworth House), Mr Donald McLachlan, Major C. J. D. Haswell, Lt. Col. J. G. O. Whitehead, Mr David Chandler, Mr A. S. Bennell, Dr Roy Strong (Director of the National Portrait Gallery) and Mr H. V. T. Percival (Director of the Wellington Museum); the staffs of the National Military Museum, the Household Cavalry Museum, the Imperial War Museum, the Indian Section of the Victoria and Albert Museum, the India Office Library, the French Embassy, India House, the National Library of Ireland, the Irish State Papers Office, the Public Record Office of Northern Ireland and Mr A. P. W. Malcomson, the Public Record Office, Somerset House, the London Library, the British Museum, Chelsea Public Library, Kent County Archives, the British Medical Association, the Jockey Club and Madame Tussaud's.

I would also like to thank all those who have put me in touch with material for this first volume: Sir Michael Adeane, Sir Martin Charteris, Mrs Jean Braddell, Professor Edmund Ford, Mr Martin Gilbert, Reverend C. C. Ellison (Meath Historical Society), Reverend R. J. Kent (St George's Church, Dublin), Reverend Edwin Starke, Mr Frederic Raphael, Mr Richard Buckle, Miss Margery Weiner, Mrs E. de Winton, Mr John Betjeman, Major-General John Sheffield, Mr John Kerslake, Dr John Roebuck, Mr David Colville, Mr G. Handley-Taylor, Mr M. C. Farrar-Bell, Mr Joseph Bryan III, Captain Gerrard, Miss Joan Cooley, Mr A. P. Ryan, Dr Patrick Kelly, Lord Head, Mr Michael Glover, Mr Francis Boyd, Commander Burrows, Mr Alan Tillotson, Mr R. W. Houssman, Mr W. G. Constable, Mrs Fortescue-Hitchins, Mr R. Bucknall. To those friends who have read all or part of the book I express my sincere appreciation, especially Mr Harold Kurtz whose criticism was invaluable at every stage, Sir Basil Liddell Hart, Mr Paul Johnson, Mr Ian Robertson and my sister-in-law, Lady Violet Powell, who once more brought her expertise to bear on the proof-reading. I am greatly indebted to Mrs Agnes Fenner both for her inexhaustible typing and helpful criticism.

Lastly I must thank all my family for their support, including Antonia for devising the title, Thomas for sharing Irish nuggets and Judith and Valerie for cutting and shaping. To my husband I owe the inspiration of his lifelong devotion to the subject, not to mention his having been born a great-great-nephew of Kitty Pakenham, first Duchess of Wellington.

A CALENDAR OF EVENTS IN WELLINGTON'S CAREER 1769-1815

1769	1 May	Birth of Hon. Arthur Wesley, Dublin.
	15 August	Birth of Napoleon Bonaparte, Corsica.
1781		Death of father, 1st Lord Mornington. Enters Eton.
1784	Summer	Leaves Eton. At Brighton with tutor.
1785		Brussels with mother.
1786	16 January	School of Equitation, Angers, France. Returns England end of year.
1787	7 March	Ensign.
	25 December	Lieutenant.
1788	February	Arrives Ireland as A.D.C. to Lord-Lieutenant.
1789		French Revolution.
1790	April	M.P. for Trim, Ireland.
1791	30 June	Captain.
1792	September	Courting Kitty Pakenham.
1793	1 February	France declares war on Britain.
	30 April	Major.
		Proposes to Kitty Pakenham; rejected.
	30 September	Lieutenant-Colonel.
1794		Commands brigade Flanders; withdrawn 1795.
		Napoleon commands French artillery, Toulon.
1796	3 May	Colonel in the army.
	June	Sails for India in command of 33rd.
1797	February	Arrives Calcutta; next eight years in India.
1798		Richard, 2nd Lord Mornington, arrives as Governor-General, having changed family name back to Wellesley. Irish Rebellion.

1799	Spring	Invasion of Mysore.
	4 May	Storming of Seringapatam, death of Tipoo Sultan.
		Governor of Mysore. Richard created Marquess Wellesley.
1800		Union of Great Britain and Ireland. Defeat of Dhoondiah Waugh.
1801		Resignation of Pitt, Addington Prime Minister. Arthur Wellesley superseded.
1802	March	Peace of Amiens ratified.
	29 April	Major-General.
1803	May	Renewal of war against France.
	6 August	Outbreak of Second Mahratta War.
	12 August	Capture of Ahmednuggur.
	23 September	Battle of Assaye.
	29 November	Battle of Argaum.
	15 December	Surrender of Gawilghur.
1804	1 September	Order of the Bath.
		Napoleon crowned Emperor; Pitt Prime Minister again.
1805	10 March	Embarks for home; calls at St. Helena.
	10 September	Reaches England.
	20 October	Napoleon defeats Austrians at Ulm.
	21 October	Nelson's victory at Trafalgar.
	2 December	Austerlitz; Austrians and Russians crushed.
	December	Arthur Wellesley takes a brigade to the Elbe.
1806	23 January	Pitt dies; succeeded by coalition Ministry of 'All the Talents'.
	30 January	Succeeds Cornwallis as Colonel of the 33rd.
	February	Returns home; posted to Hastings.
	1 April	M.P. for Rye, Sussex; later for Mitchell, Cornwall; Newport, Isle of Wight.
	10 April	Marries Kitty Pakenham in Dublin.
		Napoleon decrees blockade of Britain (Continental System).
1807	3 February	Birth of Arthur Richard Wellesley, son and heir.

	March	Tory Ministry of Duke of Portland.
	3 April	Arthur Wellesley joins Government as Chief Secretary of Ireland.
	9 July	Treaty of Tilsit between Napoleon and Tsar Alexander of Russia.
	31 July– 30 September	Copenhagen expedition.
1808	16 January	Birth of second son, Charles.
	Spring	Risings in Iberian Peninsula against Napoleon.
	25 April	Lieutenant-General.
	12 July	Arthur Wellesley in temporary command of expeditionary force to Portugal.
	1 August	Troops begin landings in Mondego Bay.
	17 August	Battle of Roliça.
	21 August	Battle of Vimeiro; Arthur Wellesley superseded.
	31 August	Convention of Cintra; later recalled to England for Court of Inquiry.
1809	16 January	Death of Sir John Moore at Corunna, Spain.
	April	Arthur Wellesley resigns Chief Secretaryship, sent in command of force to defend Portugal.
	12 May	Crossing of the Douro and capture of Oporto.
	27 June–4 July	Enters Spain.
	6 July	Marshal-General of Portuguese Army.
	27–28 July	Battle of Talavera.
	4 September	Viscount Wellington of Talavera.
	Autumn	Retreat to Portugal; orders secret construction of Lines of Torres Vedras (September).
		Withdrawal of Walcheren expedition; Portland resigns; Perceval Prime Minister.
1810		Wellington perfects his 'defensive system'.
	April	Napoleon foresees trouble with Russia; marries Marie-Louise of Austria; cancels plan to command in Peninsula himself.

	10 July	Ciudad Rodrigo, Spain, surrenders to French.
	28 August	Almeida, Portugal, surrenders to French.
	27 September	Battle of Bussaco, Portugal.
	8 October	Wellington enters Lines of Torres Vedras.
	14 October	French discover Lines and refuse to attack.
1811	5 March–8 April	French retreat to Spain.
	11 March	Surrender of Badajoz to French.
	3–5 May	Battle of Fuentes de Oñoro.
	5–12 May	First siege of Badajoz.
	11 May	Surrender of Almeida to Wellington; garrison escapes.
	16 May	Battle of Albuera.
	19 May–10 June	Second siege of Badajoz.
	31 July	General (local rank).
	Summer–autumn	Retreat to Portugal.
1812	8–19 January	Siege and storming of Ciudad Rodrigo.
	February	Earl of Wellington; Grandee of Spain with title of Duque de Ciudad Rodrigo.
	16 March–6 April	Third siege and storming of Badajoz.
	11 May	Assassination of Perceval; Lord Liverpool Prime Minister.
	May	Napoleon begins invasion of Russia.
	17 June	America declares war on Britain.
	22 July	Battle of Salamanca.
	12 August	Entry into Madrid.
	18 August	Marquess of Wellington; Generalissimo of Spanish armies (22 September).
	19 September–21 October	Siege of Burgos.
	22 October–19 November	Retreat to Portugal; French retreat from Moscow (October–December).
	December	Wellington visits Cádiz and Lisbon; Portuguese title of Duque da Victoria.
1813	1 January	Colonel of the Royal Regiment of Horse Guards.
	4 March	Knight of the Garter.

	21 June	Battle of Vitoria. Field-Marshal.
	25 July	First assault on San Sebastián abandoned and city besieged by Wellington; same day French invade passes of Pyrenees.
	28–30 July	Battle of the Pyrenees (Sorauren).
	31 August	Second assault and fall of San Sebastián; same day Battle of San Marcial.
	7 October	Crossing of Bidassoa into France.
	16–19 October	Napoleon defeated at Battle of Leipzig.
	31 October	Surrender of Pamplona.
	10 November	Battle of the Nivelle.
	December	Battles of the Nive and St Pierre.
1814	February	Crossing of the Adour and investment of Bayonne.
	27 February	Battle of Orthez.
		Bourbon Prince at Wellington's HQ.
	4 February– 19 March	Abortive peace negotiations with Napoleon at Châtillon.
	1 March	Treaty of Chaumont against Napoleon (Quadruple Alliance).
	31 March	Entry of Allies into Paris.
	6 April	Abdication of Napoleon.
	10 April	Battle of Toulouse; end of Peninsular War.
	16 April	Treaty of Fontainbleau with Napoleon.
	24 April	Louis XVIII returns to France.
	28 April	Napoleon sent to Elba.
	3 May	Wellington created Duke.
	4 May	In Paris for Review of troops by King.
	24 May–8 June	Mission in Madrid.
	30 May	First Peace of Paris signed with France.
	14 June	Farewell to troops at Bordeaux.
	23 June	Returns to England for celebrations.
	5 July	Ambassador to the French Court.
	August	Leaves for Paris, surveying defences of Low Countries on the way.
	22 August	Arrives Paris Embassy.
	15 September	Congress of Vienna opens informally.
	24 December	Treaty of Ghent; end of American War.

1815	3 January	Secret Treaty between Britain, France and Austria.
	8 January	Battle of New Orleans.
	3 February	Wellington arrives Vienna as British Plenipotentiary.
	1 March	Napoleon lands in France.
	7 March	Congress hears of Napoleon's escape from Elba.
	13 March	Congress outlaws Napoleon.
	19 March	Louis XVIII flees from Paris.
	20 March	Napoleon enters the Tuileries. The Hundred Days.
	25 March	Treaty of Chaumont against Napoleon renewed.
	28 March	Wellington leaves Congress of Vienna.
	4 April	Enters HQ in Brussels.
	April–June	Assembly of Allied army under Wellington.
	9 June	Final Act of Congress of Vienna.
	15 June	Napoleon crosses Belgian frontier; captures Charleroi.
		Duchess of Richmond's ball.
	16 June	Battles of Ligny and Quatre Bras.
	17 June	Prussians retreat to Wavre; Wellington follows to Mont-Saint-Jean.
	18 June	Battle of Waterloo.

PART I

PART I

1 Retained for Life

Wellington is a national hero. His countrymen today, whether they feel exalted or irritated by the breed, cannot deny that he belongs to it. His name still issues a challenge. The challenge may change with time and the password need renewing. But there is still an encounter —or a collision.

A century ago the great Duke, riding in metal or stone above crowded British cities, reminded Europe that here was something hard, gleaming and strong. An Empire that had been threatened, an Empire victorious, an Empire on the march. Now the challenge has turned inwards. The bronze horseman points his baton not across the Channel but at his own countrymen. Let them question themselves: what makes a national hero today? Is it still the deliberate sense of duty which once formed the spine and dynamic of that commanding presence? Where do they find their heroes now?

When Wellington was in his seventy-fifth year, Thomas Carlyle discovered that all heroes had to be warriors. Cromwell and Napoleon, Luther and Knox, he squeezed them all on to his bed of Procrustes, leaving the first pair with only minor mutilations, but trimming Luther into 'a right piece of human valour', and stretching Knox to cover 'a right sore fighting life'. Even Shakespeare, it seems, was a born swashbuckler: 'This man too,' wrote Carlyle brazenly, 'had a right stroke in him, had it come to that!'

Nonsense apart, the search for national heroes does not generally lead far from the fighting. Drake, Marlborough and Nelson all shine forth under the floodlights of a nation saved in war. Infection killed more British women in childbed than ever Napoleon's invasion troops could have destroyed by rape. The *Grande Armée* was a clumsy amateur compared with killers like fever and smallpox. Yet some may not quite remember now whether there were two Jenners or one— or was it all Lister and Pasteur?—while Wellington stands, the one and only.

But why among the war-leaders, soldiers and statesmen, do some hold their places and others slip? A collection of Boer War generals once had their busts reverentially enshrined, peaked caps, moustaches and all, inside green glass doorstoppers. Few would recognize today a single one of these heroes by name. 'We left Pitt [the Elder] in the zenith of prosperity and glory,' wrote Macaulay, 'the idol of England, the terror of France, the admiration of the civilized world. The wind, from whatever quarter it blew, carried to England tidings of battles won and fortresses taken . . .'. And all too soon after Macaulay left him, Pitt subsided, honourably but inexorably, into the history books. Wellington's battles and fortresses, his Vitorias and Torres Vedras, are still living names. As one of Wellington's contemporaries, Sir Jonah Barrington,[1] wrote with the slight inaccuracy but great verve which envy imparts: 'I knew his Grace when Captain Wellesley—Sir Arthur Wellesley—Secretary Wellesley—Ambassador Wellesley— and Duke of Wellington. In the first stage of his career, I was his equal, in the last, nobody is.' Where did he get his magic?

It is possible of course to examine the Duke item by item. He had brilliant brains, an antagonist of genius and Europe for an arena. The green glass generals had none of these advantages. Pitt the Elder was highly neurotic. The Duke possessed almost supernatural balance. But an itemized hero explains nothing. Somehow he must be caught in action, in flight like a great meteorite wrenched off from the mass of humanity: blinding, molten, irresistible. No doubt he will cool in time, like the meteorite, and then rough edges will begin to appear; cracks, excrescences and other eccentricities. The Duke had his share. There is nothing unheroic about that. The British even find it endearing. 'England expects every man to do his duty'—and every great man to do much else besides, some of it, as the Duke would have said, 'rather curious'.

*   *   *

At first sight, one of the Duke's more curious traits was a studied indifference to his own history. 'The Duke of Wellington has nothing to say to the forty or fifty Lives of Himself which are at present in the course of being written', were the words with which at the age of seventy-one he dismissed one of these hapless authors. The author in question, Sir J. E. Alexander, was in process of apologizing for the

---

1. Sir Jonah Barrington (1760–1834), Judge in the Court of Admiralty, Ireland, until deprived of his office in 1830 for acts of peculation in 1805, 1806 and 1810. His most famous and racy book was *Personal Sketches of his Own Times*.

fact that his script had been pirated by some blackguard and was now being advertised in London on a large placard as *The Secret Memoirs of the Duke of Wellington*. Far from accepting this apology, the old Duke concluded his terse reply with some acid advice about future Wellingtoniana: 'If the writers thereof would adhere to the golden Rule for an Historian viz. to write nothing which they did not know to be true, the Duke apprehends that they would have but little to tell; and he believes that there would be nothing worth pirating.' No doubt the present biography, like so many of its predecessors, would have received the same unfailing discouragement.

As for the Duke's pedigree, he liked to represent it as something unknown and unknowable. When he was seventy-four and had long been the most famous member of a leading family, a certain Samuel Gordon wrote from Aungier Street, Dublin, to ask for the name of a book dealing with Wellington's ancestors, the Wellesleys, in the days of Cromwell. Wellington replied as if the Wellesleys of County Meath were no more or less traceable than the Sam Gordons of Aungier Street: 'He has no knowledge of any person from whom or place at which Mr Gordon could procure Information on the matter referred to. . . .' A fuller knowledge of the great man's character would have warned his correspondent what to expect. His taboo was no aberration but an expression of principle. It can only become intelligible, therefore, as his life-story unfolds. Meanwhile, his picture of a family tree shrouded in the mists of history, with which he loved to baffle enquirers, must yield to more recent research.

*   *   *

The Wellesleys came from Somerset. The earliest document in which their name appears, a charter dated about 1180, is still in the archives of Wells Cathedral. When did the family go to Ireland? No documentary evidence has survived, but a respectable authority, William Lynch, implies that it was with Henry II in the 1170s. Writing in 1830, Lynch stated that the Wellesleys had held the hereditary office of Standard Bearer to the King 'since time immemorial'—meaning, apparently, since the reign of Henry II.[2] He described how Henry's

2. *A View of the Legal Institutions, Honorary Hereditary Offices, & Feudal Baronies, established in Ireland during the Reign of Henry II. Deduced from Court Rolls, Inquisitions, and other original records.* Lynch had access to documents since burnt in the Four Courts fire, 1922. His book is dedicated to the Duke of Wellington whose family records he examined.

former Standard Bearer had thrown down the royal banner during a battle against the Welsh and run away. He was superseded by a Wellesley whose conduct on the battlefield was more reliable. The new Standard Bearer would, of course, accompany King Henry when he invaded Ireland.

By the reign of Henry III there is documentary evidence of a Wellesley in Ireland. He went over in 1226 on 'King's business' and bought property in Dublin. From the latter half of the fourteenth century onwards these Wellesleys lived entirely in Ireland, steadily amassing land by marriage or services rendered. There was Sir William, Member of Parliament in 1372, Keeper of the Castles of Kildare and Carbery, Justice of the Peace for Kildare and Kilkenny, Sheriff of Kildare. A Patent Roll of 1400 recorded that he was retained by the King for life with a salary of £20 a year'. There was his son Sir Richard, who by marrying Joan de Castlemartin founded the family fortunes in County Meath. During the reign of Charles I, however, the Wellesley property was confiscated, probably for Roman Catholic backslidings by Valerian Wellesley, head of the family. His successor, Gerald Wellesley, or 'Garret [the Irish form of Gerald] Wesley' as he now called himself, successfully petitioned Charles II for return of his estates on the ground that he was 'an innocent Protestant'; he ended his days respectably on the Grand Jury at Trim in Meath. His wife was Elizabeth Colley. Their son, Garret Wesley II, lacked one advantage—an heir. On whom should he bestow the Wesley name and fortune?

Ever since the Wellesleys settled in Ireland they had been intermarrying within that restricted circle of Anglo-Norman families of the Pale among whom they lived: Plunkets of Dunsany, Fitzgeralds of Dangan and Kildare, Cusacks of Dangan and Trim, Colleys of Castle Carbery. Joan de Castlemartin, the heiress, was herself the daughter of a Cusack heiress, Catherine, and the widow of a Fitzgerald. The Ascendancy names chimed together over the centuries, and when Garret Wesley I married Elizabeth Colley he was echoing already familiar harmonies. For Elizabeth Colley's great-great-grandmother was another Catherine Cusack, granddaughter of Alison de Wellesley. The Colleys in fact had Wellesley blood.

How could the childless Garret II do better than choose his first cousin Richard Colley, younger son of his maternal uncle Henry Colley of Castle Carbery, only fifteen miles away? This Henry Colley who died in 1719 made Garret one of his trustees, confessing in his will that he left 'several daughters unmarried (I thank God not for want of my endeavours)'. However, he was able to bequeath his elder unmarried daughters £2,000 in the 6 per cents each, perhaps because Garret had made such splendid provision for Richard.[3]

Richard Colley, a man approaching forty when his Wesley bene-factor died in 1728, could look back on his own Colley pedigree with satisfaction. The first Sir Henry Colley, Cowley or Cooley of Castle Carbery, a soldier in Queen Elizabeth's army, Deputy Lieutenant and Steward of King's County, was picked out for being 'so good a servitor, so careful a man in his charge'. The Lord Lieutenant of Ireland, Sir Henry Sydney, described him as valiant in youth and loyal in maturity, having kept the King's County 'well ordered, and in good obedience'.[4] Unfortunately he became 'blind and impotent', but not before he had produced two sons to marry two daughters of Adam Loftus, Primate of Ireland. Archbishop Loftus, it was said, 'bringeth up his children well, and matcheth his daughters all as

3. According to an unsubstantiated tradition, Wellington's great-great-uncle, Garret Wesley II, had originally wished to adopt the young Charles Wesley, brother of John Wesley the founder of Methodism. The reason was said to be similarity of name. The matter was not raised, however, until a century later, first by Adam Clark in his *Wesley Family* (1823) and then by Thomas Jackson, *Life of Charles Wesley* (1841). An unpublished MS of John Wesley's was said to describe payments made by Garret for Charles's educa-tion and a subsequent adoption offer. John was also said to have called his brother's refusal of the offer, 'a fair escape'. But the Wesley Concordance logs no such phrase; nor do the Methodist Archives contain any such MS. Then came C. J. Stevenson's *Memorials of the Wesley Family* (1876) stating for the first time that Garret and Charles Wesley were actually blood relations. As a result of this new claim various Victorian genealogical tables depicted Charles Wesley's great-great-grandmother as a Colley, while his great-great-grandfather appeared as a direct descendant of Sir William de Wellesley. Each part of this allegedly *double* relationship (itself suspicious and a sign that the Victorians were over-egging the pudding) was a figment of Victorian imagination and has been separately demolished by Mr Charles Evans in his 'Ancestry of the Wesleys' (*Notes and Queries*, June 1948) and Mr Malcolm Pinhorn working in 1966 for the Methodist Research Centre. Thus, despite a contrary statement in the *Dictionary of National Biography*, no relationship has been established between the Methodist Wesleys and the Duke of Wellington.

4. Bearing in mind that Arthur Wellesley, Duke of Wellington, was to marry a Pakenham, it is perhaps worth noting that Sir Henry Sydney's mother was a Pakenham: Anne, daughter of Sir Hugh Pakenham of Lording-ton, Sussex.

well with the sons and haires of good Englishe possessioners, as Sir Harry Cowley'.

Sir Harry's heir, the second Sir Henry Colley or Cowley, was another 'good Englishe possessioner' whose great-grandson Richard took his M.A. at Trinity in 1714 under the name of Cowly. Richard Cowly, Cooley or Colley never had to decide which way to spell his name, for in 1728 he was to change it to Wesley by adoption, and in 1746 to Mornington by ennoblement. Here in Richard Wesley, an Irish Georgian gentleman born about 1690, civilized and eccentric, was the Duke of Wellington's grandfather.

What did these six centuries of a strikingly homogeneous past mean for Wellington? Behind him stretched an embattled English race who had occupied an alien land, marrying strictly with their own kind and becoming not only a ruling caste but a ruling garrison. Knights of the Pale *par excellence*, they kept order and exacted obedience, usually faithful to their sovereign, always to their caste. It would be hard for Wellington to escape from such a heredity. Especially from that William de Wellesley, Knight, who had been 'retained by the King for life' at a salary of £20 a year. The phrase was to be echoed almost word for word centuries later by Arthur Wellesley, Knight, Viscount, Earl, Marquess, Duke. Though the retaining fee was to change amazingly, the spirit would remain the same.

'Retained for life. . . .' The Duke of Wellington heard his ancestral voices. Remote yet insistent, relevant though archaic, the voices prophesied a lifetime of service for this descendant of the first Henry Colley, 'so good a servitor, so careful a man in his charge'.

*   *   *

Richard Wesley, with plenty of money, a wife (Elizabeth Sale, descended from a family of ecclesiastical lawyers), adequate daughters but no son, moved in 1728 into his new home at Dangan, County Meath.

The Dublin he left behind seemed more like a provincial town than a capital city. No public body had as yet decreed the magnificence of wide, well-paved streets. True, Stephen's Green could rival any square in London, while Phoenix Park, where the English garrison manoeuvred, already outshone Hyde Park or St James's. But the Dubliners, with their heartiness and oddities, reminded an English visitor, Mrs Pendarves, of the dwellers in some warm-hearted region like Cornwall—much 'tittle-tattle', great 'civilities', overcrowded ballrooms and positively enormous meals.

'Convivial indulgence', admitted an Irish patriot, was the besetting sin of eighteenth-century Ireland. Both Dean Swift and John Wesley, founder of the Methodists, denounced it. The majesty of the law itself was not exempt. One judge, described as 'a scarlet pincushion well studded', drank his brandy even in court, from an inkstand: he would 'bow down his head and steal a hurried sip . . . through a quill that lay among the pens'. Lesser mortals might be bad farmers and blundering magistrates, but they were 'great at potation'—like the ex-naval man who carried a boatswain's whistle on his waistcoat button and, when potation robbed him of a word, he filled the gap with a shrill blast. The Duke of Wellington's severe abstemiousness bewildered his contemporaries. One wonders if reaction against the bacchanalian Ireland from which he sprang was partly responsible.

*   *   *

It was Mrs Mary Pendarves, future friend of Dean Swift, who left behind the gayest picture of the Wesleys at Dangan. Richard, while over in London in summer 1731, had invited her to stay:—'my hero', she wrote ecstatically in her journal, '. . . so much goodness, friendliness and cheerfulness joined'. At first she was not impressed by the 'flat country' of Meath; but her hero was remedying it by planting trees and digging canals. They lived in the handsome stone mansion 'magnificently', but 'without ceremony', meeting in the 'charming' hall, with its organ and harpsichord, when they had a mind for company. Possibly Irish houses were under-furnished, 'but they make it up in *eating and drinking*!' A year or so later she was back at Dangan, to find landscaping, good living and above all liberty in greater profusion than ever. Battledore and shuttlecock, breakfast and harpsichord now went on in the great hall simultaneously without infringing one another's rights, while the ornamental water gleamed with the sails of real ships and the groves with statues of every deity from Bacchus to Fame. Perhaps one shrine had been neglected, for there was still no son; nevertheless her hero improved his estate as if he had one, his only ambition being 'to make all about him happy'.

The diarist Isaac Butler saw Dangan about eight years later. Now there was 'a noble piazza of seven curious turned arches', at least

twenty-five obelisks, a Rape of Proserpine weighing three tons, 'a
regular fort' down by the lake with four bastions, curtain walls and
forty-eight cannon which fired salutes on family birthdays. Three
vessels rode at anchor in the lake, a twenty-ton man-of-war, a yacht
and a packet boat.

When Mary came again in 1748 there had been some changes. A
famine in 1740 had prevented Richard from making quite all about
him happy; but no doubt he had pleased his family by becoming in
1746 the first Lord Mornington. Mary herself had married Swift's
Chancellor at St Patrick's Cathedral, Dr Delany. And Garret
Wesley III had been born at last on 9 July 1735, the musical prodigy
who was to be Wellington's father.

While still in his nurse's arms the baby had listened attentively to
his father's playing—for Richard 'played well (for a gentleman) on
the violin'; and though 'indolence' prevented the child from com-
posing until the advanced age of nine, the next four years saw
amazing progress.

Young Garret's godmother, Mrs Delany, reported enthusiastically
on this 'most extraordinary' thirteen-year-old. He was already com-
posing, excelled at the violin, the classics, and the theory and practice
of naval and siege warfare, offering as Governor of the fort and Lord
High Admiral of the man-of-war on the lake to salute his godmother
with every gun from both.

While indulging his son's tastes Richard Mornington had not
curbed his own, so that when he died in 1758 the Wesley fortune was
somewhat impaired, though his heir still had the substantial income
of £8,000 a year. Garret, the new Lord Mornington, was twenty-
three. Having settled £15,000 on the younger members of the family,
he married next year Anne Hill, eldest daughter of Arthur Hill
(afterwards Lord Dungannon), a strong-minded girl of sixteen with
no fortune.[5] His godmother saw them both at the play, Garret
looking solemn and Anne not so solemn as an engaged girl should—
perhaps because he had generously made her a jointure of £1,600 a
year and £500 a year pin-money.

Mrs Delany later decided that the young Morningtons '*seemed*'

5. Arthur Hill was a banker, brother of Lord Hillsborough. Garret had
courted Lady Louisa Lennox in 1758, daughter of the Duke of Richmond,
Lord Lieutenant; but though at first well received he was cut out by Mr
Connolly of Castletown who, according to Mrs Delany, had double Garret's
fortune and half his merit.

very happy, though their future was doubtful. Anne lacked 'judgement' (as her son Arthur was also to discover), while Garret's upbringing had certain 'disadvantages'—a reference possibly to hereditary obsessions with Dangan's landscape. When Arthur Young, the famous agriculturalist, visited Dangan in 1776 he found acre after acre under ornamental water instead of under the plough, and an archipelago where there should have been turnips.[6]

Joyfully saddled with this romantic incubus, Lord Mornington advanced in rank, the arts and paternity if not in the six per cents. He was created an Earl in 1760,[7] Doctor and then Professor of Music at Trinity in 1764 for his sacred compositions, madrigals, catches and such enchanting glees as '*When for the world's repose my Chloë sleeps*', '*Come fairest Nymph*' and '*Here in cool grot*'.[8] In 1760 his son and heir, Richard Colley Wesley, was born, followed by William in 1763, Anne in 1768, and in 1769 his third surviving son, Arthur. Then came two younger boys, Gerald Valerian born in 1770 and Henry in 1773. All the boys were destined to have distinguished careers, some brilliant, Arthur the most dazzling of all.

* * *

The 1760s were not a prosperous time for Ireland. The poor in their squalid cabins, existing on a diet of potatoes and milk, were increasing as fast as the Wesleys and there were far more of them, so that the population, which had been under 2 million in 1706, would be $4\frac{1}{2}$ million by the end of the century. Yet only the coastal areas had a market or cash economy. The whole hinterland depended on a subsistence economy where high rents, arrears and evictions—that eternal but unholy Irish trinity—spawned endless miseries and gangs of peasant desperadoes to give the misery a voice. In the south 'Whiteboys' and 'Shanavests' appeared, and in the north, round

6. Naturally, there is no open criticism in the single paragraph devoted to Dangan, but Young's copious enthusiasm for the wheat, fallow, 'bere' (barley), turnips and above all drainage of neighbouring estates, contrasts with his cool tone in summing up Dangan's floodings—'the effects pleasing'.

7. The reasons for his elevation are not obvious, though he took a prominent part in Dublin life, raised large sums for charity and was Chairman of the Governors of the Lock Hospital.

8. His unpublished MSS included a cantata, '*Caractacus*', and a march for the installation of the Duke of Bedford as Lord Lieutenant.

Anne Hill's Dungannon, 'Hearts of Oak' and 'Hearts of Steel'.[9]

Ireland's first Coercion Act was passed just four years before Arthur Wesley's birth. Charter schools had been founded in 1733 by well-meaning people like the Wesleys to teach Catholic peasants a Protestant catechism:

> *Is the Church of Rome . . . uncorrupt?*
>
> *No, it is extremely corrupt, in Doctrine, Worship and Practice.*

In 1750 Catholics had none the less been allowed to join the Army. With Coercion since 1765, you could now have an Irish 'Whiteboy' tied to a triangle, being beaten by an English sergeant while an Irish soldier was forced to look on. The presence of countless Catholics in an army whose duty consisted in holding down Catholic Ireland was to cause Wellington concern many years later.

Flogging on the triangle (strictly a tripod to whose apex the prisoner's hands were bound) was by no means the most barbarous punishment available in the 1760s. A priest, Father Nicholas Sheehy, was hanged, drawn and quartered in 1766 for expressing sympathy with the wretched peasants, though a more refined taste now dictated that the four limbs should only be cut, not cut off. And the year before, 'Darkey' Kelly, a brothel-keeper of Dublin, had been burnt alive in Stephen's Green.

Even so, Arthur's birth year, 1769, showed some hopeful signs. No doubt the spending of absentee landlords abroad had risen from £621,499 in 1730 to £1,208,982 in 1769; but the Lord Lieutenant was no longer permitted to be an absentee, so that there was a chance of enlightened rule from Dublin Castle. Maritime commerce in the Irish ports was growing and a fraction of its benefits trickled inland. Inventiveness was rife among individuals, if not yet among governments. Richard Lovell Edgeworth, father of 'the great Maria' as Sir Walter Scott was to call the celebrated novelist, invented a telegraph system, a turnip-cutter, a wagon and trailer, 'a wheel *in which* a man should walk' (nearly killing the walker by dashing unexpectedly into

9. This subsistence economy is described by Lynch and Vaizey in *Guinness's Brewery*. A cow and potato patch could feed the entire family at subsistence level; smallholdings were easy to get; the landlord system discouraged improvement or saving; a large family was an insurance against personal disaster. The net result was national disaster—a huge rise in population but no way for the masses to rise above their low estate.

a chalk pit), a light phaeton with springs, a one-wheel chaise for narrow lanes and a large umbrella for haystacks. He won a gold medal from the Irish Society of Arts in 1769.

The lucky stars, meanwhile, looked down on the hero's birthday —though on precisely which day has never been agreed. Wellington himself always kept his birthday on 1 May. His biographer cannot do better than follow him, dismissing with Wellingtonian brusqueness the four rival dates, 6 March and 3, 29 and 30 April.[10]

The place of his birth is also disputed. There is evidence based on local tradition, but only on tradition, for Dangan Castle. There is ingenious support for a premature birth on the road between Dangan and Dublin. And there is no valid argument whatever for a variety of suggestions including Trim, Laracor, Mornington, Athboy, Athy,[11] 114 Grafton Street, Dublin, Molesworth Street, Spring Gardens, a house opposite 6 Merrion Square and the Dublin packet-boat at sea.

Dublin weekly and bi-weekly newspapers, however, which were published at the beginning of May, announced the birth of a son to the Countess of Mornington 'a few days ago' in Merrion Street, where, at No. 6, stood Mornington House. Despite Wellington's own inveterate distrust of newspapers, in this case they must be assumed to know best. At 6 Merrion Street (now 24 Upper Merrion Street) on 1 May 1769 the future Duke of Wellington was born.

More relevant to his story than any local legend is the fact that on 15 August of the same year was born Napoleon Bonaparte.

10. For a full discussion of this question, see Philip Guedalla, *The Duke* (1931), and the Rev. C. C. Ellison, '*Riocht Na Midhe*', *Records of Meath Archaeological and Historical Society*, vol. III, no. 4, 1966. The main problem is posed by an entry in the register of the Mornington's parish church, St Peter's Dublin, giving 30 April as the baptismal date.

11. Athy, a town in Kildare, perhaps deserves a special word, since it is the only name which Wellington himself apparently gave as his birthplace. When, as an old man of eighty-two, he was asked to fill in the census form for 1851, he is said to have written for his place of birth, 'In Ireland—believe Athy' (letter in *The Times* from Mr Stanhope Kennedy, Basingstoke, 3 June 1926). Unfortunately the original census forms of this and several following decades were destroyed in 1913.

2 *Odd Man Out*

The childhood which has almost no annals is not necessarily happy. Wellington's grim reticence about his youth fits into the impression of a frustrated fourth child, conscious of latent powers but inhibited by two clever elder brothers and two promising younger ones.

No one bothered to leave behind a description of the child's appearance, though one surviving contemporary portrait, a silhouette, gives the impression of a delicate, even poetic face. The nose already has a faint downward curve, unusual in childhood. The lips, far from pouting, form a line that is almost sedate. His eyes were always of a brilliant light blue; his hair was brown, or possibly at this date fair.

As a small child, Arthur attended the Diocesan School, Trim. This medieval stone building was known as Talbot's Castle, in honour of the warrior whom Shakespeare called 'the scourge of France'. It seems appropriate that an even greater 'scourge' should have done his first mental arithmetic (at which he shone) in that castle; less appropriate, perhaps, that the only anecdote which Trim's historian, Dean Butler, could unearth about Wellington was a tearful one.

One of Arthur's schoolfellows, and incidentally a cousin, was the redoubtable Richard Crosbie, later to be known as 'Balloon Crosbie' because of his flying exploits. For a wager, young Crosbie climbed to the top of Trim's 'Yellow Steeple', as the gaunt tower of St Mary's Abbey was called, from which could be seen the rushy River Boyne below and, on its farther bank, facing the Abbey, the huge ruins of Trim Castle. With nearly 500 feet of walls still standing, ten flanking towers, a moat and the remains of a barbican, this grim fortress dominated Arthur's childhood. When young Crosbie's last will and testament suddenly came fluttering down from the top of the Yellow Steeple, the future Iron Duke, as Butler relates, burst into tears because nothing, not even one gamecock, had been bequeathed to him.

> *Alas, this is a child . . .*
> *It cannot be this weak and writhled shrimp*
> *Should strike such terror to his enemies.*

*   *   *

Trim was Arthur's first and last experience of Irish education. By moving to London his father prevented him and his brothers from acquiring what Arthur's future brother-in-law, Edward Pakenham, called 'a singularity of pronunciation that hereafter might be a disadvantage . . . in society'.

The London preparatory school, of which Wellington himself sometimes spoke, was Brown's establishment in Chelsea. He did not speak well of it. The shilling tip he once received while a pupil there from his eldest brother Richard, was well-matched by the school's modest educational provisions. They ensured that Arthur would enter Eton singularly ill-equipped. He admitted to his future biographer, the Rev. G. R. Gleig, that he was 'a dreamy, idle and shy lad'. Indifferent health, explained one of his schoolfellows, gave Arthur a careless and lethargic manner. He would never take part in playground games but 'lounged' against a large walnut tree watching the players and picking out those who cheated. If set upon by the victims of his scrutiny, he would fight himself free but always return to his tree, 'as quiet, dejected and observant' as before. A black-and-white drawing, published in 1852 to illustrate the Duke of Wellington's schooldays, shows the hero standing under his tree, but instead of lounging, he is actively directing the troops in the playground with an outstretched hand in which one almost sees the shadow of a baton. The illustration seems to have owed more to Wellington's celebrated tree at Waterloo than to events in Chelsea forty years earlier.

The Mornington parents were 'frivolous and careless personages', according to Arthur's brother Richard. It is unlikely that Arthur heard much about current affairs during these early school years. Yet there was much to discuss both abroad and at home.

American colonists were not losing their War of Independence as expected; by 1778, in fact, they had gained allies in Spain and France. Irish Protestants sprang to arms, spreading wild rumours of a French invasion and pouring their money into costly volunteer corps in return for which they fiercely demanded commercial equality with England. 'Free trade or this!' they cried—'this' being a cannon on which they had hung their slogan, equally ready to fire on English or French. Irish Catholics in 1778 were placated with another partial Relief Act, to lure them into the Army.

The destructive Gordon Riots of 1780 broke out in London against an imaginary papist threat, and even the children of 'frivolous' Lord

Mornington must have picked up something of what everyone was talking about—'black Wednesday', and the troops who were called in too late. These events seemed to teach the lesson once for all that prompt counteraction alone could stop rioting.

By the end of 1781 General Cornwallis had surrendered to General Washington, the partnership of George III and Lord North was on the point of collapse and Arthur Wesley's father was dead.

*   *   *

The loss of his musical parent in May 1781 can scarcely have improved Arthur's prestige in the family. So far, his sole outstanding gift was intense love of music and skill in playing the violin. It was not a gift to be prized by his widowed mother. The late Lord Mornington's orchestra, famed for its noble personnel and charitable performances, had filled no mouths at Dangan, indeed his obsession with 'cool grots' had led to the family's present extremely cold comfort. Under a cloud of family indebtedness which compelled refulgent Richard, now Lord Mornington, to leave Oxford without a degree, Arthur entered Eton in autumn 1781, carrying his shyness with him.

At Eton, Gleig was surprised to learn, he became distinctly 'combative'. A boy named 'Bobus' Smith, brother of Sidney Smith the wit, used to boast wryly, 'I was the Duke of Wellington's first victory'. Smith was swimming one day in the Thames when Arthur started throwing stones at him from the bank. The swimmer threatened to thrash the aggressor—'I had a fight,' related Smith, 'and he beat me soundly.'[1] A game of marbles, however, during the school holidays at Brynkinalt, the home of Arthur's grandmother, Lady Dungannon, in north Wales, ended in a stand-up fight with Arthur getting thrashed. His opponent, a young blacksmith, afterwards delighted in having 'beaten the man who beat Napoleon', adding that 'Master Wesley bore him not a pin's worth of ill-will'.

There were no compulsory, organized games at Eton and even the most casual cricket or boating did not attract Arthur. Lonely and

---

1. In later years Smith was to be famous for his ugliness. He once bored Talleyrand by expatiating on the beauty of his mother. 'Monsieur Smith,' interrupted the great diplomatist who was no beauty himself, 'c'était donc Monsieur votre père qui n'était pas beau?' Arthur's apparently unprovoked aggression may have been a protest on behalf of aesthetics.

withdrawn, he preferred the grounds of the Manor House where he boarded, playing at the bottom of the garden and jumping over a broad black ditch. He had no aptitude for the classics and his younger brother Gerald, who had, was soon his scholastic superior. Richard, having given up his own dazzling academic career felt no compunction about settling with their mother to remove Arthur from Eton, in order that all the available funds might be concentrated on Gerald and the next little academic star, Henry. This she did at the end of the summer half, 1784.

Wellington did not choose to set eyes on Eton again until 22 January 1818, thirty-four years after his own schooldays. By then he was visiting his two sons who were boarding in his old house. First he looked at his old room; then, opposite, at a work-room for the boys' maids, nicknamed 'Virgins' Bower'. When the cook began rounding up the 'virgins' to come forth and curtsey to the Duke of Wellington, he marched into the kitchen saying, 'The Duke is coming to see *you*.' Next into the garden—but what had become of the broad black ditch over which he had jumped so often? 'I really believe I owe my spirit of enterprise,' he said with his laugh like a war-whoop, 'to the tricks I used to play in the garden.' The stream, with its banks of black mud, had been filled in, but a subsidence in the lawn must have indicated— as it still does—where Arthur Wesley had played his tricks.

The Duke visited Eton once more while his sons were pupils there. General Hardinge also once brought him down from Windsor Castle. The Duke made a bee-line for the work-room at the end of the passage. 'That,' he said pointing, 'we called "Maidens' Bower".' Despite the charms of Maidens' (or Virgins') Bower, Eton did not see him again until duty called him to his brother Richard's funeral in 1842; he left immediately by a back exit after the ceremony in College Chapel. His last visit was in 1844, when he was commanded to attend upon Queen Victoria and her guest, Louis Philippe, King of the French.

It seems odd that an alumnus so lukewarm when young, so indifferent when old, should have paid to his *alma mater* the highest tribute in his power: 'The Battle of Waterloo was won on the playing-fields of Eton.' Of all Wellington's alleged *obiter dicta*, this is perhaps the best known. Yet probably he never said or thought anything of the kind.

This 'laconic' (as Wellington's epigrams used to be called) did not make its first appearance until three years after his death. In 1855 an eminent French writer and parliamentarian, Count de Montalembert, visited Eton in search of material for his projected book on the political future of England. The writer picked up something which the orator in him turned to good account: ' . . . one understands the Duke of Wellington's *mot* when, revisiting during his declining years the beauteous scenes where he had been educated, remembering the games of his youth, and finding the same precocious vigour in the descendants of his comrades, he said aloud: *"C'est ici qu'a été gagnée la bataille de Waterloo."* '[2]

Note, first, that there is no mention here of 'playing-fields'; therefore no justification for later attempts, based on this passage, to praise (or deride) Wellington for advocating organized games. Note, second, the difficulty of deciding on which of his later visits he made his oracular *mot*. None seems appropriate. His remark, in 1818, that jumping over the broad black ditch had produced his own 'spirit of enterprise', could only be used, if at all, to prove that the battle of Waterloo had been won by a small, odd-man-out in the Manor House garden.

Nothing daunted by these difficulties, a successor to Montalembert, Sir Edward Creasy, soon carried the 'Waterloo–Eton' legend another stage forward. As the aged Duke passed the 'playing-fields', wrote Creasy in *Eminent Etonians*, he paid a tribute to the 'manly character' which they nurtured: 'There grows the stuff that won Waterloo.'

By 1889 that excellent club raconteur, Sir William Fraser, had capped both his predecessors. In his *Words on Wellington*, he not only repeated for the first time in English Montalembert's original 'Waterloo' epigram, but added for good measure Creasy's tribute to 'playing-fields' and 'manliness'.[3]

Meanwhile, over one hundred years earlier, in 1784, the subject of these debates, Arthur Wesley, had left Eton after his three inglorious

2. The present Duke of Wellington has pointed out that the tone of this epigram is Napoleonic, rather than Wellingtonian: it has affinities with Napoleon's 'Soldiers! from the summit of these Pyramids forty centuries look down on you . . .'

3. The amiable fantasy was further embellished in 1915 when Dr J. E. C. Welldon pointed out in his *Recollections and Reflections* that if Richard, Arthur's eldest brother, had not been expelled from Harrow for 'barring out' an old Etonian headmaster, Dr Heath, Arthur would have followed him there and the Battle of Waterloo have been won on the Philathletic Ground at Harrow.

years, having been neither happy nor successful. He never returned, as has been shown, except when he had to. And when, as Chancellor of Oxford University, he was asked in 1841 for a subscription to Eton's new buildings, he bluntly told his fellow-chancellor and fellow-duke (Northumberland, Chancellor of Cambridge) why he had refused:

> I am called upon to subscribe to build Schools, Churches, Temples, Mosques, etc. in all parts of the World. . . . I had determined that I would not subscribe to defray the Expense of addl. buildings at Eton College. If these are required the Publick should provide them, or they should be provided out of the means already at the disposition of that Royal Foundation. I fill an honorary Office that of Chancr. of the U. of Oxford which gives me a great deal of trouble and costs me a great deal of money. I cannot in that capacity enter into further subscriptions to maintain and increase other foundations.

The cold reference to Eton as just another foundation, comes oddly from one who is supposed, as it must now seem wrongly, to have laid his greatest victory at her feet.

*   *   *

Arthur was now fifteen; an awkward age, and the word 'awkward' seemed to stick to him like a burr. With his polished sister Anne, product of a French governess, and his admirable brother Gerald, he visited the famous 'Ladies of Llangollen' that summer of 1784, and made a poor showing. These two ladies, Lady Eleanor Butler and Miss Sarah Ponsonby, described as 'the most celebrated virgins in Europe', had rejected the vanities of eighteenth-century Ireland and fled together to what Wordsworth called 'a low-roof'd Cot' in the mountains of north Wales, there to cultivate a romantic friendship. When Arthur first saw them they had powdered curls and black habits over the cut of which they spent much thought; nevertheless many people found their clothes 'somewhat ludicrous'. He was to remember them fifty years later looking like two little old men or benevolent witches, as they stood side by side outside their cottage with hair cut short, mannish jackets, top hats, and a cat and a dog.

When their rather odd neighbour, Lady Dungannon, brought over her three grandchildren, Miss Sarah regaled her cousin, Mrs Tighe, with an account of Arthur's backwardness. Arthur revenged himself on the world by spreading a rumour that elegant Anne had run off with the footman.

A few weeks later the London home broke up. Lady Mornington, like many another financially embarrassed Briton, decided to live in Brussels until the tide turned. Arthur was packed off to Brighton for some much-needed tutoring with the Rev. Henry Michell. He must have liked the man and the solitary life, for he was to choose Michell's grandson, the Rev. Henry Michell Wagner, to tutor his own sons. At the beginning of 1785 he went with his mother to the home of a Brussels advocate, M. Louis Goubert. Again he seems to have liked his host: after Waterloo, when Brussels was overrun with troops, he put a special guard on old M. Goubert's house. He was friendly, too, with a young fellow-boarder at Goubert's, John Armytage, son of a rich Yorkshire baronet. In Armytage's journal Wesley appears as the possessor of exceptional musical skill but no other 'species of talent' whatever. Nor did Armytage know of any plans for sending Arthur into the Army; Arthur's wishes, 'if he had any', were for a civilian life.

But a year with Arthur in Brussels and in civilian life, which meant a year with Arthur's violin, was enough for Lady Mornington. She returned home herself and sent him to France, to prepare for that last refuge of square pegs—the Army.

Prejudice against the Army was almost universal. At home there was no police force, so that the strong arm of the law was represented by companies of red-coats whose discipline, behaviour, pay and billets even by eighteenth-century standards were deplorable.[4] While the privates were feared and disliked by the people, their officers were distrusted by the government. 'Fit and necessary objects of the jealousy and vigilance of the House of Commons', was the best Charles James Fox could say of British officers. Fox was a Whig; but even Tories, even Wellington himself would never cease to feel a deeply historical, thoroughly British reserve towards the standing

4. After the Gordon Riots, for instance, Fanny Burney heard that 'much slaughter has been made by the military among the mob. Never, I am sure, can any set of wretches less deserve quarter & pity; yet it is impossible not to shudder at hearing of their destruction.' Her father, however, replied, 'I bless every soldier I see—we have no dependence on any defence from outrage but the military' (*Diary and Letters of Madame D'Arblay*, vol. I, pp. 343, 348).

army. Sir John Fortescue, its distinguished historian, makes the further point that the years 1783–93 were among the worst in the Army's history, since they occupied the trough between the wars against America and France, the latter of which ultimately forced the 'Horse Guards' and War departments into a programme of army reform.[5] What a career to choose for a son growing up in precisely that abysmal decade. But what else could be expected, with Arthur's sorry record? Richard had in fact written to the Lord Lieutenant of Ireland about a possible commission as soon as Arthur left Eton. And now there had been this fruitless year in Brussels.

'I vow to God I don't know what I shall do with my awkward son Arthur,' complained Lady Mornington to her daughter-in-law, William's wife. He was 'food for powder and nothing more'.

*   *   *

To prepare himself for this uninviting future Arthur was dispatched to the historic Royal Academy of Equitation at Angers in Anjou. Here the young sons of the nobility and gentry from all over Europe had been trained for two centuries in the art of horsemanship, in swordplay and fencing, in mathematics and 'the humanities'. Angers was no mere riding-school. Among past pupils had been George Villiers, 1st Duke of Buckingham. Gauche, sixteen-year-old Arthur Wesley was hardly a reincarnation of George Villiers, who had descended on Angers aged nineteen, 'loving everybody and avid of amusement'; but Angers was just the place to give Arthur the civilized *politesse* if not *panache* he needed. After the cloak-and-dagger period of Villiers and Alexandre Dumas, the Academy reached its zenith under the Pignerolle family, who had constructed a monumental new edifice only thirty years before Arthur's arrival. Its classical façade

5. These years looked back directly to the disgraceful American War of Independence, whereas the reforms made by the Duke of York, Sir Ralph Abercrombie and Sir John Moore in response to the subsequent French war were still in the future. But throughout Wellington's career the British Army was subject to a confused and confusing system. On purely military matters the highest authority was the Commander-in-Chief's department, and since his office was in the Horse Guards' building it was generally known as 'the Horse Guards'. There were also (1) the Secretary *for* War and the Colonies who planned campaigns and raised recruits; (2) the Secretary-*at*-War who was Parliament's watchdog, presiding over the War Office administration; (3) the Ordnance Department. See Richard Glover, *Peninsular Preparation*, pp. 28–40.

and mansard roof, two vast courtyards, pavilions and stables, gave it more the air of a palace than a riding-school.

Arthur's name headed the list of entries for 1786: '*Mr Wesley, gentilhomme Irlandais, fils de Mylaidi Mornington, pensionnaire, entre le 16 Janvier*.'[6] With two sons of Irish peers for boon companions, Mr Walsh, son of Lord Walsh, and Mr Wingfield, son of Lord '*Portscowz*' (Powerscourt), this '*groupe des lords*' as they were called, would make for the eating-houses of the town centre in the evening, where their college uniforms of scarlet coat, yellow buttons and sky-blue facings mingled with the blue or silver-grey of the French garrison. Otherwise Arthur might join in games of chance, played under the supervision of Mme de Pignerolle, who would confiscate the stakes if too high and put them in a poor-box. One day she was touched to find that Arthur had purposely persuaded everyone to play for gold.

The *groupe des lords* were sometimes entertained by the French nobility: the Dukes of Brissac and Praslin and the Duchess of Sabran. Wellington used to laugh in after days at the Duke of Brissac's habit of reserving special delicacies for himself. 'Only think what would be said . . . if at Belvoir Castle, or any other great house, there was one set of dishes put on the table for the master of the house, and another set not so good for his guests!' Brissac was guillotined.

Angers must have been largely responsible for the change which was soon noticed in Arthur. Admittedly the English colony (108 out of 334 Academicians during his year) tended to keep aloof, and he and his friends had a tiresome habit of dropping small change out of their windows on to the heads of passers-by. He was still often unwell and spent some of his happiest hours playing on a sofa with his white terrier 'Vick'. This is perhaps the reason why his later feats as a rider were to excel in valour rather than grace, despite the Academy's motto of 'Grace and Valour'—in that order. Nevertheless, the impression given by many of his biographers that he left Angers with nothing much more than a good French accent, because nothing much more was available at a place like Angers, cannot be accepted. Is it a coincidence that Angers trained two English Prime Ministers, Chatham and Wellington? It is certainly ironical, as the people of

6. At the head of the year before stood the name of '*Mr Frotteskiou*', also an Irish boarder and probably one of Arthur's Fortescue cousins, through the marriage of his aunt, Elizabeth Wellesley, to Chichester Fortescue of County Louth.

Anjou are today quick to point out, that each in due course became France's most formidable enemy in time of war.

Wellington would certainly have preferred a university education, as he was himself to make clear. But short of that, Angers did him proud. Years later, as the supremo in Paris, he was able to renew his acquaintance with at least one of the grandees from Angers, the Duchess of Sabran. Nor did his knowledge of the French language acquired at Angers merely provide a passport to duchesses. It was to make him one of the most cosmopolitan of great Englishmen. M. de Pignerolle, a Frenchman, was the first to detect the signs of brilliance which had been invisible to Arthur's countrymen. Towards the end of Arthur's residence a young Irish peer and his governor were entered as boarders. The latter enquired of Pignerolle if he had any English boys of promise. Pignerolle replied that he had 'one Irish lad of great promise, of the name of Wesley . . .'.

Arthur left Angers with his governor, Mr Mackenzie (afterwards General Sir A. Mackenzie of Fairbairn), and drove to Paris. The carriage broke down outside the city and they had to walk the rest of the way, Arthur no doubt complaining, for Mackenzie remembered him as a boy who could not stand much exercise. At any rate, he passed through the pre-Revolutionary city. To him, the Bourbons' capital was then and always the only true Paris.

If Angers had a weakness it was one which Arthur himself would have been the last to admit. In Marcel de Pignerolle the Academy had a director dedicated to the *ancien régime* who, in the savage days ahead, would prefer to die rather than reach a compromise with the Revolution. Under the care of this man Arthur Wesley spent an impressionable year. Who was to warn him that Pignerolle and his friends were glorifying a ghost? In Wellington's mind the old French Court always stood for reality as well as romance—the 'real thing', in a world given over more and more to shams. Lord Stanhope,[7] with his unerring nose for a significant story, tells how one evening at dinner in 1840 in the dining-room at Apsley House, the Duke fixed his eyes on a pair of portraits of Louis XVIII and Charles X in their royal robes. 'How much better after all,' he reflected smiling, 'these two look with their *fleurs-de-lis* and *Saint-Esprits,* than the two

7. The 5th Earl Stanhope, author of *Conversations with the Duke of Wellington*, did not in fact succeed until 1855 and was known as Lord Mahon throughout the Duke's lifetime; but for the sake of clarity the name under which his work was published, i.e. Stanhope, will be used wherever possible.

corporals behind, or the fancy dress in between!' The corporals were Europe's royal war-lords, Alexander of Russia and the King of Prussia in uniform, while the fancy dress was George IV painted by Wilkie in Highland kilt and bonnet.[8]

*   *   *

The new Arthur made an instantaneous impression. His mother is said to have caught sight of him for the first time at the Haymarket Theatre, after he returned to London towards the end of 1786. 'I do believe there is my ugly boy Arthur,' she exclaimed incredulously, for he had shot up, his hair was well powdered and his cheeks were bright. Not that the military prospect could now be allowed to recede. Richard dashed off a letter to the Duke of Rutland, Lord Lieutenant of Ireland, the moment Arthur arrived:

> Let me remind you of a younger brother of mine, whom you were so kind as to take into your consideration for a commission in the army. He is here at this moment, and perfectly idle. It is a matter of indifference to me what commission he gets, provided he gets it soon.

If Arthur saw this brotherly message he would not have felt unduly resentful. No doubt he would have preferred civilian life, but it was never his way to carry opposition beyond a certain point. His temperament and philosophy allowed him to argue, but always in the end to make the best of a bad job, not to throw it up. His later letters were to ring with trumpets sounding a good-tempered retreat.

However, two words applied to him by Richard might have disconcerted him in later life—'perfectly idle'. For there is evidence which will appear in due course that not long after his unsatisfactory schooldays were over he developed an active if spasmodic interior life, unknown to his family. At the same time the process of forgetting the disagreeable aspects of his youth was set in motion. Like many a brilliant younger son who fails at first and then makes good, the last thing he wanted was the gift of total recall. In the end he achieved a degree of total obliteration which can only make one gasp; for having reached the age of seventy-eight in a state of indomitable vigour, he

8. The pictures still hang today in the dining-room at Apsley House— now the Wellington Museum—except for the portrait of Charles X which is at the top of the main staircase.

was able to say unblushingly to one of his younger friends: 'I have never been, and never am at this moment, listless or idle.'

*   *   *

Arthur's family were able to give him a suitable if unostentatious present in good time for his eighteenth birthday: on 17 March he was gazetted Ensign in the 73rd Highland Regiment. Many boys younger than he were already higher up the military ladder, and he himself was not too young to appreciate that 'since I have undertaken a profession I had better try to understand it'. Indeed, if a favourite part of his legend is to be believed, he took his new military career so seriously that he at once performed an act of dramatic significance: he had one of his privates weighed in full kit.

Years later, his Irish-born friend, John Wilson Croker, remembered, or thought he remembered, the Duke telling him about this unique incident and decided to put it in his own *Memoirs*.[9]

> Can you spare me five minutes [he therefore wrote to the old Duke on 15 November 1850], to tell me whether my recollection of one of the most remarkable passages of your life (as I think) is correct? Did you once tell me that the very day (or week) that you *first joined the Army* you had a private soldier & all his accoutrements & traps separately weighed, to give you some insight into what the *man* had to do & his power of doing it?

Croker concluded that his memory could scarcely have deceived him on so characteristic a fact.

Wellington's reply was certainly no less characteristic than the story he was asked to vet:

> I have frequently calculated the weight of each of the articles which the Soldier carried. . . . But I don't think that I made this calculation on the day I joined a regiment or ever said that I had made it at that period! In the orders respecting the examination of Officers for Promotion I have required that this knowledge should be attained.[10]

9. John Wilson Croker (1780–1857). M.P. for Downpatrick, 1807, founded the *Quarterly Review*, 1809, secretary to the Admiralty.

10. Order signed by Wellington on 14 May 1850: '[Officers] should know the weight of the knapsack, the weight of the soldier's firelock, of his pouch with or without the ammunition . . . of his accoutrements with or without the bayonet, of the bayonet with or without the scabbard.'

Some such order may well have given rise to a legend like Croker's; on the other hand, Wellington's answer to Croker may be a vivid example of his passion for what today would be called 'debunking', buttressed by a selective memory and genuine humility. Either way, the whole episode throws a fascinating light on the making of a hero; in which must be included Croker's bland decision to go ahead with his story regardless, and not even to mention the Duke's own denial.[11]

*　　　*　　　*

No one could live on an Ensign's pay alone. He must either move rapidly through the various stages of promotion, or acquire additional patronage, or both. On 24 October 1787 the Duke of Rutland died and the Morningtons promptly closed in on his successor, Lord Buckingham, the Viceroy designate, whose fat red face expressed kindly greed and who had already got Richard a seat on the English Board of Treasury. He at once yielded to this new clamour: by 4 November Lord Mornington was already thanking him for having appointed Arthur one of his aides-de-camp at 10s. a day. His private income was £125 a year. 'I can assure you sincerely,' wrote Arthur's brother, 'that he has every disposition which can render so young a boy deserving of your notice; and if he does not engage your protection by his conduct, I am much mistaken in his character.' Auspiciously on Christmas Day Arthur was gazetted Lieutenant in the 76th Regiment.

The new year brought a hitch. In his best vein of sarcasm Lord Mornington wrote on 8 January 1788 to Lord Buckingham denouncing a monstrous attempt by Hobart, the Secretary at War, to put all the aides-de-camp on half-pay.[12] Arthur was about to leave for Ireland, having arranged an exchange into the 41st Regiment which, unlike the 76th, was not booked for service in the East Indies. But he might as well go to India as try to live on half-pay among the *bon ton* of Dublin.

This business is very unfortunate for Arthur, as his men are now all raised [fumed Richard], and he . . . only waits the mighty fiat

11. The Wellington–Croker correspondence forms part of the *Wellington MSS* at Apsley House. Croker's version occurs in his *Correspondence and Diaries*, vol. I, p. 337, and has been repeated as fact in every subsequent biography of the Duke.

12. Robert, Lord Hobart, 4th Earl of Buckinghamshire (1760–1816). Appointed Governor of Madras, 1793. See below, p. 60.

of the Secretary at War. I fear he must wait for the decision of that great character; for I think under the present circumstances he cannot safely leave England. However, I hope the Secretary will deign to temper his grandeur with a little common sense in the course of a few days, and then I will consign your aide-de-camp to you by the first mail-coach.

Common sense, or at any rate some equally powerful pressure, duly operated upon the over-zealous Secretary and the half-pay idea was dropped. On 23 January 1788 Arthur was transferred into the 41st and a day or two afterwards Lady Mornington 'consigned' him to his new lord and master, from their London home in Henrietta Street, Cavendish Square. She sent the Ladies of Llangollen two lyrical letters to prepare them for the new Arthur who would call on his way to Holyhead: 'there are so many little things to settle for *Arthur* . . . and when you see him you will think him worthy of it as he really is a very charming young man, never did I see such a change for the better in any body . . .' Before this letter arrived, Arthur and his grandmother, Lady Dungannon, had already visited the Ladies. Eleanor Butler noted in her journal that they had dropped in shortly after breakfast on 28 January, adding: 'A charming young man. Handsome, fashioned tall and elegant.' His charm had worked even upon his problem grandmother, for the journal continued, 'She was in the best Temper'.

On 1 February 1788 he sailed into Dublin Bay. All seemed set fair for the legendary return of the younger son to his native country, from whose shores he had departed wrapped in a sombre disguise of reserve and silence, only to reappear, at least in the eyes of his family, as the prince destined to cut through the cobwebs and briars that choked the citadel, win his princess and seize his place in the sun.

Or was Ireland, alike in her frustration and her poetry, her despair and her rapturous hopes, to remain forever inimical to his kind of genius? 'The Irish politicks are vastly too intricate for a *volume* to describe,' wrote Lady Sarah Napier a year before he arrived. 'There is no *system* or regularity here.'

As it happened, regularity was to be Wellington's guiding star.[13]

13. *Life and Letters of Lady Sarah Lennox*, vol. II, p. 61. Sarah Napier (1745–1827), *née* Lady Sarah Lennox, daughter of the 2nd Duke of Richmond, married as her second husband Colonel, the Hon. George Napier. She was mother of three of Wellington's most famous officers, Charles, George and William Napier.

3 Food for Powder

The Ireland to which Arthur Wesley returned was quiet—the quiet before the storm.

This happy state dated from 1782 when the Irish orator, Henry Grattan, had risen to his feet under the magnificent chandeliers of Parliament House and saluted Dublin's first independent Parliament: 'Ireland is now a nation. In that character I hail her, and bowing in her august presence I say, *Esto perpetua*.' The 'perpetuity' was so far only six years old; but it was a beginning. Since then a wave of national confidence had swept over Dublin inspiring Protestants and Catholics, Whigs and Tories alike to build, to drain, to trade, to 'frolic' (a favourite word) and in short to make their city the most beautiful in Europe. Everyone was in perpetual motion. The humbler Dubliners jostled one another in whiskeys, *chaises marines*, noddies, *pochays*, one-horse chairs and gigs, while the nobility's glorious coaches rolled inviolate through the widened streets and squares like state apartments on wheels. Even in the unkempt countryside a few valiant landlords were stepping up their campaigns for improvement. Richard Edgeworth had just invented estate railroads to carry manure to his fields, having tried unsuccessfully to waft it uphill by means of a fire-balloon. He was spreading lime far and wide, as was another ardent landlord near by, his cousin, Lord Longford.[1]

Dublin Castle alone, the seat of all power, was in no state to lead an Irish renaissance, nor to impress a young aide-de-camp with the sublimity of his duties. Arthur Wesley found an arrogant junta installed whose one aim was to bind the upper classes to themselves and to the British connection by four golden chains: titles, pensions, sinecure posts and highly paid jobs. Once past the Captain of the Guard at the Castle gates, splendid in powder, gorget and sash, Wesley entered the busy world of placemen which the Dublin poor regarded with a mixture of hatred and jest: of a fountain erected for the poor at public expense in a magnificent square where no poor lived—'And there it is to this day, a great job, by Jagurs, why wouldn't it?'; of expresses to be dispatched hourly to the host of sub-sheriffs, surveyors and minor officials up and down the country; and

1. Lord Longford's grandmother was the half-sister of Edgeworth's father.

of 'place ladies'—the boisterous daughters of government officials —to be entertained and handed down from Viceroy to Viceroy and regiment to regiment with the state chairs and barrack fixtures.

There is a glimpse of Arthur Wesley and his entourage in Lady Morgan's *The O'Briens and the O'Flahertys*, an Irish novel of the period. The Vicereine, surrounded by the Castle Irish, who include huge and clumsy Lord Kilcolman and flashy O'Mealy the 'reglar' with his *chevaux de frise* of powdered whiskers, turns to the youngest aide-de-camp in waiting.

'So, Arthur, order supper and gather up those flowers, which Lord Kilcolman has thrown down with his Atlas shoulders.' Arthur flies to execute his lady's commands—to order supper and to pick up prostrate flowers, until destiny sends him to order armies and restore fallen dynasties.

The Vicereine unkindly called Arthur and his colleagues her 'awkward squad', for Pitt had just sent her over a new batch of younger sons to find places for. But despite their inexpertise supper would be duly served in the Round Room where the rompers, dashers and rattlers of the *bon ton* flocked to eat the Castle roasts and ragouts, washed down with Tokay, burgundy, champagne and iced sherbet, to the sentimental measures of a German band. When the Lord Lieutenant, his Privy Council and aides at length rejoined the ladies, having endlessly toasted everything from the glorious and immortal victory of William III to the no less glorious and immortal victory of the favourite race-horse of the day, 'the Keeper of the Seals could not keep his legs—the Speaker could not articulate a syllable—the King's Solicitor suffered judgement to go by default'— and the aides were in no state to help anyone.

Wesley's most pressing danger was not to become food for powder but food for sharks. Gambling, whether in clubs or as private wagers, was an obsession. He is heard of betting 'Buck' Whaley 150 guineas that he would walk the rutted six miles from Cornelscourt outside Dublin to Leeson Street inside, in a specified time. He did it in fifty-five minutes and won his wager. But success did not always turn on grit and fibre, so that soon he was borrowing money wherever he safely could, for instance from his landlord, a boot-maker on Ormonde Quay. Nor did certain financial misfortunes of his grandmother and elder brother warn him to live quietly. News came in November 1788 that Lady Dungannon, having quit Wales for a jollier life at Hampton Court, had been arrested for debt, conducted by two bailiffs and six

'Marshall Men' to a sponging house, where she met and entered into lively conversation with a Mr Cavendish's mistress, until a horrified Lord and Lady Mornington arrived and bore her away, the latter 'shocked and provoked by her mother's want of feeling or shame'. She was forthwith shipped abroad to a French convent with her granddaughter Mary, William's eldest child, as chaperone.

This débâcle did not encourage Richard to keep Dangan afloat. His whole estate was mortgaged in any case, and there were debts of £16,000. A generous spendthrift himself, he was living with a French courtesan, Mademoiselle Gabrielle Hyacinthe Rolland, by whom he constantly had children. He paid all Lady Dungannon's debts, nonetheless, and brought her home again within six months, just beating the French Revolution. Of his brothers, William at least was no problem, since he had acquired the fortune and name of his rich cousin William Pole of Ballyfin in County Meath.

On both sides of Arthur's family there was thus a spendthrift strain, balanced by a flair for harsh rectitude in his mother and 'a little pepper' noted by Mrs Delany in his mother's father. Which was to be his master, the frivolous or the serious and fierce? The anecdotes which survive of his Irish life when he was between nineteen and twenty-one show the two elements evenly matched.

There were stories of picnics outside Dublin to which ladies refused to go if 'that mischievous boy' Arthur Wesley was also invited. (He specialized in twitching out the lace from shirt collars.) A young Mrs St George, however, who had been lent Dangan for her honeymoon, noticed him favourably. He was 'extremely good humoured and the object of much attention from the female part of what was called "a very gay society" '. The Napiers of Celbridge thought him a 'shallow saucy stripling', though Colonel George Napier, father of generals, is credited with one of those prophecies which great men tend to attract. 'Those who think lightly of that lad are unwise in their generation: he has in him the makings of a great general.' There was the story of an unruly Arthur fined for beating a Frenchman and seizing his stick in a Dublin bawdy-house. The narrator of this incident was inclined to forgive the young offender, since he later made a habit of beating Frenchmen and taking their batons. Arthur's appearance before the magistrates was scarcely worth noting, considering the plague of duelling and fighting in Dublin all through this period. Sir Jonah Barrington was the first to point out its astonishing incidence at the bar alone: a Lord Chancellor fought a Master of the

Rolls, a Chancellor of the Exchequer fought Henry Grattan and three others and the Provost of Dublin University fought a Master in Chancery. Lord Chief Justice Norbury was said to have '*shot* up into preferment'.

In another episode, again at a picnic, Arthur has become a curiously muted figure. The fashionable Lady Aldborough had given him a lift on the way there, 'but he was so dull that I threw him over and brought back *le beau* Cradock.[2] All the other carriages having started or being full, he had nothing for it but to return with the band.' The explanation of this 'dull' Arthur may be found in the last, most striking episode.

A casual visitor to Dangan Castle, John Ruxton, uncle of Maria Edgeworth, happened to enter the room which the reputedly 'idle Castle aide-de-camp' had just left. Mr Ruxton picked up the book Arthur Wesley had been reading and was amazed to find that it was Locke's *Essay Concerning Human Understanding*. Well might the society beauty consider a young man 'dull' who immersed himself in the problems of 'innate ideas', truth and reality, faith and reason. Locke's celebrated demonstration that all knowledge derived from *experience* was well calculated to appeal to the future Duke of Wellington.

If Arthur was engaged upon improving his own understanding, who or what had inspired him? Marcel de Pignerolle may have started it. Very likely the Ladies of Llangollen had introduced the new, elegant young Arthur, fresh from Angers, to the little room leading out of the salon which was their library. Eleanor Butler was to present Arthur with a rare Ormonde prayer-book in Spanish, before he went to the Peninsula in 1808. Lastly, it is possible that the Castle aide-de-camp had already met a bookish and extremely charming girl, three years younger than himself, who was destined to play a bitter-sweet role in his life.

Kitty Pakenham, Lord Longford's second daughter, lived about thirty miles from Dangan Castle at Pakenham Hall, Castlepollard, in County Westmeath. She and the future authoress, Maria Edgeworth, were friends and distant cousins, Maria being five years older than Kitty and as uncompromisingly plain as Kitty was pretty. Indeed, according to the Edgeworths Kitty had 'an indefinable

2. Wellington got his own back when he superseded Cradock as Commander-in-Chief, Portugal, 1809. Through his influence the disappointed 'beau' was created Lord Howden in 1819.

beauty'. Wellington's biographers usually put his first meeting with Kitty sometime in 1792 when he was twenty-three and she twenty. It may have been earlier. New responsibilities had brought him more and more to Trim since 1789, which was nearer than Dangan to Pakenham Hall. During the previous year he was always dropping in on Dangan to keep an eye on his brother Mornington's estates. (Richard had been a Member of the English House of Commons since 1784.) Kitty at seventeen or eighteen, that is in 1789 or 1790, would certainly have been presented at the Viceregal Court where Arthur, from his place of vantage behind the throne, would have seen her. Her gaiety and glowing complexion, her bobbing curls and exquisite figure made her a great favourite up at the Castle.

Even if Arthur's excursions into the *Essay Concerning Human Understanding* were not the result of a budding literary friendship, they would surely have promoted one. For how could Kitty, always retiring with a book to the window-seat of the library at Pakenham Hall, fail to be interested in a most unusual young cavalry officer who in public clanked his spurs and in private read Locke?[3]

The struggle within Arthur Wesley was to take place over the next five or six years against the background of a viceregal court which had brought dissipation to a fine art. From 1789 onwards it had to face the growing tremors caused by the French Revolution.

*   *   *

To the supporters of Pitt, among whom Arthur's family numbered themselves, it seemed that France in 1789 had gone mad.

'Aren't you sorry for poor dear France?' wrote his sister Anne to the Ladies of Llangollen; 'I shall never see Paris again.' At Angers Marcel de Pignerolle was advising his dwindling band of pupils to return to their homes immediately, since he had haughtily refused to conform to the new order. When Bastille Day came round again on 14 July 1790 the Ladies of Llangollen gazed apprehensively at a crimson sunset and Eleanor wrote in her journal:

> The sky like a sea of Blood. Have never beheld anything like it but once before: that was the evening of the fire kindled by Lord George Gordon in London. I tremble for France.

*   *   *

3. Wesley transferred to the cavalry (12th Light Dragoons) without promotion in June 1789.

The Wesley interests steadily moved away from an Ireland again becoming disaffected. Anne Wesley, now a regular beauty, was seen by Fanny Burney in a stage-box in London with her mother and their Irish relative, Lord Mountnorris.[4] His Lordship told Fanny that 'the spirit of the times' would reach even England. Fanny was incredulous.

'In what could be its pretence?'

'The *game-laws* and *the tithes*.'

What hope, then, of Ireland escaping the revolutionary spirit, when its tithes were far more onerous and were paid to an alien Church? In January 1790 Anne married a safe Englishman, Henry Fitzroy, son of Lord Southampton.

A Wesley must of course still sit for the family seat of Trim, but the up-and-coming William, who had succeeded Richard as M.P., wanted to move on. It was agreed that he should transfer like Richard before him to the English House of Commons, while Arthur cut his political teeth on Trim, by standing as its candidate. He cut some remarkably sharp ones in the March of 1790, blackballing an attempt by Trim to present the Freedom of the Corporation to the nationalist leader, Grattan.[5] Grattan's proposer extolled the hero's 'respectability', and Wesley anxiously noted the growing enthusiasm of the burgesses to honour him. He must 'risk everything' to stop this 'disgrace'. When his moment came he routed the benches opposite with a homely mixture of sarcasm, common sense and geniality:

> I therefore got up & said that the only reason given why Mr Grattan should get the freedom of the Corporation was his respectability . . . .

If everyone said to be respectable was to get the Freedom of Trim, they would soon have the whole community freemen.

> Mr Grattan could never be of any use to us & never would attend. . . . I would certainly object, however great my respect for him. . . .

4. Arthur Annesley, 1st Earl of Mountnorris (1744–1816), married Sarah Cavendish, daughter of Sir Henry Cavendish. See below, p. 433.

5. By conferring the Freedom of the Corporation, a town enabled the man thus honoured to enjoy certain privileges, such as the Parliamentary vote, exemption from tolls and a share in the corporate revenue.

Wesley then proposed a short adjournment, which he used to tell his side that they must stick to the party and not be swayed by their 'inclinations' for Mr Grattan. Arthur won hands down—forty-seven votes to twenty-nine, as he reported to Richard with a sigh of relief:

> I hope you'll approve of all I have done, really I was in the most difficult situation I ever experienced & only got out of it by sticking up manfully to what I first said.

Just as manfully he turned down the usual requests for land and loans (not to mention the repayment of £70 owing by Richard), on the ground that these transactions would 'vitiate his return' at the coming General Election.[6] Altogether, his supporters had behaved as handsomely as possible. 'They are all fine fellows.' But it was not his kind of life, and he knew it. He ended his letter pointedly with an enquiry after Richard's health and a suggestion: 'I am still of the same opinion with regard to your going abroad & hope you will accept my offer to accompany you.'

All this gives more than a hint of the future man and politician: of the life-long determination to act rightly if possible, 'manfully' in any case; of dislike for jobbery; and of fondness for both 'fine fellows' and sarcasm. Political manoeuvre, on the other hand, did not turn out to be his forte, and the adroitness which he had shown at Trim was sometimes to desert him at Westminster.

Election day duly arrived on 30 April 1790. If it was anything like the usual run of Irish elections, Wesley had a gruelling time. Richard Edgeworth was to recall scenes of riot, hubbub and drunkenness in which electors could fill themselves ten times over with beef and claret in the streets. Arthur, having been successfully declared M.P. for Trim, reported to his brother that it had gone off much better than he expected. Slim and pink-cheeked, he sat for two years under the splendid cupola of Dublin's Parliament House without opening his mouth. Today he and his friends would be called lobby-fodder;

6. In *Castle Rackrent* Maria Edgeworth describes how Sir Condy tried to collect votes by promising freeholds for the sons of voters or places as excisemen and high constables; the burgesses themselves were promised new leases and abated rents; while to get them to the poll there were more promises of liquor, straw, beds, ribbons, silver buckles, horses and postchaises. Agents, lawyers and secret servicemen also had to be paid and as the gentlemen who had promised subscriptions never paid up, Sir Condy Rackrent was left with a load of debt.

in 1791 Wolfe Tone had another name for them—'the common prostitutes of the Treasury Bench'.[7]

Wolfe Tone was the intense, white-faced young nationalist leader whose 'United Irishmen', founded in this year, soon eclipsed Grattan, with their double demand, issued at pike's point if necessary, for Catholic Emancipation and Parliamentary Reform. Richard Mornington, meanwhile, was content to leave Grattan, Tone and all other Irishmen to the growing bigotry of the Castle, for he himself was pulling still further out of Ireland. In 1791 he sold Mornington House in Merrion Street to the father of Lord Cloncurry for the substantial sum of £8,000; the son later remembered having seen 'among the *notabilia*' at a house-warming party, the future Duke of Wellington.

Arthur wrestled with his problems in the country like a glorified estate manager. He acted as umpire throughout 1792 between the family agent, John Page, and a tenant named Locker who occupied some cabins on the Dangan estate and was in arrears of rent. Through Page, Wesley was in touch with the most hated class in Ireland. As absenteeism grew among landlords, pretensions grew among agents. Their clever sons entered the professions and they themselves were gradually received into society, though despised for their alleged 'stubborn, intractable, incorrigible vulgarity'. The stubborn John Page wished to evict Locker. Eviction was a problem which was to concern Arthur deeply in the years to come. In July 1792 he restrained Page but by August Locker 'positively refused' to pay his rent, and Arthur rather wished he had taken him to court earlier; 'although I think we should have been inexcusable,' he told Page, 'if we had omitted to try fair & friendly means, before we proceeded at law.'

A major problem was to sell the Kildare estates profitably and to hold crumbling Dangan together until it too could be sold—for Mornington had decided to sever even the tenuous links with Ireland of an absentee landlord. There was also Lord Mornington's nameless 'friend' and her child.[8] Arthur saw them when 'pay-day' approached in May and wrote to John Page's son: 'I have determined that I will

7. Tone's inimitable phrase is quoted by Guedalla, p. 33.
8. This was not one of Richard's many children by Mlle Rolland, but may have been an illegitimate son named Johnston who many years afterwards became Richard's private secretary when he was Lord Lieutenant of Ireland.

not send the child to school until I return to town which will be in about a month. Thank you for the money.'

Money was not only required for Mornington's friend. Arthur himself was always drawing on the agent for loans, as countless Irish families have done before and since. During 1792 there were new debts to Page totalling 79 guineas, but considering that Arthur had only recently achieved a captain's pay (in the 58th Foot in 1791 with an exchange into the 18th Light Dragoons in 1792), it was almost to his credit that his debts were not larger. Moreover, Lord Buckingham had been replaced as Viceroy in 1789 by Lord Westmorland, of whom the Buckingham clique wrote disparagingly that he had only 'a few good points', among which economy did not figure. Arthur soon found himself serving in a court whose extravagance reminded people of the Sun King.

Debts were perhaps inevitable. They were not a good springboard for matrimony.

*   *   *

By 1792 Arthur Wesley and Kitty Pakenham were openly courting. Even John Page knew about it, for Captain Wesley's letter to him dealing manfully with Locker's case was mailed from Castlepollard, 16 September 1792, and headed 'Coolure' the day before.

Castlepollard was the Pakenhams' nearest village. Its market square always smelt of cow-dung and turf-smoke and its cabin-lined road led to 'the Castle', as everyone called Pakenham Hall. Coolure was the home of Kitty's uncle, Captain Thomas Pakenham, R.N., half an hour's walk from 'the Castle' and standing, three-storied and alone like a house which had lost its street, on the wild shores of Lough Derravaragh.

No more delightful setting could have been found for young love. Thomas Pakenham had all the geniality of a naval captain and the lake was enchanting, especially in the evening, with its islands dotted here and there, its flotillas of wild-fowl and its echoing hills, echoing perhaps to the sound of Arthur's violin. Unlike Garret Wesley in his flat Meath, Kitty's grandfather had had no need to slave away creating hills and dales in this lovely country; nevertheless the park had been duly landscaped in its time, and now Arthur could escort Kitty home by the short cut round the lake and up through her father's 'black red bog', whose draining and cultivation Arthur Young had

admired. Lord Longford was not brilliant like the Professor of
Music, but Young had found it exhilarating to meet 'so spirited an
improver', and Maria Edgeworth's father greatly respected the
character and book-learning of Lord Longford's wife. In any case,
Captain Wesley did not have to deal with him, for he died that very
year and was succeeded by Kitty's brother Tom.

Tom saw no reason to throw away his popular sister on a penniless
suitor. Tom himself was young, and a bachelor; he may also have
been suffering from incipient ideas of grandeur, for when his grandmother died (in January 1794) he was to become an Earl;[9] he would
do nothing to encourage the Castle aide who, now that Mornington
House was sold, found his way more and more often to the Longford
town house in Rutland Square.

Arthur did his best, none the less, to raise himself in the eyes of
Tom and his sister during the first months of 1793. Suddenly he
became articulate and began to speak in Parliament. In January he
seconded the Address from the Throne, deploring the imprisonment of Louis XVI and the invasion of the Netherlands by the
French, and congratulating his own Government on what he hoped
would be a reasonably liberal attitude towards the Roman Catholics.
By February Louis XVI was dead; England and France were at
war; and Ireland, in the manner of high politics, was again placated
with a substantial measure of Catholic Relief. Liberal opinion was
appeased by the abolition of various 'jobs'; but as an antidote to too
much progress the Government suppressed the Irish Volunteers,
so that the green banner with its harp and motto, 'I am new strung',
was again a mockery.

*   *   *

In the spring days of 1793 the thoughts of Arthur Wesley turned to a
more tangible harp and harpist, in Pakenham Hall. Mildly burdened
by debt and as mildly flushed by debate, he decided to try his luck
with Kitty Pakenham. He failed. His offer was rejected because he

9. How a baron could inherit an earldom from his grandmother is explained below for those interested as well as puzzled by the peerage. Thomas
Pakenham (1713–66) married Elizabeth, daughter and sole heiress of Michael
Cuffe, grandson of Alice, sister and co-heir of Ambrose Aungier, 2nd and
last Earl of Longford of the 1st creation. Thomas Pakenham was created
1st Baron Longford (1756) and his widow was created Countess of Longford
(1785). Her son Edward Michael became 2nd Baron Longford (1766) and
his son Thomas became 3rd Baron on his father's death (1792) and 2nd Earl
on his grandmother's death (1794).

could not keep her on a captain's pay in the 18th Light Dragoons, nor on the pay of a major in the 33rd Foot, nor even of a lieutenant-colonel in that same regiment: for thanks to loans from Richard he managed to buy two promotions in the crisis year of 1793. His promotions were not remarkable compared with those of wealthier young men. Kitty's brother Ned bought his majority at seventeen. Kitty Pakenham, in fact, of the 'sweet disposition' and 'well bred politeness' praised by the Edgeworths, was not for him. No doubt she said good-bye to her lover softly and civilly. For him it was the parting of the ways.

This year was also to be the parting of the ways for France and for Europe. Nothing would be the same again. Fanny Burney heard that 4,000 refugees had arrived in England after the 'September Massacres' of the year before, among them Mme de Staël and Fanny's future husband, the Chevalier d'Arblay. M. de Pignerolle had clung on at Angers, but the magnificent establishment which Arthur remembered was reduced by 1792 to five horses. Now, in 1793, the Terror swept France. The *ci-devant* Director of Angers Academy was only one among many hundreds to lose his life: he was arrested at his home and taken to the dungeons of Doué-la-Fontaine. There he died, probably shot, on 27 December.[10]

Arthur could not go back to picking up spilt flowers for the Irish Vicereine, when the European order which he had learnt to love at Angers was being overturned. Could he go forward to being a soldier? His exploits as a Member of Parliament did not encourage him to persevere along the political line. One day in 1793 the Speaker, Sir John Parnell, took him and another young Member, Robert Stewart (afterwards Lord Castlereagh), to dinner with Jonah Barrington, who found Arthur frank, open-hearted and popular, but afterwards recalled his juvenile appearance and unpolished address: 'he occasionally spoke in Parliament, but not successfully, and never on important subjects; and evinced no promise of that unparalleled celebrity and splendour which he has since reached . . .'.

He faced the truth about himself. His problem was not just being a younger son. Part of him was still standing aloof, a dilettante, under the walnut tree in the school playground, but with a violin bow, not a

10. The buildings of the School of Equitation were used as infantry barracks until the beginning of the twentieth century. '*Un peu plus tard* [1944], *une nuit, surviendront les avions anglais qui, derrière eux, ne laisseront que ruines.*' *Le Pays d'Anjou* (1967). Extract from the *Courier de l'Ouest*.

shadowy baton in his hand. With Kitty, he had made one serious attempt to become committed. That had been positive. Now he must take negative action, destroy everything that stood in the way of his military vocation. First, the card-playing in the Dublin clubs. Next, the violin.

He burnt it in the summer of 1793 with his own hands: burnt the hours strolling beside the little waves at Coolure, the bouquet of wine at Angers, the dozing in Brussels, the mooning by the Thames at Eton and the lingering on the ancient bridge over the Boyne at Trim; burnt all the dreams and poetry going back to his childhood when he had listened enraptured to his father's playing.

What was to take their place? Regimental accounts. From now on they took up much of his time, though not unpleasantly, for he was a master of detail. As a lieutenant-colonel with war at hand he had to make payments for recruiting and tracking down deserters: John Oxley for instance, recruited on 20 April, a deserter on the 26th. Then there were the regiment's Military Agents, complaining of the 'enormous Balance' of £3,039 9s. 1¼d. due to them from the elderly Colonel, Lord Cornwallis: 'we never had a Regiment that left this Establishment with their accounts in so unsettled a manner.'[11]

Arthur bent himself to making all these rough financial paths smooth, as he had done (and was still doing) for Richard's affairs in Meath. Figures had no terror for him; indeed, as Duke of Wellington he often told his friend, Robert Gleig, about his special talent for 'rapid and correct calculation'; another future biographer, Sir Herbert Maxwell, thought that he might have been a great financier if his destiny had not driven him to soldiering and politics.

Only a few of his friends touched in their memoirs on the loss of a musician and his violin. One added sombrely that Wellington always disliked any mention of this 'circumstance'.[12]

11. Charles Cornwallis, 1st Marquess (1738–1805), Colonel of the 33rd Foot. Surrendered at Yorktown in American War of Independence, 1781. Governor-General of India, 1786, of Ireland, 1798–1801; returned to India, 1805, as Governor-General in succession to the Marquess Wellesley and died there.

12. Lord Francis Leveson-Gower, afterwards Earl of Ellesmere and author of *Reminiscences of the Duke of Wellington*, p. 80. J. W. Croker in his *Correspondence and Diaries*, vol. I, p. 337, footnote, says that he heard the story from Wellington's friend in India, Colonel Shawe. 'Some circumstances occurred,' Shawe told Croker, 'which made him reflect that this was not a soldierly accomplishment and took up too much of his time and thoughts; and he burned his fiddles and never played again.'

He had made the break. Now, as so often after a climax, there lay before him not the immediate vision of the promised land, but the frustration of asking and asking for the means to get there.

*   *   *

He found himself compelled for the next two or three years to do the very thing which in later life he could not endure in others. To beg for favours. To write polite letters requesting patronage, including those necessary but humiliating paragraphs in which he declared himself totally unworthy of the favours requested. There was still a certain amount of darting between military and civilian corridors, according as doors seemed to open or shut in his face; but the trend was always towards the Army.

Would Richard request Mr Pitt to desire Lord Westmorland to put him in one of the flank corps being formed that summer of 1793 to support the Dutch? 'If they are to go abroad, they will be obliged to take officers from the line, and they may as well take me as anybody else. . . .' But somewhere between London and Dublin the cup slipped and he was still a Castle aide-de-camp.

Another autumn came and another expedition was planned, this time to the Normandy coast. The 33rd were to join it under the command of Lord Moira. An affluent linen-draper agreed to service Arthur's debts, and he resigned his Trim seat. Dangan Castle had also been disposed of. Neither had the old pull, since he was no longer allowed to ride over to Pakenham Hall on a September day and pay his court to Kitty.

1793 passed gloomily into 1794. Nothing had come of Lord Moira's expedition. Anti-Jacobin madness engulfed England. *Habeas corpus* was suspended in May 1794. It became a crime to advocate constitutional change or to hold large meetings. Botany Bay was filling up with 'felons' who, if they had been active forty years later, might have become respectable leaders of Reform. In the garrison that was Ireland, government informers were busy. Lady Morgan remembered that the Castle authorities 'ordered out more troops and ordered up more wine. The state butler and the first aide-de-camp were kept in perpetual activity. The wine was declared prime and the times perilous.' Wolfe Tone was trapped and exiled to America, while his United Irish Society followed the Volunteers into liquidation. There were no spurs to be won in the battened-down island.

At last Lord Moira's army was ready to sail again. He was to reinforce the Duke of York in Flanders with 10,000 new men including Arthur Wesley and his 33rd.

Some time before he sailed a brief but far from unimportant letter was sent to Kitty Pakenham, dated bleakly 'Barracks *Tuesday*'. Arthur had just received Lord Longford's final determination against their marriage. This was punishment enough, he said, for any offence he might have caused by having written to her recently and by writing again now. Nevertheless he could not accept that all was over. As Lord Longford's decision was founded upon 'prudential motives', an improvement in Arthur's situation could alter everything. There followed a sentence of which the last phrase was decisively to alter Arthur's life. If something did occur to make Kitty and her brother change their minds—'my mind will still remain the same'.

To an honourable man, those seven words would be binding.

In June 1794 he left Cork for Ostend, privileged to see active service for the first time—and under the worst possible conditions.

* * *

Nothing could have turned out more fortunately. He saw the effects of a divided command, of a winter campaign in a bitter climate, of no properly organized food supply or winter clothing, of local inhabitants who preferred the enemy to their allies, and above all of a prolonged and undisciplined retreat. In short, as he told Stanhope forty-five years later when his friend was suggesting that the Dutch campaign must have been very useful to him: 'Why—I learnt what one ought not to do, and that is always something.'

Lieutenant-Colonel Wesley's initiation began at Ostend, where he was put in command of a brigade which he brought round, as a rear-guard, by sea to Antwerp. Then came a chaotic and hopeless attempt to hold Belgium, followed by an autumnal retreat into Holland. He had never been particularly robust and his health began to crack. A letter to his doctor, Alexander Lindsay, brought back an anxious reply on 2 August, with full instructions for dealing with this return of his 'aguish complaint from fatigue, damp etc.'. All aguish illnesses were bilious in origin, wrote Lindsay; he must therefore repeatedly take a pill containing three grains of calomel combined with three grains of the Cathartic Extract—'you may recollect the time you was attacked . . . you took two or three doses . . . &

afterwards took the saline mixture . . . & I believe you took a vomit before taking either . . .'. The letter ended by recalling that after all this the patient 'got quite well'. It sounded reassuring, and seems to have been as good a preparation as any for an arduous stand upon the River Waal from October 1794 until January in the new year.

General Winter arrived in November 1794 with ferocious frosts and fought on the side of the French. When Colonel Wesley thought the enemy were about to go into winter quarters until the spring— 'I think it impossible for any troops (even the French) to keep the field in this severe weather'—they came speeding down the frozen canals, rolled up the Dutch, seized all their ports and sent the exhausted red-coats staggering towards Hanover into a new intensity of cold and wretchedness.

Arthur had planned to go home on leave for the sake of his health. His personal *malaise* was matched by general disillusionment. Prince Ernest, later Duke of Cumberland, wrote to his brother the Prince of Wales in November: 'I openly declare to you I wish myself most sincerely back to Pall Mall.' In order if possible to silence the rumbles in Parliament against Pitt and his bungled campaign, the chief command was withdrawn in December from the Duke of York. 'To say that I shall not feel this as a severe blow,' protested the Duke vehemently to his royal father, 'would be contrary to my own character . . .'. The public, however, viewed His Royal Highness's character rather differently:

> *The noble Duke of York*
> *He had ten thousand men,*
> *He marched them up to the top of the hill,*
> *And he marched them down again.*

As one of the unhappy ten thousand who had done the marching, Arthur also hoped for home in December. But he was kept an extra six weeks on the banks of the Waal by the French, sleeping in his clothes and turning out once or twice every night. It was no compensation that they were 'perpetually chattering' to his men across the river and offering to dance the *carmagnole* for their amusement.

Nor was there any encouragement from the high command. 'I was left there to myself with my regiment . . . thirty miles from headquarters,' he later told his friend, Lord Ellesmere, 'which latter was a scene of jollifications, and I do not think that I was once visited by the

Commander in Chief.' One scene of jollification Arthur never forgot.
A despatch from allied headquarters was brought in while the port
was circulating.

'That will keep till tomorrow,' laughed the officer in command,
airily waving it away. Another kind of 'jollification' was described by
Prince Adolphus to the Prince of Wales. 'The life we lead here is not
the most amusing; we are however now pretty well off for girls, &
this renders it less tiresome.'

'The infantry regiments,' continued Wellington to Ellesmere,
'were as good in proper hands as they are now [1837], but the system
was wretched.' The system, in fact, was a scandalous traffic in
commissions developed over the past ten years by which army
brokers ("rascally crimps") created a flood of new field officers out
of anyone who could pay, from schoolboys to keepers of gambling
dens and worse.[13] The military historian, Sir John Fortescue, is
more severe than Wellington and says that the new recruits were as
bad as the new officers: 'They were the off-scouring of the nation,
who could be purchased at a cheap rate by the crimps—criminals,
decrepit old men, raw boys, the half-witted, the feeble-minded,
even downright lunatics.' The wagon-train was named after London's
most notorious prison, 'The Newgate Blues'.[14]

It is significant that Arthur did not at that time find anything
radically wrong with an army invigorated even by this appalling
material. 'Many of the regiments were excellent', he recalled to
Stanhope; it was the man in authority who was generally 'quite an
imposter; in fact, no one knew anything of the management of any
army . . .'.

At headquarters no one knew anything at all. Those fighting in the
field had to depend for information on letters from England. 'The
real reason why I succeeded in my own campaigns,' concluded
Wellington to Stanhope, 'is because I was always on the spot—I saw
everything; and did everything for myself.'

Miserable and hungry, Arthur's brigade marched doggedly

13. Sir Walter Scott stated that baby boys and even young ladies might
have commissions bought for them: 'We know ourselves one fair dame who
drew the pay of captain in the dragoons, and was probably not much less
fit for service than some who actually did duty' (*Memoir of the Duke of York*,
1827. Quoted by R. Glover, p. 148).

14. However, Glover's *Peninsular Preparation*, which is in part an apologia
for the Duke of York, points out that it was something to have a wagon-train
at all and without the Duke's efforts there would have been none.

towards the River Ems and so to Bremen and the Weser, more and more often breaking rank to loot, or to add their frozen bodies to the snowy heaps of dead men and horses which lined the roads. A certain old Colonel Watson of the Guards had warned Wesley back in Belgium what to expect:

> You little know what you are going to meet with. You will often have no dinner at all. I mean literally no dinners, and not merely roughing it on a beefsteak or a bottle of port wine.

The Duke of York, languishing at home, received a horrifying report from General Walmoden in February 1795 that the English army was destroyed, except for the officers, their carriages and huge baggage trains. (Prince Ernest, however, insisted that he too, as an officer, had 'very nigh kicked'.) This was another thing which Arthur Wesley learnt not to do: not to save the officers' carriages first. Indeed, in the Peninsula officers would be amazingly lucky if they possessed any carriages to be saved.

Emphatically there had been no spurs to win; though Lieutenant-Colonel Wesley was at least congratulated by headquarters on an action he had fought at Boxtel, in Holland, on 15 September 1794. This was the first military engagement of his life. There had been a charge by a French column. With commendable steadiness his infantry obeyed Wesley's orders to hold back their fire until the last moment. Then, at his command, they drove off the enemy with rolling volleys of musketry. Thoughts about these tactics, about a proper supply-service, and about officers who looked after their men, accompanied Wesley on his voyage home at the beginning of March 1795, and remained with him for the rest of his life.

*   *   *

When he arrived back in Ireland a palace revolution with nation-wide consequences was about to sweep the Castle.

The old junta had successfully opposed a fresh attempt by Pitt to introduce Catholic Relief. Fitzwilliam, a reforming Lord Lieutenant who had replaced Lord Westmorland, was recalled to England on 25 March. Dublin went into mourning, shops closed and his carriage was drawn by the people to the waterside through streets draped in black. So ended the 'Fitzwilliam episode', as it was called. But it was an episode which started a gale.

'Here is a whirlwind in our Country,' wrote Maria Edgeworth in April 1795 to her aunt, Mrs Buxton, 'and no angel to direct it, though many booted and spurred desire no better than to ride *in* it.' Within six months the whirlwind had become uncontrollable. The prohibited United Irishmen burst up again like dragon's teeth, sworn now to bring off a French invasion of Ireland followed by an armed rebellion. 'All that I crave for my own part,' Maria wrote again in January 1796, 'is that if I am to have my throat cut, it may not be by a man with his face blackened by charcoal.'

Amid this excitement, home for Arthur merely meant yet another round of begging and rebuff. Everything seemed to be repeating itself—Arthur back at the Castle as a frustrated aide-de-damp, Arthur M.P. for Trim again, lodging at Fosterstown, Arthur speaking in Parliament, on 13 March, immediately upon his return. But gay Lord Westmorland, the Viceroy who had particularly favoured himself and Kitty, had gone. Who could tell whether Fitzwilliam's successor, Lord Camden, would show any interest in the absent Lord Mornington's younger brother? There was a new urgency in Arthur's pleas for something to do.

With desperate optimism, probably inspired and certainly backed by Richard, he decided to open with a bumper request: to become Secretary at War—no less. It was a forlorn hope but worth trying, for as Secretary at War he would leap from scarcely £500 a year to £1,800. And to show that he could fight in Parliament as well as in the field, he defended his old chief, Westmorland, against an attack by Grattan. He had still not decided whether he was a soldier or a politician. Lord Camden was unimpressed, and in June Arthur had lowered his sights to a civil department—something either at the Revenue or Treasury Boards. 'I assure you nothing but the circumstances under which I labour would induce me to trouble Your Excellency's Government,' he began miserably, and then went on to flog himself into the necessary posture of abasement:

> . . . I hope I shall not be supposed to place myself too high in desiring to be taken into consideration . . . [but if these Boards] are considered too high for me, of course you will say so . . . . You will perhaps be surprised at my desiring a civil instead of a military office. It is certainly a departure from the line which I prefer.

Beggars can't be choosers. He ended as he had begun with a bitter reference to 'the necessities under which I labour'. Nothing came of it. The last wild throw, made by Richard possibly without Arthur's knowledge, was to offer his brother as Surveyor-General of the Ordnance—a position already occupied by Kitty's uncle, Captain Thomas Pakenham of Coolure. Lord Camden agreed, but Arthur himself turned it down for obvious reasons. An indignant Tom Pakenham attributed the attempt to oust him to 'a deep laid scheme of Mornington's.'

This embarrassing affair seems thoroughly to have shaken Arthur's confidence and health. At any rate, he is next heard of at Southampton in September 1795, resolved to sail to the West Indies with the 33rd, but laid up with a bout of fever. His physician, Dr Hunter, found it necessary to prescribe four kinds of pills ('A. is the bark, B. is calomel and opium, C. is quassia and D. is another mixture of calomel') besides 'the Strasberg liniment' consisting of strongly camphorated spirit of wine, tincture of cantharides and tincture of opium for local rheumatic pains, and a change of air if only ten miles away from Southampton. Should the bark prove purgative he must add three drops of laudanum to each dose, and if the Strasberg liniment should fail to effect a cure ('Can be used with the best success for dogs and horses') he must strengthen it with two table-spoonfuls of melted grease or the fat of a freshly killed fowl.

While Richard and Dr Hunter thus worked hard on Arthur's behalf, Lord Camden wrote that he would be 'very glad' to make some arrangement satisfactory to Colonel Wesley 'against you come back from the West Indies'. There was a genial touch of humbug in the Viceregal phrase, 'against you come back'. If Arthur was not killed either by the French or by a tropical fever it would probably be because he was drowned before either of the other enemies had a chance to attack; and in fact it was from this last fate that he was saved by a miracle.[15] Of his convoy, seven transports were wrecked by a storm on Chesil Beach soon after they had left Portsmouth. After waiting a few more weeks until December, the fleet again put out to sea, this time in the teeth of a winter gale which not surprisingly dispersed them for good. Wesley's ship was among the lucky ones which after seven wild weeks on the ocean were blown back to England. It was by now February 1796. The 33rd wintered at Poole. In April they were turned round again and sent in advance of Wesley to India.

15. In the annual return of casualties, 1 January 1793 to 31 December 1798, the 33rd lost 430 men dead but only six of them killed by the enemy.

India! In contemporary jargon, a switch from the West to the East Indies meant stepping out of the white man's graveyard into the treasure-house of the Orient. Richard felt that after so many setbacks he could not advise Arthur to decline such an 'advantageous station'. As soon as his constituents, his debts and his health—the last two still troublesome—made it possible for him to sail, he must catch up with his regiment.

So on 20 June 1796 Richard wrote to his cousin, Sir Chichester Fortescue, Ulster King of Arms, with all the warmth and cynicism of which this strange man was capable:

> My dear brother Arthur is now at Portsmouth waiting for a wind for India. . . . I shall feel his loss in a variety of ways most bitterly and none more than the management of Trim, where by his excellent judgement, amiable manners, admirable temper and firmness he has entirely restored the interest of my family.

Perhaps Sir Chichester might temporarily stop the gap? He would be required to attend only two meetings at Trim annually, and Richard's 'Trimmers' could be beguiled with a deceptive *au revoir*:

> Pray remember me kindly to all my friends at Trim, do not let them suppose that Arthur is not to return to them, and talk of my intentions of going to visit them.

There was to be no visit and no return—or so Lord Mornington devoutly hoped. After Arthur had gone Richard firmly guided Sir Chichester into the family seat, writing to him a year later with graciousness if not tact:

> I am happy to have you safe seated for Trim, a seat which I hope you will fill for the remainder of your life, as I think if Arthur has good luck he will be called to act on a greater stage than dear Dublin.

Richard himself had parted from dear Dublin some time ago; now his dominating role as Arthur's lofty superior ceased also. Next time they met their relationship was to be more balanced and in some senses even reversed. But whatever his faults, Richard had put his back into the problem of Arthur. King George III might complain to

Pitt that Lord Mornington's 'total want of attention' to his Windsor constituents had 'rendered him really obnoxious to them'. He had not been inattentive to Arthur.

Once the decision to leave England had been taken it was mainly a question of how the colonel should deal with his debts—for Arthur, through rapid transfers, was a full colonel at twenty-seven. Lord Camden had seen him before he sailed from Ireland (as he told Lord Mornington) and been so much impressed with his 'propriety and spirit' in going to the East Indies that he longed to relieve his mind over his debts. On the other hand, there were persons who had prior claims on the Viceroy's patronage. If consistently with those claims he could give Arthur a sinecure office, 'he might depend upon my doing it . . .'.

Fortunately Arthur had decided to depend upon himself and choose a soldier's life. A valedictory letter from the Viceroy shortly before he sailed for India showed how right he was. Should a seat at the Revenue Board fall vacant wrote the slippery Camden he would certainly try to earmark it for Arthur—except that Arthur was unable to accept it and it could not be kept open.

As Arthur waited at Portsmouth for the fair wind his debts were still outstanding but under control. There were substantial loans from Richard, and £955 14s. 8½d. owing to the agent, John Page, who thought this 'serious sum' ought to be mentioned to Lord Mornington in case Colonel Wesley never returned. But if the colonel felt the slightest 'delicacy' about speaking of the debt, let him just leave a written paper with my Lord; 'may all happiness & success attend you wherever you go'.

*   *   *

How, then, did Arthur Wesley stand with himself and the world at this crucial point in his life?

There were no regrets for Dublin or Meath: he had called Ireland when overseas two years earlier, 'that country of scoundrels'; now it was rushing headlong into rebellion. Indeed, as Arthur Wesley sailed for India, Wolfe Tone sailed for France, to raise help for the rebels. To leave Ireland seemed sane, to go there inexplicable, as George III made clear when he enquired about the whereabouts of Fanny Burney's young nephew:

'He is—in Ireland, Sir.'

'In Ireland! What does he do in Ireland? What does he go there for?'

'His father took him, Sir.'

'And what does his father take him to Ireland for?' Fanny was cornered.

'Because—he is an Irishman, Sir!'

Arthur was twenty-seven years old, chronically frustrated and in constant ill-health. No doubt the two were connected. His income was paltry, and his debts, though 'of a size that would not much disturb a person of less scrupulous honor', had necessitated odious begging letters which made an indelible impression. Two years later he wrote to Richard from India that he expected nothing from Camden, having long determined 'if possible not to think upon that subject . . .'.

Indigence and indebtedness had killed young love. If Lord Longford, Kitty's brother, had adopted Arthur Young's advice on how to assess a prospective husband—' 'Tis true I hear many excellent things of him; but does he farm hugely? Are his turnips clean? . . . these are points much more to the purpose than the common rubbish of character ye common mortals attend to'—the answer must have been that there was not a turnip, clean or unclean, to offer Kitty. Nothing but the 'rubbish of character'.

Among the 'rubbish' lay a secret resolve to read. The voyage to India gave it a fine excuse. From Dublin Arthur brought his small library, to which he added in England over fifty pounds' worth of books. Among the Oriental dictionaries, grammars and maps, the military manuals and histories of India, were works of a more general interest. Voltaire, Rousseau, Frederick the Great, Maréchal de Saxe, Plutarch's *Lives* and the *Caesaris Commentaria*—in Latin; for law, Blackstone's *Commentaries*; for economics, Adam Smith's *Wealth of Nations*; for philosophy, Locke and *Human Understanding* reappear; for theology, five volumes of Paley gilt; and for the good of his Anglo-Irish soul, twenty-four volumes of Swift at 2s. 10d.[16]

At least one person had an inkling of something else which lay

16. In *The Duke*, pp. 54–65, Mr Guedalla has studied in fascinating detail the books which Arthur Wesley took to India. He includes a comparison between Arthur's list of 1796 and Napoleon's '*Bibliotèque du Camp*' of 1798. Briefly, the two lists had only five volumes in common, namely the first five titles named in Arthur's list above. Napoleon excelled in the classics, for instead of Caesar (Arthur's sole representative) he could boast of Tacitus, Livy, Thucydides, Homer, Virgil and Polybius.

among the 'rubbish'—something rare but not yet definable. There was a Dr Warren (probably Richard Warren the court physician) whom Arthur had consulted as well as Dr Hunter before leaving England. 'I have been attending a young man,' said this Dr Warren to a friend, 'whose conversation is the most extraordinary I have ever listened to . . . if this young man lives, he must one day be Prime Minister.'

What was it in Arthur's manner which told Dr Warren that he had the necessary sense of direction, critical understanding, vigour, personality and vision? Or was it in the subjects he talked about that he revealed the mystic trade-mark? One guess is as good as another. But if this slight young man, recently sick and battered by the incompetence of his superiors, held forth on his prospects in India— his chance to emulate Clive's victories, to extend the settlement of Cornwallis without the controversy, and to achieve the power of Warren Hastings without his suspected corruption—the doctor may well have thought himself in the presence of either brain fever or genius.

Arthur and his trunkload of books followed the 33rd at the end of June. Ireland was already a month away. It had been high time to break out from the Castle, where his spirit had been a prisoner for more than nine years. Perhaps, indeed, he had never yet known what it was to feel truly free.

4 Ascendancy in the East

The Colonel of the 33rd had one consuming idea: to reach India and begin his career in earnest.

The voyage to the Cape he found tolerable, as he raced to overtake his regiment in a cruiser. Cape Town itself was enlivened by the presence of two sisters, Jemima and Henrietta Smith, also on their way out to India. Jemima was 'a satirical and incorrigible flirt'. He paid court to Henrietta who had a 'pretty little figure and a lovely neck'. ('Neck' was the polite term for bosom.) No doubt she was glad to receive it, for young Captain George Elers who noticed the lovely neck also remembered that her admirer was 'all life and spirits . . . with a remarkably large aquiline nose, a clear blue eye . . . remarkably clean in his person . . . spoke at this time remarkably quickly'—in fact, a remarkable person.[1]

The second half of the passage, confined to a slow troop-ship and lasting from September 1796 to mid-February 1797, was in Wesley's own words 'most tedious'. Neither his travelling library nor the impact of strange continents and oceans—the whales and flying-fish, the coral and palms, the wafts of perfumed air from spice islands and of oven-hot offshore winds from Madras, the final voyage up the Hooghly River into the Garden Reach and at length Calcutta itself—none of these novelties could take the edge off his impatience. He never wasted time on descriptive prose. 'Most tedious' remained his first and last comment on a passage to India which must be regarded as one of the most significant in British history.

*   *   *

Fortunately there was a resident in Calcutta when Arthur arrived who did not share his reticence. William Hickey had gone to India as a servant of the East India Company to get rich. 'Cut off half a dozen rich fellows' heads,' had been a friend's parting advice on presenting

1. *Memoirs of George Elers*, pp. 46–7. G. Elers (1777–1842), Captain in the 12th Foot. He has much to say of Wellington that is interesting and amusing, but in later life was prejudiced against him. Elers was a cousin of Maria Edgeworth.

Hickey with a sword, 'and so return a Nabob.' Twenty years older
than Wesley, Hickey had made the Coromandel coast below Madras
on the very day that Arthur was born—1 May 1769. His India diaries,
though capricious in their judgements of people, fill with welcome
gossip the gap which Arthur left.

With the beginning of the hot season only a month away, Calcutta
immediately whirled the 33rd and its colonel into hectic festivities.
There were gentlemen's 'seats' all round the city and where there
were seats there were feasts—'glorious dishes of Calipash and Calipee'
with fat venison, turtle and rich savouries. On St Patrick's day
Colonel Wesley, as a newly arrived Irishman, was asked to preside
at the usual dinner, which he did, notes Hickey, 'with peculiar credit
to himself'.[2] Three days later another Irish soldier arrived, famous for
the race he had founded at Doncaster, Major-General John St Leger.
Hickey gave a house-party for him at his 'little château' at Chinsurah,
an imposing brick and stucco mansion with verandahs and Doric
pillars, to which Colonel Wesley was invited. They rose early every
morning with keen appetites for breakfast, then played trick-track
(back-gammon) until 3.30 when they dressed for dinner at precisely
4 P.M. Thereafter, 'we pushed the claret about very freely'. What
with St Leger being a notorious associate of the Heir Apparent and
all Calcutta wishing to do him proud, Hickey fell into a state of
continuous excess, for 'I never could flinch from the bottle when in
jovial society'. A time came, however, when Hickey not only flinched
but tried to flee. The most 'dangerous' parties, he found, were those
held by the 33rd. Hearing that Colonel Wesley 'with a few other
equally strong heads' was to be present at one hard-drinking session
to which he had been invited, he at first declared himself too ill to
join their 'jovial crew'. Unwisely he later yielded to the 33rd's
persuasion and found himself round a table with 'eight as strong-
headed fellows as could be found in Hindostan'. Twenty-two healths
were drunk in large goblets, after which guests were permitted to
continue in glasses of a more moderate size. At 2 A.M. the jovial crew
staggered out to their palanquins and were carried back to town.
Hickey's excruciating headache lasted for two days and nights.
'Indeed, a more severe debauch I never was engaged in in any part of
the world.' He had not been trained at Dublin Castle.

2. Hickey puts these and subsequent events in 1799, but all or most of
them must have occurred in 1797. He wrote his memoirs at Beaconsfield in
1813.

And so the stifling spring passed into summer. They celebrated the King's birthday on 4 June with yet another glorious debauch. With General St Leger seated on Hickey's right and Colonel Wesley on his left, they enjoyed the very best champagne, hock, claret and Madeira, followed by 'several choice songs' from junior members of the 33rd including catches and glees, and to crown all a solo rendering of *The British Grenadiers* by the General himself. Next morning at breakfast all but the General's young aide-de-camp, Captain De Lancey, complained of 'slight sickness'. A 'hair of the same dog' soon set them to rights.

Despite this haze of jollity the 33rd were supposed to be preparing for an autumn campaign.

*   *   *

Once again, Arthur had plunged into a land crying out for change. India was full of troubles, among them being multiple corruption. Rapacity was not the prerogative of any one man, institution or colour. Warren Hastings was picked out for special notice:

> *And heron Hastings . . .*
> *So wont to cram on Asiatic fish;*[3]

but in fact every grade of the East India Company, from its Court of Directors at Leadenhall Street in the City of London to its network of military and civil servants out East; every rank in His Majesty's Army; the numerous independent merchants living in the three British Presidencies of Bengal, Madras and Bombay; and the whole array of native Indian rulers ranging from Moslem sultans and Hindu rajahs to hordes of freebooters scouring the villages—all alike expected to make their fortunes quickly and easily out of India. Pitt's creation of an India Board and Cornwallis's systematic reforms in 1793 had been intended to demonstrate that India was no longer the Company's private Eden. Cornwallis's successor, however, Sir John Shore, was in Arthur's opinion too 'timid' for the times.[4] There had

3. Hasting's trial had ended in acquittal the year before Arthur sailed. 'Peter Pindar', the author of this couplet, was Dr Walcot (1738–1819), a physician who afterwards took Holy Orders and published several volumes of immensely popular satiric verse.

4. John Shore, 1st Baron Teignmouth (1751–1834), son of a supercargo (marine superintendent) to the East India Company. On his return to England, he was elected to the Committee for the Abolition of the Slave-Trade, and joined the Clapham Sect.

been trouble in Oudh. Arthur admitted that Shore's recent negotiations with the Nabob of Oudh to increase his annual tribute and
dismiss the French sympathizers among his ministers had been
successful. But it showed a poor spirit to resign immediately afterwards, as Shore did, 'lest another Storm should arise of which he
would be obliged to see the End'. The spectacle of a 'timid' Governor-
General must have contributed to the Wellingtonian idea of duty as
it took shape in his maturing mind.

The affair of the Nabob of Oudh illustrated the complexities of the
Indian game. Incomparably larger than all the European territories,
the Indian princely states, including Oudh, covered most of the huge
sub-continent. There had been a time when the Mogul Empire,
centred in Delhi, imposed some kind of unity on these states. But
by 1797 the 250-year-old Empire had fallen into decay, and the
Europeans, having inserted themselves into the interstices, were
pushing their way through the ruined fabric like banyan or peepul
trees in a crumbling fort, until nothing remained but heaps of loosened
stones and spreading trees. Britain had her powerful root-system.
French influence, despite Clive's victories, remained strong in its
trading centres; and there was a largish piece of Portugal at Goa.

The problem was, how could the two main European rivals
strengthen themselves against each other in India, now that war had
broken out between them in Europe?

One way was by getting control of an Indian princely state. The
French had done so in Oudh. Another was by attacking the Dutch
colonists in Java or the Spanish in the Philippines, if the shifting
alliances and hostilities in Europe changed them from harmless
planters into springboards for French invasion. News from the
European battlegrounds always reached India long after the event,
like light from a star. So in this war-game the most dashing schemes
were often absurdly out of date.

*   *   *

Almost on arrival Colonel Wesley found himself in the thick of it. He
wrote with suppressed excitement to Mornington on 17 April 1797
that there was to be a large expedition against the Spanish colony of
Manila in the Philippines. (Spain by 1796 had dropped out of the
coalition against France.) The 33rd was to sail with the contingent
from Bengal; his own name had been mentioned as the Deputy

Governor's choice for chief command. As for the alternative names suggested, to put 'such people' in command, he wrote witheringly, would be to throw away our ships and soldiers. Better to leave the Spaniards in peaceful possession.

His contempt for his rivals was matched by a consummate though reasoned confidence in himself, founded on the large force which would be at his disposal and the equally large dose of 'pusillanimity' at the disposal of the enemy. His own 'exertions' would compensate for his want of experience.

Here was a great commander in embryo.

At the back of his mind there were also his debts. 'Of course the Chief Command of this expedition would make my fortune,' he burst out at the end of this candid letter. 'Going upon it at all will enable me to free myself from debt, therefore you may easily conceive that I am not very anxious for the conclusion of a peace at this moment.'

His half-serious fears of peace were premature, since negotiations initiated by Pitt with the French Directory had foundered on the question of the return to France of her lost colonies, and were broken off in September 1797. But by 20 May he knew that his misgivings about the chief command were justified. He was not to lead the Bengal force after all. Lord Hobart, the Governor, despite the 'entreaties' of his friends, had selected General Braithwaite on grounds of seniority. With a good adjutant-general, a good quarter-master-general and a good army, Lord Hobart argued, the Commander-in-Chief did not matter. 'But he is mistaken,' wrote Arthur severely, with the authentic accents of the future, 'if he supposes that a good high-spirited army can be kept in order by other means than by the abilities & firmness of the Commander in Chief.'

Two months later Arthur informed Richard that he had not heard from Lord Hobart lately, as 'between ourselves' Hobart had written him a very angry letter, 'such as I have been unaccustomed to receive & will never submit to'. Arthur professed not to know what he had done to offend. But if he had lectured Hobart on how to run an army in the manner of his letter to Richard, Hobart's irritation was scarcely surprising. A snub delivered to General St Leger by Colonel Wesley about the same time confirms the impression of a new, sharp intellect at work in India; one crackling with pent-up energy, bold enough to say No to anybody, but less ready than formerly to take No for an answer.

Whether or not because of his horsy enthusiasm, St Leger supported a memorandum to establish Indian Horse Artillery. 'Without
being regularly bred to Artillery,' commented Colonel Wesley, 'it is
not difficult to perceive the advantages which would attend such an
establishment. . . .' It was no more difficult, however, to see the disadvantages. There was no supply of horses. The most Colonel Wesley
would consider was an emergency unit of eight horse-drawn guns and
four howitzers; for the rest, bullocks were best.

There was probably more to it than St Leger's horses versus
Wesley's bullocks. Wesley's letter gives a feeling that he was not
going to have anyone, even the man destined to assume supreme
command of the whole Manila expedition, careering about the East,
smoking 'sagars', roaring out patriotic songs and turning his battlefields into Doncaster races. Indeed, small things were happening
under Wesley's nose to cause him reservations about the rip-roaring
society of which he was now an ornament.

*   *   *

After three months 'entirely free from ague', he had contracted a
slight fever in June. Then there was the gambling of the 33rd.
Captain Norcott, a young relative of his friend General Cunninghame, was suddenly ruined. He had played for the first time and
lost £600. Arthur paid Norcott's debt, making him promise never
to gamble again. Now he asked the general to take over his debt.
The wretched Norcott had contributed two-thirds of his pay, but
this only accounted for £160. Arthur could not wait, 'more particularly as I am obliged to borrow myself'. Another young protégé in
the 33rd, brother of Edward Cooke, a prominent politician at Dublin
Castle, broke down in health and was ordered home. But he bought
so many 'curiosities of the east' for his lady-friends that Arthur had
to lend him £100 before he could embark.

At last in July 1797 came news from Arthur's family. Mornington
was to be Governor of Madras at once and afterwards Governor-
General of India. Congratulations poured from Arthur's pen—so
glad Mornington was coming—sure he would manage to preserve
his health—would do everything possible to help.

Having indirectly heard of the possibility of Mornington's appointment a fortnight earlier, he had already sent home some blunt views
on the Indian scene. Taking the 'natives' and the climate together,

India was 'a miserable country to live in, and I now begin to think that a man well deserves some of the wealth which is sometimes brought home, for having spent his life here.' Among the class of 'mischievous' and 'deceitful' agents and dealers whom he mostly met, he had not come across a Hindu with one good quality—'and the Mussulmans are worse . . .' One could not punish offenders with imprisonment or whipping, as at home, for this would cause loss of caste; in any case their learned men (if Arthur's Indian histories were to be believed) taught that God punished crime which was in their eyes quite sufficient. 'Notwithstanding all this,' he assured Mornington, 'being here for a few years would place you in so high a situation for the remainder of your life, that I should like to see you Governor-General.' Not that he himself expected to derive more advantages from his brother's appointment than he would from any other Governor-General, owing to 'rules on patronage in India'. (If the brothers intended to obey these rules, they were the only people in India who did.) It was sad that Mornington had to leave his wife and children behind. This was perhaps mitigated by the news that their mother had at length visited her daughter-in-law, Richard's former mistress and since 1794 his wife. Arthur believed that 'nothing but absurdity prevented it being done sooner'. On the other hand, their mother had only taken her absurd line from a desire to do right, so the Morningtons need no longer feel any uneasiness on this delicate subject. 'It must be a pleasant thing for you,' added Arthur warmly in his role of family adviser and peacemaker, 'upon coming away.' He had to confess, however, that he was 'a bad judge of the pain a man feels on parting from his family'.

Compared with the heavily burdened Mornington—five children for ever illegitimate, despite their mother having been made an honest woman—Arthur seemed bleakly free from family cares. He may have intended a rueful reference to his own failure to become a married man. It is more probable that he was presenting himself rather cynically as one absorbed in the here and now who neither felt nor wished to feel the pain of partings. How far he was really like that is another matter. Part of him felt bitterly about his adolescence, rejecting sentiment. On the other hand, he complained more than once during this summer of 1797 of not having received a single letter from home since he had left in the previous June.

*   *   *

Meanwhile preparations for the Manila expedition kept him sweating at his desk. He was aware that 'the higher classes of Europeans' kept healthy by taking more care of themselves and using more 'conveniences' and 'luxuries' than the lower orders. Before embarkation he therefore issued thirty-six paragraphs of hygiene drill, to be observed by the men on board ship.

> No. 3. Each man's hammock to be scrubbed at least once a fortnight.
> No. 15. On Sundays the men to draw up in their hats, coats, gaiters and accoutrements to hear Divine Service.
> No. 21. The men to wash their feet and legs every morning and evening and if possible every day to have water thrown over them.
> No. 31. A quart of spirits between 8 men but (No. 32) diluted always with three parts water.

In the event, it was a member of the 'higher classes' who failed lamentably to add his three parts of water. William Hickey had persuaded Arthur to take on as chaplain to the 33rd the nephew of his friend Mr Scawen, a young man named Blunt. They sailed in August. After only three days at sea the unfortunate clergyman got 'abominably' drunk and rushed out of his cabin stark naked among the soldiers and sailors, 'talking all sorts of bawdy and ribaldry and singing scraps of the most blackguard and indecent songs'. Such was his shame on afterwards hearing of these 'irregularities' that he shut himself up and refused to eat or speak. Colonel Wesley was informed. He instantly rowed across to Blunt's vessel and sent for him. The wretched man declined to appear. Wesley then descended to Blunt's cabin and talked to him like a father:

> . . . what had passed was not of the least consequence as no one would think the worse of him for the little irregularities committed in a moment of forgetfulness . . . the most correct and cautious men were liable to be led astray by convivial society, and no blame ought to attach to a cursory debauch. . . .

Colonel Wesley's broad-minded and kindly attempts to 'reconcile Mr Blunt to himself' were not successful. In ten days he forced himself to die of contrition.

Apart from the occasional tragi-comic failure, Arthur at twenty-eight had become the successful father, physician, welfare officer and banker to his men. The Manila expedition, however, did not prove a major test of his new skills.

He had got as far as the Malay Archipelago and was writing an encouraging letter to the patient John Page in Ireland—he had *not* been wrecked coming out of the Hooghly River as reported and would pay off two years' interest in four or five months—when disastrous news reached Bengal. There had been, in Hickey's vague but agitated words, 'an alarming mutiny of our seamen'. Lord Spencer, First Lord of the Admiralty, put it with spine-chilling precision: 'The Channel fleet is now lost to the country as much as if it was at the bottom of the sea.' On top of these momentous mutinies at Spithead and the Nore which, until settled, were a threat to England's life-line, came the news that yet another of her allies, Austria, had followed Prussia and Spain into a peace treaty with the enemy. Vast French armies had been released from Europe for aggression round the world, while the defenders of the British Empire in India were standing off Manila, a thousand miles away. The Bengal and Madras armies were abruptly ordered to return at once to their respective headquarters at Fort William and Fort St George.

By the end of December Arthur, who had last written to Page expecting to capture Manila 'with ease', now had to think instead about captivating the ladies of the Residencies with some dazzling new shirts. Would Page send him eight pieces of the best Irish linen? And 'let it be very fine'.

*   *   *

It was hard to associate fine Irish linen with the horrors being perpetrated in that unhappy land.

Wesley had lately wished 'joy' to his Irish friends on the literal ship-wreck of French invasion hopes in December 1796 in Bantry Bay—'the best news I have heard from Ireland for some time'. But the ham-handed and mail-fisted 'disarming of Ulster' by General Lake in 1797 (to be followed by murderous and provocative arms-raids in the south), were no joy even to Lake's own colleagues.[5] Sir

5. Gerard Lake, 1st Viscount Lake of Delhi (1744–1808). A member of George III's Household, 1782, and intimate friend of the Prince of Wales whose marriage to Mrs Fitzherbert in December 1785 he had managed to postpone for a brief period by persuading the intended clergyman not to perform the ceremony.

Ralph Abercromby, the Commander-in-Chief and a soldier who anticipated Wellington in many aspects of greatness, could not forever remain silent on these outrages. The Irish Army, he announced in a memorable General Order of February 1798, was in a state of 'licentiousness which rendered it formidable to everyone but the enemy'—a quotation which apparently stuck in Wellington's head. Such words were intolerable to the bigoted Government of Ireland. Abercromby was forced to resign.[6]

The Irish emergency had already in 1797 had its repercussions in India. General Lord Cornwallis, who had been intended to replace Shore at Calcutta for a year or two while Mornington followed Hobart at Madras, could not now be spared from home.[7] At the end of this chain of reaction Lord Mornington emerged as Governor-General of India, appointed on 4 October 1797. To the unconcealed mortification of Lord Hobart, he had soared past the Madras Presidency straight to the top.

*   *   *

There had been one or two things for Richard to clear up in County Meath first. 'With respect to the Linnen at Trim,' he wrote to his cousin Sir Chichester Fortescue, 'if it be mine and not Arthur's let it be sent immediately to me in London, if it be Arthur's I wish you to take charge of it. The same direction to be applied to the Books. I positively ordered that nothing should be sold at Trim.'

Not so at Dangan. A note in Richard's handwriting survives dealing ruthlessly with the disposal of Dangan's fixtures and fittings. 'The remainder may be sold for old brass or *firewood*.' The private chapel was dismantled, its east window of St Paul preaching to the Athenians going to the parish of Agher.[8]

Englishmen had preached the unknown God of the Protestant Ascendancy to the benighted Irish. Now once again England's sons were to perform their mission in a land full of darkness but also of promise. The Ascendancy had failed in Ireland. In India, on the

6. This fine commander—a type all too rare in the British Army at that date—was eventually posted to Egypt. He defeated the French at Alexandria, 21 March 1801, but was himself mortally wounded.

7. He became Commander-in-Chief of the army to put down the Irish Rebellion in 1798.

8. Painted by Gervaise from a cartoon of Raphael. It may be seen in Agher Church today.

contrary, might not creative minds like those of the three Wellesley brothers—Richard, Arthur and Henry, Richard's secretary—be welcomed? Those were the days before racial prejudice had poisoned the British Raj. Soon after the Wellesley triumvirate was formed the celebrated Indian, Rajah Rammohun Roy, was predicting with enthusiasm that 'forty years of contact with the British would revivify Indian civilization'. The three brothers were about to embark on their first period of brilliant cooperative effort. But for a start, Arthur had to adjust himself to a small change in his style.

$$* \qquad * \qquad *$$

Plain 'A. Wesley', as he had been accustomed to sign himself tersely from birth, had to go. Richard had spent some of his last leisure at home in persuading his ever-obliging cousin Sir Chichester Fortescue, Ulster King of Arms, to allow him to impale the de Lacy Lion Rampant in his escutcheon. This armorial *coup* had been projected with a view to a step in the peerage. Pitt loyally advanced 'the strong claims of the closest personal friendship' to press a marquessate for Mornington upon George III. The King resisted; but meanwhile Richard had put a finishing touch to his reconstructed lineage.

The family name had been 'Wellesley', not 'Wesley', for many hundreds of years; 'Wellesley' it should be again.[9] Three extra letters were not to be sneezed at, in the acquisitive fairyland of heraldry. Richard would become 'The Marquess Wellesley' if the King relented; his young brother Henry was already 'Henry Wellesley'. There was nothing for it but that 'A. Wesley' should change too.

A letter dated 19 May 1798 and signed 'Arthur Wellesley' for the first time, was posted to General Harris in Madras.[10] It informed him briefly that the Right Honourable the Governor-General, the Earl of Mornington, had arrived at Calcutta in good health the day before yesterday.

On this same 19 May a tragic event shook nationalist Ireland. Young Lord Edward Fitzgerald, gallant leader of the rising planned for 23 May, was shot and arrested in Dublin. He died on 4 June—a macabre birthday present for George III. Cornwallis put down the rebellion in May and June with some attention to humanity, while Maria Edgeworth, who had just redecorated the house, hoped the

9. It was still 'Wellesley' in Edmondson's mid-eighteenth-century *Peerage*.
10. George, 1st Lord Harris of Seringapatam and Mysore (1746–1829).

rebels would show the same consideration for her new wallpapers:

> O rebels! O French! spare them! we have never injured you, and all we wish is to see everybody as happy as ourselves.

The token French force sent to support the rebels arrived too late and was defeated in October with the help of various Pakenhams; exactly six months to the day after Lord Edward's arrest, on 19 November, the captured Wolfe Tone committed suicide. For Ireland, prostrate and numb, there was to be another brief chance of progress and reconciliation.

For Arthur Wellesley also a short period of tantalizing opportunity, culminating in bitter disappointment, opened.

5 Tigers of Mysore

The interval between the Manila fiasco and Lord Mornington's comet-like arrival at Calcutta (with a long, glittering tail of baggage which provoked some unfavourable comment) had not been wasted by Arthur. He nosed around the southern Carnatic, staying in 'humdrum' Madras, whose gardens Hickey had found inferior to 'the most barren part of Hounslow Heath.' Wellesley's attention, however, was directed to a character who lived beyond Madras, in Mysore, bearing no small resemblance to the brigands of the Heath itself.

All reports, including Arthur's to Richard, made it clear that the formidable Moslem ruler, Tipoo Sultan, the Tiger of Mysore, was in alliance with the French.[1]

*   *   *

Lord Mornington reacted more violently to this news than even the alert Colonel of the 33rd expected. He decided that the Tiger of Mysore should learn once for all who was king of the jungle. He would gather an army forthwith and settle Tipoo early in 1799. The last great battle had been fought six years earlier when Cornwallis had defeated Tipoo in his capital of Seringapatam, two hundred miles west of Madras. It was not a happy precedent. Cornwallis had stormed the city on a dark and tempestuous night and though in the end victorious had lost a vast number of men. Arthur, with his cautious diplomatic instincts, and fortified by the frantic pleas of Madras officials not to stir up tigers unnecessarily, strongly counselled Mornington to have patience and negotiate. But the Governor-

1. Among the documents found in Tipoo's palace after his death was a letter of April 1797 to the French: 'Happy moment! the time is come when I can deposit in the bosom of my friends, the hatred against those oppressors of the human race. If you will assist me . . . we will purge India of the villains' (Marquess Wellesley's *India Despatches*, vol. V, p. 1).

Wellington's *Despatches* will be generally followed in the spelling of Indian names, partly to avoid confusion, partly because an agreed modern spelling is not always easy to find.

General had not left his brilliant London circle to sit idly under the punkas of Fort William waiting for stalling messages from a 'deceitful' Oriental. He determined to use his brother as a go-between in selling his forward policy to Madras. By July Arthur was doing his best in singularly distasteful circumstances.

The new Governor of Madras, Lord Clive, proved to be an awkward customer.[2] Richard nicknamed him Puzzlestick, and Arthur found that though mild and moderate, he had a 'heavy understanding' which enabled his officials deliberately to mislead him over the Governor-General's intentions. It took Arthur five hours to convince Lord Clive that Richard did not intend to 'precipitate the country into war'. (If Clive's understanding had been brighter Arthur might have taken even longer.)

Arthur was ordered in August to bring the 33rd from Calcutta to Madras, ready for the fray. The voyage was a disaster. They ran on to a reef and were saved from drowning only by their own 'bodily strength' in refloating their ship. Then Captain Frazer supplied them with contaminated water, so that the whole regiment including Wellesley got 'the flux'. Such criminal neglect was 'inconsistent with the principles of the Christian religion,' wrote Arthur angrily, on 19 August, adding a few days later, 'I am afraid I must make a public complaint of him.' He did so, informing the adjutant-general, Colonel Close, that dysentery had caused the deaths of fifteen men— 'of 15 as fine men as any we had . . .'.[3]

A note of restiveness invaded Arthur's letters to his younger brother Henry during that autumn, due to the endless diplomatic intrigue needed to keep the peace with Clive and prepare for war with Tipoo. His policy involved isolating Clive from his officials, particularly his secretary, Josiah Webbe.[4] Most of Arthur's letters to Henry on this delicate subject were written partly or wholly in what passed for code. On 19 October he advised that the 'S.G.' (Supreme Government) should avoid disputes with Clive even on petty subjects, as disputes would erect 'the little men such as 10 [10 = W =

2. Edward, Lord Clive (1754–1839), eldest son of the great Clive; Governor of Madras, 1798–1803. He returned to England, 1804, and was created Earl of Powis.

3. Sir Barry Close, Resident at Poona, 1801–11, a Persian and Arabic scholar admired for his Roman virtues. He died in 1813.

4. A dedicated civil servant who died in 1804, during the tensions of the Second Mahratta War. He had meanwhile become one of Arthur Wellesley's closest associates.

Webbe] who have to handle them, into great ones'. Arthur's furtive job was not made more palatable by the fact that he still half agreed with 'the little men'. When Richard wrote to him on 21 October for his opinion on the crucial question of war or no war, he had to reply that there were strong reasons for simply making Tipoo accept a British ambassador and expel the French; he would willingly go as envoy himself.

His ambivalent attitude to the war did not prevent him from working overtime to organize supplies of bullocks, grain and money. On the last day of October he was too busy to put a letter to Henry into code, though one sentence was an obvious case for the treatment:

I have likewise prevailed upon Lord Clive to appoint a commissary of stores. . . . Matters then will be brought into some shape, and we shall know what we are about, instead of trusting to the vague calculations of a parcel of blockheads, who know nothing, and have no data.

Corruption was even worse than stupidity. Colonel Lindsay had done more 'dirty business' in the way of 'durbar jobs' than anybody in India, and was 'a disgrace to the King's army'.[5]

As hard to bear as the jobbing officers and un-Christian gentlemen was the fate which tied Arthur down in a post where he could do nothing to reduce his debts. The Court of Directors had cut all officers' allowances just as he was preparing to take the field and would have to buy plate for his military 'family'—a soup tureen and dishes for twelve. In an Indian camp, he explained to Henry, everyone brought their own cutlery and plates to eat off, the 'hosts' providing eatables and dishes. At one point he had thought of the Governorship of Ceylon if there were no war, though Henry was warned, 'I don't wish that this should be mentioned to Mornington.' While assuring Henry that he would stay at Fort St George as long as required, he could not help rubbing in that his position was a very awkward one.

I should not however wish M to know that I feel it at all. I cannot but consider myself, & I am afraid that if all were known

5. 'Durbar jobs' were transactions in the courts of independent Indian princes.

others would consider me as 9. 23. 5. 12. little 20. 23. 7. 7. 23. 5. 7. 26. 19. 1. 19. 6. 3. 12.

Which, when decoded, meant 'very little better than a spy'.[6]

*   *   *

Within two months of Arthur's last groan the tension was relaxing. Lord Clive responded to his blandishments and supported the war policy. Most of Arthur's own doubts were repressed. He summoned Richard to Madras for personal supervision of the final rupture with Tipoo. Up till the end of November 1798 there had been a risk that fresh troops sent to reinforce the Madras army might snatch the 33rd's place on the battlefield from under Arthur's nose. But on the 29th he received a reassuring note from the Commander-in-Chief. The Colonel of the 33rd was in fact destined to hold an extensive command.

His good fortune arose out of a disgraceful death from duelling. Colonel Henry Harvey Aston of the 12th had been ordered to prepare for the war a strong force of 16,000 infantry and cavalry belonging to Britain's recently acquired ally, the decrepit old Nizam of Hyderabad.[7] Before Aston set off, one of his junior officers, Lieutenant Hartley, thought fit to complain to him that some articles ordered by Hartley from Europe had been charged to his account while still in the quartermaster's store. A Major Allen, who was responsible, got wind of the fact that Aston considered him 'illiberal'. His friend, Major Picton, thereupon demanded a Court of Inquiry into this grand quarrel; innumerable meetings were held over which Wellesley had to preside and Picton, having been rebuked by Aston for causing so much trouble, challenged his colonel to a duel.[8] Luckily his pistol misfired, Aston fired in the air, they shook hands and went home. Major Allen, however, profoundly dissatisfied with this tame dénouement, rushed round next morning to Aston's house and handed in his resignation from the regiment. Aston asked him to

6. The whole of this passage from *Supplementary Despatches*, vol. I, p. 110 is omitted.

7. The alliance had been achieved by a British *coup* in October 1798. The Nizam's French military advisers were forced to surrender and get out without a blow.

8. Major Picton was a brother of Wellington's future Peninsular general, Sir Thomas Picton. See below, p. 255.

reconsider it. A hot argument followed culminating in a fantastic exchange:

'Colonel Aston, what is your private opinion of me?'

'I am not obliged to give you my private opinion upon any subject.'

'Then will you give me a private meeting?'

'Yes!'

They met on the duelling ground where Aston offered to state that his use of the word 'illiberal' had been intended for Hartley's private ear. This apology was not acceptable to the inflamed major.[9] He put a ball through Aston's shoulder, who died on 23 December after a week's agony, leaving to Wellesley his fine grey Arab, Diomed. And that was the end of a gallant officer who had just been appointed to prepare a force to fight Citizen Tipoo, but was killed by his own side instead.

Weeks of Wellesley's precious time had been wasted on this squalid affair, indeed towards the end of the Inquiry he had had only four hours' sleep in forty-eight. After Aston's death he still had to see that the widow was informed through a whole series of society ladies, for Aston had been a prominent member of London society and a dandy who never bought less than twenty shirts at a time. Minutely recorded by Wellesley, this episode and others like it helped to mould the future Commander-in-Chief. He has often been trounced for doing less than justice to his gallant officers, even re-marking on occasion that gallantry and stupidity marched together. Here was an early instance of besotted behaviour appropriate to tribal rituals, perhaps, but not to his idea of British officers on the eve of battle.

Meanwhile with Colonel Aston dead it fell to Colonel Wellesley to supply the Nizam's army for its march on Seringapatam.

*   *   *

'The plot thickens so quickly,' wrote Arthur to Henry from the Nizam's camp on 28 December 1798, that he would not have time to meet the Governor-General in Madras before marching. If information were needed Henry must come to him, where incidentally he would get his first sight of an Indian camp—'a curiosity of its kind'.

9. Duellists arrived on the ground primed with spirits and spiced ginger nuts.

In this cool phrase Arthur described the vast, ungainly cara-vanserai he was preparing to shepherd southwards. His own silver-plated tableware was a drop in the ocean of oriental finery displayed in tents and bazaars, his loud commands a whisper among the shouts of camel drivers, the braying of asses, trumpeting of elephants and din of 150,000 camp followers advancing inside a hollow square around which circled a guard of 6,000 cavalry. His grocery bill for the last three weeks seems strangely unexotic: candles, hair powder, three pots of pomatum, a dozen vinegar, a dozen sauces, four bottles of mustard, two capers, two pickles and an innocent supply of sugar candy. Also from the grocer, three dozen brandy, presumably for cooking, though this is not certain. Wellington's biographers agree that his palate was so insensitive (either by nature or deliberate training) that he could not tell bad wine from good.

*   *   *

Lord Mornington gave the order to invade Mysore on 3 February 1799. Tipoo was still sending civil messages which ended with the wish, 'Continue to rejoice me with happy letters'. But though the letters continued they became progressively less happy. British preparations were far advanced. So was the season. And the news of Nelson's victory on the Nile, still comparatively fresh, made them suddenly feel a match for the French in Mysore or anywhere else in India. As Richard wrote euphorically to Arthur on the day before he gave the order to march:

> The Irish Rebellion & French invasion, & Bonpte. expedition are gone to the Dogs. . . .[10]

So let Arthur stop his 'croaking', especially his 'fears & fancies about money' (Richard had just raised a loan to finance the expedition) and take heart from the universal praise which had been lavished on his own late command of the Nizam's contingent.

> I wish to God the whole were under your direction; but even as it is, I think our success is certain. . . .

10. The French army in Egypt had begun diminishing under the British Naval blockade since September 1798, but Bonaparte did not make his secret escape from Egypt until August 1799. During his 'Alexander the Great' phase, Bonaparte glanced towards India from time to time, encouraged by the Tsar Paul I of Russia; the Tsar, however, was assassinated in 1801.

His 'croaking' brother was not so sure. But he had at least achieved one success already—against Richard himself. The over-excited Governor-General cherished a design to take the field in person. Fortunately he asked Arthur's advice first who replied bluntly:

All I can say upon the subject is, that if I were in General Harris's [the Commander-in-Chief] situation, and you joined the army, I should quit it.

Arthur himself did not get on with Harris nor did he admire his talents. But to upset Harris at this juncture would damage the 'public interest'.

Ironically, Richard got wind a few days later that the Governor of Madras, Lord Clive, was contemplating the very action which he himself had so reluctantly dropped. Would Arthur somehow stop Clive's 'ill-omened visit' to the army? 'I cannot tell you how uneasy this strange indelicate measure makes me. . . .' Arthur's knowledge of human nature was growing apace, though with a somewhat cynical slant. He had had to face multifarious vexations in the Nizam's camp. General Harris's ungenerous attitude to his work above all gave him the mulligrubs.

Having left for Hyderabad at a moment's notice to take up his command, he had naturally asked Harris for some assistance. All he had got were two wash-outs, one 'so stupid that I can make no use of him & the other such a rascal that half my occupation consists in watching him. . . .' Another man who needed watching was Colonel Richardson, the officer in charge of the troops' arrack.[11] Wellesley pointed out to the colonel that as superintendent of bazaars, it was his duty to check the consumption of arrack, but as employer of the man who sold arrack it was in his financial interest to increase its sale. 'This clashing of duty and interest,' wrote Colonel Wellesley frostily, 'I conceive it to be desirable to avoid wherever it is possible.' There were also Majors Picton and Allen to be delivered over to the authorities under close arrest.

Nevertheless, he managed to get the whole hungry camp supplied with grain 'through bullying day and night', without costing the public a single shilling. 'I bustled through the difficulty,' he explained to Henry in a graphic sentence. Yet General Harris had not 'sufficiency of spirit' to give credit where credit was due; and as 'there is nothing to be got in the army but credit', Harris's neglect was hard

11. A strong spirit distilled from rice, date or coconut juice.

indeed to bear. 'I was much hurt about it at the time', he wrote a month later. He had even contemplated asking to join his regiment but for the thought that Harris wanted to get rid of him. Now, however, 'I don't care . . . and shall certainly continue to do every thing to serve General Harris, and to support his name and authority'.

Virtue had its reward. The Nizam's Prime Minister decided that as a European officer had to command his army in the field, it had better be the Governor-General's brother. So after supplying it, bringing it south and at last being praised for his efficiency in a General Order from Harris, he was delighted to find himself at the head of this large force, with his own 33rd added to it as a European stiffener.

*   *   *

One officer was not pleased. David Baird, twelve years older than Wellesley and a major-general, had been captured by Tipoo's father, Hyder Ali, on the bloody field of Perambaukum, 10 September 1780, and kept in irons for over three and a half years at Seringapatam.

He had hoped to forget his past sufferings in some glorious new action, such as Manila. Arthur Wellesley had been picked for it. That was Baird's first grievance. Now Wellesley was to command the Nizam's contingent. Baird sent General Harris 'a strong remonstrance'. It did him no good. Indeed, by annoying Harris he sowed the seeds of yet another disappointment.

*   *   *

As was to be expected, Wellesley's few letters *en route* for Seringapatam were totally devoid of scenic comment. Not a word of the luxuriant rice-fields and sugar plantations round Bangalore, nor of the hilly, dense country as they turned south for the capital.

Things had not gone altogether well. Early on the march it was apparent that Major Shee of the 33rd was neglecting his duties. Some of his men were marching without arms or equipment. When Wellesley remonstrated, Shee replied rudely that he was 'extremely sorry', not for any misconduct but for Colonel Wellesley having been 'so much misinformed' as to censure him. And a lot more in the same strain. Wellesley's reply was coldly furious.

This is not the first time I have had occasion to observe that, under forms of private correspondence, you have written me letters upon public duty, couched in terms to which I have not been accustomed.

Next time he received such a letter he would send it straight to the Commander-in-Chief. Not that he wanted to do anything 'unpleasant to your feelings'; but once for all, the welfare of the 33rd was his responsibility. Shee's Irish blood boiled. 'You conclude with a threat of laying my letters of that kind before the Commander-in-Chief.' Nothing could be more welcome. In case of further reproof he himself would be obliged to submit his conduct to the decision of a general court martial.

Apart from these disturbances in the 33rd, general progress was retarded by mismanagement and misfortune. The Nizam's army had started out so over-loaded that Arthur christened it 'that monstrous equipment'. Its 120,000 bullocks made matters worse by dying in droves. On 9 March Arthur reported to Henry that his friend Captain Malcolm, in charge of the Nizam's sepoys, 'leads the life of a cannister at a dog's tail'.[12] By the 25th he himself was 'not a little fagged'. Finally, there was a lack of harmony among the High Command. 'We have had much blundering and puzzling,' Arthur wrote to Mornington on 5 April, 'and I have been present at many strong & violent discussions. . . .'

It was Tipoo who made them pull themselves together. As they struggled out of thick jungles into Mallavelly on 26 March, they were suddenly confronted with a ridge crowned by elephants. This was the first sign of Tipoo's brave bid to defeat the invaders before they reached his capital. Colonel Alexander Beatson who was present with the allied army and became the enthusiastic historian of the Mysore campaign, paid tribute to the dash of Tipoo's attack next day.[13] Two thousand of his French-trained troops advanced in column on the 33rd who held their fire 'with the utmost steadiness' until the enemy

12. Sir John Malcolm (1769–1833), one of Wellington's closest friends. He was the Governor-General's representative at headquarters in Mysore, 1803. Known as 'Boy' Malcolm for his gay temperament, he became a distinguished administrator, linguist and historian of the East. He retired in 1831 and entered Parliament as an opponent of Reform.

13. Beatson, as a former aide-de-camp of Lord Mornington, was an enthusiast for the Wellesley family as well as for the campaign. His account is not always complete or objective.

were sixty yards away; then came the deadly British volleys tearing
holes in the close-packed columns; confusion spread and Wellesley's
cavalry easily scattered them. There were equally successful skirmishes all along the front. Well pleased with themselves the Allies
continued their march. Colonel Wellesley, however, felt that if
Tipoo had used his troops better before the action, the Allies would
still be penned in the Bangalore jungles.

By the 5th the Allies had completed a sweeping arc round Seringapatam and were encamped two miles beyond it to the west. Arthur
sat in his tent and finished a rather carping letter to Mornington on a
buoyant note: there was no more squabbling, 'and we shall be masters
of this place before much time passes over our Heads.' He was right;
but first he had to go through one of the most unpleasant experiences
of his life.

*   *   *

Though the Allies outnumbered Tipoo their position was in one
respect hazardous. Numerous enemy outposts were concealed between the Allied camp and the city, mainly in five great 'topes'
(thickets) of cocoa, bamboo and betel. Enemy rockets were already
dropping among the Allied tents.[14] No siege-works could safely
begin until this dangerous ground had been cleared. Wellesley, partly
as a diversion, was ordered to 'scour' one of the thickets known as the
Sultanpettah Tope.

The ground inside this tope was scored with irrigation canals from
four to six feet deep. Even after a thorough reconnaissance it would
have been difficult terrain to negotiate in stifling darkness. But there
had been no chance to reconnoitre. As soon as the enemy realized
that Wellesley's attack was in progress they punished his staggering,
groping men with a hot fire of musketry and rockets. It was impossible
for Wellesley to locate the quarter from which the counter-attack
was coming or even to rally his own troops for a disciplined withdrawal. He had certainly achieved a diversion, but that was all. Lost,
separated from the unfortunate 33rd and dismally aware that he had
failed, he stumbled into headquarters several hours later to make his
report to General Harris.

14. This was Wellington's first experience of a type of missile which was
later produced in Europe, notably by Sir William Congreve. See below,
pp. 287 and 401.

'Near twelve,' wrote Harris in his journal, 'Colonel Wellesley came to my tent in a good deal of agitation, to say he had not carried the tope. It must be particularly unpleasant to him.' Wellesley's second-in-command made sure that it was even more unpleasant than necessary by circulating a story that he had eventually been found fast asleep with his head on the mess-room table. Word went round that 'Wellesley is mad'. Some said that but for his relationship to the Governor-General, 'he never would have had a chance of getting over this affair.'[15]

Twelve soldiers (eight of them from Wellesley's 33rd) who had been taken prisoner in the tope were carried into Seringapatam and killed by having nails driven into their skulls or their necks wrung by Jetties (Hindu 'strong men'). Then they were all rolled up in mats and buried outside the fort, where their graves were discovered by their comrades a month later. Those who were killed outright during the fighting, like young Lieutenant Fitzgerald, turned out to have been the lucky ones.

The whole horrible episode of the tope and the killings made an indelible impression on Wellesley. He wrote to Mornington on 18 April from camp:

> I have come to a determination; when in my power, never to suffer an attack to be made by night upon an enemy who is . . . strongly posted, and whose posts have not been reconnoitred by daylight.[16]

The fact that Lieutenant Fitzgerald's brother, the Knight of Kerry, was one of his closest Irish friends, would have helped to keep the memory alive. As in 1794, events had taught him 'what not to do'. This time he was learning from that rare phenomenon, a failure of his own.

15. As late as 1839 a *Life and Exploits of Wellington* by G. L. Hutchinson was advertised at 2*d.*—'Splendid original work'—'Embellished with beautiful engravings'. Part of the 'originality' consisted in giving full weight to Wellington's 'mistakes' and Tipoo's courage at Seringapatam. By these means the author hoped to find his 'well thumbed pages in the hands of the Peasant and the Artisan' rather than 'in the ringed fingers of the most spruce dandy'. Captain George Elers relates that Wellesley waited in 'despair' until dawn, Harris's servant having told him, 'Master, General Sahib gone to sleep' (*Memoirs of George Elers*, pp. 102 and 293).

16. Wellington wrote on 1 April 1814 that Sir Thomas Graham had been very unfortunate in his attack upon Bergen-op-Zoom. 'However, night attacks upon good troops are seldom successful' (*Despatches*, vol. XI, p. 618).

On the following morning, 6 April, all the enemy outposts were cleared. Wellesley again led the attack against the ill-fated Sultan-pettah Tope, this time with complete success. After the action, Colonel Barry Close, always a good friend of Arthur's, rushed jubilantly into Harris's tent. 'It has been done in high style and without loss.'[17]

*   *   *

Now at last the siege-works could begin, following each other with rhythmical precision according to the hallowed ritual of the master, Vauban[18]—batteries, parallels (trenches), zigzags (connecting lines) to more advanced parallels and batteries, the enemy guns silenced, and then—the breach. At Seringapatam nothing was allowed to break the relentless, scientific pattern.

On several occasions Tipoo put out peace-feelers:

I have adhered firmly to the treaty; what then is the meaning of the advance of the English armies . . .? Inform me. What need I say more?

He 'needed' to say that within twenty-four hours he would surrender the fort and large areas of Mysore, send four sons as hostages and a huge indemnity. Instead he waited six days and then offered to dispatch vakeels (envoys) and hold a conference. 'What more can I write?' Nothing more. On Mornington's instructions Harris refused the vakeels and pressed on with the siege.

There was a shattering roar on 2 May. A shell had fallen on a rocket magazine inside Tipoo's fort. Black smoke belched up in a huge plume laced with fiery stars, plunging into ominous shade the fort's long, low white walls, the shining roofs of Tipoo's palace, the sugar-

17. According to Baird's biographer, Theodore Hook, the 'high style' so much praised by Close was marred by Colonel Wellesley keeping the troops waiting an hour so that Harris ordered Baird to lead the morning attack on the tope. 'Don't you think, Sir,' remonstrated Baird, 'it would be but fair to give Wellesley an opportunity of retrieving the misfortune of last night?' (T. Hook, *Life of Sir D. B. Baird*, vol. I, p. 174). Hook was as hot a partisan of Baird as Beatson was of Wellesley and his account must be taken with equal reserve. Wellesley was late because the message ordering him to attack had miscarried.

18. Sébastien de Vauban (1633–1707), the most celebrated of all military engineers. He built or strengthened 150 fortresses and conducted forty sieges.

white minaret of his elegant mosque, the flat boulders of the River Cauvery which encircled the island of Seringapatam, and the shell-shattered trees, banks and aloe hedges which concealed the British siege-works.

By noon next day the breach was 'practicable' and bamboo scaling-ladders were silently carried into the trenches at dusk.[19]

On the morning of 4 May 1799 the order went out for the assault. David Baird, mindful of his lengthy sojourn in the black hole opposite, volunteered to take command of the 4,000 storming troops. Wellesley was in charge of the reserve in the trenches. At 1.10 P.M. the towering Baird leapt from his trench and bellowed,

'Now, my brave fellows, follow *ME* and prove yourselves worthy of the name of British soldiers!' The defenders smashed into them with muskets and rockets; but the leaders of the attacking force, always known grimly as the 'forlorn hope', were already across the almost dry river-bed. They reached the summit of the breach within six minutes, where they planted a British flag. An officer's hat suddenly waved on his sword as two more flags appeared, while thousands of defenders fled, some of them tearing off their turbans to use for sliding down into the inner ditch. All Tipoo's elaborate outer defences, built under French supervision, were abandoned. On the northern face there were heavy losses on both sides, but Allied reinforcements poured in through the breach and soon the attackers had joined up at the fort's far corner. Ten French officers surrendered. All was over bar the looting.

* * *

When news of the Allies' victory reached the Governor-General it drew from him an avalanche of congratulatory eloquence: consummate judgement, unequalled rapidity, animation, skill, humanity, honour, splendour, glory and lustre—all were theirs. In England it seemed as if the days of the great Clive had returned.

* * *

A search meanwhile was made for Tipoo in the palace, which it was thought would be his last refuge. The Tiger of Mysore was not there.

19. The term 'practicable' mean wide enough and sufficiently full of debris for the storming party to scramble up and over into the fortress.

The day had opened gloomily for Tipoo with an ominous report from his astrologers. Alarmed, he made oblations of an elephant, a black bullock, two buffaloes, a black she-goat, a black jacket and cap and a pot of oil in which he first looked at his own reflection to avert evil. Ascetic, cruel, brave and profoundly religious, his habit had been to study the sacred books and make notes on them, except when personally training his recruits to avenge their national defeat by Cornwallis. Seated on a throne shaped and striped like a tiger, with a pearly canopy crowned by the gold and jewelled 'Uma' bird, he would say it was better to live like a tiger for two days than for two hundred years like a sheep. He died like a tiger.

Fighting and killing to the last in a bloody mêlée at the North Gate, he fell wounded, was lifted by his attendants into the soft palanquin which he had always scorned, and was then shot dead by a British soldier who fancied the jewel in his turban. At dusk Baird, accompanied by Wellesley who had earlier joined the troops inside, tracked him down. In the macabre torchlight his body was recognized by an amulet on his right arm and dragged out from a huge pile of corpses. It was so warm that Wellesley felt the heart and pulse. The dark eyes were open, the expression stern but dignified as in life. He was buried next day beside his father, Hyder Ali, in the Loll Baug garden of cypresses, with the river rising in a tigerish storm which, if it had come sooner, might have saved him. The lashing rain made the Cauvery too deep to cross, and the sky was striped with lightning which killed several British officers. In his pocket-book was found a prayer: 'I am full of sin; thou art a sea of mercy. Where thy mercy is, what became of my sin?' With all his sins he was a remarkable man and had gone where mercy is.

*   *   *

Utterly exhausted by the tension, heat and violence of the assault, Baird asked General Harris for his troops and himself to be temporarily relieved. Arthur Wellesley was therefore appointed acting Governor of Seringapatam. Next day, 6 May, he was confirmed in his onerous but lucrative post.

The first intimation of this change came to Baird in an unfortunate way. While leisurely breakfasting in Tipoo's palace with his staff, he was presented by Colonel Wellesley with a sheet of official paper and the awful *fait accompli*:

'General Baird, I am appointed to the command of Seringapatam and here is the order of General Harris.' The huge Scot rose to the occasion. Ignoring Wellesley, he turned to his dumbfounded subordinates and roared out the word of command.

'Come, gentlemen, we have no longer any business here.' Breakfast, however, was business of a kind and Governor Wellesley intervened graciously.

'Oh, pray finish your breakfast.'

Once outside the palace, Baird hit back with a rasping letter to Harris: 'Before the sweat was drying on my brow, I was superseded by an inferior officer.'

This was his third grievance and the first ill-fated reference to supersession. It was to haunt Baird and Wellesley by turns for months.

Harris replied angrily that Baird had better go back to Madras: his conduct was insubordinate and his letter 'very improper', showing 'a total want of discretion and respect'.

The fact was that Harris's choice had been between the lion-hearted general who had captured Seringapatam, but was disliked by the Indians he would have to rule, and the colonel who was well liked and had demonstrated his efficiency, but was the Governor-General's brother. The colonel was chosen. As he himself wrote many years later: 'I was the *fit person* to be selected.' This well-merited triumph for Wellesley, however, led eventually to undeserved humiliation.

* * *

To restore order among the inhabitants and to keep order among the victors was Arthur's most urgent task. The congested island (only $3\frac{1}{2}$ by $1\frac{1}{2}$ miles) was an appalling scene of chaos—loot, murder and Tipoo's live tigers, which were habitually chained up outside his palace, 'getting violent'. Only too glad to avail himself of Harris's order to publish by beat of drum or tom-tom that he would instantly put down tigers of all species, he soon had four looters swinging from gibbets in key streets. Not that he particularly blamed them; for what could you expect, as he wrote to Richard on 8 May, from troops who had been through so much? These drastic measures ended the crisis, brought the peasants back to the city and got the bazaars open again to feed the army. The head of the Hindu royal family, a child whose throne had been usurped by Hyder Ali, was restored.

Distribution of prize-money was always a sordid and rapacious aftermath of victory, whether on sea or land. The Admiralty Prize Courts were 'a public scandal' and prize-money was the cause of endless bickering between officers. Similarly in the Army. Arthur called the prize-agents 'sharks', and explained to Richard that the sooner the distribution was made the better:

> A successful army which has nothing to do is very inflammable, and I never saw one so near a ferment. . . .

The Governor-General, no less inflammable, jumped to the conclusion that Arthur was describing a mutiny and reprimanded him for an alarmist letter. In the end the total treasure was estimated at £1,143,216. General Harris got £150,000, the sepoys and Indian surgeons about £5 each and Colonel Wellesley £4,000.

Arthur at last was solvent. That is, unless he paid back all he owed to Richard. For his prize-money by no means covered his expenses. These had quadrupled since the campaign began and the Government had not yet made any allowances.

> The consequence is that I am ruined . . . I should be ashamed of doing any of the dirty things that I am told are done in some of the commands. . . .

Knowing the 'quite scandalous dilatoriness' of the Government, Richard handsomely insisted on postponing his own repayment.

> I am in no want of money and probably never shall be: when I am, it will be time enough to call upon you.

The need came, but not for many years.

To thwart the 'sharks' Arthur sent Tipoo's robes and turbans, which they planned to auction, to Fort William, and as a gift for Richard, Tipoo's musical tiger. Who knows how many happy hours Tipoo spent feeding his hatred of the British on the sight and sound of this horrible toy? Pinned beneath the carved claws of a royal tiger lay a man, presumably a servant of the Company, whose left hand waved helplessly while a shrill, intermittent scream came out of his mouth, to the accompaniment of the tiger's savage growls. A pipe organ inside the tiger and his victim was responsible for this hideous concert, which could be varied by playing eighteen ear-splitting notes on a keyboard in the tiger's belly. Richard presented 'Tipoo's Tiger' to the Court of Directors and the famous 'Uma' bird to George III.[20] He added the same bird, looking appropriately like a peacock, to his own coat-of-arms.

The question of his public reward sadly inflamed the peacock strain in his nature. Declining a gift of £100,000 from the Court of Directors for fear of seeming to rob the army, he jibbed at sharing with Lord Hobart any honours which the army might spontaneously proffer. As Governor-General, he was 'the sole fountain in the Civil Service from which the success of our arms and the glory of our army have flowed . . .'. Arthur would surely agree that he could accept nothing 'if Bobby Hobart is to be put in the same triumphal car as me'. Arthur promptly punctured his brother's vanity.

> Lord Hobart will not stand in the same rank with you in the public estimation. . . . But in any case I don't think it is right for a man to refuse to receive a mark of respect, because one is offered to another person or that he can conclude . . . that his actions are undervalued because those of another are considered.

So Lord Mornington was persuaded to accept from the army a Star and Badge of St Patrick made from Tipoo's jewels.

Another honour with an all too distinctively Hibernian flavour was bestowed on him on 2 December 1799. Having been from the age of twenty-one an Earl in the Irish peerage he was raised, with the same limitation, to a Marquessate. The Directors added an annuity of £5,000 a year for twenty years, to keep it up. But to the friend of the English Prime Minister an *Irish* Marquessate was just 'a double gilt potato'.

* * *

When Harris's army departed in July 1799 Colonel Wellesley took command of the remaining troops in Mysore, while his friend Colonel Close became Resident at Seringapatam.

Two things stand out in Wellesley's Mysore command: the

20. The Uma bird is at Windsor Castle while the tiger is a favourite exhibit at the Victoria and Albert Museum, though today its growl is somewhat asthmatic.

military experience derived from pacifying brigand-infested new territories, and the resolve, carried out over three years, to give its peoples a firm and just rule. This fitted in well with his brother's revolutionary plans for India, by which he proposed to replace the unsatisfactory 'double rule' of Company and princes by 'subsidiary alliances' established by treaty. But when Richard tried to include an article in the new treaty of alliance with Seringapatam giving the Company the right to take over the Rajah's authority at any time, Arthur strongly objected. The natives, he wrote, were bound to feel that 'improper advantage' would be taken of such a clause; after all, the conduct of the British Government in India had not always been such as to give them complete confidence. The Governor-General bowed to Arthur's judgement, changing the clause to cover emergencies only. Even so, the Rajah of Mysore was to discover there was 'a price for entering the ring fence of military security' which the Governor-General offered to the Indian princely states. Henceforth even the Rajah's own Prime Minister regarded him as a British puppet.

*   *   *

As for Arthur's military task, the Governor-General suggested that he might begin by collecting anecdotes for a history of the siege; Colonel Kirkpatrick, his own military secretary, would make a good compiler, 'but he has an Iron pen'. The future Iron Duke never had any love for such histories, with their certainty of provoking controversy. Fortunately he was soon engaged upon more congenial business.

A Mahratta freebooter, one of the smaller tigers of Mysore named Dhoondiah Waugh, had been lying in Tipoo's dungeon awaiting a horrid end. The assault on Seringapatam enabled him to escape. Gathering round him Tipoo's wild men he lived off the defenceless villages of the Deccan, at first eluding capture by Wellesley's troops through swift movement and local intelligence.

Later on in the Iberian Peninsula, the French armies were to enjoy the same speed, given by freedom from baggage, and Wellington a counter-balancing effectiveness from the Spanish guerrillas' intelligence system.

Pushed inexorably northwards, Dhoondiah at last vanished out of the Deccan into Mahratta country, while Wellesley turned to other trouble spots—a rebellious Rajah of Bullum, border areas where Mahratta raids were endemic and the eternal quarrels in Malabar between a race of high caste, militaristic Hindus, the Nairs, and fanatical Moslem traders, the Moplas. Arthur was intrigued by the fighting Nairs, whose customs perhaps appealed to a bachelor lacking family life. 'No Nair knows his own father,' he wrote, 'and every man considers his sister's children as his heirs.' Brahmins alone, who were a higher caste still, might approach within ninety-six steps of a Nair.

The Nairs spoke only to Brahmins and the Brahmins spoke only to God. Richard would have appreciated this even more than Arthur.

Suddenly, early in 1800, Dhoondiah's name cropped up again. There were rumours of a Dhoondiah plot to kidnap the royal family while out hunting with Colonel Wellesley, and a skirmish took place with Dhoondiah's bandits in which, as Arthur remarked, 'the gentlemen succeeded against the blackguards'. By April there could be no doubt: 'our old adversary Dhoondiah Waugh is in force'. Indeed, he was now calling himself the King of Two Worlds.

* * *

At this crucial juncture a letter reached Arthur from the Governor-General which raised both his hopes and his hackles. King George III, it appeared, had personally ordered an expedition from India against the Dutch colony of Batavia (Java) to demand its surrender, since the mother country, Holland, had been forced into alliance with France. The British were to sail under a flag of truce, in order that the surrender might be voluntary. And to help the Dutch make the right decision there was to be a token force. Richard informed Arthur that he had assigned the principal conduct of this expedition, including command of the token force, to Admiral Rainier. Would Arthur like to serve as the Admiral's military commissioner? It would involve no fighting, no responsibility. Or as secretary Josiah Webbe put it, who wanted Arthur to remain in Mysore, 'neither fame nor prize money'. Arthur was torn. He had been in the Deccan for over a year. On the other hand, his position under Rainier would be ambiguous. Webbe knew his man when he wrote:

> I have no doubt, therefore, that you will prefer your present independent and extensive command, to being stationed in Batavia.

To clinch it Webbe ended his letter:

> You are to pursue Dhoondiah Waugh wherever you may find him, and to hang him on the first tree.

Though Arthur prized the continuation of his independent command more than the permission to hang, he was convinced by Webbe and refused the Batavia offer.

So the king of earth and heaven was chased through Mahratta territories and back into the Deccan, where he was gradually squeezed between the troops of Wellesley and his second-in-command, Stevenson. In July his camp was captured, and on 10 September 1800 he was caught unawares, his 5,000 cavalry routed and he himself slain. His four-year-old son was found afterwards cowering among the baggage. The soldiers picked him up and galloped after the colonel, who at once made himself responsible for little Salabut Khan's future.

Another personal note struck on 10 September was the 'great swift charge' of four regiments headed by the Colonel of the 33rd himself. This was the first and last time that Arthur Wellesley led a cavalry charge. A colleague at Fort St George congratulated him for showing 'what has never yet been shewn in this Country, that is, what cavalry can do'; 10 September was 'the brightest day the Cavalry has seen in India'. This tribute is interesting in view of Wellington's later criticism of the cavalry arm.

Wellesley's hunting down of Dhoondiah brought him widespread recognition, notably from the Commander-in-Chief, General Harris, who thanked him publicly for his judgement, gallantry and 'peculiar and progressive energy'. It also seems to have sharpened the Governor-General's awareness of his brother's military distinction. The admirable settlement of Mysore had led him to believe that dear Arthur was after all destined to shine in the civil rather than the military sphere. Possibly he was also reflecting the still strong prejudice against soldiers, and paying Arthur the compliment of considering him too good for the Army.[21]

21. While Arthur was chasing Dhoondiah, Lady Holland wrote in her journal how much she regretted that Lord George Leveson was raising a regiment in England, for 'he throws away very excellent abilities upon a profession where so little is required . . .' (*Lady Holland's Journal*, vol. II, p. 33).

Now all this was over. A new approach was to be made to Arthur. It would demonstrate that the Governor-General considered his brother the best man in India for a military assignment of the most urgent and special nature.

*   *   *

Two papers marked 'Private & Secret (A)' and '(B)' were addressed to Arthur by his brother, the Governor-General, on 5 November 1800. They were to prove gunpowder to Arthur's equanimity.

The great man informed him that owing to the French threat to India from Egypt he had decided to improve on H.M.'s instructions regarding Batavia. Instead of engineering a bloodless victory over the Dutch, he proposed to attack the Isle de France (Mauritius), the only French naval base in East Indian waters. The idea had come to him in consultation with a friend, ex-captain of a merchantman, named Charles Stokes—thoroughly reliable fellow, 'chosen to escort Lady Wellesley to India'—who together with Admiral Rainier would meet Arthur at Trincomalee, Ceylon. Arthur would there take command of the invasion force, set off secretly, and having arrived, capture the Isle de France in one night. On no account must Arthur mention the plan to anyone, not even Lord Clive.[22]

As the weeks passed Richard's passion for the expedition and for having Arthur in command seemed to increase. Prepared to face all criticism, he wrote on 1 December:

> Great Jealousy will arise among the General Officers, in conse-
> quence of my employing you; but I employ you, because I rely
> on your good sense, discretion, activity and spirit; and I cannot
> find all these qualities united in any other officer in India who
> could take such a command.

If successful, the Marquess Wellesley intended to appoint his brother Governor and Commander-in-Chief of the Isles de France and Bourbon, with absolute freedom to return to India if he wished. Stokes was to be his Intendant.

---

22. Clive had long been strongly in favour of an expedition against the French in Egypt, not Mauritius, as were others at that date both in India and at home. Stokes had not escorted Lady Wellesley to India after all, since Richard was advised that owing to her past she would be unacceptable. When he returned the marriage broke up. See pp. 188 and 237.

His ardour will not displease you; *but he is somewhat inclined to a little too much magnificence which you will manage.*

Magnificence in a marquess or a merchant captain—Arthur could manage both.

Five days later a letter from Fort William ran to fifty-nine paragraphs of instruction 'for your guidance', all breathing the utmost urgency and reiterating the need to give Mr Stokes 'a distinguished reward'.

This looked to Arthur like his chance at last. No subservience to Admiral Rainier, no sailing under a flag of truce. A surprise attack on the true enemy, the French. He promptly got himself recalled from Mysore and wrote enthusiastically to Richard that he expected to reach Trincomalee on 22 December 1800. In case of victory he would leave Mornington (as he still called his brother) to decide whether he should remain in Mauritius or return to Mysore.

It is absolutely indifferent to me which I do, and I shall be glad to be in that place in which I can be of most service.

Within three weeks Arthur had become far from indifferent. For while he was at sea the Governor-General sent him a disquieting letter which he received in Ceylon on 7 January 1801. If after all, warned Richard, he decided that the armament assembled by Arthur at Trincomalee must be used against Egypt instead of Mauritius, the force would have to be commanded by a general, not a colonel.

Arthur reacted hotly. The general would almost certainly be Baird. Lord Wellesley himself admitted that Arthur's position under Baird, after all that had gone before, would not be 'very eligible'; yet how could Arthur withdraw just as the troops were going on active service? It was an intolerable dilemma. And why had it occurred? Because, concluded Arthur fiercely, 'you have altered your mind . . .'. He felt sure that when Richard had given the first orders he intended him to command the army *at all events*.

His embarrassed brother could not deny it, though he was to make several ingenious attempts. Since his decision to appoint Arthur he had been personally confronted by a furious Baird resolved not to be passed over a fourth time in favour of the Governor-General's brother. But the Governor-General had spoken so fast at the interview and changed the subject so often (though always with the utmost urbanity) that Baird had never managed to broach his grievance at all. Next morning, however, he returned. There were stormy exchanges, at the end of which Baird shouted hopelessly,

'Then I am to consider your Lordship's answer final and that I am *not* to command on this expedition?' To his surprise Lord Wellesley ordered him to wait. On the following day he was summoned to a third interview.

'I have finally arranged matters,' said the Governor-General with positively startling urbanity, 'so that *you* shall command.'

When Arthur heard of Baird's protest he sympathized. But that was no reason, as he was to repeat obstinately over and over again, why the wrong done to Baird should be righted at his expense. On three counts his own sense of grievance was to become almost fanatical. He had let down his best officers in Mysore by inviting them to serve on his staff in Ceylon and then handing them over to Baird, 'a man they all dislike'. He had been given the drudgery and expense of preparing the expedition on false pretences: if he was fit to equip he was fit to command. His reputation had been irreparably damaged: for it would be said that if the Governor-General, who was known to favour his brother, superseded him, there must be something very wrong with him.

The Governor-General's first instinct was to deflect Arthur's wrath by blaming Rainier. It was true that Rainier had declined to serve under Arthur on the hair-brained Mauritius venture (since Stokes, its lynch-pin, turned out to be a pompous ass and his plan, as Arthur agreed, 'the greatest nonsense'). The expedition had therefore been switched back to Batavia—but with Baird in command. Why Baird, not Arthur, for Batavia?[23]

At the end of January an overland despatch arrived from home which seemed to answer Arthur's last question and to provide Richard with an even better scapegoat than the Admiral. Writing on 6 October 1800 from Downing Street, Mr Secretary Dundas announced that the forthcoming expedition from India was after all to be part of a grand joint affair against the French in Egypt. Batavia was off. General Abercromby's forces from the west would meet 3,000 Indian troops from the east in the Red Sea—and command of those

23. This was the crux. Arthur wished to *command*, but not necessarily in Mauritius. While preparing his Indian Despatches for publication he wrote to Gurwood on 6 December 1833; '. . . I never entirely approved of the Expedition to Mauritius.'

Indian troops 'should be given to some active and intelligent officer
. . .'. So it was all Dundas's fault that Colonel Wellesley could not
command.

Arthur was not appeased. As he pointed out later, the Dundas
despatch mentioned neither Baird's name nor that of any other
general. In fact its phrase, *some active and intelligent officer*, might
have been made to fit Arthur himself.

*   *   *

Everything now seemed to conspire against him. Henry, who would
have proved a safety valve and champion, did not return from leave
in England until too late. 'Had I been here in time,' he wrote to
Arthur in March 1801, 'I think I could have prevented [Baird's]
appointment.' Worse still, the formal confirmation of his 'supersession' did not reach Arthur at Trincomalee in time to save him
from plunging yet further into the mire.

The date was 10 February 1801. Unwisely assuming that he was
still in command of the Trincomalee troops but aware from a copy of
Dundas's despatch that they were to go to the Red Sea instead of
Batavia, he decided without any instructions to provision them forth-
with in Bombay. His good friend Frederick North, Governor of
Ceylon, was horrified.[24] If Dundas's despatch meant that he should
go anywhere, it meant that he should go to Suez. Full of foreboding,
North dashed off a note to Arthur:

My dear Colonel—For the love of heaven do not go to Bombay.

North himself and their mutual friend General McDowall would see
that the bullocks from Malabar were dispatched to Suez and old
'Jonathan' (Jonathan Duncan, Governor of Bombay) could not fail to
send the rest however much he 'dawdled'.

Our friend General McDowall is fretting his guts to fiddle
strings, as I am mine, at the thought of this Bombay scheme.
Cosseir & Suez are your objects. . . . If there were any thing to say
more but go, go, go, I would.

24. Born 1764, third son of George III's Prime Minister, Lord North;
died unmarried in 1829 as Earl of Guildford.

If the worst came to the worst, North added, and the Bombay bullocks failed, Colonel Wellesley could always pick up some horses and camels from Arabia instead.

Fiddle strings? It was all fiddlesticks. This was not the way Arthur was accustomed to talk about his precious bullocks. *Horses* instead? He was aboard the *Suffolk* ready for the Bombay passage by 15 March, informing North firmly from his cabin that 'Articles of provision are not to be trifled with, or left to chance'. The friendly Governor had to wait till 30 March to hear from the headstrong but irresistible Colonel the tale of his adventures. Not that he did not know already, like everyone else, that Colonel Wellesley had received a very sour welcome in Bombay.

After the usual 'extremely tedious' passage, wrote Arthur, he had arrived to find that Lord Wellesley was 'not pleased at my having quitted Ceylon without his orders . . .'. In fact, his supersession had been made public while he was still at sea and an eager Baird had arrived in Ceylon to take over his troops, only to find they had been spirited away. Shocked and angry, Baird was forced to chase them to Bombay. Arthur meanwhile had explained the bullock problem and other reasons for his unprecedented initiative to his brother in an official letter of 23 March. That he should thus attempt to justify himself angered Fort William further, and even Henry told him his letter was 'unnecessary'. All in all, Arthur was lucky eventually to receive an imprimatur for his action. He had at least shown 'alacrity', wrote the Governor-General, and this he could 'entirely approve'.

Strangely enough, it was the culprit, Arthur, who could by no means approve. He still considered Lord Wellesley's conduct indefensible. His supersession still rankled. From Bombay he wrote to Henry: 'I was at the top of the tree in this country. . . . But this supersession has ruined all my prospects. . . . However, I have lost neither my health, spirits, nor temper in consequence thereof.'

This was brave but untrue. As he continued feverishly to probe the wound the next thing he knew was that he had been attacked by a genuine fever of some unidentified Indian species. After various treatments, the famous Dr Helenus Scott of Bombay decided it was the Malabar Itch, caught by sleeping in a strange bed on the way from Ceylon. Arthur was ordered to plunge himself into baths of nitric acid so strong that the towels on which he dried were burnt. As for his letters, large sulphurous yellow stains on the flimsy rice paper seem to this day an all too appropriate background to the caustic accounts of his wrongs.[25]

Paradoxically it was Baird himself who, on reaching Bombay on 31 March in the *Wasp*, turned out to be a much needed dove of peace. Such had been Arthur's spleen that he had made up his mind to quit the Army and India for ever—a Hercules throttled in his cradle by the serpents of envy. But Baird showed himself so sympathetic to his stricken junior—'the General behaved to me as well as a man could' —that Arthur decided to go to Egypt after all as Baird's second-in-command. He was able to write to a friend:

> My sense of the original injustice is somewhat blunted. . . . I must ever look back upon the last five months as the most interesting in my life.

This sudden swing from despair to cheerfulness—part disposition, part will-power—was characteristic of him. He was never a man of iron, in the sense of lacking temperament. The Iron Duke had even a certain volatility all his own.

Despite this upward swing, he had not really 'got the better of' (a favourite phrase) the fever, nor of the grievance. By writing a long recapitulation of his supersession on 18 April to Lord Wellesley, he seems to have caused the fever to strike again. He confessed this time to being 'very ill'. Because of the renewed eruption on his skin he had finally to cancel his '*laudable*' intention of catching up Baird in Egypt. (The sarcastic italic was Arthur's and underlined his bitterness.) Fate decided that he should remain aloof in the villa, Surrey Cottage, he had hired from a parsee rice contractor, with its porch, double carriageway—useless, alas—and tantalizing panoramic view over the Fort and Back Bay. It was just as well, for the ship in which he had intended to sail went down with all hands.

He himself put down the recurrence of his illness to the spring tides at Bombay, just as he had attributed the first attacks to his sedentary life in Ceylon and on the tedious *Suffolk*. His friends,

25. Malabar Itch, a form of ringworm entitled *Tinea imbricata*. The fungus spreads in concentric rings of scales, involving large areas of the body surface; 'a fully developed case presents a system of parallel wavy lines which at first creates the impression that a complicated series of figures has been tattooed on the skin . . .'. The irritation is severe. One modern treatment includes the application of glacial acetic acid. See Dey and Maplestone, 'Tinea imbricata in India', *Indian Medical Gazette*, January 1942.

especially Henry who was the estranged brothers' go-between, knew better. It was the Supersession Itch.

*   *   *

There was one redeeming factor, Mysore. When more or less recovered from the physical itch, Arthur had taken up his old command again in May 1801 at Lord Clive's urgent request. In Mysore things were as prosperous as they were dark elsewhere. Many a barren area had become what he called 'a sheet of cultivation', thanks to his enthusiasm, and he hoped to 'make Potatoes as flourishing in Mysore as they are in Ireland'. The place was quiet, apart from the Bull Rajah, and even the followers of the King of Two Worlds he now found to be satisfied with one, and 'very peaceful inhabitants'.

It was true that the army, officers and men alike, had deteriorated during his absence. The men's health at Seringapatam he quickly put right by rebuilding the verandah at the Green Palace where they were quartered. Certain villainous proceedings among the officers were another story and would require his more lengthy attention.[26] Nevertheless the picture was gratifying. India needed him. He took Henry's advice, given with some reserve since Henry himself was ill, not to leave 'this hateful country' just yet. Arthur felt qualified, out of his own bitter experience, to give some advice in return.

I know but one receipt for good health in this country and this is to live moderately, to drink little or no wine, to use exercize, to keep the mind employed, and, if possible, to keep in good humour with the world. The last is the most difficult, for as you have often observed, there is scarcely a good humoured man in India.

The uses of moderation, including therapeutic good temper, were of course not the discovery of Arthur Wellesley, but he was well in advance of most Anglo-Indian thinking, including that of William Hickey who boasted in 1802 of having saved the life of a fevered friend by pouring four bottles of claret down his throat every twenty-four hours. The Colonel of the 33rd had finally thrown off the social tyranny of the heavy debauch and the jovial crew.

*   *   *

26. See pp. 94–6 below.

How does he come out of the ordeal of his supersession? In many respects he was the victim of his elder brother's mistakes. 'The great Governor-General,' writes G. M. Trevelyan, 'had the impatience and the autocratic temper that often accompanies real genius not quite of the first order,'[27] and impulsiveness, a variant of the same flaw, had led him to boost the egregious Stokes and promote 'dear Arthur' over Baird's head, without considering the consequences. But when every allowance is made, Arthur's conduct can only be called obsessional. He finished by driving himself into a blind alley: Baird's appointment, he admitted, was just and unavoidable; his own supersession was unjust and unnecessary. Where was the way out?

His admirable recipe for health—good temper—he could not yet follow, despite valiant efforts. Indeed, ill-humour drove him to a step (the passage to Bombay) which even Fortescue describes in a hushed voice as 'a very bold one for a mere colonel to take', and which he himself in later years would have regarded as rank insubordination.

He and the Governor-General were still corresponding after mid-1801 through intermediaries. Great events were needed—peace in Britain and war in India—to bring these two remarkable brothers together again in a new alliance.

This time it would have to be a true alliance between equals. Arthur Wellesley was emerging as one who did not suffer superiors gladly. 'We want no Major-Generals in Mysore,' he remarked on hearing that an officer of this superior rank had landed in India. Team-work with 'such people' as seemed likely to come his way gave him the itch. As he wrote to Henry during the wretched aftermath of his supersession:

'I like to walk alone. . . .'

27. G. M. Trevelyan, *British History in the 19th Century and After*, p. 107.

6 *That is all India*

Strange things were happening in England and Ireland, though the news trickled through in the usual haphazard way, through merchant captains in Madras. 'I never reads a newspaper,' said one lately arrived; 'I have a large family and I never suffers such a thing to come into my house.' Arthur nevertheless learnt the fact of Pitt's resignation on 5 February 1801, as early as June that year. His immediate reaction was dismay. Things looked 'very bad indeed': for a new administration would be too weak to carry on the French war.

He did not yet realize that this was precisely what the majority at home desired. Wheat at £6 a quarter, causing bread riots, had temporarily dimmed the heroics of England's stand against Napoleon. The satirists chanted:

> *O Lord our God arise,*
> *Send us some new allies*
> *That we may treat.*
> *And should their amities*
> *End in fresh perfidies*
> *Send back our subsidies*
> *That we may eat.*

Pitt's successor, Henry Addington, a portentous mediocrity, was already beginning to 'treat' when Arthur first heard about the change of government. By 1 October a preliminary treaty with France was agreed amid public rejoicing. Up went the fireworks, down went the price of bread. In March 1802 the Peace of Amiens was ratified. It was to prove a curious entr'acte lasting only fourteen months, at the end of which, in May 1803, the great drama would reopen with Pitt's return, a fresh declaration of war and the majority again wanting nothing so much as a chance to get at 'Boney'.

What seemed curious to Arthur in June 1801 was the immediate cause of the Government's resignation that February, which was not war-weariness but King George III's refusal to let Pitt honour his pledges to Ireland on Catholic Emancipation. Arthur tolerantly put it down to royal madness.

I conclude that the derangement of the King's mind was the cause of his opposition. . . . He must have known of [his Minister's] intentions respecting the Catholicks when they . . . carried through the Union.

The full story was more squalid than he guessed. The Irish Parliament, following the 1798 Rebellion, had been induced to abolish itself and declare for Union with Britain during the previous year (1800) on the understanding that Catholics would henceforth be eligible for the new, united Parliament. This *douceur* had been more than matched by a golden rain of titles and cash for the Protestants who would, through the Union, lose their Dublin seats and patronage. The rate for the job was £8,000 a seat, and Lord Longford, with whom Arthur had crossed swords over Kitty Pakenham, was one of those who collected this tidy sum.

In the end only the Protestants got their *quid pro quo*. While Pitt's benign intentions towards the Catholics were still unknown to the King, the Lord Chancellor took it upon himself to warn His Majesty. George III put his foot down and Pitt resigned. Despite his victory the King apparently became violently deranged ten days later.[1] When he recovered in March Pitt promised never again to propose Catholic Emancipation during His Majesty's lifetime. 'Now my mind will be at ease,' said the King. But temporary ease of the royal mind (for Pitt's strange sacrifice did not save the King from recurring attacks) was to be won at the cost of Ireland's lasting relief.

*   *   *

The East India Company pounced with joy on the opportunities given by peace and the removal of Dundas, Lord Wellesley's friend, from the India Board. They set about putting Wellesley's policies into reverse. Urgent despatches sped from Leadenhall Street in the City of London to Fort William announcing the new era—cuts in military expenditure and stepped-up investment. There were also to be changes in personnel.

Officials, some of them with dubious even criminal records, who

1. The King's attacks are not now considered to have been madness but the disease of porphyria. See Ida McAlpine, M.D., M.R.C.P., Richard Hunter, M.D., M.R.C.P., Professor Rimington, etc., 'Porphyria—A Royal Malady', *British Medical Journal*, 1968.

had only recently been swept out of their grimy corners by the Governor-General's stiff broom and sent packing to England, were suddenly returned to sender, without compliments, by the Company. Josiah Webbe, now an ardent convert to the Wellesley system, found himself superseded and even Lord Wellesley felt the nick of the axe. One of his most creative projects, a college for civil servants in Calcutta, was summarily wound up and the chance to re-educate the ignorant young men who came out to govern India in a state of habitual 'indolence and dissipation', abandoned.[2]

The abrupt demise of the college affected Arthur also, for he had hoped that a somewhat rakish and very junior Company secretary, Tom Pakenham, son of his old friend Admiral (formerly Captain) Pakenham of Coolure, would be knocked into shape at this very institution. All he could do now for young Tom was to ask friends to keep him out of bad company and himself lend him the large sum of 9,182 rupees.

The struggle against 'our Honourable masters', as the Wellesleys sarcastically called their Directors, was reflected in the flights of letters which passed between the brothers and their loyal officials. Webbe informed Arthur drily that the Directors had made him a present of 10,000 pagodas for his services against Dhoondiah, '& it has done you the further honor of reducing your table allowance from 6[00] to 400 p[agoda]s'—the reward to operate in 365 days' time and the deduction 'on the 1st instant'.

Arthur predicted a wave of 'greediness' and 'dishonesty' among the Company's new placemen:

I have determined that as soon as . . . I find that it is intended to introduce the new system of dubashery[3] and rapacity into this country, I shall withdraw, and I believe every honest man . . . will do the same.

He himself knew a good deal about 'dubashery and rapacity' in Seringapatam and how, if unchecked, they could spread like a plague.

*   *   *

2. Macaulay derided the ignorant secretaries of the India Board who did not know whether 'the Mahrattas were Mahometans or Hindoos' (*Essay on Pitt*).

3. A *dubash* was an Indian secretary, agent or middleman, and *dubashery* meant corrupt dealings by European officials through these agents.

The trouble had begun while Arthur was away campaigning. Soon after he returned to Seringapatam in 1801 he forwarded to the Commander-in-Chief 'an interesting account of the sale of the Company's salt petre by Lieutenant-Colonel Mandeville & his lady, etc., etc.,' in their private house.[4] The 'etceteras' stood for the fact that the saltpetre was part of Tipoo's captured stores, that Colonel Wellesley had assembled a Commission of officers to inquire into the embezzlements, and that there would be a determined effort by the Europeans to make Nellahtomby Dubash, the Lascar storeman, the scapegoat.

Almost at once, however, it emerged that 'Nelly' (as the men called Nellahtomby) and his mates had committed all their enormities under orders, and when he made a statement implicating the commissary, Captain Macintire, the Commission refused to enter it on their minutes. Next morning they were forced to record something far worse—that Nellahtomby's desk had been broken open during the night by Captain Macintire and all the incriminating evidence stolen or destroyed. Even Lieutenant-Colonel Saxon, elderly and hitherto respected, was 'not quite clear'. Macintire, wrote Arthur to the Commander-in-Chief, 'must inevitably be ruined', even though he had been 'a brave and active officer'—a bit too active. Besides stealing the saltpetre, he had bought up cheap from dealers old fire-locks and gun barrels, placed them in the arsenal and sold off seven loads of new ones. Arthur himself had warned Macintire against this arms traffic, 'but as soon as I have turned by back' Macintire started operations. Old Saxon at least showed some shame: before his arrest he had been seen driving in Vellore with his palanquin closed up to hide his face. In the end all three officers were convicted, Colonel Mandeville and his lady being the worst offenders. While others were merely stealing cannon and brass pigs from the arsenal and mint, the Mandevilles had stripped the copper bands from the pillars of the Mysore palace.

Reorganization of the whole arsenal was undertaken by Wellesley, Macintire being replaced by a Captain Freese, of whom more will be heard. By the end of the year Arthur had closed 'a scene of villainy' which he believed 'would disgrace the Newgate Calendar'. Sickened though he was, humanity urged him to seal the affair with an en-nobling act. He wrote to Lord Clive on behalf of 'an old man', the

4. The British Army largely depended on India for the saltpetre used in ammunition.

former Lieutenant-Colonel Saxon, who was now completely destitute and had therefore become 'an object of charity'. In view of his long service and previous good conduct, Colonel Wellesley recommended Lord Clive to order him a small pension.

Stealing from a Company itself highly rapacious was by no means the gravest offence which Colonel Wellesley had to deal with. The very lives of the civilian inhabitants were endangered by types like Captain Shuttleworth, a dissolute Assistant-Surgeon, and a Lieutenant Dodd. Shuttleworth had tied up and flogged Chimbusa Chitty for refusing to give him straw without payment for his horses but a court martial (of which incidentally Colonel Saxon was the President) had 'honorably' acquitted the culprit of 'ungentlemanlike behaviour', letting him off with a reprimand. If such conduct was not 'ungentlemanlike', wrote Wellesley, it was a poor comment on 'the character of a British officer and gentleman, and I never can approve a sentence which describes it in other terms than those of the strongest reprobation'. The lenient sentence was nonetheless confirmed by General Braithwaite; whereupon Wellesley boldly retorted with a General Order to his troops. 'Execration,' he announced, would have been 'a more proper sentence', but since he was allowed only to lecture the offender, he would point out that troops were in Mysore 'to protect the inhabitants, and not to oppress them'. The oppressor was 'hereby publicly reprimanded'. Colonel Wellesley also took the opportunity to criticize the Commander-in-Chief, Braithwaite (though in a private comment to Close), for his 'very extraordinary' conduct.

Here was a touch of iron, likely to create devoted admirers but also personal enemies.

The case of Lieutenant Dodd was even more deplorable. This officer had forcibly obtained money from Indians by torture— making them stand in the sun with boxes of stores on their heads. Wellesley felt certain that Dodd had flogged Basur, a goldsmith, to death and then made the villagers swear that Basur had poisoned himself. And Dodd's sentence? Six months' suspension of rank and pay and—a reprimand. Once again Wellesley implored the authorities to 'reflect on the disgrace . . . to the whole army' if Dodd were not discharged. It was Dodd himself, however, who made sure that justice should not catch up with him. In the New Year of 1802 the shamefaced authorities had to inform Wellesley of Dodd's desertion. His description had been circulated—straight and well made (alas, in limbs only), sandy hair, small blue eyes, thin lips, spoke Moorish tolerably well and had 'a good deal of the Irish accent in his speech'; last seen on a Bombay boat at midnight, 3 February, 'carrying with him a tall stout Bay horse'. It was thought that William Dodd and his tall horse intended to offer their services to the Mahrattas.

*   *   *

The turbulent Mahrattas were being vigilantly watched by Wellesley. On 29 April 1802 his command was strengthened by his promotion to the rank of major-general (though only on the India list). And that spring, as if to clear the decks, Major-General Wellesley was freed from two encumbrances.

One of these was Colonel Shee, under whose erratic surveillance during Arthur's absence his precious 33rd had become a nightmare of drunkenness and brawling. There had been a ludicrous Christmas row between a lieutenant-colonel and a major, because the latter's *dubash* had overcharged the former's servant by two-thirds, for fifty raisins in his plum pudding. There had been an officer 'staggering on parade' through 'indisposition', and another in the 77th who wanted to change into the 33rd because, having been severely wounded, drink went to his head. Saddest of all was the case of young Lieutenant Goodlad who organized cricket and sent Colonel Wellesley pages of light gossip which he rightly called 'my nonsense'. At a dinner in honour of the new major-general Goodlad had said in his cups something so awful that his brother officers refused to serve with him. 'These drunken quarrels are certainly very bad,' agreed Arthur with one of Goodlad's outraged superiors, 'but give me leave to ask, are they worse in a subaltern than in a commanding officer?' If not, the regiment must pass over Goodlad's offence, since for many months it had condoned Shee's. Wellesley himself had never condoned Shee's offences. He had in fact been quietly trying to get him moved when death, heralded by a 'spasmodic fit' lasting several days, anticipated his wish.

The rebellious Rajah of Bullum was another long-term obstacle to be at length dislodged. Arthur hoped that he would give himself up, in which case he would try to get him a government provision. But the Rajah fled into the Western Ghats and was last seen with 'only a handkerchief on his head and short drawers on his *breach*'; on 9 February a reward of 1,000 pagodas offered by Major Munro accomplished his betrayal and capture. A specialist on military history and Indian government, Munro did not agree with the Wellesleys'

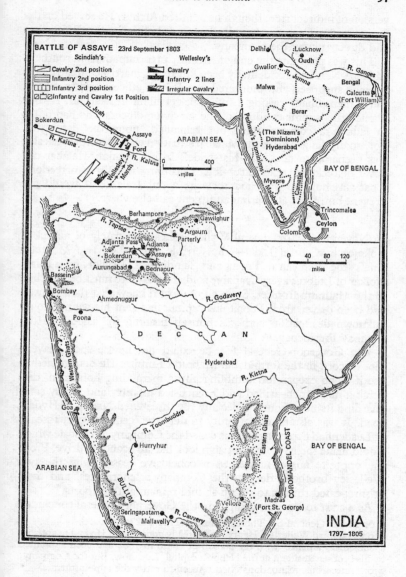

BATTLE OF ASSAYE 23rd September 1803

Scindiah's

Cavalry 2nd position
Infantry 2nd position
Infantry 3rd position
Infantry and Cavalry 1st Position

Wellesley's

Cavalry
Infantry 2 lines
Irregular Cavalry

Bokerdun
R. Juah
R. Kaitna
Assaye
Ford
R. Kaitna
Wellesley's March

ARABIAN SEA

0   400
miles

Delhi   Lucknow
Oudh
Gwalior   R. Ganges
R. Jumna
Malwa   Bengal
Calcutta
(Fort William)
Berar
(The Nizam's
Dominions)
Hyderabad
Peshwah's Dominions
BAY OF BENGAL
Mysore
Malabar Coast
Carnatic
Trincomalea
Ceylon
Colombo

Berhampore
R. Taptee   Gawilghur
Argaum
Adjanta Pass   Parterly
Adjanta
Bokerdun   Assaye
Aurungabad   Bednapur
Bassein
Bombay
Ahmednuggur   R. Godavery
Poona

0   40   80   120
miles

D E C C A N

Hyderabad

R. Kistna

Western Ghats

Goa

R. Toombuddra
Hurryhur
Eastern Ghats
BAY OF BENGAL

ARABIAN SEA

BULLUM
Seringapatam   R. Cauvery
Mallavelly
Vellore
Madras
(Fort St. George)
Coromandel Coast

INDIA
1797–1805

version of indirect rule, though he admired Arthur. He served on the
Seringapatam Commission and advocated abolition of that Rajah also,
and direct rule by the Company.[5]

This was not quite the end of Arthur's preoccupations in southern
India. A Nair had accidentally been killed; his martial compatriots in
revenge surprised and murdered two British officers and twenty or
thirty men, finally raising a full-scale rebellion in Malabar. Arthur
blamed the 'supine conduct' of the surviving officers who had failed
to launch a counter-attack but remained 'upon the defensive'.
Potentially dangerous as the Malabar situation was, General Wellesley
was prepared to take it in his stride. 'In my opinion Malabar can
never be reckoned upon excepting as a country ripe for insurrection.'
That was how he was later to write about Ireland. It would not
prevent him from answering an urgent call elsewhere.

*   *   *

In November 1802 General Wellesley heard privately of an act of
violence in Central India—'the terrible defeats' of two Mahratta
chiefs, the Peshwah of Poona and Scindiah of Gwalior, by a third,
Holkar of Indore; every available soldier in Mysore must be marched
to the Mahratta frontier. Soon all the world knew that the Peshwah
had been driven from Poona, his capital, had sent his women to an
unknown destination and was himself heading for asylum in the
Bombay Presidency.

The Governor-General felt he could not ignore such heaven-
sent discord in the formidable Mahratta Empire. He determined to
use it as an excuse for humbling all its marauding horsemen, dis-
persing its French-drilled and French-led infantry and finally safe-
guarding its neighbours, especially the threatened Nizam of Hyderabad. It was also an opportunity to defy the 'cent per cent rascals'
of Leadenhall Street, as Webbe called the Company, on a scale which
would make the Mysore campaign look like an economy drive. From
the opposite angle, it seemed a conclusive reason why the two
Wellesley brothers, despite the Company's 'enormities' and their
own repeated threats to resign should remain at their posts.[6]

As a start to the new campaign, the Governor-General concluded

5. Major-General Sir Thomas Munro (1761–1827).
6. The third Wellesley, Henry, had already gone home. He had negotiated
a 'subsidiary alliance' with the Nabob of Oudh in 1801 and been appointed
by his brother Resident at the Nabob's capital, Lucknow. But the Company,
with 'indecorous insinuations', had refused to ratify the appointment.

yet another 'subsidiary alliance' in December 1802—with the Peshwah. This treaty, called after the Peshwah's refuge at Bassein, a handsome coast town near Bombay, with an old Portuguese fort, just like many others which Arthur was soon to see in Portugal itself, shifted the whole balance of power in Central India. Until the Treaty of Bassein, the Peshwah had been titular head of the Mahratta Confederacy. Now he was a 'protected prince' or, like the rulers of Hyderabad, Mysore and Oudh, a British puppet. The other principal members of the Confederacy, Holkar, Scindiah and the Bhoonslah (Rajah) of Berar, who had hitherto spent much time fighting one another, now had a reason for uniting against the provocative British.

Arthur had always been alert to the dangers of 'subsidiary alliances', but if there was to be a second Mahratta war he intended to be in it. And not only in it, but with his scope greatly increased because of it.[7] 'You are dying of the cramp,' Addington had once told Richard before he went to India. All these talented Wellesleys tended to die of the cramp and Arthur in particular constantly needed fresh chances to develop the strength that he felt was in him. The Mahratta command seemed made for him. He also took it for granted that he would retain his command in Mysore. It was therefore with consternation that he heard privately from Webbe of Baird's appearance on the scene, bent at long last on reoccupying the seat of power in Seringapatam.

But General Wellesley's authority in Mysore was confirmed, an act which finally reopened direct communication between the two brothers. Arthur's luckless rival moved off towards the Mahratta frontier, only to find that his troops there had been reduced by drafts made upon them by—General Wellesley. Having protested to Madras in vain, Baird left India for ever, taking his fifth and last grievance home with him. Arthur's subsequent fame, however, and Baird's own sense, eventually exorcized the ancient rivalry. 'It is the highest pride of my life,' Baird said in 1809, 'that anybody should ever have dreamed of my being put in the balance with him. . . . I know both him and myself now.'[8]

* * *

7. First Mahratta War, 1761; second, 1803–5; third, 1817.
8. Baird's biographer took the line that all soldiers have the right and indeed duty to regard every appointment and promotion with 'honorable jealousy'. Perhaps it was the climate of India, where Arthur himself could find 'scarcely a good humoured man', which turned honourable jealousies so sour.

The next thing was to get the Peshwah back into Poona. At once, the piecemeal lessons which Arthur had learnt from sporadic Mahratta outbreaks on his borders were brilliantly integrated. He brought his army safely across the fords of two rivers, the Toombuddra and Kistna, in March and April 1803, and in order to be ready for the rise of these and the other great rivers which criss-cross India, he ordered Major Doolan to start immediately making basket-boats. He had both studied his Caesar and acted 'much as Alexander the Great seems to have done'.

Two things had produced a superb commissariat on the long march from Seringapatam: a lovingly perfected bullock-train, and successful if ferocious measures to prevent the troops from plundering the friendly villages on whom Wellesley depended for supplies. A smooth advance brought him within sight of his goal by 8 April. News reached him on the 19th that the Mahratta Governor of Poona intended to burn it down before evacuating. To restore the Peshwah to a smoking ruin would have been a fatal blow to prestige. So Wellesley, with 400 cavalry, covered forty miles that night—in all, sixty miles in thirty-four hours—expecting every moment, as they galloped over the last range of hills, to see a black pall above the city. When he dashed into Poona on the 20th it was in turmoil but untouched.

*   *   *

By the middle of May the Peshwah was back on his musnud (throne) receiving nuzzers (tribute) from his ministers, as Colonel Close, the Resident, exultantly if somewhat technically informed the Court of Directors. The question was now whether the other Mahratta powers could be induced to leave him there.

In General Wellesley's urgent opinion, a relentless 'harrying' of the Mahrattas by troops who could move with 'celerity' was the best tactics. But the Governor-General was so much harried himself by Company criticism that the chance to rush the Mahrattas into speedy peace was lost. Only Holkar was satisfactorily accounted for by early summer: he had discreetly withdrawn, loaded with booty, into Hindustan and on Arthur's forceful advice was allowed to get away with it. If only Arthur's advice to ignore Holkar had been followed during 1804 also, Lord Wellesley's great pro-consulship might not have ended, as it did, under a cloud.

On 4 June 1803 General Wellesley marched out from Poona.

During the next two days the armies of Scindiah and the Bhoonslah gathered menacingly on the Nizam's frontier. Nevertheless Arthur continued to negotiate, resisting Close's advice to give Scindiah a time-limit for withdrawal. This, he wrote, would smack of 'harshness and hostility'. Close retorted by denouncing (to Webbe) Arthur's lack of his usual spirit and confidence.

While angry 'epistles', as Arthur called them, dripped from moist pens and uncomradely abuse hung in the humid air of Residencies, the Governor-General took a step which finally put his brother above controversy. On 26 June General Wellesley was given plenary political and military powers. Whether by negotiations or war, his orders were to 'restore the tranquillity of the Deccan'.

Once again the Governor-General had over-ridden 'jealousy' (this time 'among the Residents') in favour of his brother.

*   *   *

The breakdown of negotiations and declaration of war took place on 6 August 1803.

The first necessity was to seize Scindiah's great hill-fortress of Ahmednuggur, among the strongest in India and plumb on the Nizam's frontier. After a 'brisk and gallant contest' on 8 August 1803 the outer fortifications of the town were captured. Two days later a battery of four guns, skilfully placed, opened fire on the fort and continued pounding away until on the 12th the garrison surrendered. So expeditious had been the performance that a bemused Mahratta chief is said to have exclaimed: 'These English are a strange people. They came here in the morning, surveyed the wall, walked over it, killed the garrison and returned to breakfast.'

Inside were found ample provisions and 'trifling articles' belonging to Scindiah—swords, dirks and pistols, looking-glasses and bawdy pictures. The picture which had made most impression on Wellesley had been that of a young soldier knocked from the highest rung of a scaling-ladder who picked himself up and immediately raced to the top of the town wall again, to be first over. Who was he? asked the General. A volunteer from the 78th, he was told, named Colin Campbell.[9] Wellesley promoted him to brigade-major and before he

9. Sir Colin Campbell (1776–1847). Not to be confused (as has happened in the editing of Ellesmere's *Reminiscences*) with Sir Colin Campbell, Lord Clyde (1792–1863), hero of the Indian Mutiny.

left India made him his private secretary. It was to be a favourite joke that he had first seen Sir Colin Campbell, Governor of Ceylon, 'in the air'.

The success of Ahmednuggur may have led Wellington later to underrate the infinitely more formidable problems of reducing Peninsular fortresses when defended by outstanding and resolute Frenchmen. Napoleon's attack on him as merely a 'Sepoy General' was false from the start and finally proved the most deadly boomerang. Wellington's Indian sieges were a different matter. The quality of resistance put up was not very relevant to Badajoz or Burgos in Spain. In conversation with Lord Ellesmere, Wellington later confessed that he had in fact thought his Indian experiences relevant, until bitterly disillusioned.[10] If Napoleon had called him a 'Sepoy siege-master' it would have been crude propaganda but less ludicrously wide of the mark.

*   *   *

While the Governor-General was as usual commending his brother's 'alacrity', Arthur had already marched from Ahmednuggur, resolved on bringing Scindiah and the Bhoonslah to a decisive battle. His second-in-command, the slow-going Stevenson, was causing him some concern. Instead of 'dashing at' the rebel horsemen, he got drawn into long defensive operations 'in which he must be a loser'. Wellesley did much galloping over grey-green or ochre hills and through muddy fords, to urge Stevenson onward. By crossing another great river, the Godavery, he managed to manoeuvre Scindiah northward away from Hyderabad. On 20 September he and Stevenson separated at Budnapoor, Stevenson advancing through a valley some fourteen miles west of Wellesley's line of march. Wellesley planned to join forces again at a village twelve miles from Bokerdun. In the neighbourhood of Bokerdun he would bring the enemy to battle on 24 September.

But on the 23rd, with Stevenson unaccountably not yet emerging from the hills, Wellesley received intelligence that Scindiah's cavalry had already escaped him, though there was still time to catch his infantry in their camp, which was only six not twelve miles away. Wellesley at once made a swift reconnaissance on a good horse, entailing a circuit of four miles. He was astonished by what he saw.

10. See below, p. 350.

Instead of infantry alone opposing him, Scindiah's whole army was still there, spread over seven miles of shimmering plain, where the green parrots, bee-eaters with copper linings to their emerald wings, vultures and kites flashed, circled or hovered in the incandescent light above the small shrubs and tangled banyans. Thousands of cavalry stretched from Bokerdun on the left to merge into infantry and artillery in the centre and round the village of Assaye on the right. A river, the Kaitna, protected their front. This was a position of considerable strength. The two brilliant French commanders, Boigne and Perron, who had been responsible for transforming the Mahratta hordes into relatively modern armies with European equipment and officers, had done their work well. The General had to think quickly. There was still no Stevenson (he had lost his way); it was a case of Wellesley's 7,000 of all ranks against six times that number. Counting cavalry alone he was outnumbered by twenty to one. He had only twenty-two cannon to the Mahrattas' hundred and more. If he retreated he would risk his baggage being seized by swarms of horsemen, besides incurring a severe blow to prestige. If he attacked it must be with troops who had already marched twenty-four miles that day. He turned to an Indian vakeel (envoy) and asked what he thought would be the result of a battle. The man replied with Oriental politeness that 'the battle was not always to the strong'. The gamble was in fact prodigious, such as only a fool or a genius would dare. General Wellesley ordered the advance. The vakeel privately decided he was mad.

The first crisis came when they heard how steep and rocky were the Kaitna's banks and the guides declared there were no fords. At once Wellesley's genius took over. Still pressing on, he saw through his glass, below Assaye, to the right, two other villages facing each other on opposite banks of the Kaitna.

> I immediately said to myself that men could not have built two villages so close to one another . . . without some habitual means of communication . . .

There must be a ford, whatever the guides said. He sent a staff officer on ahead who duly found the ford. How did Wellesley come to make his inspired guess?

> When one is strongly intent on an object, common sense will usually direct one to the right means.

Strongly intent though he was, his inevitable delays over the ford problem had given the Mahrattas time to strike camp and form into a dense line behind the Kaitna. Fortunately for him they failed to occupy the ford. But as his men marched diagonally towards it they fell under a hot cannon-fire. The head of Wellesley's orderly was blown off while he was actually crossing. The headless trunk, spouting blood, remained in the saddle for a few moments while the terrified horse plunged and reared among the general's staff, scattering them far and wide, until at last its ghastly burden slid into the water.

Once across, Wellesley calculated that the ground would favour him, or rather that he could force the enemy to conform to his idea of its most advantageous use. A tributary stream the Juah flowing parallel to the Kaitna but behind Assaye until it joined the main river well below the village, presented him with a tongue of land under a mile wide, which he could just fill with his small army. This would deny 'the overwhelming deluge of native cavalry', as he called them, any space for manoeuvre. As his men came up from the river he began forming them into three lines: infantry in the first two, cavalry as a reserve in the third, with his left and right flanks on the Kaitna and Juah respectively. There was no slackening in the Mahrattas' cannonade, but Wellesley intended to attack their left immediately, where it lay along the Kaitna, roughly at right angles to his position.

All at once it became clear to the staring British that something strange was happening. The Mahrattas had forestalled them. They were changing front, not scientifically perhaps, but with breath-taking Gallic precision. Such expertise was totally unexpected even in a French-trained army. The Mahratta infantry and guns were soon face to face with the British, between the two streams, with their left on Assaye. Every minute more and more cannon-balls came bounding across. Despite this hazard Wellesley could not avoid a corresponding adjustment in his own front line on the extreme right, nearest Assaye; for the Mahratta manoeuvre had dangerously lengthened his front. He still intended to open his attack against the infantry on the Kaitna (now the Mahrattas' right), correctly reckoning that once their right and centre had been pushed back to the Juah their left and Assaye would fall. Now, however, he must first order his pickets on the right wing to move outwards and make room for detachments coming up on their left to fill in the gaps. With this order went a specific warning to the pickets' commanding officer,

Colonel Orrock, on no account to swerve still further to the right during the coming engagement, or he would get within range of the Mahratta artillery grouped round Assaye. The order was sent. Meanwhile the murderous cannonade had redoubled. Wellesley could wait no longer. With the adjustments not yet quite completed he gave the word to attack.

We attacked them immediately, and the troops advanced under a very hot fire from cannon, the execution of which was terrible.

Terrible it was; but not enough to save Scindiah's artillery from the fury of Wellesley's centre and left. There was no resisting them. They captured or cut down the first line of brave Mahratta gunners at their posts and went on to destroy the second line, despite an audacious ruse of some of the first-line gunners. These feigned dead until the victorious British had swept over them, when they sprang to life again, turned about and fired into their captors' backs, only to be shot down in their turn. Deprived of their guns the Mahratta infantry showed no mind to stand and fight. This was what Wellesley had foreseen. This should have turned directly into his irresistible push from the left towards the Juah. And so it would have, but for the sudden intervention of dire calamity on his right.

Colonel Orrock, whether dazed by the fire or unable to halt his rightward movement, or simply misunderstanding Wellesley's warning, had led his pickets, followed by the 74th Highlanders, straight at the guns under Assaye. Theirs not to reason why. It was one of those 'unlucky accidents' for which Wellesley could never blame Orrock, though it accounted for half his total losses. The issue trembled in the balance.

With no thought but to save the remnants of their comrades, the 19th Dragoons under Colonel Maxwell and the 4th Native Cavalry dashed in together, the latter brought forward from the reserve by Wellesley himself in the nick of time. The rescue was made. The tide turned. Wellesley went on to drive in the Mahrattas along the Juah, while Maxwell and his 19th charged down upon the remaining infantry under their German commander, Pohlmann. At the moment of striking Maxwell was shot dead. His dying convulsion accidentally reined in his horse so that his men, imagining a deliberate check, wheeled aside from Pohlmann's front with shouts of 'Halt! Halt!' Whereupon Pohlmann and all his followers took the opportunity to make off. Some suspected him of treachery to Scindiah; if so it was understandable, since both his Mahratta masters had fled early in the day. Last to leave the field were the Mahratta horse who, in Fortescue's words, 'rode sullenly away'. Victory was complete.

Assaye had been a close run thing. The day was all but lost in a stupendous massacre under its walls. It was won in rivers of blood— 'the bloodiest for the numbers', as Wellington was to recall grimly, 'that I ever saw . . .'. To the enemy's 1,200 killed and 4,800 wounded he lost 1,584 killed, wounded and missing, 650 of them Europeans. In one company the officer and forty-four men out of fifty were killed. Every mounted field and staff officer lost a horse, Colin Campbell three. Wellesley's bay was shot under him and 'Diomed', the grey Arab left him by Colonel Aston, was piked. Moreover Wellesley's emergency introduction of the reserve cavalry so early in the battle prevented them from pursuing and wiping out the enemy. Thousands of Mahrattas, having fled across the Juah, were able to escape into the Adjanta Ghat, though 'in great consternation' and leaving the field littered with their magnificent brass guns.

> *The sun of the evening looked down from his throne,*
> *And beamed on the face of the dead and the dying,*
> *For the roar of the battle, like thunder, had flown,*
> *And red on Assaye the heaped carnage was lying.*

On the darkening battlefield the victors dropped exhausted and slept among the ungathered dead. Arthur, at first sleepless and mourning, sat for a time with his head on his knees. Visions of his heroic Sepoys, of his vital European regiments, of the officer who had lost one arm against the Bullum Rajah and broken the other hunting but who had charged with his bridle in his teeth waving his sword in his single, mutilated hand—all the courage and the carnage floated before him. When he at last slept it was only to be awakened by a recurring nightmare—'a confused notion that they were *all* killed . . .'. Had it been worth it? Less than a month later he was writing to Stevenson:

> I acknowledge that I should not like to see again such loss as I sustained on the 23rd September, even if attended by such a gain.

This was to be by no means the last time that melancholy would follow a great victory. Talavera, Badajoz, Vitoria to a lesser and

Waterloo to a far greater degree—they all brought their reaction. But years later, when his battles were distant memories, his friend, little Mr Chad of the diplomatic service, asked him what was 'the best thing' he ever did in the way of fighting.

'Assaye,' replied the Duke of Wellington sombrely. He did not add a word.

*   *   *

It was his victory. Without his nerve and willpower it could not have happened. Colin Campbell of the 78th, writing to the father of a dead comrade, was the first to pick out the quality which made Wellesley such an incomparable leader on the field:

> The General was in the thick of the action the whole time . . .
> I never saw a man so cool and collected as he was . . . though I
> can assure you, till our troops got the orders to advance the fate of
> the day seemed doubtful. . . .

The echoes of Assaye were to roll on triumphantly into Wellington's middle and old age, and after.[11] A visitor to the battlefield in 1829 sent him a poetic account of the mud fort overgrown by peepul trees, the fragments of shattered cannon and the sacred banyan which sheltered a fakir in its hollow trunk while its branches shaded an officer's grave. The mango under which Arthur Wellesley directed the battle had died of its wounds and been carried off for firewood. But would his Grace accept a box made from wood hewn from its roots by his Lordship's humble servant, Lieutenant J. E. Alexander? The Duke, as was his custom, would not.

A century later an Indian writer, J. R. Jeejeebhoy, eloquently declared that the victor of Assaye 'rose in his tent . . . on the 23rd of September, 1803, and before sunset found himself universally famous'. This was suitably Byronic. But in his next words the writer's enthusiasm overreached itself. 'His path thereafter,' he added, 'was ever strewn with the sweet flowers of a nation's gratitude.'

Looking no further than Arthur's last full year in India, 1804, the flowers in some places would have seemed to the hero of Assaye thinly strewn.

*   *   *

11. A monument was erected to the battle and a sum lodged in a local bank for its upkeep which produces twelve rupees a month.

By the end of 1803 the various British armies had between them won a whole series of victories.

Wellesley's army entered Berar on 25 November. At 3 P.M. on the 29th he and Stevenson, after marching in burning heat since 6 A.M., joined forces at Parterly, six miles north of the River Purna, a tributary of the great Taptee. Wellesley had detected Stevenson's approaching troops before anyone else.

'How can you tell Colonel Stevenson's dust from any other dust?' asked an admiring Indian on his staff. Immediately after Stevenson's arrival Wellesley climbed a tower to look for the enemy. Only five miles to the north, on an absolutely flat plain in front of the village of Argaum, he saw a seething mass of enemy horse and foot. He had ten or eleven thousand to put against them. Nevertheless he marched straight for the plain.

A great sea of high corn made the enemy invisible to his vanguard until the very moment when they emerged into the plain, a moment made terrible by the sudden concentrated fire of fifty Mahratta guns. Even Wellesley was at first somewhat alarmed by this development and rode forward to investigate. He was quickly reassured.

'We shall have time to take these guns before night,' he remarked confidently. His advance-guard, however, were of a different mind. Their one idea was to escape from the deadly cannonade. Already in some confusion, they and their gun-bullocks plunged backwards into two Sepoy battalions behind them, both composed of the heroes of Assaye who notwithstanding their fine record panicked and fled. Once more this was a moment of crisis on which the fate of an army hung.

Wellesley, who happened to be in the forefront of his troops, first tried showing himself to the fleeing Sepoys. He waved his sword and shouted encouragement in a vain attempt to rally them. At last he gave up, calmly sent them to the rear to be re-formed and then brought them forward again himself, under cover of his own far fewer guns, into their original positions. After it was all over he said frankly:

'If I had not been there to . . . restore the battle, we should have lost the day.'

By 4.30 P.M. all his troops were in line and he gave the word to advance. A fierce collision between Sepoys and a wild horde of screaming Arabs caused the enemy's defeat in one part of the field and rapidly expanded into the headlong rout of all the rest. Wellesley's cavalry at the battle of Argaum leapt after the Mahrattas, killing, capturing and rounding up men, horses, camels, elephants and thirty-eight cannon under the hectic light of the moon. His total losses were 562, hardly one-twentieth of his force.

Gawilghur, a vast, impregnable fortress if ever there was one, high up between the headwaters of the Taptee and the Purna, gave the Bhoonslah's defeated infantry an incomparable chance to make a last stand. They were perhaps 30,000 strong. For some reason they failed to seize it.

The siege necessitated the most violent exertions on Wellesley's part. In order to direct his ailing second-in-command, he had to ride over to Stevenson's camp every day by a circuitous mountain road, a matter of fifty miles there and back in the blazing heat.

According to the history books the place was taken by assault in a few hours on 15 December 1803. Stevenson certainly stormed the northern wall of the outer fortification in fine style. Did he really have to assault the main fortified area to the south-east, the base of whose rampart would have defeated a mountain goat? And how did Wellesley's column in the south-east corner manage to get in, *if opposed*, despite an exhausting, twisting, at times almost perpendicular climb, followed by a passage through two narrow heavy doors in a little gate tower, and then an advance for sixty yards in a chute only eighteen feet wide between high walls? The problem has mystified one of the very few military historians (if not the only one) to explore this fantastic fastness. 'Three reasonably effective troops of Boy Scouts armed with rocks could have kept out several times their number of professional soldiers.'[12] The only possible answer is that resistance collapsed before a general assault became necessary. The affair cost Wellesley only fourteen killed and 112 wounded, a small price indeed compared with Assaye. He was reaping the benefit of the moral ascendancy he had established at Assaye and Ahmednuggur. Ten years later, in Spain, he was to reap the benefit of Gawilghur, in launching troops and guns through mountains which the French considered impassable.

12. Mr Jac Weller made a unique examination of the sites of Wellington's Indian battlefields and sieges in 1968, and most kindly informed the present writer of the results of his topographical discoveries, including the deductions to be drawn from them. As well as suggesting that the all-out assault was unlikely, Mr Weller argues that the alleged slaughter of the whole garrison of many thousands was probably an exaggeration also, since Gawilghur was a hill-fort of such immense size that most of the able-bodied garrison could have escaped.

All the unfortunate Mahrattas who were either wounded or trapped on the battlements of Gawilghur were ruthlessly butchered or hurled alive on to the jagged rocks below. At such a cost were the Peshwah and Nizam saved and Scindiah and the Bhoonslah finally subdued.

*   *   *

Treaties negotiated by Arthur with Scindiah and the Bhoonslah vastly extended the 'subsidiary alliance' system and convinced the sanguine Governor-General, against Arthur's initial doubts, that 1804 would see the last Mahratta fish, Holkar, in the net. But the system was already showing its weakness. The pivotal alliance with Scindiah proved a delusion and Holkar, certain of no danger from that quarter, inflicted a defeat on General Lake's army under Colonel Monson in Malwa of such appalling dimensions that 'the national military character' seemed to have been plunged back into the bad old days when Hyder Ali and Tipoo chained up Baird.

Arthur had originally been ordered to take part in the grand drive against Holkar, but famine in the Deccan made it impossible. He put down the Monson débâcle to three things: no attention to supplies, no boats and failure to 'make a good dash at Holkar' and get it over. 'Would to God I had come round here in March,' he wrote to Malcolm, 'and Holkar would have been in the tomb of all the Capulets!'[13]

Besides Monson's 'retreat, defeat, disgraces and disasters', Arthur saw many things in the India of 1804 to make him wince. Never a devotee of 'subsidiary alliances', he wrote acidly in December that they had turned the Indian princes into 'mere cyphers', unable to organize their own defence or to rely on the Company to do it for them. His recent treaty with Scindiah he felt had been dishonoured by his brother's refusal to let Scindiah keep his capital of Gwalior:

> I would sacrifice Gwalior, or every frontier of India, ten times over, in order to preserve our credit, for scrupulous good faith. . . . What brought me through many difficulties in the [Mahratta] war, and the negotiations for peace? The British good faith and nothing else.

His position as major-general on the Madras (i.e. the Company's)

13. Monson started for Malwa in April.

staff he considered to be 'of an ambiguous nature', since it had never been confirmed in England by the Duke of York.[14]

Finally there was the question of his health. William Hickey had once commented with a mixture of relish and commiseration on a Dutchman's tombstone to be found on the Coromandel coast:

> *Mynheer Gludenstack lies interred here,*
> *Who intended to have gone home last year.*

Was this to be Arthur's fate? He suffered more and more often now from spasms of rheumatism, lumbago and ague; and when not physically feverish was consumed with a burning desire to go home: 'I am anxious to a degree which I can't express to see my friends again.' At last, after many doubts and disappointments, he made up his mind on the night of 16 February.

Imminent departure suddenly made India seem dear and he counted on Malcolm's letters to keep him in touch. Parliament had sent thanks for 'memorable services' in the Deccan; his old friend 'Beau' Cradock, now Sir John, brought out the Order of the Bath for him to Madras, and quite in the spirit of bygone Dublin pranks, pinned it on his coat, like Santa Claus, while he slept. His fortune amounted to over £42,000; enough, as he told Cradock, to make him independent but not a Nabob.[15] That was what he wanted: for as Henry had once written to him, 'you care less about money than any man I ever yet knew'.

A golden vase worth 2,000 guineas, a sword worth £1,000, besides

14. Captain Elers remembered that as long ago as 1801 Arthur had confided to him that his *'highest ambition'* was to be a major-general 'in his Majesty's service'. It seems likely that the Duke of York did not favour him, and had backed Baird for both Seringapatam and Mauritius. George Elers had a story that when General Harris, Arthur's supporter, returned to England the Duke of York snapped at him, 'Pray, General Harris, what reason had you for superseding General Baird in the command of Seringapatam and giving it to a junior officer?' Harris stammered miserably and H.R.H. turned his back on him (Elers, pp. 103, 122). On 24 December 1822 Charles Greville recorded in his diary a 'confused' conversation with the Duke of York about Wellesley and Harris which showed the Duke's hostility to Wellesley.

15. 'I am not rich in comparison with other people, but very much so in comparison with my former situation, and quite sufficiently for my own wants . . . those sums have rendered me independent of all office or employment' (*Supplementary Despatches*, vol. IV, p. 483, Wellesley to Cradock, 15 January 1805).

countless addresses from gallant officers and illustrious civilians, expressed praise and thanks. His most heartening address had come from Mysore on 16 July 1804.

> We, the native inhabitants of Seringapatam, have reposed for five auspicious years under the shadow of your protection. . . . May you long continue personally to dispense to us that full stream of security and happiness, which we first received with wonder . . . and, when greater affairs shall call you from us, may the God of all castes and all nations deign to hear with favor our humble and constant prayers for your health, your glory, and your happiness.

Here was one timeless memorial left behind in India to the 'Sepoy General'—the impress of his work and character. Another was of that whimsical kind which is sometimes bequeathed by the great to a countryside. A huge jutting peak above the village of Khandalla in the Western Ghats, known locally as the Cobra's Head, was to become The Duke's Nose.

*   *   *

On 10 March 1805 Sir Arthur Wellesley sailed thankfully in H.M.S. *Trident*, the flagship of Admiral Rainier. Her captain, Benjamin Page, in time to come presented the Corporation of Ipswich with a bust of Wellington, surprisingly designated 'The Napoleon of India'. Apart from sea-sickness, the voyage was refreshing, especially the month's stay in St Helena. Its climate seemed to him, as it did not to Napoleon, 'the most healthy I have ever lived in', restoring his physical health. 'I am now convinced that if I had not left India,' he wrote to Malcolm from the island, 'I should have had a serious fit of illness.' The old Governor, a comical 'quiz' two hundred years out of date, afforded him much needed light relief from his brother's *avant-garde* schemes. The next inhabitant of the island to interest Arthur would be neither old-fashioned nor modern, but as timeless as absolutism itself. Oddly enough Napoleon was to occupy the very house where Arthur had stayed, The Briars, while Longwood was being prepared for him.

On 10 September 1805 the *Trident* dropped anchor in the Downs, off Dover. It was the twenty-fifth anniversary of Hyder Ali's victory over the British and the fifth of Wellesley's over Dhoondiah.

*   *   *

Some time after 1815 Arthur's old governor at Angers, General Mackenzie, who had known his youthful lack of stamina, asked him to explain his extraordinary endurance on the field of Waterloo. What had caused this change? The Duke replied promptly:

'Ah, that is all India.'

It was indeed all India—the ability to live for three years on end in tents, to remain for hours in the saddle, to train troops not naturally good at marching to set up record after record. 'Marches such as I have made in this war, were never known or thought of before.' And it was all 'fair marching' measured on a wheel pushed along with the army, and sometimes called a 'perambulator'.

From physical toughness sprang prodigies of industry with the pen. His *Indian Despatches,* stiff with memoranda and enlivened with letters on all subjects from war and peace to women and potatoes, were to entrance the whole world, including their author, when they came to be published. 'They are as good as I could write now'— 'the same attention to details'—'fresh'—'amusing'. *The Times* was awed and delighted by the incessant tramp of transport bullocks through the thick volumes.

How did he manage to write so many letters in the midst of active operations? asked Stanhope. The Duke gave one of his great replies:

'My rule always was to do the business of the day in the day.'

Industry was backed by 'alacrity' which made him always seek out 'forward' officers with 'dash'. It was inexorable necessity which afterwards introduced caution into a naturally bold temperament. Indeed, his friend Colonel Thomas Munro, while congratulating him on Assaye felt bound to point out the risks he had run: 'Your mode of attack though it might not have been the safest was undoubtedly the most decided & heroic.'

From regimental experience in India he learnt how to handle large bodies of men, his command having risen to 50,000 in 1804. 'I have often said that if there were eight or ten thousand men in Hyde Park, it is not every general that would know how to get them out again. . . .' But he would have known. He also knew the value of theoretical study. He wanted some of his infantry to be taught gunnery. He still believed 'that the main strength of our armies consists in British infantry. But I think that a soldier cannot know too much.'

From the combination of experience and study came his famous 'attention to detail', which gave to the sick their cots and quilts, to the healthy an exact mixture of arrack and water, and to the bullocks a precise speed and load. But vital as his army in India was, he knew where its influence must stop. 'Although a soldier myself, I am not an advocate for placing extensive civil powers in the hands of soldiers. . . .'

Many of these concerns were material. What had India taught him about human beings?

The 'native inhabitants of Seringapatam' were not alone among Indians in regarding his justice and fairness with 'wonder'. Native customs were always to be respected, whether it was a question of who owned dancing girls 'as long as their persons are worth having', or of insisting that the search of Tipoo's zenana for arms should be 'as decent and as little injurious to the feelings of the ladies as possible'. He would not even remove from Tipoo's harem the Christian women carried off by him, despite a request from 'a very respectable priest'. For he had promised to take all Tipoo's family under the Company's protection, and 'it is not proper that anything should be done which can disgrace it in the eyes of the Indian world.'

Notwithstanding this and many other signs of sympathy, he felt no particular sentiment in favour of black skins, such as Thomas Clarkson, William Wilberforce and the Anti-Slave Trade Society were expressing in England. He would not have two half-caste officers said to be 'as black as my hat', in the 33rd. They might be 'intrinsically as good as others', but the 33rd was not a Sepoy regiment. Nor did he approve of the Resident of Hyderabad residing with an Indian princess. 'His conduct for a length of time has really been a disgrace to the British name and nation.' A place for everything and everything in its place. That was regularity. That was the ideal.

Government and Company officials often infuriated him, but he in turn was not above recognizing his own faults. The Mahratta war had caused many violent disagreements with Bombay, and on 7 January 1804 he wrote disarmingly to the Governor:

I don't know whether I ought to regret the disposition which I feel to consider nothing impossible, to suppose that everything can be effected by adequate exertions, and to feel deeply and to complain of the disappointment . . . I really believe that I may sometimes have complained without much cause.

His officers he exhorted to remember that they were 'gentlemen and soldiers'—in that order. Gentlemen did not accept bribes. Major

Doolan once naïvely reported that the Rajah of Kittoor had offered him 4,000 pagodas and Wellesley 10,000 to take Kittoor under the Company's protection. Arthur soundly berated him:

> ... I am surprised that any man, in the character of a British officer, should not have given the rajah to understand that the offer would be considered an insult. ...

The crestfallen Doolan replied that he had merely thought a cash payment would test the Rajah's sincerity. He would in future invariably comply with all his colonel's instructions, 'as my only Wish, is to Merit your approbation'. He was forgiven.

Colonel Wellesley practised what he preached.

'Can you keep a secret?' he said to a Rajah who had offered him £50,000 for information about his negotiations with Scindiah.

'Yes!' replied the Rajah eagerly.

'So can I.'[16]

It was Wellesley's firm belief that faction, or what he called 'party', was the greatest of regimental evils; but if, despite all efforts, factious critics attacked their commanding officer, he must not be swayed by them: 'do your duty as you would, if they were where they ought to be, and I daresay will be hereafter'.

To the rank and file he gave two watchwords, 'discipline and regularity', which would protect them against their besetting sin—intoxication.

*　　　*　　　*

His own besetting sin, according to Captain Elers, was certainly neither 'party' nor intoxication nor anything else of that kind.

> Colonel Wellesley had at that time a very susceptible heart, particularly towards, I am sorry to say, married ladies. ...

Elers's sly verdict was coloured by disappointments over patronage in later years; nevertheless there seems no doubt that Arthur's

16. A similar story is told of Moltke in the 1870 war:
'Can you keep your mouth shut?'
'Yes.'
'So can I.'

interest in women and theirs in him had grown while in India. With his quick speech, ready laughter and muscular, well-built figure, rather over middle height (five feet nine inches), he was an attractive man who lost nothing from his 'strongly patrician countenance' and the glitter of 'something strange and penetrating' in his clear blue eyes. Letters from fellow-officers occasionally mention his feminine admirers—the two belles of Calcutta, one of whom favoured Arthur; Mrs Coggan, who drew Arthur's portrait and was so lovesick that the Governor of Bombay begged him to 'take pity on this good lady, & ask her to pay you a visit, after the monsoon . . .'; Mrs Gordon, wife of Arthur's paymaster, who with her husband and 'the young paymaster' were kindly given rooms in Arthur's house while their own was being built. In the emotionally charged atmosphere of Anglo-Indian society, full of 'great hospitality and conviviality, seasoned with some female jealousies of attention & etiquette, & squabbles for precedence', not to mention a shared passion for amateur theatricals, the handsome major-general might well have been tempted to act as a Don Juan. Perhaps in imagination he did sometimes play that role. For an exhilarating collection of romantic fiction was listed for his voyage home. including *Love at First Sight*, *Illicit Love*, *The Rival Mothers*, *The Supposed Daughter* and *Lessons for Lovers*. But for the most part Arthur Wellesley stood out as a chivalrous though somewhat detached figure, more likely to make aphorisms than to make love.

The attention of both the Calcutta belles was soon diverted to Lord Mornington. Mrs Coggan was in fact an old lady who enjoyed flirtations with the great, and had turned to Arthur from Governor North because of certain scandalous stories about North and a Malay Princess at Colombo. The Gordons left Arthur's house in a slight huff because he was too busy to pay Mrs Gordon proper attention. Two months later she was regretting Arthur's departure on business: 'Since your absence Seringapatam has not been half so gay, no dinner partys [sic], at least I have been at none.' After the Mahratta war the gay Gordons were in great demand again. In May 1804 she was executing commissions for him in Bombay—'the oysters were excellent'—and he was astonished she should hesitate to send him notes, or doubt whether they would be acceptable. They always would be, '& what is more I'll answer your letters when I have time, which I assure you I would not do for Every body'. She had permission to detain the 'susceptible youths' of his staff—'my champions as you call them'—for three days' gallivanting at Bombay as long as she did not let them marry. 'After that they would not answer my purpose.' Better still, she could visit his headquarters at Chittendore, 'to enliven us'.

> There is excellent galloping ground in the neighbourhood of the camp; & the floor of my Tent is in a fine state for dancing, & the fiddlers of the Dragoons & 78th & Bagpipes of the 74th play delightfully.

Back in Seringapatam the following December, he writes that there is not much doing, 'indeed you seem to have tired people out'.

One more relationship with a married woman may have been of a more serious nature.

Captain John William Freese of the Madras Artillery, whom General Stuart had appointed Commissary of Stores at Seringapatam in July 1802, had a young and very pretty wife, General Stuart's daughter.[17] She had given birth to a son, Arthur, on the seventh of that month, to whom Arthur Wellesley stood godfather. Poor little Mrs Freese lost her eldest son in the following October, which may have drawn her and Arthur together, for he loved children. At any rate, he lost his heart to the captain's wife and shocked his censorious aide-de-camp, Captain West, not to mention an officious married lady, the natural daughter of an earl, a situation guaranteed to make anyone starchy. But Mrs Freese's husband, according to Captain Elers, did not object.

Arthur rode it out. Mrs Freese received a long letter from St Helena describing 'all our adventures, etc.', and Arthur's friend John Malcolm continued to send him brief news of 'little Mrs Freese' until, in 1807, his small godson was brought home from India by General Cunningham to live with an aunt. But when Arthur Freese arrived his aunt was dead. General Cunningham at once thought of the boy's godfather. Would Wellesley have him? Little Arthur was four; the same age as Salabut Khan when Colonel Wellesley rescued him from the Deccan battlefield. (One of Wellesley's last acts in India had been to leave money for Salabut's education.) Of course

17. Arthur had written to Webbe soon after the rascally Macintire was suspended as Commissary (*Wellington MSS*, 14 August 1801) to say that Captain Freese had arrived at Seringapatam to take temporary charge of the stores.

he took in Arthur Freese, and on 20 June 1807 Malcolm wrote to him from India of Mrs Freese's intense relief.

> I never saw Mrs Freese better, and your accounts of Arthur which she read today have made her mad with joy. Why do you shave the poor boy's eye-brows—& endeavour to alter God's works—In Scotland red hair is a *Beauty* at least it was *five centuries* ago.[18]

Two years later another close friend in India, Captain Barclay, reported that Major Freese had been lucky not to be in command during a mutiny at Seringapatam, while Mrs Freese had been equally lucky in her own way:

> The little lady has got over another confinement since the suppression of the Mutiny.

This is the last reference to 'the little lady' in the Duke of Wellington's correspondence, though her son was to grow up and flourish in his home and incidentally to throw some interesting new light on its inmates. For many years the portrait of a dark-haired beauty with shining eyes hung in Apsley House, whether to remind Arthur Freese or Arthur Wellesley of a lost gleam may never be known.[19]

*   *   *

It remains to round off the Indian story with a better documented affair of Arthur's 'susceptible heart', but one on which the knowing Captain Elers was silent.

Two well-meaning intermediaries had combined in 1801 to re-awaken the memory of Kitty Pakenham. The first was Colonel Beresford, lieutenant-general of the Ordnance at Dublin Castle under Thomas Pakenham of Coolure, the master-general, who wrote:

> I know not if Miss Pakenham is an object to you or not—she looks as well as ever—no person whatsoever has paid her any

18. Mrs Freese's next three sons were sent to an uncle in England who never reported on their health or progress so that Mrs Freese, through fretting, developed a liver complaint.

19. The portrait of dark-haired Mrs Freese is now at Stratfield Saye. Both Arthur Freese and his father had sandy hair.

attention—so much I say having heard her name and yours mentioned together—I hear her most highly spoken of by Mrs Sparrow. She lives so retired that nobody ever sees her—one night Tom Pakenham took me to sup at Lady Longford's—I could not avoid looking with all my eyes at the lady and thinking of you and former times.

He was thinking particularly about Arthur because a letter had just arrived from him written during the Dhoondiah campaign—'but I had not nerves to say anything about you . . .'. Beresford did have 'nerves', however, to enclose a letter for Arthur from the charming Mrs Sparrow—'she talks so handsomely of you, you ought to be flattered'—whose message, though now lost, is not hard to guess. For Arthur replied fully to Olivia Sparrow, who was the wife of General Sparrow, daughter of Lord Gosford and Kitty's best friend:

> August [1801]
>
> You may recollect a disappointment that I met with about 8 years ago, in an object in which I was most interested. Notwithstanding my good fortune, and the perpetual activity of the life which I have led, the disappointment, the object of it, and all the circumstances are as fresh upon my mind, as if they had passed only yesterday. How much more would they bear upon me if I was to return to the inactivity of a home life?
>
> Upon the whole I think that for many reasons referable as well to another person as to me, I am better away; but I acknowledge that I am very anxious to go home. . . .
>
> I have answered your question candidly, and have stated facts which tend rather to my own humiliation . . . because I wish to shew you that the merit of your friend is still felt, and because I know that you will not mention them (to more than six full assemblies).
>
> Fortune has favoured me upon every occasion and if I could forget that which has borne so heavily upon me for the last 8 years, I should have as little care as you appear to have.
>
> When you see your friend do me the favour to remember me to her in the kindest manner.

Which was it that bore so heavily upon him? Love or humiliation? Whether or not Mrs Sparrow broadcast Arthur's 'facts' to six full assemblies, she certainly forwarded his letter post-haste to Kitty. Poor Kitty's often unmanageable emotions broke loose in her reply to Olivia:

> Dublin *May 7th* [1802]
>
> God Almighty forbid he should either remain an exile from his country or be unhappy in it. Olivia you know my heart . . . as well as I know it myself you know how sincerely I am interested in his happiness, and you can imagine what gratitude I feel . . . for his kind remembrance. My dearest Olivia you know *I* can send no message, a kind word from me he might think binding to him and make him think himself *obliged* to renew a pursuit, which perhaps he might not then wish or my family (or at least some of them) take kindly. My first wish if I was not taking care not to wish about it, would be that he should return and feel himself perfectly Free (I do not mean free from regard for those who sincerely regard him, but to act as he pleases) and then—I hardly know what to wish then for fear of nursing a disappointment for him, for myself, or a vexation of my friends. Yet they all speak of him with kindness particularly Aunt. . . .

As Kitty wrote on, she gradually reined herself in and with the punctuation signs appeared three steady facts: that she still loved him, that her family were still lukewarm about him (except for Aunt and Uncle at Coolure under whose cheerful roof the courtship had begun), and that despite Olivia's assurances she desperately feared Arthur was becoming lukewarm about her.

> He now desires to be kindly remembered, but do not you think *he* seems to think the business *over*, in a former letter to you his words were I believe 'You cannot say more to her than I feel'. Do you recollect? Olivia I am afraid of saying a word ever since your letter arrived for fear it should be his name. So then the sooner I hear from you the better pray write soon.

Like all intermediaries, Kitty's dearest friend both acted as a safety-valve and kept up a good head of steam.

Letters continued to pass between Olivia Sparrow and Arthur Wellesley until at last in 1805 the time came to put it all to the test. One thing at any rate was clear. His longing to get home was not only due to ill-health or bad relations with the Horse Guards and Leadenhall Street. Nor was there any doubt of whom he was thinking when he told Lord Wellesley, 'I am anxious to a degree which I can't express to see my friends again.' Nor to what he referred when he wrote to Cradock, 'I am not rich in comparison with other people, but very much so in comparison with my former situation. . . .' Even the Mrs Gordons and Mrs Freeses now fell into place. They were the way in which he chose to learn his *Lessons for Lovers*. More effectively than Mrs Sparrow they sharpened the soldier's nostalgia and desire for family life. And being married ladies, they preserved him in that interesting state which Kitty had described as 'Free'.

INTERLUDE

7 *My Dearest Kitty*

Arthur Wellesley was home after nine years, if home was the word. His mother was still living in a house off Cavendish Square; but there was no intimacy here. Her letters to India had been so impersonal that every page, as Henry said, might have been cried aloud from Charing Cross. A Dublin acquaintance, Sir Jonah Barrington, meeting Arthur again in the Strand, did not recognize the 'sallow' stranger, and Arthur had to stop him with the words, 'Have you forgotten your old friend?' He had been fêted all over India; in England he was hardly known, and the 'rattles' of the *bon ton* were ill-equipped to discuss Assaye. Yet he must still bend his mind to the East. There was urgent work to be done for his brother: the defence of the whole 'Wellesley system' in India to a sceptical Whitehall and hostile Leadenhall Street.

Richard was no longer Governor-General. On the voyage home Arthur had learnt of his abrupt and ignominious dismissal. He was even now on his way back, having been replaced by the old, low-spirited and ailing Lord Cornwallis. The choice by the Company of this broken-down servant was in itself an insult to the Wellesleys. 'Send me all your commands to England,' Arthur had written to his brother before leaving; 'I shall have nothing to do excepting to attend to them. . . .' He had not then visualized how irksome his task would be, and there was also other business to occupy him.

From September 1805 onwards the hope of serving in a European war absorbed him. He had arrived home to find a Third Coalition just concluded by Pitt—Britain, Russia and Austria against the newly crowned Emperor Napoleon—and there was the prospect of a British expeditionary force to support it. Less than half his mind can now have been on the empire of the Mahrattas. As for his being rich enough to live 'independent of all employment'—that only meant he could afford to wait for the right post. Meanwhile, by a historic coincidence, his first encounter with the civilians of Whitehall brought him face to face with the very heart and genius of the war.

At the Colonial Office in Downing Street, on 12 September Arthur Wellesley was waiting to see Lord Castlereagh, who had lately been moved from the India Board to become Secretary of War and the Colonies.[1] Also waiting in the little ante-room for an interview was a naval gentleman with only one arm, whom Arthur immediately recognized. The gentleman could not be expected to know the crop-haired, sunburnt major-general from India, nine years younger than himself. But neither did the major-general expect to be treated to quite such a display of Nelson's notorious egotism:

> He entered at once into conversation with me, if I can call it conversation, for it was almost all on his side, and all about himself, and, really, in a style so vain and silly as to surprise and almost disgust me.

No doubt the victor of Assaye managed to convey his impatience; or, as Arthur himself suggested with engaging simplicity,

> I suppose something that I happened to say may have made him guess that I was *some-body*. . . .

At any rate, Nelson left the room for a moment, found out who the general was and returned to dazzle him with a very different version of the Nelson touch.

> All that I thought a charlatan style had vanished, and he talked . . . with a good sense, and a knowledge of subjects both at home and abroad, that surprised me equally and more agreeably than the first part of our interview had done; in fact, he talked like an officer and a statesman. . . . I don't know that I ever had a conversation that interested me more.

What did they discuss? Posterity is indebted to John Wilson Croker for an account of this interview written down from the table-talk of the ageing Duke of Wellington when he himself had become the world's most famous living 'officer and statesman'. Wellington recalled that Nelson had dwelt on 'the state of this country' and 'affairs on the Continent'. An article in *The Edinburgh Review* of 1838 was more specific. Wellesley apparently contrasted the feeble action of Vice-Admiral Calder that July against the French Admiral Villeneuve,

1. Mr Oliver Warner writes that the ensuing event 'almost certainly' took place on this date. See 'The Meeting of Wellington and Nelson', *History Today*, February 1968.

with the conclusive victories which Nelson had 'taught the public to expect'. Like certain Indian officers known to Arthur, Calder was one of those who failed to 'make a dash at' the enemy.[2] Nelson in turn expressed the hope that Wellesley might be appointed to attack the French in Sardinia—strategic 'good sense' compared with the expedition to Hanover which Pitt was actually planning.

Nelson undoubtedly helped to form the future Duke of Wellington's ideal of the great captain who could see far beyond his own flagship or headquarters. It would be interesting to know whether Nelson also gave Wellington a clue to his secret as a leader—the delightful impression of consultation, of welcoming advice, of taking the younger colleague into his confidence and spontaneously disclosing what he hoped to achieve. If he did, Arthur Wellesley was unable to benefit. Sensitivity to the responses of others could produce, as in Nelson, both a unique grace of leadership and the weakness of vanity. Neither that particular grace nor that failing were among Wellington's endowments.

By the narrowest of margins providence had succeeded in bringing together the heroes of Trafalgar and Waterloo for the best part of an hour. On the following day, 13 September 1805, Nelson left London to join H.M.S. *Victory* at Portsmouth, and at the cost of his life to win the resounding triumph which Calder had missed. Wellesley had only just arrived in London after a quarter of his life spent abroad. During the years of battle ahead he became fond of invoking 'the finger of Providence' to explain extraordinary pieces of good fortune. On this earlier occasion he felt that Lord Castlereagh's keeping his two visitors waiting long enough to discover one another's worth, had been a matter of luck: '. . . luckily I saw enough to be satisfied that [Lord Nelson] was really a very superior person. . . .'[3] It is by no means impossible that Castlereagh did it on purpose.

*   *   *

2. Calder was sent home just before the battle of Trafalgar for having failed to pursue Villeneuve on 23 and 24 July, after capturing two of the Spanish ships on the 22nd. One reason for Calder's failure was his wish to secure the two prizes. His active career came to an end.

3. The full passage runs: 'Now, if the Secretary of State had been punctual & admitted Lord Nelson in the first quarter of an hour, I should have had the same impression of a light and trivial character that other people have had, but luckily I saw enough to be satisfied that he was really a very superior person . . .'.

Arthur's loyal efforts during that autumn of 1805 on his brother's behalf, were rewarded. Not of course by converting Castlereagh to the belief that Lord Wellesley had after all acted according to instructions. Castlereagh obstinately insisted that the Governor-General should have found some 'middle way' of saving India without a Mahratta war. 'From this supposed project,' wrote Arthur sadly to his brother, 'I could never drive him.' Yet, while Castlereagh resisted the advocate's pleas he came to believe in the advocate's personality and skill. At a crucial moment in Arthur's career this was to make all the difference.

Pitt was visiting George III at Weymouth when Arthur arrived in England, but within a few days of returning home he invited General Wellesley to ride with him from Wimbledon Common to London. Arthur continued to his brother:

> We rode very slowly [Pitt's health was crumbling] and I had a full opportunity of discussing with him and explaining all the points in our late system in India, to which objections had been made, which were likely to make any impression upon him. . . . Upon all these his mind appeared to be satisfied.

It was fortunate that Pitt seemed satisfied, for Arthur had arranged to leave London next day. He proposed to take the cure in Cheltenham. It was a cure which he hoped would lead to his recovery from rheumatism and possibly also from many deeper-seated ills, such as loneliness, disappointment and humiliation.

* * *

A week or more before his journey Arthur had received a letter from Olivia Sparrow (which he did not keep) dated 17 September. Overwhelmed as he was with business, he found no time to answer it until the 24th. But on that day he sent her an interesting reply.

Kitty Pakenham had lost her brother-in-law, Mr Hamilton. She was in Ireland, presumably leading a life of unselfish seclusion; mourning for the deceased and comforting the widow, her younger sister Helen. This, it appears, was not an excuse in Mrs Sparrow's eyes for Sir Arthur's failure to communicate with her. These facts, or something like them, emerge from Arthur's reply to Olivia.

. . . I see evidently that you imagine that I am unworthy of your friend & I have not vanity enough to assert that I am otherwise. All that I can say is that if I could consider myself capable of neglecting such a woman I would endeavour to think of her no more. I hope that you will find that I am not quite so bad as you imagine I am.[4]

So Arthur was going to have a chance to prove himself. But where and when? Clearly in Cheltenham, whither Mrs Sparrow must have summoned him.[5] It was after the meeting in Cheltenham that he hoped Mrs Sparrow would find him 'not so bad'. Mrs Sparrow herself had been neglectful in one respect, for he continued:

You have not told me what is to become of your friend in the Winter. Does she remain in Ireland? Shall I go over to see her? How long has Mr Hamilton been dead?

Arthur then went on to break to the eager go-between some unpleasant news. Through no fault of his own, all might yet come to nothing.

The Government were about to dispatch a force to the Elbe, hoping to rescue the King's ancestral Hanover from the French. He therefore ended his letter to Mrs Sparrow on a subdued note:

I am very apprehensive that after having come from India for one purpose only I shall not accomplish it: & I think it not impossible that if the troops under orders for embarkation should be sent to the Continent, I shall be ordered to go with them, & possibly never see you or her again. . . .

4. Sir Arthur Wellesley to Hon. Mrs Sparrow, 24 September 1805 (*Wellington's Private Correspondence*). It is possible that Mrs Sparrow had heard Arthur's name linked with someone else. Kitty's niece, Mrs Foster, wrote many years later that after his return all the gay and fair 'flocked admiringly round the gallant & attractive young officer' and rumour at once selected for him one whose smiles he was supposed to return. But he 'answered all such gossip by the silencing step of proceeding directly' to ask for the hand of his first love (*Wellington MSS*).

5. See Mrs Arbuthnot's Journal, 27 June 1822, where she noted that the Duke of Wellington had told her Lady Olivia Sparrow (as she then was) 'sent for him' on his return to England.

If Arthur really believed that he had left India 'for one purpose only'—to see Kitty Pakenham again—his mood was more romantic than he afterwards admitted. More important than his mood, however, was the letter which he had written to the young Kitty about 1794 before leaving Ireland, containing a phrase which he was not likely to forget: 'my mind will still remain the same'. Now that he was well-off, Lord Longford's 'pecuniary motives' for refusing his consent to the marriage would no longer operate. If Kitty still wanted him, his old pledge stood and he was hers. Only the lady herself, or death somewhere on the foggy Elbe, could release him.

Fortunately for the success of his chivalrous enterprise, the first detachment of troops for Hanover (which did not include Arthur) was not after all destined to embark until the end of October. But there was still one country visit to be fitted in before he could take the road to Cheltenham.

*   *   *

On the way there, he had to call in at Stowe, the seat of Lord Buckingham, where he 'underwent a bore for two days' discussing Lord Wellesley's future with his fat old friend. 'Bucky,' reported Arthur in due course to his brother, 'is very anxious that you should belong to the opposition'.[6] With this in mind Bucky urged Arthur to 'inflame' Lord Wellesley against Pitt for not having given him the Garter. Furthermore, Arthur should emphasize that the Government depended on the support of an old, sick King, whereas the Opposition were backed by the future, in the shape of the Prince of Wales. In short, argued that connoisseur of self-advancement, 'to join the opposition was the best political game of the day'.

The boredom of life at Stowe did not incline Arthur to these views. Instead he recommended his brother 'to remain neutral for some time, and observe the course of events'. As for Parliamentary attacks upon Lord Wellesley, they were inevitable. No one in England, Arthur complained, understood India or even tried to.

*   *   *

6. (*Wellington MSS*, 21 December 1805). The so-called New Opposition whose leader was Lord Buckingham's brother, Grenville. Lord Grenville became Prime Minister of the coalition 'Ministry of all the Talents' after Pitt's death and the consequent fall of his Tory Government.

When Arthur at last reached the agreeable spa of Cheltenham it would have been as well if he had remembered his own sage advice delivered to Richard in another context—'remain neutral for some time'. His love for Kitty was far from compelling. Indeed it is fairly certain that, with other young men about town, he had been drawn to the company of London's most bewitching courtesan, Harriette Wilson.[7] Nevertheless he met General and Mrs Sparrow at Cheltenham by arrangement.[8] Olivia was 'very charming', as Colonel Beresford had long ago discovered. The atmosphere was agreeable and there was much to talk about, Olivia's brother-in-law being Lord William Bentinck, Governor of Madras when Arthur left India. Arthur's sister-in-law, Mrs William Wellesley-Pole, had given him an introduction to a French *émigrée* countess and her friend Miss Upton; and there was a moment of wit and drama worthy of his favourite amateur theatricals. The countess's garter fell off as they left the Pump Room, Arthur picked it up with the appropriate words, '*Honi soit qui mal y pense,*' and Miss Upton whispered sardonically in the countess's ear, 'Lucky it was a new one.'

Mrs Sparrow's task was not difficult. She must have already written to Kitty giving her a glowing account of Arthur's faithful love, together with his letter of the 24th. An answer from Kitty would arrive soon. All she had to do meanwhile was to go on being charming, while Arthur went on proving that he was 'not quite so bad' as she pretended to imagine.[9]

Kitty's answer was sent to Olivia on 8 October. It is clear from the

7. See below, pp. 191–6.

8. It is quite clear that Wellesley was in touch with Mrs Sparrow and replied to her letter on 24 September *before* he left London for Cheltenham. See *Diaries and Correspondence of G. Rose*, vol. II, pp. 198–9, which show that Pitt went to Weymouth on 17 September (before seeing Wellesley), was there at least till the 22nd and was back in London on the 29th. Wellesley was writing to Colonel Freese from Cheltenham on 18 October (*Supplementary Despatches*, vol. IV, p. 533). Sometime therefore between 23 September and 18 October he left for Cheltenham, taking in Stowe (two days) on the way. A likely date is the end of September, since he wrote to Lord Wellesley that he had gone to Cheltenham 'shortly after' his arrival in England (*Supplementary Despatches*, vol. IV, p. 535).

9. Sir Herbert Maxwell's account (*Wellington*, vol. I, p. 78), on which others, including Mr Guedalla's are based, describes how at Cheltenham 'an amiable busybody', Lady Olivia Sparrow, twitted Wellesley with heartlessness to her bosom friend. Wellesley exclaimed, 'What! does she still remember me? Do you think I ought to renew my offer? I'm ready to do it.'

long, distraught sentences that *she* was Olivia's problem, not Arthur.

> Your letter arrived just as I was leaving Langford Lodge. Olivia it does agitate me. . . . What can I say, I can know nothing of his mind but what you have told me you assure me he still regards me he has authorized you to *renew the proposition* he made some years ago but my Olivia I have in vain sought in his letter for one word expressive of a wish that the proposition should be accepted of.

She continued, like the good creature she was, to insist that if he were proposing to her 'from any cause *whatever*' but a thorough conviction that it would contribute to *his* happiness, she would be 'most truly wretched'. Then she proceeded to show a degree of shrewdness and sensitivity sadly lacking in her Olivia:

> It is quite impossible for me to express the apprehension that preys upon my heart. . . . I think he wishes to be ordered abroad and perhaps he is right for I am very much changed and you know it within these last three years, so much that I doubt whether it would now be in my power to contribute [to] the comfort or happiness of any body who has not been in the habit of loving me for years like my Brother or you or my Mother. Read his letter again my dear Olivia is there one expression implying that *Yes* would gratify or that *No* would disappoint. . . . Perhaps when I hear from you again . . . this most painful doubt will be removed till then what can I say?

This pathetic cry from the heart at last petered out in disjointed comparisons between mutual and one-sided love, in the reflection that if she had disobeyed or deceived her mother, 'he must himself have disapproved of my conduct', and, significantly, in an agonized reference to the oppression of her mind which prevented her from writing intelligibly.

But Kitty's predicament was intelligible enough. To read her letter right through is to receive the impression of some sense, much sensibility, but above all of emotional unease. What had happened three years ago to make her write that she was 'very much changed' and—almost accusingly to Olivia—'you know it'? Her friends declared she had lost her round pink cheeks pining for Arthur. 'She is now very thin and withered (I believe pining in his absence helped to make her more so),' wrote the Hon. Mrs Calvert in the following

May.[10] Others asserted that she had been scarred by smallpox. This was not true and was contradicted in writing after the death of Wellington by her beloved niece Catherine Foster, *née* Hamilton, only daughter of Kitty's sister Helen.

Often had the Duchess [Kitty] been heard to laugh at the impudent and ill-natured untruth, which soon became a current report, that she had been disfigured by the smallpox, an invention which was the more daringly absurd from the impossibility of its falsehood not being evident to all who personally knew her. The unblemished texture of her skin and the extreme beauty of her teeth, together with the extraordinarily youthful appearance of her delicate little figure were always too remarkable . . . to leave any possibility of any *mistake* representing her personal appearance excusing the *misstatements* which were very generally made.

Nevertheless the irresistibly sentimental lyric by Tom Moore was said to have been inspired by Arthur Wellesley's love for his 'dear ruin':

> *Thou would'st still be adored, as this moment thou art,*
>   *Let thy loveliness fade as it will;*
> *And around the dear ruin each wish of my heart,*
>   *Should entwine itself verdantly still.*[11]

The beginning of the 'change' in Kitty, precisely dated by herself to 1802, had another cause, and a clue is found in the brief love-story of Kitty Pakenham and Galbraith Lowry Cole.[12] This young man, who was to become one of Wellington's Peninsular officers, proposed to Kitty 'two or three years before' Arthur's return from India. According to Cole's family, Kitty 'played fast and loose with his affections'. In proof, his granddaughter quotes a letter of 20 October 1802 from Lowry's brother William, Dean of Waterford, to another brother, Arthur:

10. Hon. Frances Pery (1767–1859), daughter of Edmond Sexton Pery, Viscount Pery.
11. Another version of the Moore story is that the poet was in love with Kitty himself.
12. 1779–1842, second son of the Earl of Enniskillen. Married in 1815 Lady Frances Harris, daughter of Lord Malmesbury.

> . . . Lowry since that love affair with Kitty Pakenham seems like
> a burnt child to fear the fire. . . .

and again on 1 July 1803 to the same brother:

> Kitty is at Cheltenham. I am beginning to think she wishes to
> bring on the subject again with Lowry, but he fights shy. She will
> deserve it as she treated him cruelly. . . .

Suppose the fire had burnt Kitty also? The affair was certainly no
flash-in-the-pan, for Kitty's brother Ned returned on sick leave from
the West Indies early in 1806, just in time for her wedding, but
expecting to find her engaged to—Lowry Cole.

The pieces of the jigsaw begin to fall into place. *1801*: Colonel
Beresford reported to Wellesley that Kitty looked 'as well as ever—
no person whatsoever has paid her any particular attention'. *May
1802*: Kitty wrote to Olivia that 'he' (Colonel Wellesley) seemed to
think 'the business *over*', and anyway a renewal might cause 'vexation' to her family. *Mid-1802*: Kitty herself considered the business
was over and therefore allowed Cole to court her. He proposed and
was accepted. *Later 1802*: Mrs Sparrow intervened. Citing Arthur's
letter from India as proof of his continued attachment, she begged
Kitty to remain faithful to him. Olivia won, as she always did, and
the Cole engagement was broken off. But the unfortunate Kitty,
torn between the conflicting pressures of her beloved mother and
eldest brother, her present lover and her best friend, fell into a
decline.[13] (Three years later Mrs Calvert was remarking that 'she
looks in a consumption' and her doctor, Sir Walter Farquhar, advised
her to take great care of herself.) Today we should probably say that
she had a nervous breakdown.

Gradually and painfully she struggled back to health. By the time
Olivia told her that Arthur was on the way home at last, she seemed
almost her old self again. 'I never saw her look more animated or more
pretty,' wrote Maria Edgeworth four days before Arthur reached the
Channel, 'than when she was speaking of herself.'

But ever since 1802–3 her temperament had been different, as Mrs

13. Kitty's niece Mrs Foster (see footnote p. 129 and text p. 133) mentioned in her apologia for the Duke and Duchess that after Arthur departed
for India Kitty's brother was induced to 'press upon her' the advisability of
accepting some other admirer.

Foster made clear towards the end of the passage already quoted:

> An air of dejection and melancholy paleness was all that could have been wished otherwise in the amiable Duchess. . . .

Self-critical and anxious to a degree, though at the same time curiously opinionated, she may well have given rise to the nineteen-year-old Annabella Milbanke's strange remark on turning down Ned Pakenham in 1812: 'all the Pakenham Family have a strong tendency to insanity'.[14] Not that Miss Milbanke was a good judge, if she thought that in choosing Byron instead she was uniting herself with a pillar of normality.

Kitty's agitated letter of 8 October clearly gave Mrs Sparrow the chance to draw back before it was too late. But the assiduous scheming of five years could not be reversed. She showed the letter to Arthur. Without having set eyes on Kitty for at least eleven years, he sent her a formal proposal of marriage.[15] It was a strange reflection of his fatalistic state of mind, in which the study of personal happiness found so little place.

The other female friend, Mrs Calvert, heard afterwards that 'when someone told Sir Arthur he would find her much altered, he answered that he did not care; it was her mind he was in love with, and that could not alter'. Alas, the mind, too, had changed. Though Kitty was still a bookworm, the delightful little toast of Dublin Castle, gay, carefree and winning had vanished.

Within three weeks or so Arthur received from Kitty a joyful if still somewhat nervous acceptance:

> I should be the most undeserving of beings were I capable of feeling less than gratitude in return for the steadiness of your attachment. . . . To express what I feel at this moment would be quite impossible. I will therefore only say that I am conscious of a degree of happiness of which till now I had no idea.

But ought they not to meet first? asked Kitty.

14. There was also Robert Pakenham, an invalid twin of Henry who died aged sixteen and whose name was not included in later genealogical tables. Ned Pakenham referred to 'our Robert's heavy disposition' in a letter home in 1807. By then 'our Robert' was dead (*Pakenham Letters*).

15. His actual letter has not survived but Kitty's reply (see below) proves that he sent it.

It is indeed my earnest wish to see you, besides the pleasure it must give me to meet again an early and truely valued friend, I do not think it fair to engage you before you are quite positively certain that I am indeed the very woman you would chuse for a companion a *friend* for life. In so many years I may be much more changed than I am myself conscious of. If when we have met you can tell me . . . that you do not repent having written the letter I am now answering I shall be most happy.

Kitty had thus conscientiously repeated the offer to release him. More than ever now he was bound to ignore it.

A copy of this letter was dispatched by him to Mrs Sparrow—he could not 'bear to part with' the original—together with two other letters which he had received on the same day, presumably from Kitty's brother and mother giving their consent. 'Now my dearest friend,' he wrote to Mrs Sparrow, 'you may wish me joy for I am the happiest man in the world. Nothing could now prevent my happiness but this expedition'—the forthcoming expedition to the Continent. If, however, he could get leave before it, without seeming to shirk active service, he would be in Ireland very soon.

*   *   *

The war in Europe was still on Arthur's mind. He had received his answer from Kitty on 4 November. It was a date of private satisfaction neatly sandwiched between national tidings, first of disaster, then of a tragic triumph. On 20 October Napoleon had eliminated the Austrian army at Ulm. The dreadful news reached England on 2 November. Pitt would not believe it until next morning his friend, Lord Malmesbury, translated an account from a Dutch paper. Then 'his countenance changed'. The day after Ulm came Nelson's victory on 21 October at Trafalgar, and on 6 November its announcement in England, together with the heavy news of the hero's death. Despite the almost unbearable loss—how could they defeat Napoleon without him?—the nation recognized that it was Pitt's energy which had made Nelson's triumph possible. The effect of Ulm was wiped out and on 9 November, Lord Mayor's Day, the Great Commoner was thanked at the Guildhall Banquet for saving Europe. It was Pitt's day. Arthur Wellesley was present to hear the Prime Minister's reply, unforgettable in its brevity and grandeur.

I return you my thanks for the honour you have done me; but Europe is not to be saved by any single man. England saved herself by her exertions and will, as I trust, save Europe by her example.

The Duke of Wellington described it with enthusiasm but equal brevity to his friend Stanhope thirty-three years later: 'That was all; he was scarcely up two minutes; yet nothing could be more perfect.'

It was the supreme lesson of much in little. But though Wellington applied it brilliantly to his own conversation and despatches, the gift always fled from him when he rose in Parliament.

*   *   *

One more memorable encounter took place between Pitt and Arthur Wellesley before each set out on his travels—Arthur to the Continent, Pitt to eternity. Taking the young soldier into his confidence, the Prime Minister predicted that Napoleon would be checked as soon as he met with 'a national resistance'; that 'Spain was the place for it, and that then England would intervene.' Ten years later, at a dinner in Paris after Waterloo, Arthur Duke of Wellington recalled this remarkable prophecy.

Was the whole story apocryphal? It originated with the Spanish general Alava who was present at the dinner in 1815, and was repeated by Lord Acton in his *Lectures on Modern History*, 1906. An unpublished letter from Wellington seems to support it. 'I happen to know', wrote the Duke in 1847, 'that Mr Pitt before he died was in communication with the Spanish government.'[16] The extraordinary thing was that Pitt's young confidant was to become the instrument through which his prophecy was fulfilled.

*   *   *

There was no chance to get to Ireland and back before the Continental expedition sailed. Arthur was waiting about for his turn to embark. He filled in the time by accepting an invitation from the

16. *Wellington MSS*, 2 March 1847, Duke of Wellington to J. W. Croker. On the 22nd of the same month the Duke added that 'with Mr Pitt himself, I had been on the most intimate Social relations from the time I landed in England in September till I went from Deal to join the Army on the Weser ... in the last days of December'.

East India Company to one of their 'Wednesday dinners'. There were also Lord Wellesley's children to be visited—one of his few entirely pleasurable duties. All the boys were fine fellows and the girls handsome and accomplished. 'This is some consolation,' he added, 'even if your services should not have been . . . treated as they deserved.' Arthur concluded a very long letter with, for him, an unusual outburst of eloquence. Richard had the final consolation of reflecting that

> by your firmness and decision you not only saved but enlarged . . . the invaluable empire entrusted to your government at a time when everything was a wreck, and the existence even of Great Britain was problematical.

With its unmistakable echoes of Pitt, this letter, dated 21 December, was left to await Lord Wellesley's arrival. Arthur was now at Deal, on the point of taking a brigade of infantry to reinforce the thousands of British troops already in north Germany, wasting their time in supporting a Prussian offensive which never came off. He only hoped this expedition would be more fortunate than its predecessor in November—'but it does not look like it'.

He was right. Contrary winds had prevented the Government from learning that three weeks earlier, on 2 December, Napoleon had finally crushed the Austrian and Russian armies at the battle of Austerlitz. The news, when it came, broke the Third Coalition and Pitt's heart. The change in his expression that had followed Ulm now returned in a permanent and more harrowing form. For the few weeks that remained to him, his face was stamped with what his friend William Wilberforce called 'the Austerlitz look'.

Among the grim wastes around the River Weser, full of disagreeable memories of 1795, Arthur heard the grimmer news. It seemed ironic that on 30 January of the new year, 1806, in the midst of such complete and comfortless inactivity, he should be appointed to the post of colonel of the 33rd. But that was his fortune. For old Lord Cornwallis, his predecessor, who had caused so much trouble to the military agents by not paying the regiment's bills, had died in India three months after becoming Governor-General. That February Arthur Wellesley, without having fired a shot but with a greatly augmented salary, was brought home again.

*   *   *

The outlook seemed grey. Pitt had died on 23 January 1806, just over a week after receiving his friend Lord Wellesley, the newly arrived ex-Governor-General of India, at his bedside. The dying minister gasped out a few words in praise of Lord Wellesley's brother—'He states every difficulty before he undertakes any service, but none after he has undertaken it'—and then fainted.[17] This distinguished tribute, however, could not assist Arthur's immediate career. He was put in command of 'a few troops' at Hastings—'the old landing place of William the Conqueror', as he explained to the historically-minded Malcolm in India. But there was no prospect of it becoming the landing-place of Bonaparte, for he had dismantled his invasion camp at Boulogne a full month before Arthur Wellesley arrived back in the Channel. As Arthur sailed by, he may have seen Napoleon's unfinished obelisk on the hills above Boulogne, begun in good time to commemorate a conquest which never took place. How could Sir Arthur Wellesley, K.B., submit to such paltry employment? asked one of his friends. His answer became famous.

I am *nimmukwallah*, as we say in the East; that is, I have eaten of the King's salt, and, therefore, I conceive it to be my duty to serve with unhesitating zeal and cheerfulness, when and wherever the King or his Government may think proper to employ me.

This was the first time that Arthur Wellesley had expressed an idea so familiar to his ancestors of the Irish Pale—'retained for life'. That it came to him first from India was significant, for India was his most formative period. At a later date he was heartily to approve of his friend Barry Close's success in restoring order among some mutinous Sepoys by reminding them that they were *nimmukwallahs* and had eaten the Company's salt.

Wellington was a man in whom an idea, once it had taken root, struck wide and deep. He became possessed by it. The idea of the retained servant, the *nimmukwallah*, was to send up marvellous shoots.

*   *   *

17. These words have been described by Pitt's biographer, J. Holland Rose, as his 'swan-song' (*William Pitt and the Great War*, p. 556). See also Gleig, *Life*, p. 8, who claims to have received Pitt's opinion of Arthur Wellesley direct from Lord Sidmouth (Addington). Pitt considered Wellesley 'quite unlike all other military men. He never made a difficulty, or hid his ignorance in vague generalizing. If I put a question to him, he answered it distinctly; if I wanted an explanation, he gave it clearly. . . .'

Hardly had Arthur accepted the fact that he was to be retained at peaceful Hastings, than he was faced by high excitement elsewhere. The trouble which he had predicted in Parliament over the 'Wellesley system' blew up in the person of a retired Anglo-Indian merchant named James Paull. This strange character had made a large fortune in Oudh, partly through 'ingenuity', and partly through the benevolence of Lord Wellesley. In the course of two years Paull's initial gratitude to the Wellesleys had turned into profound vindictiveness. While in Oudh he had researched into the details of Henry's unpopular treaty with the Nabob. He was now busy exposing it in Parliament. His indictment was that the Wellesley administration had squandered public money, including a grant of 30,000 rupees to Arthur in the Deccan. His aim was to have Wellesley impeached. With the very recent precedent of a former First Lord of the Admiralty, Lord Melville, who had been successfully impeached for investing naval balances with Messrs Coutts for his own indirect profit, things did not look too good for Lord Wellesley.

If Nabob Paull had temperamental difficulties, so did the ex-Governor-General. He was vain and imperious. Like a later Viceroy, Lord Curzon, after Lord Wellesley returned home he always walked 'as if accompanied by elephants'. In India his luxury had pleased, amused and irritated. The sumptuous town-planning lavished upon Calcutta was admirable; but what about the reception he gave to his successor, Lord Cornwallis? At the waterside were paraded a dense array of carriages, servants and staff officers. The amazed Cornwallis turned to his secretary:

'What! What! what is all this, Robinson, hey?'

'My Lord, the Marquis Wellesley has sent his equipages and attendants as a mark of respect. . . .'

'Too civil, too civil by half. Too many people. I don't want them. . . . I have not yet lost the use of my legs Robinson, hey?'

In the splendid new palace Cornwallis was horrified to find dozens of sentries posted outside his apartments. It felt like a prison, 'for if I show my head . . . a fellow with a musket and fixed bayonet presents himself before me'.

Paradoxically, it was the other Wellesley, Arthur, who was to surprise and delight his comrades in the Peninsula by posting only one sentry outside his tent when the generals of his allies posted their dozens. As contemporaries never tired of pointing out, no two brothers were ever more different.

Nevertheless, Arthur's clan loyalty was stronger than any reservations he may have felt about his brother's magnificence or the ultimate wisdom of 'the system'. When Lord Castlereagh advised him to enter the House of Commons and defend his brother from the back benches, he agreed. He was offered the seat of Rye, a few miles along the coast from Hastings, by Lord Grenville, Prime Minister of the Whig–Tory coalition, and on 1 April declared elected. The Army had granted him leave. A supper, tea and cold collation for the burgesses cost him £269 16s. 0d., with an added £50 for the poor instead of bunting. He used the remainder of his leave to make the journey, so familiar in youth, to Ireland, there to marry Kitty Pakenham.

*   *   *

He had been warned. But the sight of his faded, thirty-four-year-old bride, chaperoned by her maiden aunt, Lady Elizabeth Pakenham, was a shock all the same. 'She has grown ugly, by Jove!' he whispered into the ear of his clergyman brother, Gerald, who was to marry them. Arthur decided afterwards that he had not been 'in the least' in love with her. As he was to tell his friend Mrs Arbuthnot in 1822:

> I married her because they asked me to do it & I did not know myself. I thought I should never care for anybody again, & that I shd. be with my army &, in short, I was a fool. I will tell you the whole story if you like.

But the whole story is an integral part of his life, and must await events.

The ceremony took place on 10 April 1806, in the Longfords' same drawing-room in Rutland Square which had been the scene of his early, unsuccessful courtship. It was in the parish of St George's, Dublin, where to this day the church register can be seen, containing their two names:

> The Honble. Sir Arthur Wellesley, K.B., to the Honble. Catherine Dorothea Sarah Pakenham of this parish by the Rev. G. Wellesley.

To Maria Edgeworth and Kitty's other country friends the marriage was 'one of those tales of real life in which the romance is far superior to . . . fiction'. Maria hoped that 'the imaginations of this hero and heroine' had not been so much 'exalted' that they would find their happiness, 'so long wished for', fall short of expectations. Waking or sleeping, 'the image of Miss Pakenham', declared Maria to her cousin Margaret Ruxton three days after the wedding, 'swims before our eyes'. But one thing was wanting: 'a description of the person of Sir Arthur. . . .'

The honeymoon was short (Arthur's leave expired after six days) but not too short for Maria's curiosity about his appearance to be satisfied. She wrote to her stepmother on 1 May (his thirty-seventh birthday) that he had been seen at Dublin Castle.

> Sir Arthur is handsome, very brown, quite bald and a hooked nose.

They were right about the good looks and the nose. But the baldness must have been an illusion caused by Arthur's close-cropped hair. At a time when powdered hair and *queues* tied with ribbon were the fashion (and obligatory in the services), the eccentric Wellesley kept his hair unpowdered and cut short. His friends understood it was for reasons of hygiene. But he was always remarkable for his plain common sense.

At the end of a week—for Arthur took an extra day's leave—he returned alone to his duties in England. His bride was escorted home at leisure by her brother-in-law, Gerald, so like Arthur as to features but without the great nose and look of decision. As a newly married woman Kitty was presented at Court to Queen Charlotte, who made the most of a romantic opportunity.

'I'm happy to see you at my court, so bright an example of constancy. If any body in this world deserves to be happy, you do. But did you really never write one letter to Sir Arthur Wellesley during his long absence?'

'No, never, Madame.'

'And did you never think of him?'

'Yes, Madame, very often.'

There was no need to mention to Her Majesty the indefatigable pen of Mrs Olivia Sparrow.

They came to live at 11 Harley Street, a part of London much frequented by French *émigrés*, who had been settled there by Arthur's old friends the Buckinghams. There had been a moment when the

Wellesleys might have removed into the more spacious house opposite. For Kitty was expecting a baby. But Arthur's careful instincts forbade him to take a more expensive place than necessary. So the agent received a polite note of refusal:

Hastings, *September 14th, 1806*

Sir,

I have received your letter of the 13th. It appears to me that the house you mention in Harley Street opposite No. 11 is very dear. I shall therefore be satisfied with No. 11 unless you should hear of one that will suit me better at a reasonable expense. Your most obedient Servant

Arthur Wellesley.

The truth was that Arthur found the cost of living in England far higher than he had expected. In July he was even advising Malcolm, whose return he personally desired, to stay a little longer in India:

Expenses here are very heavy and fortunes very large. Notwithstanding all the taxes and the rise in price of every article in life, there is more luxury than ever . . . and more persons with large fortunes and fewer with fortunes of a moderate extent, than there were formerly. You could not exist in the way you would like. . . .

Arthur himself was not existing in the way he would like. On 19 September he wrote to Richard that his regiment had marched to Portsmouth to embark; 'Yet I have heard nothing of being employed.' So he had asked Lord Grenville to chivvy the Duke of York. 'It is such an object to me to serve with some of the European armies. . . .' Even if it meant leaving Kitty. The earliest surviving letter written to Kitty by Arthur after their marriage shows already the tip of the iceberg floating towards this ill-assorted couple. 'Domestic annoyances' was the name he was later to give to this small, visible manifestation of incompatibility.

Deal. *December 6th 1806*

My Dearest Kitty

I send underneath, an order for 50 Pounds; but I wish you would not send it till you want the Money as the Bankers will not have it in their hands, till they have disposed of some stock of mine. George [an unspecified manservant] is to have 14 Shillings a week Board Wages, & if he should want more, or not be satisfied give him Warning; for it is high time to draw a line.

Ever Your's most affectionately
A.W.

Time to draw a line. . . . Wellington was a great man for drawing lines. But Kitty, unlike the rational French, did not know a line when she saw it. Or if she did, she still obstinately led on her pathetic detachments of servants and children. On into a forbidden country, bristling with guns, *têtes de loup* and *chevaux de frise*, as formidable as any in the Lines of Torres Vedras.

8 The Gilt Potato

The year 1807 began with Arthur still playing his 'most difficult and unpleasant game' on the back-benches. Difficult, because the Ministry he supported—the coalition now called with increasing sarcasm, 'All the Talents'—contained Whigs who were attacking his brother. Unpleasant, because this was precisely the kind of ambivalent situation against which his straightforward nature revolted. Perhaps that was why he was never able to turn confused states of political warfare to his own advantage. Rescue came from an unexpected quarter.

Unhappy Ireland was once more poised to fulfil her ironic role in British politics—the destruction of British Governments. In the aftermath of Emmet's rising, Bonaparte's defeat of Prussia at Jena and England's total isolation, there was a violent reawakening of Catholic passions. The Talents Ministry proposed to soothe them by throwing open the Services to all 'Dissenters'. King George III intervened with a resounding No, choosing St Patrick's Day, 17 March 1807, to demand from his Cabinet a pledge never again to raise the Catholic spectre. The Cabinet replied by resigning on the 25th, the very day on which one of their only two really 'talented' measures passed into law—abolition of the slave-trade. The other was the introduction of short term service into the Army; a reform designed to help recruitment and symptomatic of the nation's resolve to defy Napoleon. For the 'Talents', especially Charles James Fox at the Foreign Office, had tried hard and yet failed to make an acceptable peace.

The King sent for the aged 3rd Duke of Portland whose infirmities, though different, were scarcely less disabling than his Sovereign's: he controlled the agonies of the stone with quantities of laudanum, slept prodigiously and hardly ever spoke. He formed a Tory Government with Castlereagh back at the War Office and Canning as Foreign Secretary. From this eminence Canning lamented the demise of the late Ministry in his favourite medium, satiric verse:

> *The demon of faction that over them hung,*
> *In accents of horror their epitaph sung;*
> *While Pride and Venality join'd in the stave,*
> *And canting Democracy wept at the grave.*

The Tories had no doubt shaken themselves free from 'canting Democracy'. But who was to rid the ailing Prime Minister of a turbulent Ireland? Two dukes, Rutland and Beaufort, as well as Arthur's old friend Lord Clive, were approached in vain for the post of Lord Lieutenant. At last the Duke of Richmond, everyone's boon companion, made the sacrifice. As his Chief Secretary he selected Arthur Wellesley.

This was the end of Wellesley 'neutrality'. With Richard still under fire from the Left, Arthur had no hesitation in accepting. From now on he was a Tory, though still with a soldier's aversion to 'party'. The situation in Ireland would prove demanding. But at least the potato this time was suitably gilt. No less than £6,566 a year was earmarked for the Chief Secretary's salary.

* * *

Arthur had changed his constituency from Rye to Mitchell in Cornwall after the dissolution of 1806, and was to change it again in 1807 to Newport, Isle of Wight.[1] But these electoral shufflings, which were entirely untainted by 'canting Democracy', affected his life and everyone else's a good deal less than an event which took place at 11 Harley Street on 3 February 1807.

Kitty gave birth to a son and heir, Arthur Richard. Sir Arthur was hanging about as fathers do, when Mrs Calvert called on Kitty and her 'nice little boy'. Lady Salisbury also looked in with her daughters, and took the opportunity to invite a by no means reluctant Arthur to hunt at Hatfield. The only surviving letter which refers to his son's birth was written three days afterwards from Hatfield to his mother-in-law, Lady Longford. Arthur expressed his thanks for her attention to Kitty's health 'in the late disturbing & critical moments'.

His frail wife was now in her thirty-sixth year. It was something of a miracle that she had produced a child safely, especially in the prevalent conditions of lying-in chambers. Her mother would have seen to it that all the well-fitting Georgian casements at No. 11 were tightly closed and the room kept stiflingly hot by a roaring fire in the efficient grate. But Kitty survived. And if she was soon again

1. He had first been elected for Tralee in 1807, but Irish seats were very expensive—usually £5,000 each for a whole Parliament—and Henry had found Newport for him at about £800 for seventeen months. The Irish Secretary's salary was reduced by 1825–6 to £1,500.

becoming a little querulous, it was no wonder. She was pregnant in May, a month after they moved to the Chief Secretary's lodge in Phoenix Park.

Arthur's robust method of allaying her various fears was kindly meant but more suitable to a subaltern with a slight scratch than a properly anxious mother. When baby Arthur caught measles at only five months old, his father wrote cheerfully from London where he had returned to his Parliamentary duties,

> I have no apprehensions for the Meazles being convinced that it is a mild disorder, & one that has no bad consequences, if the Patient is well taken care of as it is going off.

To Wellington, illness was always something to be 'got the better of' with as little fuss as possible.

A week later an outcrop of 'domestic annoyances' caused a few mild protests from Arthur to his 'dearest Kitty'. There was an unpaid bill.

> I enclose a letter from a Bricklayer. I thought you had paid him. Let me know whether you have or not.

Was the bricklayer dishonest or Kitty at fault? Judging by a subsequent letter, it was the latter.

Rather more serious was the sad case of Kitty's maid who had drowned herself for love of Arthur's gardener. Sir Arthur hoped that,

> the remainder of the Maids of the Park will put up with the misfortunes of this world, & not destroy themselves. Let the Gardener be taken back. It is evident that he had nothing to say to the death of the woman.

Writing again on the 18th he was glad 'the Children'[2] were getting over measles, as he had always expected. As for the gardener, unless the law proved him guilty, 'it would not be very charitable to dismiss him from my Service: & I shall certainly not dismiss him'. Arthur believed in the law, not sentiment. By the 25th the bricklayer affair was not going so well.

2. Probably Arthur Freese and the Hamilton children as well as little Arthur Wellesley.

London *July 25th 1807*

My dearest Kitty

... I am much concerned that you should have thought of concealing from me any want of money which you might have experienced. I don't understand now how this want occurred, or why it was concealed; & the less there is said or written upon the subject the better; for I acknowledge that the conclusion I draw from your conduct upon the occasion is that you must be mad, or you must consider me to be a Brute, & most particularly fond & avaricious of money. Once for all you require no permission to talk to me upon any subject you please; all that I request is that a piece of work may not be made about trifles ... & that you may not go into tears because I don't think them deserving of an uncommon degree of attention.

Once for all—trifles—tears—mad—Brute. The approach seemed somewhat formidable. Kitty was not mad nor Arthur a brute. But his forthright attempts to set her on the right road 'once for all' merely scared her into further incompetence.

Three days later another note on the gardener affair showed a new set of warning signals: Kitty refusing to be dictated to and Arthur becoming a little hopeless.

London *July 28th 1807*

It would have been imagined that I had acted harshly by you in desiring that the Gardener might not lose his place, from the answer which I received this day upon that subject; & certainly nothing was ever farther from my thoughts. But it is to be hoped that at some time or other I shall be better understood ... it appears that your letter is written purposely to give me to understand that I had not allowed you the authority to act, & that I had expressed my *desire* upon it. This will never do ...

The bold, masculine 'Once for all' had deteriorated into the fatalistic, 'some time or other'. And he was already 'misunderstood'.

*   *   *

The Ireland to which Arthur had returned as Chief Secretary was not the country he had left. On the personal side, for instance, there was now no reason why he should ever want to set eyes on Dangan again. A few days before the battle of Assaye, on 12 September 1803, the nationalist Dr Brenan was writing to his sister: 'Mr Roger O'Conner has purchased *Dangan*, the Marquis of Wellesley's Place, & pays 2000£ a year for 700 acres, when he is to commence Farmer on a large scale. . . . This is an odd time for making such large purchases.' It was indeed.

Emmet's rising had just been suppressed but agrarian unrest was far from subsiding. Roger O'Connor, however, had no intention of 'commencing Farmer'. He was a dedicated United Irishman, like his brother Arthur who had escaped to France and been created an honorary general by Napoleon. It was said by those in the know that Roger had rented Dangan in order to have a mansion for entertaining Napoleon, when the latter came to liberate Ireland. (Roger's loyalist brother Robert had prepared a cage for Bonaparte in Cork.) By 1807 Dangan was no longer kept up like a gentleman's residence. Its fine trees were hacked down, their stumps left standing like grave-stones, its walks overgrown, shrubberies gone wild and plantations run into bare poles. None of this was quite in keeping with the idea of a Chief Secretary's early home.[3]

Indeed, if Wellington was ever chaffed for being an Irishman and replied with a notorious quip, it was probably during this period:

Because a man is born in a stable that does not make him a horse.

*   *   *

Mornington House had fared better than Dangan, but like all great places after the Union, its value had dropped catastrophically by 1802 to £2,500. Antrim House in fashionable Merrion Square had been an hotel since 1801, while Dublin's Parliament House was now the Bank. As a Dubliner in *Florence Macarthy* says to a young Irish nobleman who has returned to Ireland after the Union, in disguise:

'That's the ould parliament house, Sir. Why, then, there was grate work going on there oncet, quiet and aisy as it stands now, the cratur! . . . Och, the trade was ruined entirely . . . and that's what the Union has brought us to . . .'

3. In the ordnance survey map of Dangan, 1837, the Castle is approached by 'Ruins of Drives' and 'Old Canal', but two obelisks have survived and the 'Quay' and 'Gibraltar Battery' are still marked.

'And what use is made of that magnificent building?'

'What use is it they make of it, your honour? Why, then, sorrow a use in life, only a bank, Sir; the bank o' Ireland; what less could they make of it?'

Though Arthur Wellesley had not returned to Ireland in disguise, there was no lack of people to tell him how Dublin had been ruined by the Union. When he studied the problem he rightly concluded that the damage due specifically to the Union had been exaggerated. All the same, he agreed with Kitty's friends, the Edgeworths, in deploring the landlords who had removed themselves to England after the Union and thus increased the evils of absenteeism.

Only the wretched cabins remained eternally unaltered, with the same ragged families inside, the same sprouting weeds on the roof, and the same holy pictures on the walls, mingled with the prints of the exquisite singer, Mrs Billington, who had taken Ireland by storm in 1783 and was reputed mistress of the Duke of Portland in his heyday.

*   *   *

In this familiar yet changed scene, it was Arthur Wellesley's overriding task to distribute the Irish patronage. It had to be done so as to produce the maximum number of bought-up Government supporters in Parliament. For patronage in both parties was still the great adhesive, as Wellesley recognized:

We must keep our majority in Parliament, and . . . that can be done only by a good use of the patronage of the government.

The proper application of patronage involved the Chief Secretary in many interviews, much smooth and some rough correspondence, for none of which Arthur had a relish except perhaps the last. But there was a job to be done. *Dubashery* no doubt, but of the most hallowed kind. And when a job-hunter went too far (like a certain Mr Meeke, whose name belied his nature) Arthur could always show a touch of the old iron:

You are rather high in your demand of an office . . . but I hope to place your friend if he be more moderate than you are.

The new Chief Secretary had arrived at the Castle just in time for the 1807 elections. Wexford, after great exertions, produced an unexpected Tory success. The first Tory candidate, it is true, got rid of his Whig opponent by killing him in a duel; but as this was 'reckoned fair in Ireland', wrote Arthur, 'it created no sensation' and another Tory candidate was elected. A hard-pressed colonel in Clare, however, could see no hope of being elected unless Sir Arthur took a hand in the removal of the hostile local sheriff. But again the Chief Secretary had to draw a line. 'I am sorry to tell you,' he wrote, 'that there is no precedent whatever for the dismissal of a sheriff . . . excepting for gross misconduct.'

In agreeable contrast to these and many other difficulties was the contest for Downpatrick in Ulster of the young lawyer, John Wilson Croker. Croker, with his fleeting resemblance to Wolfe Tone, his alert grey eyes, long nose and intellectual forehead, the whole marred only by a weak mouth and ugly voice which he used incessantly, was a great find on Arthur's part.

On 21 May the Tories of Down were in the lead and Croker wrote: 'The popery war-whoop was sung against us but we out-sang them.' By the 23rd they were home and dry—with a majority of twenty-five out of 141.

And so entered into Parliament, into history, literature and above all into Wellington's life-story, John Wilson Croker. Posterity must do him a kind of homage for the incomparable memory which enabled him to record so much of Wellington's conversation in his master's authentic voice. Gratitude of a perverse literary sort is also due to the man who furnished Lady Morgan with her model for Mr Conway Crawley in *Florence Macarthy*, the abominable agent's clever son; and Disraeli with Mr Rigby in *Coningsby*, leader of 'that fungous tribe' of whom Taper and Tadpole were button-mushrooms:

There was nothing profound about Mr Rigby. . . . He was, in short, a man who possessed, in very remarkable degree, a restless instinct for adroit baseness.

Though Croker did indeed develop some odious characteristics, his portraits in literature maligned him. A man of such unmitigated 'baseness' could never have become Wellington's lifelong friend.

*   *   *

The joy of Croker's victory was somewhat impaired by the threat of a petition against corrupt practices and an avalanche of solicitations. Lady Elizabeth Pakenham, Kitty's spinster aunt, requested a job for a friend. Arthur explained his 'delicate situation' and suggested she should apply instead to her nephew, Lord Longford; to which she answered that Longford, alas, had a rule never to solicit except for his own brothers. Lord Wellesley desired a post in the Revenue 'at an early date' for Tim Hickey, his boatman in India; Arthur's mother sent four pages of demands; his sister Anne's irrational wish to nominate someone as captain of the Dublin packet got a tart refusal. It was almost a pleasure to receive his brother William's more relaxed appeal:

> I hope the other applications I have made will be attended to in time. I am getting into disrepute with my *Rascals*, for not having done anything for them since we came in. . . . Sydenham[4] was discovered viewing Blenheim the other day with a whore—they went by the names of Mr and Mrs Thompson—O the Profligacy of the Age! ! !

How did Arthur Wellesley defend the profligacy of political practices? He was never very convincing and indeed admitted that they could not be defended 'in the abstract'. Bribes and the bribable were anathema to him personally; nine-tenths of English politicians, he believed, did not need bribing but supported their party on some sort of principle. In Ireland, on the contrary, 'in my day at least, almost every man of mark in the state had his price'. Wellington would be finally driven by his mildly liberal friend, the Rev. G. R. Gleig, to defend this situation by results—through patronage the constitutional monarchy was preserved and 'canting Democracy' curbed. Surely it was better to let the rich and educated jostle for jobs, and having got them, become the bought-up champions of law and order, than to have a 'scramble' among the needy and ignorant?

When Wellington came to tackle these problems in the age of reform, his Irish experience was decisive. Always at the back of his mind was the thought that without the price-system, not a man in Ireland could be relied on to support the British connection.

Fortunately for Arthur, patronage was not his sole concern. The

4. Thomas Sydenham, Lord Wellesley's aide-de-camp in India and a family friend.

Government's road was also paved with good intentions towards the Catholics.

*   *   *

In an interview with a Catholic nobleman, Lord Fingall, Wellesley promised that the Catholic laws, though not at present open to reform, would be administered by him 'with mildness and good temper'.

The Yeomanry of Enniscorthy were forbidden by Arthur to celebrate the anniversary of the Vinegar Hill victory over the rebels of '98. Such 'disputes' should be forgotten, not revived. Again, the Dean of Winchester was turned down for the bishopric of Cork because of his ultra-Protestantism. Disturbances in Sligo and Mayo were excused as the work of agitators who 'deluded' the people, instead of being punished under the Insurrection Act. As a result, twenty lads from these counties abjured the 'Thrashers' (a violent agrarian group), cursed it, and after testifying to 'the mildness of government', joined the Army.

Nevertheless, despite all the mildness and good temper, an aggressive young Catholic lawyer named Daniel O'Connell began to organize the disaffected. There was plenty of material to hand. At country fairs maypoles were being set up as 'trees of liberty', and even among those too old to fight, the Castle found 'a deep rooted antipathy to Great Britain'. Arthur O'Connor was 'looked to as a leader, and many expect that Bonaparte will make him king of Ireland'.

A resounding new triumph for Bonaparte abroad had as usual fanned Irish hopes. On 29 June 1807 Wellesley heard of 'a great action' having taken place on the 14th. It was the rout of Russia at Friedland. In July the two Emperors, Napoleon and Alexander, met on their celebrated raft in the River Nieman at Tilsit, lavishly decorated with eagles.

'I hate the English as much as you do yourself,' said the Tsar as he stepped aboard.

'If that is the case, then peace is already made,' said Napoleon. They proceeded to divide the Continent between them.

The defence of Ireland had always been one of the Chief Secretary's duties and the 'summit conference' at Tilsit turned Wellesley's thoughts, nothing loth, towards his true profession. Ireland, he knew, had been for some time in a jumpy state. News had been flashed in April by General French at Cork of a hostile fleet sighted off the coast. The invaders turned out to be West Indian merchantmen. This false alarm nonetheless prompted Wellesley to write a memorandum on Ireland's exposed coastline. He had toured from Dublin to Cork with his brother William in July and August of the year before, visiting martello towers, barracks and rivers.[5] Among other things he had suggested a proper 'watering wharf' at Berehaven to save the men getting wet when filling their casks. Now he used his experience to rule out more martello towers and simply recommend a larger naval station at Bantry Bay.

> I lay it down as decided that Ireland, in a view to military operations, must be considered as an enemy's country. . . .

This was precisely how he had written about Malabar in India. Throughout his adult life he had moved between two British ascendancies, in the East and the West, each, as he was honest enough to admit, maintained by force. Of the army in the East he had written:

> They feel they are a distinct and superior class to the rest of the world that surrounds them; and their actions correspond to their high notions of their own superiority . . . and they show in what manner nations consisting of many millions are governed by 30,000 strangers.

Irish Protestants had the same 'high notions', being possessors of the soil, as he often said, 'by right of conquest'. While he had been away in India, many liberalizing ideas had percolated from France to Britain, even to the ruling classes. They had not reached India. Indeed, one reason for establishing the new college in Calcutta had been to decontaminate any young civil servants arriving tainted from Europe. Arthur Wellesley was untouched by French heresies. This was his misfortune. But he was compensated by remaining throughout the gloomiest years of England's struggle against France,

---

5. The chronicle of Wellesley's tour was written in a small brown leather pocket-book with alternate white and mauve leaves, which is now in the National Library of Ireland. Wellesley admired the 'most beautiful rivers', liked a sprig of lemon-scented verbena given him by a lady, but was disappointed with Blarney Castle—'everything in ruins'.

completely free from any uncertainties, feelings of inferiority or fears. At all times he was prepared to fight. Now, in mid-1807, with Ireland 'an enemy's country', it would be more rewarding to fight the enemy direct. The results of Tilsit were to make that possible.

*   *   *

Some time before the end of May 1807, Arthur Wellesley heard that the Government were yet again planning an expedition to the Continent, though its object was secret. Immediately he determined to leave Ireland. Otherwise people would say that he had avoided active service 'in order to hold a high civil office'. Castlereagh was given no choice. 'I positively cannot stay here,' wrote Wellesley on 1 June, 'whether I am to be employed on [the expedition] or not.' There would be no difficulty in finding a successor. The Chief Secretaryship was a highly gilt potato.

Castlereagh gracefully accepted the inevitable. Within ten days it was settled that Arthur should leave Ireland at once but carry on his Irish business in London until the expedition actually sailed. Whether he would retain his office and salary after that was unknown and a matter of indifference to him.

Several letters went to Admiral Tom Pakenham, one asking him to settle with Kitty about her going to Coolure. There were to be no 'tears over trifles' in this quarter. He told the Lord Lieutenant:

> I have not written to Lady Wellesley upon [the expedition]; and it is as well not to say anything to her about it till it will be positively settled that we are to go.

Keeping his excitable wife in the dark until the last moment was to become his rule. Kitty knew in June 1807, however, that her husband might not return to Ireland as Chief Secretary after his Parliamentary session, in which case she would have plenty to occupy her mind—accounts to pay off; wines, hay and the curricle to be sold at a correct valuation; the silver and carriages to be brought to London; the cows belonging to Mr Pakenham in Phoenix Park to be sorted out from Arthur's herd and returned. No doubt Arthur still fondly hoped he had a domestic quartermaster-general in the making.

Another letter to Tom informed him that the troops from Ireland for the expedition must be in England by the 22nd, so would he help 'hurry the fellows away'? If any of the 'fellows' were Marines, Arthur was responsible for a proposed reform in their sleeping-quarters. He had written the year before that if their numbers were to be kept up, some arrangement would be needed 'for stowing them in the Barracks'. Hammocks would be the best mode, since

> the beastly practice of two great hulking fellows stark naked sleeping together would be done away with.

The texture of canvas used for hammocks must also be improved. This was a reform which Arthur was to press for continually. In the army there were wooden cribs in which *four* great hulking fellows slept together.

His last message on sailing from Dublin was to say that he had noticed a cracked pier in the harbour. Would his secretary tell the ballast-office to repair it? There was also one parting shot at the military establishment in Dublin, delivered via General Littlehales, the Irish Military Secretary: 'Your Judge Advocate is an *Ass.*'

He was to go on the expedition, and Kitty had to be told at last. Just before embarkation he sent her a loving note from Sheerness to say that Lord Longford was at Deal to see off his young brother, Hercules Pakenham, who would come under Arthur's command. Edward Pakenham also was going. 'God Bless you,' he ended, 'my dearest Kitty.'

Thankful to be rid at least temporarily of placemen, informers, asses and tears, he embarked on 31 July 1807 in the *Prometheus*. His destination was to all but the Government and Service chiefs, unknown.

*   *   *

Through channels kept strictly to himself George Canning, the exceptionally active Foreign Secretary, had discovered certain 'secret articles' in the Treaty of Tilsit which left England with the stark choice of either submitting to Napoleon or being strangled. The Emperor had already decreed in 1806 the closure of all Continental ports to British trade. After Tilsit, the noose was to be fatally tightened by the surrender to him, if necessary, of Europe's remaining neutral fleets, those of Portugal and Denmark. Napoleon might even use the fleet at Copenhagen to invade England. With brilliant foresight—

or unethical effrontery, depending on how the total situation is regarded—Canning ordered neutral Denmark to place her excellent fleet in Britain's safe custody until the end of the war. Otherwise he would get it on the same terms by force. The indignant Danes refused and the British Navy set sail.

At the time, Canning's 'courage and initiative', as Professor Asa Briggs calls it, struck many Whigs and Radicals as being utterly reprehensible. 'The English have behaved like shabby thieves,' roared Samuel Whitbread the Radical in the House of Commons. Charles Napier, a serving soldier of twenty-five, wrote, 'now every one says— *Poor Danes!* A soldier cannot fight an enemy he pities with proper spirit.' But to Wellesley and the majority then, and to the majority of historians now, Britain's desperate necessity was rightly Canning's law.

The actual operation was quick and fairly clean, for British regulars were fighting the Danish militia. Wellesley had counted on the satisfaction of meeting the French again at last—'it may be depended upon that the Danes will be joined and assisted by the French'— but this crowning excitement was still to come. Lord Cathcart led the expedition with 'a steady old guardsman' named Sir Harry Burrard as his second-in-command. Sir David Baird commanded a division and Sir Arthur Wellesley a brigade. The latter was to play a crucial part, even though the Horse Guards pointedly gave him what he called a 'dry nurse' in the shape of a second-in-command, General Richard Stewart.

On 16th August he was ordered to land with an advance guard not far from Copenhagen; the army followed and the city was duly invested. Ten days later, while the siege was proceeding, a sudden danger loomed in the shape of a relieving force of Danish regulars. Wellesley was given the task of cutting it off. This he proceeded to do, but not until he had cut off his 'dry nurse' first. Stewart had been allowed entire charge of organization during the voyage; when he came up with ideas for the attack also, Wellesley stopped him short.

'Come, come, 'tis my turn now.' The dry nurse subsided with good humour into his proper place, while Wellesley went on to clear the enemy out of their entrenched positions at Kiöge, a town south-east of Copenhagen. There were no further attempts to relieve the city.

Wellesley's whole action cost him only 172 casualties, though the Danes fared a good deal worse. 'We are very unpopular in the country,' he wrote on the 28th, admitting sadly that though his men fought very well, they had behaved only 'tolerably well in other respects'. Pillage was to be a problem in Europe as well as India.

Now it was a question of whether to bombard and storm the beautiful city, if, as seemed certain, it would not surrender. Wellesley felt they ought to find some less barbarous way of reducing it. All his life he was to oppose the bombardment of cities. Fortunately after three days of a sporadic cannonade, the garrison surrendered on 5 September. To Bonaparte's rage, the British had thus narrowly forestalled his own army of 30,000 men waiting at Hamburg to take over Denmark themselves.

Major-General Sir Arthur Wellesley, K.B., as a reward for gallantry was appointed one of the three British Commissioners to arrange the terms of capitulation. When Parliament met in February 1808, he was publicly thanked for 'genius and valor', 'zeal', 'intrepidity' and 'exertion', not forgetting references to 'paths of glory', 'seat of Empire' and 'the throne of his King'. For all these, in India and in Denmark, his sword had not been 'drawn in vain'.

*   *   *

Arthur had in point of fact presented one of his finest swords to the Lord Lieutenant of Ireland as a parting present, under the firm conviction that he would not return there. During the Danish campaign, however, he heard that the Lord Lieutenant insisted on having him back. He was still Chief Secretary. Reluctantly his own sword must be turned once more into the office quill.

Three consequences of this brief martial interlude were important to him. Further experience in handling the population of an invaded country, assertion of his own authority, and the association of his name at last with service in Europe. (He was still inclined to say that Indian victories positively damaged a man's chances with the Horse Guards.)

His kindness towards the luckless Danes brought him a rewarding letter from one of his Danish opposite numbers:

> Penetrated with gratitude for your human and generous conduct. . . . I beg leave to repeat what my words were unable to express. . . . It is a great pitty [sic] that political views should counteract the private feelings of the individuals, but, as soldiers, our lot is to obey.

One other event connected with the Copenhagen campaign was to prove of some importance to Wellesley. Lord Grosvenor had taken with him on the expedition a favourite mare named Lady Catherine, got by John Bull out of a mare by the Rutland Arabian. She was found to be in foal and sent home. When her offspring, a strong chestnut, was born later in England, he was called Copenhagen.

*　　　*　　　*

Kitty had received several reassuring notes from Arthur, the last undated but hoping, after an interview with Lord Castlereagh, to leave for Ireland 'tomorrow'. He had reached England on 30 September.

For the next eight months it was back to the old Irish treadmill, with intervals for performing his duties in London or cosseting Kitty. 'Lady Wellesley,' he informed the Irish Chancellor on 7 December, 'is in a situation which will not permit her to go from the neighbourhood of Town at present.' On 16 January 1808 she presented him with a second son, Charles.

The threat of invasion had once more receded, making Ireland a little less of 'an enemy's country'. During that autumn of 1807, with the Danish fleet safely in English harbours, the Portuguese navy had also been rescued at the eleventh hour from Napoleon's clutches. He had declared war on Portugal on 20 October. As the French conquerors—General Junot and his tatterdemalion troops—staggered into Lisbon from Spain, they heard that the coveted ships, with the Portuguese royal family on board, had vanished over the horizon to Brazil two days before.

So Wellesley was able to devote himself again to 'mild government'. He considered how reforms in schooling might draw Catholic and Protestant children together; he wondered whether the tithe and rent problems might not be solved by eradicating absentee clergy and landlords; he produced statistics to show that Maynooth College needed to train twenty-five per cent more priests a year; he reformed the Dublin police; he prepared an embargo on corn exports in case of a potato famine; and he refused to arrange a little matter of patronage for the Duke of Kent.

But his heart was not in it. Or rather, the task of reforming Ireland was too heart-breaking. You could not 'make a dash at' peculators, as you could at Mahratta robbers, since sudden and hurried reforms in

Ireland, he believed, 'invariably ended by making matters worse than they were'. Of course that was 'no reason for not making a beginning', and he hoped he had indeed achieved 'some effectual progress in every department of the state'. All the same, he wanted to leave.

'I shall be happy to aid the government in any manner they please,' he had written to Canning somewhat desperately on 17 October 1807, 'and am ready to set out for any part of the world at a moment's notice.'

Successive British governments had not been backward in devising wild-cat assaults all over the world. To take only this year, there had been a fiasco in Buenos Aires, when the captors were captured and the commander cashiered, a severe defeat in Egypt, a crazy expedition to Sweden, and now Canning had a scheme for bringing in the New World to defeat the tyrant of the Old. Luckily, Wellesley also was brought in. He was required to co-operate with the emissary of Venezuelan revolutionaries, General Miranda, in planning an insurrection in his native Spanish America against Napoleon's ally, Spain. Wellesley at once pointed out some of the project's more disastrous flaws. Besides, there was a philosophical objection to sowing revolutionary oats where none grew before:

I always had a horror of revolutionizing any country for a political object. I always said, if they rise of themselves, well and good, but do not stir them up; it is a fearful responsibility.

Yet as the youngest lieutenant-general in the Army, promoted in April 1808, Arthur Wellesley wished as ardently as any Minister to take advantage of a crack in Napoleon's colossal empire. Even fighting shoulder to shoulder with Miranda would be better than not fighting at all. In June 1808 he gladly accepted the command of 9,000 men assembled at Cork to invade Spanish America.

Meanwhile the genuine crack, the chasm, the abyss into which Napoleon was ultimately to fall, had opened in old Spain the month before. Early in May 1808 the popular Spanish king, Ferdinand VII, who had been set on the throne by the people after his miserable father had been deposed by them, was summoned with his parents by Napoleon to Bayonne, forced to abdicate, abducted and finally replaced by the King of Naples, Joseph Bonaparte. Patriotic Spain spontaneously burst into flame. This was high-toned insurrection. This Wellesley could applaud—'there was advantage to be derived from the temper of the people of Spain'. This was Napoleon's crack of doom.

All of which would be 'much facilitated', as Wellesley wrote dryly but with true vision, not by sailing away to South America but by 'alarming' Bonaparte at home.

> Surely this is not impossible; and the manner in which his armies are now spread in all parts of Europe . . . afford [*sic*] an opportunity which ought not to be passed by.

The arrival of a Spanish deputation in England the very next month, June 1808, and a Portuguese one in July urging joint attacks on the common enemy, made sure that the opportunity should indeed not be passed by. The destination of Arthur's whole force at Cork was switched to the Iberian Peninsula. 'A strange piece of scene-shifting,' remarked Creevey the Radical, sarcastically. But this time the Government had made no mistake.

In a state as near to euphoria as Arthur ever reached, he made his last preparations in London. They included a stormy interview with General Miranda, held in the street to prevent him 'bursting out'. When the general heard that South America must take second place to Spain, he bellowed a parting malediction, 'You will be lost. . . .'

An even more extraordinary interview was held by Arthur with Father James Robertson, O.S.B., the monk who became a British secret agent. Arthur had already interviewed him in Dublin about the possibility of sending him out on a very special mission. A distinguished Spanish general, the Marquess de la Romana, and his impressive army were being used by Napoleon as part of his occupation forces in Denmark. If someone could only get a message to Romana describing the new situation in Spain and the need for him there (four spies had already tried and died), the British Navy would do the rest. Arthur invited the monk to Harley Street on 31 May and broached the subject with characteristic force.

'Tell me, Mr Robertson, are you a man of courage?'

'Try me, Sir Arthur.'

'That is what we mean to do.'

'Romana' Robertson, as he came to be called, carried out his mission brilliantly after many thrilling adventures. As a result, the fleet was able to conjure 9,000 excellent soldiers out of Denmark and into Spain and to present Arthur Wellesley with his most valued Spanish general.

Sir Jonah Barrington, who had last seen Arthur looking 'sallow' and 'worn out' in 1805, gave the radiant general a farewell party, taking the opportunity before supper to denounce the Copenhagen expedition as 'robbery and murder'. Arthur was too happy to argue. He just laughed.

John Wilson Croker attended another farewell dinner, an intimate one at 11 Harley Street alone with Sir Arthur and Lady Wellesley. He was to be caretaker of the Irish Office for the duration, and after Kitty had withdrawn and the new Dublin water supply had also been disposed of, Croker found that his host had fallen into a brown study. What was Sir Arthur thinking about?

> Why, to say the truth, I am thinking of the French that I am going to fight: I have not seen them since the campaign in Flanders, when they were capital soldiers, and a dozen years of victory under Buonaparte must have made them better still. They have besides, it seems, a new system of strategy which has out-manoeuvred and overwhelmed all the armies of Europe. 'Tis enough to make one thoughtful; but no matter.

Sir Arthur had been thinking aloud. Now he made a memorable prediction.

> My die is cast, they may overwhelm me, but I don't think they will out-manoeuvre me. First, because I am not afraid of them, as everybody else seems to be; and secondly, because if what I hear of their system of manoeuvre, is true, I think it a false one as against steady troops. I suspect all the continental armies were more than half beaten before the battle was begun—I, at least, will not be frightened beforehand.[6]

Six months earlier Croker had kindly made it his business to deal with Sir Arthur's lapsed membership of the exclusive Kildare Street Club in Dublin. The subscription was five guineas a year, he wrote,

6. Croker, vol. I, pp. 12–13. Charles Greville heard a shortened version of Arthur's reply to Croker from Croker himself on 14 December 1839: 'Sir Arthur, you don't talk; what is it you are thinking about?' 'Of the French. I have never seen them; they have beaten all Europe. I think I shall beat them, but I can't help thinking about them.'

and Sir Arthur had been a 'defaulter' since 1794. Croker, however, could get him readmitted for only three guineas.

It was a favour of which Arthur secretly hoped to make little use. He had faithfully served his apprenticeship in India and Ireland. Through all he had been *nimmukwallah*, though he was beginning to call himself instead, a shade bitterly, 'the *willing horse*'. Friendly Ministers had helped him to get 'pretty high up on the tree' at home.

Now, in his fortieth year, he was ready to leap on to the world stage. His aims were limited to what was termed 'a particular service' —the 'absolute evacuation of the Peninsula by the troops of France'— his army was small but good, his energies only waited to be released. Napoleon, about to enter his fortieth year, was master of that stage and had been for years; his armies were enormous, his ambition megalomaniac. In the year 1808 each took a decisive turning: Napoleon towards his downfall, Wellesley towards fulfilment.

PART II

PART II

9 *My Die is Cast*

'Nothing but a first-rate is fit to go alongside a first-rate,' wrote Nelson to George III, trying to convince his Sovereign of the need to match French men-of-war with British ships of equal strength. Translated into military terms, the same problem faced Wellesley at Cork. The impression made by his armament was a mixed one.

His 9,000 men were to be reinforced on landing in the Peninsula by 5,000 troops now afloat off Spain, under his future second-in-command, General Sir Brent Spencer.

In this person Wellesley at once recognized another 'dry nurse' chosen by authority to keep an eye on him. Spencer, however, was to prove the least of his anxieties. 'I came to an immediate explanation with him. . . .' If only all generals had proved equally reasonable.[1]

The last minute 'scene-shifting' from South America to the Peninsula had meant that the very few horses collected for the long voyage were never properly increased. Wellesley was desperately short of them for cavalry, artillery and supplies. His small wagon-train had to be deflected from its original duty of putting down 'Thrashers' and 'Liberty Rangers' in Ireland, and he could count on less than 350 cavalry sabres. But at least there were 229 drummers and trumpeters. It was to be hoped that the cities of the Peninsula would resemble Jericho.

Wellesley's infantry on the other hand—the 'steady troops' of his last talk with Croker—were the best England had assembled in memory. While Napoleon had provoked in Spain and Portugal the flashback of nationalism, in England and Prussia he was stimulating

1. Wellesley's 'immediate explanation' consisted, even in his own recollection, of a long formidable harangue: 'I told him I did not know what the words *"second in command"* meant, any more than third, fourth, or fifth in command; that I alone commanded the army . . . that . . . I would treat . . . him . . . with the most entire confidence, and would leave none of my views or intentions unexplained; but that I would have no *second in command* in the sense of his having anything like . . . superintending control; and that, finally and above all, I would not only take but insist upon the whole and undivided responsibility of all that should happen while the army was under my command' (Croker, vol. I, p. 343).

military reform. Jena was less surprising when it was remembered that four Prussian generals were over eighty, thirteen over seventy and sixty-two over sixty when Napoleon and his young marshals thrashed them. Britain had young champions in John Moore and Arthur Wellesley. The Government had also increased the militia to 200,000 men, some of whom would volunteer for the regular army serving abroad and make the best of soldiers, and had added 45,000 new recruits to the regular army in 1807–8.[2] In that army there was henceforth to be short hair. Pigtails were cut off, sponges issued and heads washed. Not all soldiers approved, as young Arthur Shakespear of the Dragoons discovered: 'many were indignant', since pigtails, if properly looked after, could have 'a very military appearance'. At any rate, Arthur Wellesley's cropped head would no longer be mistaken for baldness.

At the famous Shorncliffe camp, Sir John Moore had trained his unique Light Division of highly disciplined men in whom individual initiative was at the same time encouraged. At Woolwich, Colonel Shrapnell had invented a secret new weapon officially known as spherical case shot, though it was later called by his name, generally minus the last letter ('shrapnel'). When exploded in the air by several consecutive fuses, it had a long range and wide spray of bullets which the enemy were to find 'very dreadful' and Wellesley 'of great benefit'. Among Wellesley's files for January 1807 was a booklet and letter from Colonel Shrapnell recommending new siege-guns made by the Carron Company on the principle of Nelson's 'carronades'.[3] Within a few years Wellesley wanted no other kind.

By no means all the great Peninsular names were as yet with his army, but there was Rowland Hill, the beloved 'Daddy' or 'Farmer' Hill who looked like a benevolent coachman and with whom Wellesley expressed himself extremely rejoiced to be serving again:

> and I hope that we shall have more to do than we had on the last occasion [Copenhagen] on which we were together.

On his staff was Lord Westmorland's son and heir, Lord

2. The militia was an auxiliary force for home defence raised by ballot, for which substitutes could be found, at a price.
3. The famous Scottish ironworks were founded in the eighteenth century by the inventor, Dr John Roebuck, at Carron, where these large calibre guns were cast. Nelson's 'carronades' were shorter in the barrel than Wellington's. The name was a play on the words 'cannonade' and Carron.

Burghersh, a dashing aristocrat of twenty-four with a mop of wavy hair.[4] He had been dispatched to Wellesley by Lord Castlereagh with the caution that if there was 'nothing interesting' for him at headquarters he should be sent into the interior to gather intelligence, Wellesley meanwhile kindly seeing that his zeal did not lead him into 'Embarrassments that make no part of his Military Duties'.

For aide-de-camp, a handsome, apple-cheeked young man of nineteen had been recommended by the Duke of Richmond, a young man who was to make smooth, as far as possible, the path of Wellesley's whole life.

> O'Hara used to say [wrote Richmond] he had rather have a wife recommended to him than an aide-de-camp, notwithstanding this, I will venture to say that Fitzroy Somerset is an active and intelligent fellow, and is anxious to go on service.[5]

It was not only Fitzroy Somerset's intelligence, but his phenomenal truthfulness and exactitude in describing a situation and carrying out an order, which Arthur prized. Fitzroy was widely liked for his equanimity and complete dedication.

Dr Hume, another man destined to play no small part in his life, public and private, was in charge of the wounded.

*   *   *

Up to the very end Wellesley was still wrestling with Irish patronage —who should be Deputy Warehouse Keeper of Stamped Goods? The Warehouse Keeper of Unstamped Goods, to be sure—but at last the time came for his waiting troops to be brought back to their transports from excursions, exercise and billets ashore, thoughtfully organized by Wellesley and Hill. On 12 July, one day ahead of his army, Wellesley put to sea in the *Donegal*, whose captain, the superlatively handsome Pulteney Malcolm, brother of his friend

4. Lord Burghersh (1784–1859), eldest son of the 10th Earl of Westmorland, was to become a diplomat, not a general. During the winter of 1813–14 he was Wellington's correspondent and Allied Military Commissioner at Frankfurt. In 1811 he married Wellington's favourite niece, the clever graceful and feminine Priscilla Wellesley-Pole.

5. *Supplementary Despatches*, vol. V, p. 453. Lord Fitzroy Somerset, youngest son of the Duke of Beaufort (1788–1855). Commander-in-Chief after Wellington's death, created 1st Lord Raglan, died in the Crimea.

John Malcolm, was 'in high style' and in charge of the fleet. He intended to employ part of the passage in learning Spanish from Lady Eleanor Butler's prayer book, a sensible parting gift from the Ladies of Llangollen.

*   *   *

Having transferred on the 13th into the fast cruiser, *Crocodile*, General Wellesley was soon in contact with the Spanish Junta at Corunna, where he found high spirits, requests for money and arms and a strong patriotic disinclination for British officers or men. Wellesley could not yet be expected to recognize this as a danger signal. He wrote home enthusiastically: 'It is impossible to describe the sentiment which prevails throughout the country.' On the 24th he reached Oporto, where there was an ardent British 'factory' based on the historic port wine trade, and a no less ardent bishop, head of the Supreme Junta of Portugal. To him Wellesley allotted the pastoral task of collecting hundreds of oxen and pack-mules for his transport, while the Portuguese general, Bernadin Freire, was persuaded to march south to Leiria on the Lisbon road, and there meet Wellesley's army with stores of food and 6,000 troops. Wellesley left behind Colonel Trant as Freire's liaison officer, a spirited Irishman whom he was to recall nostalgically after he was dead:

> Trant, poor fellow! a very good officer, but as drunken a dog as ever lived.

Wellesley departed on 25 July. Five days later one of the French generals in Portugal, Loison, massacred the whole insurgent population of Evora, men, women and children, thus making sure that any Portuguese disagreements with the British should be totally obliterated by Loison's cruelty.

Meanwhile Wellesley had sailed southwards to confer with Admiral Cotton, near Lisbon, on the proposed landing of his army in Mondego Bay. Anchorages were strictly limited on 'this iron coast', as Wellesley called it, while Lisbon was defended by a string of seventeenth-century but still 'respectable' forts in the Tagus estuary, not to mention a squadron of eight Russian ships sheltering there which, since Tilsit, were also probably hostile. At Figueira da Foz, on the other hand, where the River Mondego poured into the

Atlantic, there was an ancient fort of golden stone which the valiant students of near-by Coimbra University had seized from the French. Admiral Cotton put in some of his marines, and Wellesley decided to land there. It was 100 miles north of Lisbon and there was the usual calamitous surf beyond the bar; but it was the best they could do.

Wellesley reached Mondego Bay on 30 July. Here the old demon of supersession caught up with him once more.

A letter from Lord Castlereagh awaited him marked 'Secret'. It informed him that the French army in Portugal under General Junot was much stronger than at first suspected; that the British expeditionary force was therefore to be increased by 15,000 men including Moore's troops returning from a (bizarre) mission to Sweden; that, finally, the command of such a large armament would have to pass from Wellesley to Sir Hew Dalrymple, with Sir Harry Burrard as second-in-command. There was one bright spot. Wellesley was to continue his preparations against Lisbon without waiting for the arrival of Sir Hew and Sir Harry, attended, incidentally, by four other lieutenant-generals all senior to himself. A list of new commanders, in fact, issued by the Horse Guards on 20 July opened with Dalrymple and Burrard, worked through Moore, Hope, Mackenzie, Fraser and Lord Paget (the last of whom was shortly to run off with Henry Wellesley's wife) and finished with Sir Arthur Wellesley at the bottom.

Sir Hew Dalrymple, nearing sixty and descended from the noble Scottish family of Stair, had only once seen active service—in the disastrous Flanders campaign of 1793–4—but he had made an irreproachable Governor of Guernsey and, until this month, of Gibraltar. He sent Wellesley a report of affairs in Spain no less damping than his own presence was soon to be in Portugal: the 'Fanatical Fury' of the Juntas was worse even than the French Revolution, the Spanish would not admit their British Allies to any of their fortresses, and General Spencer had failed signally to conciliate them. 'Of Buonaparte we hear nothing, his armies seem to be left to their fate.'

Sir Hew's last sentence, at any rate, proved to be almost clairvoyantly correct. On 23 July 18,000 French soldiers were surrounded by the Spanish General Castaños at Baylen and forced to surrender. So brilliant was the victory and so alluringly simple the encircling manoeuvre, that Wellesley later on had great difficulty in getting

'Baylen' out of the Spaniards' system. He used to say jocularly before every engagement: 'Now this is not a battle of Baylen: don't attempt to make it a battle of Baylen!'

Wellesley's reaction to Sir Hew's and Castlereagh's letters was characteristic. Without obviously moving off in indecent haste, there was clearly a good chance of defeating the French armies before Sir Hew, Sir Harry, Sir John or any other senior lieutenant-generals appeared on the scene. 'I hope that I shall have beat Junot,' he wrote to his confidant, the Duke of Richmond, 'before any of them arrive, then they will do as they please with me.' Since he reckoned Junot's army (mistakenly) at only 18,000, his relatively slender resources seemed no reason for cooping his men any longer in their hot, cramped transports. On 31 July, in anticipation of an immediate landing, he issued his first General Order of the Peninsular War:

> The troops are to understand that Portugal is a country friendly to his Majesty. . . .

This uncompromising assertion was to stand between the soldiers and a multitude of favourite sins, beginning with robbery and ending with rape. It was to be repeated endlessly and disobeyed as often; it was to cost many soldiers a brutal flogging and not a few their lives. But without Portuguese co-operation the war would have been lost.

The Order then recommended, in a spirit of detached tolerance acquired in India, respect for Portuguese 'religious prejudices'— officers to remove their hats, soldiers to salute and sentries to present arms when the Host passed in the street. Lastly came announcements on some traditional British prejudices. There were to be six women to every hundred men (drawn by lot before embarkation amid screams and swooning), the men to have one pound of biscuits and one pound of meat every day, with wine added if the meat was salt; the women to be on half-rations and no wine, however salt the meat.

The landings began on 1 August. As was feared, several boats capsized in the roaring surf and a number of unfortunates were drowned including two M.P.s from prominent familes, a Cavendish and a Waldegrave. The rest scrambled over the red granite rocks, burning and bare except for tufts of samphire. Next day Wellesley issued a stirring proclamation to the inhabitants:

PEOPLE OF PORTUGAL
The time is arrived to rescue
your country; and restore the
government of your lawful Prince.

*   *   *

The landings were all completed by 8 August. On the 10th Wellesley
struck camp and entered Leiria next day after a twelve-mile march
made intolerable to his unhardened troops by deep sand, blistering
sun and the celebrated nerve-racking shriek from the wheels of
wooden ox-carts.[6] Under the lofty magnificence of Leiria Castle,
built by the medieval King Diniz of whom it was said '*que fiz tanto
quiz*'—he did as he liked—Wellesley and Freire met in fierce dispute.
Each wished to be a King Diniz; neither succeeded. Freire insisted
that the march to Lisbon should be through the protecting mountains
to the eastward, Wellesley by the exposed westward road which
alone would keep him in touch with his store ships. Nor could
Wellesley supply Freire's 6,000 men as well as his own, as Freire
wished, since his chief commissary, James Pipon, had fallen down
badly on the job.[7] In the end it was agreed, though still with many
growls, that Wellesley should arm, feed and take with him just
seventeen hundred light troops under Trant.

*   *   *

Junot meanwhile had sent a French veteran, General Henri François
Comte de Laborde, to hold up Wellesley's advance on Lisbon at the
first suitable battleground. He allowed the British to pass through
Batalha, the site of King John I of Portugal's crucial victory over
Spain in 1385, on the actual anniversary of the ancient battle, 14
August. There in the abbey built as a thank-offering, John's English
Queen Philippa of Lancaster still lay beside him on a romantic
marble tomb holding his left hand in her right—to be taken perhaps

6. Virgil spoke of '*stridentia plaustra*'; the Portuguese had an onomato-
poeic word for it, '*chiar*'.
7. Wellesley wrote angrily to Castlereagh on 8 August that 'the people
who manage [the commissariat] are incapable of managing any thing out of
a counting house'. He had to show them every detail himself (*Despatches*,
vol. IV, p. 59).

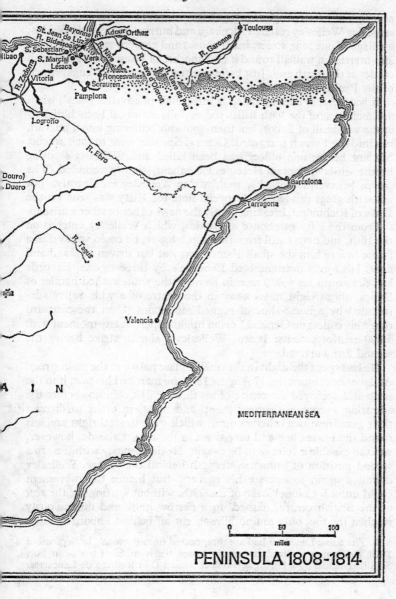

PENINSULA 1808-1814

as a sign of better Anglo-Portuguese relations in the future.[8] On the same day Wellesley reached Alcobaça and hurried on towards Obidos, a village of one long street, small houses and gardens gay with lemons and myrtles, a wall all round it and another of King Diniz's Moorish castles at the north end. Just before he reached it the first engagement of the Peninsular War took place.

It was what Wellesley called 'a little affair of advance posts', when a detachment of the 95th Rifles successfully drove off French pickets at the windmill of Brilos, but then 'foolishly' entering into a pursuit, ran into the French rearguard. General Spencer went to their rescue, but not before one officer had been killed and Wellesley's young brother-in-law, Captain Hercules Pakenham, slightly wounded. 'The troops behaved remarkably well,' wrote Wellesley indulgently, 'but not with great prudence.' A special note for Kitty was sent via the Duke of Richmond, breaking gently the news of her brother's mishap.

From the lofty gatehouse of Obidos, which Wellesley entered on the 16th, and better still from its church tower, he could see as if in a frame before him the small French army at last driven to stand and fight. His forces outnumbered Laborde's by three to one. Laborde had drawn up his 4,000 men in front of the whitewashed hamlet of Roliça, about eight miles away in the centre of a wide valley surrounded by a horse-shoe of rugged mountains. Over the eastward range his colleague General Loison might appear at any moment with 5,000 reinforcements. It was Wellesley's aim to strike before the second army arrived.

He had spent the night in the small square palace in the main street. At dawn next morning, 17 August 1808, he marched his men into the plain and deployed the centre of his three scarlet columns before the admiring French with great pomp and noise, in order to distract their gaze from two other columns which were to steal right and left round the horse-shoe and take them in the rear. Laborde, however, was too capable a veteran to be caught. He dexterously withdrew to a second position of immense strength behind the village. Wellesley intended again to operate his pincers. But before the movement could unfold, Colonel Lake of the 29th, without waiting for the rest of the British centre, dashed up a narrow gully and miraculously reached the top, only to find himself cut off behind Laborde's lines.

8. The name Lancaster had not disappeared from Portugal. In September 1810 Wellington received an enquiry about the number of troops in Fort St Julian signed by a Portuguese officer named Don Rodrigo de Lancaster.

He himself was killed and almost all his men were casualties before help could reach him. His action changed the battle of Roliça from an inconsiderable occasion to a perilous drama.

On realizing the disaster, Wellesley at once abandoned his abortive pincer movement and ordered a general advance. A swarm of British skirmishers doggedly fought their way up the mountain clefts, smoke from their muskets marking their violent ascent and shouts of triumph or anguish echoing through the ravines. The infantry followed close behind and took over the whole westward half of the ridge, while the British left also began to close in. Laborde clung on with his right to the last moment, hoping in vain for Loison. There was no option but to retreat. For a time, with the help of his cavalry, he withdrew in good order. Suddenly the dams of discipline burst and his army poured away, abandoning three of their five guns.

Nevertheless it was not a decisive success for the British. Wellesley had not enough cavalry for a pursuit and Laborde, though wounded, got all his survivors back to the mountain fastness of Montachique near Torres Vedras. His losses were about 700 to Wellesley's 487, more than half of the latter in the tragic 29th. Wellesley himself described the battle with awe rather than triumph. It was 'a most desperate' action; 'I never saw such fighting as in the pass', and the French showed 'their best style'. Clearly it would need something more than Roliça to drive the French out of Portugal.

*   *   *

Wellesley awoke from a night in the open near Roliça to hear that 4,000 reinforcements from England were off the coast. He at once marched to cover their disembarkation at the mouth of the River Maceira from the hills round Vimeiro, a peaceful village with a hundred small houses, some pine woods, a stone bridge over the Maceira and a plain little church colour-washed in blue and white. The landings took place in the pink-bouldered estuary on the 18th, 19th and 20th, not without the usual drownings. On the evening of the last day, the sloop *Brazen* brought in the first of the lieutenant-generals destined to supersede Wellesley, Sir Harry Burrard.

Wellesley immediately rowed out through the surf to propound to Sir Harry his plan for next day—a swift march south to Mafra, the important royal town north of Lisbon whose palace Byron was to describe next year as 'magnificence without elegance'. From Mafra he

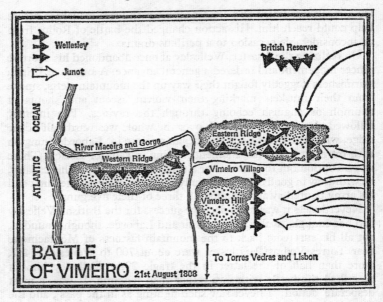

BATTLE OF VIMEIRO 21st August 1808

would outflank Junot's army which he had learnt was drawn up before Torres Vedras.

But the passenger on board the *Brazen*, full of elderly caution, objected that the British army, though now raised to 17,000 men, still fell far short of Junot's 30,000 (counting in Junot's forces miles away on the Spanish frontier). Therefore, until Sir John Moore's contingent had also arrived, Burrard proposed to take no action whatever.

Burrard proposed but fortune disposed. While Sir Harry prepared to spend a quiet night on board the *Brazen*, leaving Wellesley still in charge of the camp at Vimeiro, Junot was on his way from Torres Vedras to take them all by surprise.

Not long after midnight reports of a French movement began to reach Wellesley. To the Commander-in-Chief, reprieved from supersession for twelve hours, the news was wonderful beyond dreams. Before dawn he was up on a long ridge covered with myrtle and gum cistus above his camp which ran at right angles to the sea, watching for the French army to appear from the south. But it was from the east, at 9 A.M., that the first clouds of tell-tale dust appeared and the shifting glint of arms.

This was an unlooked-for crisis. The French were now turning his left; and he must redeploy his whole army so that, instead of facing south and west to withstand an attack on Maceira Bay, it would be ready to meet the French from the opposite direction. Coolly he led some thousands of his men into their new positions, unmoved by hectic messages pouring in all the while from agitated scouts. One cavalry vedette, he recalled, was in such a state of terror that his hair literally stood on end, raising the helmet from his head!

On a second, easterly ridge, lying end on to his original position and divided from it by the Maceira gorge, he drew up the bulk of his army, ordering the men when posted to lie down out of sight of the enemy. Trant's Portuguese with a supporting British brigade occupied a smaller parallel ridge behind, in case Junot tried a flanking movement to the north. All these troops were behind Vimeiro. South, or in front, of the village rose a round green hump with a flat top, known on the campaign maps as Vimeiro hill. Here Wellesley posted the rest of his army, which included the famous light troops of the 43rd and 52nd. And here began the battle of Vimeiro on 21 August 1808, with the advance of four dense French columns, their right led by the wounded hero of Roliça, Laborde, their left by Loison, the villain of the Evora massacre.

In front of the Grenadiers, according to hallowed Napoleonic practice, swarmed a darting mass of *tirailleurs* (skirmishers), supported by guns, whose ritual act consisted in stinging, flustering and confusing the enemy lines until they were sufficiently distraught to fall an easy prey to the solid infantry behind. This time none of the magic worked.

Wellesley knew all about the peril of French *tirailleurs*. Instead of asking his 'steady troops' to face them unprotected, he posted a strong skirmish line of his own at the foot of Vimeiro hill, armed with rifles. Most of his infantry waited behind the crest, with orders to hold their fire till the last moment. In front of them twelve guns were drawn up against the first French group of seven. As the French went in they were met in rapid succession by obstinate rifle-fire, a brief cannonade and then, suddenly, a thin red line of British infantry—'thin' because only two deep, so that every weapon could fire—delivering its 'rolling' musket-fire company by company down the whole line and gradually wrapping itself round the head of the leading French column, until its deadly hail poured into the French flanks as well as front. The French general tried in vain to form his huge rectangular column (thirty men broad by forty-two deep) into line, and thus bring the rear ranks of his muskets into play. The British fire was too hot for this manoeuvre. His column began to disintegrate. The British bayonets thrust and thrust again. All at once, like a panic-stricken herd of sheep (or so it seemed), the French bundled themselves headlong to the bottom of Vimeiro hill. After the battle a pair of victims of this savage fight, one French and one British, were found in deathly embrace skewered together by the same bayonet.

A second thick French column, and then two more, advanced against the hill, only to meet the same lapping, murderous fire from the thin red lines, a fire which even the indomitable French could not endure. They lost eleven guns and had a first taste of the new 'shrapnel' fired from British howitzers. Half-way through these four French attacks Sir Harry Burrard arrived on the ridge. Generously he ordered Wellesley to finish what he had so well begun.

The next stages, however, gave Wellesley some bad moments. After a bout of unpleasant street-fighting in Vimeiro village, he decided to try a cavalry charge on the disordered French columns. The 20th Light Dragoons accordingly dashed forward at a breakneck gallop which ended in fiasco, the horses bolting, most of their riders casualties, the colonel dead and little damage inflicted on the enemy. This was the first but far from the last time that Wellesley saw British cavalry go out of control.

On the ridge behind Vimeiro fighting had broken out at 10.30 A.M., half an hour before the assaults on the hill collapsed. Here the British repeated their earlier tactical triumphs but in such a clear-cut and complete manner as almost to render this part of the action a curtain-raiser for Wellington's great victory two years later at Bussaco. Springing up unexpectedly from behind a precipitous crest, 3,000 British muskets, some of them belonging to the survivors from Roliça's 29th, drove three French brigades down into the valley and away to the north of the ridge. Here there was a temporary setback, when the French were reinforced, but by bringing the 29th round himself to attack the French right flank, Wellesley again managed to establish a column *v.* line duel, which ended for the fifth time that day in a mob of broken French infantry fleeing down a blood-stained slope. More men, more guns captured; no French reserves left; no spirit either. It was still only noon. This was the moment to turn a defeat into a rout.

Wellesley galloped impetuously up to Burrard and raised his hat. The soldiers watched him intently. One of them, Rifleman Harris, remembered it twenty-one years later: 'Methinks it is something to have seen that wonderful man even do so commonplace a thing as lift his hat to another officer in the battle-field.' Then in a loud voice clearly audible to his staff Wellesley exclaimed:

'Sir Harry, now is your time to advance. The enemy are completely beaten, we shall be in Lisbon in three days.'

Sir Harry hesitated and Wellesley pressed him again, adding the bait of Sir Harry himself taking part in the victorious campaign:

'We have a large body of troops which have not been in action; let us move them from the right to Torres Vedras, and I will follow the French with the left.'

The French had in fact fled eastwards, leaving Torres Vedras and the road to Lisbon open. It was Sir Harry's chance.

But Sir Harry had said No once and he said it again. Enough was enough. He had been created a baronet for doing nothing much at Copenhagen in 1807. Before Junot's attack he had said to Wellesley, 'Wait for Moore.' He repeated it. It was not a pun but a fatuity. Wellesley turned away in disgust, remarking to his officers that they all might as well go and shoot red-legged partridges.

The glow of Vimeiro nevertheless hung over Wellesley for another few hours. In jubilant letters to his brother William and the Duke of Richmond he described himself as 'the Child of Fortune' and 'the most fortunate man in the world'. Thanks to Junot he had been able to prove, what he had long suspected, that the fabled French shock-tactics would melt before steady troops, well led. As he was to say to Croker with a smile many years later, the French came on with more confidence at Vimeiro, 'seeming less to *feel their way*', than ever again. Richmond responded in due course with equal zest. There was 'something whimsically providential', he reflected, in Junot forcing a glorious victory upon Arthur at the very moment the command was passing. 'You must have bribed him to attack you when he did.' Lady Wellesley was highly delighted, as Arthur could imagine, and his own small daughters kept saying that 'as you have killed all the French, you must now come back'.

By the end of next day the glow had vanished. The heat tortured the wounded. One of the army doctors, Adam Neale, found he could do nothing for them but offer words of consolation and 'a little opium'. The vultures and the effluvia from the dead made the whole army yearn to march. From having been 'the most fortunate of men', Wellesley suddenly found himself, as he told Richmond, in a 'very delicate' position. On 22 August the army's third Commander-in-Chief in twenty-four hours, Sir Hew Dalrymple, took over. Instead of consulting Wellesley on all points, as Castlereagh had naïvely suggested, he totally ignored his young subordinate's plans for an advance. To make matters even more 'delicate', the army still came to Wellesley on every detail, refusing to take orders from anyone but 'their old General'. In fact, the two men were from the start at loggerheads.

Junot now deftly intervened. Choosing his subtlest negotiator, the remarkably ugly General Kellerman whose face was covered with black sticking-plaster of odd shapes, he sent him under a flag of truce to propose a treaty for the total evacuation of Portugal by the French. As the Frenchmen galloped into Sir Hew's camp there was a sudden flurry of alarm at what was thought to be a surprise attack. From Wellesley's point of view an attack would have been better than the morass of intrigue into which he now slithered.

*   *   *

To cut a long and dismal story short—the kind of story which Wellesley always detested and often mishandled—terms for a forty-eight-hour armistice were agreed to on 22 August, which greatly benefited the victorious British army, moderately assisted the defeated French and desperately shocked the uncomprehending peoples of Portugal and Britain. All the French-occupied fortresses were given up and the royal flag of Portugal waved once more on St George's Castle, Lisbon, above the ochre battlements, ancient brass artillery and white peacocks. Since Burrard had thrown away the chance of annihilating Junot immediately after Vimeiro, every responsible man, and more especially Wellesley, welcomed this as the only other way of freeing Portugal at once and absolutely.

Scarcely anyone, however, and certainly not Wellesley, accepted Kellerman's detailed interpretation of the main agreement. While it was inevitable that the French army should be repatriated, together with their property, and in British ships (though this last clause choked the public with rage), it was a peculiarly disagreeable shock that French 'property' was found to include church plate melted down, two state carriages belonging to the Duke of Sussex and the Portuguese royal family's cambric sheets from Mafra run up into shirts for Loison. Kellerman even inserted a clause to have the Russian ships in the Tagus repatriated also, though Admiral Cotton afterwards dismissed this grotesque item out of hand.

The proposed armistice terms of the 22nd were read over to Wellesley at Sir Hew's request and criticized by him; they were then drafted by Sir Hew and Kellerman alone, Wellesley having left the room. Kellerman signed. Sir Hew was about to sign also when Kellerman astutely suggested that Wellesley should sign instead, since he and Kellerman were of corresponding rank. Kellerman's more devious reason was to get the actual victor of Vimeiro thoroughly involved in a treaty which he knew would be unpopular and might be rejected.

Against his better judgement, without even reading the final draft, Wellesley complied with Sir Hew's request to put his name to a document for which he was in no sense responsible. He was afterwards to regret his action deeply. Why did he do it?

His first motive was one of principle: he agreed with the armistice in principle (though not in detail) and did not wish to raise a 'faction' against his lawful commander on the very day he arrived. Second, 'good nature', as he himself wryly called it: a wish to do what 'they' asked; almost a fatalistic acquiescence in what would give 'them' pleasure without too much inconvenience to himself. Similarly he had become a youthful soldier because 'they' wanted it, and Kitty's husband for the same reason. It was a weakness of character, perhaps, though an endearing one; and one that seems strange and inconsistent in a so-called Iron Duke. That is, until it is remembered that only machines, like the steam-boat of the same name, are made of the same metal throughout.

*　　*　　*

The armistice was duly transformed into a convention. It was ratified on 31 August by Sir Hew at parched, stony Torres Vedras and by Junot at Lisbon, where it had been negotiated. Next day the British headquarters were moved nearer Lisbon to Cintra, Byron's 'glorious Eden' in the hills. Wellesley neither negotiated nor read a word of the final document (though of course he knew the gist) until it was published in the *London Gazette Extraordinary* on 16 September 1808, as the Convention of Cintra.[9] It created a furore.

A very popular radical journal, the *Political Register*, launched a bitter attack on all three generals, asking whether they could even be described as curs who allowed a mastiff (Junot) to carry off their bone? 'No, not so; for they complacently carry the bone for him.' Wordsworth wrote a tract against the Convention and proclaimed in a sonnet that 'selfish interest' had led a brave army astray. Three stanzas of Byron's best invective in *Childe Harold* were devoted to it:

> *And ever since that martial synod met,*
> *Britannia sickens, Cintra! at thy name;*
> *And folks in office at the mention fret,*
> *And fain would blush, if blush they could for shame.*
> *How will Posterity the deed proclaim!*

Posterity has in fact proclaimed the deed extremely sensible, though in September 1808 everyone was feeling 'sickened', even the old diehard Sidmouth—'every British heart must sicken at this break-down of the country's honour'—and none more so than Arthur himself. 'I am sick of the state of public Affairs,' he wrote to William on 6 September, and three days later to Richmond, 'I am sick of all that is going on here, and I heartily wish I had never come away from Ireland.' These outbursts were the culmination of progressive disillusionment, in which confusion over his own future played a growing part. Already on 24 August he had told William, 'I wish that I was away from this Army,' and Richmond on the 27th,

> since the arrival of the great generals, we appear to have been palsied, and every thing has gone wrong.

He added, with memories of Baird and India:

> But I don't like to desire to go, lest it should be imputed to me that I am unwilling to serve where I don't command.

On the 30th, however, he was contradicting himself in a letter to Castlereagh:

9. Sir Hew's despatch sending home a copy of the Convention was dated from Cintra, hence its name.

I have been too successful with this army ever to serve with it in a subordinate situation. . . .

There was in any case one audacious thing he could still do for his devoted army before he went home to face the music. He could make sure they had a commander worthy of them. Sir John Moore was now in Portugal and clearly the man. First the political breach between Moore and the Government, who sensed in him a taint of Opposition, must be healed. Wellesley, believing himself to be the ideal go-between, wrote to Moore offering his services. His letter contained sentences not only relevant to the immediate situation but also to the whole direction of his own life:

. . . the Commander in Chief must be changed, and the country and the army naturally turn their eyes to you. . . . Although I hold a high office under Government [Chief Secretary of Ireland], I am no party man; but . . . I think I have sufficient influence over them, that they may listen to me upon a point of this description. . . . In times like these, my dear General, a man like you should not preclude himself from rendering the services of which he is capable by an idle point of form.

The *nimmukwallah* was at work again. But now a new ingredient had appeared in the developing concept: the need for some measure of neutrality within the party system. 'Party' and 'points of form' were set against 'services'. A man needed a certain amount of elbow-room to do his duty in full.

Moore, touched by Wellesley's unexpected overture, agreed to meet him at Queluz, the charming little rose-pink palace outside Lisbon. Wellesley told Moore that the army had confidence in only two leaders, the two whose unorthodox conference was now taking place at Queluz. One or other of them must stay to liberate Spain.

And you are the man—and I shall with great willingness act under you.

But for the Convention of Cintra and its humiliating and protracted effects, he would no doubt have done so—and perhaps lost his life, like Moore, or his arm, like Baird.

The day after the meeting Wellesley embarked for England. His

brother William's more and more hysterical letters, begging him to
return and defend himself, had at length decided him to obtain leave
of absence from the army. He and his officers landed at Plymouth on
4 October. His first concern was to make the landlord of their inn
borrow a London newspaper. 'We are very anxious to know what
people are saying about us.' He was looking, according to a stray
observer, 'low and nervous', and expecting, as he said cheerfully,
'to be hanged drawn & quartered; or roasted alive', or at any rate
'shot like Byng'.

> However, I shall not allow the Mob of London to deprive me of
> my temper or my spirits; or of the satisfaction which I feel in the
> consciousness that I acted right.

Arthur was putting a bold face on it, as had been his fashion ever
since he sailed from Trincomalee without orders, seven years before.
He talked blandly of devoting his talents to hunting and shooting if
the Army, Ireland, and all else failed. Nevertheless there was a chill
feeling of having been sent back to start.

Confidently as the Child of Fortune had told Croker three months
earlier, 'my die is cast', where was he now? The dice was back again,
rattling disconsolately in the box.

10 *Cintra and Charybdis*

Politically conscious London vented its wrath on Sir Arthur, and for good measure included his whole family in the attack. For he was the only politician among the three culprits of the Convention. Samuel Whitbread, the leading Radical M.P., though he deplored Cintra and 'all the lost opportunities for national glory', could not help rejoicing 'to see the Wellesley pride a little lowered'; while Cobbett[1] wrote to Lord Folkestone, who had acted for James Paull against Lord Wellesley over India:

> How the devil will they [Wellesley and friends] get over this? now we have the rascals on the hip. It is evident that *he* [Arthur] was the prime cause—the only cause—of all the mischief, and that from the motive of thwarting everything *after he was superseded.* Thus do we pay for the arrogance of that damned infernal family.

Though the Duke of Richmond begged Arthur not to mind 'the whispers of those who dislike the name of Wellesley', his mother and his three brothers minded very much.

Lady Mornington wrote to her eldest son on 8 October:

> Thank God, I have seen dear Arthur in good looks and Health and am more delighted than I can express at his conduct and high spirit in leaving those persons to their own intentions who have so basely injured him. . . . I trust they will ere long be confounded and punished . . . for the disgrace they have brought upon Dear Old England.

William managed to relieve his feelings in 'cursing and swearing' but Henry, whose 'fibre' was described as 'of the most excitable nature',

---

1. William Cobbett (1763–1835), the famous Radical author and politian with a huge following, published the *Political Register* every week from 1802 until his death. Imprisoned 1810–12 by the Government for denouncing the flogging of mutineers. Beneath his Radicalism were many conservative emotions, as expressed in his *Advice to Young Men* (1829) and *Rural Rides* (1830).

had been taken ill with vexation. Richard's behaviour was pitiable.
When Lord Grenville assured him of unabated affection in this time of
family misfortune, he cried for half an hour. The persistent attacks on
his Indian government had received their quietus in April that year
when James Paull, having lost £300 at a gambling club, blew out his
brains. But if Paull had lost £300, he had lost Lord Wellesley a
hundred times as much in the huge costs of his defence—indeed, his
whole Indian fortune. While waiting to be cleared, Richard could not
hold office; frustration produced indolence and indolence carried
him unresisting into a life of indiscreet sex. 'In spite of his Idleness,'
Arthur had written to William two days after Roliça, 'he would have
been in Office before now if he had not taken to whoring.' A friend
of Lord Buckingham's confirmed that Lord Wellesley 'goes to Ramsgate again . . . where . . . he has a fresh *amour*, after his manner, with
a very stale inamorata, but with which he is intoxicated for the
present'. Richard added to Arthur's anxieties by tactlessly urging
the King to create his brother Viscount Vimeiro. The wrathful
monarch, who a short time ago had been quoting the wonderful
Vimeiro despatches from memory, now declared the conduct of Sir
Arthur, Sir Hew and Sir Harry to be all equally 'disgraceful'.

London was raucous with the partisans of the three generals,
Arthur's friends putting into his mouth excuses he had never made,
while those of Sir Hew and Sir Harry tried to involve Sir Arthur in
responsibilities he had ceased to hold. He refused to be drawn.

> I have not read one word that has been written on either side,
> and have refused to publish, and don't mean to authorise . . . a
> single line in my defence.

He was right. For the Government had been forced to recall Sir
Arthur's two successors and announce a military inquiry into the
Convention to open on 14 November, when all three generals would
be examined. True to what was to become a lifelong principle, he
would say nothing excepting through the channel of a 'regular'
inquiry. But in private he rarely described the other two generals
more warmly than as 'These People', 'the great generals', 'the
Gentlemen', or even 'these poor creatures'. And he was quite ready
to risk a public scene with the London mob, against his friends'
wishes, by attending the King's levee. 'I will go to Court tomorrow
or never go again,' he announced. He went, and with some cynicism

noted that not only did the Royal Family receive him 'most graciously', but a deputation who had come to petition the King to have him tried for treason, recognized his hawk-like profile and promptly asked after his health with 'fawning civility'. He concluded stoutly, 'I think I may defy the mob of London.'

Next day he took Richmond's advice to remove himself temporarily to Ireland—'All in this country but the rebels,' wrote Richmond, 'are anxious for your return'—and he was back at the Castle by 20 October. His departure did not escape Cobbett's malicious notice. The *Political Register* took the opportunity to remind its readers of how ignominious had been the recent arrival in London of the victor of Vimeiro:

> he had the discretion not to make any noise upon his landing. He snugged it in, in the Plover sloop, and off he went as fast as post-horses would take him to that place where one man is not known to another; and where a man may walk about, and be hidden at the same time. This must, however, have been a little mortifying to the high Wellesley. It was not thus that he used to enter Calcutta. . . .

Having sarcastically mentioned Indian 'triumphal arches' and 'thousands of gilded barges', Cobbett went on to ask why Arthur Wellesley, this 'Chevalier de Bain', this conqueror of 'Monseigneur le Duc d'Abrantes [Junot] en personne' had come home. Could it be that 'he is come home for the purpose of avoiding another meeting with the Tartar Duke, or any of his like'? This imputation of cowardice stung Arthur into thoughts of a libel action. William dissuaded him, though deluging him with frantic entreaties to return from Ireland immediately in order to counteract Sir Hew's 'most artful and assiduous' propaganda, which had made even Castlereagh 'a little shy' when William saw him on Arthur's behalf. William promised to put nothing in the papers—'But be sure your cause will go to Leeward if you do not come here to watch and guide it.'

This gloomy prediction crossed a letter from Dublin full of Arthur's usual cheerful cynicism and self-confidence. He felt 'quite at ease' about the inquiry, for his case was stronger than William seemed to think:

> I declare I read the abuse of myself with as much indifference as I do that of Sir Hew . . . they have now found out that I corrupted the officers of the Army, & wrote the address myself! ! !

This was a reference to the generous thanks and piece of plate presented to him by his officers after Vimeiro.

At last the Court of Inquiry assembled, in the Great Hall of Chelsea College (now Hospital). Sir David Dundas, known as 'Old Pivot' from his prolific writings on drill, who was very soon to supersede the Duke of York as Commander-in-Chief in circumstances highly discreditable to the Duke, presided. Under him sat six other generals including Peter Graig, once a candidate along with Baird for superseding young Wellesley at Trincomalee. When the result came it was a fumbling anticlimax. Since the Court were determined not to blame either Sir Hew or Sir Harry and could not in justice blame Sir Arthur, everybody was right, though in violent mutual contradiction.

Wellesley's own performance was completely convincing. Since Sir Hew had had no confidence in him and consistently rejected his advice, he could not now be saddled with responsibliity for what Sir Hew had done. Sir Harry he admitted frankly had a military case for not advancing after Vimeiro, though he himself strongly opposed it. But once Sir Harry had prevailed, the expediency of *a* Convention was 'as clear as day'. This was the only point on which Wellesley considered himself answerable. The public, he agreed, had not obtained the results from the victories of Roliça and Vimeiro which they had a right to expect. This was nothing to do with him: 'my signature is a mere form'.

By six votes to one on 22 December 1808 the Court approved the Convention. By four to three they reluctantly accepted its details. But neither Dalrymple nor Burrard ever held command again; a blessing for which the much maligned Convention has since been given credit.

Wellesley himself ended by despising the whole affair. He considered the Report 'most extraordinary':

> I say nothing of opinions; for opinions in these days are like colours, matters of taste. But as far as respect me [*sic*] they have not stated even the facts correctly, and . . . garbled the whole most terribly.

*   *   *

Arthur Wellesley was back yet again in Ireland. His mood fitted the glum spirit of the times. In answer to Lord Enniskillen's innocent enquiry after a small sinecure for a relative, he snapped back that there were no sinecures left in Ireland. If the Earl's relative would not take an office with constant duties attached, 'he will get none'.

Kitty cannot have found this thwarted hero easy to please. Throughout the Cintra episode he had frequently stressed his need for 'patience and [good] temper', a sure sign of strain.

The marriage had jogged along fairly happily for the first two years but in 1808, with another year of Arthur's constant travels between Phoenix Park and Harley Street, Kitty began running to her various Irish cousins with tales of his coldness and neglect. Sorry as they all felt for her at first, she eventually alienated some of even this faithful band by her complaints.

It was during these difficult days that London's most aspiring courtesan, Harriette Wilson, claimed in her *Memoirs* to have consoled 'the Duke of Wellington'.

Harriette was the darling of the dandies. Among her lovers were, or soon would be, the Honourable Fred Lamb, Tom Sheridan, Lord Alvanley, Beau Brummell, the Marquess of Lorne, Lord Ponsonby, William Ponsonby, the Marquess of Worcester, son and heir of the 6th Duke of Beaufort, and many other glittering Regency names. She was queen of the 'demi-reps', mistress of the Game of Hearts and altogether an extremely vivacious if not beautiful London-bred *gamine*.

'The Duke', as she consistently called Wellesley, was said one day to have approached a certain Mrs Porter's notorious establishment in Berkeley Street on foot, 'rapped hastily' on her door, and as 'one of her oldest customers' demanded a meeting with Harriette Wilson. When Mrs Porter made some practical difficulties, enlarging upon Harriette's 'wildness' and 'independent' life, he interrupted impatiently.

'Nonsense! it is very well known that the Marquis of Lorne is her lover.'

Mrs Porter surrendered to superior generalship and agreed to approach Harriette. Picking up his hat, he gave a final brief command.

'And make haste about it. I shall call for your answer in two days.'

Harriette, burdened by debt (for Lorne was stingy and anyway going to Scotland), arranged to receive 'the Duke' a few days later. She described how he arrived punctually at 3 P.M., bowed, said 'How do you do?' and then in silence tried to take her hand. She withdrew it.

'Really, for such a renowned hero, you have very little to say for yourself.'

'Beautiful creature! where is Lorne?'

'Good gracious—what come you here for, Duke?'

'Beautiful eyes, yours!'

'Aye, man! they are greater conquerors than ever Wellington shall be; but, to be serious, I understood you came here to try to make yourself agreeable?'

'What, child! do you think that I have nothing better to do than to make speeches to please ladies? . . . You should see me where I shine.'

'Where's that, in God's name?'

'In a field of battle.'

'*Battez-vous, donc*', retorted the accomplished demi-rep, '*et qu'un autre me fasse la cour!*'

According to the *Memoirs* he now became her constant visitor, but 'a most unentertaining one' who seemed to her in the evenings, when he wore his broad red ribbon of the Bath, to look 'very like a rat-catcher'. On one of these occasions she claimed to have teased him about Cintra.

'Do you know . . . the world talks about hanging you?'

'Eh?'

'They say you will be hanged, in spite of all your brother Wellesley can say in your defence.'

'Ha! what paper do you read?'

'It is the common talk of the day.'

'They must not work me in such another campaign,' the hero of Vimeiro is said to have replied smiling, 'or my weight will never hang me.'

*   *   *

What is to be made of all this? Harriette Wilson's use of the anachronistic title, 'Duke of Wellington', is not in itself sufficient to discredit her story, for it was her practice to call peers indiscriminately by any of their titles, usually the highest one. Lorne, for instance, she often referred to as Duke of Argyll before he had succeeded to his father's dukedom.

In the passage just quoted she certainly has caught Arthur Wellesley's quick, peremptory speech, noted by all his friends, as well as the paternal touches and wry humour. Even the taciturnity broken by rather naïve gestures of homage sound perfectly authentic.

During his friendship with 'Miss J' in the 1830s, many of these characteristics were described in Miss J's diary with striking similarity.[2] However, in contrast to the genuinely 'Wellingtonian' touches, her account is full of equally remarkable improbabilities: his wearing the Order of the Bath to visit a *cocotte*, his boasting of battle honours. It is time to extricate Wellington from her little claws.

Harriette Wilson was writing her *Memoirs* in 1824. She was living in Paris with a disreputable Colonel Rochfort, harbouring a grudge against the Beaufort family who she felt owed her a pension in return for not having married Lord Worcester. Driven by chronic shortage of money and smarting under lack of recognition, she decided to try her hand at authorship as a solution for her troubles. Her impresario in the enterprise was a rascally publisher named Joseph Stockdale, who published works of scandal and pornography, as well as excellent maps of the south of France which Wellington's army found very useful. Each of Harriette's former beaux was to be given the chance to buy himself out of the *Memoirs* by the payment of £200.

On 16 December 1824 Stockdale dispatched one of these charitable offers to the Duke of Wellington:

24 Opera Colonnade.
My Lord Duke,
   In Harriette Wilson's Memoirs, which I am about to publish, are various anecdotes of your Grace which it would be most desirable to withold, at least such is my opinion. I have stopped the Press for the moment; but as the publication will take place next week, little delay can necessarily take place.
                    I have the honour to be,
                         My Lord Duke,
                    Your Grace's ever attached Servant
                    John Joseph Stockdale.

The Duke of Wellington's reply to this unpleasant document has disappeared, but not without leaving a resounding echo behind which is now a part of the English language:
Publish and be damned.

2. 'Miss J', as the Duke always addressed her, was an evangelical young beauty named Miss Jenkins, who besieged him, soul and body, from after Mrs Arbuthnot's death in 1834 until nearly the end of his own life. See Volume II.

According to legend, Wellington wrote these words in flaming red ink right across Stockdale's letter and posted it back to him. How much truth is there in this cherished tradition?

Stockdale's actual letter is at Apsley House and has nothing on it except the blackmailer's own slime.[3] A second letter from Opera Colonnade, however, shows that the Duke had indeed told Stockdale to go to hell and take Harriette with him. Stockdale's reply to the Duke's defiance was dated 28 December 1824.

Mr Stockdale was certainly not aware that the Duke of Wellington had been written to, much less threatened by Harriette Wilson now Rochfort. . . .

Mr Stockdale has purchased one half of the property of Harriette Wilson's Memoirs; his chief motive in which was to protect, as well as he could, any friend, who might be disagreeably implicated in them. Instead of exulting, he was grieved & pained, far, very far beyond what he shall attempt to describe, in the discovery of the prominent figure which the Duke of Wellington & the Marquess Wellesley cut, in those pages, from which S. [sic] was anxious to obliterate them, though it would diminish the interest of the work, & its consequent produce, perhaps, not less than £5,000. Indeed as a friend of that illustrious house, S. does not hesitate to say that twice that sum would be a cheap purchase of the destruction of those details, which, a few hours will place beyond the possibility of redemption. . . . If a Jury can now be worked upon, to declare the facts stated in these memoirs, libels, the work does not contain one page, which would not be sufficient to overwhelm, in its consequences, any publisher whatever.[4] Mere Justice, however, compels Mr S. to say that there is scarcely a line which does not carry . . . the fullest conviction of its veracity, & the unequalled number of fashionables, implicated in it all named at full length without reserve, combined with the dramatic air which the author flings over the whole cannot fail to give it an interest & circulation exceeding all which was anticipated of the suppressed Memoirs of Mary Anne Clarke.

3. Wellington frequently drafted his answers on the blank spaces left by his correspondents; occasionally he crossed the original writing; sometimes he used pencil instead of dark ink, but never red ink.

4. Wellington's apparent threat to go to court was not carried out, but other victims of Stockdale's unscrupulousness brought a series of libel actions which eventually ruined him.

When published early in 1825 Harriette Wilson's *Memoirs* took by storm a shocked, mesmerized, incredulous world. The Duke of Wellington figures prominently eight or nine times. Mrs Arbuthnot, his greatest woman friend of this period, could not believe these slanders and asked him on 19 February whether he had really known 'this woman' who dared to ridicule the great Duke as well as claiming him for one of her innumerable lovers. As she recorded in her diary, he replied frankly:

he had known her a great number of years ago, so long tho' that he did not think he should remember her again, that he had never seen her since he married tho' he had frequently given her money when she wrote to beg for it. . . .

Thanks to Mrs Arbuthnot, it is now possible to see the outlines of what really happened through the mists of Harriette Wilson's fund-raising fiction.

The 'great number of years ago' (dating back from 1825) when Wellington knew Harriette Wilson represented the months between September 1805 and March 1806—a matter of twenty years earlier. He had just returned from India and was somewhat at a loose end (until firmly whipped in by Olivia Sparrow). Since Harriette did not appear on the scene until about 1803, he cannot have met her before he went to India. But he almost certainly paid earlier visits to Mrs Porter's house in Berkeley Street, from which Harriette later conducted her affairs. These would have taken place between 1795 and 1796, while he was gloomily hanging about London, rejected by Kitty Pakenham and waiting to set sail. Captain Elers, the friend of Indian days, told the story of a beautiful Mrs Sturt who, when stranded in Madras on the way to join her husband, had appealed to 'her old friend Colonel Wellesley'. Generously and characteristically he at once made out an order on his banker for £400. Captain Elers added that Mrs Sturt had originally emanated from 'the establishment of a notorious woman living in Berkeley Street'. Surely none other than the procuress, Mrs Porter.

What more natural than that Major-General Wellesley should have returned to his old haunts in 1805? Or that he should have ordered Mrs Porter, as 'one of her oldest customers', to produce for him this new talk-of-the-town called Harriette Wilson? Or that the actual hero of Assaye should have been conveniently transformed into the future hero of Portugal, Spain and Waterloo? Or that he should have sent Harriette money when the Lornes, Ponsonbys or Worcesters failed her, just as he had salvaged Mrs Sturt when let down by Major William Sturt?

*   *   *

So the Stockdale–Wilson combine published, hoping that the Duke would be damned. Everything necessary had been done. For it was obvious that a caricature of the great Duke of Wellington would have far better box-office and revenge value than an accurate account of Sir Arthur Wellesley.

Or should we question Wellington's own veracity? Did he conceal from Mrs Arbuthnot some of the truth in February 1825? His confidence in Mrs Arbuthnot was complete. Why should he lie to the keeper of his conscience? He had revealed to her only three years earlier the story of his marriage to Kitty, even admitting that he had been 'a fool' to propose. Why then pretend to her that he had not seen Harriette Wilson since his marriage if in truth Kitty's inadequacies had driven him back to her?

Nor were the winter of 1808 and spring of 1809 when Harriette Wilson says she saw so much of 'the Duke', seasons favourable to courtesans. This was the time when the celebrated Mary Anne Clarke scandal broke over the head of the Duke of York.

*   *   *

The very day after the Royal Commander-in-Chief had signed the report on the Convention of Cintra and sent a copy to Dalrymple (20 January 1809), Colonel Wardle, M.P., stood up in the House of Commons and moved for an inquiry into the Duke of York's conduct as Commander-in-Chief.

For weeks to come Cintra and all Wellesley's troubles, not to mention the predicament of the British army in Spain in those freezing winter months, were driven out of the public mind. Colonel Wardle's inquiry was instituted. As if in an earthquake, a mass of underground corruption at the Horse Guards suddenly became exposed to the country's horrified gaze. It was shown that another clever, witty and conscienceless London *gamine*, Mary Anne Clarke, had used her position as the Duke of York's mistress to augment the irregular allowance he made her by selling under the counter and at cut prices, commissions, promotions and exchanges.

You'll be treated with Honours if you secrecy mark, Sir,
For my Master is Noble and I am his Clark, Sir.

The burning question was whether the Duke of York had known that this criminal traffic was going on.

Though Mary Anne entranced the Members of Parliament who questioned her, the ravishing gown of blue silk barely concealed an implacable little fury. She had been dismissed by her royal lover in 1806 and had found a quick and sure way to revenge. How amusing to be able to tell goggling Members that she sometimes had had to remind the Commander-in-Chief of his nefarious promises by pinning a note on their bed-curtains.

Arthur Wellesley was in his place at Westminster during Mrs Clarke's examination and began by being 'positively certain' the Duke of York was innocent. When Mrs Clarke later had the bright idea of dragging Arthur's own name into the scandal, accusing him of having known about the sales of commissions, he would have liked to dismiss her allegations against the Duke as equally slanderous. A letter to his friend Richmond described the noisy scene:

The House was in a roar when she mentioned my name; but I was happy to find that not a single man, not even Folkestone, imagined that I knew anything about the matter.

But Arthur Wellesley was no longer so 'positively certain' of the Duke's ignorance. He was still optimistic enough to believe, however, that these revelations would actually enhance Britain's reputation abroad, instead of giving a handle to revolutionaries and republicans as many people feared:

as it will be manifest to the whole world that not one of any party . . . has had any concern, direct or indirect, in the sale of an office; and that these transactions, which have deservedly created so much indignation, have been carried on by the scum of the earth.

Indignation against the Duke of York continued to mount. His effigy was burnt in Suffolk and Yorkshire. It was 'the immorality of his life', reported Arthur Wellesley to Richmond, which outraged the country areas. That aspect of the affair made 'no impression in town'. By 19 February Wellesley was convinced that the Duke could not remain in office, though he had loyally testified on the 22nd to his interest in the Army's welfare. If the Government tried to support him it too would fall. During the following month Wellesley came to believe with the vast majority—which today no one can doubt—that York 'must have suspected Mrs Clarke's practices'.

More important, Wellesley endorsed the general view that certain moral standards were necessary in public men. He put to Richmond on 6 March the question whether

> a Prince of the blood, who has manifested so much weakness as he has, and has led such a life (for that is material in these days), is a proper person to be entrusted with the execution of the duties of a responsible office.

The answer was clearly No. On 17 March the Duke of York resigned from the Horse Guards and next day was replaced as Commander-in-Chief by old Sir David Dundas. An *Epistle to Mrs. Clark* registered Peter Pindar's entire satisfaction with this denouncement.

> *No longer now the Duke excites our wonder,*
> *Midst gun, drum, trumpet, blunder bus and thunder;*
> *Amidst his hosts, no more with rapture dwells*
> *On Congreve's rockets, and on Shrapnell's shells;*
> *But quits, with scornful mien, the field of Mars,*
> *And to Sir David's genius leaves the wars.*

None of this boded well for General Wellesley. Though the Duke of York had never favoured him since India, Dundas's 'genius' was to prove no less irksome than York's coolness to his future command. For an atmosphere of timidity, especially as regards promotions, now pervaded the Horse Guards.[5] It was understandable; but intensely annoying to a general who wanted nothing more than to collect the best possible staff.

5. George Napier gives an account of his asking, or trying to ask Dundas for promotion. Having enquired after George's health, Dundas replied to every question on promotion, 'Wear flannel, Major, wear flannel' (*Early Life of Sir George Napier*, p. 81).

Finally, the relevance of Mary Anne Clarke to Harriette Wilson should now be clear. Arthur Wellesley, it must not be forgotten, had arrived back in England under heavy fire. Scarcely had the Cintra guns been silenced before the great Clarke cannonade opened. So powerful was it that one stray ball at least came bounding towards Arthur. Was it likely that he would choose these months of crisis to renew relations with another member of Mrs Clarke's dangerous sisterhood? His own comment on Richard's 'whoring', written before the Clarke bomb burst, was almost answer enough. Quite conclusive were the remarks he made after the Clarke affair, about the unfitness of men who led raffish lives for responsible office. 'For that is material in these days.'

It happened that at this very time Arthur Wellesley himself, after a long, painful interlude, was once more expecting a responsible command.

*   *   *

During November 1808 Spanish resistance had collapsed under a tremendous French onslaught directed by Napoleon in person. Madrid was again in French hands. Wellesley's new friend, Sir John Moore, was driven from Spain in December, and though he heroically evacuated all but a few thousand stragglers from his suffering army and saved both Cádiz and Lisbon, he himself fell at Corunna on 16 January 1809.

Sir David Baird lost an arm, young Harry Burrard, Sir Harry's son and Moore's aide-de-camp, was killed and General Anstruther, who had led a division at Vimeiro, died of dysentery. Whig support for the war died too. 'I hope my country will do me justice,' Moore murmured as he lay mortally wounded. The Whigs believed that 'all all all all all all all all all all will be laid on his shoulders, for "dead men can tell no tales"'. Beginning with the Grenvilles and going right through to Cobbett, the Left was totally disillusioned. Napoleon had not even bothered to stay in Spain but handed over to Soult. By the end of March 1809 Soult was in Oporto and the Portuguese of Lisbon clamouring once more for aid; this time, it would seem, in vain. All, all, all was ten times worse than before.

Arthur Wellesley had followed with horror the story of the retreat to Corunna. 'I was certain that nothing could save the army but an attack by the French,' he wrote to Colonel Gordon in India on 22

January 1809; 'and it is only to be lamented we have lost two such valuable men as Sir John Moore and Sir David Baird. The latter, I conclude, cannot live.' The sturdy Scot survived but not to command in the Peninsula. There, 'Beau' Cradock had assumed chief command but was clearly unfit for it. General Beresford, at the invitation of the spirited Portuguese[6] whose language he spoke, had taken over the whole south wing of the palace at Mafra and was reorganizing the Portuguese army. But as nearly all their officers had gone to Brazil and Junot had finished off what remained of the rank and file, Beresford had a long way to go before Portugal could defend herself. Worst of all the hero Moore, before he died, had said that if Spain fell Portugal could not be held. Who now dared draw the sword?

Arthur Wellesley, rehabilitated but only just, used the month of March to cut through all obstructions with his pen.

*   *   *

'I have always been of opinion that Portugal might be defended whatever might be the result of the contest in Spain. . . .' These were Wellesley's challenging words in a memorandum of 7 March to Lord Castlereagh. They challenged Moore's pessimism, though Wellesley entirely dissociated himself from Tory attacks on Moore's conduct. The conditions of success, he continued, were 20,000 British troops including 4,000 cavalry; a reconstituted Portuguese army; and the Spaniards to keep at least some of the huge French armies pinned down in their country. 'As soon as this shall be done, the General and Staff officers should go out. . . .' On the basis of these brave words Castlereagh battered down the Cabinet's resistance, first, to another expeditionary force, second, to Wellesley commanding it. Castlereagh believed in him.

Wellesley's orders from the Government, nevertheless, reflected a certain stringency in the situation:

> The defence of Portugal you will consider as the first and most immediate object of your attention.

Any combination with Spain would be left to his discretion, but he

---

6. The Portuguese approached Wellesley first who, unable to accept, suggested his friend, William Carr Beresford.

should on no account undertake it without the express authority of the British Government.

*   *   *

On the day before Wellesley's memorandum of 7 March, a sensational event had scandalized London society. Arthur's sister-in-law, Lady Charlotte Wellesley, wife of his brother Henry and mother of four young children, eloped. She went off in a hackney coach with Henry, Lord Paget, probably the best cavalry officer in the Army, son and heir of the Earl of Uxbridge, and himself the father of numerous children by his wife Lady Caroline Villiers, daughter of the Prince of Wales's former favourite, Lady Jersey. Paget's relatives denounced Lady Charlotte as a 'nefarious damned Hell-hound' and '*maudite sorcière*'; Lady Charlotte called herself 'a Wretch'; but nothing would induce her to return to Henry Wellesley, sick with grief and a liver complaint he had contracted in India. It was not a good send-off for Arthur, apart from the fact that he was devoted to his youngest brother. 'The people in the streets talk of it—even the mob,' lamented Paget's horrified brother-in-law, Lord Graves. With the names of Wellesley and Paget linked in such a way it was inevitable that the Peninsular expedition should be deprived of Paget's skill in the arm where Arthur would need it most—the cavalry. This on top of Cintra and Mary Anne Clarke seemed enough anxieties to go on with. Another family convulsion, however, this time still nearer home, was to agitate Arthur's last weeks in England.

Kitty's youngest brother, also named Henry, had run into debt through gambling and persuaded her to lend him the necessary money. The trouble began when she made over to Henry the house-keeping money given her by her husband to pay the tradesmen. Arthur's imminent departure for Portugal brought in all the unpaid bills, Kitty could not settle her accounts and one of the tradesmen dunned Sir Arthur. His anger was unforgiving. So much so that it is hard to believe this was poor Kitty's first offence. Indeed, something of the kind may have happened over the unpaid bill two years earlier. On that occasion Sir Arthur had suspected the tradesmen in question of 'cheating'. This time it was clearly Kitty's fault and he did not choose that particular word. But he used one not unlike it—mis-appropriation. She had misappropriated his funds.

This painful episode spoilt the last days together of husband and wife. Its echoes were to haunt Kitty's journal during the long months ahead, and Arthur's memory for the rest of their married life.[7]

*   *   *

By the beginning of April his preparations were almost complete. The friendly Richmonds offered Kitty a little house at Goodwood, under sixty miles from London, 'with good medical people'. But she was thinking of Malvern Wells, when the weather was warm enough. In return, Arthur took one of Richmond's protégés as assistant adjutant-general.[8]

Sir David Baird, now one-armed, regretfully handed over his own favourite aide-de-camp, Captain Alexander Gordon, on 2 April to General Wellesley, wishing Arthur success in his command 'wherever it may be'. (The public did not yet know.) Gordon, wrote Baird, though young, was very intelligent and active. Arthur's personal requests for aides-de-camp went fairly well, despite the new Dundas regime. 'But old David is so costive,' he wrote to Richmond on 7 April, 'that it is difficult to get anything out of him. . . .' Finally, there was the usual paternal entreaty from Lord Westmorland, which followed him out to Portugal. Would he see that young Burghersh's 'disposition to be a great General' did not run him into unnecessary hazards?

There is a strong impression that the ardent young soldiers who made up Arthur's 'family'—as the general's staff were always called— gave him a good deal more pleasure than the family left behind in England.

His Irish business still had to be concluded. Lord Rosse, assuming no doubt that any British expedition would be driven out within the usual few months, kindly offered to keep the Chief Secretaryship of Ireland warm for Wellesley until he returned. But either the recollection of a recent attack by Samuel Whitbread on his dual office in

---

7. Henry Pakenham afterwards became Dean of St Patrick's and there is a story that he tried to persuade the Duke of Wellington to use his influence for further promotion.
'One word from you, Arthur, and I could be a bishop.'
'Not one word, Henry, not one.' Five letters from Wellington to Lord Longford, Henry's brother, covering 1828–30 (*Longford MSS*) show that if the actual dialogue was apocryphal its tone was authentic. The tone recurred whenever Lord Longford pleaded on Henry's behalf.

8. James Bathurst who went mad and was replaced by Ned Pakenham.

1808, or his own second-sight, warned Wellesley to refuse. He resigned his seat in Parliament and office in Ireland. Croker was left to handle the routine business until a successor was appointed. In due course Croker became his successor.

The spring of 1809, as it turned out, was to be the last time Wellesley held office in Ireland or indeed set foot in that country. It is therefore all the more agreeable to find that his work there ended on characteristic notes of personal affection and social constructiveness. On 2 April he asked Richmond to allow the Irish-born Ladies of Llangollen pensions of £50 each. And the last letter from him now lying in the Irish State Papers Office is a plea to start draining 'the Bogs & Morasses of Ireland'. One bog at least stood no chance of being drained until Wellesley himself became Prime Minister—the anti-Catholic laws. Meanwhile, the 'enemy country' showed that he had not gone altogether unappreciated. One of the Dublin guilds, gave him a new-year present—a silver box containing its Freedom, for his 'private worth' and high military talents, 'highest amongst the heroes that this your native land has given birth to'.

* * *

Yet it is possible that conventional tributes and silver caskets are not the best notes on which to send abroad this most spontaneous and least grandiose of generals. As it happens Harriette Wilson claims that 'the Duke of Wellington' paid her two farewell visits before he left.

Early one morning before she had finished breakfast he called, but proved to be 'impenetrably taciturn'. At length he broke the silence.

'I wonder you do not get married, Harriette!'

'Why so?' He did not answer. Since the Convention of Cintra she professed to have noticed that he never gave any reasons for anything he said unconnected with fighting. He began again.

'I was thinking of you last night, after I got into bed.'

'How very polite to the Duchess. Apropos to marriage, Duke, how do you like it?'

'I was thinking—I was thinking that you will get into some scrape, when I go to Spain. . . . I must come again tomorrow, to give you a little advice.'

'Oh, let us have it all out now, and have done with it.' But he took a hasty leave. Harriette affirmed that she was not sorry, for she had found him 'very uphill work'.

His last alleged visit took place a few hours before he 'betook himself again to the wars', and was more to her liking. She burst into tears at the thought that she might never see this man again, who had relieved her from 'many duns'. He kissed her cheek, told her to look after herself, to leave her address for him at Thomas's Hotel as soon as he returned, and if she wanted anything in the meantime to 'write to Spain'.

'Do you hear?' wiping her eyes and kissing them; 'God bless you!' He hurried away.

Harriette had no doubt been through many a parting scene with soldiers going to the wars and knew how to describe one. But if it is incredible that Arthur Wellesley ever figured in this touching interview, it is equally unlikely that Harriette and her duns let him go without one anguished appeal. The last words of the alleged visit recounted above may have been the end of a real letter from him to her. In which case it is pleasant to think of the departing hero leaving behind not only vellum and silver tributes to himself but a charitable order on his banker for her.

He never once returned on leave during the five years of his Peninsular campaign, beginning in 1809. Therefore Harriette's next circumstantial account of his turning up 'unexpectedly' and providentially on short leave from the Continent was another of her inventions. But she was certainly ill, penniless and broken-hearted at this period, after Lord Ponsonby, the only man she truly loved, had deserted her. In her distress she doubtless wrote to Wellington in Spain, through Thomas's Hotel, and he replied with the usual banker's order and letter. Perhaps that letter even contained something like the three remarks which were attributed to him by Harriette during the invented visit he paid her while on an imaginary leave. These specimens of 'Wellingtoniana' it would be sad indeed to lose.

'I always dreaded your getting into some scrape. . . . How much money do you want? . . . I have thought of you, very often, in Spain; particularly one night, I remember, I dreamed you came out on my staff.'

11 *The Hideous Leopard*

Napoleon's orders were that Wellesley's army like Moore's was to be driven into the sea. With his usual flair he had hit upon a peculiarly offensive name for his opponent. Not a British lion, king of beasts, but an emaciated leopard, hideous and heraldic. The innovation was effective (though somewhat overworked by Napoleon), ridiculing as it did the creatures on the Royal Standard and the English character. Every sepoy general who had served in Seringapatam, like Arthur Wellesley and his second-in-command, John Sherbrooke, appreciated the image. Tipoo Sahib's hunting leopards had given them all the creeps. 'The hideous leopard contaminates by its very presence the peninsula of Spain and Portugal,' declared Napoleon to his soldiers in 1808. 'Let us carry our victorious eagles to the Pillars of Hercules. . . .'

Wellesley's task, in reverse, was to drive those eagles, broken-winged, back over the sierras and if possible to the Pyrenees. There were plenty of Gillray cartoons to make them appear equally unprepossessing. For a moment, however, it looked as if the leopard would be driven into the sea without any help from the French.

One of those storms which Arthur believed always accompanied his travels almost wrecked his ship, the *Surveillante*, during his first night at sea, 14 April 1809. His aide-de-camp, Colin Campbell, was sent by the captain to request Arthur to put on his boots and come up on deck, for the end was near. Wellesley replied that he could swim better without his boots and would stay where he was. Neptune subsided, and another touch was added to the legend of imperturbable calm.[1]

*   *   *

He arrived on 22 April in the Tagus to find Lisbon *en fête* in his honour. Its magnificent Black Horse Square was crowded with merry-

---

1. Broughton, *Reflections of a Long Life*, vol. III, p. 254. The exact reverse of this story (though with the same moral) was published by A. Dyce, *Recollections of the Table-Talk of Samuel Rogers*, where the captain informs Wellesley that all will soon be over, to which Wellesley replies calmly, 'Very well, then I shall not take off my boots.'

makers who had banished Cintra from their thoughts. There were groups dancing to castanets and drums, plump ladies in painted litters or sedan chairs with white head scarves and fichus, short handsome gentlemen in tricorne hats decorated with bunches of ribbon and a motto across the front—'Conquer or Die'; peasants in long straw cloaks, white shirts, blue drawers and black shovel hats, pilchard dressers, lemonade sellers, chestnut roasters blowing grains of salt with a palm leaf on to their nuts to give them a bloom; beggars carrying round written accounts of their sad stories for the charitable Portuguese to read, and mendicant friars with Saint Anthony's image to kiss; ballad singers thumping out future triumphs for Arthur Wellesley on guitars, and special tableaux at the theatre where Victory placed a wreath of laurels on the head of a noble figure with a splendid nose, now to be Marshal-General of all the forces in Portugal. After the torches had been extinguished, mud-carts creaked back and forth collecting dirt, and last of all house-holders threw their slops out of their upper windows with cries of '*Agoa Vai*'—'Water, beware!'—so that stray revellers might put up their umbrellas in time.[2]

Arthur Shakespear, cornet in the 2nd Dragoons, was one among thousands of British soldiers who saw Lisbon for the first time in 1809. He was shocked that such a 'fine town' should be so 'horribly dirty', and even more by finding something cold in his bed, a lizard. The countryside enchanted him.

The other Arthur as usual ignored all such things. He was pre-occupied with a 'delicate' matter on which he had become something of an expert. Supersession. This time he himself was superseding an old friend, 'Beau' Cradock. It was a measure of his own sensitivity on this subject that ten years later, when bombarded with a hundred worthier claims to his patronage, he got the 'torpid' Cradock a peerage.[3]

*   *   *

2. The future chaplain-general to the forces, the Rev. Samuel Briscal (see below, p. 286), was unlucky during his first visit to Lisbon. 'The odious custom in Lisbon of turning out into the street for a certain necessary purpose has been of serious consequence to me, for in my great bustle and confusion I made use of some paper in which I had wrapped a £20 note, & the note is lost to me, I suppose for ever' (Michael Glover, 'An Excellent Young Man', *History Today*, 1968).
3. Created 1st Lord Howden, 1819. The descriptive word is Oman's.

Only two days after his arrival, when another man would have been still taking stock, Wellesley made one of his quick decisions. He would march north immediately and rescue 'the favourite town of Oporto', as he called it, from Marshal Soult. Having succeeded, he proposed to return south leaving Marshal Ney (now in the Spanish province of Galicia) 'to the war of the peasantry which has been so successful . . .'.

This was Wellesley's earliest tribute to the gallant Spanish guerrillas who first made their spontaneous appearance on the scene that year.[4]

Half-way down the rugged Portuguese border he would cross into Spain, bringing his army of 26,000 to co-operate with the septuagenarian Spanish captain-general, Don Gregorio García de la Cuesta, against Marshal Victor in a drive on Madrid.

His plan was by no means lacking in dash and optimism. His Peninsular allies, though intensely patriotic, had recently shown their ardour in somewhat alarming ways. His old enemy, the Portuguese General Freire, had been murdered in March by his compatriots for cowardice; and in the same month the Spanish General Cuesta was routed at the battle of Medellin, having been knocked down and ridden over by his own cavalry who in turn were shot for desertion in large numbers by the Junta at Seville. An English official on 26 April testified to the continued energy of this Junta. They were working even on Sundays.

> You hear of no turtle feasts, haunches of venison, or country seats; no expense for messengers carrying the red box at an enormous expense as in England, from one watering place to another.

Despite this hyperactivity, Wellesley was careful to detach General Mackenzie with 12,000 men from his small army to guard Lisbon against Victor while he himself was in the north, instead of relying on Cuesta.

To complete the sense of melodrama in the Peninsula, a French officer named Captain d'Argenton had secretly slipped into the English lines and on the night of 25 April revealed to Wellesley an impending mutiny against Marshal Soult. Soult was suspected of

4. In Spanish a '*guerilla*' means a little war and those who wage it are '*guerrilleros*'. The word 'guerrillas' is used here and throughout in the accepted English sense.

regal ambitions, like Junot before him—'Nicholas Jean de Dieu Soult, King of Northern Lusitania'—and it seemed that his despotism, and even Napoleon's in due course, might end in a Night of Long Knives. Wellesley was neither entirely sceptical nor credulous. Lord Castlereagh advised him to 'act cautiously' in regard to Argenton's *'projet'*. He supplied Argenton with passports to carry on his conspiracy, but informed Castlereagh that he would not 'wait for revolt, but shall try my own means of subduing Soult'.

His initial 'means' were in their own way no less dramatic than Argenton's and a good deal more effective.[5]

He joined his troops at Coimbra on 2 May and spent the inside of a week revolutionizing the Anglo-Portuguese army. For the first time he introduced into the British Army autonomous divisions. He toughened his Portuguese infantry by putting one battalion into each of five British brigades. He strengthened his skirmish line by giving every brigade a permanent company of riflemen. All this was the practical result of Vimeiro. He had digested its failures and successes—the raw Portuguese troops who had not been able to stand alone; the British infantry who had held back their fire so steadily when protected by the riflemen's screen. It was lucky for him that the French, lapped in the luxury of contempt, did not learn the lesson of Marshal Junot's failure. A series of piecemeal assaults on Wellesley's line was the classical error, which Marshal Victor was soon to repeat at Talavera.

Thanks partly to Argenton, Wellesley now knew that Soult's army was 23,000 strong (rather more than he had reckoned, and all veterans) against his own 17,000 supported by Beresford's 6,000 Portuguese. An attempt to trap some of Soult's forces between Coimbra and Oporto failed, though with little loss. On 12 May he reached the suburbs of Oporto itself. His troops were on the threshold of the greatest adventure of the Peninsular War.

*   *   *

At 2 A.M. on that morning of 12 May 1809 Wellesley's men had heard a thunderous roar over the River Douro, which flowed majestically through steep hills between them and the city. It was Soult blowing up the bridge. Through the temporary capture of Argenton (he soon

5. Argenton's plot collapsed, he escaped to England, returned to France to collect his wife, was taken and shot.

made his escape) Soult knew that the British were advancing in force. He did not guess how quickly. The marshal sat up all through the night of the 11th putting the last touches to a methodical plan for evacuation. He had ordered every craft on the river to be destroyed, and had posted troops to watch the long westward curves of the great Douro as it wound towards the Atlantic. He ignored the south and east. It never crossed his mind that the hideous leopard would not come in from the sea. At 9 A.M. next morning, exhausted but well satisfied, the tall French marshal went to bed.

The leader of the leopards, meanwhile, stood on the terrace of the Serra Convent opposite the city, training his glass intently upon the deep, forbidding river at his feet. Above its precipitous banks to the left he could see tiers of houses crowned by the twin-towered Cathedral and his friend the Bishop's palace. On the right the cliffs were steeper still; but a narrow path zigzagged up towards an isolated square stone building behind a high wall.

Wellesley looked unostentatious enough in his plain blue coat, short cape and plumeless cocked hat; hardly a match for the starred and beribboned champions opposite. But the quiet dress and figure concealed a thirst for action, however spectacular, to surprise the enemy.

At this crucial moment one of his scouts made his way into the silent group on the Serra hill. The scout was Colonel Waters, a famous daredevil of the future. His present proposal suited his temperament.

The River Douro, which according to Soult should have been bridgeless, boatless and totally impassable, could in fact be crossed. A Portuguese barber had noticed four large wine-barges lying unguarded on the French side, but concealed from their view by overhanging cliffs. He had also managed to find a solitary skiff, paddled it over to the south bank, and having hidden it in the rushes under the Serra slopes, reported to Waters. Should he paddle back for the barges?

Waters was promptly ordered to collect volunteers. He organized a splendidly mixed party of six brave Portuguese—a barber, a Prior and four peasants—to help him bring these sitting targets across the three hundred yards of sunlit, open water.

Not a sentry noticed, not a gun fired. Soon the makeshift transports, shaped like clumsy gondolas, lay hidden with the skiff under the south bank, ready to take the first soldiers over. The time was 10.30 A.M. Now it was up to Wellesley.

'Well, let the men cross.' No histrionics. No hat-waving. Yet the command he had given so informally, so 'phlegmatically' as it seemed to the historian Fortescue, was in fact a cry of 'Death or Glory!'

The perilous ferrying began. Thirty by thirty, the soldiers filed into their barges. At the end of an hour only 600 had got across. But led by a company of the Buffs (3rd Foot) they had made good use of their time and numbers.

The square building to the right in which Wellesley had shown such interest turned out to be the Bishop's Seminary, now standing empty. Into it ran the first small boat-load. They banged the iron gates shut and proceeded to fortify their heaven-sent, ecclesiastical bridgehead. It was covered by British howitzers which Wellesley had brought into place on his hill opposite.

At noon he put down his glass for a moment to scribble a note to Beresford. 'My advance Guards are crossing in Boats; & the French Picquets are evacuating the Town.' He would follow them as soon as possible but the bridge would not be repaired till tomorrow, '& the passage by Boat goes on but slowly'. Moreover, the troops under John Murray, an incompetent soldier, failed to cut off any French higher up the river.[6] When, after a full hour, French artillery and infantry at last launched fierce attacks on the Seminary from the hill behind, they were all scattered—by the same rolling volleys and shrapnel which had caused havoc at Vimeiro.

Soult meanwhile was sleeping. An orderly rushed four steps at a time up the stairs to the room where his staff were still at breakfast, shouting that the English were coming over the water . . . were in the town. Soult, roughly awakened, refused to believe it.

'Bah! It's a party of red-coated Swiss who've been down to bathe.'[7] But already the northern banks of the Douro were spotted with British red-coats clambering up into the steep, narrow streets, and a stream of French fugitives was pouring helter-skelter out of the town

6. This note is now among the Raglan Papers with nine others like it. Its peculiar interest lies in the fact that a carbon copy was sent to Beresford, this being Wellesley's original pencilled note. The pencil is so faint that the present writer found it easier to read from the copying ink on the back of the paper, with the help of a mirror. Sir Charles Oman, who saw these notes in 1922, said they were the earliest examples of copying he had seen. Wellesley may have got the idea from his brother William, who wrote to him in the Peninsula saying he had decided to make copies of all his own letters in order to follow Arthur's replies.

7. According to another, rather unlikely version, Soult was watching Wellesley's crossing of the Douro from a 'high tower' and made his remark about the Swiss soldiers on seeing the red-coats himself.

into the rugged country beyond. Those who were supposed to guard the mass of barges on the north bank fled with the rest, so that a throng of Portuguese citizens swarmed down and ferried over the British in mounting numbers. Soult's personal attempts to rally his men failed. He was forced to follow the stampede, abandoning a thousand sick and wounded in his hospitals and a very fine meal on his table. General Wellesley had the pleasure of sitting down to it at four in the afternoon.

Oporto was liberated. For the remainder of that evening the British residents, wild with joy, threw open the doors of their factory house and drowned themselves and Wellesley's men in port wine. Next day, when all the troops and guns were across the Douro, the pursuit began.

So did torrential rain. Up into a wilderness of crags, mud, tossing pines and hissing torrents the exhausted Allies dragged their mules and guns. In vain. Soult's fleeing army, always just ahead, jettisoned more and more of their baggage, cannon, arms and even wounded whenever their pursuers showed signs of gaining on them. It was nauseating for the British soldiers and their leaders to have to follow in the train of such havoc. Sodden carcasses of horses and mules and piles of human debris choked the eddies under every rickety bridge. Nauseating for the majority, that is. There was always a coarse-grained minority of British soldiers eager to splash down among the bodies and dredge up booty with much shouting and laughter.

French reprisals against the Portuguese peasants encountered on their flight stirred Wellesley to his coldest fury.

> . . . I have seen many persons hanging in the trees by the sides of the road, executed for no reason that I could learn, excepting that they had not been friendly to the French invasion . . . the route of their column on their retreat, could be traced by the smoke of the villages to which they set fire.

In retaliation, no savagery seemed too terrible to their Portuguese victims. They tortured French stragglers, burnt the abandoned wounded alive and were known to have sawn an officer in half.[8]

8. Colonel René returning from a pre-war mission (Londonderry and Gleig, *Story of the Peninsular War*, footnote p. 38). One British soldier described how he found a wounded Frenchman in a circle of blazing straw; every time he tried to crawl out the peasants pushed him back with pitchforks (*Autobiography of Sergeant William Lawrence*, p. 146).

In the face of such atrocities Soult only fled the faster. Even with
Beresford and his Portuguese out in the mountains to the east,
gallantly trying to head them off, Soult and his desperate ragamuffins
managed to stagger over the Spanish border on the fifth day of the
pursuit. Slightly earlier young Marshal Victor, away to the south,
had at last bestirred himself and raided over the same border in the
opposite direction. Wellesley turned to face this new, not unexpected
threat, and to open the second phase of his planned offensive—the
drive into Spain.

On 22 May 1809 he was back in Oporto and taking a breather to
write to William among others. He had lost his sword and wanted
William to send him 'a straight regulation Sword, with a plain black
belt', and not to forget 'some black tea'. His mood, however, was far
from black. 'You will see the accounts of our proceedings for one
month,' he wrote confidently to William, '& I hope you will like
them.'

Would the whole country this time share his satisfaction?

*   *   *

Once more Portugal was clear of the French. (Victor had quickly retired again.) In less than four weeks the leopard had come in from the
sea and driven Soult's mud-stained eagles into the mountains. The
whole incredible affair of Oporto had cost Wellesley only twenty-
three killed, ninety-eight wounded and two missing. Something like
another 400 were added to his casualty list by the pursuit, 200 of them
sick. Soult lost altogether 4,000 veterans. This heavy toll, added to
the deplorable state of those who survived, has convinced at least
one modern historian, Jac Weller, that Wellesley's defeat of Soult
in effect avenged Soult's defeat of Moore.

> The French most directly connected with Moore's disastrous
> retreat had in turn been even more soundly beaten.

Nevertheless Soult's retreat made nothing like the stir of Moore's.
That was mainly a matter of national propaganda. When England's
small and precious army lost 5,000 men it was rightly a matter for
public lamentation. To Napoleon, whose stupendous victories were
only achieved by even vaster sacrifices, the loss of Soult's 4,000 was
quite endurable.

More than that, the same sour feelings which had spoilt the aftermath of Vimeiro developed in England after the crossing of the

Douro: disappointment that the results of such gallantry were not more brilliant. Wellesley's failure to catch Soult was indeed to cost him dear in two or three months' time. Those of his admirers who argue that he never intended to wipe out the whole French army, but only to liberate Portugal, are going beyond the facts as stated by Wellesley himself. In his letter to William of 22 May he showed that he meant to catch Soult and would have done so but for 'three accidents'—unlucky affairs of mistaken orders, undefended bridges and failed rendezvous in rain-swept defiles. If he had succeeded, on the other hand, it would have been beyond the Government's hopes and indeed instructions. 'From the force I had & the force opposed to me what right had they to expect that I should do so much?' he wrote angrily to William on 1 July, having by this time heard that the Government had actually encouraged the public to think that he had got himself into a 'scrape'. Why had they failed to explain that his orders were 'not to go outside the Portuguese frontiers unless in an operation which had Portuguese objects & was for Portuguese Defence'?

Wellesley's real concern, however, was not with the Government's latent disloyalty but with the Opposition's scathing abuse. They had never whole-heartedly backed this second Peninsular expedition, nor the choice of commander. They expected him to fail as their hero Moore had failed, and when Samuel Whitbread read Wellesley's Douro despatch, especially his reference to a 'large body' of French cavalry, infantry and artillery which had fallen upon the Seminary from Oporto, he rudely declared in Parliament that Sir Arthur's account was 'an exaggeration'.[9]

Even Creevey, Whitbread's close friend, admitted that the Opposition's outstanding personality had no 'manners, no taste or talent for conversation'. In Wellesley's irate opinion he had neither manners, taste nor talent for debate, since he had accused the British general in so many words of having '*lyed*'. It took a long exchange of letters, promoted by the antagonists' common friend General Ferguson (a brigade commander at Vimeiro) to bring the strife temporarily to an end. Creevey himself wrote a characteristic postscript:

I hate Wellesley, but there are passages in his [latest] letter which made me think better of him. . . .

9. It was in fact a force of 10,000 supported by many cannon, every one of which the French lost.

To Ferguson he was 'a very fine manly fellow'; and to the modern student, the only one among them all who showed a spark of humour. Winding up the correspondence in September 1808, Wellesley wrote to Whitbread:

> I will not enter into any statement of our affairs in this part of the world; I daresay that you will hear and read enough, and speak more upon them than some of us will like. . . .

*   *   *

Now that the dust of contemporary faction has settled, the crossing of the Douro stands out for the triumph it was. Wellesley had acted with audacity but without rashness. His infallible eye for ground told him that a passage could be attempted and the Seminary—a natural fortress—defended long enough for his purposes. The advice he gave to Beresford on this, Beresford's first independent command, put one side of his military faith in a nutshell:

> Remember that you are a commander-in-chief and must not be beaten; therefore do not undertake anything with your troops unless you have some strong hope of success.

When that strong hope existed, as at Oporto, his philosophy was always to 'make a dash at the enemy'. To Sir Charles Oman the Oporto campaign was 'one of his strongest titles to fame', and proved once for all that 'he was a safe general and not a cautious one'.

To those whose lives were in his hands it might even seem enough that he could offer them safety so far as was possible. In fact he had far more to give them.

*   *   *

For the time being Marshal Victor relapsed into dilatoriness. There was no need after all for Wellesley to hurry to the border. He used the pause to deal with defects in his army. There were plenty of them. Indeed it was soon hard to believe that this was the same man who had written on the night after Oporto:

> I cannot say too much in favour of the officers and troops.

Less than three weeks later he was writing:

The army behave terribly ill. They are a rabble who cannot bear success any more than Sir John Moore's army could bear failure. I am endeavouring to tame them. . . .

Admittedly the first of these letters (both written to Castlereagh) was for publication and the second private. Even so they emphasize the defects of Wellesley's character as well as those of his army. He tended to rush to extremes. His practical judgements were cool and moderate but on paper imagination and temper were apt to take control.

His army's besetting sin was plunder. He intended to 'tame' them by sending the worst corps home and punishing individual offenders on the triangle. Three or four hundred lashes were calculated to tame even the most spotted leopards, except perhaps the ironically named 'Belem Rangers', who were convalescents in Belem hospital and presumably too weak to be lashed but not too weak to rob. Since a new method of court martial had been introduced by the Horse Guards it had become almost impossible to get the necessary evidence even against notorious looters. Wellesley's solution (apart from the introduction of grimmer deterrents such as executions, which were not resorted to during the early months of the War) was to be a new system of military police based on the experience of foreign armies. Meanwhile his summary of the situation for Castlereagh's benefit on 17 June was not exactly an encouraging one from a commander on the eve of a fresh advance.

We are an excellent army on parade, an excellent one to fight; but we are worse than an enemy in a country; and take my word for it, that either defeat or success would dissolve us.

After all this it was not to be supposed that his other military departments should escape censure, or even the Higher Command and Government itself. 'Our Commissariat,' he wrote, 'is very bad indeed'; the chronic emptiness of his military chest caused serious trouble; while certain initial jealousies among his officers used up already short supplies of time and patience.

Beresford was marshal of the Portuguese Army. Like Wellesley, he had been jumped up over the heads of his seniors, but unlike Wellesley, he rode about Lisbon in regal state with a long train of glittering staff. The same thing went for field officers who had been transferred from British into Portuguese regiments. They automatically gained rank by transfer, leaving behind many dissatisfied colleagues who saw themselves permanently superseded. Dissatisfaction as Wellesley pointed out ominously to the British Minister in Portugal, John Villiers, 'once excited, works in a British army'. Wellesley then went on to develop one of his curious but revealing theories about the military life.

> We are not naturally a military people; the whole business of an army upon service is foreign to our habits, and is a constraint upon them. . . . This constraint naturally excites a temper ready to receive any impressions which will create dissatisfaction; and when dissatisfaction exists in an army the task of the commander is difficult indeed.

Before all these dissatisfactions could be removed the 'impecunious' state of his army, as he called it, had become a major scandal. He had found only £120,000 in the chest when he reached Lisbon that April, having been promised £400,000, and by the end of May things were far worse. He wrote bitterly to Villiers from Coimbra:

> We are terribly distressed for money. . . . I suspect the Ministers in England are very indifferent to our operations in this country.

Ironically, the 'indifferent' Ministers sent him permission to enter Spain just about this time, together with reinforcements—but still no money. He wrote again to Villiers on 11 June:

> the ball is at my foot, and I hope I shall have strength enough to give it a good kick: I should begin immediately but I cannot venture to stir without money.

Bonaparte of course would have kicked forthwith. His armies lived off the country, by forcible requisitioning amounting to robbery. Wellesley would not kick off until he could pay cash.

The problems of paying for the War had in fact only just begun. They were not to be solved until a financier with prominent blue eyes, light reddish curls and an astute humorous expression, took a hand. This was Nathan Mayer Rothschild, founder of the London House of Rothschild in 1803–4. In one year alone he was to transmit £11 million in Continental subsidies and remittances to the Penin-

sula, his brother James in Paris being rumoured to possess suits of
female clothing in which he personally smuggled bullion to Wellington through the French lines.

*   *   *

The Treasury's failure in 1809 did not help him in settling on a joint
plan of campaign with his difficult Spanish colleague, General
Cuesta. Two days after his letter about the football he was writing
gloomily to John Hookham Frere, Minister at Seville, that but for
'the obstinacy of this old gentleman', the British and Spanish armies
could between them have intercepted Victor after Soult's defeat—
'the finest game that any armies ever had . . .'. It was true that old
Cuesta had refused to undertake such sophisticated operations, preferring a simple, knock-out blow nearer to Madrid. But could the
British have marched without money, even if Cuesta had agreed?

Part of the delay, at least, was due to the 'torpid' Cradock. He had
been sent by Wellesley to Cádiz at the end of April to change
£100,000-worth of Spanish gold into Portuguese dollars and was
expected back in mid-May. 'Beau' Cradock stopped nearly a month
and 'amused himself' (as Arthur informed William sarcastically),
not returning until 15 June.

The rest of the money arrived at last on 25 June. Wellesley marched
on the 27th. His infantry began crossing the border into Spain on
4 July. By this time it was too late for manoeuvring, since Victor was
far up the Tagus at Talavera, only seventy miles from Madrid and in
touch with the main French forces under King Joseph and Marshal
Jourdan. Obstinate or not, old Cuesta was going to get the 'great
Battle' on which he had set his heart.[10]

*   *   *

A detailed plan of campaign had still to be agreed. On 10 July there
took place at the Fort of Miravete, Almaraz, the famous first meeting
between the Allied generals. It was not a success. Thanks to a
chronic dearth of good maps and an incompetent guide, Wellesley

10. Wellesley wrote to William on 15 July that to fight 'great Battles' was
not the best plan for the Spaniards. 'But at present I believe it is necessary
they should do so; & they would not hear of any proposal of mine . . . to
move the Enemy from Madrid by Manœuvre' (*Raglan Papers*).

kept Cuesta waiting five hours. Though Cuesta showed all the courtesy of a Spanish grandee, it was not very convenient to have his troops reviewed by torchlight. The flickering gloom, however, was all too symbolic of the Spanish evolutions. Wellesley could see no sign of professionalism among the officers, no manoeuvrability among the men. Courage was their one shining feature, shared to the full by Cuesta himself.

Despite the injuries he had received from his cavalry riding over him at Medellin he had the tenacity to fight on, just like old Marshal Blücher who was to be ridden over at Ligny in June 1815. But whereas Blücher could at least sit a horse, poor old Cuesta led his armies from inside a huge coach drawn by nine mules until he reached the actual battlefield, when he submitted to being hoisted into the saddle and held in place by four Sancho Panzas.[11] Blücher insisted on marching towards Waterloo because he had pledged his word to Wellington. Cuesta felt pledged only to the cause; he also felt a harsh and not altogether empty suspicion that at Seville John Hookham Frere was conspiring with the Junta to have him removed. Above all, Cuesta's unbounded self-confidence was not based as in the case of Wellesley, on a matchless capacity for taking pains, but on a peculiarly touchy form of traditional conceit.

A four-hour discussion between Cuesta and Wellesley followed the torchlight review. General Odonoju, the Spanish adjutant-general of Irish descent, acted as interpreter. Cuesta, at any rate, gave him the minimum of work to do, for his invariable answer to all Wellesley's suggestions was No. Priorities having thus been established, an agreement was reached to join forces on 21 July at Oropesa and from there to advance on Victor together, while the Spanish General Venegas intercepted the French from the south-east. As soon as Victor heard of the Allies' arrival at Oropesa, he realized that with only 20,000 men against their combined 55,000, he must hastily retreat behind the River Alberche a few miles to the north-east of Talavera. His position was still weak. The Allies decided to attack him simultaneously at dawn on the 23rd.

Wellesley was up at 2 A.M. When no Cuesta appeared he rolled himself in his cloak and took one of his celebrated pre-battle naps. At 6 A.M. there was still no Cuesta. Wellesley rode over to his camp

11. Sergeant Nicol, however, who was present at Talavera with the Gordon Highlanders described Cuesta as 'a fine stout rough-looking old man' (*With Napoleon at Waterloo,* p. 95).

and found the old man reclining disconsolately on his loose carriage cushions by the Alberche bridge. His army was too tired, he said; he had not reconnoitred sufficiently; the bridge might not bear his artillery. They would attack next day.

Next day there was no Victor to attack. He had flitted eastwards during the night. Wellesley's scouts warned him that other French armies in Victor's direction were concentrating. Nor had the movement of Venegas materialized.

It was now Wellesley's turn to refuse to join Cuesta in a foolhardy chase after Victor on the 24th, especially as the Spanish commissariat had let him down as badly in July as the British Treasury had in June. Supplies and transport had failed. His troops were on half-rations. 'I have never seen an army so ill-treated in any country,' he wrote to Frere that day. If this went on he would have to bring his excursion into Spain to an end. Cuesta, he added, became 'more and more impracticable every day', and he had lost the whole day of the 23rd through 'whimsical perverseness'.

Was Wellesley being unfair? A modern Spanish historian, Pablo de Azcarate, points out that Wellesley himself seemed far from sorry at Cuesta's failure to attack on the 23rd.[12] His letter to Frere of 24 July concluded with the words:

> that omission I consider fortunate, as we have dislodged the enemy without a battle, in which the chances were not much in our favor.

It would be unfair to Wellesley to take these words as his considered opinion. In military matters (though not in politics) he tended to look on the bright side until he knew the worst. In this case he knew the worst all too soon, and the word 'fortunate' was not repeated. He had already modified his opinion on the 25th, when he wrote to William that he was 'not sorry' to see the enemy gone next morning, for though they would have beaten them there would have been heavy losses. His final opinion was expressed to Lord Stanhope in 1833. After rather handsomely giving Cuesta credit for being 'sensible' as well as brave, he admitted that his obstinacy of 23 July had proved fatal.

> If he had fought when I wanted him to at Talavera, I have no hesitation in saying that it would have cleared Spain of the French for that time.

12. Pablo de Azcarate, *Wellington y Espana* (1960).

There can be no doubt that the Allies missed a unique chance, nor that the people of Britain, when they heard the full story, were right to look upon 23 July as the blackest day of the campaign. But they were wrong in attributing Cuesta's recalcitrance to the fact that it was a Sunday. As Wellington remarked of this *canard* to Stanhope: 'he made many other foolish excuses, but that was not one of them . . .'.

Kitty Wellesley, however, evidently swallowed the story, for she noted in her journal with asperity:

> Sir Arthur intended to attack Victor on the 23rd but was prevented by Genl. Cuesta. His reason is said to have been that it was Sunday. . . . Thus was a glorious opportunity lost.

★   ★   ★

Kitty had made a romantic resolution when her husband said goodbye on 8 April 1809. She would keep a journal in which their respective activities, recorded on opposite pages, would afterwards tell her exactly what her hero had been doing at every moment of her daily round. But as usual Kitty's good intentions were betrayed by her sad temperament. It was mid-July before she could summon up energy to begin.

> *London. July 16th. Sunday.* Very late this morning. Heard Arthur a lesson. Arthur Freese his catechism.
> *July 17th.* Rose very late from fatigue. Wrote to Sir Arthur. . . . I heard to-day that Sir Arthur was proceeding to Madrid, Heaven prosper them! Longford and I dined early and went tête-à-tête to the play, 'Killing no Murder.'[13]
> *July 18th.* The British Army on its March.

Her physician, Sir Walter Farquhar, had advised her to try the invigorating Channel breezes at Broadstairs. She and her 'darling boys', protected by '*dear Longford*', stopped one night at Sittingbourne on their way to the coast.

> Lord Chatham, who is going to Ramsgate to take command of the Expedition, slept also at Sittingbourne.

This was the ill-fated Walcheren expedition. It was eventually to

13. By Theodore Hook, a popular writer of light comedy; later author of Baird's *Life*.

destroy Portland's moribund Government and to put even Wellesley's prospects in jeopardy.

In conception, Walcheren was sensible enough. It had been Castlereagh's inspiration. After the Spanish catastrophe of Moore he was eager to transfer some of Britain's eggs into another basket. When the Austrians defied Bonaparte yet again, Castlereagh sent a force under Lord Chatham and Admiral Sir Richard Strachan to support them. But Chatham and Strachan were no quicker than Kitty Wellesley in getting off the mark.

> *Great Chatham with his sabre drawn,*
> *Stood waiting for Sir Richard Strachan;*
> *Sir Richard, longing to be at 'em,*
> *Stood waiting for the Earl of Chatham.*

The Austrians had already been defeated at Wagram (5–6 July) before Chatham sailed.

Kitty went over to Deal from Broadstairs on 21 July to gaze upon the immense Walcheren convoy still in the Channel.

A more magnificent [sight] cannot be conceived than that of the Fleet now in the Downs, above 500 sail of transports including 50 Men-of-War. God Almighty protect our brave Men, success attend them!

Next day she was at Deal again and wrote hopefully:

July 22nd. . . . the cheering of our Men as they passed really went to my Heart, God bless them!

—but less confidently in the domestic pages of her journal during the following two days:

July 23rd. Sunday . . . I propose beginning a regular plan of occupation to-morrow.
July 24th. Began the day wretchedly. God forgive and strengthen me!

Kitty's entries for 23 and 24 July would not have done badly for General Cuesta.

*   *   *

He had plunged after Victor on the 24th in the deluded conviction that the French were fleeing before him. In fact Victor had retired *pour mieux sauter*—having joined forces with General Sebastiani and King Joseph. Cuesta was in a 'scrape', as Wellesley had predicted. He made a precipitate retreat to the Alberche. It was then Wellesley's task actually to go down on his knees to the arrogant old anachronism and persuade him to bring his troops right back to a strong position at Talavera, from which Wellesley knew they could best receive the coming French onslaught. But before Victor's attack had fully developed, Wellesley himself was in a 'scrape', due to the negligence of a British brigade.

Wellesley had gone out with two divisions to cover Cuesta's return to Talavera. On 27 July, while on the way back, Donkin's brigade took an unorthodox siesta and were surprised by stealthy French skirmishers. The unlucky British had laid aside their arms in order to repose more peacefully; many of them were slaughtered before they could get up. Wellesley happened to be at the top of the Casa de Salinas, an isolated stone building, from one of whose twin towers he was making his customary investigation of what lay on the other side of the surrounding olive and cork groves. Suddenly he caught sight of French light troops under the Casa's walls. With a wild clatter he and his staff dashed down the steep stairs, leapt on to their horses and spurred out of the courtyard, peppered by the desultory bullets of French soldiers who fortunately did not know at whom they were firing. This was Wellesley's narrowest escape of the Peninsular War, and one of the rare occasions on which he drew his sword—perhaps the 'short regulation' article sent out to him by William after Oporto.

Wellesley rallied Donkin's brigade himself and then retreated to Talavera 'in face of both armies'. Two British battalions had been broken, losing 440 men to the French 100. It was not an auspicious beginning.[14]

*   *   *

The battle of Talavera has always caught men's imagination since Byron wrote his ominous lines:

14. The Casa de Salinas or Serranillas can still be found by the traveller, though the present inhabitants of Talavera do not easily recognize either name. After many enquiries by the writer in 1966 it was at last identified by an ice-cream vendor as the block of agricultural flats which he supplied.

Three hosts combine to offer sacrifice,
To feed the crow on Talavera's plain.

Two of the hosts, Spanish and British, were already being posted
while Wellesley was emerging from the Salinas affray. Talavera's
plain, the site he had chosen, lay parched and dusty between the
walled city on the Tagus, backed by an outcrop of red barbaric rocks
to the south, and a range of blue mountains three miles to the north.
The plain was a mile wide, divided in half by a shallow stream, the
Portina, which flowed from the northern mountains, across grass-
land, through a lower ridge which it cut into two hills, over more flat
grass, behind a redoubt, across a stretch of cultivation and into the
town. The battle was to be fought on either side of the Portina line,
almost as in a game of French and English, mainly between the two
ridges and the redoubt. Wellesley posted all his forces to the west of
the stream, so that the road to Portugal was behind them. Of the two
key ridges, the higher was called the Medellin, a name of ill omen.
This he occupied, leaving its opposite number, the Cascajal, to the
French. In the exposed sector between the Medellin hill and the
redoubt he placed mainly British troops; the bulk of Cuesta's army
was given the cultivated area extending from the redoubt to the
town, defended by breastworks. The battle was not expected to begin
until next day. But another 'chance-medley' affair (as Napier called
the Salinas episode) acted as a dramatic curtain-raiser on the evening
of 27 July 1809.

It happened by stages. First, some distant French dragoons indulged in casual shooting at Spanish pickets in Cuesta's sector. No
one was harmed. Nevertheless Cuesta's whole front line suddenly
responded with an enormous reverberating salvo. No Frenchman was
harmed (they were too far off) but next moment 2,000 raw Spanish
soldiers, terrified by their own thunder and shouting 'Treason!',
were shocked into headlong flight, sweeping along General Odonoju
and Cuesta's coach part of the way to the rear, where they sacked
Wellesley's baggage-wagons in company with some British pay-
masters, commissaries and stragglers. The extraordinary rout then
poured down the road to Portugal, spreading alarm and despondency,
including the news that the French had won.

Wellesley was his imperturbable self. At the sound of the giant
Spanish volley he had turned to a British liaison officer.

'If they will but fire as well tomorrow, the day is our own; but as

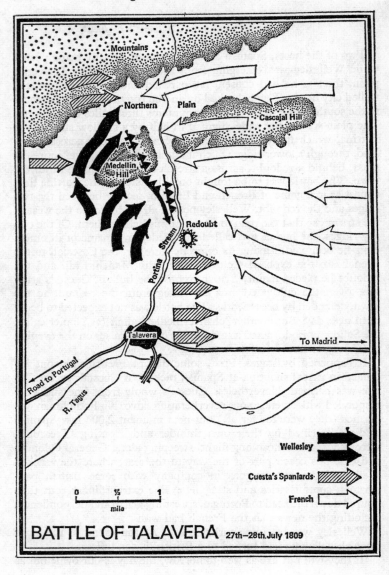

Mountains

Northern   Plain

Cascajal Hill

Medellin Hill

Portina Stream

Redoubt

Talavera

To Madrid →

Road to Portugal

R. Tagus

Wellesley

Cuesta's Spaniards

French

0   ½   1
mile

BATTLE OF TALAVERA 27th–28th.July 1809

there seems nobody to fire at just now, I wish you would stop it.'
When the four Spanish battalions took to flight he added,

'Look at the ugly hole those fellows have left,' and ordered it to be
filled from the second line. Thanks to Cuesta's speedy action, the gap
was soon closed but it made a lasting breach in Wellesley's trust. It
was not that he ever minded troops running away—'They all do at
some time or other,' he explained to Croker—as long as they came
back. The Spanish levies had not come back and they had robbed his
baggage. He did not mention the episode in the early Talavera
despatches, but when things began to go wrong between him and the
Spanish later on, he remembered that panic flight.

Cuesta had his own reaction. He ordered a decimation: two hundred of the captured deserters to be executed after the battle in cold
blood. On Wellesley interceding for them, Cuesta reduced it to forty.

At sunset on that day, Wellesley's army could see huge masses of
French rolling in from the east like banks of indigo cloud. Some of
the British rank and file began to look pale even in that rosy light,
but their officers had no doubt they were as steady as ever. The test
came before it was quite dark.

*   *   *

Marshal Victor, aware that the lines opposite were still disturbed by
the Spanish exodus, like the sea after a storm, determined to chance
his arm on a night attack. It was a bold, if not reckless bid, but nearly
succeeded.

Hill's reliable division, which should have been in the front line on
the Medellin, had inadvertently been assigned to the rear while
Wellesley was over at the Alberche. There was a sudden uproar and
shouts of 'The hill! the hill!' 'Daddy' Hill heard the turmoil in front
but thought it was 'the old Buffs, as usual making some blunder'.
In fact it was the 9th Léger swarming up the shadowy slopes with
drums beating and cries of '*Vive l'Empereur*', to overwhelm a force
of Hanoverians who, believing themselves to be in the second line,
had eaten their few wheat grains and settled into an uneasy sleep
without posting pickets. Both Wellesley and Hill rode up in the darkness to investigate the firing. Before Hill knew where he was, he had
plunged into the thick of the fighting and almost been dragged from
his horse by a French skirmisher. He galloped himself free, ordered
forward his division including the 29th, and had the satisfaction of

hearing, if not seeing, this gallant regiment, heroes of Roliça and Vimeiro, topple the enemy off the Medellin crest into the Portina gulley below. Both sides lost over 300 men; and but for the 29th the British might have lost this crucial ridge and so the battle. With difficulty Wellesley restored his positions. He then lay down on the ground, wrapped in his cloak, for a few hours of sound sleep before the murderous dawn. No one else had much rest. Throughout the night there was a constant crackle of fire as jumpy soldiers shot at shadows.

*   *   *

Broadstairs. July 27th. Took my Children to Ramsgate. They were delighted walking on the Pier. They proposed to make a necklace for me of the Cannon Balls.

*   *   *

As the red sunrise of 28 July 1809 spread behind the huge black silhouette of the French army, 40,000 men could be counted with ease by the watchers on the Medellin, facing their own force of 20,000. (The Spanish regiments behind their breastworks were scarcely attacked by the enemy, though they were essential for the security of Wellesley's right flank.) All at once a signal gun on the Cascajal opposite opened up the French barrage. Fifty-four cannon, aided by swirling smoke and mist which an easterly breeze blew across the Medellin, prepared the way for three dense French columns to advance in portentous order. 'Damn their filing!' exclaimed Hill nervously, when he suddenly saw them move upwards as if on parade; 'let them come in anyhow.'[15] They came in, column against line, as at Vimeiro. Wellesley had made his infantry lie down or wait behind the crest until the French were in position to take the full blast of close-range, rolling volleys. In less than two hours of bloody fury all three attacks had failed and the Portina valley between the Medellin and Cascajal was filling up with corpses.

A truce was called during the fierce glare of the early July morning while soldiers from both sides drank from the fouled stream. The British were ordered to bury their dead on the Medellin immediately and not to leave them out in the burning sun. On the Cascajal the

15. This is said to have been one of the only two occasions when 'Daddy' Hill swore. See below, p. 398.

French held a council of war, Marshal Victor angrily demanding one more assault on the Medellin. If this failed it would be time for him 'to give up making war'. Joseph and Jourdan were for withdrawal, leaving Soult to take the Allies in the rear, but Victor's bad temper triumphed. Afterwards, his colleagues were able to mock him unmercifully. When was he going to resign?

At 11 A.M. the French drums beat a recall to the eagles. Blue and scarlet uniforms, mingling down at the Portina, drew apart; there were nods and smiles, a final hand-shake here and there, and they were ready once more to be foes.

This strange scene at Talavera was the rehearsal for a regular procedure throughout the Peninsular War. With no lust for killing between the French and English, a civilized by-play developed on both sides, encouraged by at least some of their leaders. Wellington described to Croker in 1828 how the advance-posts would always give each other notice of an imminent attack, the French calling out, *'Courez vite, courez vite, on va vous attaquer.'* Wellington added:

> I always encouraged this; the killing of a poor fellow of a vedette [scout] or carrying off a post could not influence the battle and I always . . . sent to tell them to get out of the way.

Around noon Wellesley could see a formidable dust-cloud raised by fresh French troops—the corps of Sebastiani and Lapisse, 15,000 strong. He sent over to Cuesta for reinforcements, who responded promptly.

There followed in fierce succession two immensely powerful French assaults upon the British centre—the third and fourth attacks of the battle. The first of them, an advance in column of 4,500 infantry and eighty cannon, was received, absorbed and broken by British and Spanish artillery-fire combined with what can now be called Wellesley's usual infantry method: a screen, a tense holding of the breath behind it, the triumphant exhalation. After Wellesley's death-volleys had done their work not a single piece of artillery was still in French hands; nor had they fired a shot.

Now came the half-hour which was to decide the battle. The fourth French attack, though heavier than the rest, since 15,000 veterans were involved, looked certain at first to meet the fate of all its predecessors. From his post on the Medellin, Wellesley could see his long, raging lines battering the heads of the French columns, which gradually disintegrated. The end seemed near; until he realized that one brigade of Guards and two of the King's German Legion, mad with excitement, had hurled themselves right over the Portina and far into the second, unbroken mass of French columns beyond. Six hundred out of the Guards' 2,000 fell, and the 'ugly hole' (to use Wellesley's earlier expression) which they had left in their own front was about to be filled with a roaring tide of French cavalry and guns, ready to burst back into and break up the whole shallow British battle-line from the rear. The fate of the day depended on how Wellesley handled this crisis.

Though weak in reserves and threatened everywhere, especially on the Medellin, he somehow contrived to lay his hands on 3,000 heroic men; enough to do the trick. Hill was ordered down from the Medellin with the 48th, and Mackenzie up from the redoubt with the 24th, 31st and 45th. Into the gaping centre marched the resolute 48th, opening their ranks for a moment to allow the remnants of the Guards to pass through to the rear and then, in Napier's words, 'resuming their proud and beautiful line'. To the exhilaration of all, the Guards and the King's German Legion reformed behind them with a loud hurrah. The French, on the verge of superlative victory, were held. Their commander, Lapisse, was killed, Sebastiani retired. Their spirits flagged; thousands of horribly dripping bayonets thrust ever more feebly until it was clear that the ghastly combat in the centre had petered out. Victory at Talavera had been plucked from their grasp.

Wellesley, it is true, was not quite easy about the position in the northern plain, and sent Anson's Light Brigade against a French infantry division there. His cavalry ran into the usual pitfalls of over-excitement producing uncontrollable speed; to which on this unhappy occasion was added a physical booby-trap in the form of a fifteen-foot-wide chasm concealed by long grass. Some cleared it, some tumbled in headlong breaking necks and legs. A few reined up in time. Of those who got across the majority raced on and on, only to be cut down by the dreaded Polish lancers. The rest wheeled northwards under cover of Spanish infantry, into the sheltering mountains.

Nevertheless the 23rd Light Dragoons, who suffered most, did not charge in vain. After the English whirlwind had spent itself it was found that the French, too, had retired.

*   *   *

No regular pursuit of the beaten French could be undertaken. Only Cuesta's troops were fresh enough and Wellesley would not move them. The tactful reason he gave in his official despatch (29 July) was that the ground they already held was too 'important'. In a private memorandum of 28 July he revealed the true reason: 'the Spanish troops are not in a state of discipline to attempt a manoeuvre . . .'.[16]

Next morning, 29 July, when Wellesley might have reformed his armies, the French had all gone. They knew, though he did not, that Soult would be there in command of another French army within a week. There was nothing for Cuesta to do but to march out his forty thieves dressed in white, and shoot them.

* * *

In the late afternoon after the battle a running flame had caught the grass on the Medellin, making a horrible roast of dead horses and scorching the wounded, as if to offer a final 'sacrifice', in Byron's words, to the god of war. 'I never saw a field of battle,' wrote George Napier, 'which struck me with such horror as Talavera.' 'Never was there such a Murderous Battle!!' said Wellesley. He had been outnumbered two to one in the fighting and had lost over 5,000 men, a quarter of his force engaged; the French over 7,000. He himself had been bruised by a spent bullet, Mackenzie killed and all his staff wounded or their horses shot. It sounded like Assaye. Wellesley decided it was worse.

The battle of Talavera was the hardest fought of modern times. The fire at Assaye was heavier while it lasted; but the battle of Talavera lasted for two days and a night.

* * *

Kitty received the news of her husband's victory on 14 August. Her reactions were entirely characteristic.

16. The date of this memorandum, 28 July, is not given in *Despatches*, vol. IV, p. 510, where it is printed, but occurs on the copy in the Raglan Papers. The date is important, since Professor Azcarate argues that Wellesley criticized the Spanish for indiscipline only *after* he had broken with them towards the end of August.

Thank God his exertions have been crowned with the success they deserve and, tho our loss has been dreadful, yet the events of the 27th & 28th July will ever be thought of with pride by this country, and ought to fill the Spanish nation with gratitude.

If Arthur had seen that last line he would have laughed sardonically. Kitty continued:

Hearing the servants disclose their intention of repairing to a Public House to rejoice, I thought their rejoicing had better take place at home, I therefore gave them some Spirits and liberty to make themselves as happy as they could without being quite Drunk. . . .

Spirits and liberty. What else could anyone want to make them happy? But Kitty's diary showed that after her shaky start on 15 July she had quickly relapsed into total inadequacy and self-reproach.

July 31st. I fear indolence is again creeping about me. I am fatigued by a regular course of insignificant occupations & dissatisfied with myself when idle.

August 2nd. Ill & idle. I have nothing to say to this languid day.

August 5th. Much as yesterday, languid and dawdling.

August 6th. Too late for Church.

August 7th. Very shamefully late. This will never do. Finished my accounts of the Week.

August 8th. Still too late.

August 10th. I am tired. This unvaried life fatigues but must be endured.

Her 'unvaried life' had consisted in devoting herself to her boys, persuading the cook to take the Sacrament, teaching Arthur Freese to give up the 'odious vice' of fibbing, walking on various piers and making galoshes. Then, on the day before the news of Talavera arrived, a piece of good news brought on an emotional crisis. She heard that her brother Edward had arrived safely in England from the West Indies. The sudden joy only made more intolerably vivid the memory of how she had forfeited Arthur's love.

August 13th. This was as unexpected as it was delightful. How ungrateful I am conscious of being. It has pleased God to deny me one blessing: on that one I had fixed all my hopes of happiness, and every other blessing, which Heaven has so liberally bestowed fails to make me even easy. Perhaps in time God will pity the agony I suffer: perhaps it is inflicted for my ingratitude. Oh Merciful Father, forgive and pity a very weak and suffering Being. My fault is great, but my punishment is most severe. God Almighty, look on me with mercy! I will not again give way to these unavailing regrets . . . from the time my Children go to bed, I find my mind torn with the most painful recollections, but I will not so soon break the resolution I have thought it prudent to form: I will therefore write no more tonight.

Next day, with the Talavera despatch. poor Kitty got her reward. She was able to finish her diary for 14 August on an ecstatic if still somewhat distracted note:

I was myself incapable of anything. Walked up & down the room till, quite exhausted, I went to bed with feelings most different from those which afflicted me yesterday. . . .

*   *   *

The King and Prime Minister, though each racked with personal gloom—George III over Princess Amelia's illness and Portland over his own—decided to rejoice the hero of Talavera with a peerage which, but for Cintra, would have been his after Vimeiro. Arthur's brother William discussed the news in a long letter of 22 August, complaining mildly about his difficulties in finding a suitable title. Why had not Arthur left instructions before he went abroad? William of course was joking. He knew his brother too well to suppose that he, unlike Richard, would ever ponder a title before it was conferred. The College of Heralds could not allow time for Arthur to be consulted, so William had to plump. He plumped for 'Wellington'. How he reached his decision was explained in the same letter:

after ransacking the Peerage and examining the map, I at last determined upon Viscount Wellington of Talavera and of Wellington, and Baron Douro of Welleslie in the county of Somerset—

Wellington is a town not far from Welleslie . . . I trust that you will not think that there is anything unpleasant or trifling in the name of Wellington. . . .

Arthur found it neither trifling nor unpleasant. Instead he expressed the highest approval:

> . . . Viscount Wellington of Talavera is exactly right. You could not take for me Lord Wellesley's title . . . you were quite right in not taking Vimeira; & in that situation I think you have chosen most fortunately.

Kitty, on the other hand, was not enthusiastic.

> *Broadstairs. August 26th*—Lord Henniker called in the evening to congratulate me on Sir Arthur's Peerage. I regret his former stile [*sic*] and title—that of Wellington I do not like for it recalls nothing. However, it is done & I suppose it could not be avoided.
> *August 31st*—I have now received several letters directed to me 'Lady Wellington' so I must assume the name . . .

Arthur casually 'assumed the name', in the sense of signing it for the first time, on 16 September 1809, his elevation to the peerage having been gazetted on 4 September. At the end of a dry letter about finance to John Villiers he wrote:

> Believe me, etc.
> Wellington.

> This is the first time I have signed my new name. Would the [Portuguese] Regency give me leave to have a *Chasse* at Villa Viçosa?

It would be an honour to have Viscount Wellington hunting anywhere.

Croker composed a poem on Talavera for which Arthur sent somewhat ironical thanks—'I did not think a battle could be turned into anything so entertaining'—and he was painted by a Portuguese. Under his name on the engraving they wrote the single glorious word, *Invicto*. Premature shouts of triumph were anathema to

Arthur. He hastily scribbled under the offending epithet: 'Don't halloo till you are out of the wood.'

Talavera was indeed to set him wandering for fourteen long months until the moment came, on Bussaco ridge, to challenge the eagles once more.

12 Retreat to Portugal

For the space of just one day after the Talavera victory all seemed well and the road open to Madrid. Next day, 30 July 1808, came an alarming report. Marshal Soult had evacuated Galicia, and once more with properly equipped soldiers instead of tatterdemalions was at the Pass of Baños ready to advance. On 8 August Wellesley (as he still was), wrote that he now had 'the whole host of Marshals' against him in Estremadura—Soult, Ney, Mortier, Kellerman, Victor, Sebastiani—as well as the King and 5,000 men from Suchet's corps. Unless Soult, in particular, was stopped, he would cut Wellesley's life-line with Portugal. This was the real crisis of the Talavera campaign. It was this which was to change Wellesley's victory into retreat.

An Anglo-Spanish conference was called, nerves taut on both sides. Cuesta proposed that one half of each army should jointly hold off King Joseph from Talavera while Soult was handled by the other half. Wellesley felt he knew which half would bear the brunt. He vetoed any division of his army and chose to deal with Soult. Cuesta promised to look after the British wounded in Talavera until they could be moved. Harrowing scenes took place as Wellesley's army marched out, some of the sick crying to their comrades not to desert them, others limping or even crawling along the road until the last British baggage-wagon and camp-follower had vanished, leaving them behind under a pall of dust.

Wellesley duly reached Oropesa on 3 August, only to be met by two pieces of bad news. Austria was rumoured to have made peace with Napoleon. This event, if true (as indeed it was), would drastically affect his Spanish campaign, perhaps the whole war. For Napoleon would be free personally to hunt the leopard. The second event was in the short run more devastating. Cuesta, threatened by Joseph, had packed up his baggage as soon as Wellesley left Talavera and was marching to join him. Fifteen hundred British wounded were left to the French. It was not that Wellesley feared for their safety. The French would (and did) care for them well.[1] It was what he

1. Sergeant Nicol of the Gordons who was among the wounded said that the French kindly shared their Spanish loot with their British prisoners (*With Napoleon at Waterloo*, p. 106).

called 'the disgrace'. Part of his triumph over Soult at Oporto had lain in compelling him to abandon a thousand wounded in the town. Cuesta had now caused Wellesley to lose half as many more. There needed only the Junta's utter failure to supply his army with food and transport, for him to wash his hands of Spain and fulfil his threat to return to Portugal.

To do Wellesley justice, he did not pretend that his own army was blameless. The plundering which he had tried to put down after Oporto broke out with redoubled fury now that his men were hungry, short of carts and in retreat. The women were an especial problem. One General Order had to be issued against their buying up all available bread before the commissaries could get at it, and another to prevent them 'clambering' on to the clothing carts at Lisbon and holding up the regiments' clothes. George Napier wrote that it was far more difficult to control the camp-followers after Talavera than soldiers of ten times the number. The only way, he added,

is to have plenty of provosts, to hang and flog them without mercy, the devils incarnate.

The flogging of women was later to land Wellington in trouble. But as he explained to Lady Salisbury:

It is well known that in all armies the Women are at least as bad, if not worse, than the men, as Plunderers! and the exemption of the Ladies would have encouraged Plunder!

'The Ladies', their husbands and babes-in-arms would dive into the cellars of plundered houses and paddle up to their middles in seas of wine, until the 'Bloody Provost' interrupted them in what Wellington called their 'Sports'. Then there would be a drunken dash for safety and the women, who could not run as fast as the men, would be caught, in the words of a Highland soldier, with 'sax and thirty lashes a piece on the bare doup'.

Among the soldiers, robbery of beehives was a favourite crime, the 4th Division being known for their prowess as 'honeysuckers'. Wellington told the story of a beehive-robber he himself caught red-handed.

'Hillo, sir! where did you get that beehive?' The soldier, misunderstanding his intention, replied obligingly that the beehives were just

over the hill but he'd better hurry or they'd all be gone. This time
Wellington had not the heart to punish. What could you expect from
a starving army in a land flowing with wine and honey, if nothing
else? As he himself said, 'a starving army is actually worse than none'.

Enormous bitterness was generated on both sides by the supply
question; indeed, the echoes can still be heard today. In Spain it is
argued that Wellesley's army was well-fed until he announced his
withdrawal, when the Spaniards naturally ceased to feed soldiers who
were abandoning them. But in face of Wellesley's complaints of
hunger and half-rations *before* Talavera, this argument has only
limited force. On the other hand, Wellesley was mistaken in believing
as he did that his Allies deliberately starved him, while living off
the fat of the land themselves. There was no fat left in the plains of
Estremadura after the French had scoured them. Nor would the
ordinary diet of Spanish peasants have seemed anything but starvation to British beef addicts. (Wellington once observed that the Irish
were happiest in a wine country, the Scotch on pay-day and the
English when there was plenty of beef.) Kitty sent her Arthur a copy
of the widely-read *Letters from Portugal and Spain* by Dr Adam Neale,
published that year. From this book Arthur would have learnt that
the Spanish people lived on 'an execrable mess' eaten three times a
day, consisting of 'vinegar, garlick, lamp-oil and Cayenne pepper,
mixed with boiling water poured over a dishful of bread'; bacon or
sausage on Sundays only. Spanish 'enthusiasm'—a trait which
Wellington tended to distrust—had led them blithely to undertake
his provisioning; Spanish inefficiency and sheer poverty made it
impossible for them to keep their promise.

*   *   *

On 4 August Wellesley crossed the Tagus at Arzobispo and began his
circuitous, painful and long-drawn-out exodus from Spain; an exodus
punctuated by occasional good news but more often bad (such as a
grave defeat of the Spanish forces left as a rearguard to defend the
bridge of Arzobispo); an exodus sometimes brought to a halt but
never reversed.

One of the brighter interludes occurred on 8 August when the
Junta rewarded him for Talavera with the captain-generalship of
their forces—too late—and six beautiful Andalusian horses. His
letter of thanks included a dignified refusal to 'become a burthen upon

the finances of Spain during this contest for her independence' by accepting the captain-general's salary. Two contrasted events quickly followed, both on 12 August; General Cuesta left and Lord Wellesley arrived. A paralytic stroke deprived Cuesta of the use of his left leg. With one foot now almost in the grave, he resigned. Neither of the only two Spanish generals whom Wellesley trusted and admired, La Romana and Castaños, was appointed in his place. In place of John Hookham Frere, however, the retiring British Minister, arrived the man who should have been a tower of strength to Arthur's cause: his brilliant eldest brother. Kitty's great friend, Mrs Calvert, heard that Lord Wellesley's reception was delirious. The cheering people took out the horses from his carriage and drew it into Seville, one large lady eventually seizing 'his little lordship' in her arms, covering him with kisses and depositing him as 'saviour of the country' in front of the delighted Junta. But the most that Lord Wellesley could do for them was to persuade his brother to halt for two or three months at Badajoz, just inside the Spanish border, in order to lessen the Junta's 'ill-temper and alarm', not to say 'consternation' at the British army's retreat.

Arthur did not greatly welcome Richard's arrival. 'He will not be able to do any good,' he had written to William in July. Apart from the inherent difficulties of the Spanish situation, Arthur was thoroughly disgusted with his brother's personal record.

*   *   *

Richard was trying to separate from his wife who, however, refused to vacate the Wellesley mansion, Apsley House at Hyde Park Corner. William described the situation to Arthur with his usual verve:

> *Commissioner* Sydenham [Lord Wellesley's friend] is vested with full powers to arrange a Treaty of Separation, but Madame declines the proposal, and swears nothing shall ever induce her to quit the House. . . . There never was such a Devil—nothing can be more handsome than Wellesley has been to her in all his conduct, or more liberal than his proposals. But she is as vindictive as a fiend, and as hard and indelicate as those of her old profession can be.

Unfortunately the incorrigible Richard was involved with another lady practising his wife's 'old profession'. His arrangements for bringing this friend to the Peninsula caused a long delay in his departure (officially put down to his being ill) and an even greater scandal. Samuel Taylor Coleridge recalled the details to his fellow-writer, Robert Southey, in November: how the Marquess Wellesley had

> stayed a full month in town in consequence of a squabble about his taking out in great pomp—in a separate vessel hired for the purpose, a common whore called Sally Douglas whom he has in keeping—the King heard of it and expressed his displeasure and the Marquis took huff—at length, however, consented to take her more *clandestinely*, she went however and with a grand establishment, and is now with him in Spain. . . .

Added to the vexation of Richard's flamboyant presence was the burden of Henry's apparently crepuscular future. Henry had already gone through the ecclesiastical preliminaries of his divorce in June, but was once again living with Charlotte. 'I understand that she is already *under his protection*,' lamented Arthur to William. He could not understand how Charlotte's brother, Lord Cadogan, could allow his sister to live '*& perform*' with a man from whom she had been divorced by the Church;

> & I conclude that Poor Henry will again be dragged through the Mire, & will marry this blooming Virgin again as soon as she will have been delivered of the consequences of her little amusements.[2]

But since the deed had been done and Henry had also returned his elder children to her, Arthur devoutly hoped William and the rest of the family would not 'give or even look an opinion on the subject', which would only add to poor Henry's unhappiness.

This was right and charitable. The situation, however, was not quite as Arthur imagined. Remarriage was not contemplated. The handsome Lord Paget had gone to Walcheren, leaving Charlotte in need of 'protection'. Moreover, the misery of Henry's motherless children was more than he could bear, as Kitty's journal made plain, and he had grasped at even temporary comfort for his elder ones.

2. A daughter, born to Charlotte in 1810, of whom Henry Paget was the father (Marquess of Anglesey, *One-Leg*, p. 109).

As for the baby, Gerald Valerian, born in 1809, Henry refused to admit that he was his son. It was left for Kitty, with Arthur's blessing, to adopt this 'miserable little Being', as Kitty called him, out of the motherliness of her heart. 'The wretched infant is rejected by every body.'[3]

The sight of these woebegone children had a salutary effect on Kitty. She invited them all to dinner on 23 August and wrote that night in her journal:

> they are strong instances of the dreadful evils which the loss of a Mother inflicts upon Children. . . . Let no degree of Suffering, O my God, tempt me to forsake my Children!

And again on 6 September:

> . . . [Henry] is miserable, and the Children daily suffering from their loss. My darling Children, may no degree of suffering tempt me to forget my duty to you. I little imagined the extent of my crimes when I so earnestly wished to die.

The memory of Arthur's unkindness, however, had no effect on her present love and solicitude for him. Two days later it was his suffering (from dysentery) that wrung her tender heart:

> My dearest Arthur has been ill and shamefully treated by those people for whose sake he is hazarding his life. He has been distressed for provisions of every kind, while the Spaniards have had plenty of every thing: it is impossible not to abhor such ingratitude.

Throughout the rest of that year Kitty's diary continued to reflect Arthur's opinions (as above), her own shortcomings—'I have spent most evenings at the Library at work. It is not pleasant, but I am conscious I am not to be trusted quite alone'—occasional improvement— 'settled the accounts of the week. Forgot nothing!'—and the strange rush of public events.

3. Gerald Valerian Wellesley (1809–82). He became Queen Victoria's much loved Dean of Windsor and was one of the few people whose sympathy and advice did her good after Prince Albert's death (G. Battiscombe, 'A Victorian Dean', *History Today*, 1968, and *Victoria R.I.*, pp. 326–7).

In mid-September thousands of the sick, dying and dead from
Walcheren were being landed at south-east coast ports. Kitty dared
not go near her favourite Ramsgate pier for fear of catching the awful
'Walcheren fever'—dysentery. 'The sight of the Fleet is dreadful as it
was magnificent some weeks ago,' she mourned. The Whig Opposition were in a fury over the Walcheren débâcle and their mounting
wrath spilled over on to Wellesley and the Talavera campaign. 'I am
convinced that in six weeks' time,' said Lord Grey, 'there will not
remain a single British soldier in the Peninsula except as a prisoner.'
He denied that Wellesley had won a victory; the captured guns did
not prove anything; the French might have found it 'convenient' to
leave them behind. The most that *The Times*, a keen Opposition
paper, would grant to the newly-created Viscount Wellington was
courage and activity: he was no Black Prince, as his adulators suggested, nor Talavera a Crécy or Agincourt. Even the future General
Sir William Gomm, then a captain in Walcheren and a devoted
admirer of Wellington, feared that his 'ardent spirit' had blinded him
to the consequences of his victory; he ought to have studied Moore's
troubles, which would have taught him not to trust 'these degenerate
Spaniards'. Today there are eminent critics, like Sir Basil Liddell
Hart, who consider that he took a great risk with the campaign;
while Fortescue believed that though the risk was justified, the
motive—to show Castlereagh he was a better man than Moore—
was not.

Be that as it may, the faith of the Peninsular army in their leader
remained unshaken. It was reflected in the objective remarks of a
young Swiss officer who had served under and loved Sir John Moore.
Lord Wellington, he decided, seemed rather more than his age,
despite his tall, neat figure, expressive features and piercing glance.
He was said to be very energetic, prompt in decision, and 'always on
his own at that. . . .'

He has the liking and confidence of the Army, who agree in
thinking him resourceful, enterprising, and ambitious. I have
heard him—wrongly, I think—accused of hauteur, though he is
far from having the attentive affability we so admired in poor Sir
John Moore. . . .

Nor could the Swiss officer quite approve of the fact that Lord
Wellington was 'utterly heedless' of forms and regulations regarding

dress, over which poor Sir John had been so extremely particular. But there was one matter where Wellington had the distinct advantage. As a good Swiss, the writer held that English public opinion was as fickle as it was ill-informed. Moore had minded desperately the attacks made on him, whereas 'Lord Wellington laughs at all the calumnies the papers publish'.

Castlereagh himself was in dire trouble that September. He discovered that after a long intrigue Canning had persuaded Portland to oust him from the Cabinet by laying on him all the blame for Walcheren and the Talavera retreat. Portland's dilatoriness in not moving Castlereagh at once caused the fall of the Government and incidentally snuffed out his own life. Canning, Castlereagh and Portland all resigned, and Castlereagh sent Canning a blazing protest at his duplicity—'the best production he has ever framed', according to William, giving the news to Arthur; 'It is bitter, and it is also true'—a protest which concluded with a challenge to a duel.

'I'd rather fight than read it, by God!' said Canning. They fought on Putney Heath on 21 September, Castlereagh wounding Canning in the thigh ('as neatly as possible', said Creevey) and Canning shooting a button off the lapel of Castlereagh's coat.

Kitty's journal reflected the deep shock to Tory society:

> every proof of discord in our governors affords a triumph to our enemies, & he who exposes such discord acts as an enemy to the country.

The old King turned his back on the horrid event.

'I know two Cabinet Ministers have fought a duel,' he said, 'but I don't want to hear any more about them.' He was not so mad as they thought.

Discord was also present in the Wellesley family. Richard's political sympathies were with Canning; Arthur owed everything to Castlereagh; Henry was embarrassed by Canning asking him to be his second in the duel; William said he 'adhered to' the Cabinet 'through all this crooked and intricate business'.

When the news of the duel reached Wellington on 6 October he too was shocked.

> It will confirm in the minds of all men despicable opinions which they have had of the publick servants of the state.

Nevertheless he told William in a most significant letter of 22 October that he would continue to support the Tories, with one important proviso.

> . . . I don't conceive that I ought to embark in politics to such an extent as to preclude my serving the Country under any administration that may employ me.

Wellington in fact did not expect the Tories to last and was prepared to serve under the Whigs. The war came first. He must not be asked as a party politician to surrender the command he held as a soldier. This line of thought, briefly unfolded to Sir John Moore in the *tête-à-tête* at Queluz, now inspired him to a full-scale and masterly attack on the party mentality.

> . . . I never felt any inclination to dive deeply in party Politics; I may be wrong but the conviction in my mind is that all the misfortunes of the present reign, the loss of America, the success of the French revolution etc. etc., are to be attributed in a great degree to the Spirit of Party in England; & the feeling I have for a decided party politician is rather that of contempt than any other. I am very certain that his wishes & efforts for his party very frequently prevent him from doing that which is best for the Country; & induce him to take up the cause of foreign powers against Britain, because the cause of Britain is managed by his party opponents.

Throughout the Peninsular War Wellington was expected to put up with the party dog-fight at home. Tentatively and temperately he proposed a war-time reform:

> It may be true that the country cannot be served in Parliament excepting by people acting in Parties; and I acknowledge that I don't understand the subject sufficiently to be able to make up my mind upon that point. What has passed lately however has increased my doubts . . . & my opinion is that the best result of the late confusion would be a . . . compounding of all parties to support the Government against the Jacobins.

The new Tory Government, described by Mrs Calvert as 'a set of dolts', was headed by a lawyer, Spencer Perceval, Portland's Chancellor of the Exchequer. He was an evangelical, fanatically opposed to Catholic Emancipation. The best his admirers could say of him was that he was clever and an 'honest little fellow'; Cobbett, an enemy, called him 'a sort of under-strapper . . . to the Attorneys-General . . . a short, fair, pale-faced, hard, keen, foul-looking man with a voice well-suited to the rest', but very hard-working. History has been less than kind to him, for he was to prove courageous also, especially in handling the Prince Regent. The two most distinguished members of the former Government—Canning and Castlereagh—were both out, Lord Liverpool was War Minister, William Wellesley-Pole was Irish Chief Secretary and the Marquess Wellesley was haled back from Spain to cast his lustre over a dull crew by becoming Foreign Secretary. Henry was another to benefit. The news of Talavera, according to Kitty, had caused 'a gleam of pleasure' to 'animate his sad countenance'. Now the gleam must have been brighter, for he was appointed in place of Richard at Seville, to work closely with Arthur as in India. For Arthur himself there was a new and serious challenge.

He must convince a shaky Government, battered by the Opposition and what William called a 'perfectly diabolical' *Times* newspaper, not to throw in its hand at Lisbon as well as in Walcheren. From Walcheren the last of the British troops were withdrawn in December 1809, to the accompaniment of more poetry:

Friend: 'When sent fresh wreaths on Flushing's shores to reap, What didst thou do, illustrious Chatham?'

Chatham: 'Sleep!'

Friend: 'To men fatigued with war repose is sweet, But when awake, didst thou do nothing?'

Chatham: 'Eat!'

Was ignoble withdrawal to be the fate of Wellington also? The Opposition had no doubt. Abercromby told Creevey on 12 November, 'the Wellesleys will now be beat if they are attacked properly . . .'.

*   *   *

Wellington was operating on a knife-edge. It was his delicate task to convince the Government that retreat from Spain had been inevitable while evacuation of Portugal would be disastrous. As regards the first proposition, his troops were with him to a man. 'There is not a man in the army,' he had written in August, 'who does not wish to return to Portugal'. Hunger and fever since then, in the unhealthy Guadiana valley around Badajoz, had not changed their mood. Only the sunny-tempered Ned Pakenham, newly arrived as assistant adjutant-general, thought the Spanish people unfortunate rather than disloyal. 'I am one of the few,' he wrote home on 20 December, 'who exceedingly regret leaving Spain.'

Wellington had taken two steps in the interest of his second proposition—the defence of Portugal—one secret and successful, the other open (since it involved the Spanish army) and in his eyes a failure, though paradoxically it was to turn out a success also.

On 10 September, as unobtrusively as possible, he visited Lisbon. The citizens had wished to receive him 'handsomely' but he declined in a firm letter to Villiers.

> I will arrive at Lisbon in the dark so there must be no ceremony, this can be postponed for another time.

The next few weeks he spent in riding all over the 'Lisbon peninsula', as the hilly quadrilateral between Lisbon, Torres Vedras, the coast and the Tagus is called. With him rode his chief engineer, Colonel Richard Fletcher, who on 20 October received a twenty-one-point memorandum full of references to 'damming', 'redoubts', 'barriers' and 'signal posts', and introduced by a thousand-word essay on how these mysteries would enable the position they had surveyed to be held against any sweep by Napoleon's eagles, winter or summer. It was a classic case of Wellington seeing for himself; what one of his officers, Sir Harry Smith, was to call his 'old practice with the army'. When any problem was reported or question put to him he would always reply:

'I will get upon my Horse and take a look; and then tell you!'

The result of these particular rural rides would be seen in due course, when thirteen months of closely guarded secrets came to an end and Wellington was ready to astonish the world with his Lines of Torres Vedras. Meanwhile he used his evenings in Lisbon to pull up sharply some of those officers whom he had earlier described as almost as bad as the men. Alleged convalescents were going to the Lisbon theatres, sitting on the stage and misbehaving behind the scenes.

ATLANTIC OCEAN

(1) Pero Negro
(2) Montachique
(3) Senhora do Porto
(4) Monte Agraço

Leiria
Batalha
Alcobaça
Abrantes
R. Tagus
Peniche
Roliça
Obidos
Vimeiro
Santarem
R. Zizandre
End of 1st Line
Torres Vedras
Sobral
Alenquer
Ericeira
End of 2nd Line
Arruda
Mafra
Alhandra
Bucelas
Cintra
Lisbon
Queluz
Fort St. Julian

0   10   20
miles

1809-1810

PORTUGAL AND THE LINES OF TORRES VEDRAS

The officers of the army can have nothing to do behind the scenes. . . . They must be aware that the English public would not bear either the one or the other and I see no reason why the Portuguese public should be worse treated.

Admiral Berkeley reported that the commissaries and medical staff, instead of being with the army were in Lisbon,

keeping their houses, horses, and whores, and the Commissary-General at Cintra, taking his diversion.

Wellington had to issue a General Order requesting these officers to cease their misconduct towards the Portuguese inhabitants. It was generally believed that he had limited all official Lisbon leave to twenty-four hours, since no one required to stay longer than that in bed with a woman. This grim good humour seems to have pleased his army though it shocked Sir Charles Oman, who in general found Wellington's relations with 'the other sex . . . unedifying'. It is too early in this story to judge Oman's hard saying. It may be noted, however, that Wellington himself found unedifying the procedure of a court martial in October 1809 which '*honorably*' acquitted a certain Lieutenant Pearse of unofficerlike and ungentlemanlike conduct during an affray in a brothel.

> I believe that there is no officer upon the General Court Martial who wishes to connect the term Honor with the act of going to a Brothel. . . .

An honourable acquittal should be a subject for 'exultation'; visiting a brothel was hardly in this category. He therefore strenuously recommended the court to omit the word '*honorably*' from its verdict.

Before leaving Lisbon he wrote cryptically to his mother that he had come here 'on business' and was sending her some antique china.

> It is long since I heard from you. But I hope that you are in good health. I was not very well some time ago; but I am now quite recovered.

*   *   *

While thousands of palisades and fascines were being secretly indented for at Torres Vedras, Sobral and Lisbon, Wellington set off again at the beginning of November from his headquarters at Badajoz to visit Seville where he said good-bye to Richard, and to Cádiz where he had more exacting business.

In the interests of Portuguese defence, it seemed important to save the Spanish armies from annihilation. This might prove impossible. There had been a 'September Plot' against the inept Junta. Richard felt it his duty to warn these 'caitiffs' and 'curs', as he politely called its members, of their enemies' designs, and they fled to Cádiz where Wellington found them planning a string of autumn victories to rehabilitate themselves. Aghast at such suicidal folly, he tried to dissuade them, but in vain. In sour mood with Spain, he bought his mother a shawl, 'which bad as it is, is the only manufacture of Spain I have seen', and then wrote to William prophetically from Badajoz:

I have but little news for you. The Spanish Army of La Mancha has moved forward & is upon the eve of a General Action & I think of destruction. . . .

Not many days later, in November, this Spanish army was utterly broken to pieces at the battles of Tamamès and Ocaña. After weeks of more plots and counterplots, arrests and manifestoes, the Central Junta abdicated on 29 January 1810, preparatory to handing over to an elected Cortes. On 1 February King Joseph Bonaparte, bent on acquiring the easy wealth of Andalusia, entered Seville. Except in Cádiz, open Spanish resistance had collapsed. So, it appeared, had Wellington's hope that Spain might yet do something to stem the new French flood now being released against the Peninsula by Napoleon.

*   *   *

This was where the paradox of Peninsular warfare came in. Wellington himself was the first to appreciate it. From his new headquarters at Viseu, high up on its breath-taking plateau among the mountains of Portugal, he wrote to Lord Liverpool on the last day of January 1810 about Spain's last hope.

It is probable that, although the armies may be lost and the principal Juntas and authorities of the provinces may be dispersed, the war of partizans may continue.

Spain was to be saved, in fact, not by grape-shot, greybeards and grandees, but by hardy guerrillas and the sudden flash of the knife. These peasants spontaneously organized themselves into small, do-or-die bands, at least one to each province headed by folk heroes: Juan-Martin Diaz called 'El Empecinado', the dweller-by-the-stream in the Guadalajara mountains; Julian Sanchez, the farmer in Old Castile whose family had been murdered by the abhorred French dragoons; El Marquisito in the Asturias; El Medico; the Minas, Elder and Younger. The heroic elder Mina in Navarra was held to be a model of humanity because he did not kill his prisoners unless they were badly wounded. One chieftain named Moreno killed and wounded nine Frenchmen with a single discharge from his enormous blunderbuss which dislocated his own shoulder. When he shortly afterwards presented some captured silver plate to his native town, he enriched it with a handful of French ears, some with ear-rings.

By a special kind of nemesis, the ease with which Napoleon's armies flowed right over the country gave the partisans their chance. The enemy were spread far but spread thin. Even the basic force of 200,000 veterans which Napoleon was compelled to keep, year after year, in Spain, would never be safe from the noon-day ambush and the things that went bump in the night.

Wellington despised 'enthusiasm' in the Spanish army and government; he prized it in the irregulars. Indeed the partisans represented the one form of 'irregularity' which he not only prized but paid for, whenever an intercepted French despatch, often gruesomely blood-stained, was brought into his camp. Furious partisan warfare against Napoleon's couriers helped to perfect Wellington's intelligence system. The partisans in turn were gradually trained for the regular army by Wellington's British scouts. Longa in Aragon became a first-class Spanish general.

Most of these picturesque British scouts were either killed or captured in the end, including the greatest of them, Major Colquhoun Grant: 'he was worth a brigade to me', said Wellington when he heard that Grant was a prisoner; 'I wish he had not given his parole. . . . I should have offered a high reward to the guerrilla chiefs for his rescue.' The guerrillas were devoted to him and nicknamed him '*Granto el Bueno*'—the Good—to distinguish him from the unpopular John Grant known as '*Granto el Malo*'. Wellington preserved among his papers some of Grant's original intelligence reports. Neatly marked No. 1, No. 2 and so on in Grant's precise, spiky hand, they looked more as if they had been penned in some commodious office or factory house than by candlelight behind the enemy lines. Every one of them came direct to Wellington.

Grant was in fact not given the proper treatment of a prisoner on parole and made a fabulous escape in 1814, to handle Wellington's intelligence before Waterloo.[4]

4. Grant endured the handicap of his scarlet uniform rather than wear the civilian clothes of a spy. It caused his capture in 1812 by glowing brightly through the trees where he was hiding (C. J. D. Haswell, *The First Respectable Spy, The Life & Times of Lt.-Col. Colquhoun Grant, 1780–1829*).

The main weakness of Wellington's intelligence seems to have been in cracking the French codes. He told Sir William Napier after the war that he would have given £20,000 to anyone in the Peninsula who could decipher King Joseph's letters as Lady Napier had done for her historian husband. During the early years of the war there were no decoding specialists, but anyone in Military Intelligence, including Wellington, could have a go. By 1813 there was some specialization at headquarters—and also many bright ideas from home. Lord Bathurst sent Wellington a box of shoes with false soles 'for conveying written intelligence in an unsuspected manner'.

One more group which deserved (and received) well of the Commander-in-Chief were his religious 'irregulars'. James Warren Doyle, an Irish student for the priesthood at Coimbra University who was called up into the Portuguese army and refused the rank of major or any uniform beyond his Augustinian habit, volunteered to collect information. The Irish College at Salamanca, under its remarkable rector, Dr Patrick Curtis, ran an even better known intelligence service.[5] During the war the College practically shut down. In 1809, for example, there were only four names on its books—Burke, Shea, O'Grady, O'Kelly—and these four, having gone off as guides and interpreters in Sir John Moore's army, remained with Wellington's. Relays of young Irish novices, previously known as somewhat 'turbulent students', became spirited intelligence officers. After the war both Doyle and Curtis, the former as the famous 'J.K.L.' (James, Bishop of Kildare and Leighlin) the latter as Archbishop of Armagh, were to retain close but sometimes 'turbulent' relations with Wellington.

It was not surprising that Napoleon, feeling all these sinister drains on his resources, should have later come to speak with loathing of 'the Spanish ulcer'.

* * *

5. Curtis had entered the College as a student in the year of Wellington's birth, under the name of 'Don Patricio Cortés' and later, as a chaplain in the Spanish Navy, was captured by the British. He did not return to Ireland till after the Peninsular War. A note dated 1813 from the Bishop of Valladolid mentioned that either Wellington or his Director-General of Hospitals, Dr McGrigor, would pay back '275 dollars own [sic] to Dr Curtis'. This was the rent for the Irish College in Salamanca which had been taken over as Wellington's main hospital. Curtis also asked Wellington for a few hundred pounds for his own subsistence, as he had lost his post as Regius Professor of Astronomy and of Natural History at the University (*Maynooth College Archives*, Dublin).

1810. London. January 1st. Began this year by wishing every happiness to my Husband, comfort to those who need it, and a continuation of happiness to the happy.

Kitty's husband was one of the happy. He had laid his plans and was ready to take on all comers. When the French reinforcements arrived, he told William on 4 January, he would be

> in the way . . . & I hope we shall do tolerably well even if *Boney* should come to drive the Leopards into the Sea.

The first new wave of attacks actually came from the Opposition. They seized the occasion of Parliament's reassembly and vote of thanks for Talavera to accuse Wellington of having 'fought for a peerage'. His title was described by the indefatigable Whitbread as 'a premium on rashness'. What did it matter? Creevey had to confess 'All our indignation against him ended in smoak [*sic*].' Better still, his army under his eagle eye—and nose—was at last 'improved'. Though its plundering could be 'infamous' at times, and though he admitted it might still 'slip through my fingers as it did through Sir John Moore's', beehives and all, these were reasons for exertion not dejection. Nor were his exertions all disciplinary. He would do anything to get his army their legitimate supplies. There was one occasion when a staff-officer visited a large estate to procure forage. He returned empty-handed. Wellington asked why.

'I was told I would have to bow to the noble owner, and of course I couldn't do that.'

'Well, I suppose I must get some myself.'

A few days later the forage began pouring in. How did he do it? 'Oh, I just bobbed down.'

In February 1810, when Wellington was voted a pension of £2,000, Creevey organized a petition from the Common Council of London against it. Wellington believed that the petitioners were hoping to have him once more, as after Cintra, '*en spectacle* at Chelsea'; but again he did not care:

> they may do what they please, I shall not give up the game as long as it can be played.

The petitioners failed. William reported that they had not made the smallest impression'. There was no Court of Inquiry into Talavera at Chelsea. The war went on.

*   *   *

It remained to strengthen the morale of the British Government before the French armies arrived.

Blunt accounts by William of Richard's love-affairs had convinced Arthur that no help was to be expected from the Foreign Secretary. In March William understood from Lord Wellesley's Cabinet colleagues that he hardly ever visited his office or spoke in the House of Lords, that nobody could get access to him,

and that his whole time is passed with Moll [William's generic name for Sally Douglas], for whom I hear he has bought Henry's House, and who it is said is rapidly ruining Wellesley—His colleagues never name him to me. . . .

The only good news was that 'Milady' [Lady Wellesley] had at last been 'driven out' from Apsley House, though at the cost of £4,500 a year clear of income tax, plus £5,000 'to pay what she calls her debts'. Arthur replied to William in April with equal bluntness:

I wish that Wellesley was castrated; or that he would like other people attend to his business & perform too. It is lamentable to see Talents & character & advantages such as he possesses thrown away upon Whoring. . . .

By May, it was true, William heard that Richard had 'entirely got rid of the expense of Moll which must have been considerable—almost boundless'—but now he was flirting with the outcast Canning, a liaison not much better in William's eyes than the one with Moll.

At the War Office, Liverpool was more industrious but scarcely less irritating. He had sent Wellington an extraordinary private letter on 27 February 1810. The Government, he said, were unable to give him 'any positive instructions' but left everything to his 'discretion'. (This was feeble though not unwelcome.) On the other hand, Napoleon had made another leopard speech on 4 December 1809:

When I shall show myself beyond the Pyrenees the frightened leopard will fly to the ocean, to avoid shame, defeat and death.

Liverpool therefore pointed out that in view of Napoleon's forth-coming arrival in the Peninsula, the possibility of Portugal's fall and the consequent need for an army to defend His Majesty's own dominions, 'the safety of the British Army in Portugal is the first object which his Majesty has in view'. This, as Wellington remarked hotly to William, was 'ludicrous enough'. The British Army had gone to Portugal—in order to be safe! He hoped such a letter would never be published. (William's reply to Arthur, however, showed signs of the same disease: 'I cannot bring myself to believe,' he quavered, 'that the French are not moving upon you with Gigantic strides.') Finally and inconsistently, Wellington was instructed by Liverpool not to evacuate Portugal until it was 'absolutely necessary'.

A steady flow of letters from the War Minister on similarly futile lines reached Wellington's headquarters during March and April 1810: flutterings about 'the Enemy's superiority', pleadings against 'any desperate resistance', assurances that Wellington would be 'excused for bringing the army home a little too soon rather than too late', and a queasy suggestion that it might be better to embark furtively from Peniche rather than openly from Lisbon. Of Wellington's many robust replies the most effective was sent on 2 April.

First, he was not going to be driven out of the Peninsula by the ghost of Sir John Moore, who, he stated, did not and could not know the situation in Portugal a year after his own death. Second, he was not so keen on 'desperate battles', as the Government seemed to imagine: he had stood in two positions for six months, despite his Allies' impatience to strike and his officers'—or some of them—to quit. 'I believe that the world in the Peninsula begin to believe that I am right.' Third, if he did have to evacuate it would be from Lisbon not Peniche.

> . . . I feel a little anxiety to go, like gentlemen out of the hall door . . . and not out of the back door, or by the area.

*　　　　　*　　　　　*

A month after this manifesto, Napoleon handed over his 'Army of Portugal' to the fifty-two-year-old Marshal André Massena, the 'old fox' who had been winning spectacular victories for France ever since he led the attack on Arcole in 1796 carrying, as they all did, his cocked hat on his sword. 'Massena, the Spoilt Child of Victory, is in our front,' wrote Wellington grimly to Lord Wellesley on 4 June.

A major shift in the French Empire's foreign policy during late 1809 and early 1810 had precluded Napoleon from taking on the Spanish command himself. The Austrians, defeated at Wagram, offered the Corsican usurper their Emperor's daughter, Marie-Louise, in marriage. The barren Josephine was accordingly divorced and Napoleon married Marie-Louise, 1–2 April 1810. At the same period Tsar Alexander openly sabotaged Napoleon's Continental system. The Emperor of the French saw war with Russia loom ahead and left the Peninsula problems to Massena. On the face of it, there was much solid ground for Napoleon's confidence in this second best solution.

There were 350,000 French soldiers in Spain, 100,000 of them fresh troops. And Massena's reputation alone would suffice to win the war, as Napoleon assured his redoubtable lieutenant in a flattering effort to dispel a touch of war-weariness. Massena modestly relayed this heartening compliment to his staff at Salamanca, where they waited to burst through the twin northern gateways into Portugal: Ciudad Rodrigo on the Spanish side of the frontier, Almeida on the Portuguese. The 'world in the Peninsula' would soon know whether Wellington or Napoleon was right.

*   *   *

Marshal Ney, Massena's brilliant second-in-command, appeared with 30,000 veterans before Ciudad Rodrigo on 2 July 1810 and invested it. Immediately there was a universal outcry. Wellington must march to the relief of this key fortress and its valiant old Governor, General Herresi. Wellington did not move. The white-haired Governor was compelled to surrender on 10 July. Ney gallantly gave him back his sword, congratulated him and shook hands. At that moment there was no doubt which leader commanded the Spaniard's greater respect, Ney or Wellington.

It had been the hardest of decisions for Wellington. Fully intending to relieve the place, he wrote to William as early as 13 September 1809 that though he suspected the French 'had an eye on the siege of Ciudad Rodrigo' he would prevent their success, please God, provided the garrison held out till he could reach them. The garrison did hold out; but he could not yet risk a general action.

The Walcheren fever had made havoc of Lord Liverpool's efforts to reinforce him, and he could not trust his 33,000 troops, many of them raw recruits, against Ney's soldiers. He stood at Celorico in Portugal, while the English press angrily reprinted in their columns the abuse of the 'Sepoy General' appearing in Napoleon's newspaper, the *Moniteur*. Those nearest to Wellington, however, such as his brother-in-law, Edward Pakenham, understood and admired his strategy and 'steadiness'. On the day after Herresi's surrender Ned wrote to his mother regretting that 'this Noble resistance' could not be rewarded, but predicting that the French, by dividing their huge forces, had not

> reserved that commanding power to make the Leopard jump into the Sea—for my part I think it will take the Emperor (after His family Efforts) to move us at all.

They were all beginning to enjoy the leopard business, and Ned ended:

> Lord Wellington looks as well as possible and I never saw him in such spirits.

*   *   *

General Robert Craufurd of the Light Division made up for Wellington's 'steadiness' at Celorico by a month of extreme audacity on the line of the River Coa.[6] Contrary to Wellington's instructions he held up the French advance into Portugal by daredevil skirmishing, only just giving himself time to dart back to safety, after losing over 300 men. His rashness provoked two contrasting reactions. Wellington, who desperately needed brilliance in his generals and had found it in Craufurd, though marred by wildness and a savage temper, could not bring himself to have Craufurd court-martialled. As he wrote to William:

> if I am to be hanged for it, I cannot accuse a man who I believe has meant well, and whose error was one of judgement, not of intention.

6. Robert Craufurd (1764–1812), commanding Sir John Moore's Light Brigade in Spain and affectionately (and sometimes angrily) known to his fellow-officers and men as 'Black Bob'.

Perhaps his own good spirits, noticed by Pakenham, helped him to be forgiving. It was not always so. Nor was General Thomas Picton of the 3rd Division forgiving, to whom Craufurd had ridden up and personally appealed for rescue. Picton, according to Wellington, though a fine soldier was 'a rough foul-mouthed devil as ever lived', and on this occasion he had some slight excuse for telling Craufurd, with appropriate embellishments, to get himself out of his own mess.[7]

* * *

Wellington could put up with rows between firebrands, especially when they were first-class officers, but there were more serious staff problems to be faced as well.

Few of the new officers sent out to him by the Horse Guards possessed the solid ability and agreeable temperament of an Edward Pakenham or a Lowry Cole. Though Kitty had jilted Cole in Arthur's favour, Cole served his brilliant rival with devotion and skill, writing to his sister in February 1810:

I never served under any Chief I liked so much, Sir J. Moore always excepted, as Lord W. He has treated me with much more confidence than I had a right to or could be expected from anyone.

There was General Sir William Erskine, drunken, 'blind as a beetle', according to a fellow-officer, and probably mad, whom he had sent home 'indisposed' the year before. Back he came in 1810, along with other known disasters such as Generals Lumley and Lightburne and Colonel Landers. Landers had also been sent home once already, by Sir John Moore from Sicily. Wellington would at least keep Landers off the battlefield by appointing him 'perpetual President of General Courts-Martial', with Lightburne, if Wellington had his way, as the perpetual President's first customer—Lightburne's conduct having been 'scandalous'. Wellington gave Colonel Torrens, Military Secretary at the Horse Guards, the full blast of his indignation:

7. Sir Thomas Picton (1758–1815). His family was Welsh and apparently irascible, for his brother was Major Picton of the notorious Aston duel in India. Captain Elers believed that Picton never forgave Wellington for his brother's death, though it had nothing to do with him. (Major Picton fell ill soon after the duel and died.)

Really when I reflect upon the characters and attainments of some of the General officers of this army . . . on whom I am to rely . . . against the French Generals . . . I tremble: and, as Lord Chesterfield said of the Generals of his day, 'I only hope that when the enemy reads the list of their names he trembles as I do.' Sir William Erskine and General Lumley will be a very nice addition to this list! However I pray God and the Horse Guards to deliver me from General Lightburne and Colonel Landers.

Wellington always liked to give his favourite quotations a good run. The Chesterfield epigram would have often sparkled at his dinner table, enhanced with characteristic 'By Gods!' and divested of references to authorship, until in due course his enchanted aides-de-camp handed it down to posterity as the great man's own work.

He was eventually delivered from Erskine when the unfortunate general committed suicide at Lisbon in 1813. Meanwhile there was the further problem of his second-in-command, Sherbrooke having gone home. Poor Lord Liverpool racked his brains. He had four good candidates all of whom declined (Lord William Bentinck because he was 'so despondent about the cause in the Peninsula') and it had to be Sir Brent Spencer again. The news brought no joy to Wellington. Sir Brent was a great courtier, supposed to have made a secret royal marriage to George III's daughter, Princess Augusta, known as 'Puss', and Wellington did not trust him to support the cause when on leave:

On the contrary the Royal Family at their dinners or their Card parties would make him say what they please, & he would swear to it afterwards.

To Lord Liverpool, an unrelenting Tory, he sent a special request for no generals with political prejudices.

I only beg you not to send me any violent party men. We must keep the spirit of party out of the army, or we shall be in a bad way indeed.

Another dangerous weakness was 'croaking'—the contemporary word for grumbling and defeatism. In spreading doubts about Wellington's strategy the croakers incidentally gave away intelligence to the enemy about the numbers and positions of his army, through letters home which got into the newspapers. The ups and downs of a long war would not matter, he believed, if only people minded their own business,

> instead of writing news and keeping coffee houses. But as soon as an accident happens, every man who can write, and who has a friend who can read, sits down to write his account of what he does not know. . . .

Wellington often suggested some kind of censorship, but the nineteenth century knew nothing of Official Secrets Acts. Secrecy depended on individual discretion, as when Colonel John Colborne of the 52nd, Wellington's best officer in the Light Brigade, wrote to his sister in 1810, 'Remember, my letters are sacred and must not be repeated'.[8]

One arch-croaker, in Wellington's view, was Charles Stewart, adjutant-general and half-brother of Castlereagh. Stewart developed into 'a sad *brouillon* and mischief-maker', whose 'petty intrigues' turned many officers against the Commander-in-Chief's policy. He had to be got rid of after much friction, including at least one scene when the Commander-in-Chief reduced the adjutant-general to tears. But with a remarkable talent for management, Wellington never allowed their relations to be completely severed. Nor did he let himself brood too much over croaking and criticism. Some years after the war he was telling Croker:

> I believe there was a good deal of this sort of spirit at one time, before I had laid hold of the public opinion, both in the army and the country, but I kept never-minding it, quite sure that all would come right in good season.

One result of 'never-minding' and remaining friendly was that Wellington was able to buy from Stewart before he went home his young charger, Copenhagen.

8. (Moore-Smith, p. 147, 9 November 1810.) Field-Marshal Sir John Colborne, 1st Baron Seaton (1778–1863). A brilliant product of the Shorncliffe training under Sir John Moore. Governor-General and Commander-in-Chief, Canada, 1838. He was over six feet tall, had an aquiline nose second only to Wellington's, and a winning nature.

It would not have been the British Army without some complaints of the Naval arm also, and Wellington told William he was 'teazed to death' by the interference and ingenuity of Admiral Berkeley in all matters from the commissariat to the artillery, but especially in planning for an emergency embarkation.

> I tremble when I think I shall have to embark the Leopards in front of Bonaparte aided by such a man, who has already twenty new invented modes of putting Leopards into Boats. . . .

As usual, Wellington learnt in the end how to handle an awkward human phenomenon—'I think I have managed him rather better lately'—though he still wished that the Admiral 'was not so great a General'. The culmination came on 2 December 1811 when he actually wrote to Liverpool asking *not* to be relieved of the Admiral: 'it is impossible for two officers to be on better terms than we are. I have always found the Admiral not only disposed to give us every assistance, but to anticipate and exceed our wishes in this way.' The last, ironic touch was truly Wellingtonian.

*   *   *

So great a general. . . . There were some who would have turned the tables on Wellington, declaring that the faults were not all on one side; that he did not give enough encouragement to his subordinates; that he himself, in short, had got too big for his boots, particularly since becoming a Viscount. Even the tactful William had found something amiss with the Talavera despatch.

> . . . I never read so clear or so modest a statement. I have but one fault to find with it—you are not warm enough in Praise of your officers. . . . I think you are particularly cold in praising the Artillery. I have heard that Howarth had two Horses shot under him, this might have been thrown in and would have gratified his friends and the Corps. I mention these little things because I think it is a pity that in such great exploits as yours any thing should be left ungratifying to all interested.

Another of the 'little things' was said to be a certain haughtiness at his own table. Only young Lord March, Lord Fitzroy Somerset and

Captain Burgh, later Lord Downes, were thought to be completely happy members of his military 'family'.

It was quite true that Wellington, in looking for able young men for his personal staff, preferred ability with a title to ability without. All commanders were accustomed to select their military family from their actual families or close friends, most of whom in Wellington's case were members of the nobility. Lord March, whom Wellington called 'the best fellow I ever saw', was the eldest son of his great friend the Duke of Richmond. The Beaufort family, from whom Fitzroy Somerset sprang, was to be allied three times over with Wellington's, Fitzroy himself marrying one of Wellington's nieces, while his eldest brother, Lord Worcester, having been rescued from the arms of Harriette Wilson and sent out to Wellington in the Peninsula, married another of his nieces, and after she died, yet another.

Wellington always liked the young, and in these examples of a *jeunesse dorée* he found some of the family satisfactions he had missed in his own youth. No doubt the obvious delight he took in their dashing style and uninhibited spirits created jealousies. But when ability was missing no youth, however golden, was permitted to remain. The only son of his devoted brother William Wellesley-Pole, another William of whom more will be heard, was returned smartly to his father. Wellington had more than once to 'speak sharply to him for doing things he has no right to', such as going off without leave.

Failure to take his senior staff officers into his confidence was one more of the 'little things'. Two modern historians have studied this trait in action but reached conflicting conclusions. Sir Charles Oman discovered that of all his generals, Craufurd, Beresford and Hill were the only ones with whom he 'condescended' to talk freely, so that Picton and Cole complained; while Sir John Fortescue found he wrote freely only to Hill, Cotton and Cole, so that Craufurd and Picton complained. The discrepancies in these two lists, only Hill and Picton maintaining their respectively high and low estates in both, suggests a lack of first-hand evidence about Wellington's personal relations. Nor is there the slightest reason to suppose that a viscountcy would have turned a Wellesley's head.

The fact is that for a public man he had astonishingly little of that desire to love or be loved by the many, to win wide affection by giving it widely, such as Nelson possessed to a delectable degree. With years, responsibilities, croakers and busybodies all increasing, Wellington's innate reticence developed into something which ill-will could mistake for pride. Reserved he undoubtedly was, by both design and temperament. But whatever Wellington's officers may have lost through his cool gestures and contracted human sympathies, they gained immeasurably from his super-human composure and reserves of strength at a crisis. The army had need of all Wellington's magnificent resources during that August and September of 1810.

*   *   *

After the fall of Ciudad Rodrigo it was known that Massena would besiege Almeida. The two fortresses stood facing one another like the castles across a chess board, with Elvas and Badajoz as the corresponding pair in the south. Once Massena had captured the two northern castles his road to Portugal would be open. He would be a long step nearer to saying checkmate. On 26 August 1810 he began shelling Almeida. With reasonable luck, however, Wellington could expect the town to hold out until possibly the end of September. It had a staunch Governor in William Cox, quantities of ammunition and half a million rations of bread. After September the rains would begin. Massena's advance would become water-logged and meanwhile Wellington would have completed the assimilation of his reinforcements, the training of his Portuguese troops and the secret transformation-scene inside Portugal itself. But the 'child of fortune', as Wellington liked to call himself, was not to be in luck this time. Indeed, what Oman calls 'the greatest accident of the War' was about to befall him.

Barrels of gunpowder were being carried from the main powder magazine inside Almeida Cathedral on Sunday 27 August to the cannon on the walls. One keg happened to be leaky and left a long trail of gunpowder behind it. A French shell accidentally ignited this trail; the flame ran all the way back to the great Cathedral doors, open for lading, where more ammunition caught fire and in turn set off the main magazine inside. Suddenly, in a tempest of fire and smoke and crashing masonry, like a nineteenth-century print of Judgement Day, the whole Cathedral, castle and town-centre vanished. Hundreds of the garrison died. The survivors forced Governor Cox to surrender, which he did at noon on 28 August 1810. Wellington, posted not far off, had tried to contact Cox by telegraph—bladders run up and down on long poles—but the weather was too bad. When it cleared he could see quite enough through his glass: 'the steeple of the church was destroyed, and many of the houses unroofed'. Next day he was again out early and scribbling a note to his cavalry commander, Sir Stapleton Cotton.

> *On the top of the hill at Marçaldo Chaõ,*
> 29th August, 1810, $\frac{1}{2}$ past 7 A.M.
> My dear Cotton,
> I came out here to see if all was quiet, and I am glad to see it is so.

He knew it would not remain quiet for long. The moment had almost come to put his secret plan for the defence of Portugal into action. It was to centre round a compact, deliberate retreat into a gigantic fortress which would make Ciudad Rodrigo and Almeida look like open villages. And if possible—if that 'old fox' Massena could be lured into committing such a *bêtise*—there would be one great battle on the way there in a position of his own choosing. Fought partly to hearten the croakers, it would be a battle of prestige.

By the middle of the first week in September he had moved his headquarters back from Celorico to Gouveia. There he stood until the third week, receiving accurate information from his intelligence service about Massena's advance, and bargaining with Massena through an interchange of scrupulously polite letters for the lives of each other's prisoners caught sniping or straggling in the Beira mountains.

The snipers were Wellington's. Known as the *Ordenanza*, these Portuguese peasants wore no uniforms but operated in their traditional woollen caps, short brown cloaks and breeches 'negligently drawn over their bare legs', carrying old blunderbusses, pikes, pruning knives and quince poles whose wooden tips were hard and sharp as iron. In vain Wellington insisted to Massena that the *Ordenanza* called up under ancient Portuguese law in times of national emergency, were as much serving soldiers as those in the militia or line regiments. Massena refused to recognize their status and had them all executed at the price, in reprisals, of his own stragglers' lives.

There was an incipient feeling of confidence in Wellington's camp, even though the fall of Almeida had caused the Whig Opposition and the Portuguese Regency Council to redouble their croaking in the expectation of instant evacuation. Indeed Charles Stuart, Villiers's successor in Lisbon, reported that the Council's leader, Principal Sousa, was trying to get Wellington's defensive strategy reversed through the influence of his brother, the Portuguese Ambassador in London, and Wellington had better write at once to the London Sousa in cypher if he wanted 'to break the neck of an Intrigue'.[9] To which Wellington replied agreeably with a loud but harmless bark:

> It appears that you have had a good smart contest with the Portuguese Government respecting our plan of operations. They will end in forcing me to quit them, and then they will see how they will get on.

A defensive strategy of which the core at Torres Vedras was still invisible could not be expected to win applause. Therefore criticism did not spoil Wellington's new sense of pleasurable anticipation, as he began to collect his divisions and post them for the battle they devoutly desired but could not yet count upon, in the wild hills north-east of Coimbra. Edward Pakenham was one of those who felt happy: 'nothing would surprise me less,' he assured the family party in Ireland, 'than eating my X'mas dinner in Portugal. I drink the health of all my friends in good Porto daily. . . .'

*　　　*　　　*

Which road would the 'old fox' take to Coimbra, and so onwards with 'Gigantic strides', as William put it, to Lisbon? Wellington heard to his amazement on 17 September that Massena was advancing by the road through Viseu. 'There are certainly many bad roads in Portugal', he wrote to Stuart with grim satisfaction, 'but the enemy has decidedly taken the worst in the whole kingdom.'

Besides the hazards of the road itself which included vengeful *Ordenanza* behind every rock, Massena had to face a rugged country-side stripped of all food and stores by Wellington's orders. 'Not a soul anywhere; all is abandoned,' wrote Massena glumly; 'our soldiers find potatoes . . . and only live to meet the enemy.' Massena had touched the fringe of a 'scorched earth' policy which was in due

9. Charles Stuart (1779–1845), later created Lord Stuart de Rothesay, one of the ablest British diplomats of the period. Not, of course, to be confused with Charles Stewart, Castlereagh's half-brother and future 3rd Marquess of Londonderry.

course to be unrolled before him like miles and miles of threadbare carpet. Even with the 350,000 pounds of bread found in Almeida, it was not a well-fed army which invaded Portugal.

Massena's extraordinary choice of route (due to misleading maps and ignorant guides), though more than welcome, meant a sudden and swift change of plan for Wellington. The divisions of Hill and Leith were ordered back at once from the fortified heights above the River Alva, a southern tributary of the Mondego where Massena had been expected at the Murcella bridge, to an equally strong position to the north. This was the famous ridge of Bussaco. All along Bussaco's towering hog's back, running north and south for almost ten miles, Wellington stationed his sixty cannon and army of 51,000 men, half British and half Portuguese—a somewhat thin barrier of men perched upon a mighty barrier of mountain. A staff officer, on being asked by an artillery officer for a map of Bussaco to send to England, replied: 'You only have to draw a damned long hill, and that will be sufficiently explanatory.'

Past Bussaco's southern end wound the beautiful Mondego, under a strange, perpendicular cliff of grey granite, its surface fractured into countless shelves and known as 'The Library'. Deep heather covered its sides and summit, broken by spiky aloes, boulders of black basalt and pink and grey limestone, or pine trees springing from precipitous ravines. Solid stone windmills stood here and there on high plateaux. At the loftiest point of all, two miles from its northern end, Wellington established his headquarters in the wooded and walled Convent of Bussaco. Every room was occupied by his staff, except for the Prior's and that of one monk who managed to fill his up with lumber. From a narrow, cork-lined cell with white-washed walls and brick floor, Wellington issued his final orders of 26 September 1810. His soldiers, most of them concealed behind the *massif*'s crest, were to eat a cold evening meal and lie down without fires in total darkness and eerie silence. He knew that Massena would force a head-on collision next day. No flanking movement to north or south. Head-on, against the mountain. It had been almost too much to hope for, but it was going to happen.

*   *   *

Massena had unaccountably delayed at the village of Mortagoa, eight miles from Bussaco, between the 19th and 25th. He explained to

Napoleon that he was waiting for supplies; others believed that he was resting his mistress 'Madame X'. Wife of a Captain Heberton on his staff and sister of an earlier mistress, she rode everywhere with him dressed in an aide-de-camp's uniform. Ney had to shout the results of a very inadequate reconnaissance through Massena's bedroom door. No doubt she had found the Viseu road rough going. By the 26th, however, Wellington could see Massena's army of over 65,000 men assembled on the eastern hills opposite; the most distant of them not more than three miles away.

As black night fell in tense stillness over Bussaco, innumerable French bivouac fires across the valley sprang into cheerful life.

13 They Shall Not Pass

At daybreak on 27 September 1810 Wellington reconnoitred his out-posts. One commanding officer was found to be drunk through nerves and was quietly removed. 'A man gets nervous,' Wellington explained years afterwards, 'thinking of his own responsibility; and then he takes to brandy—want of confidence in himself, there's the evil.' It was an evil from which Wellington himself never suffered, to the inestimable advantage of his army.

He also found that fog had moved in even more decisively than Massena. From his high command-post outside the Convent walls he could see nothing of the three French corps below, whose bivouac fires had made them so distinct the night before: the IInd Corps under General Reynier occupying the hamlet of San Antonio de Cantaro opposite Wellington's centre; then the VIth under Marshal Ney in the village of Moura to Reynier's right, perched on the main road which wound through the houses of Sula on Bussaco's north-eastern slopes, up over the great mountain, past the Convent and down again to the Coimbra highway—altogether a vital road in Wellington's scheme of defence; lastly the VIIIth Corps under Junot in reserve. Wellington could not even see his own riflemen on the lower slopes, though ever since dawn ominous sounds had been coming up from below. First a rustling; then a growing confusion of muffled shouts and shots. Skirmishers of both armies were in contact. All at once, about 6 A.M., the heads of four French battalions under General Heudelet burst upwards through the mist.

This was the start of Massena's dawn attack. It had been assigned to Reynier, whose 14,000 troops were to assault the central section of the ridge, using a cart-track from San Antonio which crossed it from east to west.[1] Having broken what Massena thought to be Welling-ton's thin line on the crest, they were to wheel right and take him in the rear. During a long, hectic hour it looked as if Reynier might

1. Today this old track can be seen clearly from Bussaco as it leaves the hamlet of San Antonio and begins to climb the ridge; but about half-way up it becomes a mere jumble of loose rocks, until it finally hits a new forestry road, running laterally along the ridge, and disappears.

succeed. Not through General Heudelet's force, however. After marching swiftly upwards with their left flank guided through the mist by the cart-track, they ran into a wall of fire from the Allied 3rd Division under Picton. Powerful Portuguese artillery, the strong 74th regiment, half of the 45th and a large force of Portuguese infantry drove them off to their right, where the survivors could do no more than stoutly cling to the heights they had gained. A mile to the north there was a different story.

Eleven battalions under General Merle had started out a few minutes before Heudelet. At first they made towards Lightburne's brigade on Picton's left, where Wellington himself stood, plain and workmanlike in his usual plumeless cocked hat and a grey great-coat. He soon had two six-pounders trained on them, though at long range. Distracted by fog, the guns and Allied skirmishers away to their left, they swerved diagonally in that direction and accidentally hit on a weak spot in Wellington's line. It was a lucky accident for Merle. The Allies' light troops were easily driven in. Some of Merle's *voltigeurs* (special companies of skirmishers) dashed ahead and reached the rocks on the summit. If they could be supported, the whole tide of Reynier's powerful 1st Division would soon be rolling over the crest.

Wellington ordered down two more six-pounders to blast the French flanks with grape and canister. Picton, splendidly eccentric in his undiscarded night-cap, personally rallied the disordered light companies and brought them back to support the brave men who, from right and left, were fighting the battle of the gap. These were the 8th Portuguese, Major Gwynne's half of the 45th and above all that great fighting regiment of Irishmen, some of whom only knew enough English to get by on parade, the 88th Connaught Rangers. Into the enemy's front the Portuguese musketeers poured their steady volleys, while Alexander Wallace, the Connaught Rangers' fiery colonel, used a modern variant of his famous ancestor's speech before the battle of Falkirk—*I haf brocht you to the ring, hop if you can*—to inspire his men for the charge.

'Now, Connaught Rangers . . .' he shouted, 'when I bring you face to face with those French rascals, drive them down the hill—don't give the false touch, but push home to the muzzle!' The long, sharp bayonets went home, as he drove obliquely into the French column.

Though there were eleven French battalions against only four Anglo-Portuguese, Merle's men were exhausted by their steep, fast

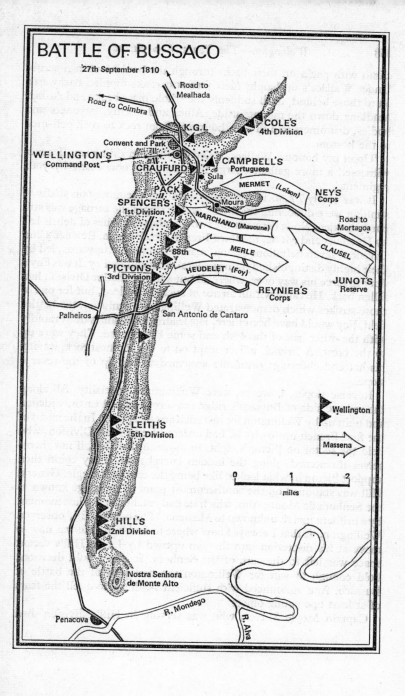

BATTLE OF BUSSACO

27th September 1810

Road to
Mealhada

Road to Coimbra

K.G.L.

COLE'S
4th Division

Convent and Park

WELLINGTON'S
Command Post

CRAUFURD

CAMPBELL'S
Portuguese

Sula

PACK

MERMET (Loison)

NEY'S
Corps

SPENCER'S
1st Division

Moura

MARCHAND (Maucune)

Road to
Mortagoa

68th

MERLE

CLAUSEL

PICTON'S
3rd Division

HEUDELET (Foy)

JUNOT'S
Reserve

REYNIER'S
Corps

Palheiros

San Antonio de Cantaro

Wellington

Massena

LEITH'S
5th Division

0   1   2
miles

HILL'S
2nd Division

Nostra Senhora
de Monte Alto

R. Mondego

Penacova

R. Alva

climb with packs on their backs through the boulder-strewn scrub. Under Wallace's onslaught their foremost ranks toppled backwards on to those behind, until suddenly the whole mass broke and rushed headlong down the mountainside, Allies and enemy, bayonets and bodies, drummers and drums, bouncing from rock to rock pell-mell to the bottom.

'Upon my honour, Wallace,' cried Wellington riding up, 'I never witnessed a more gallant charge than that just now made by your regiment.'

It was nearly 7 A.M. In the pearly air above the mountain shafts of sunlight were dissolving the mists; on the slopes the carnage was still partly hidden. Now, between the two bloody avalanches of debris left by Heudelet and Merle, the third French attack began. Reynier's 2nd Division, seven battalions strong, marched superbly upwards, led by their highly distinguished young general, Maximilien Foy. It was Foy's duty to force his way over, where all but a few of the 1st Division had fallen back. He came within an ace of success. Indeed, but for one of those strokes which demonstrated Wellington's genius on the battle-field, Foy would have been there. His leading companies dealt rapidly with the other half of the 45th and some Portuguese. They were up to the crest. A French officer leapt on to the topmost rock, waving his hat and cheering; *tirailleurs* swarmed to the lip of the reverse slope.

Reverse slopes, however, were Wellington's speciality. All along the reverse side of Bussaco's ridge ran a road of red earth, widened and built up by Wellington for just such an emergency. In the midst of the first French upthrusts he had ordered Leith's 5th Division, who held the sector on Picton's right, to move to their left, if not themselves threatened, along the hidden lateral road. They could then support Picton in what looked like being the crucial struggle. General Hill was stationed on the southernmost point of the ridge known as the Senhora da Monte Alto, which he had reached at the last moment by a brilliant march unknown to Massena. 'The best of Hill,' observed Wellington, 'is that I always know where to find him.' He was now to move at his discretion into the gap opened by Leith. Hill's vacant space was left to the care of the Senhora. It was a bold decision; bold enough to win for Wellington the first part of the battle of Bussaco. And announced with sufficient boldness to quell the fears of at least one young officer.

Captain Moyle Sherer, who was serving in Hill's division had recognized in the three columns of 'black enormous masses', in the glittering steel and clouds of dust, his first sight of a French army. (He had previously served in India.) Thoughts of Boney's invasion camp at Boulogne, of Italy overrun, of Austerlitz, of Jena flooded his mind. Suddenly he heard a loud, deep voice issuing orders:

'If they attempt this point again, Hill, you will give them a volley, and charge with bayonets; but don't let your people follow them too far down the hill.'

The style of this order—'so decided, so manly'—was just what Sherer needed. It filled him with confidence, leaving him in '*no doubt*' that he and his comrades would repulse any attack. Yet at the same time Lord Wellington's manner was simplicity itself, without a touch of bludgeoning or bombast:

> He has nothing of the truncheon about him; nothing foul-mouthed, important, or fussy: his orders on the field are all short, quick, clear, and to the purpose.

Just as the French hat appeared aloft, Leith, having covered the last stretch of the lateral road at the double, advanced on to the plateau with his 9th and 38th formed into line and waving his own plumed hat in answering defiance. Rolling volleys tore into Foy's column, Foy himself was wounded, and another chaotic mass of fugitives, sweeping along with them Heudelet's survivors, again streamed down to the bottom of the mountain and the shelter of their guns.

Marshal Ney meanwhile had seen through the thinning mist Merle's first *voltigeurs* crowning the heights. This was his signal to launch his VIth Corps from Moura, and after capturing Sula opposite him, to rush the paved road to the Convent so that Wellington would be caught in both front and rear. General Loison marched out with twelve fresh battalions against the north-eastern face of the mountain, between two wooded ravines. Inexorably they pushed a tough force of 1,400 British and Portuguese Rifles (*Caçadores*) out of Sula, and then climbed on towards two targets high above them, Ross's battery of twelve guns and the round, white, Allied command-post, Sula Mill. The British general who held this post was Robert Craufurd of the Light Division. Black Bob sat his big charger on a narrow plateau in front of the guns, a little man in a huge saddle with a loud, strident voice, soon to be heard.

Twenty yards from the top the French prepared to run in upon the guns. But Ross's artillery, having duly expended their last shot, galloped off to the rear. In their place, drawn up by Wellington on the Sula road behind Craufurd's solitary figure and totally invisible even to the front ranks of climbers below, nearly 1,800 infantry of the 52nd and 43rd (Light Division) waited, motionless and silent. Suddenly Craufurd swept off his hat and sent his great voice clanging among the rocks. 'Now, Fifty-Second! Avenge the death of Sir John Moore!' The echoes rolled back to him. 'Charge! charge!' he shouted. 'Huzza!' In a moment, 'eighteen hundred British bayonets went sparkling over the brow of the hill'. William Napier's thrilling words must find a place in any story of Bussaco, even though they managed to associate an unutterably horrible charge with the haunting beauty of a Wordsworthian waterfall. The Napier brothers were there to see the awful tornado of bullets, discharged at ten paces, slice off the heads of the leading French columns, while broad tongues of fire curled round their flanks. Down, down into the valley, sprawling and slithering over boulders streaming with blood, went thousands of Napoleon's soldiers the fourth time that day. Yet for this cruelly exposed army, four times was not enough.

Three-quarters of an hour after his 1st Division had started, Ney sent in eleven more battalions under General Marchand on the left of the two ravines. To them, at least, an easy victory seemed assured, for only four battalions, and these all Portuguese, faced them on the summit. They knew nothing of what a small nation in arms, inspired by Wellington and organized by Beresford, could do. Its young soldiers delivered a fire as steady and deadly as its veteran British allies. For all his resolution Marchand had to retreat from an impossible enterprise. Two hours later his troops were all back on the Moura foothills.

Massena's first trial of the despised Portuguese army and its leopard partners had resulted in 4,600 French losses to 626 British and 626 Portuguese—an exact Allied sharing of casualties as of valour. Wellington had resoundingly beaten the man he was afterwards to consider Napoleon's ablest general. 'Soult was not the ablest general ever opposed to me,' he said to Stanhope; 'the ablest after Napoleon was, I think, Massena.' And to Samuel Rogers: 'When Massena was opposed to me, in the field, I never slept comfortably.' But Wellington could have slept comfortably in Bussaco Convent, with Massena so grossly miscalculating the three forces opposed to him—brown uniforms, scarlet uniforms and grey granite. He was soon to meet all three again.

*   *   *

What happened next day was scarcely surprising, since part of the 'old fox's' army was still untouched. Wellington heard on 28 September that his left flank had been turned in the defiles north of Bussaco. Though in private he hotly blamed the Portuguese commander who had failed to get Colonel Trant's troops into the passes in time, the blow was to prestige rather than strategy. Though ready at any moment to go on the offensive according to the fortunes of war, he had envisaged an ultimate withdrawal into the heart of the fortress that was Portugal—now ready and waiting to receive him. There he would stand and defy the French invaders until, in good time, he was strong enough to push them out. A great victory, such as Bussaco had been, was an uncovenanted blessing. It would hearten the politicians, British and Portuguese. It would also give the Portuguese troops, in Wellington's words:

> a taste for an amusement to which they were not before accustomed; & which they could not have acquired if I had not put them in a very strong position.

But victory had never been counted upon to hold up Massena beyond the Mondego indefinitely. On the evening of 28 September Wellington resumed his retreat.

With Bussaco as brightly lit by deceptive camp fires as it had been dark the night before, Wellington's first troops slipped away past Penacova and its ruined Moorish castle at the southernmost tip of the ridge, and marched out on to the Coimbra road. Behind him on the mountain he had left 400 French wounded to be cared for by the Prior, an olive tree in the Convent garden planted with his own hands, and a legend of Anglo-Portuguese glory which has not yet disappeared. His look-out point, now shut in by plantations, is marked by a flat, inscribed stone.

> *Posto de Comando do Marechal General Arthur*
> *Wellesley, Duque de Wellington Comandante em*
> *Chefe des forcas Anglo-Lusas na Batalha do*
> *Buçaco Travade em 27 de Setembro de 1810*

Two sail-less windmills, one by Moura and the other on Sula hill, carry plaques stating that they were the command-posts of Massena and Craufurd respectively. At the Sula gate outside the Convent park a tall obelisk has been raised topped by a glass star (switched on for the anniversary) and surrounded by a railing of cannon barrels standing on their muzzles. Nearby is the Chapel of Our Lady of Victory and a museum where maps, weapons and life-size models of the valiant Allied soldiers can be seen, all the Portuguese brown-eyed, all the British blue. For the Peninsula, such a wealth of historic memorials is both inspiring and surprising—until one remembers that 27 September 1810 was the coming-of-age of the Anglo-Portuguese army. In the splendidly fantastic palace (now a hotel) built beside the old Convent by a cousin of Queen Victoria, King Ferdinand II, huge battle scenes in blue and green tiles keep fresh the legend of 'Lord W'. Inside the cell where he slept for the last time on the night after his victory is a plaque to 'The Glorious General'; outside the door is a little coloured shrine depicting Paradise. His tree still holds out its olive branches to posterity.

*   *   *

The Allies went through Coimbra with the French at their heels. Massena wrongly expected to have them beaten and flying for their ships in a week. Wellington rightly believed he was making for safety, but he kept his secret still.

The citizens of wealthy Coimbra had failed to take the 'scorched earth' measures which the frontier towns had so heroically achieved. A torrent of wretched families loaded with baggage which should long ago have been removed or destroyed, struggled over the Mondego bridge with Wellington's army, while their abandoned houses flamed behind them. Terrified inmates of prisons and asylums, smelling the fires, screamed from barred windows to be let out. The British soldiers freed them, so that among the desperate horde which poured down the Lisbon road was a quota of murderers and madmen. Some of the victors of Bussaco made their own crazy contribution to the scene. Despite Wellington's incessant orders against plunder, one soldier staggered out of Coimbra laden with a huge gilt mirror. He and the mirror were hung up together on the roadside by the 'bloody Provost'—a ghastly confrontation. Other malefactors who

belonged to regiments which had particularly distinguished themselves at Bussaco were reprieved by Wellington.

Massena's army rampaged through the deserted city looting everything they could lay hands on, from rings on the fingers of corpses in
graveyards to the priceless scientific instruments in the University.
Though Ney tried to stop the sacking, Junot did not hesitate to help
himself. Finally Massena deposited in the city's hospital 5,000 of his
sick and wounded, leaving them to be guarded only by a few sailors
brought along, hopefully, to man the leopards' ships. Hardly had the
French army marched out to continue its depredations in the great
monastery of Alcobaça farther down the road, than a strong force of
Portuguese under Trant rushed in. Some of these unfortunate French
wounded paid dearly for the frustration of Trant's troops in the
passes north of Bussaco.

Besides losing his wounded, Massena lost his communications
with France. As he raced south the militia and *Ordenanza* closed in
behind him, sealing all the exits. His couriers could no longer get
through. The besieger was besieged; though he did not yet know it.
Nor did he yet know that when Wellington's army made their usual
day's march on 8 October 1810, they were in fact entering the Lines
of Torres Vedras. The leopard had been driven into the hills instead
of the sea. There was a great difference.

$$\ast \qquad \ast \qquad \ast$$

People at home reacted to recent events much as Wellington expected. William assured him on 27 October, 'Your Battle of Bussaco
is universally admired.' But in a letter to William of 4 October
Wellington had shown himself prepared for Talavera-type criticism:

> The Croakers about useless battles will attack me again about
> that of Busaco; notwithstanding that our loss was really trifling.

Many otherwise friendly newspapers veered wildly from defeatism
to frustrated optimism. Why had not Massena been annihilated? For
a whole month they kept the public 'in trembling expectation', as
Wellington put it, of an imminent Peninsular Armageddon to destroy
the tyrant for ever. Even William was deceived and waited for news of
another 'glorious victory' by every packet. He concluded that by 27

October the next battle had already been fought and rhapsodized over its probable results:

> If you conquer—Europe—the World may be saved. If you are defeated Portugal is lost—probably Spain—certainly Ireland most likely Great Britain—and the Continent must be Bonaparte's. Conquer them, and notwithstanding the habitual gratitude of the United Kingdom, you must be a second Marlboro'.

None of this was to budge Wellington an inch.

> I shall either fight a battle or not as I shall find it advantageous.

The Prince of Wales, still under the influence of the Opposition for a few months longer, gave the news a peculiarly nasty reception. 'I condole with you heartily, my dear lord, upon poor Arthur's retreat,' he sneered to Richard, who had arrived at Windsor bursting with family pride; 'Massena has quite outgeneralled him.'

Kitty also was to receive her share of Bussaco aftermath. Life as usual had not been treating her very well.

> *Tunbridge Wells. August 27th* . . . wasted a great deal of time in arranging my flowers. No letters. Walked with my Children, which I find very fatiguing: they stop and turn and look at everything. . . .
> *September 18th* . . . I never saw a less inviting residence than Brighton [the Prince of Wales's Pavilion].

His Royal Highness's taste in houses, she decided, was 'not manly'.

She tried reading *Letters from a Spaniard*, Robert Southey's anonymous work, but found its critical tone smacked too much of Arthur's implacable enemy, Cobbett. So she read aloud Scott's *Lady of the Lake* to her mother and went to a book auction in the Pantiles, Tunbridge Wells's fashionable arcade, where she bought Spenser and Milton. On 4 October, while Arthur was describing to William his difficult operations against Massena, Kitty wrote in her journal: 'am now going to the most difficult of all operations, sitting for my picture'. Lady Longford, Kitty's mother, showed the finished portrait to Miss Edgeworth who commented: 'Lady Wellington is not like: it is absurd to attempt to draw Lady Wellington's face; she has no *face*, it is all countenance.' Kitty left Tunbridge Wells on the

13th after getting up at the unheard of hour of 7 A.M., packing before breakfast and hurrying to the Pantiles to buy her boys 'two more rabbits'. Having a good conscience, for once, may have helped her to face the shocks awaiting her in London.

London. October 13th. After a sick journey we arrived in town, where I found a letter which has indeed most deeply wounded me. No matter—I was originally to blame, but I think I could have felt more forgiveness, more indulgence: it is now, however, at an end for ever.

Wellington's wounding letter was mercifully destroyed. But from Kitty's remarks it is clear that something had again raised in his mind the sad affair of her housekeeping money. What could it have been? Wellington was writing just before Bussaco. He would have given directions in case he did not return. Among them was possibly some financial arrangement which would prevent poor Kitty, as a widow, from repeating her offence. Whatever it was, the antidote arrived next day.

October 14th. A very wretched night. Certainly gave no presentiment of the happiness which this day was to bring. My Husband and brothers safe and victorious, thank Almighty God.

The weeks after Bussaco were again trying.

October 23rd . . . I do not know for what reason I feel such terrible oppression every evening after dinner. I fell asleep, hardly woke to make tea and remained in a kind of stupor all evening. . . . No intelligence since that of the 13th: this is indeed an anxious time.

A few days later she screwed herself up to reply to Arthur.

October 26th . . . Wrote a most painful letter.

At the end of the month she gave General Nightingall, who was going out to Portugal, some shirts for Arthur, and to a soldier's wife and child who had just returned home from Portugal, money and flannel.

Her story, the gratitude and regard she expressed for my Husband, went to my heart.

Kitty's oppression was increased by the pitiful death of young Princess Amelia from consumption, which affected the King's reason beyond recall and urgently raised the question of a Regency. Kitty wrote on 3 November:

> He is worse to-day. What will become of this Kingdom? No news yet from Portugal. This prolonged anxiety is very, very wearing.
> *November 11th* ... The desperate dejection, which has oppressed me for some days past, will destroy me. I must pray for a calmer mind. ...

Like everyone else, Kitty was daily expecting news of another battle. While struggling for calm, however, she received a message during dinner to say that up to 1 November no battle had been fought. She contrived to turn this good news into yet another tearful scene:

> On first reading the note I imagined that a Battle had taken place and was indeed much agitated. Never, never shall I forget the feeling expressed for me by my Children, my little Arthur who was nearest to me, held me in his arms. Charles, who had been moved to a greater distance, in the most melancholy voice cried out, 'I am too far from you, Mama.'

Perhaps it was inevitable that Kitty should batten on tenderness when she found it. But the situation augured ill for her great Arthur, who would some day return and have to break into this magic circle. After more days of idleness, enlivened only by the news that Henry Wellesley's divorced wife had married her lover, Lord Paget—'What a complication of infamy & vice!'—Kitty decided yet again to turn over a new leaf.

> *November 30th.* As my object in writing this journal is merely that I may know exactly in what manner I have been occupied ... while my Husband is engaged abroad, I must not again forget to write each day.

She could have got her parallel into one sentence. They were each enclosed, she by deadly depression, he behind his immortal Lines.

*   *   *

Among the many captured documents brought to Wellington's camp after Bussaco were Massena's despatches taken off a French officer making his way to Paris disguised as a Spanish peasant. One paper consisted of a question and answer prepared by Massena to assist the officer through an awkward interview with Napoleon's chief-of-staff.

Q. What is the spirit of the French army?

A. Good, particularly after the manoeuvre of the General-in-Chief [Massena himself] who turned the enemy's position. . . .

Q. Do you think you will get to Lisbon?

A. Everything makes us hope so; the English being in full retreat, and the French full of confidence in their General-in-Chief.

Massena did indeed expect to reach Lisbon within a week. Nevertheless, if Wellington had been asked, 'Do you think you will halt Massena short of Lisbon?' he would have answered with better reason, 'Everything makes us hope so.'

One of the propitious things was the rain. It started, as if symbolically, on 8 October, the very day that Wellington began to shepherd his long files, two by two, into their Ark. In a few days the rains would turn streams into rivers, rivers into torrents. Like Noah, he had hit off precisely the right moment.[2]

The entry into the Lines of Torres Vedras on that first day went as smoothly as a machine.

Not that these so-called 'lines' greatly resembled the continuous lengths of stone wall or earthworks which might at first spring to mind. The Lines of Torres Vedras were essentially groups of hill-forts commanding all highways and passes to Lisbon. Yet though this is broadly true, it misses their full subtlety; for where the scarping[3] of long mountain ranges provided continuous barriers, the Lines were indeed lines.

Each contingent was met and led to its appointed defence post. By evening many progress reports had reached Wellington. Picton, for instance, wrote that he had entered Torres Vedras itself, the town which was to give its name to the whole defence system.

2. One British soldier made a small ark of his own against the torrential downpour, a barrel in which he slept on the mountainside. The first time he turned over it bounded with him to the bottom.

3. Scooping away earth to make a more or less perpendicular rampart.

Torres Vedras—the old towers—was one of the most ancient towns of Portugal. It had its river, the Zizandre, its aqueduct, its Moorish castle high on a hill and on another hill opposite, at the top of a serpentine road, the fourth-century Chapel of St Vincent. Its inhabitants were employed on the military works. All trees which might give cover to the French invader were felled and the wood used for revetting (facing) gun embrasures and ditches, while the tops of the trees formed *abattis*—twig entanglements on forward slopes. The Moorish castle had become Redoubt No. 27 in Wellington's total of 152 forts. And the little Chapel of St Vincent was inside a perimeter wall a mile long containing three separate redoubts, Nos. 20, 21 and 22, protected by a dry ditch ten feet deep and linked by wide roads and scientifically placed parapets and breastworks for the use of the garrison. Redoubt 20, where the Chapel's dome mingled incongruously with Battery 1, with two mills converted into powder magazines and a signalling post, was the largest and most important of the three. It lay at the fort's eastern end and covered the western road from the north into Lisbon, a road which gave Torres Vedras its strategic value. Five thousand troops were stationed here and the silhouettes of other forts could be seen on the skyline. Some of the hills had odd rectangular contours, where detachments of the 10,000 peasants employed by Colonel Fletcher had scarped them into formidable barriers. To the west, around the flat Zizandre estuary, wide inundations glittered and gleamed over the marshes. But for all its elaboration and fame, the first line of fortifications of which Torres Vedras formed a part, was not the strongest of Wellington's five.[4] Running for twenty-nine miles from the sea coast to the Tagus at Alhandra, it was originally intended only to hold up Massena until the army could fall back into the impregnable defences of the second line behind.

This second chain of fortifications extending for twenty-two miles from the coast to the Tagus, was roughly parallel to the first but began six miles to the south. Even on a still, thundery day the surf below the westernmost fort of all, No. 97, ran far out to sea in milky bars and came boiling into narrow ravines between inaccessible cliffs. No enemy could land here, but there was an estuary not far off. Therefore here, high up above the Chapel of the Senhora do Porto, among stunted gorse and juniper, thistles and rock rose, Fletcher's

4. Five, counting the defences on the left bank of the Tagus estuary in case of a French attack from the south.

peasants had hacked out a ditch, scarp, counter-scarp and traverse, with gun embrasures for many batteries covering the estuary and Ericeira just up the coast. Every few moments came a defiant boom from the sea; the redoubt's own guns could boom in cross-fire with Forts 96 and 95, the latter being another Torres Vedras on a small scale.

Fort 95 stood on an S-bend in the Mafra road, at the head of a great valley scarped into a deep moat. Where there should have been a few sparse fields of maize and potatoes there was a long ditch with high counter-scarp and again room for plenty of cannon. A tunnel with a wide masonry arch, securely revetted, joined the infantry above to the artillery below. The gigantic pile of Mafra itself still 'shot its gilded cupolas to the sky', as Dr Neale remembered, but it had become an entrenched camp. Twenty redoubts bristled with guns round the *tapada* (royal park). Between Mafra and the Tagus many hills were 'already Maginot' (to quote a modern Portuguese historian, Colonel Eduardo Francisco Baptista of the Engineers) before Wellington came, in particular nature's prodigious masterpiece of the Pass of Montachique. From the pinnacles of its enormous crags Neale had surveyed the 'lunar mountains of Cintra' and all the rugged pattern of 'scorched rocks' relieved by lustrous orange orchards. Now the orchards were scorched too, and the pass was ringed by a dozen ingenious redoubts, each different, to suit the terrain, but each with its similar cross-fire to control another of the north–south roads to Lisbon. The second line wound on eastwards, with a thick knot of forts at the next pass, Bucelas, until it reached the green Tagus valley where there were rice-fields, salt-pans and breeding grounds for bulls and tiny red dragon-flies. At the end of this line a strong group of redoubts had established a potent cross-fire with Admiral Berkeley's gun-boats on the river. Stone traverses were needed in these forts to protect each garrison—between three and four hundred men— from stray naval shells. A French cavalry officer, General Saint Croix, was not so lucky. A shell from the Tagus severed his head. He was one of the best generals and his men reported that he went galloping on without it.

And so southwards again to the third line. An embarkation point in case of dire necessity was the real purpose here, and the third line centred on two miles of shore round Fort St Julian, in the Tagus estuary between Lisbon and the sea. This was also the main landing-place for the army's and population's food. Everyone, including

Wellington, preferred to emphasize the latter aspect of the third line. Too much activity at Lisbon tended to cause panic in Portugal, especially among the rich, who aimed to leave not later than the leopards.

*   *   *

Back in the first of Wellington's lines the entry of troops continued throughout 8, 9 and 10 October, according to plan. General Lowry Cole was in Sobral by the 9th. On the same day Colonel George Murray of Hill's division was ordered to fall back from Arruda of the Wines, a once cheerful village full of fountains and floral friezes, past the euphemistically named Mill of Heaven, the huge powder magazine of Redoubt No. 17 on a hill crest, to the thickly fortified hills above Alhandra at the far eastern end. At Alhandra, Moyle Sherer's men were cantonned in the sacristy of a church. Finding their cloaks and blankets too wet to use, they wrapped themselves in vestments. From Alhandra Tom Sheridan, aged seventeen, asked permission to serve as a volunteer with his brother in the 57th; Wellington simply wrote across his request in thick pencil, 'Granted'.

Still on the same day General Sontag of the King's German Legion took over from Picton in Torres Vedras. Sontag did not approve of quite all Wellington's plans. The Portuguese militiamen in the fortress, he complained, did not understand their weapons, while their officers, mostly Lisbon shopkeepers, though personally willing to do everything in their power, would fall back at the first shot.

Sontag had in fact blundered into uninformed criticism of his chief's cardinal principle in manning the Lines. Wellington rejected static defence in favour of maximum mobility. To achieve his object, Portuguese militiamen were drafted into all his forts, thus freeing almost his entire regular army to circulate among the hills in two main masses, right and centre, and to move rapidly to any threatened spot. The fact that his redoubts formed independent knots or ganglions without Roman- or Chinese-type linking walls, added to his army's mobility. Mobility plus scorched earth were the distinguishing features of the whole Torres Vedras system.

A few days later Sontag was sorry to have to report that the midshipman who put up the telegraph in Redoubt 20 had not got the signal book so could not explain how it worked; the midshipman at

Sobral was in the same predicament. Could Wellington send for the book from Mafra immediately?[5]

Queries flowed in from all over the Lines about bread, reinforcements, cavalry support, when to destroy bridges, how to replace soldiers' clothes falling to pieces in the deluge of rain. Wellington replied to everything like a father reassuring an agitated family. Across one of Sontag's moans about the Portuguese militia he wrote in his habitual thick, rather illegible pencil for the attention of the military secretary, James Bathurst:

Tell him that I will attend to the enemy's movements & take care to have troops sufficient in any quarter likely to be attacked; & that I am responsible that the troops I lead in any situation are of a sufficiently good description and sufficiently numerous to defend their fort; & to do what I require of them.

They had Wellington and that was sufficient.

By 10 October 1810 the Allied army was all inside the Lines, apart from cavalry patrols. It was from one of these patrols, captured near Alenquer, that the French cavalry commander, Montbrun, received a puzzling piece of news. They had been on their way back, said the British prisoners, to 'the Lines'. The Lines? It was the first Montbrun, or any other Frenchman, had heard of them.

On the 12th Massena's vanguard, leaving General Sontag undisturbed in Torres Vedras, drove in Wellington's outposts at Sobral. Wellington at once withdrew his forces from the village to the place appointed for them three miles to the south—the immensely strong, fortified camp on the heights of Monte Agraço, a fastness towering above all other mountains in the Torres Vedras peninsula.

He had had one of his paved roads built from the foot of the mountain to the series of redoubts on its crest—a long, steep, straight road made of rectangular stones about twelve inches by four, between low walls to prevent his ox-carts from falling over the edges. Of the four redoubts, Fort 14 was the main work and contained 1,590 infantry, fourteen twelve-pounders, six nine-pounders, four six-pounders and one howitzer. Forts 15–17 were advanced works requiring rather fewer men and cannon but two howitzers each.

5. Some of the signals were not exactly drawn up with Torres Vedras in mind. 'I have sprung my bowsprit but cannot fix it at sea' (*Wellington MSS* and S. G. P. Ward, *Wellington's Headquarters*, p. 126).

From the top, looking to the left, a chapel standing on a nearby eminence, the Pero Negro, marked Wellington's headquarters. Looking due north could be seen the white houses of Sobral where the French, in turn, sat looking at Monte Agraço. This was where Wellington decided to make his stand. This was where he hoped Massena would launch his second Bussaco.

This also happened to be where Massena discovered what the captured cavalry patrol had meant by 'the Lines'. On 14 October, the day that Massena at last arrived himself at Sobral, Junot overran some light defences at the foot of Monte Agraço—and suddenly laid bare the hidden strength behind. He retired to Sobral and informed Massena.

That old fox wanted no second Bussaco. Instead he gave a rocket to the stupid officers who had not told him about the Lines. When he asked them why, they replied lamely, 'Wellington has made them.' 'The devil,' shouted Massena, 'Wellington didn't make the mountains!'

So Massena had to do what Wellington did always: get upon his horse and see for himself. On that same 14 October he made an extensive reconnaissance ending with a symbolic incident. Towards the eastern end of the Lines stood Fort 120 on a long, scarped ridge above Bulhaco. It was only a small fort with two twelve-pounders and 130 men. But someone inside was alert enough to notice Massena, followed at a distance by an imposing staff, standing on a low hill by the village of Cotovios, leaning his telescope on a wall. A warning shot was fired. Massena recognized the '*Non Ultra*' sign, raised his hat ironically and rode off.[6]

Massena re-entered Sobral merely to sit down for a month and await reinforcements. Wellington and his officers were much disappointed. To cheer them and the leading Lisbon citizens, he gave a 'grand Ball, previous dinner, and concluding supper' at Mafra on the occasion of Beresford being created Knight of the Bath. Edward Pakenham agreed that to indulge in such 'an amusement' with 50,000 of the enemy a few miles off might seem like 'madness', but on the contrary, it was only another example of 'the comprehensive

6. J. T. Jones (*Sieges*, vol. III, p. 34) points out that if the Allies had wanted to kill Massena they would have used one of their cannon. Jones had been much shocked at Bussaco when Massena, seeing Wellington on the ridge after the battle, thanking his troops, ordered the French to fire at him.

mind of Wellington'. The Mafra ball had given confidence to the
capital and pride to the Portuguese army—'*Viva!!!*'

Ned's '*Viva*' was not misplaced. For when the French turned
back from Monte Agraço on 14 October 1810 the tide of French
conquest in Europe turned also. The skirmish at the foot of the
mountain had caused only sixty-seven Allied and 120 French
casualties. Such a limited action; such prodigious results.

Sickness among Massena's troops, besides acute shortage of all
supplies, soon made a further retreat necessary. Taking advantage of
a blanketing fog during the night of 14 November (exactly a month
after the skirmish of Sobral) Massena's army silently decamped.
They left a line of straw dummies with shakos on poles to look like
sentries opposite Craufurd's outposts at Arruda. Craufurd informed
Wellington. As soon as the fog cleared, at 10 A.M., Wellington climbed
Sobral hill to see for himself. There was nothing at all. Massena had
retreated into lines of his own thirty miles away, beyond Santarém,
without having to fire a shot. Who was the Child of Fortune now?

For a few days Wellington attempted a pursuit. On 24 November
he called it off, leaving Marshal Massena to be dealt with by General
Starvation. He had no doubt in his own mind (mistakenly as it
happened) that another few weeks would see Massena out. He himself was not short of teasing problems, present and future; and if he
had been too weak to attack Junot at Sobral, he would feel even more
impotent against Massena at Santarém.

*   *   *

No less than for Massena, reinforcements were a major problem for
Wellington. The fact that sitting down in the Lines caused nearly all
his generals to ask for leave, did not help matters. An angry conviction grew in his mind that the Government's failure to reinforce
him, or to settle arrears of army pay, was due to lack of confidence
in his Peninsular campaign. Lord Liverpool, he told William, was
'dabbling in a game separate from that to be played in this country'
and had never acted on any 'broad or liberal principle of confidence'
towards him; indeed he had lately sent out a liaison officer of his
own, so that the Commander-in-Chief was 'cut off entirely'. Even his
request to '*borrow* 10,000 Men from England and Ireland' had been
refused. When England herself was invaded, 'we shall heartily repent
all the little dirty feelings which have prevented us from continuing

the contest elsewhere'. He had pressed Liverpool for Government changes to strengthen it. This had only annoyed the War Minister. Yet, concluded Wellington gloomily, as soon as the Prince of Wales became Regent, he would 'change everything'. In other words, he would bring in his friends the Whigs, who would promptly withdraw the army and leave the Peninsula to Napoleon.

This unusually violent spasm of croaking at headquarters was duly allayed by William's soothing mediation—'I have positive proof that the whole Cabinet have the most unbounded confidence in you as a General'—and by the march of events. When the Government at last passed a Regency Bill on 5 February 1811, those Tories, like young Palmerston, who were ruefully saying, 'We are all on the kick and go,' were proved wrong. The Prince Regent turned against the Whigs. William gleefully reported 'chop fallen faces' among the Opposition, 'who were all cock-a-hoop before'. Portugal would not be abandoned.

As for Wellington's generals and their eternal requests for leave, this problem was temporarily solved by news that the French had received reinforcements in December and Loison had got 'beastly drunk' toasting 'Lisbon in Twelve days'. Ned wrote to Tom Longford: 'The arrival of this reinforcement brought back all our fliting [*sic*] Generals. . . . *Viva*!' Wellington nevertheless sent a stern message to Colonel Torrens at the War Office:

> I shall be very much obliged to you . . . if you would tell any General officer who may come out in future to settle all his business before he comes out, for that he will get no leave to go home.

Of the generals who had neither gone home nor were 'fliting' to Lisbon, at least two were childishly at loggerheads by November, Picton and Leith. Each denounced the other for falsely claiming the glory of Bussaco. Picton informed Wellington it was all due to the gallantry of the 88th and 45th; Leith put it all down to the coolness and spirit of the 38th and 9th. Wellington was probably not sorry for once when Leith requested two months' leave, after a return of Walcheren fever.

*   *   *

Fevers of a different kind still raged in the Portuguese Regency Council. It is not easy to see exactly why relations between Wellington and the Sousas remained so bad for so long, despite some obvious reasons for friction. The Sousas, a great city family, were not able to persuade every peasant to carry out the scorched earth policy.[7] The French found some mills with sails still on and grain hidden instead of burnt. They were able to subsist in Portugal for longer than Wellington had calculated. From the other angle, scorched earth meant scarred people. Despite all efforts to feed the refugees, fifty thousand died of hunger behind the Lines, munching the yellow thistles which grew among the redoubts. It was a large number out of a population of two and a half million. And what were they suffering for? Wellington's 'cautious system' or 'defensive system', as he himself called it, did not at first seem worth such sacrifices. Finally, there appears to have been some religious and political distrust, which still finds an echo in Portugal today.

The Sousas naturally abhorred all anti-clericals from Liberals to Freemasons, especially the latter who had been instituted in Portugal by the French invaders with the help of Marshal Lannes and afterwards Junot. Wellington found this out almost too late. Enormous scandal was caused by his officers staging their customary masonic activities while in Lisbon. One procession in particular, of January 1810, narrowly escaped being shot at and stoned. Wellington at once issued a General Order requiring his officers to refrain from

> an amusement which, however innocent in itself, and allowed by the law of Great Britain, is a violation of the law of this country, and very disagreeable to the people.

Unfortunately the Portuguese were under the impression (and still are) that Wellington himself was a Freemason in more than a purely technical sense. This was a mistake. True, he had been initiated at Trim Lodge as a very young man. He never went near that or any other Lodge again. At first this was probably because of the close links between the French Revolution and Continental Freemasonry. Later on he developed a powerful antipathy to anything and everything which might conceivably be regarded as a secret or subversive society.

From this point of view both Methodist preachers and Catholic

7. Half of Portugal, from the frontier westwards, was, in a way, trained to carry out the scorched earth policy, through centuries of bickering with the Spaniards. The people living by the coast were not.

priests were suspect. They might do the soldiers good; but they served societies within Society, tempting soldiers to divide their allegiance. His troops were forbidden to enter Catholic churches during Mass except to take part in the service; he was well satisfied to learn that none attended. To 'get the better of Methodism' he mainly relied on his favourite young chaplain, the Rev. Samuel Briscall, whose personal example would strengthen 'true religion'.[8] Wellington realized the matter was delicate. But he felt he must warn his staff, as he did in a letter to General Calvert on 6 February 1811. After all, Methodism, if only in the form of one meeting a week, was already alive in the Guards, and the thought of Methodist privates exhorting their officers to lead more virtuous lives was not altogether reassuring.

> The meeting of soldiers in their cantonments to sing psalms, or hear a sermon read by one of their comrades, is, in the abstract, perfectly innocent; and it is a better way of spending their time than many others to which they are addicted; but it may become otherwise....

As with Freemasonry, so with Orange societies, anti-Reform clubs and of course all left-wing associations in the future—they were either dangerous or unnecessary and therefore slightly unconstitutional; however innocent at present, they might 'become otherwise'. The Freemasons were to persist throughout Wellington's life in trying to attach the lustre of his name to their cause. They received many a brusque rebuff for their pains. It would have saved the Regency Council much anxiety if they had comprehended Wellington's unusual but quite consistent principles.

Wellington's own dislike for the Sousas, whom he referred to

8. Samuel Briscall (1788–1848), head of the chaplains' department in Wellington's army; Wellington's domestic chaplain, 1814; afterwards curate of Stratfield Saye from 1819 to 1836. He died as chaplain to the garrison at Chatham.

The Methodists had to wait for their chaplains to the forces until 1881 and the Jews until 1892; the Roman Catholics got theirs in 1836. (See Sir John Smyth, V.C., *In This Sign Conquer*).

During the year 1811 the position of Church of England chaplains in Wellington's army fell to rock bottom. One modern authority says he had only one. There were to be nine at Waterloo, headed by Briscall, thanks to Wellington's efforts.

predictably as 'these gentry' never got much beyond colourful language. 'Nothing can be worse than Principal Sousa,' he wrote to Admiral Berkeley on 27 October 1810; and on the same day to Lord Liverpool, 'I hope that Lord Wellesley [still Foreign Secretary] will relieve me from Principal Souza [sic]. I cannot act with that gentleman. . . .' Yet he did. Having tried and failed to get rid of Admiral Berkeley he had accepted a bad job and settled down to work with him. Something of the same kind happened with the Sousas. Both the furious bark and the philosophical decision not to bite too hard, were typical of Wellington. Moreover in this case every one was deeply aware at bottom of fighting for the same cause.

*   *   *

Christmas Day 1810 in the Lines. Fog as usual. A message from Craufurd's advance post, the same one that had come almost every day for weeks said that it was too thick to see anything but the sentries, though 'the Drums were heard as usual'. As usual, desertions. Two men from the Brunswick Corps went over to the French, while two boys, one a scullion in Soult's house, deserted to the Allies. Then there were invitations from the French in Santarém to watch amateur theatricals, invitations from the English to watch football and horse-racing. A message from General Graham in Spain, on the 28th: the new Congreve rockets were no good. They had tried to shell the enemy's flotilla but 'tho' the shells and Congreve rockets went home, the boats sustained no injury'. Wellington was not surprised. He had come across rockets in India where they had not saved Tipoo from defeat. But he insisted on giving them a fair trial in the Peninsula.

The French were hungry, as usual; but not yet hungry enough.

*   *   *

New Year's Day 1811 in London. Kitty's journal seemed to echo the muted atmosphere of an advanced post in the Lines: all listening and waiting. Yet the journal was not quite as usual. There was a new note of asperity. At least it showed that she had some spirit. Unfortunately there was no guarantee that she would not use it against Arthur's friends when he came home.

January 1st . . . Lady Liverpool kindly asked me to spend the day with her. I did so: the company a set of stupid Lords who were anything but pleasant. I behaved very ill and expressed what I thought of them.

Next day Lady Olivia Sparrow and Lady Hood, wife of the Admiral, visited her.

Olivia & Lady Hood taken separately are extremely agreeable, together are perfect Romps.

The state of Lady Hood's room, she added later, was like that of an untidy girl. With Kitty's censoriousness went social timidity.

January 17th . . . Dined at 5 o'clock with Olivia, with the intention of going to Astley's in the evening but finding there was a probability of Ld. Wellington's name being introduced, I did not wish to encounter the public gaze. Returned home when they went.

An evening at Mrs William Wellesley-Pole's would have been 'very pleasant if there had been less of the Harpsichord'. She tried dining with old Opposition friends, but it was no good. 'I felt myself a restraint upon every mouth in the room.' A party at General Stuart's was no better.

Immediately after dinner the Ladies retired to their rooms till a few minutes before the gentlemen came up, tip-top quality breeding!

Then came a worse set-back—more criticism from Arthur.

March 12th. At last my letters are arrived and, if I have not done all that was expected of me, at least what I have done was not wrong. Must try to make up my mind to repeated disappointments.

When Arthur was kind Kitty was suspicious.

February 7th. . . . Lady Liverpool brought me a shawl from Ld. W. I hope it really was from him!

April began badly with everyone discussing the Peninsula and Kitty tongue-tied.

> *April 4th.* This is the day of Olivia's Ball: I do not go. I cannot bear the questions and observations to which I am subjected.
> *April 5th.* No news from Portugal.
> *April 13th.* Letters from Portugal: all well to the 27th. Spent the day at home alone. I will at last observe the advance of my Children, I will at last rise in tolerable time, I will at last keep resolutions so often repeated, so often broken.

Needless to say, Kitty's 'at last' was still a dream. Her journal broke off abruptly a week later and did not begin again for seventeen months. Something else, however, had actually happened—at last. On 5 March, in yet another dense fog, Massena struck camp and was off.

*   *   *

Suddenly everything moved fast again. The French had a start of thirty miles over Wellington, whose staff had given up all hope of Massena ever going. Indeed, but for a brave Portuguese having secretly crossed the misty River Mayor to warn the Allies of the French move, Massena's start might have been longer.

In the great race north, each commander had his difficulties. Massena's wretched army had been reduced to under 46,000 and even little luxuries for Madame X, such as sugar and coffee, had to be smuggled through the English lines. His corps commanders, especially Ney, were disloyal to a general-in-chief they no longer trusted. When there was a rumour (false) during the hectic retreat that Massena himself had been taken prisoner, Ney shouted, '*Pardieu! Tant mieux!*'

Wellington's soldiers were still plundering, and in January 1811 he had had to make a reasoned plea for a reform in the recruiting system, to get a better type of regular soldier.

> In respect to recruiting for the army, my own view is that the Government have never taken an enlarged view of the subject. It is expected that people will become soldiers in the line, and leave their families to starve, when if they become soldiers in the militia, their families are provided for.

What was the result of this inconsistency?

That none but the worst description of men enter the regular service.

Wellington's own 'enlarged view' was to transfer the family allowances from the militia to the regulars, presumably leaving the dependants of militiamen to starve instead; but this parsimoniousness was in deference to Lord Liverpool's lamentations about the country's financial plight.

Granted that Wellington's army was not perfect, it was improving as fast as Massena's deteriorated. 'We are becoming a more efficient and better army every day,' he wrote to Liverpool just before the pursuit began.[9]

A series of exciting rear-guard actions, in the course of which two of the gallant but accident-prone Napier brothers were wounded and either Massena or Ney was always in danger of being cut off, lasted until the middle of March. Up till then Massena had intended merely to break through into an unscorched district, and having pleasantly gorged himself there, to renew the march on Lisbon. Thanks to Trant's militia, however, and Wellington's tactical skill, Massena was manoeuvred away from the Mondego and forced to make a dash for the Spanish frontier.

On 15 March he gave the crucial order. All impedimenta including ammunition were flung away and pack-animals hamstrung. The pursuing Allies were reminded of Soult's ghastly retreat from Oporto, only this time it was far worse. Ravines, pits, ditches, huts and chapels revealed their sickening collections of skeletons and decomposing or fresh bodies, some of them half burnt or mangled by torture, to extract information about hidden food and wine. Certain French soldiers swore they could smell out caches of food; woe betide the peasant who failed to produce any, after one of these 'diviners' had begun snorting. 'Mothers were hung up with the children by their sides, and fires lighted below them,' wrote General Robert Long.

9. The change in the British Army was to be reflected in Maria Edgeworth's new novel, published 1812, *The Absentee*: 'The life of an officer is not now a life of parade, of coxcombical or of profligate idleness—but of active service . . . military exploits fill every day's newspaper, every day's conversation . . . in the present state of things, the military must be the most honourable profession, because the most useful. Every movement of an army is followed, wherever it goes, by the public hopes and fears.'

If Massena called the British 'barbarians' for their scorched earth policy, the British found that they were fighting against demons. Ned Pakenham described to his brother Tom on 16 March, in the midst of the pursuit, 'the acts of horror actually committed by these fiends of hell'. It seemed hardly possible that these were the same civilized Frenchmen who had once warned them, while still in the Lines, not to worry if they heard 101 cannon-shots: it would only be a *feu de joie* in honour of the birth of Napoleon's son, the King of Rome.

Despite Ney's defensive brilliance, Wellington felt so sure of victory by 20 March that he sent his troop-transports home. The front and back doors out of Portugal were thus voluntarily closed. Two days later Marshal Ney was sent involuntarily back to France. Massena had ordered a ludicrous swerve to the south against Placencia. Ney rightly called it madness and wrongly defied his superior. At 8 P.M. on that 22 March Massena asked:

'Please inform me whether you persist in refusing to obey my orders . . .?' At 9 P.M. Ney answered:

'I persist in refusing . . . .' At 10 P.M. Massena took away Ney's VIth Corps and gave it to Loison.

A week's agonizing tramp through barren mountains soon forced Massena to turn east again. On 3 April Reynier's IInd Corps narrowly escaped extinction at Sabugal on the River Coa. But for the fog on the battlefield and the denser fog in General Sir William Erskine's mind, the Light Division and cavalry would have taken the French in flanks and rear.[10] Even as it was they caused 760 French casualties to 179 of their own and according to Wellington, who was watching from a hill, they fought 'one of the most glorious actions British troops were ever engaged in'.

That night Massena ordered a general retreat on Ciudad Rodrigo, across the River Agueda. Five days later he and Madame X entered Salamanca, his base. The Governor gave a dinner in honour of Massena's aide-de-camp but ungallantly declined to pay his/her arrears or allowances. 'What a mistake I made,' admitted Massena at last, 'in taking a woman to the war.' Apart from this mistake, however, Massena's faults had really been Napoleon's. With an army of only 65,000, Napoleon had given him an impossible task. Portugal

10. Erskine temporarily commanded both cavalry and light infantry, their own generals, Cotton and Craufurd, being on leave. Erskine launched his troops at Sabugal in various directions but always the wrong ones.

could not be subdued by less than 100,000, as Wellington had always said. But since Napoleon insisted that there were never more than 30,000 leopards—Portuguese being a species of animal which he simply did not count—65,000 French soldiers seemed plenty. Considering these handicaps and the assistance of Madame X, Massena's extrication of his army from Portugal was a triumph of skill.

On 10 April 1811 Wellington issued a proclamation:

> The Portuguese are informed that the cruel enemy ... have been obliged to evacuate, after suffering great losses, and have retired across the Agueda. The inhabitants of the country are therefore at liberty to return to their homes.

Massena's 'great losses' amounted to 25,000; Wellington's to less than a sixth of that number.

*   *   *

From almost all sides applause rained down on Wellington. 'I now most heartily congratulate you,' wrote William on 8 April, 'on your astonishing success in driving Massena out of Portugal.' Everyone, even the Opposition, rejoiced 'except the *great* Genl. Tarleton who I understand says—It may yet turn out, that this may be a great manoeuvre of Massena's'.[11] On the same day young Hercules Pakenham gave the army's reaction: 'even in Retreat the Spirit of the Army was integer [unbroken]'; now its sentiments 'in respect to Lord W. cannot be expressed'. Three weeks later when a vote of thanks was passed by both Houses for Wellington's campaign, William felt Parliament had never been 'more unanimous'. Lord Grey was 'highly flattering', Ponsonby (another Whig leader) 'very handsome', Canning 'very complimentary'; Tarleton 'made a hobling [*sic*] recantation'. And miracle of miracles, costive old Sir David Dundas at the Horse Guards actually gave Wellington leave to *promote* six majors and twelve captains to the brevet rank of lieutenant-colonel and major respectively! Finally his old friend from India, Sir Thomas Munro, who had once criticized Sir Arthur for running risks at Assaye, fully approved his Portuguese campaign and Spanish

11. (*Raglan MSS*, No. 112) General Tarleton, M.P., veteran of the American War of Independence under Cornwallis, had been prominent in belabouring Arthur Wellesley over Cintra.

prospects in choice Anglo-Indian phrases. 'The Portuguese,' he wrote, 'must now be excellent sepoys,' while the Spanish guerillas, like the *polygars* (chieftains) of Bullum on a vast scale, would make Bonaparte's task in Spain 'herculean'.

Spain was already in Wellington's mind again. The Portuguese war represented the solid virtues of caution and economy of force by avoidance of big battles. Beside a battery whose gun embrasures framed the great white church of Alhandra far below, was to stand a monument to the Lines of Torres Vedras: a pillar surmounted by the figure of Hercules, with the inscription, NON ULTRA—*They Shall Not Pass*.

They did not pass. But there was more to it than that. After the retreat, the stand. After the stand, the advance. In the final advance against Massena, Wellington's army had shown a new talent of immense significance, manoeuvrability. On 8 April Wellington wrote to one of his engineers.

We have given the French a handsome dressing, and I think they will not say again that we are not a manoeuvring army. We may not manoeuvre so beautifully as they do, but I do not desire better sport than to meet one of their columns *en masse*, with our lines.

Did this mean that he was ready to risk big battles in the open at last? He had predicted exactly a month earlier: 'the war is now likely to take on a new shape . . .'.

14 The Keys of Spain

The new shape of war demanded radical changes in Spain. Without a secure hold on its two border fortresses of Ciudad Rodrigo and Badajoz, Wellington's war could never become properly offensive.

Up till the beginning of March 1811 the Spaniards at least held Badajoz, though under siege by Soult. But there had been bad Spanish omens ever since the uniquely dependable General Romana died in January: 'His loss is the greatest which the cause could sustain,' wrote Wellington sombrely. Only a few days later the cause had to sustain a second shock when the Governor of Badajoz was killed while making a sortie. Well aware of the fortress's increasing peril, Wellington despatched Beresford on 8 March to its relief. When Beresford arrived, it was to besiege Badajoz not to succour it. For the treacherous new Governor, José Imaz, surrendered it to Soult on the 11th. In Wellington's bitter words, Badajoz had been 'sold'.

It was true there was some good Spanish news. General Sir Thomas Graham, that hearty, honest Scot, had made Spain ring with a great victory over the French at Barrosa on 5 March.[1] The 'tremulous' behaviour, however, of his Spanish colleague General Lapena, nick-named 'Lady Manuel', had defrauded his ardent troops of their share in the triumph. Nevertheless Barrosa had taught the French a lesson. 'They will find out some time or other ' wrote Pakenham cheerfully, 'the Johneys [*sic*] can fight a trifle.' How were the Spaniards to be trained to fight like the Johnnies?

The answer to this and most other Spanish problems, thought Henry Wellesley at Cádiz, was to 'make Arthur Generalissimo'. Once the Spanish army had been disciplined and equipped by Britain, he told Richard as early as January 1811, 'I am persuaded that in a year there would not be a Frenchman in the Peninsula.' A loan of ten millions to the Cortes should do the trick.

1. Thomas Graham, Lord Lynedoch (1748–1843). A liberal-minded, gallant old warrior whose talents were not of the highest order but were entirely devoted to the public service. For a time he was Wellington's second-in-command.

Arthur agreed; but Henry was foiled by three awkward facts. General Blake, a Spaniard of Irish descent whom Henry described as very popular because he had won one battle and lost only seventeen, was desperately jealous. Richard had forfeited all influence with the Cabinet, so that the slogan 'Arthur for Generalissimo' received no powerful backing at home. On the contrary, Lord Liverpool, as War Minister, was aghast at the idea of heaping a Spanish loan on top of the unpopular Portuguese subsidy. After marshalling a dozen arguments against Henry's plan, he ended as usual by leaving everything to Wellington's 'discretion'. With deep disgust Wellington drew William's attention to the carping terms and spirit of Liverpool's letter—and then let the matter of his Spanish command drop. The problem of Badajoz could not be dropped so easily.

*   *   *

As soon as Massena had been driven back into northern Spain, Wellington decided to see for himself how Beresford was proceeding in the south. With only a staff officer or two for company, he rode off at a tearing pace on 16 April, leaving Sir Brent Spencer behind in charge. Ned Pakenham reflected the disturbed feelings of the army at this event:

> The change of leaders is very different indeed; Sir Brent Spencer has charge of this Corps, and is as good a fellow as possible to meet at a County Club, but as to succeeding Wellington it is quite Damnation to him. . . .

The northern army expected to have to fight Massena at any moment without Wellington in command. The Portuguese fortress of Almeida, standing opposite to Spanish Ciudad Rodrigo, was the only Portuguese territory still in French hands. Its garrison was on the verge of starvation. Massena would clearly make a return dash into Portugal to save Almeida and his own reputation at the eleventh hour. Napoleon himself had given him a broad hint. 'The Emperor hopes that you will soon find an opportunity to take a striking revenge.' Pakenham sincerely trusted that in the coming battle, 'the intrepidity of our Troops' would partially compensate for 'the incalculable loss of our leader'. Ned need not have worried. Having minutely instructed Beresford regarding the immediate investment of Badajoz,

Wellington started back again at a gallop on 25 April and 'returned to us', in Ned's jubilant words, 'exactly in time'.

Young Johnny Kincaid of the Rifles had been eaten up with curiosity when he joined the Peninsular army in 1810 to see the famous general. Since Wellington frequently visited the Torres Vedras outposts, Kincaid was soon satisfied. 'He was just such a man as I had figured in my mind's eye,' he wrote. A man who could be picked out from hundreds of others dressed in the same uniform. Now, on Wellington's whirlwind return to the northern army in April 1811, Kincaid spoke for all:

we would rather see his long nose in the fight than a reinforcement of ten thousand men any day.[2]

★　　　★　　　★

On 2 May 1811 Massena ordered an advance upon Almeida of 48,000 men and thirty-eight guns.[3] Wellington, curiously symmetrical with forty-eight guns and 38,000 men, stood waiting on the border at the village of Fuentes de Oñoro, on the River Dos Casas. His fire-power was for the first time satisfactory, his man-power not. Part of his army was at Badajoz; many of his troops were sick again; and one of his divisions, the 7th, was fresh from England, though it perhaps made up for lack of military experience by possessing one of the best diarists of the Peninsular war, Private W. Wheeler of the 51st. Wheeler had landed at Lisbon in March, making the Englishman's usual remarks about the excess of filth and priests. (His solution was to draft all able-bodied clergy into the forces, using the rest to clean up the streets.) The army received its reinforcements thankfully: 'of Course, the More Men, the More Means', wrote Ned in symbolically large letters, 'and we have a Man of Energy to use them . . .'.

2. The effect on the soldiers of Wellington's personality and their relief at his reappearance was even discussed in London society: 'his name alone must be equivalent to half an army', wrote Lady Bessborough, mother of the handsome young Colonel Frederick Ponsonby, 'and [gave] such security of not failing' (*Correspondence of Granville Leveson Gower, Earl Granville*, vol. II, pp. 457–8).

3. Oman gives this figure of 48,000. General Sir James Marshall-Cornwall (*Massena*, p. 240) says Massena had only 45,000, while Massena himself would not admit to more than 35,000.

(*Top*) Anne Hill, Countess of Mornington, mother of the Duke of Wellington, by Robert Healey, 1760.

(*Bottom*) Garret Wesley, 1st Earl of Mornington, father of the Duke of Wellington, aged 22, by an unknown artist.

3 (*Top*) Richard Wesley, 2nd Earl of Mornington, aged 21, by Downman.

4 (*Bottom*) Arthur Wesley, future Duke of Wellington, aged about 11, by an unknown artist.

5 Arthur Wesley as Lieutenant-
Colonel of the 33rd, aged about 26,
by John Hoppner. Given by Arthur
to his brother Richard in 1841,
who said of it: 'It is admirable;
much the best which exists of you;
the likeness is perfect, and conveys
the true expression of your
countenance.'

6 Battle of Assaye, 23 September
1803.

7   Storming of Gawilghur,
15 December 1803.

8   Major-General the
Hon. Sir Arthur Wellesley,
K.B., by John Hoppner,
1806. The portrait
represents Wellesley in
India.

9 Mrs Freese, by an unknown artist. She was wife of Colonel William Freese and mother of Arthur Freese, godson of the Duke of Wellington.

10 Sir Arthur Wellesley, by Robert Home, 1804. The star and ribbon of the Bath were added later as the news of Wellesley's appointment to the order did not reach India until 1805. 'It belonged to the poor Duchess,' wrote the Duke about this portrait, and it still hangs at Statfield Saye.

11 Catherine Dorothea Sarah ('Kitty') Pakenham, Viscountess Wellington, by Slater, 1811. Maria Edgeworth commented: 'Lady Wellington is not like: it is absurd to attempt to draw Lady Wellington's face; she has no *face*; it is all countenance.'

12   Battle of Vimeiro, 21 August 1808.

13   Capture of Oporto, 12 May 1809. On the right is the Serra Convent with Wellesley holding up his telescope; in the centre, across the River Douro, is the Bishop's Seminary.

14   Battle of Bussaco, 27 September 1810. The French, with an eagle, are driven from the ridge at the point of the bayonet, while through the smoke is seen the Convent on the crest. Drawn by Atkinson for Edward Orme's *Historic Military and Naval Anecdotes*, 1817, a publication to which Wellington subscribed.

15   Torres Vedras, the town with its fortress on the right, 1810.

16   Self-portrait of Kitty at Tunbridge Wells, *c.* 1810, sketched in water-colours to 'amuse' her brother-in-law, Harry Stewart in Ireland. Home-made slippers were her speciality. She was later laughed at for never being without an old basket. The saddle is placed well back on the animal's crupper to give the rider's liver a good shaking.

17   Battle of Fuentes de Oñoro, 3–5 May 1811. The French are attacking over the river Dos Casas; Wellington's command-post is above on the right.

18   Lord Wellington,
      by an unknown
      Portuguese artist,
      thought to be at the
      storming of
      Ciudad Rodrigo,
      19 January 1812.

19   Storming of Badajoz, 6 April 1812. Notice the spikes and sword-blades
in the breach.

20 'The Beau', 1812, by Juan Bauzit, water-colour. Wellington is shown in civilian clothes—dark blue great-coat and grey breeches.

21 Crossing the Bidassoa into France, 1813. Wellington is watching the troops accomplishing their surprise march through the water.

22 Wellington, drawn in chalk by Francisco Goya, Madrid, 1812. Wellington started up in a rage during one of the sittings, when Dr McGrigor confessed that he had disobeyed orders on the march.

23 The Duke of Wellington by Thomas Phillips, 1814.

24 The Duchess of Wellington by Sir Thomas Lawrence, 1814.

25 Princess Pauline Borghese, Napoleon's sister. When asked by friends about the pose she said it was quite all right as the studio was well heated.

26 Prince Von Blücher, Field-Marshal of the Prussian forces, a sketch from the life when on his visit to London, June 1814, by Major-General Birch Reynardson.

27 Congress of Vienna, 1815, by Isabey.

28 Napoleon's favourite flower. He always said that he would return from Elba with the violets of spring. This bouquet conceals the faces of the Emperor, the Empress Marie-Louise, and their son the King of Rome. The caption reads 'Flowers of spring so dear to the French, You will give us back our glory and peace.'

Fleurs du primtems si cheres aux ...
Vous nous rendrez notre gloire et la paix

29   The Duchess of Richmond's ball, 15 June 1815. The guests, with Wellington in the centre, receive news of Napoleon's advance against the Prussians.

30   Copenhagen, Wellington's chestnut charger, painted posthumously by B. R. Haydon. The Duke always said it was a good likeness.

31   Battle of Waterloo, 18 June 1815, by Sir William Allan, now in the
Royal Military Academy, Sandhurst. The twin of this picture, showing the
field from the French side, is in the Wellington Museum and was admired by
the Duke. 'Good—very good,' he said; 'not too much smoke.' Wellington is
seen here on the left in his civilian dress and small cocked hat.

32   Battle of Quatre Bras, 16 June 1815. The death of the Duke of
Brunswick.

33 Meeting of Wellington and Blücher at *La Belle-Alliance*. 'Mein lieber Kamerad!' exclaimed Blücher; 'Quelle affaire!' The artist, George Jones, was right to imply that their kiss was exchanged from horseback, but Wellington recollected the scene as having taken place nearer to Genappe.

34 Waterloo, late afternoon. Congreve rockets show up as the sun begins to sink. On the left is *La Belle-Alliance*, in the centre La Haye Sainte with the Observatory above, built for Napoleon but not used, and on the right Wellington's Tree.

35 The Duke of Wellington writing his Waterloo despatch. Sir Alexander Gordon is lying dead in Wellington's camp-bed next door. By the Duke's favourite niece, Lady Burghersh, 1839.

36 'A Wellington Boot, or the Head of the Army.'

The Man of Energy posted his centre in a position after his own heart. A rugged hill crowned the village of Fuentes and shaded off westward into a long plateau; behind its crest his main force could be concealed. The village ran down irregularly, tier by tier, to the boulder-strewn water. It was, and still is, a miniature labyrinth of single-storey cottages and stone walls enclosing small, odd-shaped vegetable patches and tortuous alleys. All these mazy paths converged eventually on huge slabs of rock above, where on one side stood the church with its immemorial stork's nest and on the other Wellington's look-out post. Farther north his left wing covered Almeida, while to the south his right guarded the retreat road into Portugal. Dared he hope that Massena would at last oblige with a frontal assault?

Early in the morning of 3 May Wellington was out with his glass sweeping the straight white road from Ciudad Rodrigo. He saw five of Massena's divisions emerge from the woods of cork and ilex. By 2 P.M. it had begun. Ten French battalions launched themselves across the Dos Casas, made a brief lodgement behind rock or wall and were hurled back over the blood-stained water. Again they came on, this time driving the defenders far up among the crags, until the critical moment when Wellington sent in two Scottish regiments, the 71st and 79th, and they were thrown right out of the town. As at Bussaco, Massena's head-on collision had failed. Next day, 4 May, there was a grim lull while both sides dragged their dead from the narrow entries and angles where they were wedged in their hundreds; and one side, Massena's, prepared to combine yet another frontal attack with the flanking movement which had in the end been so successful at Bussaco.

That evening, providentially, General Robert Craufurd returned to his Light Division from leave. He was just in time. For throughout the next day, 5 May, Wellington's army was to be under constant pressure with the possibility of defeat never far off.

Massena's flanking movement to the south began all too well, under cover of fog, by surprising the Empecinado's guerrillas and cutting up several battalions of the new 7th Division. There seemed nothing to stop him. A few French prisoners brought in to the Allied camp and questioned as to how many of Massena's men were in the attack, replied, 'The whole French army.' Consternation overwhelmed the interrogators and the awful news was rushed to Wellington.

'Oh! they are all there, are they? Well, we must mind a little what we are about.'[4]

His famous imperturbability had never been more needed. Two hours after dawn the crisis was desperate: Wellington's right overrun, the 7th isolated, Fuentes exposed in flank and rear, the relief of Almeida in sight. Wellington had a stark choice. To withdraw his mauled battalions on the right—if indeed he could withdraw them—and so uncover his escape route into Portugal. Or, by abandoning the siege of Almeida, to use the blockading troops for keeping open his road home. He took the bold course. He ordered Craufurd and the Light Division to go in and bring back the broken battalions into the lines. Let the road to Portugal be lost; he trusted his troops not to need it. Nothing would induce him to uncover Almeida.

Now followed under the eyes of the admiring Commander-in-Chief one of the most polished displays in military history. Surrounded by swirling eddies of French dragoons, Craufurd covered the retreat of the 7th with a series of rhythmical evolutions which suddenly transformed the deadly orthodoxy of Hyde Park reviews into a dance of life. Defying the enemy cavalry to approach his invincible infantry squares; holding off their artillery with short cavalry charges until his horses in Wellington's words, 'had not a gallop in them'; and, as his squares formed by turns into column, protecting their retirement with the six guns of Bull's Horse Artillery, he brought his own Light Division and the crippled 7th to safety. The battle of Fuentes de Oñoro might have been fought under the walls of Troy, judging by Napier's Homeric account of one incident in Craufurd's epic. Captain Norman Ramsay, commanding a pair of guns, stayed behind too long firing at the French cavalry and became totally engulfed. Suddenly there was a convulsion in the dense French mass:

> an English shout pealed high and clear, the mass was rent asunder, and Norman Ramsay burst forth sword in hand at the head of his battery, his horses breathing fire, stretched like greyhounds along the plain, the guns bounded behind them like things of no weight,

4. This anecdote is recounted by Wellington's Judge Advocate-General, F. S. Larpent (*Private Journal*, vol. I, p. 85), without date or place, simply as an example of his coolness in a crisis; but it seems to relate to the battle of Fuentes, particularly as an anecdote about Fuentes follows it on the next page of Larpent's Journal.

and the mounted gunners followed close, with heads bent low and pointed weapons in desperate career.

With cheers and shouts Craufurd's lines opened to receive the heroic charioteers.

Wellington meanwhile had realigned his army to meet the new situation. His front now lay at right angles along the plateau, one leg running back westwards, with its hinge on Fuentes church—a position not without danger. Massena did his best to exploit it. As soon as he had seen his cavalry victorious on the southern plain, he had begun again pounding Fuentes. Attack after attack carried the French up to the church; wave after wave of defenders, each new contingent sent in by Wellington in the nick of time, drove them down again to the river, while the roar of cannon from hill to hill and crash of musketry between the confining walls made a deafening background to the horrid business of hand-to-hand fighting in the alleys.

The decisive moment came at noon, when the Allies had lost the village and the huge plumes of Bonaparte's Grenadiers seemed to be everywhere, almost up to Wellington's command-post on the plateau above. Below, the piles of gory kilts showed where the flower of the Highlanders had died. All now depended on the Connaught Rangers, those 'wild Irishmen' who had been favourite butts at Dublin fancy-dress balls when Arthur was a boy. Pakenham had been sent by General Mackinnon to ask if the 88th, with the indomitable Wallace at their head, might clear the village. Wellington gave the order and Pakenham galloped back.

'He says you may go—come on!' With ferocious yells and plunging bayonets the Irishmen charged, sweeping all before them. At last, by 2 P.M., the assaults petered out. The once picturesque Spanish village was in utter ruin but victory was won. (Wellington later asked the British Government in the detached manner which concealed his feelings for a contribution to the restoration of Fuentes: it had recently become a battlefield and had not been 'much improved by this circumstance'.) Massena had fought his last battle and lost. During the next few days Wellington stood on the ridge awaiting a new attempt. For once he hastily threw up fortifications on what might be tomorrow's battlefield. They were unnecessary. Massena had ordered his subordinate, Bessières, to fetch ammunition from Ciudad Rodrigo for yet another onslaught against Fuentes on 6 May.

Bessières refused and Massena, in a passion, cancelled the whole operation. On 10 May at dawn a staff officer, Lord Aylmer, rushed into Wellington's room while he was shaving, with the news that the French had decamped. Lord Aylmer was as surprised by his chief's cool reaction as he had been by the news itself.

'Ay, I thought they meant to be off; very well,' said Wellington, and he went on scraping at his determined chin.

Having retreated to Ciudad Rodrigo, Massena later announced to the astonished world—a victory. It was a curious kind of victory, with the French losing 2,192 to Wellington's 1,545. Napoleon sent an acid comment: 'His Majesty is distressed, as we all are, to see his army retire before a British force so inferior in numbers.' Nevertheless something had happened on the night of 10 May 1811 to give Massena a shred of excuse for his claim.

*   *   *

Having written off the revictualling of Almeida by distributing its intended provisions to his own hungry army, Massena prepared to wind up the affair with a dramatic postscript. Three volunteers were paid 6,000 francs each to get a message into beleaguered Almeida. The message, in cipher, ordered Governor Brennier to break out. He should fire three salvoes at intervals of five minutes starting at 10 P.M. to indicate 'message received'. Two of the volunteers were caught and shot; the third, named Tillet, got through, mostly on all fours. Next night Massena heard the signal guns. Well satisfied, he made off for Ciudad Rodrigo.

Wellington of course had taken steps to prevent a sortie. He specifically ordered the bridge of Barba de Puerco to be guarded. By audacity and bluffing on Governor Brennier's part, however, and dismal apathy or errors on the part of five British officers, the garrison blew up Almeida and got away. Wellington was angrier than he had ever been: 'the most disgraceful military event,' he stormed, 'that has yet occurred to us.' Today the 'disgraceful event' can be perversely appreciated for what it tells about Wellington's officers, not to mention the tempestuous light it flashes upon his own character.

As usual the preposterous General Sir William Erskine was involved. He was dining on the afternoon of the 10th with Sir Brent Spencer when Wellington's instructions reached him at 4 P.M. to secure the bridge. At first he proposed sending one corporal and four men. 'Sir William,' expostulated Pakenham, who was also present, 'you might as well attempt to block up the bridge with a Pinch of this Snuff as to place such a party for such an Object.' Erskine apparently agreed to send the 4th Regiment instead, wrote out the order to its colonel, named Bevan, stuffed it in his pocket, took some more snuff —and forgot it. As a result Bevan did not get his orders to occupy the bridge until midnight. He then made the mistake of taking his own officers' bad advice: 'Oh! you need not march till daybreak.' If he had gone at once he might have waylaid the French, since Brennier was not at the bridge until 4 A.M. and Bevan had under three miles to go. Erskine made matters worse for Bevan by suppressing his own negligence and telling Wellington that the 4th had been late through losing their way. Wellington seems to have realized that Bevan received Erskine's orders late, but this of course did not excuse Bevan's own delay. He therefore turned down Bevan's request for an inquiry into the respective responsibilities of himself and Erskine, deciding instead to bring Bevan before a court martial (where in fact he would have had a chance to state his case). Bevan's tragic reaction is described in a letter from young Major Hercules Pakenham of the 3rd Division to his brother:

Campo Mayor, July 11th, 1811

My dearest Longford. . . . Poor Bevan, Lt: Col: of the 4th, on whom Campbell [he meant Erskine] unjustly threw the slur of having *lost his way*, after requesting an Investigation which was overruled, Blew his Brains out the night before last.

The army was deeply shocked by this disaster and some blamed Wellington for hierarchical prejudice, causing him to make a lieutenant-colonel (Bevan) the scapegoat for a general's sins. Over a century later a librarian at the War Office was still accusing Wellington of 'heartlessness' in this affair.[5] Was he guilty?

Wellington's passions had undoubtedly been roused. Incompetence seemed to meet him at every turn. General Alexander Campbell (a close friend of the Prince Regent) had stupidly posted his pickets at Almeida too far from the *glacis*, Colonel Iremonger had heard it being blown up but did not think the blast 'anything *Extraordinary*', while Colonel Johnson had later gone beyond his orders at the bridge thereby losing 300 valuable lives. In Wellington's eyes Johnson's

5. F. J. Hudleston, *Warriors in Undress*, p. 18.

fault—foolhardiness—was so prevalent and dangerous as to merit immediate court martial. He wrote in explanation:

> . . . The desire to be forward in engaging the enemy is not un-common in the British army; but that quality which I wish to see the officers possess . . . is a cool, discriminating judgement in action. . . .

The problem remains as to why Wellington did not seize this golden opportunity of eliminating the ludicrous Erskine at last. The answer again emphasizes the vein of fatalism or stoicism in his character. He had already tried desperately to get rid of this man and failed, for Erskine had more influence at the Horse Guards than the 'Sepoy General'. Therefore Wellington, according to his creed, must make the best of a bad job—which would hardly be achieved by telling the world that one of his generals had lapses through taking a drop too much.

William Wellesley-Pole, however, was permitted to know Arthur's true feelings. He received a caustic note from Spain on 15 May:

> . . . I begin to be of opinion with you that there is nothing so stupid as a gallant officer.

The last sentence in this same letter pointed to the core of his irritation:

> . . . I am obliged to be everywhere and if absent from any opera-tion something goes wrong.

The truth was that the humiliation of Almeida had gone far to wipe out the glory of Fuentes, and when the Government decided not to move a vote of thanks for that battle, Wellington could not but agree. 'The business would have been different if we had caught the garri-son of Almeida,' he wrote to Lord Liverpool. Yet the pill was bitter. Of all his battles up to the present, Fuentes de Oñoro seemed to him 'the most difficult one I was ever concerned in, and against the greatest odds. . . . If Boney had been there,' he admitted to William, 'we should have been beat.' It was no good William replying that the escape of the garrison was 'perfectly well understood here', and that Fuentes had brought him so much renown that 'I think you are now above any Intrigue that can be formed or initiated against you'. What with the Opposition taking up Colonel Johnson's case, and the Portuguese Sousas venting their own grievances in anonymous letters, Arthur had half made up his mind to go home as soon as the Spanish fortresses had been recaptured. On 16 May he set off southwards once more, sensing perhaps that Beresford's siege of Badajoz might be another of those operations where, in his absence, 'something goes wrong'.

*   *   *

Beresford had opened the siege at the beginning of May. His artillery was a collection of brass museum pieces from the picturesque medieval walls of Elvas, stamped with the names of long-dead kings. This pack of sick bloodhounds, for ever 'drooping at the muzzle', were expected to batter down the giant among all the many bastions and towers of Badajoz—Fort San Cristobal. Naturally no progress was made and when, after a week, Beresford heard that Soult was coming up behind him, he abandoned the abortive siege and turned to meet Soult at the battle of Albuera. Wellington was on his way south, but had not arrived.

Oh, Albuera! glorious field of grief!

The awful paradox of this British victory gained by Beresford at Albuera near Badajoz on 16 May 1811 was not likely to be overlooked by Byron, nor indeed by Wellington, who arrived at Elvas three days later on the 19th. The carnage on both sides was appalling: 4,000 Allies lost out of 10,000; 7,000 French out of 24,000. Colonel John Colborne's superb Light Brigade, blinded by a sudden hailstorm, were mown down and then annihilated by the demon lancers of Poland in a matter of minutes. Beresford lost his nerve and had actually ordered a retreat when the twenty-six-year-old Henry Hardinge,[6] attached to the Portuguese forces, took it on himself to urge upon a willing Lowry Cole the absolute necessity of throwing in the 4th Division, orders or no orders. And so the bloody tide turned. On the victorious side not enough men were left alive in some regiments to collect their dead—those terrible dead of the Peninsular battlefields,

6. Sir Henry Hardinge, 1st Viscount Hardinge of Lahore (1785–1856). Governor-General of India, 1844; Commander-in-Chief, 1852.

who, stripped of their clothes by human kites, lay buried stark naked until the kite swooped down from the sky or the wolf came down from the mountains—

> *For with his nails he'll dig them up again.*[7]

One sympathizes with the feelings which prompted Beresford to send in a report of the battle dwelling less on the glory than the grief. Wellington, however, foresaw the disastrous effect of the despatch's 'desponding' or even 'whining' tone, as he called it. It would have 'driven the people in England mad'. The whines must be omitted.

'This won't do,' he said shortly to Colonel Thomas Arbuthnot who had brought it in while he was dining at Elvas on the day of his arrival. 'Write me down a victory.' After all, it was a victory. Soult had been forced to retire.

Having changed the tone of the despatch, Wellington's next thought was to encourage his subordinates and friends. The shattered Beresford, whose trouble Ned Pakenham had diagnosed weeks ago as 'Anxiety', received a steadying message:

> You could not be successful in such an action without a large loss, and we must make up our minds to affairs of this kind sometimes, or give up the game.

To Henry Wellesley, on whose stoutness at Cádiz depended all his hopes in Spain, he wrote more frankly but still with optimism: Albuera would be justified

> if Soult goes far enough from me to renew the . . . siege of Badajoz, but . . . another such battle would ruin us.

Only William was allowed to catch a note of personal alarm. Once expressed, however, it could be forgotten.

> We have had a great battle in this quarter at which I was not present but as usual I shall be abused for the loss sustained by our troops; which is certainly very great.

7. (John Webster, *The White Devil*, Act V scene IV). Dr Adam Neale first saw Webster's line acted out by the wolves at Vimeiro. Goya immortalized, if that is the right word, the stripping of the war dead in his drawings, now in the Prado, Madrid. When Lieutenant William Bragge saw Albuera a year after the battle the ground was white with bones.

William was ready with his customary reassurances. The whole story of Albuera, he insisted, was well understood in Britain from the flood of officers' letters home, 'even to the general's loss of Head and ordering the Retreat etc., etc.'. In any case Arthur could now put the southern army back under Hill (at last recovered from fever), leaving Beresford 'to arrange the Portuguese'.

Wellington visited the awful scene of battle on 21 May, and came upon one famous regiment 'literally lying dead in their ranks as they had stood' a thing he had never seen before. The effect on his army was to make his long nose among them more prized than ever.

'Men of the 29th,' he said when visiting some of the wounded, 'I am sorry to see so many of you here.' A veteran replied,

'If you had commanded us, my Lord, there wouldn't be so many of us here.'

*   *   *

The second siege of Badajoz, opened by Wellington immediately on arrival, was to show how right the men of the 29th had been.

'Badajoz may fall,' he wrote to Charles Stuart in Lisbon on 8 June 'but the business will be very near run on both sides. . . . I have never seen walls bear so much battering, nor ordnance, nor artillery, so bad as those belonging to Elvas.' The first assault, on 6 June, had in fact already failed; three days later came the second, also a failure. When he heard that 60,000 French were closing in on him he ordered the siege to be raised. A speech to his staff explaining the situation ended with some *sotto voce* mutterings about being 'my own engineer' next time. On 17 June he retreated with the whole army across the Guadiana.

Everyone was pleased in his own way, even the more malicious Whigs, who had got wind of the siege's second failure and secretly hoped Wellington would destroy himself with another Albuera. Henry Brougham, M.P., wrote happily to Creevey:

I wish you would come to town and let us have a few mischievous discussions . . . a report is very prevalent that the siege of Badajoz is raised, previous to another fight.

Soult and Governor Philippon of Badajoz congratulated one another, for the town had been on the verge of surrender through starvation.

Wellington's soldiers were equally thankful to depart. Private Wheeler, who had fallen wounded on the *glacis*, loathed the whole siege. Work in the trenches beforehand was suffocating. Stranded in a desert of baked earth and scorched thistles, the besiegers knew that the cool Guadiana flowed only a few hundred yards away, but if anyone so much as popped up to look at it, 'bang goes half a dozen muskets at his head'. They had had to storm the breach before it was completely practicable, the ladders were too short and the main assault-party lost its way. When Wheeler regained consciousness the battle was over and he was lying shoeless and shirtless in the moonlight among the dead and wounded: 'the old black wall and breach looked terrible . . . like an evil spirit frowning on the unfortunate victims that lay prostrate at its feet'. One victim, Wheeler himself, managed to 'bound' like a deer at daybreak back into his lines—'devil take the thistles'—and his heart bounded again, no doubt, when he found there was to be no second Albuera.

On 26th June Wellington wrote firmly to a friend:

I don't know how the bloodthirsty people in England will like what I have been doing lately and am doing now but I am convinced I am right. I have all the French troops in Spain in my front; they have been looking at us for a week and the more they looked at us the less they like us and I believe that I should get over the crisis of this moment without a battle, of which we can at present ill spare the necessary loss, however confident I am of the result.

The French had finally lost their appetite for Bussaco-like engagements against Wellington, while Wellington's knowledge of their numerical superiority prevented him from attacking them. 'The devil is in the French for numbers!!!' he wrote on 12 July. The result was that he defied them from strong positions above the River Caia, a tributary of the Guadiana, for a month and then marched north towards Ciudad Rodrigo. Pakenham as usual spoke for the whole army:

Lord W's judgment in withdrawing his troops on the very day he did,—His countenance afterwards in front of very superior numbers,—His wonderful transfer under the influences of the most disappointing circumstances . . . arising out of the want of skill of another [Beresford],—have if possible raised him higher in the estimation of his Soldiers.

Soult at last returned gladly to luxurious Seville with his regal ambitions undimmed, while Massena's successor, Marshal Marmont, was left to handle Wellington.

*   *   *

It was good to be rid of Massena at any rate, even though General Foy believed that he had long ceased to be the great Massena of the flashing eyes. Napoleon was positively contemptuous when Massena returned to Paris. The unlucky general had received his dismissal a few hours after his great *coup* at Almeida.

'Well, Prince of Essling,' sneered the Emperor, 'so you're no longer Massena.'

To Wellington he would always remain the one marshal who had kept him awake at night.

His successor, August Marmont, Duke of Ragusa, was altogether different. Youngest of the marshals (only thirty-six against Massena's fifty-two), he was well educated, a good colleague, not self-indulgent; a new type of opponent for a new shape of war.

*   *   *

When Wellington moved north, sickness was his worst enemy. At one time 17,000 men were on the sick list. 'We were now in the most miserable, sickly place I was ever in,' wrote William Tomkinson of the 16th Light Dragoons. 'Scarcely a single officer enjoyed his health, & the men were becoming daily more sickly. I had my ague nearly every other day....' Young William Bragge of the 'Galloping Third' (Heavy Dragoons) staved off the dysentery for a time by wearing flannel and avoiding fruit; in the end he succumbed to 'King Agrippa'. Pakenham, who nearly died, and Charles Napier who could hardly walk, were both sent home. Wellington himself was off colour for a fortnight and had to modify his spartan regime of riding and writing, as described by Tomkinson: up at 6; 6 to 9 writing, breakfast; visit of heads of all departments until 2 or 3; riding till 6; dinner; 9 till 12 writing. He was in fact reorganizing his whole army. Enough cavalry had been accumulated at last to satisfy him and, by heroic planning which utilized river transport, he brought his first siege-train including iron guns up from Lisbon to Almeida. A letter from Wellington to Admiral Berkeley, dated Freneda, 9 October 1811, showed that he wished all his siege-guns in future to come from the famous Scottish firm which had made Nelson's 'carronades'.

> . . . I have had enough of sieges with defective artillery and I will never undertake another without the best. Therefore in all my letters I have desired to have either 29 prs. 9 feet long, Carron manufacture, or 28 prs. 8 feet long, of the same manufacture and Carron shot.

Two months later (18 December 1811) he wrote to his brother-in-law, Culling Charles Smith, second husband of his widowed sister Anne, for a travelling barouche. 'It must be a Barouche in which I can sleep': breadth of axle-trees not to exceed five feet eight inches; low on the ground or it would overturn; lined with common Russia leather. Wellington received his barouche in April 1812, sent out in the transport *Freelove*.

Next to illness, the difficulty of finding first-class generals still provoked him most. General Charles Stewart of the cavalry was short-sighted but owing to a wound could not wear glasses. Erskine at least wore glasses, and for lack of a better man Wellington had characteristically persuaded himself by mid-1811 that this unstable, dim-eyed drunkard was a cavalry officer of 'prudence and circumspection'. The man he needed was General Lord Paget. But it might make a bad impression at Cádiz to invite so soon the seducer of Henry's wife. In any case William doubted whether Paget would accept: 'If I know anything of Ld. Paget's character he will not stoop to waive his Rank to serve under you. . . .'

For the rest, he had still to solve the eternal problem of leave. Apart from fevers, many generals had 'business', one put his shoulder out, another reported his spleen 'out of order'—a complaint which poor Arthur sometimes seemed to share. His invaluable commissary-general, Robert Kennedy ('who is as well as I am'), was lured home by his wife; while George Murray, the equally indispensable quartermaster-general, was replaced by Colonel Willoughby Gordon, an industrious but gossiping Whig who had been responsible for informing Arthur from the Horse Guards that Kennedy was 'ill'. After all these trials, a major who requested leave in order to save his fiancée's heart from breaking was lucky to get off with nothing worse than avuncular irony:

> We read occasionally of desperate cases of this description, but I cannot say that I have ever yet known a young lady dying of love. They continue, in some manner, to live and live tolerably well . . . and some even have been known to recover so far as to be inclined to take another lover, if the absence of the first has lasted too long.

The major was ultimately allowed to save her from death or faithlessness by returning home to marry her; it was he who died, at Vitoria.

One agreeable change could be recorded in Wellington's staff. General Graham, victor of Barrosa, replaced Sir Brent Spencer as second-in-command, 'which I am led to hope,' wrote Pakenham, 'may induce our friend [Wellington] to indulge himself a little more, although he has proved Himself near an Iron man.'

*   *   *

There could be little indulgence for the Iron Man at this moment. In August he blockaded Ciudad Rodrigo and on the 27th cautiously repeated to Lord Liverpool his conviction that the war was entering a new phase:

> We have certainly altered the nature of the war in Spain; it has become, to a certain degree, offensive on our part.

Less than a month later Marmont came rampaging in to relieve Ciudad Rodrigo and caught Wellington, through a rare failure to concentrate, with his army dangerously strung out. There were some critical moments between 25 and 28 September. At El Bodon, in particular, Picton's 3rd Division was isolated but saved itself by a brilliant movement across an open plain swarming with French cavalry. Forty times the Connaught Rangers heard the French bugles sound the charge; forty times the horsemen drew off, thwarted. Picton's assistant adjutant-general, Hercules Pakenham, described 'this imposing force Pounding us and ready to Charge in case of confusion. However, they never dared it, after we got together.' General Craufurd of the Light Division gave Wellington a fright by continuing his outpost operations, as usual, until the last moment. Wellington received him sarcastically on the 26th:

'I am glad to see you safe, General Craufurd.'

'Oh! I was in no danger I assure you,' said Craufurd, misinterpreting his welcome.

'But I was, from your conduct.' As he left the room Craufurd was heard to murmur:

'He's damned crusty this morning.'

Wellington himself had narrowly escaped capture on the 25th by mistaking a party of French Chasseurs for his own Hussars, whom the Horse Guards had recently had the bright idea of putting into French-type caps. A year later he was laughing at this and similar incidents in his life as a soldier:

> Although I had the family eye of a hawk, I have frequently been within an ace of being taken, and have more than once been obliged to take to my 'scrapers'. . . .

Old Graham summed up the three days of September fighting as 'very pretty, but rather fine spun'—what Wellington would have called 'near run'. After Marmont's revictualling of Ciudad Rodrigo, the Allies went into cantonments for three months from 1 October, to recover their health. Wellington's own health was once more excellent. He wrote to General Campbell on 6 October: 'I have been very well during the late *bustle.*'

*   *   *

While the colder weather in the Peninsula did its healing work and the agues vanished in a round of gaiety—hunting, dinners and balls for the superior officers, dancing the fandango with village belles followed by hot chestnut suppers for the rest—there were signs that the war was again losing support at home. Creevey wrote in his journal on 31 October: 'The campaign in Portugal and Lord Wellington begin to be out of fashion with the Regent,' and next day, 'Wellington and Portugal are going down.' It was true that when someone at Carlton House had begun to praise Wellington's victories in the north, the Prince Regent burst out—

'Damn the north! and damn the south! and damn Wellington! the question is, how am I to be rid of this damned Princess of Wales?'

Caroline of Brunswick, Princess of Wales, from whom the Prince had separated (though without a divorce) as soon as their only child,

Princess Charlotte, was born, would in due course become a 'damned' nuisance to Wellington also. For the moment she was a nuisance only in upsetting the precarious balance of her husband's temper. William had already warned Arthur that the Prince had turned against his Ministers and instead of asking them to his fête, invited 'every Blackguard and most of the Whores in London.' Suddenly the help which Wellington failed to find in the English Court was furnished by none other than the Emperor of the French.

Napoleon, who would neither return to Spain after the autumn of 1808 (possibly the most fatal failure of his career) nor leave well alone in Peninsular affairs, ordered Marshal Suchet to be reinforced at Valencia with 15,000 of Marmont's best men. Wellington promptly decided to open the siege of Ciudad Rodrigo in the new year.

Christmas 1811 for Wellington's wife and in-laws was a sad season. That December Kitty's popular sailor brother, Captain William Pakenham, had gone down in his ship with all hands during a gale in Lough Swilly. Ned, now at home, reported: 'Kitty's steadiness has quite astonished me. She is calm to a degree that only could proceed from goodness and religion.' There was no gay party at Pakenham Hall, with Lord Longford telling his famous stories, as in November when Maria Edgeworth heard about his night journey in a stage-coach opposite a gentleman in a fur coat who turned out to be a performing bear.

Wellington broke the melancholy news to Hercules in the honest, unvarnished words that were natural to him. He could not pretend to offer consolation;

> I think however you will bear your misfortune like a Man; and will seek to divert your Mind from reflecting upon it, by attending to your duty in the new scene which is opening before us.

Three days after writing this letter, on 8 January 1812, Wellington formally opened the new scene by ordering Ciudad Rodrigo to be invested. The garrison had recently lost 200 of their store cattle on the *glacis* to the guerrillas, not to mention their Governor, M. Reynaud, a Swiss, who had sallied forth to recapture the cattle and been caught himself.[8] Hercules suggested that the hungry garrison

---

8. According to William Bragge's information the Governor had got himself taken prisoner on purpose, as his brother was Vice-Master of Trinity, Cambridge, and he wanted to see England.

would 'probably keep Lent early'. At any rate they were not destined
to keep it in Ciudad Rodrigo.

That night of 8 January, 450 volunteers under Colonel Colborne
seized the main outwork, situated on a dominating hill named the
Great Teson, from which they had a clear view of the town's defences.
Ciudad Rodrigo, with its system of ancient ramparts strengthened
by modern works, and its square Moorish castle facing the Roman
bridge over the Agueda, looked (and still looks) a remarkably compact, defiant fortress. Digging the trenches for the siege was an
odious business; the ground was snow-covered and the cutting-tools
sent out from England abominable. The contractors' profits always
seemed to take precedence over the army's parallels. Wellington considered the whole 'cutlery' situation 'shameful'. Working-parties
waded through the half-frozen Agueda and began each shift in
breeches stiff with ice. William Bragge heard that 'Rations of Rum
have lately been stopt . . . to have a sufficient Quantity for the Men
working in the Trenches'. In their flanks and rear Hill's division,
among them Private Wheeler, kept guard. Wheeler lit fires in caves
of snow and slept with his haversack as a night-cap, his legs in the
sleeves of his great-coat and his red jacket buttoned over his 'seat
of honour'. Listening to the growing bombardment, he and his
shivering comrades longed for the assault to begin.[9]

It began on 19 January 1812. Two breaches were by now pronounced practicable. Wellington wrote out the order to attack sitting
calmly on the Great Teson with guns booming all round him: 'the
attack on Ciudad Rodrigo must be made this evening at 7 o'clock.'
He dared not wait, for Marmont was at Salamanca.

Picton's 3rd Division was to storm the main breach to the right,
near the Salamanca gate, Craufurd's Light Division the smaller breach
to the left, supported by a minor incursion under the Castle walls and
a diversion by the gate of Santiago. Every attack succeeded. Picton
launched the 88th led by Colonel Mackinnon with the words,
'Rangers of Connaught! It is not my intention to spend any *powder*
this evening. We'll do this business with the *could iron*,' and he rode
off, pounding the sides of his hog-maned cob. The Irishmen obeyed

9. William Napier, though absent on sick leave, described the bombardment of 14 January with his usual verve: the hissing shells 'seemed like fiery
serpents leaping through the darkness, the walls crashed to the stroke of the
bullet, and the distant mountains returning the sound appeared to mourn
over the falling city'.

orders. One young volunteer addressed his bayonet after its first success: 'Holy Moses! how easy you went through him!' But just as they had negotiated unexpected obstacles in the ditch, under heavy fire, a huge, over-zealous mine exploded beneath them, blowing Mackinnon sky high, scorching Harry Smith who was as far away as the lesser breach—but incidentally laying bare the defences to the survivors. In they poured; while events no less dramatic were passing on the left.

Captain George Napier had asked and received a 'favour' of Craufurd: to lead the storming party of 300 volunteers from the 52nd headed by the 'forlorn hope' of twenty-five under Lieutenant Gurwood, future editor of Wellington's *Despatches*. In the darkness Johnny Kincaid was one of those who lost his way during the attack: 'I saw, in a moment, that I had got into the wrong box'; but the sound of shouting quickly told him where the lesser breach was. Here reigned a fiery inferno of leaping and falling figures, part of a human tide which moved inexorably forward, dependent on the resolution of each individual soldier to make up for the technical deficiencies of the engineers. Craufurd was hit in the spine, Colborne in the shoulder, Napier in the arm, Gurwood in the head; but after lying stunned in the ditch Gurwood came to and 'cut off in search of the Governor' (in Harry Smith's slightly envious words) who duly rendered him his sword. While others were groaning on their beds next day, Gurwood was having the sword buckled on by Lord Fitzroy Somerset at a ceremony in the breach.

Meanwhile the town had been captured by columns of heroic troops who promptly turned into a horde of drunken maniacs. Trigger-happy in the Cathedral square, they suddenly began shooting at doors, windows, roofs and stars until, as Kincaid wrote, some heads were 'blown from shoulders in the general hurricane'. At last the voice of Sir Thomas Picton with the power of twenty trumpets recalled them to reason, alternately addressing them as 'Men and Englishmen—not savages!' and consigning them to eternal damnation. But even twenty trumpets blaring hell, besides many brave officers bashing crazy heads together with broken muskets, could not save Ciudad Rodrigo from being sacked. Next morning Wellington, from his austere headquarters in the little Montarco palace near the Salamanca gate, with its simple façade, cobbled patio and plain columns supporting a dark upper storey, watched the victorious 52nd march out.

'Who the devil are those fellows?' he asked, as a series of bizarre apparitions passed in front of him festooned in silk gowns, garlanded with strings of pretty Spanish shoes and carrying hams, tongues and loaves on the points of their *could iron*. When they came up with Picton they had the audacity to ask for a cheer.

'Here, then, you drunken set of brave rascals,' he laughed, 'Hurrah! we'll soon be at Badajoz!'

Then came the turn of the wounded, the dying and lastly those for whom death was too good an end—deserters to the enemy found hiding in the town after its capture. 'Eleven knelt on one grave,' under orders 'to be shot to death three times', recalled Harry Smith with a shudder. Kincaid, in the same regiment, said that Wellington pardoned all with good characters up to the time of their desertion, which apparently amounted to five out of the eleven. One bold fellow demanded his arrears of pay before execution. Another, though reprieved, went mad from shock.

The gallant 'Dan' Mackinnon had been killed by the mine. He was a great athlete and popular leader who once impersonated the Duke of York at a banquet and dived head-first into the punch-bowl; another time, when Wellington was visiting a convent, he impersonated a nun. Craufurd's wound was mortal and he died in slow agony, enquiring every hour after Napier (who lay below him, saddened by his groans) and begging Wellington to forgive him for the intrigues he had carried on with Charles Stewart and other 'croakers' when Wellington was on the defensive. 'Craufurd talked to me as they do in a novel,' said Wellington afterwards. Now that Wellington had taken the initiative it was a bitter blow to lose the most brilliant commander of outposts in his army.[10] The wound in Colborne's shoulder, where the gold braid of his epaulette had been driven in, was so painful that he could only bear the ball to be dug out five minutes at a time over a period of months. In telling Lady Sarah Napier that George's arm

10. Craufurd's unpopularity seems also to have evaporated. Two years earlier Wellington had received a private note from Dundas asking him to enquire into Craufurd's 'very unusual degree of severity' towards his brigade (*Wellington MSS*, 9 January 1810). At the time of Fuentes, Harry Smith said that Craufurd's officers 'execrated him. I did not . . .' (H. Smith, vol. I, p. 49). After his burial in the breach at Ciudad Rodrigo where he fell, his soldiers marched back to camp straight through a large pond which lay in their path instead of wasting time on a detour. This had been one of Craufurd's 'severities' in training. 'Sit down in it, Sir, sit down in it,' he would roar if a soldier stepped over a puddle.

had been amputated, Wellington showed himself once again a master of the right approach:

> . . . Having such sons, I am aware that you expect to hear of those misfortunes which I have more than once had to communicate to you.

He had divined Sarah Napier's feelings perfectly, for she replied with deep emotion a month after the storming:

> I can with truth assert that *nothing* has had so much the power of consolation to me as your letter . . . for the very cool composure of mind evinced by the admirable style of a letter, written to a simple individual by a General at the very moment of a victory, shews me what firmness may be attained by those who have such an example constantly in view. . . . unalterably yours Sarah Napier.

Wellington was no less concerned about the humbler wounded. Soon after the siege, on hearing at dinner that some sick soldiers had been dumped out of doors, he rode thirty miles that night to their bivouac, ordered them to be carried into the officer's quarters, rode back next night to see if he had been obeyed and finding the sick men thrown out again, had them finally brought in and the officers cashiered.[11]

After the burials and the executions, the stock-taking. Wellington congratulated his army on 'the brilliant results of their labours and gallantry'. Allied losses were 1,100 for the whole siege. The French lost 530, besides nearly 2,000 prisoners. Ney had needed twenty-five days in 1810 to reduce it; Wellington had taken only twelve. As in the far-off days of Ahmednuggur, the siege had gone through without a hitch—the only one of Wellington's Peninsular sieges to do so.

The Government elevated him from Viscount to Earl, with a pension to suit of £4,000 instead of £2,000. William characteristically feared that Viscount Douro would be an 'awkward' title for his son, and hoped to discover a better name 'connected in some way or other

11. Bivouacs were draughty outdoor shelters made of branches. Cantonments were buildings in which the army was billeted. Wellington gradually replaced bivouacs by tents in the campaigning season. He was laughed at by the French for mollycoddling his men.

with the Family', for little Arthur. Wellington stopped him at once. Whether he liked 'Douro' or not it happened to be the name his faithful Portuguese soldiers called him by. Little Arthur became Douro and thus remained until the end of his father's life.

Exactly a month after Wellington's victory—on 19 February 1812 —William was writing urgently again to say that Richard had handed back his seals of office that morning. It was an act that was to have its full effect on the Wellesley fortunes in three months' time. At the moment no one knew exactly why he had done it. His friends said it was a protest at the inadequacy of the war effort; his enemies said he wanted to be Prime Minister himself. Creevey simply dismissed him as a 'broken down scamp and bankrupt'.

The Spanish Cortes meanwhile created his brother Duke of Ciudad Rodrigo and a Grandee of Spain. The man who carried his victory despatch to the Cortes was Don Miguel de Alava, the devoted Spanish liaison officer destined to take the dead Romana's place in Wellington's affections and to concoct the best of all epigrams on the Iron Man:

> General Alava told me [wrote Stanhope in 1831] that when he travelled with the Duke and asked him what o'clock he would start, he usually said 'at daylight'; and to the question of what they should find for dinner, the usual answer was *'cold meat'*. *'J'en ai pris en horreur,'* added Alava, *'les deux mots* daylight *et* cold meat!'[12]

Officers were not the only members of Wellington's entourage to be worn out by his remorseless energy. His horses dropped like ninepins. Culling Smith got another request about this time:

> I am very badly off for Horses, having lost some, worn others out, & others being useless. The Peninsula is the grave of horses; and I have lost 14 upon a Stud generally of 10 in three Years.

Would Smith send him some with good feet and shoulders, preferably mares, which stood the climate better? 'You'll observe that I ride about 12 stone,' so an animal not quite swift enough for the turf 'might be able to carry me'. A little later Culling Smith heard that a grey horse which had reached Lisbon in March was very fine but troublesome to ride—always neighing.

12. General Alava (1771–1843), Spanish patriot, soldier and politician; ambassador in London, 1834.

I think however that the heat of this Country, the Work & Starvation will tame him; and he will then be a very valuable Horse. ... This Devil (as my mother would call him) kicks every thing he goes near.

At daylight on 6 March 1812 Wellington suddenly slipped off quietly to Badajoz hoping, no doubt, that it would be third time lucky.

* * *

This time the army was not to hurl itself disastrously against the impregnable strength of Fort San Cristobal across the river, but to breach the city walls in the south-east by Fort Picurina and the lunette (small detached work) of San Roche, while Picton and Leith escaladed the Castle and the north-western ramparts. Wellington's guns were now iron, not brass. Time was not, apparently, so short. All this was an improvement. Nevertheless there were weaknesses still.

The required corps of sappers and miners had not been provided by the Government, and Wellington's line regiments were no better as amateur engineers than they had been before. Harry Smith, who was with the forces at Badajoz, wrote bluntly, 'soldiers hate sieges and working-parties', while Kincaid described his life in the trenches as that of a mere 'gravedigger'. The fortress itself had been given more teeth by its remarkably ingenious Governor, Armand Philippon, assisted by a garrison of over 4,000 men and many *Afrancesados* (French sympathizers) among the Spanish inhabitants. The huge ochre walls and angular bastions thirty feet high 'frowned' down on the besiegers if ever a fortress frowned. Neither the scores of nesting kestrels in the Castle tower, nor the thousands of frogs chanting in the inundations near the Picurina outwork, could cause anyone to forget that Badajoz had earned a reputation for strength through blood, ever since it was wrenched from the Moors in 1229.[13]

Badajoz was invested on 16 March. The first parallel was dug on 17 March in a tempest. Starting on St Patrick's Day seemed to the numerous Irish a good omen. But the guardian of their rain-swept isle did not prevent the Guadiana from rising on the 22nd and

13. Even today there is an eerie and intimidating waste land among the old fortifications, unpaved and dimly lit, where at night hordes of what the Victorians used to call 'street Arabs' delight in springing out to storm passing cars.

sweeping away their pontoon bridge, while the amateur engineers worked in flooded trenches. Flame became the demon on the night of the 25th, when Fort Picurina was successfully stormed in streams of fire discharged by the defenders amid a tumult of rockets and alarm bells, and the yells of the combatants. So shaken were the French by this loss, says Napier, that General Philippon had to fortify the garrison with horror stories of their future as prisoners of war on the dreaded British hulks, if they surrendered the town.

There was bad news for Wellington on 29 March. Marmont was marching westward towards Ciudad Rodrigo. At Badajoz the breaches would scarcely have been passed by the great siege-master, Vauban, as 'practicable'. Wellington was nevertheless forced to declare them so. He dared not wait. It was doubtful whether the limited skill of his technicians would ever have made them much better. The day after the storming he was forced to tell Torrens:

> The truth is, that, equipped as we are, the British army are not capable of carrying on a regular siege.

The climactic night came on 6 April 1812. William Grattan of the Connaught Rangers noticed that a desperate calm had descended on the ranks of tattered, tanned soldiers waiting in their open-necked shirts and trousers rolled up. Unlike the faces of men before a pitched battle, these faces were at once strained and ferocious—'a tiger-like expression of anxiety to seize upon their prey . . .'. Grattan had observed the same thing before the storming of Ciudad Rodrigo: 'a determined severity'—'an indescribable *something* about them' that caused admiration and awe. Here it was again at Badajoz, and Grattan repeated the telling phrase: 'a certain *something* in their bearing' that marked them both as the priests and victims of Moloch. 'In a word, the capture of Badajoz had long been their idol.'

It happened to be Easter Sunday. After the issue of twenty-seven paragraphs of instructions by Wellington, the Light and 4th Divisions were launched into hell at precisely 10 P.M.

Kincaid, for one, had been in trepidation lest the enemy should 'tamely' surrender before the assault. Now, as the minutes ticked away and the two armies lay enshrouded in a humid mist, silent except for the intermittent '*Sentinel! Gardez-vous*' exchanged between French sentries, the muffled striking of the city's clocks and a faint hum of excitement in the Allied trenches, some of Kincaid's comrades remembered pleasantly the orgy after Ciudad Rodrigo's fall while others, grown 'incredibly savage', resolved to avenge the blood of their comrades shed twice already under those sinister walls. At last, still in quivering darkness, the silent advance into the breaches began. Suddenly a single fire-ball scattered a dazzling radiance, catching the two sides in the split second before they clashed: black figures clustering thickly on the ramparts behind glinting *chevaux de frise* and enormous shells; below them the scarlet columns of the British advancing like streams of burning lava. Inky blackness again. Next moment the whole thing blew up. In the lurid glare of innumerable separate explosions, all the 'forlorn hopes' were dashed to pieces by hundreds of powder-barrels rolling and roaring from the ramparts. The storming-parties found the slope over which they should have climbed bristling with iron 'crows-feet', while the ditch, instead of being filled up with rubble from the walls, had been cleared by Philippon's orders between dusk and darkness and either spread with *fugasses* (small mines) and trains of powder or left pitted by huge holes brimming with mud.[14] Nevertheless, as if driven on by a whirlwind, the multitude behind bounded over the dead and dying and forced their way across planks studded with spikes a foot long; only to be faced on the summit by a long array of captured sword-blades manufactured, mockingly, from finest Toledo steel and set in immense beams fastened down with chains. Baffled and murderous, some of the men forced their comrades in front on to the swords, thinking to make a bridge over their writhing bodies. Not one got across. Forty times and more the bugles rang out and the doomed columns answered their officers' frenzied cries to advance with a loud hurrah. There was never an answering British shout from above; nothing but taunting enemy voices crying out, as the live shells, grenades and fire-balls were tossed over the walls, 'Come up and take Badajoz!' One soldier called it a volcano, another said the ditch was 'vomiting fire'. Robert Blakeney, a mere boy, was not too young to feel the elemental mingling of earth, air, fire and water on this cataclysmic night:

from the very earth destruction burst, for the exploding mines cast

14. General Sir John T. Jones, the expert, positively gasped at the French inventiveness: '*ballots de laine, sacs à terre, fascines, cordages, bateaux, barils foudroyants, chapelets de bombes de quatorze pouces . . .*' (Jones, vol. I, p. 193).

up friends and foes together, who in burning torture slashed and shrieked in the air. Partly burned they fell back into the inundating water, continually lighted by the incessant bursting of shells.

Wellington stood with his staff on a hillock only slightly screened from the fire, calmly, it seemed, reading the dreadful reports by candle-light. But his chief medical officer, Dr McGrigor, saw his jaw drop and his face turn deadly pale as the last appalling news came in of utter collapse in the breaches. Dully he asked someone—he couldn't see who—to take an order.

'Go over immediately to Picton and tell him he must try if he can succeed in the Castle.' Why should any of the subsidiary attacks by escalade succeed, when the stupendous massed assaults had failed? But shortly before midnight an officer dashed up on a foam-flecked horse to announce that they had. Picton's 3rd and Leith's 5th Divisions had again and again rushed up ladders which were continually thrown down or simply burst apart because the timber was green: 'it was almost impossible to twinkle an eye on any man before he was knocked down'. Picton was wounded and so was Hercules Pakenham; but an indomitable will to get over and a thinning opposition at last brought victory.

'Huzza, there is one man up!' On this frail beginning the 45th built a secure lodgment. Hundreds flew over and the Castle was in Allied hands. There was no need for the 3rd Division to batter their way into the town through the Castle gates, for the bugles of the 5th were already sounding in the streets. Taken in the rear, the great French defence at the breaches dissolved away, and the spent survivors of the Light and 4th Divisions marched into Badajoz unmolested. It had fallen in just twenty days.

The town was deathly still though the street lights were shining. Every shutter was closed, for the inhabitants knew better than to come out and welcome soldiers they had hoped would be beaten. According to the barbarously logical rules of war, a town which refused to surrender and forced the besiegers (always at a disadvantage) to storm it at enormous cost, deserved to be sacked—unless of course the inhabitants, as distinct from the garrison, were friendly. The British had never, not even in 1809, found Badajoz friendly. And so, in the small hours of 7 April 1812, pandemonium broke loose. The troops had been through hell—the inundations transformed into fiery lakes of 'smoking blood', the spikes, the shredded bodies, the flames, the blackened flesh, the din, the corpses piled so tight and high they were still warm in the morning. Sudden release from one hell only plunged them into another. Every door was battered in, old men were shot, women raped, children bayoneted. A nun dragged into the street by two soldiers prevailed on one of them to spare her; the other promptly stepped back a pace, took aim and shot his friend dead.

The awful night passed but next morning the army was still mad with drink. Wellington himself was almost killed by a drunken *feu de joie*. Rifleman Costello of the 52nd recognized him by his unmistakable profile, as he stood at the end of a street, surrounded by trigger-happy, shouting soldiers. 'Old boy! will you drink? The town's our own—hurrah!' Someone tried to fire in the air but the bullet went singing past Wellington's head.

He issued (7 April) a General Order—stern, though ambiguously worded: 'It is full time that the plunder of Badajoz should cease.' This did not necessarily mean that he approved of first-degree plunder, so to speak, though Oman thought so, and so no doubt did most of his soldiers. Even educated young men from solid English homes standing among prosperous acres, saw nothing wrong with the rules of war.

W. Bragge of the 'Galloping Third' (King's Own Dragoons): *the Survivors richly deserved the liberty of plundering the Town.*
J. Kincaid of the Rifles: *The men were permitted to enjoy themselves for the remainder of the day.*
J. Donaldson of the 94th: . . . *we were allowed to enter the town for the purpose of plundering it.*
A. Leith-Hay: . . . *the immemorial privilege of tearing the town to pieces.*
W. Tomkinson of the 16th Light Dragoons: *The dead and dying in the breach were the most shocking thing ever seen, and perhaps a little plunder was necessary to drown the horror.*

And John T. Jones, the siege historian, admitted that he had passed lightly over the pillaging, because the French were always so much worse.

It is highly unlikely that Wellington thought his troops 'deserved' to plunder. The testimony of one of his aides-de-camp, James Stanhope, is flatly against it. 'He fulminates orders,' James Stanhope wrote in his journal, 'and will hardly thank the troops, so angry is he.' Pakenham spoke of 'the most shocking licence' in the town which had enabled the enemy to escape to San Cristobal, and added: 'Wellington has been affected in the extreme.' Wellington never forgot the scenes of debauch. 'I remember,' he recalled to his friends years later, 'entering a cellar and seeing some soldiers lying on the floor so dead drunk that the wine was actually flowing from their mouths!' On 8 April the Bloody Provost was sent to stop their 'enjoyment' by setting up a gallows under the grim Cathedral walls. Did Wellington, none the less, regard a moderate sacking as a deterrent? Oman adduces a letter he wrote to Canning in 1820 as proof that he did. If he had put the garrison of Ciudad Rodrigo to the sword, argued Wellington, in this letter, he would have saved 5,000 Allied lives at Badajoz: 'the practice which refuses quarter to a garrison that stands an assault is not a *useless* effusion of blood'.[15]

Too much weight should not be attached to these words. Wellington was discussing the advantages of annihilating a stubborn garrison, not of massacring the civilian inhabitants. More important, he had mounted a favourite hobby-horse—the thesis that progress was not always forward—when he tried in 1820 to debunk for Canning's benefit 'the humanity of modern warfare'. No one could suppose that he actually favoured the slaughter of General Philippon (who incidentally surrendered at San Cristobal on the 7th) in addition to the sacking of Badajoz. What he could not resist was a superficially logical argument, however perverse in reality, which gave him an opportunity to lambaste the 'modern' world.

*   *   *

On the morning after the siege another Wellington showed himself to his deeply astonished staff. He visited the dead on the *glacis*, and seeing so many of his finest men destroyed—his total losses were nearly 5,000—he broke down and wept. They had never seen it happen before. Then, still sunk in grief, he went back and wrote to the War Minister:

15. In explaining the matter to Stanhope on another occasion Wellington said he would have been entitled to slaughter the garrison of Almeida, if he had managed to catch it, but implied he would not have done so. He thought Governor Brennier's dash for freedom was not due so much to fear of death as of having to pay back a debt of £500 he owed Wellington. 'I heard no more of the money' (Stanhope, p. 89).

The capture of Badajoz affords as strong an instance of the gallantry of our troops as has ever been displayed. But I greatly hope that I shall never again be the instrument of putting them to such a test. . . .

He had not felt like that since Assaye.

To realize how unusual for those times was Wellington's emotion, it is only necessary to compare the reactions of others on the field and at home. Picton, for one, was completely nonplussed by Wellington's tears.

'Good God, what is the matter?' he exclaimed. Wellington began cursing and swearing at the Government for not giving him enough sappers and miners. It was the best he could do to explain the inexplicable.

At home, Mrs Piozzi wrote an account of a conversation about Badajoz on 26 April.[16]

Genl. Donkin says it was a glorious sight—the storming of Badajoz; and that old John Duke of Marlbro' would have rejoiced to see the Courage of our officers & men. . . . 51 of the First Rank were knocked down from the Scaling Ladders & died cheering their soldiers.

Fifty-one leaders down at a blow. That was glory.

*　　*　　*

Yet the terrible fall of Badajoz was not without its barrack-room humour, nor even its moment of romance. That 'impudent fellow' Harry Smith, as Kincaid called him, had carried off a lovely Spanish girl of fourteen from under Kincaid's nose. She and her elder sister fled from the stricken city to the British camp, their ears bleeding where the earrings had been brutally ripped off. Everyone wanted to marry her but Harry Smith succeeded.[17] As for the traditional jokes,

16. Mrs Piozzi, formerly Mrs Thrale, friend of Dr Johnson, writing to Mr Alexander Leak, 26 April 1812.
17. Sir Harry Smith (1787–1860), has been mentioned already as a Peninsular diarist. Assistant adjutant-general to Sir Edward Pakenham, New Orleans, 1815; assistant quarter-master-general, 6th Division, Waterloo; Governor of Cape of Good Hope. Married 1812 Juana Maria de los Dolores de Leon (1798–1872), after whom Ladysmith in South Africa was named.

'You know Ben Battle,' they used to say, 'who left his legs in Badajoz breaches?' And what about Colonel Fletcher, a canny Scot, being hit where it hurt most—in the purse? A bullet from Fort Picurina had forced one of his own dollars into the groin.

Napoleon's latest orders to Marmont, written on 9 May 1812 just before he himself set out for Moscow, were also something of a joke, though a bad one. Quite unaware of the changed position in the Peninsula, he informed Marmont portentously: 'it is necessary to maintain an offensive posture . . .'. The posture was not for him to choose, now that both the keys to Spain were in Wellington's hands.

15 Grandeur and Misery

Napoleon's remote control of his marshals reached its nadir of effectiveness with the luckless Marmont, Duke of Ragusa. He had forbidden Marmont to support Soult in the south. Instead, his 'offensive posture' was to consist in a renewed attack on Portugal. Wellington's only fear was lest the Spaniards should yield up Ciudad Rodrigo and Almeida to Marmont as they had surrendered Badajoz to Soult a year earlier. He hurried north to revictual them, not without some grumbling to William:

> I never saw anything like the Spaniards yet!! I am now tied by the legs till I can get these d——d places well provisioned.

Fortunately Hill's legs were able to work for Wellington in the south. He destroyed the French pontoon bridge at Almaraz on the Tagus, thereby cutting all communication between Marmont and Soult west of Toledo. A second bridging triumph on the Tagus at Alcantára rounded off the Badajoz campaign. Wellington ordered Colonel Sturgeon, one of his best engineers, to construct a suspension bridge between what remained of the great arches built by Trajan.[1]

There was only one blot on Hill's brilliant campaign. A cavalry action conducted by the ineffable General Slade, known as 'Black Jack', resulted in a fiasco which stung Wellington beyond endurance. He wrote to Hill in a fine passion:

> I entirely concur with you in the necessity of inquiring into it [Slade's disaster]. It is occasioned entirely by a trick our officers of cavalry have acquired of galloping at every thing, and then galloping back as fast as they gallop on the enemy. They never . . . think of manoeuvring before an enemy—so little that one would think they cannot manoeuvre, excepting on Wimbledon Common; and when

---

1. Sturgeon had already distinguished himself by marrying the romantic Sarah Curran, fiancée of the dead Irish hero, Robert Emmet. She died in childbirth. See p. 403 footnote.

they use their arm as it ought to be, viz. offensively, they never keep . . . a reserve. All cavalry should charge in two lines, of which one should be in reserve. . . .

The cavalry never forgave Wellington for his 'Wimbledon Common' letter, as it was called, of 18 June 1812. Yet exactly three years later to the day something happened at Waterloo which showed that the old devil in the British cavalry was not yet exorcized.

With extensive command of the Tagus, Wellington at last had the pleasure of choosing between two almost equally inviting prospects: the freeing of southern Spain from Soult or an attack on Marmont, now returned to Salamanca in the heart of the Peninsula. A victory in central Spain, rather than Andalusia, could carry the leopards to the Pyrenees. Throughout May and early June 1812, therefore, Wellington made his multitudinous preparations for the great central thrust, including plans for diversionary attacks against Suchet in the east and Caffarelli in the north, not to mention a persuasive scheme for the Spanish General Ballesteros to keep Soult occupied in the south. It seemed enough for one man, even an Iron Man, to do. But from the end of May onwards he had to face the possibility of a dramatic challenge from home.

*   *   *

One element of drama was already a fact. On 11 May 1812, in the lobby of the House of Commons, a merchant named Bellingham whose business had been ruined by the war, shot dead Spencer Perceval. If not otherwise outstanding, Perceval now at least became the first (and so far only) British Prime Minister to be assassinated.

From Wellington's angle it looked as if the consequences would be either very bad or very good. Bad, because the Prince Regent might summon the Opposition and agree to peace with Napoleon. Afterwards Wellington confessed that this was how he had expected the crisis to end—'with the opposition in power'. That would be 'damn Wellington' with a vengeance. Good, because Richard might become Prime Minister, and among the 'Oriental dreams' of which his enemies accused him was the drive for an all-out war effort. Arthur, however, could not quite see Richard back in the Cabinet. In expressing sympathy with Richard over his resignation he had written:

In truth the republic of a Cabinet is but little suited to any man of taste or of large views.

Within a few weeks he received a long letter from William revealing that Richard had for ever 'lost the opportunity of being a Leader'. Soon after his resignation Richard had entered a crowded House of Lords, all agog to hear him 'blow Perceval and his Government to atoms'. But instead of annihilating the Prime Minister, Richard had sat absolutely mute all evening suffering from a mental black-out. Nothing could equal the appalling sensation, added William, created by the speech-that-never-was. Nothing, that is to say, until the gist of Richard's speech which had been intended to blow poor Perceval to atoms, found its way into print just after the assassin Bellingham had done the job for him. 'All parties,' reported William, were horrified by such bad taste and united against Richard. Nevertheless Richard's downfall was postponed for a few days. The Prince Regent, despite everything, sent for his old crony and asked him to try to form a new Government. Not, curiously enough, to become Prime Minister. Simply to find out who would serve.

Enquiry revealed that not a single leading figure in either party, excluding Canning, would serve if Lord Wellesley were Prime Minister. No one was surprised except perhaps the Prince Regent, whose tremendous tribute to Richard at a private party of Lord Yarmouth (later 3rd Marquess of Hertford) was listened to with awe and astonishment by Lord Yarmouth's nephew and cousin.

'You George Seymour and you Hugo Meynell,' declaimed the Prince, 'mind what I now say; that from this day you will see Lord Wellesley the greatest minister England ever had.' H.R.H. swept from the room. George immediately turned to his uncle. Did that mean that Lord Wellesley was already Prime Minister?

'No, nor ever will be,' replied the rakish but by no means unsagacious peer.[2] 'I believe he will have to *Rassle* for a Government,

2. Lord Yarmouth succeeded to the marquessate in 1822. No one could have looked more like a voluptuary than the 3rd Marquess of Hertford (1777–1842), model for Disraeli's Lord Monmouth in *Coningsby* and Thackeray's Lord Steyne in *Vanity Fair*. With his fat oval face, pouting lips and bald pate, he resembled some bursting fruit. Lord Hertford employed J. W. Croker, and Wellington often stayed with him at his home, Sudbourne. Mr Pool, editor of Croker's letters and journal, suggests that Hertford managed to keep separate his two lives of voluptuary and man of affairs. Hertford's nephew became Admiral Sir George Seymour (1787–1870).

for no one else will have him.' The allusion, as George Seymour realized, was to the celebrated Moll.[3]

By 9 June Wellington knew the truth: that there was to be a continuation of the old Tory Ministry but under Lord Liverpool, with Castlereagh still at the Foreign Office and Lord Bathurst in Liverpool's place as War Minister. Wellington was not the man to simulate more confidence than he felt, and Liverpool received a letter from the Peninsula which may or may not have encouraged him to soldier on:

> You have undertaken a gigantick task and I don't know how you will get through it.

Wellington did not believe Liverpool would succeed, unless he had both Canning and Castlereagh in his Cabinet—which seemed impossible. 'However there is nothing like trying. . . .'

A few days later (18 June) he wrote even more frankly to General Alexander Campbell, the friend of the Prince Regent.

> Affairs appear to be in a strange state in England; however, I trust that some Government will be formed. I always detested home politics, and late occurences have not given me a relish for them.

At the end of June more bad news drove him from scepticism to anger. Not only had Richard been excluded from the Government altogether but William, out of misplaced loyalty, had voluntarily stayed outside. Lord Liverpool was informed that though the Commander-in-Chief in the Peninsula was 'perfectly satisfied' with Bathurst as War Minister, his satisfaction ended there.

> I am much annoyed at the breach which prevails between your Govt. and Lord Wellesley, and particularly that Pole is no longer in office. . . .

William received an even sharper rebuke turning into a general malediction. His excuse for not entering the Government—that it would cause a quarrel between him and Richard—was nonsense: their relations would be no worse than before, whereas Arthur's

3. George Seymour called her 'Moll Rassle'. Creevey referred to 'Poll Raffee' (*Seymour MSS*; Creevey, *Journal*, 19 February 1810).

chances of getting the desperately needed money for his soldiers' and muleteers' pay were more remote than ever. Though Perceval and Liverpool were 'very honest men', they both had 'an insufficiently enlarged view of the situation in Portugal . . . .' He had more than once told Ministers that they had no real confidence in their Peninsular Policy—

and I have frequently remonstrated against the Notion that the War was maintained as a favour to me & in deference to my opinion, in which light it has always been considered by the Govt.

Wellington qualified his political tirade, as he nearly always did, with an admission that he might be wrong and his judgement clouded by William having made him 'so confoundedly vexed'. It was to take another year to convince him that Liverpool's 'steady and continued exertion on a moderate scale', as Professor Asa Briggs calls it, was in fact a war-winning policy. Meanwhile Wellington was to continue feeling both responsible and uneasy throughout his coming campaign: responsible for keeping the Cabinet straight on the war; uneasy, lest by losses or lack of victories he himself should shake their supposedly precarious power. In the midst of battles and sieges he never ceased writing letters home to try to get his 'large viewed' brothers back into the Government. Without these political anxieties it is unlikely that he would have been found at Burgos, for instance, risking both too little and too much.

$$\star \qquad \star \qquad \star$$

As usual Wellington kept his own counsel about his next moves. 'As you have left us,' he wrote on 28 May 1812 to George Murray, his valued quartermaster-general, 'I will not *tantalize* you by entering on our plans for the remainder of the campaign. . . .' If Wellington's real object was to avoid leakages rather than tantalization, it was in line with a steady policy. Leakages to the enemy via London were still a major problem, and he had developed his natural discretion into a secretiveness which was commented upon by his half-admiring, half-irritated officers. Lieutenant Bragge, for example, gave a lively account of the Commander-in-Chief's methods in one of his first letters home, dated 6 September 1811:

We hear little or nothing of Ld. Wellington, who keeps not only the Portuguese but the Officers of his Staff in the dark with regard to his Intentions, and I understand at his own Table he rattles away to the General Officers etc., and fills them full of Humbug Accounts which they have scarce time to repeat to their confidential Friends before an order arrives for the Brigades to march without Delay at least 20 Points of the Compass from the one expected.

Five months later, just because everyone expected Wellington to besiege Badajoz after Ciudad Rodrigo, the cunning Bragge suspected him of other designs:

as I know he has talked about it in every Company, I cannot help thinking that he has not the most distant Idea of going near the Place.

Wellington may in fact have been trying a bit of double bluff. After being wrong about Badajoz, young Bragge sent his father a masterly analysis on 6 May 1812 of the reasons why 'his Lordship' would not turn south and attack Soult, opening with the significant words:

Being as much in Lord Wellington's Secret as any General Officer, I have as good a right to talk about what is to be done.

Even Pakenham knew no more than the rest, though he was in constant touch with his idolized brother-in-law over Hercules's terrible thigh-wound and his own health, which seems to have depended on vast doses of 'bark' (quinine). Ned also hazarded that 'the Peer', as Wellington was now increasingly called, 'possibly may look southward again'. Contrary to all their expectations the Peer was looking eastward, and on 13 June 1812 he and his army crossed the River Agueda at Ciudad Rodrigo, *en route* for Salamanca. Forty-three thousand British and Portuguese supported by 3,000 Spaniards covered the parched plateau in four days. Next time they marched over that same ground it would seem like four years. But that June it was good to be advancing again under a commander they trusted, even if they did not quite understand him. Arty or Nosey to the rank and file, Douro to the Portuguese, the Eagle to the Spaniards,[4] the Peer or the Beau to his officers, he had become an object of keen interest to the whole army. Johnny Kincaid was watching him one

4. 'The Spanish Officers and Troops used to call me the Eagle.' (*Wellington MSS*: Duke of Wellington to Angela Burdett-Coutts, 4 October 1848).

day in earnest conversation with General Castaños, when a hare scurried past pursued by two greyhounds; Wellington immediately gave the *View Halloo* and was off—to the astonishment of the Spaniards. Lieutenant Arthur Shakespear, a contemporary of Bragge in the same regiment, afterwards recalled one awe-inspiring moment during the advance on Salamanca: 'I saw the Duke of Wellington quietly pull his boot off & scratch his foot!'

*   *   *

They reached the famous University city on 17 June 1812, where the splendid Roman bridge over the River Tormes, with its green mats of sinuous water-weed, drowsy sand-banks and ancient water-mills gave a false impression of peace. Three forts, built out of the ruins of twenty colleges and thirteen convents had been left garrisoned by Marmont when he retired from Salamanca at Wellington's approach. They would have to be reduced before the Allies could advance farther. (Bragge heard that the French would have pulled down the Cathedral as well, but for a heavy contribution paid by the agonized clergy.) An attempt to escalade the forts failed, for Wellington had not enough siege-guns to batter them. By 20 June the siege had degenerated into a blockade. 'The under Estimating of the works by those who made the secret reports,' wrote Pakenham to his brother Longford, had caused the difficulty.

While the blockade dragged on—a bad omen for future siege-operations—Wellington deliberately let pass an opportunity on 21 June to attack Marmont near the village of San Cristobal, just north of Salamanca. Why did he do so? Henry Tomkinson and many other officers, not to mention Sir Charles Oman later on, could not understand it, since the French were outnumbered and the whole object of the campaign was to destroy Marmont's army: 'we all agreed', wrote Tomkinson, 'Lord Wellington had some unknown reasons . . .'. To the old soldier, Private Wheeler, however, the reason was obvious. Wellington was too well posted on the reverse slopes behind San Cristobal to risk coming down after Marmont. Let Marmont attack him. 'The position we occupy is of vast importance,' noted Wheeler, and 'Monsieur', as he called the collective French, could not see a single man of the Allied army, unless out of 'curiosity' he climbed to the very brow of the hill. From that brow Wellington had surveyed Monsieur through his glass. For a moment his will to stand fast on the defensive wavered.

'Damned tempting!' he exclaimed to his aide-de-camp, James Stanhope, 'I have a great mind to attack 'em!' But he resisted the temptation; while Marmont for his part suppressed any 'curiosity' he may have felt to explore the ridge. Deadlock followed. At the end of four days Marmont retired behind the River Duero (as the Douro is called in Spain), incidentally picking up some much needed reinforcements on the way. This was a pity. But with a government as weak as Liverpool's to back him, Wellington did not feel justified in sustaining the 'great loss' which even a victory at San Cristobal must have entailed.[5]

And so the first part of the campaign ended for Wellington in little better than a draw, though the Salamanca forts having surrendered on 27 June he was able to drive out any regrets over San Cristobal by a triumphal entry into the city. Illuminations in Philip v's imposing Plaza Mayor were followed by a *Te Deum* in the Cathedral, and everywhere he went the Spanish ladies kissed him. The more cultured among his officers strolled blissfully through the streets comparing the lovely ochre and pink buildings with Oxford colleges to the latters' disadvantage, since in Salamanca there were no 'severe Frosts or Smoaky Chimnies' to spoil the sculpture. Many of them saw the famous guerrilla chief, Don Julian Sanchez, and his merry men for the first time, the don in a furred pelisse and immense Hussar cap with the eagle of Napoleon symbolically reversed. Was it not time the leopards made another effort to reverse that eagle in fact?

*   *   *

The situation at the beginning of July 1812 was realistically if baldly summarized by Wellington for the sick General Graham:

> Marmont will not risk an action unless he should have an advantage; and I shall certainly not risk one unless I should have an advantage; and matters therefore do not appear likely to be brought to that criterion very soon.

To the disappointment of both Marmont's and Wellington's now

5. On 7 July he wrote to William Wellesley-Pole about Lord Liverpool: 'I wish to God we had a leader again,' and severely criticized Canning for not agreeing to strengthen the Cabinet by serving with Castlereagh. People's 'extravagant pretentions and vanity will ruin everything' (*Raglan MSS*, no. 47).

evenly balanced armies the 'not very soon' turned into three tedious weeks of marching and counter-marching, the two armies sometimes parallel and within cannon-shot, each commander waiting for the other to make the first mistake. The country around the Duero was almost treeless, and the harassed troops resorted to such desperate measures as burning coffins for firewood after 'scattering their inmates'. The sun was 'scalding hot', the nights bitter. 'I never suffered more from cold,' recollected Wellington, 'than during the manoeuvres of the days preceding the battle of Salamanca.' He also suffered another narrow escape from French cavalry, when a spectator in the Light Division saw him and Beresford galloping out of a mêlée with drawn swords, the former not looking 'more than half pleased'. Wellington indeed was recovering from utter exhaustion after taking the Salamanca forts, though only his confidant William was informed.

I was never so fagged. My gallant officers will kill me.

For a fortnight he had not spent forty-eight hours in bed—always up at 4 A.M. and no rest before 9 P.M.

If I detach one of them, he is not satisfied unless I go to him, or send the whole Army; and I am obliged to superintend every operation of the Troops. However I hold out well.

If Wellington's importunate officers would not let him sleep in bed there was always the remedy of a nap snatched on a hot hill-top, aromatic with thyme and lavender. His staff well remembered one day of pitiless windings by the two armies locked together like angry serpents, when their Commander-in-Chief suddenly flung himself down with a newspaper over his head and strict instructions about calling: 'Watch the French through your glass, Fitzroy. . . . When they reach that copse near the gap in the hill, wake me.'

While Bragge began to tire of their 'wandering Life', with outpost work all night followed by breakfast of beer and onions (no other vegetables available), Harry Smith hated his Spanish girl-wife, Juanita, having to undergo 'an immense deal of marching and manoeuvring' when all she had been used to were short excursions on a donkey. The brackish water was undrinkable. The men simply rinsed their mouths and tried to wash off some of the choking dust and sweat which, grumbled Wheeler, made them look like 'an army of sweeps'.

At last this vile phase came to an end, as Wheeler knew it would: 'for two such armys cannot long remain near each other without doing something'. On 20 July there was a final grand spurt for the River Tormes near Salamanca. Marmont, whose lightly equipped troops depressed the British by always marching just a little faster than they could, was determined to outstrip Wellington and cut him off from his base at Ciudad Rodrigo. Wellington, inexorably resolved to prevent him, sketched his strategy to his staff: he would cross the Tormes if Marmont did, cover Salamanca as long as possible and fight no action 'unless under very advantageous circumstances'. This in effect meant an almost certain retreat. As he stood map in hand a round shot fell unpleasantly close; he moved a little, still talking.

The two armies crossed the river on the evening of 21 July. William Bragge, as supremely confident as most of Wellington's young soldiers, told his father that if there were a fight it would 'probably not be more dangerous than riding behind Old Major in your Buggy'.

*   *   *

No eve-of-battle has ever been more exciting than that of Salamanca. Just as Wellington's rear-guard, the Light Division, were stepping out of the river in beautiful order on to its left bank, a colossal thunderstorm broke. The brilliant lightning flickering on the musket barrels deprived Kincaid of his 'optics for at least ten minutes', while some of the 5th Dragoon Guards were even more unfortunate, being struck in their lines and deprived of their mounts and even of their lives. Major and Mrs Dalbiac of the 4th Dragoons were smothered in the folds of their tent when stampeding horses caught in the ropes, and the major saved his wife only by rushing with her in his arms and depositing her under the nearest gun-carriage.[6]

6. 'This lady,' wrote Arthur Shakespear in his diary, 'was to be seen every day, at the head of the 4th Dragoons, on the march & was constantly exposed to fire—She carried a little havresack & bottle on the pommel of her saddle—Lady Waldegrave, then living with Lord Waldegrave of the 12th Dragoons did the same—she was a most beautiful woman—I have seen her for 4 days together amongst the skirmishers.' These indomitable Amazons seem to have earned all the admiration they received, not to mention the little bottles and haversacks. After Salamanca, Mrs Dalbiac rode all over the bloody field looking for her nephew whom she found wounded and brought back into the city on a donkey.

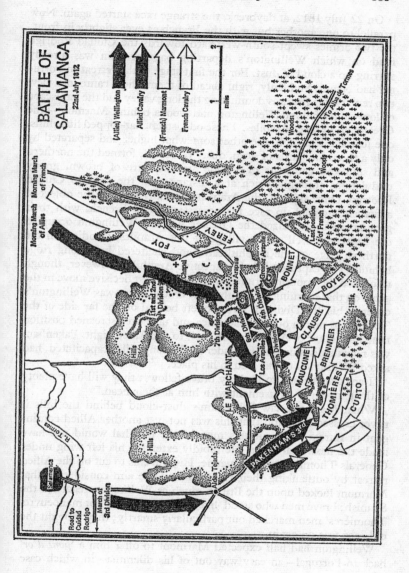

BATTLE OF SALAMANCA
22nd July 1812

(Allied) Wellington
Allied Cavalry
(French) Marmont
French Cavalry

miles

Morning March of French
Morning March of Allies
Morning March of Allies

Woods

To Alba de Tormes

Last position of French

FOY

FEREY

Chapel

Greater Arapile

Lesser Arapile

BONNET

1st and 2nd Division

BOYER

7th Division

6th Division

4th Division

CLAUSEL

Hills

5th Division

Los Arapiles

MAUCUNE

BRENNIER

LE MARCHANT

THOMIÈRES

CURTO

Hills

PAKENHAM'S 3rd

Aldea Tejada

R. Tormes

Salamanca

Hills

March of 3rd Division

Road to Ciudad Rodrigo

On 22 July 1812, at daybreak, the strange race started again. Now
parallel to one another but with the French as ever slightly in front,
the two armies swept south-westward towards the Ciudad Rodrigo
road on which Wellington's departing baggage-train was already
stirring up a cloud of dust. For the first stage of the retreat to Portugal had begun. Suddenly, right ahead of them, there came into view
two remarkable features dominating the long valley and the landscape
of low ridges behind Wellington and woods behind Marmont—the
Greater and Lesser Arapiles. These odd, steep, flat-topped little hills,
one just 400 feet high, the other somewhat higher and separated by
only a thousand yards of deep, dusty red earth, formed the northern
and southern gateposts of a wide amphitheatre of brown, grassy
undulations through which at a distance ran the road to Ciudad
Rodrigo. Once sighted, the Arapiles naturally became the object of
a fiercely stepped-up race for possession. The French, with their
greater swiftness, seized the Greater Arapile. Wellington occupied
the Lesser, as well as the village of Los Arapiles, standing on the
northern edge of the amphitheatre and sheltered by a long ridge
behind. The capture of their respective Araphiles, however, though
it focused the opposing armies, was not the most decisive move in the
game on that morning of 22 July. The crucial event was Wellington's
order to his 3rd Division, hitherto left behind on the far side of the
Tormes, to march out of Salamanca and take up a screened position
near the village of Aldea Tejada, well to the Allied right. Pakenham
was now its divisional commander for Picton, still incapacitated, had
asked Wellington to put Ned in his place.

'I am glad he had to lead my brave fellows; they will have plenty
of their favourite amusement with him at their head.'

When Marmont saw Pakenham's dust-cloud behind the hills it
never crossed his mind that this was not just another Allied contingent in retreat. Without this mistake the marshal would not have
made the next fatal move. He rapidly extended his left wing under
Generals Thomières and Maucune. His aim was to cut off the Allied
retreat by outflanking their right—a laudable aim considering that
Marmont looked upon the British much as Wellington regarded the
Spanish: brave men who stood 'like stocks' but could not manoeuvre.
Thomières' men marched out particularly smartly; they thought the
old race was on again.

Wellington had half expected Marmont to offer him a *'pont d'or'*
back to Portugal—an easy way out of his dilemma—in which case

Marmont 'would have made a handsome operation of it', driving the Allies back after less than six weeks along the road they had come. Instead his telescope showed him through the pearly Spanish light what looked like a movement against his right wing. Could this be the chance 'for which I had long been anxious'? His 5th and 4th Divisions were promptly ordered up to Los Arapiles, with the 6th and 7th in reserve. Another searching look through his glass told him there was still time—for a late breakfast. He galloped into the farmyard where his officers were picnicking, to the braying of donkeys and popping of *tirailleurs* behind outlying stone walls. Wellington told them to hurry up. He refused to dismount but bit at a chicken leg in his fingers. While he was still 'thumping about, munching', an aide-de-camp brought more news of the French left. Wellington chucked the bone over his shoulder, seized his glass, looked over the low farmyard wall and with a curt, 'By God! that'll do,' spurred his horse up the slippery shale of the Lesser Arapile. Suddenly he shut his telescope with a snap.

'*Mon cher Alava*,' he exclaimed to his Spanish liaison officer. '*Marmont est perdu!*'

The French were over-extended and a fatal gap had opened between their left and centre.

Next moment Wellington was off like the wind to Aldea Tejada where Pakenham and the 3rd Division had just arrived. No scribbled notes by aides-de-camp at this critical moment. He tapped his brother-in-law on the shoulder.

'Ned, d'ye see those fellows on the hill?' pointing to the French left.

'Throw your division into column; at them! and drive them to the devil.'

'I will, my lord, if you will give me your hand,' replied the emotional Ned. A group of staff officers standing round noticed how pale Wellington was, but he gave his brother-in-law his hand without relaxing 'his usual rigidity'.[7] As soon as Ned had gone, however, Wellington turned with a triumphant expression to his staff:

7. There are several versions of this incident, but whatever the exact words used by Wellington, his face and voice left no one in doubt that day as to what was to be done. Writing to Hercules three days afterwards Ned said, 'The Peer . . . even surpassed himself in the clearness and energy of his instructions' (*Pakenham Letters*, 25 July 1812). Napier said that Wellington's orders issued from his mouth 'like the incantations of a wizard' (vol. IV, p. 265).

'Did you ever see a man who understood so clearly what he had to do?'

At the same moment a cannon-shot flying from the Lesser to the Greater Arapile tore into Marmont's side, destroying two ribs and an arm. Napoleon's youngest marshal was out of the battle almost before it had begun. For Pakenham it was the chance of a lifetime—and Salamanca was to give him his hour of glory. 'Pakenham may not be the highest genius,' wrote Wellington soon afterwards, but his 'celerity' and 'accuracy' in carrying out orders made him 'one of the best we have'.

Having set the 3rd Division in motion, Wellington sprang into the saddle again and personally carried to each of his other divisional commanders an equally abrupt but no less effective battle order. The Opposition afterwards tried to stir up trouble over these 'Laconic Speeches'; but William Bragge expressed the younger officers' view when he wrote home:

> although not the language of the Marlboroughs . . . it is very much this modern Hero's style of addressing his Generals and is found to answer equally well.

Meanwhile at close on 5 P.M. Pakenham initiated Wellington's master-stroke. Supported by D'Urban's Portuguese cavalry on his right flank, he led the 3rd Division swiftly through the concealing dips and folds between him and Thomières, covered by some of Wellington's sixty cannon and strong in the muskets of Wallace, Campbell and 2,000 Portuguese—altogether nearly 6,000 veterans who had been fighting and winning together ever since Bussaco. The first strike was made by the Portuguese Dragoons. Through scattered bushes, smoke and swirling red dust, D'Urban all at once caught sight of the head of a French infantry column. He charged; behind him the British infantry closed in, Pakenham's generally 'boiling spirit' cool as it had never been before. Thomières' men, taken completely by surprise, managed to fire no more than one burst into Wallace's brigade before the famous rolling musketry of the 74th, 88th and 45th opened up on them. The French infantry crumpled and Pakenham shouted to Wallace, 'Let them loose!' The habitual, grim silence of the fighting British was rent by ear-splitting cheers as they went in with the bayonet. Thomières himself fell dead, two-thirds of his leading regiments and half his entire division were casualties and all his share of Marmont's seventy-eight guns taken. 'The crash was magnificent!' wrote Pakenham. After the crash, the captures: prisoners, colours and an eagle. The emblem reversed on Don Julian's cap was at last a fact on the field. 'Most Nobly,' continued Pakenham, was his own continued advance upon Maucune's Vth Corps supported by Wellington's main forces farther to the east, especially by the Heavy Dragoons of gallant General Le Marchant who lost his life: 'the Fellow died Sabre in hand', lamented Pakenham, 'giving the Most Princely Example . . .'. Even the reserved Wellington was carried away by the spectacle of Le Marchant's superb dash balanced by iron control. 'By God, Cotton,' he shouted as he rode forward beside the divisional commander, 'I never saw anything so beautiful in my life; the day is *yours*.' He was never to see that particular perfection again.[8]

At the end of the attack begun by Pakenham, two French divisions were irreparably broken and a third (Brennier's) disabled; indeed, over a quarter of Marmont's army was defeated. It was this action which inspired a Frenchman to say that at Salamanca Wellington beat 40,000 men in forty minutes.

*　　　*　　　*

No struggle against Napoleon's veterans could be a walk-over, and as Wellington shuttled in division after division diagonally from the left, there were serious setbacks on the 4th Division's front. Pack's Portuguese failed to storm the Greater Arapile, for the perpendicular wall of rock round its crest turned out to be a natural escarpment as impregnable as parts of Torres Vedras. The rest of the division, already heavily outnumbered, were now faced by a fresh corps under Clausel, who had at last come up to take over the chief command from the dead Bonnet, Marmont's unlucky successor. In a terrible confrontation General Lowry Cole was severely wounded and his men put to flight. At this critical juncture Wellington was ready, as always, to plug the hole. He brought up the 6th Division, and Clausel's

8. There were 1,000 sabres engaged in the three vital charges, the 5th and 4th Dragoons being in the first line and the 3rd Dragoons in the reserve. The total casualties were only twenty-eight killed and missing, seventy-seven wounded. Le Marchant fell in the last two minutes of the action. This famous charge stands out from General Slade's fiasco, criticized by Wellington, 18 June 1812 (see above, p. 325), and the 'heavies'' splendid though far from perfect performance on 18 June 1815 (see below, p. 544).

valiant attempt to turn the tide eventually ebbed away in the destruction of two more French corps and a desperate rush by the survivors for the sheltering woods and the bridge of Alba over the Tormes.

*   *   *

With the end of daylight, Wellington's chance to turn the pursuit into a rout also passed away. Blame could be attached to General Carlos de España who had been told to keep a garrison in Alba de Tormes and had removed it, so that Clausel's headlong flight was unimpeded. As a result the pursuit never really got going, apart from one action by General Bock's 'Heavy Germans' at Garcia Hernandez, and was called off by Wellington on the 25th. It is doubtful, however, whether pursuit-to-the-death was ever an activating idea in Wellington's army. There are no homilies on the final sprint in his General Orders to compare with the countless calls for steadiness and regularity. Nor did his men feel much urge to bayonet a fleeing foe whom they did not hate, and who at Salamanca had civilly allowed them to bathe in the Duero during the suffocating July days. In any case the haul was tremendous: 14,000 French casualties at least, to 5,000 Allied. And so Private Wheeler, with the phlegm of countless of his fellow-countrymen, dropped down on the edge of the battlefield, content to build himself a comforting wall of dead Frenchmen against the cutting wind and to fall into a sound sleep.

*   *   *

Salamanca did something for Wellington which none of his previous victories had achieved. Suddenly the world realized that this indomitable stone-waller had become 'almost a Marlborough'—to use the expression of General Foy, the only French commander to survive the battle with his corps intact.

Hitherto we had been aware of his prudence, his eye for choosing a position, and his skill in utilizing it. At Salamanca he has shown himself a great and able master of manoeuvres.

On the Allied army his personal imprint was stronger than ever. He had been ubiquitous—one moment launching the 3rd Division,

the next riding forward with the 5th, then giving the order 'Seventh
Division, advance!'—and all the time bearing an apparently charmed
life. 'Our Chief was everywhere,' wrote Pakenham, 'and Sadly Exposed himself;—in his preservation our little prayers were heard
most surely.' The little prayers at any rate seem to have saved him
from injury by a spent bullet which went through his holster and
cloak.

William Napier of the Light Division discovered a different but no
less impressive Wellington behind the endless galloping and staccato
commands.

> I saw him late in the evening of that great day . . . he was alone,
> the flush of victory was on his brow and his eyes were eager and
> watchful, but his voice was calm and even gentle . . . he seemed
> only to accept this glory as an earnest of greater things to come.

The name of 'Salamanca' for the battle was not widely used except
by the British. Abroad they called it, more accurately, the battle of
the Arapiles. On the Greater Arapile a granite obelisk stands today
commemorating the French; on the Lesser Arapile nothing. Wellington would hardly have cared. He was never addicted to the usual
means by which nostalgic human beings seek to perpetuate the past.
In any case, Salamanca was as much a ladder as a landmark.

*   *   *

The problem was how to make the most of his victory. It had aroused
a fever of hope. The Russian débâcle was still hidden in the future and
Salamanca held the world stage.[9] Arthur conveyed something of the
effervescence in Spain to William:

> The people of Salamanca swear that my Mother is a Saint; &
> the daughter of a Saint, to which circumstance I owe all my good
> fortune!!! Pray tell her this.

9. When discussing Napoleon's defeat in Russia, William Bragge wrote
on 7 February 1813 that 'Salamanca dwindles into a daily skirmish' in comparison.

He added dryly:

> The Marhattas [*sic*] formerly discovered that she was a Marhatta!

Some of his officers already saw Paris shimmering at the end of a
few days' march. And there was his own desire to keep the Government going with Peninsular successes. Militarily he might have preferred an immediate follow-up against Clausel and the 'Army of
Portugal'. But considering his own army's growing lack of food,
money, health, discipline and generals (Graham and Picton still sick,
Cole and Cotton wounded by the enemy, Beresford by an Allied
sentry), the more certain, productive and glittering alternative was
a second triumphal entry, this time into Spain's first city, Madrid.

Wellington's victorious army entered the capital on 12 August
1812, driving before them like a frightened grouse the Intrusive
King, as the Spanish nationalists called Joseph Bonaparte. (Those
Spaniards who could tolerate an alien monarch admired Joseph for
his moderate and reformist rule, calling him 'Tio Pepe', Uncle Jo.)
Wellington's soldiers found it almost impossible to describe the
ecstasy of welcome: the flowers, wine, lemonade, tobacco, songs,
dancing, and so many green boughs that the road looked like 'a
moving forest'—a kind of peaceful Dunsinane. Private Wheeler was
not unwilling to progress 'slowly' forward among 'the most bewitching and interesting little devils I have ever seen', into a city hung with
gold and silver draperies, lighted with tall wax candles and loud with
bells and '*vivas*' for Wellington, the English, the Irish and every other
deliverer, mortal and immortal. Wheeler found he had only one
penalty to pay for so much bliss: 'It was to be kissed by the men.'
To William Bragge the city's sole imperfection was its 'paltry'
Company of Comedians, whose 'most applauded Actor amused us
with using the Pot de Chambre . . . previous to going into Bed, which
Scene concluded the Play'. Wellington as usual painted no word
pictures. 'I am among a people mad with joy,' he wrote simply to his
friend Malcolm. 'God send my good fortune may continue, and that
I may be the instrument of securing their independence and happiness.'

*   *   *

There was much serious work to be done even in tumultuous Madrid, if this goal were to be attained: the enormous treasure-trove from the Retiro fortress to be distributed, including guns, shoes galore and two more eagles; the usual General Orders to be issued against plunder (Wheeler calmly stole all the English books from the Royal Library) with heartfelt requests to treat the common people 'kindly'; and preparations for the next move. Nevertheless the son of a saint was not to be let off with less than the best in the way of glory. The Cortes gave him the Order of the Golden Fleece, and he received a gracious letter from Maria Teresa de Bourbon accompanying the Collar which had belonged to her father, the Infante Luis. She wrote in English explaining that this was her contribution to 'that fraternity which ought to animate the two Nations.' Francisco Goya, supreme artist of the war, painted him incomparably, bare-headed on horse-back in his blue Spanish cavalry cloak; and if there is a restiveness in his eye and carriage more Spanish than Wellingtonian, it is not often that the cause of international fraternity is served by genius.[10]

It was while Goya was painting him that an incident occurred which threw a flood of light on Wellington's character. He had sent for his relatively new inspector-general of hospitals, James McGrigor, and in his friendliest manner asked him about the state of the wounded between Salamanca and Madrid. Now McGrigor had studied his chief. He had learnt, for instance, to make his medical reports succinctly without reading them from notes, a procedure which Wellington detested. McGrigor's reply, however, showed that he still had a lot to learn. Having explained how large the numbers were, he blandly went on to disclose that on his own initiative he had redirected the main pockets of sick, together with their supplies, on to a better route than the one fixed by Wellington.

10. This was the only painting of Wellington executed by Goya from life; X-rays have now revealed that it was painted over a portrait of King Joseph, whose dim shadow still lingers behind the Duke's head, where he hangs today in the Waterloo Gallery, Apsley House. It was exhibited in Madrid on 1 September 1812. Goya wrote to a friend: 'Yesterday His Excellency Sen Willington [*sic*] Duke of Ciudad Rodrigo was here. There was a discussion of the plan to put his picture before the public in the Real Academia, about which he expressed much pleasure . . .'. It is the only equestrian portrait. There are three others: the very fine red chalk drawing in the British Museum from life, the painting in the National Gallery, Washington (wearing blue and the only one in a hat), and the scarlet-uniformed portrait in the National Gallery, London, wearing a medal, the Peninsular Gold Cross, which was superimposed by the artist, not having been issued until July 1813. This is the picture which was stolen in 1961 and recovered in 1965.

The face Goya was studying changed. Wellington started up in a rage. How dared McGrigor alter his orders? Goya was aghast. McGrigor pleaded the danger to life, the losses at Talavera through delays. All no good.

'I shall be glad to know who is to command the army? I or you? I establish one route . . . you establish another, and order the commissariat and the supplies by that line. As long as you live, Sir, never do so again; never do anything without my orders.'

Suddenly the voice dropped and he sat down. Would Dr McGrigor dine with him that evening? The doctor saw that he must—and was seated next to his host.

*   *   *

On 22 September the end for which Wellington's brother Henry (now Sir Henry Wellesley, K.B.) had worked so long was gained at last: the Spanish Cortes created him Generalissimo of all their forces, with an estate near Granada named Soto de Roma.

Not to be entirely outdone, the English Prince Regent created him a Marquess with a grant of £100,000 by Parliament towards a future home. But when he heard that the Prince would also permit him to bear 'a Royal augmentation, *in the dexter quarter of the arms of Wellington*', he shied away from such 'ostentation', particularly as Richard wished it to take the form of an eagle. If he had to have an 'augmentation' it had better be Lord Bathurst's suggestion of the Union Jack. (It was). Nor did he wish his son to be created an earl, 'unless it should be necessary'. Bathurst agreed that it was not necessary. With the Tower and Park guns firing salvoes and Londoners almost as mad as the Madrileños, Lord Bathurst was kind enough to inform him that 'the modest and retiring conduct of Lady Wellington during the exultation of this city' had made a very favourable impression.

*   *   *

No doubt Lord Bathurst meant his compliment sincerely. It cannot have altogether pleased Wellington, if his reactions to Kitty's conduct were anything like William's.

Kitty's journal had at length restarted in September 1812. Her object as before was 'to compare in what I am engaged [*sic*] while He, the object of my thoughts, is engaged abroad'. And so on 9 September she began:

> At one o'clock went to the Poles: found Mr Pole very angry with me for not having gone to the Ball last night: it was given in honor of Lord Wellington's victory and taking possession of Madrid. . . . I could not go.

Nothing could have been less indicative of Kitty's true feelings. The diarist, Miss Berry, had a note about her on Monday, 24 August:

> I went to Lady Wellington's, the new Marchioness. She appeared to have suffered a great deal from the uncertainty which everybody had been in for more than a fortnight, and she spoke with an enthusiasm and a worship of her hero which was truly edifying.

There was also an account in the newspapers, quoted by Maria Edgeworth, of her '*running* as fast as she could to Lord Bury at Lord Bathurst's when he alighted, to learn the first news of her husband!' Maria was enchanted with Kitty. '*Vive l'enthousiasme!*' she commented: 'without it characters may be snug and comfortable in the world, but there is a degree of happiness . . . of which they have no more idea than an oyster can have.'

Three weeks after her first diary entry Kitty, with more than a touch of the oyster herself, had another crisis of confidence—and no doubt another rebuke from Arthur's brother:

> *Tunbridge Wells. September 29th.* My Mother began her journey to Ireland and I returned to my brother and my children. Being determined not to be held up *en spectacle* and finding myself totally unequal to attending the ceremony of putting up the Eagles [captured at Salamanca and Madrid] I thought my best plan was to leave town. I did so, and wrote to Lady Liverpool from Sevenoaks to excuse myself. She must receive my letter tomorrow before the ceremony commences.

Lady Liverpool was a staunch friend of Kitty's but even she must have felt this was not the way for a hero's wife to behave. Eventually the eagles had to be brought to Kitty. 'They are mine!' she cried, kissing them hysterically, and fainted away.

If Kitty felt ashamed, there were no signs of it for once in her journal; indeed it registered a sense of steady improvement.

> In the course of the last 12 months what various events have taken place: how different do I feel, altho' my situation exhibits no change—my Husband still abroad, my Children at home. My health nearly as it was: delicate, not positively unhealthy, but my mind strengthened, my habits different. I can now occupy myself and look without terror at the future.

Judging by Ned's letters, Kitty's emergence from her old state of lethargy seems to have been due to her mother giving her a new domestic 'philosophy'. The tragedy was that however fast Kitty moved, Arthur ran faster still. The gap between them was widening.

*   *   *

For the moment, however, it seemed to be Arthur who was faltering in the race. During the next three months—September, October, November 1812—the painfully frank Dr McGrigor wrote that 'everything went wrong with him'. Yet his hopes had been high.

After Madrid he started north to drive Clausel's 'Army of Portugal' out of Valladolid, capture Burgos and—who knows?—spend the winter of 1812 on the Ebro, the last great river before the Pyrenees.[11] In any case he intended to double back to Madrid and rejoin Hill if and when 'the plot thickens to the southward', in other words, when Soult's army from Andalusia joined Joseph's around Valencia and made things too hot for Hill. He needed fortune's face, not her back, to bring off such *coups*. The idea of wintering on the Ebro in 1812 was in its way as improbable as Napoleon's dream of wintering in Moscow. Possibly, if Wellington had realized how well the Government were plodding along in England, he would not have entertained it. *Il joue serre*, said General Foy approvingly of Wellington at Salamanca—he plays safe.

11. He wrote buoyantly to George Murray from Valladolid on 7 September 1812: 'Matters go on well, and I hope before Christmas, if affairs turn out as they ought, and Boney requires all the reinforcements in the North [Russia], to have all the gentlemen on the other side of the Ebro' (*Despatches*, vol. IX, p. 394).

Even now his detour to the north against Clausel was only doing what had to be done anyway, sooner or later, but at the back of his mind was the glimmer of a greater game.[12]

The town of Burgos has never forgotten that it was the birthplace of that eleventh-century ruffian, the Cid. The great Cathedral, magnificently ornate, is joyless. Its strange Santo Cristo, with human hair and limbs of rhinoceros hide, broods over rather than protects it—in the same way that the ruined Castle, on its remote eyry, broods over the city. William Bragge, who fell in love with Madrid, found Burgos 'one of the worst large Towns I have seen in Spain. . . . The People horridly ugly and what is rather remarkable for Spaniards excessively dirty'; he had no wish to go farther north, 'except to embark'. Like many another soldier in Wellington's army, he had suddenly dived headlong from exhilaration to unutterable staleness. 'I hope to God this will be Lord Wellington's last Campaign in Spain as I get quite weary of the Service,' he wrote to his father on 8 September. 'You cannot conceive half the Misery of it—we are wretched.' The misery involved sharing a house with two officers, two Portuguese, the *patron*, his wife and nine guerrillas. Next time Bragge wrote about housing conditions it would be while encamped outside the 'cursed Castle' of Burgos in open huts made of branches, without straw or palliasses, like 'Father Pigs'.

There are signs that the march from Valladolid to Burgos, and now the sight of its Castle, had much the same effect on Wellington. All his attempts to corner the 'Army of Portugal' on the way there had failed and it had escaped eastwards again. Looking at Burgos Castle for the first time through his telescope he was unpleasantly surprised by the strength of its outwork, keep, and double walls clinging to a precipitous rockface. He had been told that Burgos was

12. Military historians have not been slow to criticize his performance after Salamanca, but they seem to have under-estimated his desire to help the Government at home—a factor brought out again and again in his unpublished letters to William Wellesley-Pole (*Raglan MSS*). His (political) decision to go first to Madrid before finishing off Clausel has been particularly censured since it indirectly caused the Burgos débâcle. Fortescue thinks the dazzling range of choices after Salamanca caused him for once to lose his bearings; other writers state simply that he lost his infallible touch during the postponed pursuit of Clausel. Oman brushes aside the grand Ebro plan, apparently in an effort to simplify and thus defend Wellington's strategy, and does not mention the key letter to Murray. The truth is probably that Wellington's plans were to a certain extent pragmatical. There were many 'ifs', as he told Murray.

a relatively minor obstacle.[13] Though he captured the outwork on 19 September, thanks to the gallantry of a kilted young major, Edward Somers-Cocks, his report on the operation was symptomatic of a grey mood: 'I doubt however that I have the means to take the castle which is very strong.' These legitimate doubts, repeated at intervals throughout the siege, got through to his army and created a spreading circle of gloom. All the subsequent attacks confirmed his worst fears. The leader of one storming-party failed to understand his instructions, lost the way and was shot down with Wellington's plans in his pocket, which the French understood all too well. On 4 October a mine was successfully sprung and two breaches in the outer defences carried, but next day and again three days later the French swept down from their fastness, killed the guards and workmen in the trenches, carried off all their tools—perhaps the least of many evils, considering the tools' wretched quality— and shot Somers-Cocks through the heart while he was rallying his men.

The death of Cocks on 8 October seems to have knocked the heart out of Wellington. An outstandingly daring Intelligence officer, he was Wellington's *beau idéal* of a soldier. Nobly born (his father was Earl Somers), dedicated to his profession but even fonder of field experience than of the new military colleges, Wellington probably saw in him the young eagle who would soar above Britain's pitiful generals. Colonel Frederick Ponsonby remembered how Wellington had broken the news. Abruptly entering Ponsonby's room, he had walked up and down in silence, opened the door again, announced briefly, 'Cocks is dead,' and left without another word. At the funeral his look of sheer despair prevented his friends from speaking to him.

The loss of Cocks highlighted the deficiencies of the men left behind. Wellington already deeply regretted having yielded to the 1st Division's entreaties to take them to Burgos, instead of the 3rd and Light, who were experienced in sieges. The 1st had complained bitterly after Salamanca at not having 'Justice done them'. According to Bragge, Wellington replied, 'They had been very ill used but he would see them righted at the first opportunity.' This was unfortunately Burgos, and of these inexperienced troops only the Guards did their duty in the trenches. As the siege dragged on, the

13. So it was, given proper materials for a 'regular siege' and defenders less talented than the French.

positive contributions of some officers were as irritating as the failures of others. One Marine officer arrived at headquarters with a new bayonet exercise which would render one Briton equal to twelve Frenchmen. This reminded Wellington's staff sourly of the Marine who had earlier invented an '*artificial hill*'—a tall pole on which the Commander-in-Chief would be hoisted to survey the enemy.

'Damn me, Sir, I may tumble down and break my neck!' objected Wellington.

'Oh! my Lord, *if that is all*, you may send up one of your aides-de-camp.'

A Portuguese 'projector' wanted to burn up the French army with convex glasses. Burgos, however, was remarkable for a sunless month, deteriorating into icy deluges quite unusual even for the Spanish autumn. When all the inventions had been rejected and the last assault delivered and repulsed (18 October) Wellington miserably decided to abandon 'this d——d place'.

Looking back, it is hard to assign his failure to any single cause, so deficient was he in all the essentials of a victorious siege. He had only five engineer officers and eight men, the urgency of the Government on this question being typified by a letter from Lord Mulgrave (master-general of the Ordnance) promising that Wellington's engineers at Burgos should be supplied *before the engineers in America or the West Indies*. His assaults were piecemeal rather than smashing, partly because he refused to incur heavy losses as at Badajoz; partly because the French Governor, more brilliant even than Philippon, never gave him time to consolidate any success; partly because the essential battering-train for a knock-out blow was abysmally wanting. Wellington possessed only three long eighteen-pound guns, a few howitzers and far too little ammunition of all kinds. Pakenham wrote home on 25 September that it was 'some what provoking' to have 100 siege-guns at Madrid with Wellington so short, and military historians have differed as to whether Pakenham or at any rate Admiral Sir Home Popham and his Marines could have got siege-guns across to Burgos from Madrid or Santander in time; perhaps one of Popham's 'projectors' would have invented a way of making heavy guns move like gallopers. Wellington, however, halted Popham's eighteen-pounders when they had still fifty miles to go and time seemed too short.[14] The three siege-guns he depended on, christened

14. The arguments for and against Wellington on this count are found in Weller, *Peninsula*, p. 236, and Oman, vol. VI, p. 41.

optimistically by his soldiers Thunder, Lightning and—because it had lost one of its trunnions—Nelson, were eventually reduced to Nelson alone. Ironically, the army slipped out of Burgos after dark on Trafalgar Day, 21 October, with wheels muffled in straw. By now it was high time. Wellington was under immediate threat of being cut off by the advancing French armies, since the Spanish general, Ballesteros, had dramatically failed to oppose them in the south, as ordered. On 23 October, inflamed with jealousy of the new Allied Generalissimo, Ballesteros made a personal bid for supreme power. The Cortes promptly imprisoned him in North Africa. This was alacrity of the first order, but too late to help Burgos.

A serious though short-term result of the Burgos fiasco was a drop in Wellington's magic. Even the war-weary Bragge had expected Burgos to be captured somehow: 'as Lord Wellington in all his military Career never missed taking a Fort, I do not imagine he is going to be outdone at Burgos'. When the hero was in fact outdone, temporary disillusionment followed. One Coldstreamer decided that, much as he *revered* Wellington, he had shown unmistakable signs of obstinacy during the siege, while another declared bluntly: 'If ever a man ruined himself the Marquis had done it. For the last two months he has acted like a madman.' Dr McGrigor, whose sharp medical glances had detected the anxiety beneath Wellington's calm at Badajoz, now noticed his frequent 'bad humour'. A pleasanter thought on which to leave dark and dripping Burgos is that Wellington magnanimously faced history taking all the blame himself. Lest he should damage the very politicians he had aimed to strengthen, he wrote on 23 November to the Prime Minister:

> I see that a disposition already exists to blame the Government for the failure of the siege of Burgos. . . . It was entirely my own act.

And to a group of friends many years later:

> It was all my own fault; I had got, with small means, into the forts near Salamanca. The Castle was not unlike a hill-fort in India and I had got into a good many of those. I could get into this, and I very nearly did it but it was defended by a very clever fellow. . . .

Another very clever fellow, Napoleon Bonaparte, evacuated Moscow just three days before Wellington extricated himself from Burgos, each beginning what was to prove the most agonizing retreat in his career.

* * *

Wellington's soldiers had the advantage of plunging straight into the Spanish wine-country between Burgos and Salamanca, though for some of them the vats of newly fermented liquor were as lethal as Russian snows. Twelve thousand soldiers got drunk at Torquemada, and what looked like banks of dead bodies lined the road, only waiting to be picked up by the enemy. Private Wheeler eagerly watched a Dragoon fire his pistol into a thousand-gallon tank; next minute they were all up to their knees in wine, 'fighting like tigers'. Yet despite the gruesome crimes (and punishments) which marked Wellington's hectic retreat to Salamanca—35,000 Allies pursued by 60,000 French—he and Hill were united by 8 November on the Tormes. The wounded at Salamanca had been moved ahead of Wellington, a great *coup* for Dr McGrigor of which he took full advantage. He said boldly:

'My lord, you recollect how much you blamed me at Madrid . . . when I could not consult your lordship, and acted for myself. . . . *Now* if I had not, what would the consequences have been?'

Wellington was not going to be drawn into an argument about exceptions to his rule.

'It is all right, as it has turned out,' he retorted; 'but I recommend you still to have my orders for what you do.'

McGrigor, though he became very fond of Wellington, always considered this insistence on orders a 'singular' feature in his character. McGrigor was mistaken. What was truly singular was Wellington's desire and ability to keep the whole elaborate organization of his army in his own hands. Given this system, a fanatical insistence on orders was not singular but essential.

Against the British initiative, Soult showed less than alacrity, sailing with a wide wheel like a wary kite, said Napier, to seize a helpless prey, and losing it altogether. Wellington's evasive action, on the other hand, was brilliant. 'I fairly *bullied* the French into remaining quiet upon the Douro for seven days,' he wrote, 'in order to give [Hill] time to make his march.' He felt justified on 31 October in crowing a little: 'I have got clear in a handsome manner, of the worst scrape I ever was in.'

*   *   *

The combined armies of Soult and Marmont (the latter's now commanded by Souham) amounted to 100,000 men against the 70,000 of Wellington and Hill. Nevertheless Wellington was eager to give battle on the familiar heights of San Cristobal or the Arapiles and waited hopefully for a week. But when the old kite, refusing to pounce, began a slow, menacing circle across his route to Ciudad Rodrigo, he could wait no longer. On 15 November rain began to fall and the Allied army marched out to face the rigours of the last lap. The only man to ride was Dr McGrigor who had been kicked by a horse and was lent Wellington's carriage.

All might have continued 'handsome' but for a blunder by Wellington's new quartermaster-general, Colonel James Willoughby Gordon. This impossible colleague was already in Wellington's bad books. He had caused a garbled version of one of his chief's secret despatches criticizing the Government to reach the Whig *Morning Chronicle* and had amused himself during the siege of Burgos by writing letters 'of the most desponding cast' to Grey and Whitbread. (Wellington had generously agreed to Gordon keeping Grey in the picture but struck at Whitbread; and rightly so, since Whitbread passed on Gordon's croakings to Creevey, who in turn sent them to his wife. Gordon was married to the sister of R. H. A. Bennet, the Radical M.P.) At the same time Gordon was intriguing with the Prince Regent and Horse Guards to get himself created the Army's first ever Chief-of-Staff—an innovation which, if Gordon had possessed Berthier's talent as well as his own industry, might have proved very useful. Fortunately the War Office itself decided that Gordon would not do: '*He estimates his own good Qualities & acquirements to the highest pitch of self approval*,' wrote Colonel Torrens to Wellington on 29 September, 'and he is possessed of the most inordinate ambition. . . .'

Soon after that letter arrived Gordon showed how far his self-esteem exceeded his abilities. As quartermaster-general responsible for routing the army's supply column during the retreat, he misdirected it twenty miles wide of Ciudad Rodrigo, so that the men got no rations whatever during the last days. With the French on their heels, rain on their heads, mud sucking off their shoes and nothing to eat but the acorns which fed wandering herds of pigs, these prodigal sons fell into a 'savage sort of desperation', quarrelling, cursing, plundering, straggling, starving and dying in thousands. Order and regularity were washed away in the interminable rain. Sir Edward Paget, commander of the 1st Division who had lost an arm at Oporto, was seized from his horse by daring French skirmishers; while three other generals, Dalhousie, Oswald and William Stewart formed what Wellington afterwards sarcastically called a 'Council of War' and decided to disobey their marching instructions. In consequence they led their men into an impasse and had to be rescued by a furious Wellington.

'What did he say?' asked the diarist Charles Greville when Fitzroy Somerset told him the story.

'Oh, by God! it was far too serious to say anything,' replied Wellington's *fidus Achates*. Others present, however, remembered that after a terrible pause the Commander-in-Chief had remarked icily:

'You see, gentlemen, I know my own business best.'

It is also said that while riding in search of the truants Wellington met the officer in charge of the baggage.

'What are you doing, sir?'

'I've lost my baggage.'

'Well, I can't be surprised . . . for I cannot find my army.'

This and a hundred other anxieties gave Wellington the harassed, exhausted look which many noticed as he rode by in his glistening oilskin cape and ruined cocked hat. Despite the murmurings at Burgos, the vast majority still welcomed his familiar, plainly dressed figure with a mighty shout, 'Here he comes!' But even among these enthusiasts some cooled after an episode which had its beginnings in the bleak, hungry early hours of 17 November.

Wellington was awakened with a start by the loud rattle of musketry. The enemy falling upon his flank patrols? Not this time. The firing came from his prodigal sons, especially those in the 3rd Division, who had been agreeably disturbed by the sudden charge of hundreds of black pigs across their front. Discipline was thrown to the winds and the ravenous men scattered far and wide on an impromptu pig-shoot, incidentally wounding two Dragoons, falling in large numbers into French hands and giving Wellington his fright. Two days later, on 19 November, Ciudad Rodrigo was reached and armed guards held off the frantic rear-guard while the long-lost biscuit was at last brought in and distributed. Wellington's prodigal sons, however, were far from being welcomed home by a forgiving father.

Two of them had already been hanged for 'the shameful and unmilitary practice of shooting pigs in the woods . . .'. Now it was the officers' turn to be indiscriminately pilloried in the most sweeping and explosive circular ever issued by Wellington. He had written it, according to Dr McGrigor, in a very bad humour, apparently just before reading his copy of Cobbett's *Weekly Register*, which Kitty always posted him, presumably to keep him in touch with the worst news from home. McGrigor found him crouched over a miserable fire into which he threw the *Register* before reading his celebrated jobation to the doctor.

Never had he commanded or even read about an army, he thundered, which had so gone to pieces.

> Yet this army has met with no disaster; it has suffered no privations which but trifling attention on the part of the officers could not have prevented . . . nor . . . any hardship excepting . . . the inclemencies of the weather when they were most severe.

He did not question the gallantry of officers; what he wanted to see was 'minute and constant attention' to orders.

This tirade, running to well over twelve hundred words, did not end as so often with a disarming, 'I may be wrong,' but with an attack on the slowness of British cooking which the proud officers of Moore's old Light Division, in particular, regarded as an unfair comparison with the French. Like today's boy scouts the Shorncliffe boys prided themselves on their nimbleness in kindling a flame with a couple of wet sticks. When they remembered with what labour their men collected firewood while the French simply tore down the nearest door; and how they lugged up monstrous iron kettles from the rear while the French carried light tin kettles along with them, the comparison seemed doubly odious. Johnny Kincaid, while agreeing with Wellington that the army's sufferings were not such as to justify their terrible 'irregularities', boldly declared himself ready to make a fire as fast as anyone in France and to roast the French on it into the bargain. Arthur Shakespear found the whole thing beyond a joke and wrote resentfully that Lord Wellington thought little of their 'trials'.

Here was a new touch added to the image of what Pakenham called the 'Iron man'. Already admirably iron in his own self-discipline and endurance, he now seemed inflexibly iron in his demands upon others. Later, he was to make no bones about the right way of running an army:

There is but one way;—to do as I did—to have A HAND OF IRON. The moment there was the slightest neglect in any department I was down on them.

The notorious circular, though intended only for his commanding officers, soon found its way into regimental files and so into Opposition newspapers. It was probably true, as Tomkinson heard, that Wellington afterwards regretted his outburst, particularly as he had not known at the time of the commissariat's failure and the consequent irony of his call for instant cooking when there had been nothing to cook. Many vexations had been simmering during the retreat from Burgos and like the French kettles he boiled quickly. If he had waited a few weeks his main anxiety—the bitter disappointment at home—would have been removed. For Bathurst assured him that everything was understood and his decision to retreat honoured.[15] Foreign opinion considered his retreat the acme of fine generalship.

There were other consolations. His army recovered quickly. In their winter quarters the men revelled in cheap food and tobacco, the officers—'sporting-mad' according to Harry Smith—in beagling, fox-hunting and the occasional wolf-hunt, or 'the continual tramp up to Oporto', as Pakenham called it, to buy pipes of port for their families at home. Reinforcements kept arriving: there was even a rumour, circulated by a spy, that the Tsar was sending 15,000 men; this, however, proved false and no Russians were to be seen during the following June marching through Castile with snow on their boots. He had lost 5,000 men on the retreat but sent 20,000 French prisoners home. A less exacting commander would have lost far

15. Thomas Sydenham waggishly described to Wellington on 8 December 1812 how he had been examined by the Cabinet on the retreat. After he had been handed the Lord Chancellor's slice of turbot (for they were at dinner), the doors were locked and his interrogation began. All would have gone well but for the constant, absurd interruptions of Lord Westmorland. At last the Chancellor, seeing that they would never cross the Agueda, said, 'Come, come, Mr Sydenham, answer no more questions but pursue your march' *Supplementary Despatches*, vol. VII, p. 495).

more. All Spain south of the Tagus was free and the guerrillas elsewhere rampant.

At the end of a tremendous year he rode off to Cádiz to see what he could do for the Spanish army but with wider prospects in mind. After all, he was the Child of Fortune, and on 10 December he wrote resolutely to Beresford, 'I propose to get into fortune's way. . . .'

16 Vitoria

Cádiz gave its new Generalissimo a lyrical welcome.

Ahe Marmont, onde vai, Marmont?

They changed the popular tune composed at Cádiz when Marmont retreated from Salamanca. As always when his own praises were sung, Wellington listened coolly. As soon as the head of the landau in which he rode was lowered and the hero's face and figure became visible, a torrent of enthusiasm broke over him. 'The Eagle! The Eagle!' they shouted, seizing and clinging to his hands. A few ardent glances slid off on to the young Fitzroy Somerset riding with him, and there were renewed cries of joy at such a pair of impossibly red, English cheeks— '*Mirar el Rubio!*' On the return ride to headquarters in January 1813 Wellington described his success with the wry elation which his friends had learnt to expect:

> I was very well received at Cádiz and Lisbon and throughout the country and I ought to have somebody behind me to remind me that I am 'but a man'. I believe that I have been upon the whole, the most fortunate and the most favoured of God's creatures and if I don't forget the above mentioned, think I may yet do well— but all classes do every thing in their power to spoil me.

The next time he reviewed the troops his horse was richly caparisoned with a net embroidered in gold and purple by the ladies of Cádiz. As if all this were not enough, news came from England that the Horse Guards and Prince Regent also wished to spoil instead of damning him. He was made colonel of the Blues, and given the Garter vacated by the death of his old chief, Lord Buckingham. Unlike Richard, Arthur had neither studied nor worked for this honour; he had to ask Garter King at Arms whether the ribbon was worn from the right or left shoulder.

Official confirmation of the French disaster in Russia brought further hope that he might 'yet do well'. With his elevation since Salamanca into a European personage, he was deferentially consulted by the Cabinet as to whether in the new circumstances he should be sent to open a second front in Holland or (the Prince Regent's pet scheme) in Hanover. He had not the slightest hesitation in saying No. The fact was that by early February 1813 he had made audacious plan for driving the French right out of Spain; and from what he knew of his generals it was highly improbable that such a plan would succeed under anybody but himself. Indeed he hoped to get a dozen or so of his present generals recalled without hurting their feelings, and to prevent Colonel Torrens from sending out any substitutes: 'they really do but little good . . .'. Colonel Gordon's health conveniently broke down and he was replaced by Wellington's original and invaluable quartermaster-general, George Murray.[1]

At the beginning of March Torrens reported signs of renewed trouble on the domestic front from Mary Anne Clarke and the Princess of Wales. 'I wish both these *aimable women* were hanging at any of your outposts,' he wrote. 'We must have a victory from you . . . to put these things out of the public mind.'

* * *

Wellington was almost ready to oblige with a victory. While he seemed to be entirely absorbed in running Portuguese foxes to earth (it was said that his hounds had killed one only, by 'mobbing', but they gave him what he wanted—a lot of healthy exercise) he was in reality hunting down and remedying the many evils which had tormented his army during previous campaigns. There were to be tents to replace the hated bivouacking in the open, and prefabricated hospitals under the efficient Dr McGrigor. The suggestion had come from the doctor and been received in silence until suddenly, while walking up and down with McGrigor outside his headquarters one morning, Wellington said,

'By the by, your hospitals are ordered out and may soon be expected.' The only good suggestion of McGrigor's which Wellington rejected was the introduction of French-styled *ambulances*.[2] When

1. Wellington managed Gordon's recall so tactfully that Torrens wrote in great amusement and relief: 'Colonel Gordon *is now only anxious* upon the disappointment you will experience from *His not returning* according to the promise he made ! ! !' (Torrens to Wellington, 13 January 1813, *Wellington MSS*).
2. These ambulances were the invention of Baron Larrey, the famous surgeon of the *Grande Armée*. It was said that Wellington, at the height of the battle of Waterloo, took off his hat in salute to the gallant healer who was pointed out to him by an aide-de-camp.

William asked that a young friend of his, Dr Moseley, might be promoted, a caustic Wellington firmly turned him down: the young man was very agreeable and sang remarkably well, 'but he knows nothing of Physick . . . and he is the most negligent & inattentive attendant upon sick soldiers that we have in the Army'. Singing was no longer enough.

With the new tents to be carried on army mules, the officers were sternly ordered to find other conveyances for their own baggage; a not inconsiderable problem, since even a young subaltern like George Robert Gleig, who joined Wellington's army in February 1813, brought with him a bulky kit.

1 Regimental jacket; wings & lace; 2 grey trousers; white, coloured & flannel waistcoats; flannel drawers; 12 stockings, 6 shirts, 1 pelisse; 3 prs. boots, 1 shoes.

This, however, was nothing to Lieutenant Ker of the 9th Dragoons who according to William Bragge brought fifty boxes out to the Peninsula that year:

He is a pretty Man, remarkably neat and wears a Blue Velvet Forageing Cap, gold Tassel and Band of the same edged with white Ermine. How nice.

As at home, there was always a little trouble with *aimable women*— the Portuguese girl, for example, who ran off with Lieutenant Kelly and whom Wellington ordered to be sent home on condition she was not put in a convent. It now turned out, wrote General Cole, that the lovers had already been married by the Caçadores' chaplain; should she still be 'given back to her mother'? Wellington's soldiers generally agreed that the recent suppression of the Inquisition by the Cortes would at any rate save many Spanish girls from convents and mothers. According to the newly arrived Judge Advocate-General, Francis Seymour Larpent, there were no women at Freneda, the army's headquarters, 'but ladies of a certain description'.

Personal reports on Wellington's life during these months suggest an abstracted figure, too busy to attend to anyone but his staff or an occasional little peasant child, who would lead him by the hand to a sweet-stall in the market-place, while he hummed a short, dry tune, no doubt thinking of the new tin kettles and whether Mr Larpent would succeed in restoring the efficiency of courts martial.

Great success indeed attended Larpent's efforts to make discipline effective and fair, but it was some time before he won Wellington's confidence. By February 1813 he risked expressing surprise at the strenuousness of his work. Wellington gave a bleak smile.

'And how do you suppose I was plagued when I had to do it nearly all myself?'

Larpent was also surprised by the austerity of Wellington's table: no port wine, only thin claret, *vins du pays* and brandy. He little knew that for the coming campaign the Commander-in-Chief had ordered from Dublin forty-five dozen of the best claret and twelve dozen champagne, six of them his favourite Sillery brand—all to be shipped appropriately in the vessel *Mars*.

*   *   *

While Wellington was completing his preparations Maria Edgeworth and Kitty were visiting an exhibition of Sir Joshua Reynolds's pictures. 'Charming, amiable Lady Wellington,' rhapsodized Maria, 'as she truly said of herself she is always Kitty Pakenham to her friends.' Maria went on to compare Kitty's 'dignified graceful simplicity' with the behaviour of *'beaux esprits,* fine ladies and fashionable *scramblers* for notoriety . . .'. There is, as always, something a little defensive in Maria's praise. For simplicity was at a discount in that age of elegance.

*   *   *

At last by mid-May everything was ready. Great was the excitement among the troops in recognizing old friends again after the long months in winter quarters, from fellow-soldiers down to the very mules, Portuguese boys and trulls. Johnny Kincaid made it all sound like the beginning of a delightfully raffish new school year. Most of their grudges against Wellington had melted away in the spring sunshine, and one of his generals, F. Robinson, wrote in April:

> The former want of success has made no impression on our people, they place such confidence in their Hero, that no one questions his conduct. He is their idol, for whom they will offer their lives as freely as they will drink his health. . . .

Their idol's greatest triumph during the months of preparation had been to bring his enormously cumbersome bridging-train from the Tagus to the Douro, without the enemy catching the faintest echo of

its loud, discordant progress. This pontoon train, however, was by
no means Wellington's only secret. His evasiveness about strategy
had at once struck a newcomer like Larpent: that day for instance
when he had begun talking blandly about spending next winter in
Portugal.

'But we have eaten nearly all the oxen in the country', interposed
the commissary-general pointedly.

'Well, then, we must set about eating all the sheep,' said Wellington, 'and when they are gone I suppose we must go.'

Go? What exactly did he mean? Go forward into Spain or back to
Britain? No one cross-questioned him. But his favoured quartermaster-general, George Murray, ventured a quip.

'Historians will say that the British army . . . carried on war in
Spain & Portugal until they had eaten all the beef and mutton in the
country, and were then compelled to withdraw.'

Wellington did not care what historians would say as long as the
enemy did not guess.

*   *   *

The success of Wellington's new advance into Spain depended upon
two strategic surprises, both typical of his imaginative mind and
secretive methods. Instead of leading his whole army out along the
obvious Salamanca road, he divided it into two unequal parts, riding
personally with the smaller contingent of 30,000 men, in order to
deceive the French into thinking this was his main thrust.

Having entered Salamanca on 28 May, he coolly handed over his
command to Hill and slipped away next day towards the northern
mountains, where General Graham with the real invasion force of
60,000 men was trudging through country considered impassable by
the French. Soult, who knew it of old, no longer led a French army,
to give King Joseph the benefit of his advice. The Intrusive King
had at last succeeded in getting rid of him that February and was
now in supreme command himself with Marshal Jourdan as his
chief-of-staff. No one dreamt that Wellington would deliberately
launch his soldiers, far less guns, into the formidable wilderness of
Tras os Montes. Nevertheless it was on this secret march of Graham's
that Wellington pinned his hopes of outflanking the French line on
the Douro. William Bragge, armed with six pounds of tea, an English
cheese and a keg of brandy, was one of those who set out buoyantly
with Graham's army longing to see the 'new Route into Spain'.

A rough ride of fifty miles brought Wellington on 29 May to Miranda do Douro on the Portuguese side of the border, where the river boiled and seethed at the bottom of a ravine. Those travellers who wished to cross it clambered into a wicker basket and were wound over by a primitive system of ropes and windlass. Wicker baskets had been one of Arthur's specialities in India, and it was nothing to him to sway above the river in the spume of a cataract. The point was to go forward, not round, for time was short and Joseph must be outflanked before he had time to concentrate. Without the Army of Portugal his force was no more than 60,000.

Next day, 30 May, Wellington galloped into Graham's camp. Here all was anxiety. How get the army over the rushing River Esla, a tributary of the Douro? Bragge and his fellow-Dragoons had already decided that the secret route, the like of which had never before been attempted by British cavalry, had much better have been left alone. For days on end they had scrambled up and down precipices in single file. And then this river. . . . But though there was some croaking, Wellington's personal popularity had been too thoroughly restored to languish now. The infantry owed him their precious tents, which they took a childlike pride in erecting as if by a magician's wand, to the amazement of the peasants. One moment there would be nothing, the next—great cities white as snow. 'Jesu Maria, these English are the Devil!' The Heavy Dragoons had recently received from him 350 guineas for horses and guns captured at Salamanca, besides 1,500 dollars for an earlier success at Llerena: 'he is again a fine Fellow', wrote Bragge. He would lead them safely into Spain.

'Farewell Portugal!' cried Wellington, turning his horse round and waving his hat as he crossed the frontier for the last time. 'I shall never see you again.'[3]

Once on the Esla, it was speedily decided to send the first troops over by the ford of Almendra. The wild river, full of melted snow, swept a number of unlucky Brunswickers and ten men from Wheeler's 51st to their death; the others were dragged across clinging to a stirrup or horse's tail of Grant's Hussars. These then fixed the famous pontoon-bridge, and the rest of the army marched over it.

3. This story was told to General Donkin by Picton who was with Graham's army. Donkin considered it almost too 'theatrical' to be true of Wellington, but could not doubt Picton's veracity. Donkin probably did not know that Wellington had been an enthusiastic amateur actor in India. There seems no reason to doubt the story; indeed it is easy to overdo the picture of Wellington as the stern, silent Englishman.

The crossing of the Esla completed the first part of Wellington's strategic triumph. By 3 June his whole army of 100,000 men were united at Toro, north of the River Douro. Now began the second stage of this incredible May–June campaign. From Toro, instead of marching due east with conventional ease and deliberation along the great *chaussée* or Royal Road to France, pushing the French slowly before him, Wellington suddenly turned his army north again into more bleak hills, crowning his original flanking movement with another lightning sweep to the north-east, this time turning the French on the line of the Ebro. Such an astonishing manoeuvre, with the French border at the west end of the Pyrenees as its target, only made sense if Wellington could effect a total revolution in his supply system. This in fact he had accomplished in the second of his great surprises. Lisbon and Oporto were abandoned as his twin bases in favour of Santander on the Bay of Biscay, dependent on supply vessels using the short sea route from England. Wellington of course was taking on new burdens. He had staked his future on cooperation between the Army and Navy—an issue which rarely if ever made its appearance in British history without causing a furious paper war between the Services.

*   *   *

All 'offensive postures' had meanwhile vanished from Joseph's army, and his very name Intrusive King became more and more of a mockery as he was extruded from town after town, beginning with Valladolid, by the remorseless but invisible pressure of the enemies on his flank, whose only outward sign of existence was a cavalry screen which effectively prevented him from knowing what they were doing. As Corporal William Emmott, a Methodist in the Royal Horse Guards, put it in suitably biblical language: 'The French, with might, haste and vigour, did slip from one mountain to another before we had scarcely time to count the valleys.' At 7 A.M. on 13 June these unseen enemies were astonished to hear a tremendous explosion to the south of their march. It was King Joseph blowing up Burgos. Henry Tomkinson, young Cocks's friend, could not help sighing: if only they had not tried to destroy Burgos themselves, Cocks would have still been with them, and they would have wintered pleasantly on the River Tormes. And now as Joseph still retreated and Wellington's four great parallel columns, all streaming inexorably eastwards like apocalyptic rivers, began to descend from the barren uplands, an attempt was again made by Wellington's officers to stop him going farther.

Why not end this brilliant campaign here and winter luxuriously on the Ebro? That the march had been extremely testing no one denied. Young Captain Arthur Kennedy of the 18th Hussars, who had joined Wellington's army that spring, remembered the retreat to Corunna and considered the march to the Ebro even more tiring—'But,' he added proudly, 'the Hussars surmounted all!' The Hussars, however, had horses; it was worse still for the infantry whom Wellington, it was said, dared not question as to their well-being for fear of getting a dusty answer. Moreover there was not a man in Wellington's army who had not blinked with rapturous surprise at the fertile Ebro valley laid out below in miniature like a lotus land of vineyards and streams. But Wellington would not listen to the lotus-eaters. He knew that the majority of his army was spoiling for a fight. In Harry Smith's words, they had revelled in the 'wonderful weather' and even more wonderful supplies, not to mention their wonderful leader. Altogether it had been 'a most wonderful march'—'every man in better wind than a trained pugilist'. Those whose wind and feet did not respond quite so well to the rapidity and rough paths, were only too anxious to take it out on the French. So the advisers who begged Wellington to 'look to a defensive system' against the French armies, were silenced. 'I thought differently,' he recalled to Croker.

> I thought that if I could not *hustle* them out of Spain before they were reinforced, I should not be able to hold any position in Spain when they should be. . . .

He had risked saying 'Farewell Portugal' and did not intend to eat his words.

The hustle began on 17 June. Joseph's armies, discovering on that date that the River Ebro, like the Douro, Carrion, Pisuerga and Arlanzon before it, had been turned, immediately poured back still farther along the Royal Road into the valley of Vitoria, with the Allies on their tail. Vitoria's ten-mile-long plain, lying aslant like a diamond among the surrounding hills, was cut diagonally from corner to corner by the road and also, more waywardly, by the River Zadorra. This 'merry brawling trout-stream', as Fortescue calls it, was spanned by a dozen stone bridges and curled itself at the valley's western end into the writhing loops and bends of a whip-lash in action. The slim golden spires of Vitoria, with its famous 'White Virgin' gracefully enshrined on the outer wall of St Michael's church, stood out on an eminence two-thirds of the way across the plain to the east. The town was the centre of a five-pointed star: the Royal Road sweeping in from Madrid in the south-west and out to Bayonne in the north-east; the northern road to Bilbao, the southern road to Logroño on the Ebro, at the edge of a mountainous plateau whose sandstone rocks looked like houses and the houses like rocks; and lastly the bad road running out due east to the fortress of Pamplona in the Pyrenees.

Joseph drew up his 57,000 men and eighty guns in three defensive lines behind the Zadorra, Count Gazan commanding the first, with Generals d'Erlon and Reille in support. Almost as many more guns, besides prolific supplies were stored in Vitoria, and a mile or so beyond the city was a vast caravanserai of civilians and baggage. The King did not forget to have stands erected in the town from which the people might watch him beat the English. He did forget to break down the Zadorra bridges.

*   *   *

On 19 June the spirited Arthur Kennedy found himself bivouacked in the hills only three leagues outside Vitoria, close to 'the *great Lord*, as he is called (and certainly no one deserves the appellation more justly) . . . and thus two great personnages reposed their bones near each other!' Kennedy's hungry troops were lucky to find an abandoned French dinner consisting of seven sheep. Next day the whole army were allowed to 'repose their bones', while Wellington waited for Graham's column on the left to come up. Kennedy was dazzled by the beauty of their encampment which he found lovelier than the finest parts of Wales. That evening he climbed a hill to take a look at Vitoria. In front of it lay 'an enormous host' whose fires and torches gilded the spurs of the distant mountains. Word flew around the Allied camp that the *great Lord* would be in that glittering city next night or die on the spot.

Dawn broke on 21 June 1813 in a cold, drizzling mist. But after Salamanca, rain before battle could only be a good omen. Wellington's aim was bold and simple: with his 78,000 men divided into four columns supported by seventy guns, to cut King Joseph's Royal

Road to France and destroy his army. A flanking swoop on the left by
Graham behind the northern mountains and down the Bilbao road
was to do the actual cutting. On the right wing Hill would make a
strong feint in and above the village of Puebla, where the fact that
six centuries earlier the Black Prince had fought and won would help
to convince Joseph that this hallowed ground was Wellington's chief
concern. Wellington himself commanded the two central columns.
Part of the Allied force was guarding his rear, with Pakenham in
charge as adjutant-general. He reluctantly accepted the post, since
Picton had returned to the 3rd Division.

The French, more interested in great frontal attacks, expected
Wellington to come at them *en masse* across the Zadorra from the
west. When Joseph did suspect a feint it was in the wrong place:
half-way through the morning he was suddenly to divert a force he
could ill spare down the Logroño road, thinking that Graham's
movements in the north were bluff and an attack was developing
from the south.

At about 8.30 A.M. the first shots of the battle were fired, when Hill
sent a splendid brigade of Spaniards up the precipitous heights of
Puebla, supported by Cadogan's 71st Highlanders. Below in the
defile the rest of Hill's corps were massed under their divisional
commander, William Stewart, the same of whom Wellington had
said after the retreat from Burgos that 'he never could obey an order'.
Wellington had since come to a private arrangement with Hill that
he should in future always act as Stewart's 'nurse'. Stewart's orders
were now to advance against Vitoria by the Royal Road after the
Puebla heights had been secured. Once again, in this upland struggle
among crags and gorse, an officer in a kilt was to bring sorrow and
glory to Wellington's army. In desperate fighting, Colonel Henry
Cadogan, a former aide-de-camp of Wellington's and brother of
Henry Wellesley's runaway wife, was mortally wounded. As his
eyes began to cloud over the sun burst through the mist, and he asked
to be carried to the edge of the cliff, where he could see his Highlanders to the last. There he died with a true Nelson touch: 'I trust
to God that this will be a glorious day for England.'[4]

4. Henry Cadogan had tried desperately in 1809 to rescue his sister from
her seducer, first by offering to sell out from the Army in order to devote
himself entirely to her protection and, when she declined to give up her
lover, by challenging Paget to a duel on Wimbledon Common. It was Paget's
chivalrous refusal to fire back which probably saved Cadogan for a finer
death on the heights above Vitoria (Anglesey, pp. 100–4).

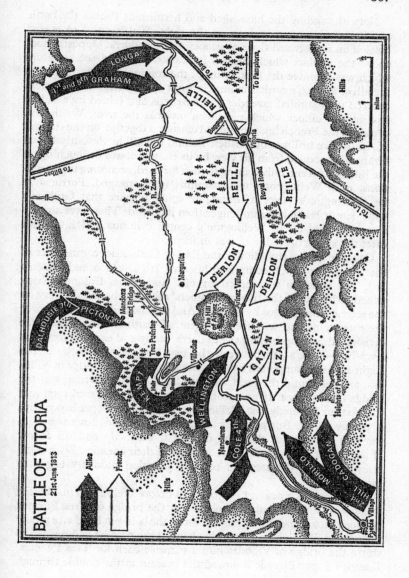

BATTLE OF VITORIA
21st June 1813

Allies
French

Notwithstanding the bloodshed and heroism at Puebla the battle of Vitoria was not to be won on the right. Wellington had posted himself on a westward slope overlooking the Zadorra. Opposite him, above the poplars which fringed its banks, he could see a feature which was to prove the focal point of the coming struggle. This was the hill of Arinez, a conical mound in front of the village of that name, covered with stunted lavender and harebells and joined by a saddle to a second hillock which ran down towards the river. Wellington could see the French high command clustered together on the summit of Arinez like brilliant butterflies. Behind the hill he devoutly hoped Graham, concealed from his view by its contours, was debouching on the Bilbao road and only waiting to rush forward, according to instructions, until Wellington's own columns were engaged. Fortunately for Wellington's peace of mind, he could not see that Graham's wide detour had taken him longer than intended. There was already a serious hold-up in Wellington's centre columns and his whole carefully synchronized plan was in jeopardy.

Cause of all the trouble was the Earl of Dalhousie, commander of the left-centre which comprised his own 7th Division and Picton's 3rd. The situation was something of a tinder-box. Dalhousie happened to be one of the two 'newcomers' who had been led astray on the retreat from Burgos by Stewart. And now he had lost his way over the mountains and was keeping them all waiting. Here were three divisions drawn up behind the Zadorra, ready and eager to force the river-line—Cole's 4th between the two bridges of Nanclares, the Light Division supported by a Hussar brigade at the bridge of Villodas, and far round the great hair-pin bend, Picton champing at the bridge of Mendoza. It was probably during these fevered moments that Arthur Kennedy saw Wellington riding by on Copenhagen with a 'pensive' look. But precisely as 'the Lord' passed along the road, the rain ceased and the mist dissolved. Kennedy and his fellow Hussars for the first time saw the masses of their enemies. With equal unexpectedness the stagnant military situation suddenly began to move.

An enterprising peasant was brought before Wellington just before midday with the astonishing news that the bridge of Tres Puentes between Picton and the extreme point of the hair-pin bend was totally unguarded. Wellington promptly changed the plan he had formed to storm the bridge of Villodas into a surprise dash for Tres Puentes. Kempt's Light Brigade followed the peasant at the double through the scrubby juniper bushes which covered the hillside down to the river's outer bend. On the far bank, a towering perpendicular cliff completely hid them from the French. They passed the bridge unscathed except for their unlucky guide, who was decapitated by a cannon-ball. Here, supported by some of the 15th Hussars, they again settled down, somewhat puzzled to be on the French side of the river, and waiting for the battle to begin.

If Wellington was impatient, Picton was beside himself. He rode to and fro hitting his horse's mane with his cane and swearing.

'Damn it! Lord Wellington must have forgotten us.' At last an aide-de-camp came galloping up, but with his eyes searching the mountains.

'Have you seen Lord Dalhousie?'

'No, sir! I have not seen his lordship: but have you any orders for me, sir?'

'None.'

'Then pray, sir, what are the orders you do bring?'

'Why, that as soon as Lord Dalhousie, with the Seventh Division, shall commence an attack upon that bridge,' pointing to Mendoza, 'the Fourth and Sixth [Light] are to support him.' Picton's passions boiled over. The idea, the monstrous idea that another division, the 7th, should fight in his front. He drew himself up and bawled at the flabbergasted aide-de-camp:

'You may tell Lord Wellington from me, sir, that the Third Division under my command shall in less than ten minutes attack the bridge and carry it, & the Fourth and Sixth may support it if they choose.' Turning to his men, he ordered them forward in language that would have made the reforming Radicals shiver:

'Come on, ye rascals!—Come on, ye fighting villains!' This grave and grand insubordination was the beginning of victory. For it in fact carried out Wellington's design, though in an unorthodox way. An onlooker watched the 3rd as it 'swept like a meteor' across the 7th's path (Dalhousie's leading columns were now up but not Dalhousie himself), gallantly defended for a time from the French batteries by Kempt's riflemen hiding at Tres Puentes; then on through grape and round-shot towards the hill of Arinez, the Connaught Rangers in the centre, the 45th and 74th to right and left and Picton cursing and yelling, dressed like a mad bonfire guy in a broad-brimmed top hat (he was suffering from eye trouble) and blue coat.

By now the whole line of the Zadorra was aflame, the 4th and Light

Divisions having been launched across their allotted bridges and fords by Wellington himself, while the French retreated from all the river bends in rolling clouds of dust and smoke. The deafening cannonade from both sides was echoed by Graham's guns at last roaring in the north-east and by Hill's quickening assault on Gazan's southern flank. By 3 P.M. or soon after, Picton had torn a great rent in the French centre; he joined forces with two more infantry brigades under Wellington's personal leadership; together they all drove at full speed for the north side of Arinez hill and the village beyond.

There is more than one personal glimpse of Wellington during the great battle for this hill, the same hill on which three hundred of the Black Prince's knights had fallen. One moment Wellington appeared suddenly at Kincaid's elbow, rebuking him for caracoling his horse.

'Look to keeping your men together, sir.' But this time it was not the usual case of a cavalry officer showing off; Kincaid's horse had been frightened by a cannon-ball. At another moment Arthur Kennedy caught sight of the familiar figure in a 'grey frock' issuing orders 'with the sangfroid of an indifferent spectator'.

Kennedy went through a gruelling experience in Arinez. His commander, Colonel Colquhoun Grant (no connection with *Granto el Bueno*), had ordered the Hussars to charge three solid squares of infantry protected by cannon. The leading squadron were almost annihilated by 'shot and shell and every delicacy of the season' until Grant, realizing too late how 'imprudent' his order had been, called them off. This fiery barrage, wrote Kennedy, was the enemy's expiring effort. For the Allied infantry led by Picton on the flank and Wellington in the centre succeeded in driving them off the hill and village. The French never managed to establish firm new lines behind Arinez. Inch by inch they gave way on all sides, 'unable to withstand the impetuosity of our British and Portuguese, who rivalled each other'.

Farther to the north, Harry Smith, brigade-major of Vandeleur's Light Brigade, managed with gay effrontery to bounce the slow Dalhousie into giving him the privilege of capturing d'Erlon's key village of Margarita.

'What orders, my Lord?' asked Smith twice in peremptory tones, for his brigade, sent up to support Dalhousie, was coming under fire. 'What orders?'

'Better take the village,' muttered Dalhousie uncertainly to his quartermaster-general, whom he was consulting before giving Smith an answer. But Smith overheard and did not wait for more.

'Certainly, my Lord,' and he made off at once in order not to hear them calling him back. After the victory Dalhousie paid him a generous compliment.

'Upon my word, sir, you receive and carry out orders quicker than any officer I ever saw.'

Smith replied with a flourish: 'You said, "Take the village." My Lord, there it is! Guns and all.'

*   *   *

There they were, guns, arms, baggage, food, money, women and all. There were so many women in Joseph's army that a French officer described it as *'un bordel ambulant'*—a mobile brothel. And now it was all abandoned. For that was the final and inconceivable end to the battle of Vitoria when, after 5 P.M., the news was shouted by the French from column to column that King Joseph had ordered a general retreat. The change from Reille's disciplined resistance in the north-east, where the French gunners were still 'bounding with frantic energy in streaming fire and murk', into unutterable chaos there and everywhere else, was a matter of minutes. *Sauve qui peut* became the order of the day. As the last shells boomed overhead, 'a dull and horrid sound of distress arose' from the dense throng of civilians choking the fields behind Vitoria and competing with soldiers and animals for a foothold on the few narrow tracks which converged on their only escape route, the Pamplona road. If only Wellington had been a commander 'like unto Joshua', sadly reflected that earnest Methodist in the Horse Guards, Corporal Emmott, and been able to gain three more hours of daylight by ordering 'the Sun to stand still on yonder mount and the Moon in yonder valley', the whole French army would have been taken prisoner.

The French artillery, released from duty at last and suddenly tearing into 3,000 jammed carriages, created confusion enough; Colonel Grant made matters ten times worse by rashly sending his Hussars pell-mell into the town on top of the fugitives and in advance of the Allied infantry. Kennedy felt this slap-bang charge in which he took part might have proved fatal if any of the French army had been able to turn on them ('I believe Lord W. thought that too'); but fortunately they managed to clear the streets as far as the

Pamplona Gate without being fired on except by snipers. Never would he forget the sight: royal coaches and generals' coaches inextricably mingled with baggage-wagons; the finest horses, mules, bullocks and donkeys he had ever seen; ladies' pet monkeys and parrots— 'in short, Noah's Ark'. The King, he heard from Joseph's captured servants, had abandoned his berline, leapt on a horse and dashed out of the town only five minutes before the 18th Hussars arrived. 'How unlucky I was,' lamented Kennedy, 'not having caught Joseph.' He and his comrades, not excluding their colonel, were to catch it from Wellington instead.

King Joseph's coach, as a matter of fact, had already been stopped by Captain Henry Wyndham of the 14th Light Dragoons and Lieutenant Lord Worcester of the 10th Hussars. Lord Worcester was using his escape from Harriette Wilson to good purpose. They discharged their pistols into the coach's nearside window and out sprang the Intrusive King on the other side, extruded yet again but still a free man. Either the British did not recognize him or his escort was too quick for them—or possibly it was the magnetic contents of the coach which held back his pursuers. From among the treasures inside, Wyndham's Dragoons acquired Joseph's lordly silver *pot de chambre*, which they christened 'The Emperor'. Their successors still use it at mess functions for drinking toasts in champagne, after which the pot is placed ceremoniously on the drinker's head.

Meanwhile the 18th Hussars could not resist the great sport which had suddenly started up under the guidance of French stragglers, by whom it had been known and honoured throughout the Peninsular War as '*le pillage*'. Spanish peasants quickly joined in the fun. Treasure-chests and ladies' bandboxes flew open and the ground was covered as if by magic with doubloons, dollars, watches, jewels and trinkets. 'Where did it all come from?' asked Kennedy. 'The whole wealth of Spain and the Indies seemed to be here.' Most of it had indeed been pillaged from the Spanish people, and who could blame them for grabbing some of it back, ably assisted by their Allies? Even Kennedy was richer by a silver brandy cup, when he and the majority of the Hussars eventually continued their delayed pursuit of the French army. Colonel Grant was generally believed to have helped himself liberally. 'Lots of Ladies Jewels [and] Lace Dresses,' wrote Bragge to his father in Dorset, describing the contents of the looted carriages, 'some of which you will probably see round *Mrs Grant* at Weymouth, as I hear the Col [*sic*] was active.' Many of

Grant's brigade were so 'active' that they never got back on to the road at all.

Joseph's captured coach fared little better at the hands of the 18th Hussars, a detachment of which Wellington put on to guard it. Inside were quantities of state papers and love-letters (for Joseph's regal intrusions were occasionally directed towards boudoirs), but above all a collection of priceless canvases, the property of the captive Spanish King, Ferdinand VII. (Wellington was not to know how valuable they were until six months later.) The pictures were probably saved from the sentries' attentions by being roughly rolled up; but it was thought that some state documents were purloined,[5] and certainly a corporal stole the gold ends from a marshal's baton which he found in an ornamental case of blue velvet embroidered with thirty-two gold eagles. The rest of the baton was promptly stolen from him by a drummer in the 87th. Next day (22 June) the 87th proudly presented their share of the trophy to Wellington; whereupon the 18th Hussars sent along the engraved ends, 'to undeceive him about the 87th'.[6] Thus the whole of Marshal Jourdan's baton—for such it was—came into Wellington's hands. He in turn was to present it to the Prince Regent, whose ecstasies over the victory had been unparalleled. 'When I went to the Prince with the news,' wrote Croker to his wife on 28 July, 'he embraced me with both arms. You never saw a man so rejoiced.' Jourdan's bauble, as Fortescue gloomily calls it, was just the thing to crown the Prince's joy.

*   *   *

Wellington's feelings in the hour of victory and the days immediately following were something less than joyful. As usual after a battle, his mood was set by the losses not the glory. The Allied casualties at

5. Wellington forwarded a selection of Joseph's state papers to Lord Bathurst with the frank remark that as Bathurst's office was 'a sink of papers' he would be glad to have these 'really curious' documents back again for his own files (*Despatches*, vol. XI, p. 76, 3 September 1813). The present Duke of Wellington has returned the private letters from Joseph's wife and daughters ('*Mon cher petit papa*', etc.) to France.

6. (Kennedy to his mother, 22 December 1813.) Kennedy's Vitoria story only gradually unfolded as he sent back replies to his relatives' questions. He was at first rather cagey about his exploits, forbidding his brother to hand his letter round 'the tea-tables in Belfast among all the old "cats" '. He was able to assure them that he personally had not got into trouble over the Hussars' misbehaviour.

Vitoria—just over 5,000 against the French 8,000—were not exceptionally heavy. But Henry Cadogan's death, in Wellington's own
words, 'diminished exceedingly the satisfaction' he felt in 'success'.
The success itself, though breathtaking in one respect, fell short of
hopes in another. The world had seen nothing like Wellington's
booty since the days of Alexander the Great. Among the masses of
captured equipment were 151 cannon, just on two million cartridges,
immense quantities of ammunition and 100 wagons: according to
Wellington himself, everything 'except one single carriage and one
single cannon'. The great haul of guns sent Wellington's thoughts
back to Assaye, and he wrote to his old friend of Indian days, Sir
John Malcolm:

> I have taken more guns from these fellows . . . than I took at
> Assye [sic], without much more loss. . . . The two armies were nearly
> equal in numbers, but they cannot stand us now at all.

Nevertheless Wellington aimed at capturing Joseph's army as well as
his armament and loot. He did not succeed.

The initial pursuit up the Pamplona road on the evening of the
battle had to be called off after five miles. Broken ground unsuitable
for horses and torrential rain provided obstacles which only a cavalry
commander of exceptional ability could have surmounted. There was
no such man on Wellington's staff. 'We would have done more, much
more,' wrote Kennedy, 'if Somerset or Lord Uxbridge had been in
command.' Meanwhile nemesis was to overtake the 18th Hussars.
Wellington happened to find some of them in Vitoria dead drunk. So
incensed was he with their junior officers that he refused to fill the
gaps caused by casualties from the ranks of their own subalterns.
'The 18th are sent to the Germans [King's German Legion] to learn
Out Post Duty . . .' wrote Bragge with just the faintest touch of
malice. He was only human, and there had been considerable rivalry
between the recently arrived Hussars and his own more experienced
Heavy Dragoons. Vitoria and its aftermath settled the score in the
'Heavies' favour. During the battle the Hussars had 'nearly galloped
their Horses to Death' according to Bragge, and misbehaved afterwards, whereas Colonel William Ponsonby's Heavy Brigade had
dashed past a heap of dollars on the Pamplona road without touching
a coin. They were all rewarded (Captain William Hay got thirty-three
dollars) and at the end of the war Wellington congratulated them on

never having a man before a general court martial. Lifeguardsman Robert Moore from Lancashire wrote home that his unit also had been complimented by Wellington: 'Well done, Life Guards, you have behaved yourselves as becoming Household Troops. . . .' The Lancashire lad had joined up expecting to see the world, but only in the shape of London—'never dreaming of leaving England'. He found Vitoria lasses 'very pretty and condescending', though in fear of mass ravishment.

Arthur Kennedy stoutly defended the 18th to his mother: after great fatigue they naturally did a little plundering and drinking. If Wellington had not happened to see some of them and stopped promotions, no more would have been heard; 'the most unfounded lies' had been propagated about the 18th, but 'Major Hughes has had an explanation with Lord W. on the subject and all is now settled . . . and his Lordship is to forget the past business . . .'.

Wellington was not able to dispose of the 18th's colonel, Colquhoun Grant, as easily as he had dealt with their subalterns. When he demanded Grant's recall, Torrens wrote back that on the contrary Grant was insisting on promotion, having been made a promise by none other than H.R.H. the Duke of Cumberland—'but of course the latter has no right or power to make one'. For a short time Wellington prevailed, and on 25 August William Bragge was able to inform his father that 'the Black Giant [Grant] has been under the Necessity of retiring to England in high wrath'.

Grant may have retired, but it was not to England. He simply waited at the Spanish port of Passages for fresh instructions from his friends at the Horse Guards. When they arrived, it was General Robert Long (also on Wellington's black list) who was recalled, so that the Black Giant might step into his shoes.

*   *   *

Mismanagement of the cavalry by some of his officers was undoubtedly one reason why Wellington could not follow up his victory. Some critics then and since, however, have blamed Wellington himself for not getting the best out of his staff. William Tomkinson, for instance, asked himself after Vitoria why Wellington's army was always so deficient in pursuit. He saw the answer in a combination of distrust and something like jealousy. 'Lord Wellington may not like to entrust officers with detachments to act according to circumstances, and I am not quite clear if he approves of much success, excepting under his own immediate eye.'

William Bragge got nearer to the truth. As a cavalry officer himself, Bragge kept his ears open to the nuances of regimental discussion and recognized the nauseous mixture of arrogance and incompetence in too many of his superiors. At the same time there is a hint that his brusque Commander-in-Chief had perhaps not found the best way of handling such touchy material. Bragge gave a brilliant picture of three stages in a vicious circle:

> At present the Minister or Duke of York order out a batch of Generals, who . . . have neither Talent or Experience.

That was stage one. Stage two soon followed:

> Some blunder is committed, Lord Wellington speaks his mind the Great Man is offended at being crossed, and never bothers to exert himself or act upon his Judgment again.

The inevitable last stage was seen in the retreat from Burgos and again at Vitoria:

> Here I think commences a slackness which is quickly felt throughout the whole Machine, occasions incalculable Mischief and has induced Lord Wellington to call this 'God Almighty's Army' a thousand times.

> If Wellington had never called the army by any worse name than that, no one would have objected. He was soon to pounce on a pithier phrase.

★   ★   ★

The exhausted infantry, some of whom had marched twenty miles since dawn, were allowed by Wellington to spend the night after the battle in rest. Unfortunately they did not do so. A tremendous, night-long bacchanalia developed out of the first lootings in Vitoria. The surrounding fields, lit up by flares and enlivened by wine, women and song, soon looked more like a fairground than a soldiers' camp on the eve of a vital pursuit. Regular auctions took place, as after

Ciudad Rodrigo and Badajoz, but now on an altogether more splendid scale. This time the happy auctioneers were able to dress up in the bemedalled uniforms of French generals, and besides the high quality of the goods for sale there was a copious supply of money. The whole of the French army's pay had arrived in Vitoria shortly before the battle. It was reckoned that five million dollars were on the field, of which only 100,000 reached Wellington's military chest. 'No officer dared to interfere.' One officer blatantly described how he himself had joined with, instead of restraining, the soldiers. The wagon of the French General Villatte was discovered stuffed with money and church plate. After a few 'awkward' moments the officer decided to take his share, later counting it out in a church belfry. He was able to send £250 home, buy a second horse and keep a nice balance. Saddler Sergeant Bennett boasted, 'I got a pair of good sheets and filled them with ladies' dresses, and some plate, snuff boxes, etc.,' the 'etceteras' being twelve pounds of butter and a sack of bread. His colonel's only intervention was to make him share his loot with his comrades. Privates Wheeler and Costello were other soldiers to be encouraged by their officers to 'make merry', though Wheeler was warned at all costs to keep sober in case of having to march 'at any moment'.

To march at any moment was precisely Wellington's idea, but one doomed to disappointment. His aide-de-camp, Colonel Staveley, recorded a peculiarly ironic little scene between the Commander-in-Chief and himself on the night after the battle.

'Tell Murray,' said Wellington to Staveley, speaking of the quarter-master-general, 'I shall march the army off myself in the morning.'

'At what hour?' asked Staveley.

'When I get up.'

When Wellington got up his army had only just begun to go to bed. Even the Light Brigade admitted to being so heavy with raw meat and flour that they could not march. So what the cavalry had begun ill the infantry made worse.

There were also mistakes in the transmission of orders by staff officers, one of them preventing General Graham from executing an important movement against the retreating French, by which Foy would have been cut off, and incidentally involving Captain Norman Ramsay, hero of Fuentes de Oñoro and the army's finest gunner, in unmerited disgrace.

Wellington found Ramsay marching up the wrong road. Someone

had blundered. Having ordered him to halt and on no account to
move on again until he had received orders from Wellington himself,
he galloped back to make arrangements for Ramsay's correct route.

When he returned Ramsay had gone. He had mistakenly assumed
that a second set of orders to advance, though not from Wellington
himself, were authorized by Wellington. Ramsay's error caused
further serious delay. He was put under arrest for over three weeks
and only released when Colonel Frederick Ponsonby wrote on his
behalf:[7]

> I am anxious to state how miserable he is at having incurred your
> Lordship's displeasure and to express a hope that his long service
> in this country may induce you to pardon him.

Wellington's draft reply was written diagonally across Ponsonby's
letter like an angry rain-storm:

> Captn. Ramsay disobeyed a positive order given to him verbally by
> me, in expectation of the circumstance which occurred, viz. that
> he would receive orders from somebody else to move as I did not
> wish him to move. This inattention (for it is nothing else) has
> occurred so frequently that I had determined to make an example
> of Captn. Ramsay . . .

Then suddenly the storm cleared.

> . . . but I have no objection to pass the matter over now & I'll
> send orders that he may be released from his Arrest.

When, however, a letter written earlier by Torrens arrived, asking for
Ramsay's promotion, Wellington not unnaturally declined to put his
'example' into exact reverse. He querulously wrote back to Torrens
'Nobody ever thinks of obeying an order . . .'[8] It was two years before

7. Sir Frederick Cavendish Ponsonby (1783–1837), father of Queen
Victoria's secretary Sir Henry Ponsonby, and second cousin of General Sir
William Ponsonby of the Heavy Brigade. He was large-featured and equally
sturdy as regards build and moral qualities.

8. Wellington had written to Torrens after the retreat from Burgos,
'Nobody in the British army ever reads a regulation or an order . . . in any
other manner than as an amusing novel' (*Despatches*, vol. IX, p. 602, 6 December
1812).

Ramsay was promoted. He took it hard. His severe treatment finally convinced him and his friends that Wellington had always been 'agin the gunners'—and when Major Ramsay was killed at Waterloo people wrote as if Wellington had fired the shot himself.[9]

* * *

To return to King Joseph. Virtually unhindered by a pursuing force, he managed to get 55,000 men safely over the Pyrenees and back into France, leaving Wellington to compose the kind of acidulated documents which too often had to form the postscript to his triumphs. Bathurst was told on 29 June that 'our vagabond soldiers' had been 'totally knocked up' by their night of plunder, and until discipline could be enforced we should 'do no good' even by our greatest victories. Three days later (2 July) the thunders pealed more loudly still.

It is quite impossible for me or any other man to command a British army under the existing system. We have in the service the scum of the earth as common soldiers—

and what with proposals in Parliament for reforms and soft-hearted officers in the field, it was impossible to keep 'such men as some of our soldiers are' in order.

The fatal phrase, *scum of the earth*, had long been and was to remain a favourite with Wellington.[10] He was to rub in his point to Stanhope in 1831 during one of his many arguments about flogging.

'Do they beat them in the French Army?' asked Stanhope.

'Oh, they bang them about very much with ramrods and that sort of thing, and then they shoot them.'[11]

9. Hudleston, p. 18, retells the story from W. H. Maxwell but more in anger than in sorrow, linking it with similar tales from Wellington's career (see above, p. 301, and below, p. 399): having kept Ramsay in arrest for four weeks (an exaggeration), Wellington later 'spoke kindly to him as he rode down the line at Waterloo. Ramsay did not answer, merely bowed his head gravely, and was shot through the heart about 4 P.M.'.

10. See the Mary Anne Clarke affair. p. 196.

11. William Bragge referred on 6 May 1812 to 'my Cat of eight Leathern Thongs taken out of a French trumpeter's Kit at Llerena. It is a worse Instrument than ours and will be sent to Mr Whitbread if I have the good Fortune to bring it to England.' Clausel admitted he shot fifty soldiers to death on the retreat from Salamanca (Oman, vol. VI, p. 7).

But the reason why the British Army needed the terror of the triangle as an ultimate deterrent, whereas the French did not, was because the French was an army of conscripts and the British of volunteers:

> The conscription calls out a share of every class—no matter whether your son or my son—all must march; but our friends—I may say it in this room—are the very scum of the earth.

Wellington then went on to analyse the volunteer material:

> People talk of their enlisting from their fine military feeling—all stuff—no such thing. Some of our men enlist from having got bastard children—some for minor offences—many more for drink; but you can hardly conceive such a set brought together, and it really is wonderful that we should have made them the fine fellows they are.

Wellington struggled hard, as has been shown, to improve his soldiers' conditions and to collect officers who could inspire obedience. He tried again soon after Vitoria to raise the level of recruits by making the Government pay allowances to soldiers' families, especially the Irish whose wives at present 'went not upon the parish but upon the dunghill to starve'. With such a fate awaiting their families, Wellington found it 'astonishing' that Irish militiamen ever volunteered at all; and those who did it for a few guineas to get drunk with 'must be certainly the very worst members of society . . .'.

When he used phrases like 'scum of the earth' or 'very worst members of society' he was not being vindictive but descriptive: stating the harsh sociological facts as he saw them. Of course he was wrong. His strictures, as so often happened, were over-dramatized. Not nearly such a large proportion of the Army was 'scum' as he implied. Many 'fine fellows' came into it for adventure or patriotism who needed no baptism of fire or flogging. Young William Lawrence, the Dorset ploughboy who ran away into the Army, regarded his plunderings as pranks: the bayoneted pig hidden under the train of the Blessed Virgin Mary in a chapel till the hunt died down; the half-strangled cock stuffed under his cap which suddenly crowed on parade. Nor could the theory be defended that the really licentious soldiers became better disciplined or less brutal by being more brutally punished. As Tom Morris, the articulate private in the 73rd Foot pointed out, 'it invariably makes a tolerably good man bad, and a bad man infinitely worse. Once flog a man and you degrade him for ever, in his own mind; and thus take from him every possible incentive to good conduct.' The scars on his back, and not only on his back, were ineffaceable.

Wellington saw no point in punishing a soldier at all except as a deterrent. But to treat a man purely as an 'example' was to deprive him of his human rights, to turn him into a cipher, an abstraction, a mere inkmark in a General Order; and this the new century would increasingly reject. 'It was fortunate for Britain that Wellington was at once a great humanitarian and a great disciplinarian,' wrote Trevelyan nobly. But the two vital principles were not always reconciled in him. And when things went wrong, as after Burgos and Vitoria, the principle of order fought down the claims of compassion.

He himself felt that the sacrifice he made in popularity was repaid in the ultimate perfection of his army. On 21 November 1813, four months to the day after Vitoria, he was able to call the army which he had so often described as the worst that ever left England, 'the most complete machine for its numbers now existing in Europe'. Years later he said to Lady Salisbury, 'I could have done anything with that army. It was in such perfect order.'

Even with this army in its supposedly unregenerate state, Wellington had carried off at Vitoria one of the greatest strategic triumphs in British history. To do so he had marched 400 miles in forty days, in itself a victory of logistics which Fortescue celebrated with no less a salute than an epigram: 'Wellington's supplies were always hunting for his army; Joseph's army was always hunting for its supplies.'

Public rejoicing at home reached a pitch surpassed only by the tumultuous revelling on the battlefield. William Wellesley-Pole described to Arthur how the Prince Regent had commanded him to take a principal share in organizing the most 'splendid and magnificent' fête ever held in England. A jubilant crowd of 8,500 had assembled in Vauxhall Gardens and there had been 1,200 at the grand dinner. As with the battle, however, William had to confess that some aspects of the fête were not perfect, notably the arrival of carriages at the doors and of guests at the refreshment and supper rooms where there was, alas, 'confusion'. Colonel Torrens dolefully informed Fitzroy Somerset, 'I am half ruined by the expense, exclusive of having had my carriage broken to pieces in the scramble.'

But these were small blemishes. In return for Marshal Jourdan's baton the Prince Regent raised Wellington to the exalted rank of field-marshal, and set about personally drafting him a letter of congratulation, and, as 'the *fountain of taste*' (Torrens's sly epithet), designing the first British baton, adorned with lions instead of eagles. The fair copy of the Prince's letter, written in his own hand, was much corrected, though it was nothing compared to the innumerable blots and deletions in the draft which, together with its feeble script, made it look like the path of a wounded soldier across a much scarred battlefield. The language was as fine as the writing was faint.

> You have sent me among the trophies of your unrivalled fame, the staff of a French Marshal, and I send you in return that of England.

The Duke of York rather unnecessarily added that he would have recommended Wellington to the rank of field-marshal earlier (it had been mooted after Salamanca) but for 'the spirit of jealousy' which it would have aroused.

Wellington's soldierly reply to the Prince Regent showed he felt more than ever that he had been 'retained for life'.

> I can evince my Gratitude for your Royal Highness's repeated favours only by devoting my life to your service.

Even Kitty had to bear her share of the glory. She was the star at a party of Lady Templetown's, where Fanny (Burney) met her. 'Her very name,' wrote Fanny to her father afterwards, 'electrified me with emotion.'

Europe's celebration was as unprecedented as the British baton. For the first time in history a *Te Deum* was sung in St Petersburg Cathedral for the triumph of a foreign army. Beethoven composed *Wellington's Victory* in honour of the battle of Vitoria, complete with trumpets, cannon, marching feet and snatches from '*Rule Britannia*', '*Malbrouck s'en va t'en Guerre*' (the original air of '*For He's a Jolly Good Fellow*'), and '*God Save the King*'. And in the corridors of Central European power, the statesmen felt marvellously strengthened in their resolution to resist Napoleon. The alliance of Prussia, Russia and Sweden against France was joined by Austria, and on 16–19 October 1813 the European campaign against Napoleon was crowned by the victory of Leipzig, to be known as 'the Battle of the Nations'.

A certain prophetic sense seemed to have inspired the Portuguese Government when, out of the blue, they created Wellington '*Duque da Victoria*' just two months before the battle.

*   *   *

Napoleon, exasperated by the defeat in Spain which he character-istically described as 'ridiculous', ordered the grand extrusion and replaced Joseph by Soult.[12]

The old kite was of course no longer expected to chase the leopards into the sea—that historic mission now looked a trifle bizarre—but only across the Ebro. Young William Bragge, for one, had hoped that when Soult was removed from Spain in 1813 he would never return: 'he is beyond Doubt one of the First Generals in the French Army and better able to cope with his Lordship than any other'. But here again, his Lordship's situation had changed vastly since Febru-ary. It was not now just a question of notching up another victory to please Torrens. With Europe united against him, Napoleon could not win. It was the problem of what came next; of the other side of the mountains.

12. Wellington was much shocked to learn that a beautiful French watch with a map of Spain on the case, presented to him by Lord Edward Paget, had been originally ordered by Napoleon for Joseph. The news of Vitoria caused the furious Emperor to cancel it. 'A *gentleman*,' said Wellington scornfully, 'would not have taken the moment when the poor devil had lost his *châteaux en Espagne*, to take away his watch also'. Apart from not behaving like a gentleman, Napoleon did not distinguish himself as a politician when he extruded his brother from Spain. Joseph's attempts to introduce a liberal régime were so successful that 12,000 Spanish families of *afrancesados* (pro-French), many of them progressive officials, followed him into exile.

17 Champagne and Coffee

'Here I am, sitting on the sand, and surrounded by a dozen little girls: one is mending my foraging cap, the rest singing "*Viva Wellington*".'

The writer was Colonel Alexander Frazer of the Royal Horse Artillery, the date 30 June 1813. He was waiting at a beach near San Sebastián for ammunition to be landed. San Sebastián and Pamplona were the last two pockets of resistance in Spain, but they were enough to keep Wellington behind the Pyrenees. Until he knew the result of Napoleon's latest confrontation with the Grand Alliance, he could not risk invading France without a secure line on the Spanish frontier. That meant capturing the two fortresses, San Sebastián by storm, Pamplona by starvation.

Meanwhile Marshal Soult, Duke of Dalmatia, had miraculously reconstituted Joseph's ravaged army in thirteen days after reaching Bayonne. Once more his columns, menacing as ever, were winding over the mountains in a bid to relieve Pamplona. The British soldiers nicknamed him respectfully the Duke of Damnation.

*   *   *

There is a sense of anti-climax about the battles of the Pyrenees, despite Wellington's perfected skill and his troops' courage. Salamanca and Vitoria are behind; Waterloo casts its shadow before; the urge is irresistible to hurry Wellington forward to the predestined end. This feeling is increased by the very success of Vitoria in stirring up Europe, which paradoxically diminished the world's interest in the rest of his war. Vitoria acted like a hurricane, driving in the huge rollers from far out to sea. Spain reverted, if not to a backwater, at any rate to what has been called 'the greatest of "side-shows" '.

Moreover, while these latter-day sieges and battles enhanced Wellington's reputation, they did not radically alter the picture he had already given of himself. The winning techniques, the personal devotion, patience and energy did not change, though they were heightened by the mature quality of the army on which he now lavished them. Nor were the calamities unpredictable: there were

outbursts of savagery among the rank and file, of imbecility elsewhere; the complaints of the Portuguese and Spanish Governments
called for no less self-control on his part than formerly. What could
be done when the French lobby in Cádiz announced that Wellington
had changed his religion to Roman Catholicism in order to usurp
the Spanish throne? Nothing, beyond his usual procedure—'despising them, and continuing one's road without noticing them'.

Only in so far as the battles of the Pyrenees sharpen the silhouette
of the man about to enter France, need they be fought again in detail
here.

*   *   *

The first attempt at storming San Sebastián took place on 25 July
1813. Though there were as many as 100 engineers and sappers in
Wellington's force and a strong siege-train, the engineer-historian,
John T. Jones, regretted that the operations should have still been
'irregular': not enough science, not an effective enough blockade by
the Royal Navy, too much talent in the French Governor, Emanuel
Rey, and too little control by the amiable old British commander,
Graham, over his subordinates. Doubts and arguments, wrote
Napier, seeped through to the troops, 'abating that daring confidence
which victory loves'.

Wellington, the supreme inspirer of confidence, was pacing up and
down in a graveyard. Why he chose this place is not known, except
that it was in Lesaca, his headquarters on the River Bidassoa which
ran northwards into the Bay of Biscay, forming the boundary between
Spain and France. At 11.30 A.M. they brought him the appropriately
gloomy news. The assault upon San Sebastián had failed. He at once
galloped over to the city, ordered the siege to be changed into a
blockade until the desperate shortage of ammunition had been made
good, and reached Lesaca again that evening—to receive disquieting
rumours of gun-fire in the mountain passes of Maya and Roncesvalles
above Pamplona.

With the evocative name of Roncesvalles and the faint thunder of
battle rolling down the valleys, came the insistent ghost of Roland's
horn, and Colonel Andrew Barnard aptly spoke of 'that Chivalric
ground', wishing he had fought there himself. Lord Dalhousie, however, who actually commanded a division not far from Roncesvalles,
was undisturbed by echoes chivalric or otherwise. He sent Wellington
a bland assurance that the French attack in the passes, though heavy,

had been repulsed. This fitted Wellington's own belief that the main French thrust would be to relieve San Sebastián. He warned Graham to stand by, ordered up reinforcements from Pamplona and went to bed. It had been a long day. It was to be a short night.

*　　*　　*

Soult with overwhelming force had invaded the passes above Pamplona at dawn on 25 July. By the morning of the 26th, after a day of incredibly brave and bloody fighting by the Allied soldiers and characteristic errors by the commanders when acting on their own, both passes were evacuated. Cole's 4th Division, supported by Picton's 3rd, retired on Pamplona. Posted originally in an extremely strong position above Roncesvalles, where the ancient monastery still claimed to harbour Roland's bones, Cole had been ordered by Wellington to hold on until the last possible moment. He did not do so. An eerie mist suddenly blotted out the battlefield on the afternoon of the 25th. Firing on both sides abruptly ceased. In the dead silence that followed, broken only by muffled voices or distant cow-bells, the gallant Cole lost his nerve. He dreaded being cut off. He had had no sleep for two nights and in his own words was 'somewhat fagged'; he was responsible for 11,000 men, the largest force he had ever commanded.

Captain Arthur Kennedy, a relative of Sir Lowry Cole, wrote home on 9 August that the talents of 'our cousin' were 'not much thought of in the army *entre nous*'. Yet Cole had been magnificent at Albuera. The point was that the only commander on whom the army could invariably rely was Wellington.

Picton, looking more eccentric than ever in his top-hat and with an umbrella for a whip, felt equally lost without Wellington and could give Cole no encouragement to stay.[1] General Sir William Stewart meanwhile, at Maya, had gone off to investigate the firing near Roncesvalles, leaving his subordinate, W. H. Pringle, to cope with an army he had joined only twenty-four hours before. As Wellington often had reason to remark, Stewart was a valiant busybody who preferred to do anything rather than obey his own orders. Nevertheless his generals' behaviour on this occasion was received with relatively genial criticism.

1. Umbrellas were officially banned by Wellington on the battlefield, though he allowed all sorts of other odd personal equipment.

They are really heroes when I am on the spot to direct them, but when I am obliged to quit them they are children.

His brother-in-law, Pakenham, was far blunter:

> ... most of them have gone mad with anxiety or alarm of [the] situation they had placed Themselves in, pursuant to [Wellington's] daring scheme. ...

Wellington afterwards confessed that his 'daring scheme' for attacking such widely separated fortresses as Pamplona and San Sebastián at the same time, was 'one of the greatest faults he ever committed in war'. He also told the Prime Minister: 'There is nothing I dislike so much as these extended operations, which I cannot direct myself.'

* * *

His chance to resume personal direction came in the small hours of 26 July, when he was roused from two or three hours' sleep by a message revealing the truth about Maya. He at once rode over the mountains towards Pamplona, issuing orders as he went to his reserves, the 6th and 7th Divisions. The news he received along the route was so bad that he finally dashed ahead of his staff and, accompanied only by Fitzroy Somerset, galloped into a village not ten miles from Pamplona —Sorauren. Here he found his army drawn up by Cole and Picton on a steep ridge with the French in the act of taking up position on the heights opposite. He grasped the situation immediately. There was only a moment in which to issue new directions to the approaching 6th Division, which was clearly in imminent danger of being cut off. Indeed, he was himself.

'The French are coming!' shouted the Spanish villagers signalling frantically up the road. Wellington, who had dismounted at the grey stone bridge over the River Lanz, seized his writing materials and resting them on the parapet scribbled thirteen lines of redirections to his quartermaster-general, Murray.

'The French are coming! The French are coming!' Fitzroy Somerset snatched the note from him, vaulted into the saddle and raced at full speed out of one end of Sorauren as the French light cavalry entered the other. Wellington, now quite alone, prepared to join his embattled lines above the village. He put his thoroughbred into a gallop, and as he flew up the scorching hillside between spicy box bushes, there were some like young Gleig who, not having yet seen the Commander-in-Chief, did not recognize the thin, muscular rider, bronzed and smiling, in a plain grey 'frock' buttoned close to the chin, grey pantaloons and low cocked hat worn 'fore and aft', covered with an oilskin and rammed down on his nose. O'Toole's Caçadores, however, knew who it was the moment they caught sight of him.

'*Douro! Douro!*' they cried, and the British regiments joined in with 'Nosey! Nosey!'

Wellington took his stand dramatically on the highest point of the ridge, opened his telescope and calmly surveyed the unpleasing visage of Marshal Soult opposite, which had been pointed out to him by a double-agent. The act was partly to complete the reassurance of his agitated 'children', partly to make the naturally cautious Soult ask himself what all the cheering was about. Had reinforcements arrived? While Soult paused and considered (he was notoriously indecisive on the battlefield) Wellington's vital 6th Division would be making its way to Sorauren, as redirected by Somerset, through the hills.

During the crucial hour that afternoon Marshal Soult did indeed take his siesta.

'Who could sleep at such a moment?' exclaimed General Clausel in an agony of impatience. When Soult was awake again a colossal thunderstorm broke over the battlefield and washed out the rest of daylight. But at midnight there were grand illuminations in Pamplona, ready for the French victors.

They never came, for Soult had lost his chance. Next day, 28 July 1813, the omen of the thunderstorm was fulfilled and it was Wellington who won a resounding victory: the first battle of Sorauren. The French columns found that they could no more capture 'Cole's Ridge', as the great hill came to be called in honour of the 4th Division's heroic stand, than they had been able to storm Bussaco; while the 6th, led by Pakenham, suddenly swooped out of the mountains and delivered what was almost another Salamanca stroke against the French flank.

'The 28th was fair bludgeon-work,' wrote Wellington. It had been no less critical at times than the battle of Talavera on whose fourth anniversary it occurred. 'I escaped as usual unhurt,' he told William; 'and I begin to believe that the finger of God is upon me.' William was horrified to hear of his brother's narrow escape on Sorauren bridge and felt that the finger of God could be overworked.

I agree with you that the finger of God is upon you; but I shudder at the risks you run, & I wish I could persuade you to feel very much depends on your life. . . . for the sake of Europe & of us all, you ought not to run unnecessary risks.

Wellington himself had to admit afterwards to Larpent that it had been touch and go.

'Why, at one time it was rather alarming, certainly, and it was a close run thing.'

★   ★   ★

The fighting at Sorauren burst out again on 30 July, after a day of utter exhaustion when not a shot was fired. On the French side, their system of non-provisioning meant that half-starved soldiers had tried to rush the precipitous slopes, while the heat was so intense that the dead were roasted black almost as they fell. At the end of the second battle every French division had been beaten and forced to retreat, Foy's by mere goat-paths into France.[2]

'We have had some desperate fighting in these mountains,' wrote Wellington to the War Minister of the battles of the Pyrenees as a whole, 'and I have never known the troops behave so well.' The Spanish regiments had defended 'Spanish Hill' with the utmost valour, and as for the Portuguese, they were now well known to be 'the fighting cocks of the army'.[3] In a confidential letter to William

2. The first and second battles of Sorauren are often known jointly as the *Battle* of the Pyrenees, while the battles at Maya, Roncesvalles and Sorauren are together called the *Battles* of the Pyrenees. The exact site of the two battles above the Sorauren used to be easily identified by the pilgrimage chapel of San Salvador in the valley between the two armies. Today it is a small heap of stones overgrown with brambles. The bridge, however, on which Wellington wrote his famous dispatch is still exactly the same, and is a favourite picnic spot for the people of Pamplona.

3. Wellington's tribute was none the less sincere for being partly political. It was included deliberately in a despatch to the Prime Minister of 25 July (*Despatches*, vol. X, p. 569) after the Portuguese Government had complained with some justice of their soldiers not being given due recognition in the British press. Ever since Wellington had moved his base away from Lisbon and Oporto to the Bay of Biscay, they had been in an unhappy state owing to the great loss to their commerce. At one point, in October 1813, Wellington wrote angrily to Stuart in Lisbon that if the Portuguese insisted on making newspaper reports the basis of a quarrel, 'I quit the Peninsula forever' (*Despatches*, vol. XI, p. 185). This was a characteristic bark with no bite.

on 18th August, however, he was unable to pay any tribute to the conduct of the pursuit:

> If I had had any others but Gallant Officers to deal with, I had Soult & his whole Army. As it was he escaped by the most extra-ordinary accident, and a number of Blunders which our people alone can commit.

William replied that he had suspected as much:

> I shall inviolably keep it to myself. It is vexatious that experience & example does not do more.

Part of the failure had been due to three drunken stragglers who were captured robbing an orchard by the French and gave away the position of Wellington's pursuing forces; in any case William well understood his brother's rule to take the blame himself.

*   *   *

A month later, on 31 August 1813, Soult's counter-offensive came to an end with a massive attempt to dislodge the Spanish army from the heights of San Marcial above San Sebastián. The battle of San Marcial is famous for being a single-handed Spanish victory under General Bernardin Freire, thanks to Wellington's psychological insight in refusing to reinforce the Spaniards when he could see that the day was theirs:

'Look . . . if I send you the English troops you ask for, they will win the battle; but as the French are already in retreat you may as well win it for yourselves.' They went on to do so in fine style as he had foreseen.

The incident does not bear out the suspicions of certain British officers that Wellington always made sure of getting the credit for every success himself.

*   *   *

That very morning of 31 August San Sebastián fell (though General Rey withdrew his troops up Monte Úrgull, and into a sea-girt castle above the town, where he held out until 9 September). The horrors, both accidental and deliberate, which attended its capture were never surpassed during the Peninsular War—unprecedented anxiety and 'senseless laughter' amounting to hysteria before the count-down; an appalling thunderstorm and darkness as the men marched into the trenches after hours of sulphurous heat; slaughter in the breaches so ghastly that there were not enough officers left alive when the town was entered to control their maddened troops; a sack more murderous than Badajoz and a fire that eventually razed the town. William Napier professed to believe that Wellington could have cured his troops of pillaging after Vitoria by giving immediate rewards of prize-money to the 'valourous' and shooting looters on the spot. If the Government had agreed (which is highly unlikely) Wellington would probably have raised no objection to this innovation, but it would not have stamped out pillaging nor civilized the minority of savages in his army. 'It is impossible to prevent it entirely' was to be his own verdict in 1837. The truth is that the public at home, while rightly recoiling from the age-old barbarities of siege-warfare, expected their soldiers to perform in ways which made an unpleasant reaction inevitable. 'The indescribable *something*' in the faces of soldiers just before an assault, already noticed by William Grattan at Ciudad Rodrigo and Badajoz, resulted from the total suppression of human feelings such as pity and terror. They burst out afterwards in a degraded catharsis of terror and drink.

The siege and storming of San Sebastián not only shocked humanitarians but embroiled Wellington with the Navy and the Spanish Government. His ceaseless complaints to the First Lord of the Admiralty that neither the blockading of the city nor the supplying of the Allies were carried out efficiently, provoked a rude retort on the First Lord's behalf from the Naval Secretary, none other than Wellington's old friend and protégé, J. W. Croker.

'I will take your opinion . . . as to the most effectual mode of beating a French army,' wrote the supposed First Lord, 'but I have no confidence in your seamanship or nautical skill.'

A hot protest from Wellington to the Cabinet caused Lord Bathurst to compose a soothing reply: 'You must not regard Croker's compositions as you would those of any other official person. He has the talent of writing sharply with great facility—a great misfortune in an official person. . . . You are the god of his idolatry.'

Wellington did not want idolatry but convoys for his supplies. He paraphrased caustically for William's benefit Bathurst's argument that, 'Mr. Croker is in the habit of writing Impertinent letters, & that I ought not to mind them! !' In fact he minded a great deal, but was able to work off his feelings against the Government through the usual safety valve of letters to William. By 24 September 1813 he had reached philosophic calm:

> However, I serve the Publick & not any administration; & the blackguard abuse of the Secy. of the Admiralty [Croker] shall not prevent me from performing my Duty to the best of my ability.[4]

*   *   *

Anti-British elements in the Spanish Government accused Wellington of burning down San Sebastián on purpose, in order to deal a blow at its commerce with France. The charge was utterly false. Wellington had always refused to add to the horrors of war by ordering a bombardment. At San Sebastián he specifically forbade it, pointing out to Graham in a Wellingtonian under-statement that it would be 'very inconvenient to our friends the inhabitants, and eventually to ourselves'. For this reason he was prejudiced against the Congreve rockets which he said were so inaccurate as to be good for nothing else. Nevertheless he was savagely libelled in the Spanish press, and then in the Irish. 'I do not know how long my temper will last,' he fumed to Henry. It had to last as long as the cause needed him, as he well knew, for he was retained for life.

In 1925 Queen Victoria Eugénie of Spain opened a cemetery in a flower garden on Monte Úrgull, facing the Atlantic, to commemorate the English soldiers who fought for Spain in 1813 and 1836. A stone was inscribed in Spanish and English:

> *England has confided to us their honoured remains.*
> *Our gratitude will watch over their eternal repose.*

4. Wellington and Croker were a finely matched pair on the rare occasions when they crossed swords. On 3 September 1813 Croker wrote to the First Lord of the Admiralty that he was sending out Admiral Martin to find out exactly what Wellington wanted changing, 'apart from the seasons, weather and localities'. The First Lord forwarded this letter to Wellington, who replied sarcastically on the 24th to Lord Bathurst that despite his 'ignorance of naval affairs' in preferring the boats of the fleet to the harbour boats of Passages, navigated by women, he had been given the fleet's assistance in landing his ordnance during the second part of the siege (*Supplementary Despatches*, vol. VIII, pp. 227, 274).

Gratitude is not, nor can it be, the currency of international affairs. The only flowers growing in the garden today are wild garlic, and of the English gunners forming a large group of heroic statuary, four out of six have lost their heads.

*   *   *

The next push into the Pyrenees had to wait for over a month. Wellington was determined neither to anticipate victories in Germany, Catalonia and Pamplona nor to overdrive his exhausted army.[5] He himself had appeared inexhaustible—until lumbago struck him after Sorauren. William Maginn, a Pensinsular diarist, noticed that his fifteen fine chargers had been reduced to skin and bone by all his riding. 'He was like a centaur,' said his courier, 'in seeming part of his horse, and he slept as soundly in his saddle as if in his bed.' A visitor to Lesaca during the blockade of San Sebastián commented on how little he talked or drank of his excellent wine; not even a toast with his guests.

By 8 August he was only just getting about again; but quite apart from illness, he intended to go forward at the correct pace dictated by circumstances, as he told William, 'notwithstanding the Clamour of our newspapers, & even of the Govt. . . . at our inactivity during the Winter'. He had heard this sort of clamour almost every year since the war began and he bore it stoically and stubbornly. Nevertheless he confessed privately to William that his relations with the Tory Government had relapsed into the bad old state of 1810 and 1811. 'I am quite certain the Govt. are tired of me & all my operations,' he wrote on 9 January 1814; 'and wish us both at the Devil.'

One piece of good news arrived from William in February 1814 to counter-balance some of these vexations. King Joseph's pictures, which he had shipped back to England on 5 October 1813, turned out to be masterpieces. William had shown them secretly to the President of the Royal Academy, who declared that a Correggio and a Giulio Romano ought to be framed in diamonds—it was worth fighting the battle of Vitoria for them alone. Lord Mulgrave, master-general of the Ordnance, added that Arthur must certainly keep them

5. Oman described Wellington's decision not to pursue Soult on 2 August as his 'grand refusal' and Napier wrote somewhat sententiously: 'Had Caesar halted because his soldiers were fatigued, Pharselia [*sic*] would have been but a common battle.'

all himself as trophies of war. Wellington knew only too well how this kind of talk would go down with the public. The pictures were not to be exhibited, he ordered William, until those belonging to King Ferdinand had been returned to him. 'The good natured World would accuse me of stealing them.' All the same it was a most agreeable surprise—'I believe I was born with *Fortunatus'* cap on my head'. Later, King Ferdinand performed one of his rare acts of generosity in asking Wellington to keep them, and they are now at Apsley House and Stratfield Saye. The collection includes works by Velasquez, Van Dyck, Rubens and Wellington's favourite Dutch and Flemish masters. In a sense the masterpieces were equally fortunate in falling into Wellington's hands. Some of them were used at first by the soldiers as tarpaulins to cover their baggage-mules. Two days after they had been safely consigned to England he was ready to reopen his Pyrenean campaign.

*   *   *

Wellington's army crossed the River Bidassoa into France on 7 October 1813. As Bragge put it, they had 'infringed upon the Sacred Territory' at last.

Everything went like clockwork. There was the requisite thunderstorm the night before; local shrimpers whispered to Wellington that the Bidassoa estuary was just fordable at very low tide and proved correct; and Soult's 'impregnable' right flank was turned by an army apparently marching through the sea. The only fault with the clockwork was that it made the clock go too fast. Soult's fortified lines on the *massif* of La Grande Rhune, above the village of Vera, fell next day so smoothly to the Allies that Wellington's gallant officers expected to clear the next river-lines—the Nivelle, the Nive and the Adour—as if they were riding in a giant steeple-chase. Harry Smith recalled that the whole army were so confident they would have tried, if ordered, to carry the moon.

A newcomer to this army, twenty-year-old Lieutenant Edmund Wheatley of the King's German Legion, got his first taste of battle above the Bidassoa: he heard the 'tune' of the French drums—'dum, dum, dum, dum, dummery dum, dum'—and was puzzled like many others by the strange hissing and plaintive whistling all around. When a shell just missed him his superior officer, Colonel Ompteda, called out,

'Vell, Veatley, how you like dat?'

'Not good for the kidneys.'

It was here that another newcomer, the youthful, amusing and dandified Welshman, Ensign Rees Howell Gronow, saw the creator of this great army for the first time.

He was very stern and grave-looking; he was in deep meditation . . . and spoke to no one. His features were bold and I saw much decision of character in his expression. He rode a knowing-looking thorough-bred horse. . . .

A corporal, however, in the same situation was less studied in his language.

'There goes the little b—— what whops the French!'

Gronow had not mistaken the decision in Wellington's character. He decided not to advance farther while Pamplona still held out. This the indomitable garrison continued to do until 31 October, when they finally emerged like skeletons from their tombs on resurrection morning. Now at last, on 10 November 1813, Wellington was ready for the next move: to force the line of entrenched mountains above the River Nivelle.

Before the battle Smith remembered Wellington sitting on the turf at the summit of La Rhune mountain, surrounded by his Light Division commanders—Alten, Colborne, Kempt—his eyes glued to his telescope and his ears alert to useful ideas on the coming assault, which was to take place against the Petite Rhune opposite.

'These fellows think themselves invulnerable,' he said, 'but I will beat them out, and with great ease.' Colborne agreed to the beating, but doubted the ease. Wellington then explained that the French would not dare to concentrate their defence as he would concentrate his attack.

'Now I see it,' said Colborne. He and his fellow-officers began to get up and go.

'Oh, lie still,' said Wellington. So the group settled down again round him on the mountain top, and had the instructive experience of hearing him dictate his exact plan of attack to his quartermaster-general, Murray. The episode is significant. That intimate, informal gathering on La Rhune preserves the memory of a Wellington who was not always the cold, uncommunicative leader of legend.

'Remember: at four in the morning,' said Wellington to Larpent, as they rose from dinner on the evening of 9 November 1813. Next day Larpent, standing high up on La Rhune, was able to follow the fall of one French redoubt after another by the advancing glint of the Allied bayonets.

The battle of the Nivelle was remarkable for personal valour: for William Napier storming the topmost fort at the head of the 43rd, with the Light Division's famous 'stern shout'; for John Colborne bluffing a strong French garrison into surrender—'You are cut off. Lay down your arms.' 'There, Monsieur, is a sword which has ever done its duty'—and for Wellington suddenly appearing at the head of this or that column, his presence signified by cheers which were invariably described as 'electrifying'.[6]

By the Nivelle action he demonstrated his ability to drive Soult eventually from any and every position. 'I did not do so much however as I wished,' he admitted frankly to William on 13 November: if there had been more daylight and less mud, 'I should have given Soult a terrible squeeze. As it is they are more frightened than hurt. . . .' William replied rather tactlessly in the same frank spirit: whereas the crossing of the Bidassoa had caused 'a great sensation here', the Nivelle had not attracted any notice nor won the thanks of Parliament. William's cold douche was overdone. The Prince Regent for one, described himself as 'quite worn out with the joy of . . . this thrice happy day' and begged his mother, Queen Charlotte, to assemble a 'Band of Musick . . . & for *good luck's sake*, at least to make them play *Landes Vater*.' The Queen, though 'almost drunk with joy' herself, promised to order Landes Vater and join in the chorus.

William continued with more truth, 'there is no doubt but that the attention of the Country has for some time been turned to Germany, Holland, etc.'. Arthur's attention was equally fixed upon Germany when he wrote to William, for he had just heard the news of Leipzig from a sulky French prisoner whom he dined, wined and finally examined on the evening after the battle. His French and his manners, both better than those of his brash young officers enabled him

6. Colborne's words to the French commander of the Star Redoubt were: 'You see you are surrounded on every side. There are the Spaniards on the left; you had better surrender at once!' The reference to the Spaniards was brought in because the French had a horror of falling into their hands. Colborne's 'bluff' consisted in concealing the fact that at that particular moment his own force was outnumbered.

without offence to extract information which they had failed to elicit. Where were Napoleon's present headquarters?

'My Lord, there are no more headquarters.'

In a flash he realized that this was confirmation of the Leipzig rumours: Napoleon had been defeated and pinned behind the Rhine by the combined armies of Europe. 'I saw my way clearly to Bordeaux and Paris.'

At the very moment, however, that he was politely entertaining a French officer, his Spanish soldiers were horribly pillaging a French village—Ascain. His way forward to Bordeaux was suddenly less clear. If these Spanish marauders raised the countryside against him, as the French had earlier raised the Spanish guerrillas against themselves, his cause would be lost. As early as July 1813 he had made a moral appeal to his Spanish troops not to plunder the 'peaceful inhabitants of France': it would be 'unmanly and unworthy'. Now that it had happened he did not blame the Spaniards: it was 'really hardly fair' to expect anything else from men whose own government either could not or would not feed them and whose country had been laid waste by French invaders. But if he could not blame them he could send most of them home. This he promptly did. It meant fighting the rest of the war with numbers inferior to Soult. He accepted the disadvantage in return for the increasing friendliness of a surprised and delighted French peasantry.

There was a new proclamation against plundering and the bulk of his army, including Morillo's crack Spanish corps which was retained, were licked into shape by Pakenham, who as head of the reorganized military police went about, said Wheatley, 'like a raving lion'. Wellington roared also when necessary. There were fierce orders against keeping horses in churches or grazing mules in vineyards. After Nivelle he met Colborne whose valiant 52nd had rewarded themselves with some French pigs and poultry.

'Though the Brigade have even more than usually distinguished themselves, we must respect the property of the country.'

'I am fully aware of it my lord . . . in the very heat of action a little irregularity will occur.'

'Ah, ah! stop it in future, Colborne.'

In the end the French peasants preferred this disciplined army to their own plundering countrymen, and welcomed Wellington as a liberator. Wheeler reported a talk with a French farmer: 'He was aware that the "Grand Marshal", meaning "Nosey" I suppose, would

protect the lives and property of the French who were not in arms. . . .'
Colonel Augustus Frazer believed that no army had ever behaved
better than the British army, even in its own country, and put it
down entirely to Wellington's 'wholesome regulations'. Sergeant
Lawrence thought the Nivelle proclamation 'much to the credit of
our noble commander'.

The rain unfortunately could not be sent back to Spain with the
unreliable Spanish regiments. As early as 2 September William
Napier was writing to his wife about 'General *Rain*' and 'Lieutenant-
Generals Thunder and Lightning'. 'More, more rain!' lamented
Larpent in his journal. Wellington's curious, four-foot, tubular
barometer, his inseparable companion on all his Peninsular campaigns (now in the National Military Museum, Sandhurst) was not
worth looking at. Yet again he had to wait for a month before, beginning on 9 December 1813, he could carry another of Soult's great
river-lines, that of the Nive, and invest the city of Bayonne. Five
days of hard fighting were remarkable for one political and one
human incident, besides a small but intriguing question.

As a direct result of Leipzig three battalions of Napoleon's
German Confederates changed sides during the fighting on 10
December, going over lock, stock and barrel to Wellington—an
ominous sign for Soult. Colonel Sir Nathaniel Peacocke, a 'newcomer' who had succeeded the heroic Cadogan, slain at Vitoria,
took an equally tempting opportunity to remove himself from the
front line at St Pierre on the 13th; General Hill found him easing
his conscience by beating some dilatory Portuguese ammunition-
carriers in the rear. 'Daddy' Hill, for the first time since Talavera
and the last during the war, cursed and swore; and Wellington,
when he heard of this phenomenon, remarked genially that if Hill
had begun to swear, they must all mind what they were about.

Wellington's own part during the protracted struggle on the Nive
has raised a query. Why did he not follow his usual practice of taking
over personally during the critical moments? There is no obvious
answer, but it has been suggested that he wished to give his two
senior generals, Hope and Hill, the experience of independent command. If so, he was only doing for them what he had done for
General Freire and his Spaniards at San Marcial, and incidentally
refuting another hostile myth which had grown up during the early
difficult stages of the Peninsular War. The episode of La Rhune
proved that he was not always secretive; the battles of San Marcial

and the Nive showed that he did not insist on winning every victory himself. After Hill's hard-fought action at St Pierre, Wellington rode up and exclaimed,

'My dear Hill, the day's your own!'

No doubt the growing perfection of his army helped to produce this new leader: 'There appears to be a new spirit among the officers ... to keep the troops in order,' he wrote cheerfully on 21 November 1813. If Wellington and his army had stayed together even longer than they did, it may be that he would have forgotten he ever called them scum, and they that he ever seemed hard, cold and autocratic.[7]

*   *   *

Storms came roaring down again over the mountains, and there could be no more advances for two months, whatever the disappointment at home. Wellington wrote emphatically to the Cabinet,

there are some things which *can not be done*: one of them is to move troop in this country during ... a violent fall of rain.

The deluge seemed to flow through Larpent's journal:

Still rain, rain, rain, all night. All yesterday, all the night before, and still continuing.

Meanwhile to Wellington's eternal winter problem of keeping fit himself and refitting his army was added an entirely new political dilemma—to fight Bonaparte without becoming permanently committed to the Bourbons. He solved them all to his satisfaction, Pakenham writing home that he had never seen him so well. His headquarters were now at St Jean de Luz, a healthy change from Lesaca which, with too large a population for the plumbing, stank, according to Larpent, like an old poultry-yard. There are many testimonies to the delectable change from poverty-stricken Spain to fertile France. Arthur Kennedy's tribute, given in a hitherto

7. There were some reported backslidings on both sides. On two occasions Wellington was said to have spoken so sharply to staff officers who had made mistakes that each of them, Colonel Sturgeon and Major Todd, deliberately got himself shot in a skirmish. Even Hudleston, however, no admirer of Wellington, admits that the similarity between these two stories casts doubts upon the second, which was related by G. R. Gleig at the age of ninety.

unpublished letter to his mother on 15 December 1813, is in the typical vein of a young officer.

> Meantime allow me to say I am about to *attack the enemy* in the following advantageous *positions*. A boiled knuckle of veal on the right, a roast shoulder of mutton on the left, and an apparently good-looking dish of calves head hash in the centre. Each flank covered with a bottle of champagne and sort of claret, not forgetting some Irish potatoes, my usual attendants. The whole commanded by a most civil landlady who quite oppresses me with her extreme attention, and probably expects to carry me by a *coup de main*.

Arthur Shakespear, who had had the privilege of seeing the Commander-in-Chief scratch his foot before Salamanca, was now permitted to lend this inveterate rider a horse. Wellington had come up from St Jean de Luz to inspect the 'Galloping Third' Dragoons, and the steep road had left Copenhagen exhausted.

> He asked me to give him another; a favourite horse of mine was walking round in front of the house; after taking a glass of wine he mounted her and rode a good hard canter for five hours over bad roads—he said he was never carried better. . . .

Such high good humour in the Commander-in-Chief prompted Shakespear to ask for promotion.

> His Grace made no promise, but that day fortnight upon return of letters from England I was gazetted! . . . I attributed my good fortune entirely to having supplied the *Great Man* with a comfortable horse! We played at whist that evening & I won 30 shillings from his Grace!

It is most improbable that Shakespear's promotion to a troop in the 18th Hussars occurred for that reason. Arthur Kennedy and his friends, who resented it, attributed it to repercussions of the Grant affair and the 18th Hussars' disgrace after Vitoria, added to the fact that Lord Wellington had recently seen a man in this troop chasing a sheep—he '*supposed*' to steal it. 'You may suppose what sort of man this same Lord is. . . .'

When not on horseback to review troops, Wellington hunted his foxhounds for his health in the mountains above the Bay. There had been a great scurrying round at home to find a suitable pack. Culling Smith, his brother-in-law, who handled these things for him, reported on 12 March 1813 that Lord March had applied to Lord Euston who had found some hounds in Buckinghamshire. He wore the sky-blue Salisbury coat presented to him by his old admirer, Lady Salisbury, a black cape and the boots he had designed himself for comfort and convenience. Larpent foolishly thought these boots were a sign of the great man's vanity, having once caught him discussing their shape with his soldier servant.

The army had its own experiments. Congreve's rockets were given another trial, this time against cavalry. It was agreed that they would have scared the horses stiff if only they had gone near them.

The political problem of how to regard Napoleon was not unlike that of the rockets. Wellington called him 'the grand disturber'. Yet he felt that once peace had been made the Emperor might still be the best available ruler for France, provided he behaved as he promised. Most of the Allied army, however, took the simpler view of Pakenham that the grand disturber must be 'dethroned and Decapitized [*sic*]'. During this period of uncertainty Wellington had the doubtful pleasure of entertaining the Bourbon Duke of Angoulême, nephew of Louis XVIII, in his camp. Angoulême frankly admitted that there was no strong popular French movement for a Bourbon restoration during the first weeks of 1814. What the people wanted was peace rather than any one particular ruler. Royalist feeling, however, would grow. (And he would intrigue to increase it.) Wellington's delicate task was to prevent a premature rash of white cockades—the royalist badge—in the towns he conquered. Otherwise the civil inhabitants, of whom Wellington constantly thought, might find themselves in serious trouble if the grand disturber came out on top. Riding about in pea-green trousers the odd little Prince was all smiles; indeed he bowed and scraped so energetically when motioned ahead at a door-way, that the Commander-in-Chief brought up the rear with an uncontrollable grin.

Wellington was quite prepared for a Bonapartist solution. 'But if you cannot make peace with Buonaparte in the winter,' he wrote to the Cabinet on 10 January 1814, 'we must *run* at him in the spring....' A month later there was still no peace. The only peace Napoleon had made, or thought he had made, was with his prisoner, King Ferdinand VII of Spain. By the Treaty of Valençay, Ferdinand agreed to stab Wellington in the back with the Spanish army if he were freed and sent home. Once he reached Madrid the Cortes promptly repudiated the Treaty.

Wellington insisted that one last pressing but delicate problem must be solved before he could run at Bonaparte—finance. A letter marked 'Secret and confidential' from the Chancellor of the Exchequer, N. Vansittart, to the Commissary-in-Chief, J. C. Herries, shows that by 11 January the solution was in sight, thanks to Nathan Mayer Rothschild. Vansittart explained to Herries that since it was essential for Wellington to get more specie than the Bank of England 'or any other usual channel' could obtain, it had been decided by the Prime Minister and himself to employ Mr Rothschild 'in the most secret and confidential manner' to collect up to £600,000 sterling in French coin on the Continent.

> Upon consideration of the magnitude of the objects in view, of the dispatch and secrecy which it requires and of the risks which may be incurred, it is not thought unreasonable to allow Mr Rothschild a commission of Two per cent. . . .

In a confirmatory letter to Rothschild it was laid down that he must load the coin on British warships in Holland and bear any losses incurred before loading. Before the end of January Bathurst informed Wellington that 'our Jew' had been successful in Paris and the army would now get a good remittance. All the omens were favourable. The password for the month at the Tower of London was 'Wellington'.

On 14 February 1814 Wellington's spring running began.

*   *   *

Between the middle of February and the beginning of March, Soult was driven remorselessly back. There was no need for Wellington to stop and storm Bayonne. He by-passed the city, leaving Sir John Hope to seal up its 17,000-strong garrison by crossing the River Adour at its perilous estuary on a bridge of boats. How were the engineers to get planks for the rafts? Cut up the siege-gun platforms, said Wellington brusquely. Then what about the platforms? Cut down trees from the pine forests when they were needed. Above all, get on. This was the same Wellington who had made them chop up wagons for scaling-ladders at Ciudad Rodrigo. He also showed himself the same man whose fondness for personal excursions had nearly landed him in captivity before Talavera, Salamanca and Sorauren. While examing the Adour he ran into a detachment of French *vedettes* and had to gallop for it.

Even the rockets acted according to form, 'skipping about the river like mad things', wrote a soldier in the Horse Artillery, 'and dancing quadrilles in every direction but the right one. Some of them came back to ourselves, but happily without doing any mischief.'

A few days after Hope's feat on the Adour, Wellington and Hill turned Soult's left wing successively on the rivers Joyeuse, Bidouse and Gave d'Oloron. This 'great game', as Oman calls it, was halted briefly when Soult faced the Allies on the River Gave de Pau at Orthez. Wellington sat down on a stone under an umbrella kindly provided by a passing officer to keep off the drizzle, and wrote out his battle-orders for Orthez, while waiting for the 3rd Division to come up. Other officers noticed the familiar figure in the short white winter cloak, and one of them pointed him out to Colborne.

'Do you see that old White Friar sitting there? I wonder how many men he is marking off to be sent into the next world?'

Next day, 27 February 1814, the white friar was up long before dawn and after all was ready he snatched a moment's sleep wrapped in the same cloak.

'Call me in time, Murray.'

After the quartermaster-general had roused him he triumphantly swept the demoralized French out of their strong positions, though error and ill-luck again prevented him from organizing a comparable pursuit. Colonel Sturgeon inadvertently allowed the guides to wander away, so that Wellington could not send a message to Hope at Bayonne, asking for troops to pursue Soult. The unfortunate colonel was reprimanded so stiffly that he rode into a skirmish and was shot dead. William Napier believed that Wellington felt the incident deeply but would not show his feelings: 'He has always kept to that system of never acknowledging he was wrong. . . .'[8] The pursuit was also hampered by an accident to Wellington himself, the nearest he ever came to being incapacitated by a wound.

8. It is a curious coincidence that when Mrs Sturgeon died in 1808 Charles Napier wrote that Sturgeon ought to go to the wars: 'The endeavour to get killed . . . would save him much anguish and perhaps cure him. . . . Yet he would be better pleased to fall, the world to him is void . . .' (William Napier, *Life of Charles Napier*, vol. I, p. 85).

He was riding with his Spanish liaison officer, General Alava, who suddenly called out that he had had a 'knock' on his bottom. Wellington could not help laughing. Next moment he was knocked himself: a spent bullet struck his sword-hilt driving it violently against his thigh and cutting the skin—a punishment, said Alava afterwards, for laughing at him.[9] As they laid him out on the grass, not knowing the extent of his wound, the same thought occurred to them all. 'Good God! Who is to get the army out of the country?' The wound was extremely painful and prevented him from galloping about in his usual carefree way for at least a week. Larpent feared that he was making it worse by riding at all, and hoped in vain that he would rest, 'as all our prospects here would vanish with that man'. Toughness learnt in India carried him through, and by the end of March he had forced Soult into the fortified camp of Toulouse and reached his last river-line, the Garonne.

Accompanied by only two of his staff, Fitzroy Somerset and Colonel Alexander Gordon, he reconnoitred its bank. His very plain uniform and oilskin cover over his cocked hat luckily prevented a French sentry from recognizing the Allied Commander-in-Chief. After an informative conversation the two parted on the best of terms.[10] Wellington's information on the political situation was not so easily come by.

Rumours were flying about during the first week of April that Napoleon's defensive action had collapsed and that the Allied armies of Blücher and Schwarzenberg were in Paris. What could Wellington believe? There were persistent reports that Napoleon was dead—of wounds, of poisoning, of the gravel. The conference between Allied statesmen and Napoleon's General Caulincourt at Châtillon, where Castlereagh was wrestling mainly with his colleagues to achieve the peace terms that suited Britain—the independence of the Low Countries, the adoption of British rules on sea warfare, return to France's 1789 frontiers and a compensating restitution of many of France's colonies—Châtillon was said to be dissolved leaving

9. Another version is that they were both laughing at a Portuguese soldier for saying he was '*offendido*' meaning wounded, when Wellington was '*offendido*' himself (Sir H. Maxwell, vol. I, p. 366).

10. Gleig gave a characteristically colourful version of this incident, saying that the sentry fired at Wellington but missed, whereupon a French officer apologized for this breach of outpost etiquette—'*Pardon Monsieur, c'est un nouveau*'—and fell into conversation with Wellington, who meanwhile made mental notes on the terrain (*Life of Wellington*, p. 238).

France in a state of insurrection. (On the contrary, though the negotiations with Napoleon had indeed collapsed, Castlereagh had won his own case with the Allies, and the future 'Quadruple Alliance' came into being with the signing of the crucial Treaty of Chaumont, 9 March 1814 backdated to 1 March.) 'Don't believe anything you hear in France' wrote Wellington to one of his officers.

Scepticism, however admirable, was not a policy. The essential fact on which he could have formed one—that as a result of the Treaty of Chaumont the Allies had triumphed and entered Paris on 31 March—did not reach him by 7 April, though the Horse Guards somewhat feebly hoped it would. 'I earnestly hope they may still have arrived in time to prevent another action,' wrote Torrens. Hope was not the means by which they brought the good news from Ghent to Aix.

It was true that further rumours of Blücher being in Paris reached Wellington's camp on 10 April. The information was too vague and too late. By that day, Easter Sunday 1814, Wellington had ordered 'another action'—the assault on Toulouse.

For those whose sons, husbands and brothers fell at Toulouse—nearly 8,000 of them counting both sides—it can have been small comfort to know afterwards that this was the closest-run thing of the whole Peninsular War. Wellington described it as 'a very severe affair'. Freire's Spaniards and the 4th, 6th and 3rd Divisions were all desperately mauled, the last because Picton disobeyed orders and pushed forward when Wellington instructed him to feint. Nevertheless Soult was driven out of the town, though with only 3,200 casualties to the Allied 4,500, so that the French proclaimed themselves the victors.

On 12 April 1814 Wellington rode into Toulouse at the head of his army. Napoleon Bonaparte had already fallen—from the roof of the Town Hall, where his statue had been hurled to the ground and smashed. His eagles were gone and workmen were busily chipping the letters N and B from the municipal stonework. Nobody except General Caulincourt knew that the real Napoleon had tried to commit suicide on that same day, but the poison, prepared two years earlier for an emergency in Russia, was stale.

An hour after Wellington's entry into Toulouse, while he was dressing for a dinner he was to give in the Prefecture, Colonel Frederick Ponsonby galloped in from the royalist town of Bordeaux.

'I have extraordinary news for you.'

'Ay, I thought so. I knew we should have peace; I've long expected it.'

'No; Napoleon has abdicated.'

'How abdicated? Ay, 'tis time indeed.'

Suddenly the penny dropped.

'You don't say so, upon my honour! Hurrah!' The Commander-in-Chief, still in his shirt-sleeves, spun round on his heel snapping his fingers like a schoolboy.

In the middle of the grand dinner Colonel Cooke brought in the official despatches and latest news. He had left Paris at midnight on 7 April. King Louis XVIII had been restored, there was a constitution, and the Emperor had abdicated on the 6th. He was granted by the Treaty of Fontainebleau a pension of two million francs for himself and more for his family. He was destined for Elba.[11]

At last Wellington's political acrobatics were over and there was no more need to suppress the white cockade while still fighting the tricolour. He called for champagne and gave the toast of His Majesty Louis XVIII with three times three. General Alava at once sprang up and proposed, '*El Liberador de España!*' In a moment everyone was on his feet acclaiming the liberator in English, French, Spanish, Portuguese and German. The cheering and shouting went on for ten minutes. 'Lord Wellington bowed, confused,' noted the observant Judge Advocate-General, 'and immediately called for the coffee.'

*   *   *

'Glory to God and to yourself,' wrote young Lord Burghersh to Wellington on 7 April 1814 from Paris; 'the great man has fallen.' For Wellington, the rest of 1814 promised to be a perpetual struggle between glory and hard fact, the champagne and the coffee. The acute

11. The treaty of Fontainebleau was ratified on 16 April and Napoleon sent to Elba in H.M.S. *Inconstant* on 28 April. The alternatives to a Bourbon restoration discussed by Castlereagh and the Austrian Minister, Metternich, were (1) Napoleon to continue; (2) A Regency on behalf of Napoleon's son; (3) Prince Bernadotte of Sweden to be King. Sir Charles Stewart, Castlereagh's half-brother, told Wellington in the despatch brought by Cooke of 6 April that (2) was ruled out because 'there is indisputable proof . . . that this child was not the son of Maria Louisa', but had been substituted by Napoleon for a girl born dead to his wife! Castlereagh and Metternich agreed that the Bourbons were the best bet if the French people would have them. Talleyrand was instrumental in bringing about this desired result, and Louis XVIII signed the Treaty of Paris with the Allies on 30 April 1814.

William Bragge showed some appreciation of the position when he heard of Napoleon's abdication in England:

> I left Passages [the Spanish port] on Good Friday, at which Time the glorious and very desirable conclusion to this terrible War was not known, and when our Army hear of it, I think all except Lord Wellington will be mad and certainly Drunk for Joy.

On the evening after the dinner in Toulouse all was indeed heady effervescence. White cockades were ordered for Wellington's theatre party and he stood up in his box between Picton, Freire, Alava and the Mayor while the audience lustily cheered the new order. At one point a man in black entered another box, between tall wax candles, and read aloud the constitution. Then they began again cheering appropriate lines in the appropriate play about Richard Coeur de Lion.

In London Mme D'Arblay (Fanny Burney), sitting beside her dying father in Chelsea, watched the fireworks shooting up from the building in whose Great Hall Arthur Wellesley had stood his trial in 1808. It seemed to her that Dr Burney was sceptical about Napoleon being a prisoner on a British brig-of-war. He gave a little shrug of incredulity and died during the rejoicings.

But there were few during that gay springtime not prepared to write off the scourge of Europe. A punning anagram appeared in April in the London press:

> '*ABLE*' *no longer human kind to curse,*
> '*ELBA*' *proclaims his exile in reverse.*

Lord Byron published a contemptuous 'Ode to Bonaparte':

> '*Tis done—but yesterday a king!*
> *And armed with kings to strive—*
> *And now thou art a nameless thing*
> *So abject—yet alive!*

The poet went on to thank Bonaparte for having taught mankind a salutary lesson: no longer would men worship warrior-heroes—

> *Those pagod*[12] *things of sabre-sway,*
> *With fronts of brass and feet of clay.*

12. Pagod, an idol or image of deity.

And Chateaubriand tried to reinstate the Bourbons in people's hearts while he took a final swipe at the front of brass:

> Bonaparte is not a genuine great man; he lacks that magnanimity which constitutes heroes. . . . Nature moulded him without a heart.

Arthur Kennedy of the 18th Hussars, who had been hostile to Wellington ever since Vitoria, now became positively indignant that 'the Great Lord' had apparently not been invited to the Allied review in Paris, with the Emperor of Russia and King of Prussia, 'for certainly no small part of the merit of having overthrown Bonaparte belongs to him'. People adored him, added Kennedy, 'like a Divinity'.

The champagne continued to flow, with a visit on 21 April from a queer figure in dirty overalls below but plastered with crosses and stars above. It was no less an emissary than Castlereagh's half-brother, Sir Charles Stewart, bringing an offer of the Paris Embassy.

Wellington's reaction was predictable. Since he could not serve in the Government owing to Liverpool's breach with his brothers Richard and William, and since he must serve somewhere, it had better be Paris.[13] He wrote to Castlereagh by return, accepting

> a situation for which I should never have thought myself qualified. . . . Although I have been so long from England . . . I feel no objection to another absence in the public service. . . .

Still the champagne popped and fizzed: Stewart told him privately that they were going to make him a Duke. It was not unexpected, for many people had mentioned it after Vitoria. When he wrote to his brother Henry a month later about Spanish affairs his letter ended with a casualness that was completely candid: 'I believe I forgot to tell you that I was made a Duke.' To his countrymen he was henceforth *the* Duke.

Henry Wellesley, as a diplomat himself, approved of Arthur's new

---

13. Richard had expected to get Castlereagh's job of negotiating the peace. William rightly thought this out of the question because of 'his rooted habits & disposition', despite Lord Yarmouth having taken over the 'protection' of Moll. William was extremely annoyed at not having been taken back into the Cabinet after he had broken with Richard. Eventually he was made Master of the Mint (*Raglan MSS*, nos. 123, 124. W. Wellesley-Pole to Wellington, 12 November 1813 and 18 December 1813).

career. 'After all you have come through,' he wrote, 'you will find diplomacy very pretty amusement.'

*   *   *

His army was reassured to learn towards the end of April that their hero would be going to Paris for the triumphal entry after all. There was a feeling that he might be too self-effacing. It was perhaps inevitable that he should now play second fiddle to the Duke of Angoulême in the south of France[14]—'He carried it off very well,' wrote Larpent—but General Clausel was astonished when, on being brought to Wellington's hotel room to be presented, the field-marshal opened the door himself, not an aide-de-camp nor a glint of gold braid being in sight. Larpent commented shrewdly:

> I own I think our great man goes to the opposite extreme; but he does not like being watched or plagued.

On the way to Paris he stopped at Cahors where the thirty-nine-year-old French General Foy was still convalescing from a serious wound received in the Pyrenees; he had reluctantly gone over to the Bourbons on 16 April. He was deeply touched by the way Wellington sought him out and wrung his hand again and again. Afterwards Foy put on paper his impressions of the hero:

> Lord Wellington speaks French with difficulty. [Foy may have mistaken Wellington's abrupt manner for language problems.] He is slim, of medium build: he has an aquiline nose. His countenance is full of distinction, simplicity and kindness; just as one pictures our great Turenne.

Foy had begun by writing, 'Nous avons beaucoup parlé batailles,' as if the battles were all over.

Within a year the two of them would be hard at it again. Someone heard Napoleon murmur as he left Fontainebleau for Elba that when the violets returned next spring he too would be back....

14. The Duke of Angoulême's entry into Bordeaux on 12 March, in a blaze of white lilies and cockades, was regarded as the true birthday of the Restoration.

Wellington rode a white horse into Paris on 4 May, in time for the parade of Allied troops before Louis XVIII, having been gazetted Duke of Wellington on 3 May 1814. His entry was characteristically sober compared with many riotous displays of high spirits. It was said that Talleyrand's niece by marriage, the ravishing Dorothea Countess of Périgord, later Duchess of Dino, had galloped in with the Russian vanguard (she was half Russian herself), riding astride behind a Cossack soldier.

There was a great shoving and whispering among the spectators when they heard that the Duke of Wellington was coming. Emperors and Kings craned their necks to catch the first glimpse of him. Young John Cam Hobhouse, friend of Byron and the Radicals, who was travelling on the Continent, had what he called 'an insatiable desire' to see 'our great man', and risked many kicks and prods to get to the front of the crowd.

'Oh, for God's sake, let me see him!' exclaimed another English visitor, frantically elbowing his way past Hobhouse: 'I know you will excuse me, sir, for this; but I must see him!'

Hobhouse described him as 'the curiosity of curiosities', riding between the half-brothers, General Stewart and Lord Castlereagh, in a plain blue frock-coat, white neck-cloth and round [top] hat. One of his young Irish soldiers who was watching the procession noticed a double contrast between the glittering clothes but sullen expression of the wall-eyed King of Prussia and his own hero's plain coat but far-seeing eagle eye and aquiline nose, the stamp of talent. 'In all he seemed the Roman of old—save in pomp.' Everyone was pleased and Larpent commented when he heard about it, 'This is quite like him.' It was also politic. He knew that he was to be Ambassador and did not wish to enter Paris as a red-coated conqueror. So he stood quietly in his round hat and was introduced to the Prussian commander-in-chief, Marshal Blücher. There was a great deal of smiling and clasping of hands; then someone began to translate while the Duke listened attentively and old Blücher twirled his moustachios.

Champagne again—cascades of diamonds, uniforms loaded with fur and frogging, a firmament of stars—for all but the new Duke. He had not seen Paris since that autumn of 1786 when his carriage broke down on the way from Angers and he had had to walk. His health had been less tough then but his outfit more showy. At a party of Lord Aberdeen's (whose younger brother, Colonel Alexander Gordon, was Wellington's aide-de-camp) an old friend found him quite unspoilt by success: 'gay, frank, and ready to converse' instead of resorting to the 'silence and reserve' which so often went with new dignities. When someone pointed out that Wellington was never opposed to Bonaparte in person, he answered instantly:

No, and I am very glad I never was. I would at any time rather have heard that a reinforcement of forty thousand men had joined the French army, than that he had arrived to take the command.

It was felt that he showed true liberality in repeating this opinion after Bonaparte had fallen. 'His presence may inspire the Marshals of France with some respect,' wrote the diarist Miss Berry, shocked to hear that Marshal Ney had dared to discuss at Lord Castlereagh's table and in front of Wellington—the invasion of England!

After only a week of fizz and sparkle (3–10 May) Wellington again called for the coffee—or rather he answered Castlereagh's call to visit Madrid and knock some sense into King Ferdinand's reactionary advisers. On the road between Paris and Madrid, near Toulouse, Wellington and Soult passed in the night. Soult woke up while the horses were changed and prowled round Wellington's carriage, training his spy-glass on his sleeping conqueror inside.

The reactionaries in Spain had brought back the régime's ancient glories with a zeal which shocked even the Tory Cabinet, and rendered Wellington's mission of 24 May to 8 June abortive. All the liberal reforms of the Cortes were reversed.

From Madrid Wellington travelled to Bordeaux, the chief embarkation centre for the Peninsular soldiers. Here the atmosphere was not all champagne. What was to be their future? The very next morning after Cooke's thrilling announcement in Toulouse the conversation had been all of half-pay, promotion or starvation. Johnny Kincaid spoke for most of the younger men when he described their astonishment at peace: they had been 'born in war, reared in war, war was our trade'. Only a man of powerful connections and happy temperament like Ned Pakenham could face the future with perfect equanimity: 'The change will be rather an experiment to me, but I shall relish the Trial.' Paradoxically he was one of those who were not to enjoy the hazards of peace.

In this atmosphere of relief touched with anxiety, Wellington issued his farewell Order to the troops on 14 June 1814. There were four terse paragraphs written in the third person, all notably lacking in champagne; indeed only the last paragraph sounded more than purely formal. It ran:

4. Although circumstances may alter the relations in which he [the Commander-in-Chief] stood towards them, so much to his satisfaction, he assures them that he shall never cease to feel the warmest interest in their welfare and honor; and that he will be at all times happy to be of any service to those to whose conduct, discipline and gallantry their country is so much indebted.

Today this message sounds both dignified and sincere, as it undoubtedly was. Simple brevity was natural to Wellington, and because he would have liked this mode of thanks himself, he believed that others would find it equally acceptable. They did not. In 1814 soldiers were accustomed to the rhetoric of 'glory', 'lustre' and 'immortal fame'. Wellington's notorious Order was unlucky in saying both too little and too much. The champagne of more lavish praise might have heartened the croakers. At the same time his promise to serve them raised quite unreasonable hopes, causing him trouble throughout his life and lingering on as a grey streak in his fame. Even intelligent officers like Tomkinson and Grattan believed that Wellington had it in his power to keep the Peninsular army together. 'In fine,' wrote Grattan, 'the commands of the great man that had so often assembled them at his beck, now separated them—and for ever.' A time was coming when the Duke would lament as keenly as anyone the dispersal of his model army, some to North America, others to the East and West Indies, Ireland or the social trouble spots in England.

Not only was the army broken up but the camp-followers also. Tomkinson saw no reason why the Portuguese and Spanish women who had suffered, marched, cooked, washed, danced, loved and plundered for the soldiers should not go home with them. The quartermaster-general, however, was only concerned with how to shake off these ministering angels most easily. He had wanted to embark the troops from Spanish ports instead of marching them to Bordeaux, as it would be easier to send away from thence 'all the *attirail* which accumulates about an army upon service'. This was not possible; and as the British transports cast anchor and the wind filled their sails, the last sound in the ears of Wellington's departing heroes was the wailing of the *attirail* abandoned on the French shore.

Wellington himself stopped in Paris for one more heady draught before returning home. On his first night, 19 June, he was invited to what he called 'a grand party' at Clichy where the amazing Mme de Staël had been holding 'soupers' three days a week since May in her reconstituted salon.[15] Acknowledged as Europe's most brilliant eccentric and the voice of liberalism returned to France, she had been aghast at her first nightmare vision of Prussians and Cossacks encamped around the church of St Denis where lay the ashes of the French Kings. 'Was I in Germany or Russia?' she wrote. But the Duke of Wellington was another matter. He was the liberator. He was her hero. As if aware of all that the moment contained and of the many enthralling encounters to come, he approached her with the gallantry and deference due; indeed it was one of those rare occasions when his latent histrionic talents found expression. He went down to her on one knee.

The tone of the evening changed somewhat, however, when the Abbé de Pradt, whom Chateaubriand referred to as 'the mitred mountebank' was called on for a speech. (As Archbishop of Malines, Pradt had been employed on some semi-diplomatic missions under the Empire and in 1814 became an unofficial member of the government team—people said, in order to make sure of Talleyrand having a foursome at whist.)

'We owe the salvation of Europe,' declared the Abbé, 'to *un homme seul!*' Before Wellington had time to summon a blush, as he himself related, the Abbé placed his hand on his own heart and added, *C'est moi!*'

No such misunderstanding occurred when the Duke reached the other side of the Channel. Waiting for him was a crowd frantic with joy. His arrival coincided with the state visit to England of the Allied Sovereigns, but it was he whom the people wished to see most. On 23 June 1814 he heard again the hoarse din of 'hurrahs' after five years of shrill *'vivas'*, his carriage was mobbed at Dover and cheered all the way to London, with its occupant sitting up straight and stiff inside.

15. Germaine Necker, Baronne de Staël-Holstein, (1766–1817). She emigrated to England in 1793, returned to Paris 1795, and was banished by Napoleon first from Paris and then from France.
Wellington apparently told the painter Benjamin Robert Haydon in 1841 that Mme de Staël's party took place on his very first night in Paris in 1814, i.e. on 3 May; but she had not returned from a visit to England by then. He must have meant his first night in Paris after Bordeaux (Haydon, *Correspondence and Table-Talk*, vol. II, p. 139, 1 September 1841).

Too much shouting was to be deprecated. If you once encouraged the mob to give tongue they might hiss you next time. He had always kept his soldiers as quiet as possible.

At Westminster Bridge there was a move to take out his horses so that his countrymen might pull him themselves to his house in Hamilton Place, Piccadilly, lift him out and deposit him, amid acclamation, in the Duchess of Wellington's arms. He was too quick for them. He galloped on alone.

18 See the Conquering Hero

With Wellington back on his own door-step, it is appropriate to pause and look at the man who had won the Peninsular War.

He was just forty-five, in the pride of manhood: lean, springy, his hair still brown, his eyes whether frozen over or sparkling as blue as ever, his laughter when it came an even more abandoned whoop, like a man with the whooping-cough, and his profile impressively Roman.[1] To his passionate admirers nothing seemed beyond him. Lady Anne Barnard, sister-in-law of Andrew Barnard, was one who had thought the Regent would want him as Prime Minister. She realized that the ten thousand new things to be settled would require 'a different ability', but of this she understood he had displayed 'a great deal in India'. Lady Anne rattled on about converting his sword into a plough-share. What sort of blade would it make, turning unaccustomed soil behind a vigorous, plebeian animal imperfectly trained to obedience? Uncomfortably sharp?

Wellington had certainly acquired the reputation for caustic repartee. He had never suffered fools gladly; as Commander-in-Chief he did not see why he should suffer them at all. The history of a Peninsular anecdote illustrates this. In 1811 the Prince of Orange accompanied by his English tutor, Mr Johnson, joined Wellington's staff. At dinner one day Wellington is said to have described a moment of danger when he was caught like a rat in a bottle, going on to explain the Indian conjuring trick in which muskrats were sucked into bottles by means of a vacuum created inside. The Prince's tutor raised his eyebrows.

'Either the rats must be very small or the bottles very large.' Next moment he regretted his attempt to score.

'On the contrary, Sir, very small bottles and very large rats.'

Wellington's retort was exaggerated by his critics after his death to prove that he was both offensive and stupid. Yet it showed nothing

1. This description of Wellington's laugh has fascinated all his biographers including Richard Aldington, *Wellington*, (1946), who went one better than it originator, Samuel Rogers, calling it the laugh of a horse with whooping-cough.

worse than pungent wit, a quality which today has come back into its own and has endeared him to many who would be as bored as he was by a pedagogue.[2]

It must not be supposed, however, that all Wellington's sharpness was cultivated. Some of it would have been regarded by him as a falling away from his own ideal of 'no asperity'. He once explained to Beresford that whatever the provocation one's letters should contain no severity or asperity—only a plain and short abstract statement of the facts. In personal interviews, as in letters, his explosive temper was generally controlled, but when it burst out, as Lord Ellesmere recalled, it was 'awful'. He did not intend to make Sir Charles Stewart cry, nor to send the Spanish General Abisbal reeling from his presence pale as a ghost, faint, and clinging to the banisters. He was not a bully. But neither was he a saint who could tame the 'devil' born in him and reduce it to meekness. Most of the time he quelled the instinct to lash out by speaking in stern monosyllables.

On the closely related allegation that he was obstinate and above either taking advice or giving explanations, Peninsular opinion differed. Brigadier-General R. B. Long, a cavalry officer, complained of unnecessary 'mystery', saying it was high treason to ask Wellington questions. Long's criticism is weakened by the fact that he was one of those generals whom Wellington privately considered incompetent. A more reliable witness was the Judge Advocate-General F. S. Larpent. He recognized the inconvenience sometimes caused in different departments by Wellington's 'great secresy [sic]', but found him easier to work with than he had been led to expect:

2. The story has appeared in various forms, e.g. in Colborne's *Life and Letters*, Haydon's *Autobiography and Table-Talk*, and Gilbert Murray's *Stoic, Christian and Humanist*. In the last two accounts Wellington is stated to have conducted the exchanges not during the Peninsular War but either in 'later days' or when 'very old' (Murray) and either with a lady or a subaltern—both helpless victims compared with a don. Haydon and Colborne each correctly mention India, but Murray makes Wellington say the rat was found in a bottle of Peninsular port! Murray also 'improves' the dialogue.

'It must have been a very large bottle,' remarked a subaltern. Wellington fixed him: 'It was a damned small bottle.' 'Oh,' said the subaltern, abashed, 'then no doubt it was a very small rat.' 'It was a damned large rat,' said the Duke. And there the matter has rested ever since.' Haydon's editor, Tom Taylor, ended his version in *Table-Talk* with an anonymous peer whispering to his neighbour apropos of the Duke, 'That is the style of logic we have to deal with from the War Office' (p. 659, 1926 edn.).

I like him much in business affairs. He is very ready, decisive and civil. He thinks and acts quite for himself: with me, if he thinks I am right; but not otherwise. I have not, however, found what I was told I should, that he immediately determines against everything that is suggested to him.

To do Wellington justice, he was not secretive just with soldiers and civil servants. He was as loth to take the Prince Regent into his confidence over military matters as anyone else. When in 1813 the Prince suggested corresponding, Wellington said to Larpent, 'I wrote to his ministers, and that was enough. What had I to do with him?' Wellington was no backstairs operator.

Good reasons for his reserve, connected with security, have already been advanced. It cannot be denied, however, that by and large there was some failure in communication. Wellington certainly did not want to create 'mysteries', as an early letter to an Anglo-Indian officer shows:

Remember, that what I recommend to you is far removed from mystery: in fact, I recommend silence upon the public business upon all occasions, in order to avoid the necessity of mystery upon any.

The 'mystery' arose despite himself and was not dispelled by his growing contempt for the press and public relations. Yet he would need good public relations even more as a statesman than as a soldier.

*   *   *

Unavoidable ignorance of home politics between 1809 and 1814 was another handicap. There had been economic distress from 1810 to 1811, a threat of class war between the Luddites and mill-owners in 1812, rising prices and dear food in 1813. The unrest happened to subside in 1814 while he was in England, but burst out again after 1815 during his last long period abroad. Compared with Irish, Indian and Spanish poverty he had known, capped by Portuguese starvation heroically borne, the English labourer's lot seemed enviable.

As for the march of ideas, he had come home from India in 1805 having missed the French revolutionary ferment; similarly he returned from the Peninsula with little or no knowledge of what Professor Asa Briggs calls 'the new morality' in England.[3] What he had seen of it, as represented by dissenting preachers in his army, he did not like. Instinct told him, correctly, that the new morality would burst the old bottles. Enthusiasm and democracy were two concepts which the gallant but occasionally ill-advised efforts of the Cortes to modernize Spain had taught him to distrust. They spelt disorder. In the same way, sudden death seemed the wrong method of ending old abuses. He criticized the Cortes to his brother Richard for 'having abolished the Inquisition, which if they had left it alone would have died a natural death', and added, 'they are casting a longing eye towards the landed properties of my Cousins the Grandees'. It was half a joke, but like all Conservatives he feared the inexorable law of progression by which one thing leads to another.

If agitation and declarations of human rights did not appeal to him, 'accommodation' was a benign star which he could recommend as a pilot. He wrote on 20 September 1809:

Half the business of the World, particularly that of our Country is done by accommodation, & by the parties understanding each other. But when rights are claimed they must be resisted if there are no grounds for them; when Appeal must be made to higher authorities there can be no accommodation, & much valuable time is lost in reference, which ought to be spent in action.

He was writing this to Charles Villiers, the Minister at Lisbon, about General Beresford's tiresome claims to stores, etc., for his Portuguese army, which were not their right. If he persisted in demanding them as *rights*, Wellington would have to appeal to the Horse Guards. Otherwise there could be accommodation.

*   *   *

Wellington's belief in accommodation was typical of his pragmatic mind. He had the English taste for improvisation and flexibility,

3. The Evangelicals did most to improve public morality during the years of the Peninsular War, through mass meetings, tracts and other appeals to public opinion, as well as through voluntary societies. Wellington was later to make many ironical references to 'the Saints' as critics called them. Among prominent individuals were Lord Teignmouth and 'Parson' Hannah More, whose pious books Kitty devoured.

highlighted by a constitution that was not written down. The coming months were bound to land him among the exponents of constitutional charters, commissions and carefully defined rights, and test the apostle of accommodation.

With accommodation went a certain permissiveness for which his army was grateful. He did not fuss about their clothes. 'There is no subject of which I understand so little,' he wrote emphatically in 1811. An officer could wear high-heeled boots, a light blue frock-coat with lace and a green velvet waistcoat with silver Spanish buttons like Captain Adair in 1812; or a totally glittering £300 outfit like Stapleton Cotton's, which earned him the nickname of 'Lion d'Or' and a place in *Vanity Fair* as 'Sir George Tufto, K.C.B.'; or an old red nightcap at a pinch like Picton. When ordering a general's coat to be made for himself in Lisbon he worried over the fit but nothing else: 'Only let it be sufficiently large about the sleeves & shoulders.'

This permissiveness was part of the distinction he drew between true discipline and nagging. It ranged him on the side of the Shorn-cliffe boys and (later) Desert Rats, against what he called the Russian Emperor Alexander's 'military discipline madness', Sir George Prévost's parade-ground fussiness in Canada, or the Duke of Kent's badgering in Gibraltar.

The system of His Royal Highness in the army was fraught with petty vexations. Thus in order that the officers should be ready on parade with their hair exactly as he fancied, the hairdresser had to attend them at 4 in the morning. Thus also, to detect intoxication the non-commissioned officers were ordered at stated times to smell at the men . . . at certain other times the officers were ordered to smell at the non-commissioned officers! One result . . . of such a system would be that whenever any officer had a common cold . . . and could not smell accurately, he ought . . . to report himself as unfit for duty!

Standards of food varied as much as clothes among him and his staff. 'Cole gives the best dinners, Hill the next best,' he once said, 'mine are no great things, and Beresford's and Picton's are very bad indeed.' He could appreciate good food when set before him, contrary to some reports, but as a soldier he had neither time nor inclination to order it. Would Kitty improve his table? In Paris the King's

First Minister, the Prince de Talleyrand, had his Monsieur Carême, the most famous chef of the age.

Over money Wellington was still the man who had surprised his brother Henry in India by caring for it so little. Throughout the war his affairs were left in William's hands, assisted by Lord Liverpool and marginally by Kitty. He rarely mentioned them in letters, his only strongly expressed wish being for an estate in Somerset, the land of his ancestors. Honours came more plentifully the less one thought about them. He advised a friend in 1813 not to ask for an honour: if the Government were wise they would give him one spontaneously; if not, no one whose opinion he valued would think the worse of him.

> Notwithstanding the numerous favors that I have received from the Crown, I have never solicited one; and I have never hinted, nor would any one of my friends or relations venture to hint for me, a desire to receive even one. . . .

*   *   *

On the intellectual side, university education held a magic for him that would have seemed plainly nostalgic if he had ever experienced it—which he never did. Instead, it was a might-have-been which glowed with a vividness brighter than reality. He wanted all officers to attend a university before joining the Army, and said so later on to Kitty's nephew, John Hamilton:

> You can afford the money and time for two educations [military college and Cambridge]; avail yourself of these advantages, be educated first, as if for the pulpit or the bar, and then you will have a double chance of making a first-rate soldier. I would give more than I can mention that I had had a university education.

Wellington's idea of a university looked back to the eighteenth century, though he was to battle with modern problems when he had sons of his own at college, and still more when he became Chancellor of Oxford University. Ideally his officers were all gentlemen, and gentlemen still approximating to the cultivated all-rounder of an earlier age who studied the past in his college library and the present on his European tour. He always said he was against promotion from the ranks because rankers could not hold their drink. This intellectual short-cut had the right touch of sardonic humour. Similarly his correspondence with William about young candidates for commissions was conducted on a semi-humorous basis. When he offered William the nomination to a cornetcy in the Blues in 1813, provided his candidate was a *'Gentleman'* this time, William replied suavely that he had the very thing, 'a *raal* gentleman'—sending along yet another of his protégés with a name that today is not quite legible but looks suspiciously like Byrne, Boyne or Doyle.[4]

But behind the short-cuts and the banter was a deep region of feeling which Wellington himself had not fully explored by the end of the Peninsular War. His own want of a university education probably came home to him only after his military career was over, since he was a 'first-rate soldier' without it. But his much loved brother-in-law Edward, 'that most delightful of all characters', as Sir George Napier called him, who had entered the Army at fifteen, may have been in Wellington's mind. The bravest of the brave if not the brightest of the bright, Sir Edward Pakenham, K.C.B., met his death through an excess of chivalry equalled only by his lack of hard-headedness.

*　　　*　　　*

Generous thanks had undoubtedly come Pakenham's way for his services in the Peninsula. He was the Commander-in-Chief's relative. Speaking for the rest of the Peninsular army, Sir Charles Oman made the sombre and sweeping assertion that Wellington was 'a thankless master to serve'. Oman did not like him and allowed himself to be unduly influenced by occasional expressions of dissatisfaction in contemporary books, diaries or letters. A striking example occurs in another unpublished letter from Arthur Kennedy, who felt sore about the disgrace of the 18th Hussars at Vitoria for months afterwards:

> A man gets no thanks for getting his head broke now-a-days. . . . This has been amply verified with us, never did a Regiment lose so many officers with so little thanks from the 'Head Butcher' as he literally is.

4. Wellington's full stipulation to his brother was: 'But he must be *a Gentleman*: and he ought to have something to live upon besides his Pay. I am afraid that your Protégés are generally of a different description!' (*Raglan MSS*, no. 60, 5 October 1813).

The most Kennedy could say for Wellington was that he believed him to be a good general but without much regard for his officer's feelings.

> He gratifies his own ambition by the gallantry of his troops, and that appears his principal object. . . .

A more recent historian who accuses Wellington of 'ingratitude' is the Spanish professor, Dr Jesús Pablón. He finds Wellington's Vitoria despatch unfair to the Spanish Generals Longa and Morillo who 'bore the brunt of the battle'. (They fought magnificently in the northern and southern sectors respectively, but the 'brunt' was also in the centre.) The fact was that Wellington took immense pains to be accurate and fair, and within the limits of his battlefield knowledge he succeeded. Napoleon used Wellington's despatches, which he read in the English papers, rather than his own generals' reports as sources of exact information.

Far from being a 'butcher', Wellington stood out among commanders for his repeated refusals to sacrifice lives unnecessarily. The tragic side of great victories, so obvious to him, was not always reflected in the diaries of the period. There were exceptions who noted repeatedly that war was a 'horrid trade'. The rest kept their spirits up with the macabre humour indigenous in all British armies.

'Shirts with nine tails!' the amateur auctioneer would shout as he sold off the bullet-torn effects of officers killed in action.

'Trousers full of holes to cool the blood!'

Quite apart from regiments like the 18th Hussars which had misbehaved and could not be praised, it was literally impossible for Wellington to mention *by name* all the units and officers who distinguished themselves in every battle, not to mention the civil departments which Dr James McGrigor had very reasonably insisted, ever since Badajoz, should also get their names into despatches.

'Is it usual?' Wellington had asked, the devotee of regularity fighting inside him with the apostle of accommodation.

'It would be of the most essential service,' replied McGrigor firmly.

'I have finished my despatch—but, very well, I will add something about the doctors.'

With the steady augmentation of his army the problem increased. Yet failure to name names continued to cause offence. Even William Napier, Wellington's ardent admirer, criticized him on these grounds.

'I don't like Lord Wellington's despatch about the Little Rhune,' he wrote to his wife after the battle of the Nivelle; 'I don't want to brag, but the best thing done on the 10th November, 1813, was the attack of the 43rd Light Infantry [Napier's regiment], and he has not done us the honour to mention our names.'

Another Napier brother greatly attached to Wellington, Charles, put down his chief's failure to give credit where credit was due not to lack of space but to lack of appreciation. Years later when both Charles Napier and Wellington were near the end, Charles contrasted his own 'kind feeling' expressed towards soldiers and consequent popularity, with the Duke's reticence:

> The duke had great success, but he repulsed the soldiers, and there are few of those who served under him who love him so much as I do. He feels that he owes all to his own abilities, and he feels that justly;—but he should not shew it, for his soldiers stood by him manfully.

That Wellington did realize what he owed to his troops is shown by his many tributes to his 'fine fellows', especially the infantry. But his stern front and curt battle-orders belied these kind feelings. Hindsight suggests that he might have got over some of his difficulties by taking a leaf out of the French book and making more use of medals and decorations. Colonel Harvey Jones, R.E., who was taken prisoner at San Sebastián, was struck by the innumerable crosses of the Legion of Honour distributed to the garrison after every sortie. Wellington, as has been shown, thought the British were above such things. He was mistaken. Time would show how much.

*   *   *

If he did not lavish praise on his soldiers, he inspired them with unique confidence. By 1813 his own self-confidence had a mystical streak. Long before Waterloo he was talking about 'the finger of God' protecting him. He spoke almost reverentially of the confidence which he in turn transmitted to his subordinates.

> When I come myself, the soldiers think what they have to do the most important since I am there . . . and they will do for me what perhaps no one else can make them do.

His soldiers were able to express the confidence he gave them less subtly. One of their favourite stories was of a new major-general visiting his headquarters and demonstrating that whichever way the French moved they would have him in a cleft stick.

'Then what would you do?'

'Give them the most infernal thrashing they have had for some time.'

In contrast to Wellington's robust attitude were innumerable examples of human diffidence, among the most poignant being General Clinton's agonized wish to avoid a large, independent command: he feared responsibility and felt such anxiety at the prospect of keeping 'this complicated machine' in order, that he knew he would have a nervous breakdown. Wellington's nearest approach to a breakdown had been long ago in India when responsibility was suddenly withdrawn from him and he caught the Malabar itch.

Self-confidence gave him decision. Even Hill, a brilliant general, was adversely compared with Wellington when he took over in the south while Wellington was at Burgos. Harry Smith wrote:

> We soon felt the loss of our decided and far-seeing chief, and we made marches and counter-marches we were unaccustomed to. . . .

Worse still, they made early starts without having been warned the night before to lay off a debauch. Their far-sighted chief always gave them a hint.

Taking him all in all, William Napier had no doubt when he came to write his *History of the War in the Peninsula* that this man's greatness as a leader touched the heights of genius:

> The History I dedicated to your Grace because I have served long enough under your command to know why the Soldiers of the Tenth Legion were attached to Caesar.

*   *   *

The Duke of Wellington returned home with the authority of character. He had no need to worry about exact degrees of pomp or simplicity, autocracy or familiarity required to keep up his position; unlike the new Governor-General of India, Lord Moira, who anxiously canvassed with the Prince Regent the merits of re-establishing 'the decorations of authority' against 'the levelling system' introduced by his predecessor, Lord Minto.

Wellington spurned the decorations of authority—the large staff, sentries, gold braid, cock's feathers—but was no leveller either. He walked alone. That phrase was still, as in India, one of which he entirely approved. When writing in June 1813 to his friend Sir John Malcolm (now home from the East) he advised him to stand for Parliament. 'I likewise recommend you not to fix yourself upon Lord Wellesley or any other great man. You are big enough, unless much altered, to walk alone. . . .'

So was the Duke of Wellington.

*   *   *

This was the man whom London idolized. Kitty idolized him too. When she kissed his trophies after Salamanca with the ecstatic cry, 'Mine! my own!', it was obvious whom she clasped in her arms. There was no reason to think, however, that he saw her reflection behind the laughing eyes and flattering lips of the ladies in Spain. Not much is known of his personal life there beyond the fact of his being in Larpent's words, a great favourite with 'the fair ones'. Larpent hinted that he objected to being watched and plagued by aides-de-camp in his house at Toulouse because he was having an affair with the owner's wife. Going back a little to the middle of the war, an aristocratic Spanish lady in French-occupied Madrid was said to have regularly supplied him with secret information. As she was also believed to detest both sides equally, longing to see the English hanged in the Frenchmen's entrails, she may not have been the same aristocratic lady whose brief but affectionate note has survived among Wellington's papers. Dated *Madrid* II *de enero*, it was a letter of thanks, from 'La D[uquesa]. de S[an]. C[arlos].' to Wellington for sending her the 30,000 *reales*. She promised to repay them '*pronto posible*' and signed herself his '*apasionada Amiga*'.

Going back still further to 1809, there is a curious entry in Lady Sarah Napier's journal in which she deplores the retreat after Talavera, quoting as its immediate causes the failure of Spanish faith and English commissaries. She goes on to ask—

Whose fault is that? Why the Commander-in-Chief to be sure

... who publickly keeps a mistress at head-quarters, does not give all the attention to the care of his army & disgusts his army, who lose all confidence in him.[5]

This sounds like Whig gossip at a time when hostility to Wellington was at its keenest. The admiration of Sarah Napier and her sons for him ever afterwards was as remarkable as this solitary attack.

Whether or not he had one or more mistresses during his five 'bachelor' years in Spain without any leave or wife, is irrelevant to the main fact: that his private life created no scandal of the dimensions which did so much damage to Richard's career. Indeed, Richard's flaunting of Moll in public may have acted as a dreadful warning, if warning were needed. It is true that Wellington's own line was that people's private lives were not his affair: '& as for Private concerns', he wrote to William on 15 December 1810 apropos of Richard, 'I never trouble my head about them!' But there are plenty of other letters showing how much he deplored the effect of Richard's behaviour on both his abilities and prospects. Three years later (2 December 1813) he said that the Government would be justified in not sending Richard to conduct the Continental negotiations: 'With more capacity than others his Indolence & bad habits bring him as a Man to do business infinitely below par. ...'

In Kitty's eyes a *chevalier sans peur et sans reproche* had returned to her at last.

*　　　*　　　*

Beside her, at 4 Hamilton Place, were the two little Cheam schoolboys he had last seen as babies of two and one; Arthur now seven and become 'Douro' through his father's victories, and Charles aged six. Every time Lord Liverpool or William Wellesley-Pole wrote to Wellington about his sons it was always to report that they were 'much improved'. Their father had no means of judging even now whether they were improved or not. At forty-five it might be said that he was becoming a parent for the first time.

Was Kitty improved? Her husband evidently believed she was the same hysterical Kitty who could not be told in Dublin when he was unwell in London, because of the fuss she made. Maria Edgeworth heard that he had written four times to her after the battle of

5. There was gossip about Wellington and a 'Lady A.C-ham' around 1809.

Orthez without mentioning his wound once. Her taste in clothes had not improved. While he was away she often passed the time in sewing home-made slippers and hats. She had a passion for 'little girl' muslin dresses which she wore, however inappropriately, on the grandest occasions. As this was June it is more than likely that the Duchess was in muslin, looking ridiculously young with her *retroussé* nose and pale skin untouched by rouge—a contrast to the flamboyant Spanish beauties to whom Arthur had become accustomed.

In her own mind, on the contrary, the improvement she had noticed in herself three years earlier was still being maintained. When Arthur wrote to her enquiring whether or not she felt equal to joining him in Paris and assuming the duties of British Ambassadress, her answer was surprisingly firm:

4 Hamilton Place. June 13th 1814

My dearest Arthur—I have received your letter of the 26th from Madrid in which you permit me to decide for myself with respect to accompanying [you] to Paris or not from the moment I heard of your acceptance of the appointment I had no other thought than that of going with you. . . . I have no hesitation in deciding to go, no other wish than to go. I think, with you, that *your* task is a most arduous one attended with, what to many people would appear extreme difficulties, but to an ambassadors Wife there are no difficulties which I do not feel myself equal to overcome, no duties which I am not willing to perform and I may venture to add that you shall *never* have reason to regret having allowed me on this subject to decide for myself.

Arthur kept Kitty's letter among his papers, the first one to be preserved since 1807. He may have felt that some day he would need to convince a tearful and inadequate Ambassadress that she had brought it on herself. During these weeks of wild celebration when Sarah Napier noted sharply that 'all went mad', Kitty was observed driving in her famous husband's carriage through the swarming streets of London, her head buried in a book. She was extremely short-sighted, and though several of her husband's staff wore spectacles, convention did not permit wives to do so. Lest she should fail to recognize a face in the crowd she kept her eyes screwed up and cast down.

*　　*　　*

For him all doors were thrown wide open, from Almack's to the House of Lords. Almack's Club, devoted since the peace to introducing fashionable dances like the waltz into English ballrooms, represented the very summit of London society. Practice of the new steps took place daily at Devonshire House. Its six patronesses were Corisande, Countess of Tankerville, Mary Isabel, Duchess of Rutland, Sarah, Countess of Jersey, Lady Castlereagh, the Foreign Secretary's wife, Princess Esterhazy, wife of the Austrian Ambassador, and Lady Cowper, future wife of Lord Palmerston—every one of them a paragon; indeed, to the foreign visitors and returning soldiers, England seemed to be full of incomparable women, whether of the *ton* or not. Arthur Shakespear described the ecstasy of his German comrade-in-arms, Baron Decker, on arrival:

'*What beautiful womens! I have not seen* such fine things in all my life! I shall not *sleep* tonight!'

On 28 June 1814 Wellington took his seat in the House of Lords as Viscount, Earl, Marquess and Duke, and was thanked by the Speaker of the House of Commons on 1 July in language that matched the occasion:

> When the will of heaven, and the common destinies of our nature, shall have swept away the present generation, you will have left your great name and example as an imperishable monument . . . serving at once to adorn, defend and perpetuate the existence of this country among the ruling nations of the world.

The Opposition were in a fix. What line should they take at this spectacular reversal of all their croakings? Henry Brougham had particularly asked Creevey to note in September 1813 that he predicted Wellington's defeat and retreat from the Peninsula before Christmas. How completely he had been proved wrong in six months. Perhaps poor Samuel Whitbread, who was to die by his own hand a year later, discovered the most generous way out. He protested that Parliament's grant to the hero was not munificent enough, and got it raised from £300,000 to £400,000, making in all half a million.[6] Speaking at a dinner of the Artists' Benevolent Society Whitbread contrasted Wellington's care for the Spanish art treasures with Napoleon's plundering. At a Guildhall banquet, the Common

6. 22 December 1812, grant of £100,000. 29 July 1814, annuity of £13,000 or up to £400,000 in lieu.

Council of London forgot the aftermath of Talavera and presented the hero with a sword. Two days before, at the great Thanksgiving ceremony in St Paul's Cathedral, 7 July, he had carried the Sword of State, riding in the Prince Regent's carriage drawn by eight cream-coloured horses, as the *Annual Register* related, and sitting in the Cathedral on the Prince's right, with the Sword of State before him. He was painted by Sir Thomas Lawrence standing in front of St Paul's with the sword resting on a pedestal. The Duke, who had a very strong wrist, insisted on holding the sword upright, though Lawrence said it would make people feel tired.[7]

Oxford University made him an Honorary Doctor of Laws in the presence of royalty. His Duchess was the only English lady to be presented personally to the Tsar (by the Prince of Orange). But when the Duke paid an almost royal visit to the Salisburys at Hatfield to receive the freedoms of Hertford and St Albans, he managed to pass rapidly from pomp to informality, even if he could not actually call for the coffee. Kitty's old friend, Mrs Calvert, watched him reaching across the park paling to shake hands with as many people as possible, while the crowd roared its approval. 'His modesty and unaffected simplicity of manner are quite delightful.' A party given for Marshal Blücher by Sir John Shelley and his pretty wife was the occasion of Wellington's meeting with a couple who were to become his close friends. The twenty-seven-year-old heiress, Frances Shelley, was so much overcome at the thought of speaking to the hero that she nearly fainted at his feet. His manner at first was somewhat daunting. 'He seldom speaks until he is well acquainted.' At the Prince Regent's subsequent Carlton House ball, Wellington felt well enough acquainted with Lady Shelley to make a revealing remark as they sat together and watched his young aides-de-camp dancing.

'How would society get on without all my boys?'

How would Wellington get on without them? That was the point. They were still his 'champions', as they had been ever since India when Mrs Gordon used to tease him about them. With the end of the war this *jeunesse dorée* would no longer gather automatically, under orders, at his table. Some of them would get married and all would be showered with invitations from other great houses besides his own. He would need the right hostess to keep them round him.

In the whirl of pleasure and business Wellington did not forget his

7. (Fraser, p. 10) The picture (which is the one shown on the jacket of this book) is now in the Waterloo Chamber, Windsor Castle.

Peninsular friends. Dr James McGrigor had been recommended for a knighthood. After breaking the good news, Wellington volunteered to present him at the levée where he would receive the accolade. Unfortunately Wellington was summoned by Castlereagh to discuss politics at his home at North Cray in Kent on McGrigor's great day. He therefore arranged for Lord Bathurst, the War Minister, to present McGrigor instead. The day came. Rather disconsolate, the doctor hung about in Carlton House not daring to make himself known to his new sponsor. Suddenly Wellington appeared from nowhere.

'I thought it as well to place you under Lord Bathurst; you are a shy fellow, and might not have found him out.' Then he hurried off to North Cray.

McGrigor, now 'Mac' to the chief who had once 'Sirred' him in a blaze of anger, was greatly touched but not surprised. 'There was in this act of the Duke,' he wrote, 'a benevolence of character of which I have observed many other instances, and which those only who had been much near him could know.' This was true insight into Wellington's nature and ways.

*   *   *

At last the summer 'craze', as Sarah Napier called the vast pilgrimages from all over the country to see Bonaparte's conquerors, drew to an end. The distinguished visitors had been the first to go: the Tsar, whom most people adored though one teenager, Maria Capel, found him '*horridly* Pink & Pudding-like'; the King of Prussia, the Tsar's poodle; and silver-haired seventy-two-year-old Marshal Blücher, who was voted the favourite with the crowd. When the ladies of Dover were all clamouring for one of those silver locks he had bowed and smiled: 'Ladies, were I to give each of you just one hair I should have none left.' With the departure of the Tsar the 2nd Life Guards lost their new black and brass ceremonial cuirasses, especially designed for them by the Prince Regent to impress His Imperial Majesty at the grand Hyde Park review. Prinney did not like them after all.

In one case, at least, there had been too much champagne. The young Prince of Orange was led astray by Prince Paul of Württemberg and got drunk at Ascot. Known affectionately to the Peninsular army as 'Slender Billy' he had become engaged to Princess Charlotte

of England during the previous winter, after having served on
Wellington's staff for nearly three years. Wellington wrote to congratulate her father, the Prince Regent, saying that he had never seen
or heard anything of him that was 'not good'. From now on Princess
Charlotte saw nothing in him that was not bad. After Ascot she
peremptorily informed him that their engagement was 'totally & for
ever at an end', at the same time returning to her father the list of
wedding guests from which her mother's name had been omitted,
with her fiancé's name crossed out.

*   *   *

White's Club had laid on the most dazzling as well as the gayest event
of all: a *bal masqué* at Burlington House on 1 July in honour of
Wellington. Two thousand people were present, among them the
Duke's future wayward friend, Lady Caroline Lamb, who on this
occasion hid Sir Lumley Skeffington's red Guard's coat and 'gesticu-
lated' at Byron with her green pantaloons. Lord Byron scowled back
in the guise of a monk. In his honour, balloon ascents were made
outside Burlington House. Spectators' tickets, half a guinea each.

> *The Magnificent* BALLOON
> *With its* SPLENDID CAR *may be*
> *seen every day at the*
> LYCEUM *in the Strand*

And J. W. Croker sought forgiveness for his impertinence as Naval
Secretary the year before, by trying to persuade the committee of the
Wellington Fund in Dublin to build a Wellington pillar which
should be the highest in the world—'*stupendously* high'—beating
Napoleon's in the Place Vendôme by some fifty feet.[8] He also com-
posed an ode in Wellington's honour which began:

> *Victor of Assaye's Orient plain,*
> *Victor of all the fields of Spain,*
> *Victor of France's despot reign*
> *Thy task of glory done!*

It was neither good poetry nor good prophecy.

8. (*Croker*, 7 October 1814.) The Wellington Monument in Phoenix
Park beat the Vendôme pillar by 306 feet to 44 metres. For once Wellington's
victory was not a close-run thing.

'It's a fine thing to be a great man, is it not?' said Wellington with a smile to Lady Shelley, as the London crowds respectfully made way for him. But when the female despots of Almack's Club (as Gronow called its patronesses) turned him away for wearing trousers instead of knee-breeches, the great man meekly obeyed orders and left.

*   *   *

The time came at the beginning of August 1814 to think of taking up his diplomatic post in Paris. The Speaker had concluded his July address with congratulations on this new mission:

> We doubt not that the same splendid talents, so conspicuous in war will maintain with equal authority, firmness and temper, our national honor and interests in peace.

Wellington's supreme talent in war was to inspire confidence through success and to win success through confidence. It remained to be seen how far he would be able to exercise this talent in Paris, in peace.

On the way there he inspected the frontier fortresses in the Low Countries. His companion, the Prince of Orange, was to command the British troops in Brussels and Brabant, if not the British Princess. But Slender Billy confided to Wellington that he did not take Charlotte's decision too seriously, and would wait until she changed her mind again.[9]

In Belgium the Duke found 'many advantageous positions' for defence, including the high road from Charleroi to Brussels, where it entered the Forest of Soignes. Here stood the village of Waterloo.

He arrived in Brussels in time for the ball to celebrate the Prince Regent's birthday. A dais at the top of the ballroom was draped in blue and silver and presided over by the goddess of Peace; she was to retain her throne for another six months at any rate.

9. Immediately after the engagement was broken off he had written to his father that he was glad to see her character in its true colours in time— '*elle s'est conduit envers moi d'une manière si révoltante . . .*'. (*Hague Royal Archives*, 10 June 1814). The engagement was temporarily revived and then broken off again for good.

A comedy was put on for him at the theatre named *John Bull*, but at the last moment he was too busy to attend, so that his fourteen-year-old aide-de-camp, Lord William Lennox, had the strange experience of entering Wellington's box without him, to the strains of *See the Conquering Hero Comes*. Possibly the hero's absence from a play with that title was his first exercise in diplomacy, the profession which Henry had recommended as 'a pretty amusement'.

Pretty women as well as pretty amusements abounded. The Richmonds were on a visit with their family, and there was a more or less permanent resident, Lady Caroline Capel, mother of Maria and sister of the eloping Lord Paget (now Uxbridge). Pagets were not predisposed in favour of Wellesleys; but the Mountnorrises, also on a lengthy visit, were distant relatives of the family from Ireland.[10] They had with them two daughters: the younger, Lady Catherine Annesley, was to marry Lord John Somerset whose brother Fitzroy was marrying Emily Wellesley-Pole, Wellington's lovely niece, in August. The elder, Lady Frances, was twenty-one, pale and appealing, but with hidden fires. She had married a Hussar officer in 1810, James Wedderburn-Webster, who turned out to be the worst kind of sexual braggart. 'I think any woman fair game,' he informed Byron at the beginning of October 1813, 'because I can *depend* upon Ly F.'s principles—she can't go wrong, and therefore I may.' Byron found that despite her piety (she was 'measured for a new Bible once a quarter') she could go wrong and in fact made an offer to him one night which he afterwards said he regretted having refused. Her involvement with Byron was now over. Webster's affairs were eternal. She was ready to be consoled again.

Another prominent family were the Grevilles. Lady Charlotte and her husband Colonel Charles Greville had been kind to Kitty at Tunbridge Wells while Arthur was in the Peninsula. They had a young daughter and two sons: Charles, the diarist, and Algernon, Wellington's future secretary. Lady Charlotte Greville, known in youth as '*La Coquette Gentille*' or 'The Chrysolite' (a semi-precious, golden-green stone), was the eldest daughter of the 3rd Duke of Portland. 'Lady Charlotte has adopted all the Foreign Fashions,' wrote Caroline Capel, '& you cannot distinguish her from one of the most *outré* of the Natives. . . .' To Wellington, on the contrary, she stood out not only from the natives but from most other women.

Brussels hummed with low feminine voices. One set whispered

10. See above, p. 33.

against the other, 'the Ladies in the Park' (as the aristocratic set were called who lived in the centre of Brussels) against the less fine ladies outside. Caroline Capel found Brussels the most 'Gossiping Place' she had ever known. The dangerous but delightful town released Wellington after a relatively short spell. But not for long.

19 The Grand Disturber

The British Ambassador to the Court of the Tuileries, His Grace the Duke of Wellington, K.G., whose titles alone occupied sixteen lines of close print in his letter of instructions, entered Paris on 22 August 1814. With his usual foresight he had already secured a home for the Embassy as suitable as it was romantic. The Hôtel de Charost in the rue du Faubourg St Honoré came into the market as a result of Napoleon's banishment to Elba. It had belonged since 1800 to his youngest sister, the beautiful and amorous Princess Pauline Borghese. She was in Naples for the moment, preparatory to rejoining her adored brother on 1 November. Wellington bought Pauline's Parisian mansion, signing the inventory for its contents on 26 August and arranging for the total price of 870,000 francs to be paid by instalments—'the number as great as possible'. He moved in before the end of his first week.[1] Its spacious garden ran down to the Champs-Elysées, gay by day and quiet at night, which the English appreciatively referred to in their own language as the Elysian Fields. (John Cam Hobhouse, however, who drove through it in April with young Grattan, son of the Irish nationalist, considered it 'a poor place' and its leafy alleys 'thin and scanty' compared with Kensington Gardens.) Wellington's diplomatic successors, down to the present day, have had increasing reason to thank him for this truly Elysian property.

He was formally received at the Tuileries during his first week by the Duchess of Angoulême. King Louis's palace was still sprinkled with Napoleonic bees and eagles. It was difficult to say which of the two emblems the new incumbent resembled least. King Louis had returned from Hartwell Manor and the deep green elms of Buckinghamshire, huge and helpless as a stranded whale. When walking was absolutely necessary he could just drag along his gout-tortured limbs, one throbbing agony from head to toe. Wellington afterwards told Stanhope he was 'a walking sore, a perfect walking sore', even his

---

1. 'I have come into her house,' he wrote to William Hamilton, Under-Secretary at the Foreign Office, on 29 August 1814 (*Despatches*, vol. XII, p. 88). The instalments were concluded by 1816.

head exuded a humour. Charles Greville recalled that when he and
his father had visited Louis in exile at Hartwell his room was like a
ship's cabin and he rocked backwards and forwards, making Greville
senior feel sea-sick. However, Mme de Staël divined a respectable
intellect inside the sore head and predicted 'a king very favourable to
literature'. His Most Christian Majesty fancied himself as a Voltairian.

The Duchess of Angoulême's manner to Wellington was as
flattering as possible. She felt proud, she said, that the first Ambassador sent from England should be *'le justement célèbre Lord Duc de
Wellington'*. One observer of this scene, the Chevalier d'Arblay
(Fanny Burney's husband), watched the Ambassador closely as he
stood on the first step of the throne, for all the world as though he
were its principal support. 'I have contributed not a little to its
restoration,' his expression seemed to say; but with so modest an
air that the idea had vanished almost before Captain d'Arblay
conceived it.

                    *   *   *

The Ambassador's duty was to hunt amicably with the royal family
while hammering away at King Louis to abolish the slave-trade in
his colonies—an international reform on which British opinion had
set its heart. Wellington's success in this delicate task showed how
much he had learnt of diplomacy through hunting with the boy Rajah
of Mysore's advisers and suppressing his polygars; or shooting in the
royal *tapadas* of the Peninsula while arguing frantically with the
Regents.

Between the French devotees of the slave-trade and its dedicated
British opponents, Wellington was the ideal intermediary. He himself naturally regarded the trade itself as 'horrible', but deprecated
the violence with which his countrymen were accustomed to 'urge
such subjects [as the existing plantations in Jamaica and the French
colonies] without consideration for the prejudices or feelings of
others'. Having missed the impact of the new morality by being
abroad, he was almost as astonished as the French by the fervour it
had generated.

He immediately made himself master of what he called 'the new
crusade'. By September 1814 the great apostle of abolition, Thomas
Clarkson, announced that the Ambassador needed no more help from
him so far as knowledge went, since he had studied all the volu-

minous literature sent him by William Wilberforce, Zachary Macaulay and himself, including his own *History of the Abolition of the African Slave Trade by the British Parliament*. While reading this famous book Jane Austen had said that she was in love with the author. Whether or not Wellington loved Clarkson, he maintained throughout the confidence of the British activists. His own intermediary was General Colin Macaulay, who was with him in Paris and had also been with him at Seringapatam.[2]

On the other side, he could well understand Louis XVIII's difficulties. In the new Constitution, his Chamber of Peers (copied from the English House of Lords) was full of men who had money or friends in the French colonies worked by slave-labour. Nothing would convince French opinion that the British campaign was humanitarian. The majority of Frenchmen believed that their conquerors, having been forced to curtail slave-labour themselves, because of the overproduction it would have caused in their colonies as long as Napoleon's 'Continental system' barred them from European markets, now sought to throttle their French commercial rivals. The French *colons* saw it as the last skirmish of the Napoleonic wars, while the Director of Marine assured Wellington that Britain wanted 'free' Africans to fight for her in America—merely an alternative form of slavery.

In face of these suspicions, Wellington's advice to his own Government was sensible and conciliatory: to create a public opinion in France as Clarkson had done in England by means of books and pamphlets. This was where the formidable Mme de Staël came in again, to assist and fascinate Wellington with her intellect and ardent spirit. The bond between them was not physical. She was the devoted attendant and mistress of John Rocca, a dashing horseman of twenty-

2. General Macaulay was brother of the reformer Zachary, and uncle of the historian, Thomas Babington Macaulay. Like David Baird he had been imprisoned in Seringapatam by Hyder Ali, and was secretary to the political commission sent into Mysore in 1799 with the conquering armies.

In Clarkson's book Wellington would have read that among the early supporters of abolition was Thomas Day, bosom friend of Richard Lovell Edgeworth; and among the early opponents, the Whig Lord John Russell, who condemned it as 'visionary and delusive'. Wellington would also have found Clarkson's answer to the sugar planters' plea that slave-labour was an economic necessity: 'a pound of sugar, which the planter now sells for sixpence, could not be afforded under sixpence ha'penny—and this is the necessity!' It was typical of the arguments with which the Jamaican planters were to bombard Wellington for many years to come.

eight who was dying of tuberculosis. Despite her voluptuous neck and arms she was no beauty; indeed, the painter Benjamin Robert Haydon was to cite her looks as proof that the difference between ugliness and beauty was real. 'Venus and Madame de Staël are not the same, nor a pug and a greyhound, nor Apollo and a chimpanzee.' Nevertheless she seemed a great deal nearer to a goddess than an ape, as she flashed her expressive dark eyes at the Ambassador while the two of them argued interminably about how to put the slave-trade down. She had met Wilberforce in England during her exile from Bonaparte's tyranny, and now assisted Wellington by translating English anti-slave-trade propaganda into French. 'If we can get those who read on our side, who are very few in numbers,' he wrote whimsically to a fellow-diplomat, 'we shall do a great deal of good.' Provided, of course, there was no inflammatory anti-French reading matter published in the British newspapers. Wellington relied on Wilberforce to keep the subject out of the press as long as necessary, and his confidence was not misplaced.

As a result of this patient generalship he prevailed upon King Louis to promise abolition of the French slave-trade in five years, and was congratulated by Wilberforce on his 'bloodless victory'. It still remained for Lord Castlereagh to put across abolition internationally, at the Congress of Vienna.

*   *   *

After the days of bargaining came the break for hunting-parties. *La chasse* with the Bourbons was an affair of almost medieval splendour and quaint, vicarious prowess. The Duke of Angoulême, an unreliable shot, was always attended by a keeper who fired his gun the moment his master took aim, and cried as he himself killed the stag, '*Monsieur tire à merveille!*' On one special day when, after the hunt, the royal party did some sightseeing in Napoleon's former retreat at Rambouillet, Wellington, in compliment to his hosts, wore the traditional fancy dress complete with gold lace, jackboots and a hunting-knife. He refused, however, to submit his horses to the indignity of trappings, but planted himself and his glorious breeches firmly on a plain English saddle. This example of the Ambassador's 'comical eccentricity' noted by Creevey, amused and amazed his hosts; they were never treated to the spectacle of Wellington riding out in gold lace again.

His young aides-de-camp loved riding as much as he did but could not afford the horses. His favourite hunter, Elmore, was lent to William Lennox and lamed. In trepidation Lennox kept the news secret. When it leaked out the Duke was kind but short.

'Can't be helped. Hope it is not as bad as you think—accidents will happen.'

After the hunting the concerts, assemblies, dinners, theatres and balls seductively opened by Weber's *Invitation to the Waltz*. Some were decorous, like the Duchess of Angoulême's soirées at the Pavillon de Flore; others were uproarious. Wellington paid his court to the duchesses of the *ancien régime* and the reigning beauties of the new.

Chateaubriand was amused to see the Imperial ladies showing the returned dowagers of the Faubourg Saint-Germain the way around the Tuileries. Paris, he noted, was full of piquant contrasts in ancient and modern: the old Duke of Havré in powdered wig and back-cane ambling along as Captain of the Lifeguards, his head wobbling on his shoulders, while Marshal Victor 'limped in the manner of Bonaparte'; the Duke of Mouchy who had never seen a shot fired in anger going to Mass with a marshal scarred by innumerable wounds; the Tuileries, once so 'clean and soldierly' under Napoleon, now reeking with the domestic odours of breakfast.

Wellington was amazed by the fat King's addiction to delicacies. When dining *en famille* he would tip a whole dish of strawberries on to his own plate, without offering any to the ladies.

'Queen Anne,' interjected Stanhope to whom Wellington later told this story, 'related that William III did exactly the same with fresh peas.'

'I hope it is not a Royal custom,' said the Crown's retained servant, laughing heartily.

Wellington liked being asked to the re-opened salons of 1814, and as an habitué showed the expected degree of gallantry. His motives were social and political rather than amorous: to support the homing *émigrés* and *ancien régime* in its new form.

Foremost among the beauties were the little Duchess of Duras, who in a year or so was to be one of Chateaubriand's 'Madams', and the gentle Juliette de Récamier—*la belle Julie*—extending her long fingers to Wellington from her Empire sofa. Her gesture was friendly rather than seductive, for she had just become involved with Benjamin Constant, Mme de Staël's literary friend, and was destined in 1817 to supersede Claire de Duras as Chateaubriand's 'Arch-Madam'.

A beauty less remote than Mme de Récamier was the famous contralto who had followed Napoleon's eagles from the Milan Opera House at the beginning of the century. Radiant, forty-year-old Guiseppina Grassini was as gracious to Wellington now as she had been formerly to Napoleon, when she was known as '*La Chanteuse de l'Empereur*'. In return Wellington was to keep a portrait of La Grassini in his room, balanced by a print of Pauline Borghese, with Pope Pius VII, who had been present when Napoleon crowned himself, between them. When the Count of Artois paid a call on Wellington and saw the strange trio he threw up his hands in horror:

'Exactly like Our Lord between the two thieves.' Mme de Staël had roughly the same idea when she wrote to her hero, 'Why expose the Pope to a situation of this sort?'

It may be that in the diaphanous glitter of Restoration Paris, Pauline Borghese herself, quite apart from her house, attracted or tried to attract Wellington. He described her to his niece Lady Bagot as a 'heartless little devil'.

Then there was Tallyrand's niece Dorothea who publicly declared her worship of Wellington, for the best possible reasons. Though partly Prussian by birth she abhorred the destructiveness of the Prussian troops and was dazzled by the Duke's skill and decision in preventing them from smashing up the Palais Royal. Dorothea was to act as hostess for her uncle in Vienna when the peace conference assembled there in September. Her blue-black eyes, said Sainte-Beuve, were always burning with 'an infernal fire' which turned night into day.

Of the marshals, Wellington met Ney almost at once, out hunting in the Bois. His handsome wife, Aglaé Ney, was beginning a romance with a young Englishman named Michael Bruce which was to cause Wellington much concern during the following year. Marshal Soult was instantaneously recognizable as a result of the telescopic examination at Sorauren; but it was December before the Duke and Massena were brought together at a party. The marshal looked very old, with only one eye. After they had quizzed one another for some time through lorgnettes as if before a parlour version of Bussaco, Massena advanced.

'My lord, you owe me a dinner—for you made me positively starve.' Wellington laughed.

'You should give it to me, Marshal, for you prevented me from sleeping.'

Apart from celebrated natives, Paris was packed with English visitors, eager to see the world after a decade of enforced insularity behind their grey-white cliffs. Some of them were full of spice and charm. Charles Arbuthnot, a Secretary of the Treasury and Henry Wellesley's staunch ally during his divorce, had brought over his second wife, Harriet, whom he had married that January, though twenty-six years his junior.[3] Harriet Arbuthnot was a first cousin of Wellington's favourite Burghershes, being a niece of the Earl of Westmorland. She possessed a strong but sympathetic personality, shrewd mind, conservative outlook and the charm of soft brown eyes and hair and an elegant, neat figure. Her infinitely gentle husband provided the perfect complement both to his dominant young wife and their equally emphatic friend, the Ambassador.

By October the Duchess of Wellington was ready to join her husband as planned. Kitty's frame of mind on leaving England was not auspicious. Maria Edgeworth received a letter from her post-marked Deal, just before she embarked. 'The whole of her letter,' noted Maria, 'was full of her children and of sorrow for leaving them.' The sorrow and tears became a flood when Kitty discovered the situation in Paris. To begin with, her husband was universally lionized while she was totally incapable of making any show as a lioness—except of course in defence of her cubs, and they did not arrive until the Christmas holidays to console her. Then there was the gossip. Kitty was not too short-sighted to see La Grassini on the Ambassador's arm. What she did not see her friends told her about. Everyone talked in Restoration Paris.

Lady Bessborough, married to the head of the great Whig family of Ponsonby, wrote to her lover Granville Leveson Gower on 13 November 1814:

The Duke of Wellington is so civil to me, and I admire him so much as a hero, that it inclines me to be partial to him, but I am afraid he is behaving very ill to that poor little woman; he is found

3. Charles Arbuthnot (1769–1850), held various diplomatic posts abroad before entering the Treasury as joint Secretary with Henry Wellesley in 1809, a year before the Wellesley divorce. Arbuthnot held the post until 1823 when he was given the department of Woods and Forests. Harriet Arbuthnot, *née* Fane (1793–1834).

great fault with for it, *not* on account of making her miserable or of the immorality of the fact, but the want of procédé and publicity of his attentions to Grassini.

A few months later John Cam Hobhouse heard the story from Lady Kinnaird, wife of a Whig peer and sister-in-law of James Kinnaird, close friend of Hobhouse and Byron. Though not perhaps the most impartial of witnesses, Lady Kinnaird held forth on 'the follies of the Duke of Wellington's public addresses to Grassini, who lived in the same house with the Duchess'—a piece of scandal possibly arising from garbled accounts of the Duke's picture of *'La Chanteuse'*.

There is nothing which could be called proof that Grassini was the Duke's mistress after having been Napoleon's. If she was, it appears to have been a distinction which she shared with the actress Mademoiselle Georges, aged twenty-seven in 1814, whose real name was Marguerite Josephine Weimer. She was seen in all her glory by Hobhouse at the *Comédie Française* that April: 'very large but with a fine face and strong lines with expressive action, so as now and then almost to remind me of Mrs Siddons'. Mlle Georges lived until 1867 and used to boast of having enjoyed the protection of both Wellington and Napoleon—*'Mais M. le duc était de beaucoup le plus fort.'*

One thing is certain. When the Duke did succumb to a genuine passion—in the early 1820s—there was a great deal less publicity and more of the *procédé* which Lady Bessborough had found wanting in 1814. Meanwhile Wellington continued to arouse the unbounded enthusiasm of women. As was his way, he made no bones about it when people questioned him. After the great days in Paris were over a lady asked him if it was true that he had received all that female adulation?

'Oh yes! Plenty of that! Plenty of that!' replied the Duke breezily.

*   *   *

Women and slaves were not the whole of the Ambassador's cares. He aroused the wrath of the English Protestant Society by explaining to their secretaries in one of his pitilessly lucid letters that Protestants in France were not really persecuted and could not be made the subject of another new crusade. Two royal personages also caused him some anxiety. The Prince of Orange loved his newly acquired capital of

Brussels, but not its native society. Belgium had been united by the peace treaties to Holland under the single rule of his father, King William I of the Netherlands. Wellington was deputed to point out to the Crown Prince that he entirely neglected the Belgians, confining his attentions to the English colony. His mentor admitted that his English education had given him that 'natural inclination';

> but a Person in your high situation must get the better of his inclinations ... for the sake of the higher Interests committed to his charge. [England would be glad to see] a marked preference in favour of your new subjects.[4]

Slender Billy replied with engaging candour that he had indeed avoided those 'Idiots the Belgians', but would do so no longer: 'from what I knew of the people I thought it better not to court them at first, but wait till they shewed an inclination to be on good terms with me'.

There was also the Princess of Wales. A private letter dated 15 September 1814, Walmer Castle, reached Wellington from the Prime Minister. The Princess might be coming to Paris. The French Court could not receive her as Princess of Wales, separated as she was from her husband. On the other hand, things should be made as agreeable as possible for her at the British Embassy, 'in order that she may have no inducement to return to England'. The Government could not forget that owing to the Princess's popularity with the mob, the Prince Regent, regarded as her oppressor, had been the only royalty not to receive a warm welcome during the summer celebrations. The throwing open of the Continent to English travellers was a wonderful opportunity to relieve the Prince Regent of this turbulent wife. Fortunately for Wellington, the Borghese Palace was spared the takeover by a siren far less seductive than Pauline.

A minor concern over which Wellington did not lose much sleep was the site for his ducal home, to be built with the money presented by the nation. Benjamin Dean Wyatt, who had been his clerk in India and Ireland, was in charge. Born a member of Britain's most prolific family of architects, Wyatt now set out to purchase an estate worthy of 'the Dignity and the Dukedom' (to quote the eloquent

4. (*Hague Royal Archives*, 12 December 1814.) Lady Caroline Capel provides independent testimony on this subject. All the Prince wanted, she wrote to her mother, was 'a little snug *English* Party', where he could say just what he thought (*Capel Letters*, p. 66).

language of Parliament) and to be 'a lasting Memorial' of the country's 'Gratitude and Munificence'. By the end of 1814, however, no sufficiently splendid mansion had been found. There were certain recurring obstacles. Chief among them was the proximity of even more stately homes which would overshadow the beauties of otherwise suitable sites. Blenheim Palace was particularly tiresome in this respect. Several attractive houses in Oxfordshire had to be turned down because Blenheim's superlative magnificence would have invited odious comparisons between the nation's gratitude to Marlborough and to Wellington. A pleasant property in Buckinghamshire was too close to the ducal estate at Stowe, while Standlynch in Wiltshire was not only too modest in itself, having no space in the dining-room for sideboards, but such charms as it possessed would be dimmed by the Earl of Radnor's neighbouring property, confusingly called Longford Castle. (It had no connection with the home of Wellington's in-laws in Ireland.) Where was Wyatt to find a place within reach of both London and a good pack of hounds, not too much enclosed like pretty Somerhill in Kent nor cut in half like so many parks by that ever-present menace, the turnpike road? After a fruitless survey of various residences respectively owned by Mr Coke of Norfolk, Lords Howe, Fitzwilliam, and Egremont among others, Wyatt was reduced by the beginning of 1815 to a Mr Clarke Jervoise's *'very imposing'* estate in Hampshire—'a *Princely Possession*, and *very much* superior to any other property' which Wyatt thought likely to be offered to the public.

Wellington himself took it all calmly. He reckoned on laying out £100,000 over four years, which should build him, as he informed William,

a very fair house, & as magnificent as it ought to be. After having built it I shall not be a very rich Man; but I hope to do pretty well; that is to say if I am not ruined at Paris.

The Duke was thinking of his entertaining as Ambassador, and the many expensive items he had to buy. A large array of uniforms was fortunately not among them. He always wore his scarlet field-marshal's uniform with gold-embroidered velvet collar, ribbons and orders (which included the Golden Fleece, Garter, Bath and Peninsular medal), white stock and white breeches. He was presented with the usual gift of ambassadorial silver on arrival. But apart from the

handsome silver 'campaigning set' made for him in Lisbon, he had
brought little but glory with him from the Peninsula. And so throughout the autumn of 1814, beginning on 22 September, bills were coming
in from the famous Sèvres china factory for a splendid set of plates,
coffee and tea cups and saucers, sugar bowls, cream jugs, milk jugs
and imposing '*glacières*' to hold ice. The Duke's taste led him to
choose a white ground decorated with garlands '*de fleurs et de fruits
polychromes et or*'. There was plenty of gold in the form of stylized
sprays and vines, but the soft pinks, blues, greens, mauves, and
yellows of the flowers and fruit prevented the effect from being gaudy
or even sumptuous. By 20 December he had laid out over 5,000 francs
on the Sèvres service and another 1,500 francs in August 1815—
a considerable sum for those days.[5]

Nevertheless, despite his fears expressed to William, he was not
destined to stay long enough in Paris to be 'ruined'.

*   *   *

'Everything goes well here,' he reported on 15 September 1814. A
fortnight later his tone had begun to change: 'I think we are getting a
little unpopular in the town but I don't think that circumstance is of
much importance.' On 4 October he had to admit a state of 'constant
uneasiness', caused by the two extremes of disbanded Bonapartists
and disappointed royalists who had expected a golden age.

The truth was that the Government of Louis XVIII had already
degenerated into 'paternal anarchy', a kind of benevolent muddling
which many people found worse than Napoleon's efficient tyranny.
Even Wellington wrote to Castlereagh, 'There are Ministers but no
Ministry', and everyone agreed with Mme de Staël that things could
not go on like this—'*Cela ne peut pas durer.*'

The French Army was Bonapartist to a man. Soldiers no doubt
wore white Bourbon cockades on their shakos but at the bottom of
each haversack was treasured a crumpled tricolour. Greedy old Louis
they called '*le cochon*', and in playing cards they referred to the 'pig'
of hearts or spades instead of the king. Those Bonapartists who
frequented cafés rather than barracks, either sang the '*Marseillaise*'

5. As much as £2,500 in today's money. Out of the original 130 plates,
120 have survived, some of them still in use at the Duke's house at Stratfield
Saye. The 'campaigning' and 'ambassador's' silver are to be seen in the
Wellington Museum, Apsley House.

and shouted '*Vive l'Empereur*' quite openly, or chose a more subtle game of symbolic acts and passwords. They would drink to '*his*' health, or ask in a low voice:

'Do you believe in Jesus Christ?' to which the answer was:

'Yes, and in his resurrection.'

At the end of October some Bonapartist bullets actually whistled past Wellington and the Duke of Angoulême during a review on the Champs de Mars.

If he could have seen his friend General Foy's diary for these days his anxieties would not have abated. On 26 October Foy noted that he spent an hour with Wellington. As soldiers, there was always one safe subject. '*Nous avons parlé guerre.*' Foy reserved for his diary the hard feelings about the Bourbons and England which had begun to rack him. The Bourbons were, and would long remain '*les trés humbles valets de l'Angleterre*'. Two days later he was invited by Wellington to a soirée at his house where there would be dancing—

a famous reunion. I shall not go. . . . Lord Wellington and the English are held in horror by everybody. Even the Bourbonists are beginning to come out against them.

Suddenly the unfortunate general's bitterness caused by divided loyalties overflowed:

We who were lately masters of Europe, to what servitude are we reduced? Lord Wellington is Commander-in-Chief of the army of occupation in Belgium. Our telegraph is at his disposal two hours daily to send orders to his troops. He signs his letters from his headquarters in Paris; he has an air of saying to us: if you sit on the fence it is me you will be up against. We see him coming away from the King *en frac* and in boots. The Princes go and dine with him after manoeuvres. *O Napoléon où est tu?*

Napoleon, as Foy had just heard, was very gay and active on Elba, thinking seriously of regaining his crown. If Foy, an honourable man who liked Wellington personally, felt like this, the Ambassador was clearly in trouble.

By November the British Cabinet were thoroughly alarmed for their Ambassador's personal safety. King Louis's scarcely established Government might be overthrown by an army of hungry ex-servicemen on half-pay. The Duke of Wellington might be seized. No longer referred to as the Duke, incidentally, but as 'Monsieur Villainton' in the hostile French press. He must quit Paris.

Various face-saving posts for him flitted through Lord Liverpool's agitated mind. A mission to the Congress sitting in Vienna to tell the British plenipotentiary, Lord Castlereagh, about the Netherlands' defences? (He would remain nominally Ambassador but never return to Paris.) Or the chief command in North America? He could 'give Jonathan one good thrashing' (Colonel Torrens's phrase) and then bring the unpopular American war to an end. William Wellesley-Pole answered for his brother accepting the American assignment 'cheerfully'; indeed it was William's own brain-wave.

This time William had over-reached himself. Far from agreeing cheerfully, Wellington would not go to America unless positively ordered to do so; and then only if absolutely free to negotiate. He had long been opposed to the war. Mme de Staël's passionate advocacy of peace with America did not make him any more favourable to continued hostilities, even though she sometimes went far beyond protocol in the violence of her partisanship. *The Times*, which was not over-friendly to Wellington, described on 14 October a startling scene in which she had 'pronounced an oration' in the presence of the Ambassador against the burning of Washington by his countrymen. This was 'a challenge to his Grace,' declared *The Times*, 'to prove that the sword is not his only weapon.' It had to credit him, however reluctantly, with yet another victory. 'The Duke of Wellington did all that Bonaparte himself could do—he silenced her.' (This was a reference to Bonaparte's earlier rebuff of her advances, both intellectual and physical.) Nevertheless this clash and others like it did nothing to damage her growing influence.

She was asked to his autumn balls. 'Lord Wellington treats me with great distinction,' she wrote to a friend, 'and I am proud of it.' She even made a hit with Kitty, as Maria Edgeworth testified. Kitty had avoided meeting Mme de Staël when in London in case the Bourbon Court, to which she was about to become Ambassadress, declined to receive the colourful exile. When on the contrary the French Court proved welcoming, an encounter between the two women took place in which Kitty's curious combination of bluntness and timidity for once scored.

'. . . Madame la Duchesse, so you did not want to make my acquaintance in England?' challenged the woman whom Byron called the greatest mind of her times. Maria heard that she had swept up to Kitty in full fig, her eyes flashing with indignation; and since she foamed at the mouth when angry, at least according to Gronow, Kitty may have had to face that hazard also. Kitty stood her ground and replied firmly, 'No, Madame, I did not want to.'

'. . . Madame, why not?'

'It's because I was *afraid* of you, Madame.'

'You *are afraid* of me, Madame la Duchesse?'

'No, Madame, I am not afraid of you any more.' Germaine threw her glorious arms round the little duchess.

'Ah, I adore you!'

On 2 November Kitty's husband was writing to Mme de Staël in his familiar tone of affectionate irony, that owing to a day devoted to *la chasse* he would be too tired to meet her that evening and 'sustain with dignity the various attacks which you will make upon me . . .'. She herself was so pleased with the cut-and-thrust over the American war that she wrote to Jefferson (former President of the United States) a year later, calling his attention to it: 'I don't know whether you saw in the newspapers that I upheld the cause of your America against a noble adversary, the Duke of Wellington?'

The noble adversary, after standing up to the formidable Mme de Staël, would certainly not cave in to a Cabinet like Liverpool's on the question of commanding in America. In any case, war or no war with America, if there was to be a *coup* in France against Louis XVIII, he must be at hand: 'they cannot now allow me to quit Europe. Nobody has confidence in anybody else'.

Lord Liverpool's letters, meanwhile, became more and more excited. Let Wellington make sure there was always a Bourbon prince resident in the south of France, to raise the standard there in case of a Paris massacre. (A standard was soon to be raised there, but not the King's.) Let Wellington slip away quietly or he might be recognized and stopped on the road. The sooner Lord Liverpool heard of his having landed at Dover the better.

As the panic grew so did the Duke's phlegm. He had agreed in September that owing to 'the daring class of men' operating in Paris against the King's party, he ought to be moved. At the beginning of November he was hardening against it: 'I entertain a strong opinion that I *must* not be lost but . . . I don't like to be frightened away.' He had noticed that the King and royal family were remarkably well received at the *Comédie Française* on the 16th. Why assume an English tragedy to follow? On the 24th he indignantly told William there was not a word of truth in newspaper stories that he was ill-treated by the marshals, who wanted the King to arrest him.[6]

> Still however it is necessary to withdraw me; but all I beg is that it may be done handsomely.

As in Portugal, he was determined not to go out by the back door. Lord Liverpool finally decided to leave the tricky question to the Ambassador's discretion, but as a hint not to dally sent him a warning he had received from a secret agent, Francis McGee.

> Unless Duke Wellington is instantly recalled from France, and in as private a manner as possible, he will be privately assassinated: a plott [*sic*] is forming to complete the horrid deed.

At last in December the solution was found. H.M. Government implored Castlereagh, Leader of the House, to return immediately to his place on the front bench for the new session (the Opposition were up in arms at the Congress's scissors-and-paste work with the map of Europe) thus giving the Duke an excuse to take over his work in Vienna. A letter dated 18 January 1815 from the Prince Regent to the King of France smoothly papered over the cracks:

> Sir, my Brother and Cousin! having occasion near My Person for the services of Lord Viscount Castlereagh . . . I have judged it expedient for the common cause to appoint Field Marshal the Duke of Wellington to be His Majesty's First Plenipotentiary at the Congress of Vienna. . . . I therefore hope that Your Majesty will graciously permit the Duke of Wellington to take leave of Your Majesty on this temporary Mission.

Lord and Lady Fitzroy Somerset would hold the fort, assisted, if that was the word, by the Duchess of Wellington, until the Ambassador returned. There was to be no Congress of Vienna for Kitty.

6. An even more unpleasant story appeared in *The Times*, hinting that he had failed to press home his mission to King Ferdinand of Spain for fear of losing his Spanish honours. This libel really hurt, for he suspected it came from Apsley House (Richard's home). 'God forgive me if I am wrong; and indeed the idea of such a thing is painful enough to carry with it its own punishment' (*Raglan MSS*, no. 77. Wellington to W. Wellesley-Pole, Paris, 8 December 1814).

Wellington had got his way. By firmness and decision he had avoided letting down the French Government and damaging his own reputation for personal courage. His departure from Paris was put off till 24 January 1815, after the rumours of his impending 'flight' had died away. His transfer was not to be to America. The Treaty of Ghent between America and Britain was signed exactly a month before he left, on 24 December 1814.

There was a tragic postscript to the American peace. Sir Edward Pakenham, already in America while the negotiations were taking place, was cut off from the good tidings of success. On Christmas Day 1814 he took over command of the British army which had been sent out to give 'Jonathan' his thrashing. On 8 January 1815 he was defeated and fell on the battlefield of New Orleans, hemmed in between the *bayoux* and the Mississippi with a bullet through his spine.[7]

*   *   *

The death of Kitty's favourite brother was another nail in the coffin of her married happiness. Wellington had always been attached to him, and the facial likeness between Ned and Kitty was so strong that it is perhaps not too fanciful to suggest that Wellington saw in his brother-in-law the looks that long ago were so attractive in his wife. Ned on his side understood Kitty's temperamental difficulties: he once wrote about the failure of her domestic philosophy to keep her calm. This sympathy for Kitty, together with his hero-worship

---

7. *Bayoux* were narrow water-courses intersecting sub-tropical swamps.

The battle of New Orleans illustrates the waste of war with peculiar vividness. The struggle of 1812–15 against America has been called *The Incredible War* (by J. Mackay Hitsman, 1966). Like Wellington, Pakenham did not want to fight in it. 'I think I have escaped America and shall consider myself vastly fortunate in having been spared from such a Service,' he wrote to his mother on 6 June 1814. He rejoiced too soon. When his body was returned to Ireland in the traditional cask of rum, she may have re-read his exhortation at the time of Salamanca: 'but why don't you Recollect, Woman, that you are the Mother of Soldiers, and you must meet our Circumstances with good Countenance as they come.' For all his gallantry, he was yet another Peninsular general who failed in an independent command. It is impossible to imagine Wellington accepting the desperate battleground on which the British Admiral irresponsibly landed the army in front of New Orleans, for the sake, according to Wellington, of plunder (*Pakenham Letters*, Preface).

of Wellington, might have smoothed the path between them, growing daily more rough.

*   *   *

Wellington was well posted by Castlereagh, and his Under-Secretary, Colonel Cooke, in what to expect at Vienna. He already had an enviable reputation as a diplomat built up over his past five months in Paris. Talleyrand later told Gronow of his 'astonishing' skill:

> He never indulged in that parade of mystification which is generally employed by Ambassadors: watchfulness, prudence and experience of human nature, were the only means he employed; and it is not surprising that, by the use of these simple agencies, he acquired great influence. . . .

Wellington's principle of 'no mystery-making', first expressed by him as an administrator in India, but not successfully practised in the Peninsula, had triumphed again in Paris. The change must have been deliberate, showing his different conception of authority when in the hands of a civil and a military leader.

The Congress had assembled in September 1814. After a fort-night's bickering since the beginning of October between the big five powers—Russia and Prussia, Austria, Britain and France (Talleyrand having insinuated himself into the group at the top table during September)—Castlereagh gave Wellington a first, sour report:

> I send you under flying seal the result of our discussions, not progress; for progress we have not made. . . .

A veteran wit, the Prince de Ligne, who at eighty odd was frolicking among the Congress visitors, put the same thing more brightly: '*le Congrès ne marche pas, mais il danse*'.

Towards the end of the month, Wellington saw the amusing but jaundiced account which Cooke had despatched to the Prime Minister: Prince Metternich, the Austrian plenipotentiary, was not playing a straightforward game and would not do so until he found that side games failed; there was still no advance, therefore, and Castlereagh was rather 'fidgety'. As for the Tsar Alexander, he 'flirts and plays the amiable from morning to night, and flatters himself with complete success by his captures'—captures of the sovereigns of Prussia and Austria. And how had he captured them? By sheer sentiment. He had invented a 'Sacred League', and the print shops of Vienna were full of portraits of the three Emperors beneath the flourishes of its text. Cooke was a cynic who had had one nervous breakdown and was due for another. He paid tribute to the Tsar's cleverness with a snort: 'All this nonsense tells.'

The 'Sacred League', better known as the 'Holy Alliance', was the Tsar's semi-mystical attempt to base the peace of the world on a Europe united by Christian principles. It was marred by his own terrestrial ambitions. Poland had been finally partitioned out of existence in 1795; the Tsar proposed to re-establish the unity of that region by swallowing Poland whole and compensating dispossessed Prussia with independent Saxony, while Austria helped herself in Italy. As Wellington commented to Castlereagh from Paris on 7 November, the Emperor Alexander's Polish schemes were 'the foundation of all the evil which was likely to result from the Congress of Vienna'.

Was there any combination which Britain could put up against the Holy Alliance, strong enough to thwart the Tsar and eventually produce a firm peace? Talleyrand persuaded Castlereagh and Wellington that there was. Were not France and Britain in the identical position of having no territorial ambitions, France because it was beaten, Britain because its needs had already been satisfied at the Treaty of Paris? In case the present disputes between the former Allies actually burst out into a new war, as Castlereagh thought most likely, Britain's policy must be armed mediation, supported by Austria, France and the Netherlands against Russia and Prussia. If, instead of breaking up, the Congress became 'totally stagnant' or even moved forward, a close collaboration between Britain and France would still be essential, in order to attract Austria.

This was where Wellington, while still in Paris, first made his mark on the Congress. At the beginning of November he persuaded Louis XVIII to order Talleyrand (whom Castlereagh had hitherto found as personally difficult as Churchill found de Gaulle) to co-operate 'in every way' with Britain against Russia's Polish plan. Talleyrand, at bottom, needed little pressure, and soon Wellington received a grateful letter from Castlereagh thanking him for inspiring in Talleyrand a much more conciliatory mood. Altogether there were 'some indications of light on the horizon'. By early December a compromise was reached over Poland, by which the Tsar got the Duchy of Warsaw but not the whole. When Castlereagh made his suggestion to Wellington from Vienna on the 14th, 'Would *you* feel a disinclination to replace me here?' he was able to say that the only dangerous problem now left was Saxony.

*   *   *

Wellington reached Vienna on 3 February 1815, after a dash across Europe which his two companions, young Lennox and Colonel Fremantle, found exciting but arduous. Though their entirely cold meals consisted of such delicacies as *foie gras* washed down with the best claret, sleep was limited to precisely four hours each night. Only the Duke undressed and dressed. The other two slept in their clothes before hot German stoves and presented themselves each morning to the spruce 'Beau', bleary-eyed and crumpled.

The occasion of Wellington's introduction into the conference chamber was chosen by the artist Isabey for his official painting of the Congress—such was the Duke's unparalleled prestige and the intense interest aroused by the coming of *le Vainqueur du Vainqueur du Monde*. There were great soldiers in Europe, such as the Archduke Charles and Barclay de Tolly, who had fought in the main theatres of war. No general but Wellington reached the council table. Nor did his personality disappoint expectant Vienna.

'What have you done, gentlemen?' he asked his colleagues on arrival.

'Nothing; absolutely nothing,' replied Prince Metternich.

According to Talleyrand, Wellington at once got the creaking machinery into rapid motion, while all the time maintaining 'his usual unassuming and nonchalant air'. A modern French writer, J. A. Chastenet, sees Wellington at the Congress as 'always alert and phlegmatic'. This rare combination of opposites has also been picked out by a recent British Prime Minister, Asquith, as a lucky possession of his own. In his case he described it as 'energy under the guise of lethargy'. It might be seen in a wider context as a peculiarly English syndrome. If so, it was first launched upon an amazed world in Vienna as a counter-irritant to merry-making under the guise of peace-making.

Despite the inordinate heat of the rooms which immediately gave

Wellington a frightful cold, he worked prodigiously hard during his first days, which overlapped with Castlereagh's last, to master the up-to-date situation. Exactly a month before he arrived—on 3 January 1815—a secret treaty had been signed between Britain, Austria and France (of which he already knew) to revert to Castlereagh's Treaty of Chaumont (1814) which the Foreign Secretary regarded as the king-post in the edifice of victory and peace. With singular skill Talleyrand succeeded in making Royal France join a coalition that originally had been formed against Imperial France. The enemy was Russia now, with her poodle, Prussia, as the immediate danger.

Wellington's own straightforward methods were in marked contrast to those of his two closest colleagues, Talleyrand and Metternich. 'With nations, depend upon it,' he assured his friends in old age, 'the only way is to go straight forward without stratagems or subterfuges.' The very appearance of the brilliant Frenchman, on the contrary, was contorted: with his crippled leg and monkey face, he was a byword for chicanery, not least because he had managed to remain Foreign Minister of France under the Republic, Consulate, Empire and Restoration, with a period of asylum in England and America only during the Terror. Cobbett had spoken for the English Left in calling him 'the lame fiend', while Tories like Lady Shelley and Croker were appalled by his craft, diabolical expression and villainous, hoarse voice. The Whig Duke of Argyll likened his skin at the Congress to a corpse's considerably advanced in corruption. In answer to an enquiry as to what Talleyrand was like, Wellington replied, 'Like Old Brag, but not so clever'—Old Brag being Scindiah's unprepossesing envoy in 1803. At the Congress he found Talleyrand's conversation neither lively nor pleasant, though occasionally memorable. But he had learnt long ago to do business with those he did not personally like. A time was to come when he would change his opinion of this intelligent if devious statesman. In England Metternich was considered almost equally slippery, and Lord Liverpool specifically warned Wellington against his '*finesse* & trick'.

Yet the three had this in common: they were all 'Europeans' seeking the magic point of 'just equilibrium', which by definition was world peace. It depended on checks and balances between all the European states, rather than on a monolithic Continental system such as Bonaparte had run. Within this formula there were of course differences. Metternich's original idea of how to realize it was more

rational than Castlereagh's, and included the forlorn hope of
Britannia climbing down a step or two from her maritime hegemony
which she loftily called the Freedom of the Seas; in the end it was
Castlereagh's concept which was adopted and later became known as
the 'Balance of Power'. All three, however, were agreed that the
'just equilibrium' must be achieved through sovereigns, not through
peoples, and through legitimate sovereigns at that. To Wellington
also the smoky torch of legitimacy, handed on to him by Castlereagh
who had received it from Talleyrand, seemed a manifestation of that
principle of order and 'regularity' which he had always revered.
Beyond that, he took his place in the trio not as a John Bull but as a
cosmopolitan by training and taste. Indeed, it is questionable whether
he was ever as much at home in the Mother of Parliaments as at the
Congress of Vienna. He would have been proud to believe that Europe
owed to the Congress her relative stability and greatness from 1814
onwards, whereas he held, at least during the Peninsular War, that
England had achieved her greatness despite Parliament.[8]

He enjoyed himself in the splendid Viennese mansion allotted to
him, while avoiding the scandals which surged and broke all round
him, acting as a tonic to many a jaded statesman. Two of Dorothea's
sisters, Pauline and Jeanne, were the mistresses of Congress personnel (Jeanne of its Secretary-General), while Dorothea's other sister
Wilhelmina, Duchess of Sagan, lived in turn with the English chargé
d'affaires, Prince Metternich and the new English Minister, Sir
Charles Stewart. Dorothea herself was relatively discreet, falling in
love only with a Count Clam. Wellington was furious that Stewart, his
former adjutant-general and now known as 'Prince Charles', should
display such folly. There were altogether some eighty English visitors,
including the Duke of Cumberland, who insisted that politics followed
the *amours* rather than the other way round.

There was also present Wellington's nephew, William Long-
Wellesley, only son of William Wellesley-Pole. Since the days when
Wellington had vainly tried to make him into a good aide-de-camp
young William had married an heiress, Miss Tylney-Long. Vienna

8. Charles Napier said that Wellington wrote to him about the time of
Torres Vedras: 'After you will have sat one or two sessions in parliament,
and will have obtained a knowledge of the mode in which questions are
discussed, time is spent, and business done there, you will probably be as
astounded as I have been, how England came by her greatness' (*Life of
Charles Napier*, vol. IV, p. 95).

was an ideal *milieu* for developing those unscrupulous talents which were later to plague his uncle.

★   ★   ★

A mild optimism began to supervene at Vienna, initiated by Castlereagh's remark to the Tsar after the American peace: '*Il commence l'âge d'or.*' Each individual settled down to promoting his own pet reform. J. W. Croker's contribution to the golden age was a uniform, international thermometer, which at the beginning of March he had high hopes of the Congress adopting. A golden age for the Africans would surely dawn when Wellington had persuaded Congress to denounce the slave-trade as unworthy of Christian civilization. Meanwhile he had just returned from a brief mission to Pressburg, where at least his own health was restored—'The hot rooms here have almost killed me'—even if the Saxon king declined to hand over as much of his kingdom to Prussia as the Congress wished.

A golden haze seemed also to hang over Elba. The Emperor's ambition was said by his official warder, the British Commissioner Sir Neil Campbell, to be peacefully sinking to its close. 'I begin to think that he is quite resigned to his retreat,' wrote Campbell to Lord Castlereagh as early as 17 September 1814. The haze, or Sir Neil and the French Ministry of Police, was dense enough to obliterate various facts and rumours emanating from the island. Elba was continually visited by bona fide English travellers and secret agents working both for and against Bonaparte. From his partisans he received many reports during the autumn of the Bourbon's unpopularity in France. In December secret information reached the French Government that Bonaparte, knowing all about the quarrels inside the Congress, had remarked, 'I see it will be necessary to take the field again.' They ignored it. Naturally they knew they had not paid Bonaparte's grant and he was consequently in financial straits. They were also aware that he feared assassination or kidnapping and imprisonment on St Helena. Here were four good reasons for escape. None was taken seriously. As for his parting shot of April 1814 about returning next spring with the violets—that was forgotten. Campbell, indeed, was so completely lulled by the Emperor's pleasant and tranquil manner that he had asked to be relieved from a post that was no longer necessary. Alternatively he would go on leave. On 16 February

1815 he courteously told his prisoner he was going to the mainland of Italy that day for an interview with the Austrian Minister. (Sir Neil's mistress, Signora Bartoli, was also on the mainland, at Leghorn.)

'Will you come back by the 28th?' asked the Emperor.

'Why the 28th?' Bonaparte explained that Princess Borghese was giving a ball on that day, to which Sir Neil was invited. The British Commissioner promised to be back in time.

Four days before this significant interview, a letter postmarked Calais was sent to Wellington by a Mr John F. Schrader, reporting an extraordinary conversation he had just had with his friend Mrs Wallace, wife of General Wallace and close associate of the Radicals Horne Tooke and Sir Francis Burdett.

'You very well know I am a friend to Bonaparte,' Mrs Wallace had begun. She went on to explain that she had crossed the Channel expressly to visit Bonaparte on Elba, for a particular reason.

'I can tell you my friend, most, most confidantly [*sic*] that his stay at Elba is but of very short duration!!! He will soon, very soon be King of Italy!!!'

Her breathless communication was received by Schrader with a smile.

'You have no occasion to smile—I have it from the best authority . . . and I am prodigious impatient to see him before he makes his Exit!!'

Schrader, convinced at last there was 'something very mysterious in this lady's journey', felt it his duty to get in touch with Wellington at the Congress. Neither Mrs Wallace nor Schrader's letter can have reached their destinations at Elba or Vienna in time. The grand disturber got his sister Pauline to put forward her ball three days, after which he completed his preparations for escape. These included the sealing off of the island from the outside world. Not a fishing boat was allowed to put to sea. On 26 February 1815, supported by 1,200 soldiers, six small ships besides his own, and Pauline's jewels voluntarily contributed, he boarded the brig *Inconstant* at nightfall for France, while his loyal Elbans stood singing on the quay in the glow of coloured lanterns. As his vessel began to move a stupefied silence fell.

      *   *   *

It was not till nine days later, on 7 March 1815, that the news reached Vienna. Three days earlier, however, the French telegraph system had conveyed it to King Louis in Paris.

The King's gouty fingers fumbled agonizingly with the envelope. After he had got it open and read it he sat with his head in his hands. At last he turned to a Minister.

'Do you know what this telegraph contains?'

'No, Sir, I do not.'

'Well, I will tell you. It is revolution once more. Bonaparte has landed on the coast of Provence.'

At Vienna, a hunt in the park at Schönbrunn was arranged for 7 March. But when Wellington's horse was brought round to his house he sent it back to the stable. He had just heard that another horse had bolted. At first it seemed to him that they would return it to its stable just as easily.

Sir Neil Campbell had arrived at Elba punctually on 28 February to find the ball and indeed the whole of his own *raison d'être* over. Next day he sailed off to look for Napoleon's little squadron on the wide seas, having sent the electrifying news to the Austrian consul at Genoa for transmission to Metternich, and to Florence for Lord Burghersh to forward to Castlereagh and Wellington.

In Wellington's own recollection he was the first member of the Congress to hear it. He at once had it announced to his colleagues. They are said to have burst out laughing.

Talleyrand's elaborately powdered *coiffure* was being performed for him as usual in his bedroom, while his niece Dorothea sat on the end of the bed discussing the afternoon's rehearsal of a comedy in the Metternichs' house. Suddenly a message from Prince Metternich himself was brought in.

'Read it,' Talleyrand ordered her casually, still occupied with his *toilette*. 'It's probably to tell me the time of today's meeting of the Congress.' Dorothea opened it.

'Napoleon has escaped from Elba! Oh, Uncle, what about my rehearsal?'

'Go ahead with it.'

Talleyrand and Wellington were soon in unusually animated discussion.

'He'll go anywhere you like to mention,' said Talleyrand jauntily, 'except France.' Wellington did not disagree. Like many others, he thought Bonaparte would land in Italy.

Lord Castlereagh wrote at once from London to the British plenipotentiary offering the choice of continued diplomatic service in Vienna or command of an army in Flanders. If he chose the latter the Government made only one stipulation: that he should not travel through the interior of France except at the head of troops.

Tsar Alexander, like Wellington himself, saw no choice. He laid his hand on the Duke's shoulder. 'It is for you to save the world again.'

PART III

20 Where is Nosey?

Bickerings, billings and cooings at the Congress abruptly ceased. They got down to work. In the past the *Morning Chronicle* had derided them:

> *We learn from high sources a project is made,*
> *How Vienna's grand Congress the Christmas will spend.*
> *Since public affairs have so long been delayed*
> *They may very well wait till the holidays end.*

Now the holidays had ended with a bang. Who could tell when Europe would be on holiday again?

The Congress soon learnt that Bonaparte had arrived in France on 1 March—with the violets, as he said he would. His standard was raised at Fréjus on the Golfe de Juan. He was marching on Paris. The Congress waited to hear that a shot had been fired to stop him. They waited in vain. Instead they learnt that on 7 March Colonel Charles de la Bédoyère and his 7th Regiment had gone over to Bonaparte at Grenoble. Two days later at Lyons the King's troops, after 'making faces' at his brother the Count of Artois who was reviewing them, spontaneously changed sides. Worst of all Marshal Ney, who had promised King Louis to bring back Bonaparte to Paris in an iron cage, decided on the night of 13 March after reading a proclamation by Napoleon brought by two nocturnal visitors, to join his returned master.

There had been many jokes at Court about the iron cage. 'I would not like such a bird in my room,' the King had remarked with a grimace. Someone suggested a home for it in the Jardins des Plantes. There was now little danger of the bird being caught. It seemed on the contrary that a sentence in Napoleon's proclamation was in a fair way to be realized: the eagle would speed through France 'from steeple to steeple to alight on the towers of Notre Dame'.

On the same decisive date, 13 March 1815, the Congress declared Napoleon an outlaw:

Napoleon Bonaparte, by again appearing in France with projects of confusion and disorder, has placed himself beyond the protection of the law [*hors la loi*] and rendered himself subject to public vengeance [*vindicte publique*].

Wellington's name appeared eighth on the list of signatories and created an uproar among the Opposition. Whitbread interpreted the word *vindicte* as an incitement to assassination: Wellington was morally Bonaparte's murderer. A letter to William Wellesley-Pole, however, showed Wellington unrepentant. The phrase *hors la loi*, he explained, had been inserted to rally the King's friends, while *vindicte* meant 'justice' not 'vengeance'. Even if it did mean vengeance, he continued, Whitbread had no right to accuse him of handing over Napoleon to the dagger of the assassin. 'When did the dagger of the assassin execute the vengeance of the Publick?' As for the Radicals calling him personally an assassin day after day in the House of Commons while he was serving abroad, instead of moving a regular vote of censure—this struck him as vindictiveness personified.

*   *   *

He was serving abroad in no easy conditions. Events had moved swiftly since 13 March. Napoleon entered Paris on 20 March without a shot being fired in anger. Indeed the only blow struck on Louis XVIII's behalf was said to have been by an old woman selling chestnuts. When she shouted '*Vive le Roi*' a man roared back '*Vive l'Empereur*'—and she hit him on the head with her ladle. Napoleon's astonishing performance stirred Byron to an ecstasy of admiration.

> *Oh, France! retaken by a single march*
> *Whose path was through one long triumphal arch!*

A wittier reflection on Bonaparte's astounding progress from Elba was supplied by a Paris broadsheet.

> *The Tiger has broken out of his den*
> *The Ogre has been three days at sea*
> *The Wretch has landed at Fréjus*
> *The Buzzard has reached Antibes*

The Invader has arrived in Grenoble
The General has entered Lyons
Napoleon slept at Fontainebleau last night
The Emperor will proceed to the Tuileries to-day
His Imperial Majesty will address his loyal
  subjects to-morrow.

The Emperor was carried shoulder-high into the Tuileries on March 20 1815, with his eyes shut and a sleep-walker's smile on his face. The Hundred Days had begun.

In the last hours of the night before, Louis XVIII had fled from his capital surrounded by his *Garde de Corps*, among them Fanny Burney's husband, Captain d'Arblay. Fanny, vowing it was the most dreadful day of her existence, headed for Brussels. Romantically christened *Louis le Désiré* on his return to France in 1814, Louis XVIII was now poor old 'Bungy Louis' once more—his undignified nickname in England during the first exile. It would have been too much to retreat to England again. Louis the unwanted occupied a commodious house in the Netherlands at Ghent, with a garden into which he could be wheeled.

An announcement on 25 March of a formal alliance between the European powers to re-cage the eagle followed the extraordinary news from Paris. Wellington was appointed Commander-in-Chief of the British and Dutch–Belgian forces in Flanders. All military dispositions were agreed by the Congress before the end of the month. Up to a million soldiers were eventually to envelop France from the Swiss border to the North Sea, and to strike probably in July. Five million pounds sterling were advanced by Castlereagh as subsidies—his *âge d'or* had begun with a vengeance—plus another million or so in lieu of the 150,000 troops which Britain was pledged but unable to provide.

Pressed by Wellington, the Government applied to the Rothschild brothers for assistance, and on 14 April a letter passed from Nathan in London to James in Hamburg:

... Brother Solomon [in Vienna] will ere this comes to hand have visited Bruxelles to meet Mr. Herries [the Government's Commissary-General] on the business of the new subsidies. Mr. H. leaves here tomorrow morning with one of the Lords of the Treasury by request of the Duke of Wellington solely for this object.

By 11 May the first instalment of the Russian subsidy was arranged and others in train. Moreover, on 4 April, the same day that Wellington himself reached Brussels from Vienna, Nathan Rothschild had despatched the first consignment of bullion and coin for his army: three ingots valued at £3,053 15s. 6d. On 1 May twenty-eight ingots at £27,958 19s. 1d. were sent and by 13 June (five days before Waterloo) the total had risen to over a quarter of a million pounds in ingots and specie. Nathan Rothschild wrote to Herries on 11 May to inform him of the successful operation so far. By one transaction 'the Public have been gainers to the Amount of nearly a Quarter of a Million Sterling', and by another, of £25,000. Nathan's success was apparently due to raising the exchange rate. Herries had found the franc standing at 17.50 when he was in Paris on 1 May 1814. 'By proper management, I was able to raise it to fr. 22.'

The country had been 'peace mad' since 1814 and the armed forces cut to the bone. Whatever could now be reassembled or hired would form with the Dutch–Belgians the right tip of the great European arc.

*   *   *

Wellington's work in Vienna was finished by 29 March. All the ladies kissed him good-bye and he set off for Brussels in his carriage with the same two companions as before. The final act of the Congress was not signed until 9 June, but when it was, a clause appeared declaring the slave-trade to be unworthy of Christian states—a tribute to Wellington's pertinacity. Louis XVIII's promise to Wellington, however, that France would abolish the slave-trade in five years' time had meanwhile been made to look rather meagre by Napoleon. On reaching the towers of Notre Dame the highly Christian eagle abolished it forthwith.

This act was only one item in an impressive scheme of liberal government which the Emperor now held out to the Allies as a reason for laying down their arms and leaving him to reign, constitutionally, in peace. Castlereagh was not prepared to take the risk. Nor was Wellington, for he like Liverpool regarded 'Boney' and all Bonapartists as 'Jacobins', i.e. revolutionaries, at heart. Whether or not he was right (historians are divided on the capacity of a dictator to change his spots) there was one area at least where peace could not have been maintained with 'Boney' on the throne. That was the country in which Wellington happened to be—Belgium.

'You will see another war for Belgium,' Napoleon had said to an English visitor on Elba: France considered Belgium to be French not Dutch. Wellington knew that many Belgians agreed. Yet the merest shred of suspicion that Belgium might again be annexed by France— a nightmare which Arthur Wellesley had first fought revolutionary France in 1794 to prevent—would start British sabres rattling. Rather than that, even a Bourbon was worth fighting for; though this in turn had its own difficulties.

When the Commander-in-Chief reached Brussels on 4 April 1815 he was looking for what he called a 'third term' between the Bonapartists and the elder branch of the Bourbons—the invalid Louis XVIII, his unpopular brother and heir, the Count of Artois, and Artois' despised sons, the Dukes of Angoulême and Berry. (William Tomkinson of the 16th Dragoons, serving with the British expeditionary force in Flanders, wrote that Berry drew rations for twelve horses per day, kept only two horses and sold ten rations at a profit.) Wellington thought he saw the 'third term' in the Duke of Orleans, son of Philippe Egalité, a Bourbon of the younger branch, who was indeed to be King of the French but not till 1830. What was Castlereagh going to do about it? In a secret reply dated 16 April 1815 Castlereagh turned down Wellington's 'third term': the King must be supported at least 'for the present'.

Twenty-eight of the Hundred Days had now come and gone. Wellington's political path had not become any less stony. The most decisive campaign of his life was to be based on a negative, though a stupendous one: no deep devotion anywhere towards the dispossessed monarchy but implacable hatred for the grand disturber of Europe. With the nations once more lying in the track of the hurricane there was only one possible answer: *Non ultra.*

*　　　*　　　*

The Bourbons were not the only problem royalties to give Wellington concern. His closest allies, King William I of the Netherlands and his eldest son, sometimes known respectively as the Old and Young Frog, caused (and suffered) much heart-burning.[1] The difficulty of getting

1. It was mainly the Prince of Orange's long thin neck which earned him the nickname of Slender Billy in the Peninsula. A miniature in the collection of H.M. the Queen of the Netherlands (Archives of the Royal House, The Hague) shows why he was also called the Young Frog. His broad, high, hairless forehead, wide mouth and prominent blue eyes gave him a comical though engaging expression.

the Netherlands fortresses garrisoned drove Wellington to distraction. King William professed to carry out all Wellington's suggestions but in fact objected to everything. What could you expect when all his Dutch officers had been in the French service and he was surrounded with ex-French officials, all passionately keen 'to get us out of Antwerp and Ostend'? Fanny Burney noticed how careful Wellington was not to offend foreign susceptibilities. At a concert for the benefit of Madame Catalani at the end of April he was 'gay even to sportiveness', applauding everything she sang—except '*Rule Britannia*'. To this he listened in silence and when his officers shouted for an encore, crushed them with a look: 'How magnificently he could quit his convivial familiarity for imperious dominion,' wrote Fanny in transports.

Nevertheless, King William was not appeased. 'I will have nothing to say to him,' wrote Wellington to Castlereagh on 28 April in one of his outbursts. As usual, however, he persevered. Heroically polite letters never ceased to pass between the Duke and King. At length on 3 May King William bowed gracefully to the inevitable and appointed Wellington Commander-in-Chief of all the Dutch–Belgian forces in the Netherlands. Two days later the Duke informed Lord Bathurst that he now hoped to prevent 'any rascality in the garrisons by the King's revolutionary ministers', without resorting to the extreme measure of forcibly replacing them by English governors. His proposal to mix the Dutch–Belgian forces with British stiffeners as he had done in Portugal, which the King had hitherto bitterly resisted, was also accepted. In Wellington's words, 'all the youth and treason of the army' was no longer in one corps. He explained to Bathurst, 'the screw with which I have operated upon the king is to threaten to make the real state of my relations with them known to the public . . .'.

The poor Prince of Orange winced under the side-effects of the screw. On the same day (5 May) that Wellington wrote home more cheerfully, the Young Frog complained to the Old Frog of having to endure '*des moments pénibles à cause de la mauvaise humeure du Duc* . . .'. Thank goodness, he added, the ration of *eau de vie* had arrived. It would greatly contribute to the health of the soldiers (and no doubt to H.R.H.'s fortitude). He himself had already been thrown into great ill-humour—Sir Henry Torrens called it his '*huff*'—over his supersession as Commander-in-Chief of the British–Netherlands forces by Wellington. Nevertheless he had written with dignity to the Duke while still in Vienna,

I will be happy to give over to you although I can not deny that I would under the present circumstances do so with much reluctance to any body else.

Before handing over, he intended to concentrate the available British and Hanoverian troops between Mons and Tournai, to prevent a *coup de main* in either of these places. (This was exactly what Wellington wished.) His letter ended on an urgent note. Where was his Grace? When would he arrive in Brussels? Napoleon was advancing rapidly. No one could stop him. He would soon be in Paris—'and he will lose no time to move down here'.

From Vienna Wellington was at least supplying the Prince with good advice of all kinds, from the advantages of tin camp kettles to the disadvantages of a forward position:

I recommend you not to have your troops too far in advance. It is easy to move forward if necessary, but very difficult and disagreeable circumstanced as we are to fall back.

The Duke was in constant terror of his impetuous young colleague beginning the war before the other Allies were ready. Some of them might not be ready for a considerable time, if at all.

Russia would have to leave security forces behind in Poland, Prussia in Saxony and Austria in Italy. From Portugal Wellington had hoped for 25,000 of his splendid 'fighting cocks' under their experienced general, Beresford. But most of them were disbanded, it seemed, and in any case Principal Sousa and the Portuguese Government were by now extremely tired of British officers and proposing to show them all off the premises.

'I wish to God you had a better army,' wrote Torrens to Wellington on 9 April. There was indeed much to be desired in the force collected so far.

Besides Beresford, other great Peninsular names were missing from his new staff. Sir George Murray was in Canada. Sir Edward Pakenham was dead and Wellington wrote to Ned's brother, Lord Longford, during these critical weeks again bewailing his loss. Sir Lowry Cole, Kitty's old flame, was tied up with his marriage to Lord Malmesbury's daughter; in congratulating him Wellington wished that he could 'bring every thing together as I had it when I took leave of the army at Bordeaux, and I would engage that we should not be the last in the race . . .'. Sir Stapleton Cotton, now Lord Comber-mere, wrote offering to command the British cavalry as in Spain but it appeared that the Prince Regent and Duke of York had promised this plum to Lord Uxbridge (Paget the eloper). Wellington was annoyed, but not because of the Paget–Wellesley divorce. Indeed he made short work of a friend who suggested that Uxbridge's appoint-ment would cause scandal.

'Why?'

'Your Grace cannot have forgotten the affair with Lady Charlotte [Wellesley]?'

'Oh no! I have not forgotten that.'

'That is not the only case, I am afraid. At any rate Lord Uxbridge has the reputation of running away with everybody he can.'

'I'll take good care he don't run away with me: I don't care about anybody else.'

Wellington's only objection to the appointment was that he had worked with Combermere in India and throughout the Peninsular War but with Uxbridge never. Uxbridge's cavalry actions though brilliant were confined to a brief period under Sir John Moore.

Then there were F. S. Larpent, prevented from being his advocate-general again by a government mission to Vienna, and Sir James McGrigor, promoted to be director-general of the Medical Board in England so that he could not, as formerly, be Wellington's inspector-general of hospitals. A gentleman who looked to Wellington 'very young' had appeared instead. How to use all the 'young gentlemen' sent out to him was one of his headaches.

'I imagine you must have heard much of the talent of Sir Hudson Lowe,' wrote Torrens hopefully of the intended quartermaster-general. Wellington had, and considered him downright stupid. For one thing, the Duke could not bear hesitant answers.

'Where does that road lead to, Sir Hudson?' he had once asked in his abrupt way, and when Hudson began fumbling with his map Wellington muttered, 'Damned old fool!' One astute general, knowing his chief's quirk, made a point of giving a prompt answer to a question whatever the state of his own ignorance.

'How many rounds of ammunition have we?' Wellington would rap out.

'Four hundred and twenty' would come back pat, a figure which could be adjusted if necessary afterwards.

So it was not surprising that Wellington insisted on having Lowe replaced by Sir William de Lancey, a Peninsular colleague, though not a patch on Murray.

Lord Castlereagh wrote just as naïvely about the egregious Sir Neil Campbell as Torrens had about Lowe. Though in no way responsible for 'the unfortunate evasion of that person from Elba' Sir Neil could not continue his services with the Foreign Office and would therefore return to his military duties under Wellington.

Two grand personages who tried in vain to make their way on to Wellington's staff were the Dukes of Cumberland and Richmond. The former was choked off by his royal brother, the Prince Regent, after declaring his wish on 25 March to serve under 'Field Marschall [*sic*] the Duke of Wellington'. Richmond's disappointment caused the Horse Guards immense embarrassment until Wellington promised to 'cooperate in setting his mind at ease'. In the end he was allowed a large number of trusty generals who were also old Peninsular hands: Hill, Colville, Clinton, Alten, Barnes, Lambert, Byng, Maitland, Halkett, Ponsonby, Edward Somerset, Vivian and Vandeleur, Kempt, Pack and Picton. Kempt was ready to serve *anywhere*, he announced, but Picton barely willing to serve at all. The temperamental Welshman resented not being made a peer, and may have lost his nerve after Toulouse. Wellington later recalled that Picton had come to see him in France.

'My Lord, I must give up. I am grown so nervous, that when there is any service to be done it works upon my mind so that it is impossible for me to sleep at nights. I cannot possibly stand it, and I shall be forced to retire.'

Picton had a presentiment of death just before leaving Wales to join the army in 1815, jumped into a newly dug grave, lay down in it and said, 'Why, I think this would do for me.'

His farewell to Hercules Pakenham, former colonel in his old 3rd Division, was in the same tone.

'God bless you! If we never meet again, you will at all events *hear* of me.' Picton took with him as an extra aide-de-camp his fellow-countryman, the future diarist Gronow, which is one reason why posterity has indeed been able to *hear* of him and much else at Waterloo.

Among the younger officers from Wellington's old army to return in time from America was Harry Smith of the Rifles. He and his men had seen the burning of Washington and, accustomed to Wellington's 'humane warfare', were horrified. On his way home, Napoleon's escape from Elba had been conveyed to Smith with British phlegm by the skipper of a merchantman in the Bristol Channel.

'Any news?'

'No, none.' Then, as the distance widened between the two ships there was a sudden halloo. The skipper remembered.

'Ho! Bonaparte's back on the throne of France.'

Wellington was soon to meet Smith at Hougoumont, just before the battle of Waterloo began.

'Hallo, Smith, where are you from last?' Smith told him and the Commander-in-Chief asked what regiment he had got with him. Smith told him he had three strong ones.

'That's all right, for I shall soon want every man.'

Wellington had been clamouring all through April for every man the Government could lay hands on but by the beginning of May he was still profoundly dissatisfied. All he asked for were 40,000 British infantry, 15,000 cavalry, 150 guns and staff of his own choosing. All he got were 30,000 British soldiers of all arms, only 7,000 of them veterans, and four pages of apology from the Duke of York on 5 May for having appointed staff officers without consulting him first; but as they had already 'indulged in expensive equipment', the Duke of York did not think it fair to countermand them. It seemed a poor reason for depriving the army of its best possible commanders at this crisis in its history.

The Duke of York's letter crossed with a dignified statement from Wellington to the Horse Guards. He was not satisfied but—'I think it much better that this correspondence upon the Staff should cease'. He had said what he wanted to say to the War Minister the day before:

> To tell you the truth I am not very well pleased . . . with the manner in which the Horse Guards have conducted themselves towards me. It will be admitted that the army is not a very good one;—

in which case the least they could do was to allow him his old generals as staff—

> Instead of that I am overloaded with people I have never seen before; and it appears to be purposely intended to keep those out of my way whom I wish to have.

In the end, however, it was not for the 'retained servant' to reason why.

I'll do the best I can with the instruments which have been sent to assist me.

Was there a whiff of sarcasm in that word 'assist'?

Perhaps it was the irritation caused by an unexpected proposal from his favourite gun-maker, John Roebuck of the Carron Company, which provoked him to his last and most famous (or should it be infamous?) outburst. On 6 May Roebuck offered to send him some of his new, twenty-four-pounder iron 'carronades', as ordered for the East India Company, instead of the usual brass $5\frac{1}{2}$-inch howitzers. The new ones, Roebuck added, were particularly good with Colonel Shrapnell's 'destructive shells'. The Commander-in-Chief replied witheringly: 'I do not consider this to be a proper period to alter the equipment of the army or to try experiments.' The guns that Wellington really needed, had repeatedly asked the Horse Guards to order and never received, were Napoleon's own favourites, the formidable twelve-pounders which the Emperor called his 'beautiful daughters'. Two days later Wellington let fly to 'Prince Charles' (now Lord) Stewart who was still in Vienna. Making use again, as was his habit, of an adjective he had previously found serviceable when applied to the unregenerate Peninsular army of 1810, he wrote on 8 May 1815:

I have got an infamous army, very weak and ill equipped, and a very inexperienced Staff. In my opinion they are doing nothing in England. They have not raised a man; they have not called out the militia either in England or Ireland. . . .

The handling of the militia question suggested that it was the Government rather than Wellington's army who were both infamous and idiotic in their dilatory cussedness, springing from fear of the Opposition. A legal scruple was allowed to tie the helpless hands of Bathurst for several precious weeks, since the militia in Ireland, for instance, could not legally be called up for duties which would free the regulars except 'in time of war or insurrection'.

But how far was Ireland from 'insurrection'? Wellington had secretly warned Castlereagh on 5 January that two dangerous revolutionaries, Professor Bonelli and Madame O'Connor, 'a most mischievous Person and a determined Enemy of Great Britain', wife of the Irish rebel Arthur O'Connor, were going to Ireland, Madame 'under pretence of settling her Husband's affairs'. Perhaps Wellington had dreamed of turning the tables on revolution by getting the militia called out 'under pretence' of settling Madame O'Connor.

And what state was Britain in between March and June 1815? Clearly not at peace. Yet until Napoleon invaded the Netherlands or the Allies invaded France, not at war either. While various ways of partially circumventing the militia law, without unduly rousing the Opposition, occurred by degrees to the British Government, a similar impasse was allowed to develop over veterans at the end of their service. The Horse Guards solemnly informed Wellington on 3 May that these men 'must necessarily be discharged'—unless retained by authority of a Royal Proclamation. It took another month to get the proclamation through. Thus Wellington's army remained 'very weak', as he said, in veterans and very dependent on Continental recruits, some of them mercenaries who were Bonapartists at heart and others totally untrained boys. 'Monseigneur!' wrote the commandant of Ath in the Netherlands to the Commander-in-Chief five days before Waterloo, 'Having in the Brigade of the Hanoverian Reserve many soldiers who have never fired a shot'—please send powder and cartridges to 'exercise' them.

*   *   *

If Wellington wanted more veterans, his veterans had all along asked for Wellington. 'Where is Wellington? Surely we shall not be led to battle by that boy?' murmured the first arrivals in Belgium, aware that Slender Billy was still their titular commander. 'Wellington is the man that must lead us on,' declared Wheeler (now a sergeant) of the 51st. 'He is looked to by the remnant of the old Peninsular army, an hundred times a day. . . .' When at last a General Order announced that the Prince of Orange had surrendered his command to the Duke, all the Peninsular veterans went mad with joy.

'Glorious news! Nosey has got command! Won't we give them a drubbing now!' They celebrated far into the night with a 'general fuddle': wreathes of tobacco, powerful Hollands gin, dancing, singing and the nostalgic recital of famous Peninsular deeds.

*   *   *

Kitty was not among the civilians in Brussels impatiently awaiting Wellington's return; she had gone home with the first rush from Paris. In London, however, she did her bit to keep up morale. At a party given by the master-general of the Ordnance she countered the many expressions of anxiety with, 'Ah! wait a little, *he* is in his element now; depend upon him'. Lady Caroline Capel in Brussels felt that *he* could not arrive too soon: 'Lord Wellington is expected every hour—His name is a Host in itself.' Another civilian family to be much fortified by his coming were Thomas Creevey, his wife and two step-daughters, the Misses Ord. Creevey, who had not seen Wellington since their violent quarrel in 1806 about 'Nabob' Paull, was amazed when the Duke at once held out his hand at a ball given by Lady Charlotte Greville. More astonishing even than Wellington's complete lack of resentment at the past was his casualness and sang-froid over Napoleon. In conversation Creevey, the Radical accustomed to a circle which made a point of verbal fireworks, could not give Wellington credit for appearing talented or clever; indeed at Lady Charlotte's his abrupt explosions of good humour had caused Creevey to think him drunk. But he certainly convinced Creevey in the course of many more balls and other encounters, that Bonaparte could not win.

The most famous meeting between Wellington and Creevey took place in the Park a few weeks before Waterloo. Creevey asked the Duke what he would make of the coming battle.

'By God! I think Blücher and myself can do the thing.'

'Do you calculate upon any desertion in Bonaparte's army?'

'Not upon a man, from the colonel to the private . . . inclusive. We may pick up a marshal or two, perhaps; but not worth a damn.'

'Do you reckon upon any support from the French king's troops at Alost?'

'Oh! don't mention such fellows! No: I think Blücher and I can do the business.'

Just then a British infantryman came in sight, peering about at the Park and its statuary.

'There,' said Wellington, pointing to the small scarlet figure, 'There, it all depends upon that article whether we do the business or not. Give me enough of it, and I am sure.'

In those words Wellington made atonement, raising the common soldier—'the scum of the earth'—into the living embodiment of British tenacity.

So great was Wellington's effect on the impressionable Creevey that his Radical friend, John Bennett M.P., found it necessary to administer a corrective. Bennett confessed in a letter to Creevey on 31 May that 'we thought the Great Lord had bit you [and made you believe] Boney was to be ate up alive . . .'. But Boney had a huge army in Paris, added Bennett more cheerfully, and would succeed.

The prospect of a Napoleonic victory was not quite so acceptable to poor Creevey now as it had been in the old Peninsular days of eagles versus leopards, situated as he was only fifty miles from the frontier with an invalid wife and one of his stepdaughters engaged to the fire-eating General Barnes's aide-de-camp, Major Andrew Hamilton. He wanted to believe Wellington.

*   *   *

For all Wellington's confidence, it was soon apparent that he could not put complete trust in another vital section of his army—the Intelligence. The great Colquhoun Grant (*Granto el Bueno*) had returned to direct this department. But as long as Britain was 'neither at war nor at peace' Wellington was not allowed to send cavalry patrols to investigate French-held territory, as the guerrillas had done so magnificently in Spain. So there was uncertainty, even contradiction in the intelligence that reached him.

On 9 May Wellington passed a report to the Prussian frontier troops at Charleroi that Bonaparte was setting out from Paris that day. Two days later an agent informed him that Bonaparte had already reached Lille on the 8th. (Napoleon in fact may not have quite decided by 8 May whether to attack the Netherlands immediately or defend Paris and Lyons in July–August.) By the 12th, however, Wellington was half inclined to believe that far from having left Paris Napoleon would never venture to do so, that his power was crumbling, and all the frontier movements were defensive. Two or three weeks later, on the contrary, the Prince of Orange sent Wellington an account from the French newspaper *Moniteur* of Bonaparte's magnificent demonstrations in Paris (the so-called *Champs de Mai*) on 1 June, which had been 'very pleasing' to Napoleon and which he thought might be 'interesting' to Wellington. Sir Charles Stuart, now H.M. Ambassador to the Netherlands, afterwards told Creevey that he 'never saw a fellow so cut down' as the Duke, when he first heard that news. On 6 June British intelligence was unanimous that

Bonaparte had left Paris and reached Laon; he was approaching the frontier towards Lille. When Lady Georgiana Lennox told Wellington that her mother, the Duchess of Richmond, was planning a picnic to Tournai or Lille for the 8th, he warned her off:

'You'd better not go. Say nothing about it, but let the project drop.' (Napoleon was still in Paris.) Meanwhile messages continued to fly between the British and Netherlands' headquarters with insistent orders by Wellington for securing the fortifications at Mons, Ath and Antwerp, where no unlicensed person was to be allowed to penetrate. He probably feared treachery from within as much or more than external attack. Indeed on 13 June he reverted to the view that Napoleon's departure from Paris was 'not likely to be immediate. I think we are now too strong for him here.' (Napoleon had left Paris the day before.) A letter to William Wellesley-Pole written a week earlier confirms the impression that Wellington was over-optimistic. 'We are getting on pretty well here', he had announced on 6 June, enumerating the total of 80,000 troops he expected eventually to march—that is, to march out against Napoleon rather than to receive Napoleon's imminent attack on Belgian soil. Perhaps because Wellington and Blücher thought so long in terms of attack rather than defence, they made the same mistake as King Joseph before the battle of Vitoria. None of the bridges over the River Sambre was broken.

*   *   *

A danger to Wellington's army more serious than his unreliable Intelligence had been caused from the start by international politics. The discord between Britain and Prussia at the Congress of Vienna drove a wedge between the embattled Allies.

King Louis's precipitate flight from Paris on 19 March had one ludicrous side-effect. All the secret French Foreign Office documents fell into Bonaparte's hands. (Fortunately Lord Fitzroy Somerset rescued those belonging to Britain.) Bonaparte had the satisfaction of publishing them. As a result, the xenophobic Prussian general, Gneisenau, likely in any case to be a difficult though clever colleague, was disgusted to read the terms of the secret Treaty of 3 January 1815 which had been directed against his own country (though as much against Russia). Since Wellington stood by the Treaty when he arrived a month later in Vienna, it was perhaps not so surprising that Gneisenau warned the Prussian liaison officer at Wellington's headquarters, Baron von Müffling, against Wellington's trickery: through having spent so long in India among deceitful nabobs, he had become as slippery as an Oriental himself.

Fortunately the veteran Marshal Blücher, Gneisenau's chief, was of radically different material. Uncouth, illiterate and belonging very much to the period before the sweeping reforms in the Prussian Army (1807–14), he was essentially a perfect soldier's soldier: brave, loyal and utterly unimpressed by his own numerous defeats. When appointed to his 1815 command he was said to be suffering from mental disturbance, as in 1811, during which he believed himself to be pregnant of an elephant. Perhaps it was a presentiment of Waterloo, an elephantine battle if ever there was one where pounding counted more than manoeuvre. Wellington liked and admired him.

'He was a very fine fellow, and whenever there was any question of fighting, always ready and eager—if anything too eager.'

Nevertheless there was much jealousy and ill-temper among Prussian officers, wrote Wellington to Bathurst on 4 April, and he was sending his trusted friend, Colonel Hardinge, as liaison officer to keep Gneisenau 'sweet'.

Sweet or sour, the Prussians were in no mood to share either headquarters or lines of communication with Wellington. Gneisenau had chosen Namur for Blücher's headquarters forty-eight miles from Wellington at Brussels. While the British communications ran back westwards and northwards to Ostend and Antwerp, Blücher's lines moved in the opposite direction eastwards through Liège and Aachen into Germany. Between the two armies there was thus a joint or hinge represented by the area on either side of the great paved *chaussée* running due north from Charleroi to Brussels. Napoleon had his eyes on the hinge. Wellington had one eye on the hall-door.

By training and experience Wellington had learnt to keep his eye at certain times on the exit rather than the ally or associate. As far back as India, when famine threatened his communications, he had rightly dropped any idea of going to the assistance of Colonel Monson against the Mahrattas. In the Peninsula he had faced every kind of unpleasantness with his Spanish allies rather than risk his hall-door at Lisbon. In northern Europe there was the special position of Belgium causing him to watch the North Sea exits with a peculiarly, though as it turned out, unnecessarily suspicious eye. Belgium had belonged to France by conquest for over twenty years. The perils which Wellington was constantly guarding against in Mons, Ath, Antwerp and Tournai of a *coup de main* from within, were things he had not usually needed to consider in the Peninsula. Even during the tension between him and the Sousa brothers there had never been the remotest chance of the Portuguese joining with the French to bang the hall-door in his face. In the Netherlands he completely trusted neither the Belgian fortresses nor the Dutch–Belgian regiments, particularly since Bonapartist broadsheets had begun flooding into Belgium.

> To the Brave Soldiers who have conquered under
> the French Eagles—
> The Eagles which have led us so often to victory
> have reappeared. Their cry is always the same:
> glory and liberty!

—or even better, glory and loot!

> You will receive the rewards with which the
> genius of France ever knows how to honour
> courage and to reward loyalty.

If national pride had caused King William to keep the Netherlands troops and fortresses under his own control as long as possible, national security forbade Wellington to weaken this vital network of Mons, Ath, Tournai, Enghien, Hal, Grammont, Oudenarde and Ghent (where the French court still clung together) by moving left away from them and towards the Prussians, before he was forced. That he might be so forced was always on the cards. Indeed, he had met Blücher on 3 May at Tirlemont, half-way between Brussels and Liège, to agree upon a joint strategy ('poor old Blücher', as Wellington wrote, having been obliged by a mutiny of Saxon troops to quit his Liège headquarters). The agreed plan involved Wellington in closing up eastwards to his left in case of an attack on the central hinge. It was for his Prussian allies, however, to warn him of the first sign of such an attack.

They failed to let him know that on the night of 13–14 June advanced Prussian patrols under General Zieten had seen the twinkling lights of innumerable camp fires in the direction of Beaumont, a few miles from the frontier on the French side of the River Sambre.

The eagles had reappeared as the broadsheets said they would, but with the swiftness and silence of night-birds.

21 Humbugged, *by God!*

From 7 June the total security measures which Napoleon knew so well how to impose had sealed off his frontiers along the Sambre, Rhine and Moselle. As at Elba before his escape, fishing boats were forbidden to move. Every stage coach was finally immobilized, every document intercepted—apart from the false information which his agents continued to circulate more industriously than ever in places like Ghent and Mons. On 12 June at 3.30 A.M. Napoleon left Paris. By the 14th he had concentrated the Army of the North, 122,000 strong with 366 guns, in a space of eighteen square miles around his headquarters at Beaumont. Here he gave the army its Orders of the Day for 15 June.

Soldats! He recalled the glorious anniversaries of Marengo and Friedland, both fought on 14 June. *Soldats!* He reminded them of other victories where the defeated enemy had been three to one, six to one. . . . (With their 122,000 against the combined Anglo-Dutch and Prussian forces of 210,000, the odds were once more heavily against him. But Napoleon had no intention of facing his two enemies combined. The hinge or joint between them was the single, weak spot at which he would drive, forcing the two halves apart and defeating each separately.) *Soldats!* They were asked to remember their own 'frightful' sufferings in English prisons, as also the twelve million Poles, twelve million Italians, one million Saxons and six million Belgians all 'devoured' by the princely enemies of the people. They would have to endure forced marches, battles, perils. For every true Frenchman the moment had come to conquer or perish.

Among the more subtle perils not mentioned by the Emperor were the suspicions of political treachery which poisoned the Army of the North, killing the confidence of soldiers in their commanders and of commanders in one another. The extraordinary events of April 1814 to March 1815, with their hysterical switches of individual and collective loyalties, could not fail to leave their mark on all the armies of Europe. The monolithic faith of nations for or against Napoleon finally died on the dissecting table at Vienna. Treason was in the air and surreptitiously caused both Wellington and Napoleon to make mistakes, though in opposite senses. If Wellington saw more treason in the low Countries than really existed and consequently glanced too often over his right shoulder, Napoleon underestimated the betrayal-neurosis among his French soldiers. More dreadful even than the cries of the wounded and dying at Waterloo was to be the nihilistic screech of the survivors, '*Nous sommes trahis*'—we are not defeated but betrayed.

* * *

Wellington on 13 June was still waiting for the incontrovertible sign that Napoleon had marched. Everything, apart from that essential knowledge, was ready. He had even received from his boot-maker, Hoby, two pairs of 'Wellington' boots specially ordered for the campaign to replace a modified half-boot which did not quite come up to Wellington's developing ideas on the subject.

Bruxelles *April 11th 1815*

Mr Hoby

The last boots you sent me were still too small in the calf of the leg & about an inch & half too short in the leg. Send me two pairs more altered as I have above described.

Your most faithful Servt.
Wellington

The great Hoby of St James's Street prided himself not only on his boots but also on his preaching—at a Methodist chapel in Islington. On hearing the news of Vitoria he is said to have remarked complacently, 'If Lord Wellington had had any other boot-maker than myself, he never would have had his great and constant successes; for my boots and prayers bring his Lordship out of all his difficulties.' The Duke certainly needed all Mr Hoby could do for him now.

Personally Wellington was more convinced than ever that Bonaparte would take the course he himself would have chosen: a sweep round the Anglo-Dutch right flank to cut them off from the sea. This favourite strategy, known to Napoleon himself as *la manœuvre sur les derrières* or the advance of envelopment, had already been employed by him thirty times since 1796, half of them with spectacular success.[1] It can be called his 'superiority strategy', for it depended on surprising

1. See D. Chandler, *The Campaigns of Napoleon*, pp. 162–72, and Appendix B. Famous victories in which Napoleon used this manoeuvre included Ulm, Jena, Eylau, Friedland, Wagram.

a single enemy, crushing him with a knockout blow and annihilating him in a whirlwind pursuit. Wellington paid Napoleon the compliment of believing he would choose this game and that the Anglo-Dutch army would be the recipient of these 'assorted delicacies', as his Peninsular soldiers used to say.

At first sight it may be thought curious that despite Wellington's constant emphasis on Napoleon's awkward position and defensive mood, he did not consider that the equally famous 'inferiority' or 'defensive' strategy of the 'central position' was more likely to be chosen. This strategy was particularly effective in dealing with more than one enemy. It depended for success on occupying a 'central point of operations' between them. Though there might not be time to pursue and annihilate completely either hostile army, as in the 'superiority strategy', at the end of several days' manoeuvres Napoleon stood to achieve a decisive military advantage in the field and a psychological triumph throughout Europe

Wellington, it is constantly said, ought to have realized that Napoleon could not possibly adopt the 'envelopment' strategy, since in doing so he would automatically drive the Anglo-Dutch and Prussian armies together and thus present himself with a single enemy of double his size. This argument was of course perfectly well known to Wellington but he rejected it. In his view he and Blücher were strong enough to 'do the business' whichever strategy Bonaparte adopted; but a flanking movement, he thought, would have given Napoleon the better chance. His chances were against his permanently separating two such generals as Wellington and Blücher—as indeed turned out to be the case, though it was a close-run thing.

Having made his analysis, Wellington continued to canton his new forces, as they arrived in a steady stream, over what he believed to be the threatened areas west of Brussels. In case of need they could be transferred into more easterly positions—with speed but not at a moment's notice.[2] If by some freakish chance those troops on Wellington's extreme right had to travel to Blücher's extreme left it would take them almost a week. Ninety-three thousand men were ready to march. Only a third were British.

2. The actual arrangement of cantonments was sometimes bizarre, probably due to Wellington's 'very inexperienced Staff' having to solve big problems of forage. In some artillery units the guns and horses were carefully segregated from one another. These and other abnormalities were to have a bad effect at Quatre Bras.

Meanwhile he carried on with simple but effective psychological warfare against those in Belgium showing Bonapartist sympathies.

*   *   *

What occupation conveyed to the foreigner a maximum sense of leisurely confidence and English phlegm? The game of cricket. On 12 June he compensated one of the pretty Lennox girls, the sixteen-year-old Lady Jane, for the forbidden expedition to Tournai by taking her to watch a cricket match at Enghien.[3] Cricket was not the army's sole distraction. That dashing young Dragoon, Arthur Shakespear, acted as clerk of the course three times at Grammont when Lord Uxbridge, Sir Hussey Vivian and all the other cavalry commanders patronized his well-organized race meetings. Shakespear's own horse Jubilee was a winner. He found Belgium 'a famous country to make war in', compared with Spain, and looked forward to giving Boney 'a most tremendous beating'. On the occasion of a grand cavalry review it was hard to decide which was more memorable—the splash of scarlet uniforms at the time or of pink champagne afterwards. Resplendent officers were not discouraged from partnering the daughters of aristocratic English visitors or Belgian families of the *ton* at many parties and balls, not a few of them given by Wellington himself. Caroline Capel was one who spotted Wellington's deliberate policy of inculcating confidence by keeping things normal, and by his care to give the impression that Napoleon had never been in such a 'scrape' nor himself so confident. His niece, Emily Somerset, who was expecting her first baby in May, was persuaded to stay and have it in Brussels. As for his own next moves, he successfully convinced everybody that his silence about them was due to his well-known secrecy, rather than to the fact that he did not yet know them himself. 'Nobody can guess Lord Wellington's intentions,' wrote Caroline Capel on 11 June, '& I dare say Nobody will know he is going till he is actually gone. In the meantine he amuses himself with Humbuging [*sic*] the Ladies, particularly the Duchess of Richmond.' To humbug the Duchess required a certain audacity, for she was notoriously quick-tempered. But as Caroline Capel observed, she was not the only candidate for the Duke's pleasantries.

3. The Rev. Spencer Maddan, tutor to the young Lennoxes, whose diary is the source of information, wrote on 13 June that Wellington took Lady Jane to a cricket match and brought her back 'at night', i.e. on the 12th (Maddan Papers, in possession of Mrs B. Brocklebank).

Caroline, indeed, became positively prim about this unconventional newcomer to their Brussels drawing-rooms, however desirable he might be as a Commander-in-Chief. 'The Duke of W——' she wrote coyly to her mother, 'has not improved the *morality* of our Society, as he has given several things [i.e. parties] and makes a point of asking all the Ladies of Loose Character. Every one was surprised at seeing Lady John Campbell at his House, and one of his Staff told me that it had been represented to him her not bein [*sic*] received for that her Character was more than suspicious.'

' "Is it, by ——," said he, "then I will go and ask her Myself." On which he immediately took his Hat and went out for the purpose.'

Lady Frances Wedderburn-Webster was another of the 'Loose Characters' on whom Brussels society cast an alert but disapproving eye. One incident in her much discussed relationship with Wellington was witnessed by a twenty-year-old subaltern on the Royal Staff Corps, Basil Jackson. He happened to be sitting in the Park with an 'elderly' Belgian lady when 'a very great man' walked past them. Next moment a carriage drove up on the opposite side of the Park and a young lady alighted. She was joined by the very great man. Jackson and his friend stood up to see better and watched the couple until they 'descended into a hollow, where the trees completely screened them.' The little drama concluded with the arrival of another carriage containing an agitated female sleuth, identified by Jackson as old Lady M.N., 'who went peering about for her daughter, Lady F.W.'. The green hollow, however, kept its secret.

Posterity must be grateful to Jackson as no doubt Jackson was grateful to providence for this glimpse of Restoration comedy. Imagination would no doubt fill the blank in the story with the seduction of Lady Frances Webster by the Duke of Wellington under the nose of her mother Lady Mountnorris—but for the inconvenient fact that Lady Frances was expecting a baby in a few weeks' time. The Duke's well-known passion in later life for giving advice to young women, advice which was to range from the care of infants with measles to the chances of curing sterility, had evidently developed already. What lay at the back of this benevolence in the way of amorousness, unsatisfied paternal instincts, or the sheer pleasure of being in the company of youth, must remain to be looked at later. Frances Webster, however, did not have to wait long—a matter of less than a year—before the 'peering' of her tiresome mother was terminated by one of the very few actions for libel brought by

Wellington against a newspaper in the course of a life much exposed to editors.[4]

*   *   *

So it was to be business and pleasure as usual during those last days of suspense. Reports of French activity behind the frontier kept arriving at Wellington's headquarters but none of them yet showed that enemy troop movements had ceased in front of Mons, key to the shortest, straightest route to Brussels. Most of the French forces seemed to be moving on Maubeuge, a town which formed the southern apex of a triangle, Maubeuge–Charleroi–Mons. Until Wellington was sure there was no threat to the Mons road he could not answer the Prussians' anxious questions as to where he would concentrate his army. His own uncommunicativeness was matched by Gneisenau's. Having been told nothing of the camp fires seen by Zieten on 13–14 June, Wellington was similarly kept in the dark about an audacious intention of Blücher to concentrate at Sombreffe and fall back no farther than Fleurus—both recklessly advanced positions—in case of sudden attack on the Prussian outposts at Thuin and Charleroi.

During the evening of the 14th Wellington visited the Richmonds' house and as part of his duty to keep the Duke's mind 'at ease' romped with the little Lennoxes. The rest of his army passed the time happily in their billets scattered over Belgium. Edmund Wheatley recorded that his amusements at Naast were 'meditative and contemplative'. Next day, 15 June, was to bring extraordinary matters for contemplation.

Long before dawn Napoleon began his advance into Belgium. Though his commanders were prevented from keeping to their timetables, he was able to drive the Prussians out of Charleroi with the help of the Imperial Guard at 11 A.M. and to watch his army entering the town at noon. He sat in a chair outside the *Belle-Vue* inn while the excited troops passing in front of him shouted '*Vive l'Empereur!*' and kissed his horse. Later it was observed that the *petit Caporal* was fast asleep. Meanwhile, the act of treason by one of his generals which Wellington had predicted took place, though it was worth more than a 'damn' to the Allies. General de Bourmont deserted to the Prussians during the French advance, a boost to Allied morale. At about the same time a crucial message from Wellington's trusted

4. The dénouement of the Wellington–Webster–Mountnorris story occurred in January–February 1816 and will be found in Volume II.

chief of Intelligence, Sir Colquhoun Grant, giving the true direction of Napoleon's advance and laying once for all the Mons ghost, started on its precarious journey to Brussels. It was intercepted by the witless Hanoverian cavalry officer, General Dörnberg, who had served as a colonel in Prince Jerome Bonaparte's army, deserted to the English in 1813 and become a general. Dörnberg returned the vital letter to sender with the remark that far from convincing him of Napoleon's advance, 'it assured him of the contrary'. The luckless Grant rode with his letter like a madman to deliver it to Wellington personally but thanks to Dörnberg it was too late. When Grant arrived the battle of Quatre Bras was in full swing.

Without Grant's essential information, Wellington can hardly be blamed for continuing to interpret the important but still inconclusive reports of French activity according to his previous analysis. Suddenly to jump to another conclusion would have been lucky, even inspired; but not logical.

The main new reports were three in number. In each case Wellington was to believe that Napoleon's move against the Prussians might be a feint, and his real intention to attack the Anglo-Dutch right.

About 3 P.M., nine hours after Napoleon's start, the Duke received his first report. A Prussian officer covered with dirt and sweat galloped into Brussels with a much delayed despatch sent by General Zieten from Charleroi at 8 or 9 A.M.[5] Wellington was swallowing an early dinner with his staff. He learnt that Zieten's 1st Corps had been attacked and the Prussian outposts driven in at Thuin. Now Thuin, though a great deal nearer to Charleroi than to Mons, was neverthe-

5. Henry Houssaye, the French historian and author of *1815 Waterloo* sharply criticizes Wellington for a dilatoriness which he himself invents by completely misinterpreting one of Wellington's despatches. Houssaye says that Wellington got a letter from Zieten announcing a daybreak attack at 8 A.M. but 'at 3 in the afternoon the same day he had not issued a single order'. Houssaye was misreading Wellington's letter to Clarke, 8 P.M. 15 June (*Despatches*, vol. XII, p. 473). 'I have received nothing since 8 o'clock this morning from Charleroi.' Wellington clearly meant he had received nothing *written* from Charleroi since 8 A.M. It was not surprising that he had not issued a single order before 3 P.M., as Houssaye sarcastically remarks, since Wellington's first information came at precisely that hour. Having started off on the wrong foot Houssaye went on to criticize Wellington for giving orders, when he did at last give them, for his troops to assemble on the 15th within a parallelogram instead of at the threatened point. 'It seemed indeed as if he were bewildered and paralysed by the vision of Napoleon attacking in person at all points at once' (Houssaye, footnote 326, Book II, Chapter I, and p. 82).

less close enough to Mons for Wellington's right shoulder to give him another twinge.

Before the diners had finished their dessert there was a second message: the Prince of Orange arrived from his headquarters at Braine-le-Comte (on the same east–west *chaussée* as Sombreffe but far to the west, beyond Nivelles) and announced that the Prussians had been pushed out from the village of Binche; what's more he had heard gun-fire around Charleroi with his own ears.

Wellington acted quickly. Feint or not, it was clearly time to alert his troops. He ordered his whole army to collect at their various divisional headquarters and be ready to march at a moment's notice. The orders went out between 5 and 7 P.M. His quartermaster-general, the newly married Sir William de Lancey, galloped back from dinner with General Alava and spent the rest of the night feeling rather weighed down by his new responsibilities, as he wrote out countless orders while his wife Magdalen plied him with strong green tea. It was to be their last happy day together—at least, it had begun happily. General Kempt rose from his dinner, also in Brussels, addressed a little speech to his officers about old Blücher being 'hard at it', and quietly ordered them to get their regiments under arms. Sir Thomas Picton, on the other hand, who had arrived in Brussels with his division only that morning, resented Wellington's peremptory personal instructions and bowed sourly in acknowledgement, at which the Duke responded in kind. The 20,000 troops of the reserve, including Picton's division, were to remain in Brussels under Wellington himself; the cavalry were to collect at Ninove under Lord Uxbridge. When the rest of the army moved to take up their prearranged positions between Grammont and Nivelles, under Lord Hill and the Prince of Orange respectively, it was clear that the balance had automatically shifted somewhat farther to the west of Brussels, i.e. away from Blücher, than otherwise. While the Mons–Ath–Ghent line in the east would be as closely watched as before, nothing whatever would be found nearer to the centre—the crossroads at Quatre Bras—than some of the Prince of Orange's Nassauers at Nivelles, seven miles away.

Napoleon's build-up of a phantom strategy by false intelligence was successful indeed, when it deceived one of his enemies into inclining outwards even before the wedge was driven home.

Fitzroy Somerset was one of those who could not understand why there was no definite order to march following the 'stand to arms'.

'No doubt we shall be able to manage those Fellows,' he said to his chief not without a hint of anxiety at the delay. Wellington was firm.

'There is little doubt of that, provided I do not make a false Movement.' By a 'false movement' Wellington meant a move which, if it turned out to be wrong, could not be rectified.

At 10 P.M. his Prussian liaison officer, General Müffling, arrived with the third important message so far that day. It was from Gneisenau, to say that Blücher had concentrated on the east–west *chaussée* at Sombreffe, only twenty-five miles from where they were sitting. What was Wellington going to do, asked Müffling with some concern, about supporting Blücher now that he was very likely as far forward even as Ligny? Wellington replied that the main attack might still come through Mons.

'For this reason I must wait for my advice from Mons before I fix on my rendezvous.' Nevertheless he issued fresh orders to streamline the previous movements and alert the reserve earlier. The slim, athletic figure standing before the starred and beribboned Prussian was in his shirt-sleeves and slippers. As at Toulouse, an important despatch had arrived while he was dressing for a party. He sent Müffling back to his own quarters promising to let him know the moment he had definite news as to which way Bonaparte was advancing.

Towards midnight the Duke's carriage drew up at Müffling's house. Wellington had received the long awaited despatch—his 'advices' from Mons. The yes–no question as to whether the attacks round Charleroi were feints or not was answered. The answer, surprisingly, was No.

'I have a report from General Dörnberg at Mons that Napoleon has moved on Charleroi with all his force, and that he, General Dörnberg, has nothing in his front.'

So that was it. The other way round from what he had guessed. The activity around Mons had been the feint, that at Charleroi the real thing. Wellington quickly assured Müffling that he had already issued fresh orders to the troops, this time to concentrate on Nivelles and Quatre Bras—to the *east* at last.

'The numerous friends of Napoleon who are here,' continued the Duke, 'will be on tip toe; the well intentioned must be pacified; let us therefore go all the same to the Duchess of Richmond's ball, and start for Quatre Bras at 5 A.M.'

*   *   *

The most famous ball in history was the climax of Wellington's psychological warfare which always involved 'pleasure as usual'. The question of holding it or not had first come up in May.

'Duke,' said the Duchess of Richmond one day, 'I do not wish to pry into your secrets. . . . I wish to give a ball, and all I ask is, may I give my ball? If you say, "Duchess, don't give your ball", it is quite sufficient, I ask no reason.'

'Duchess, you may give your ball with the greatest safety, without fear of interruption.' At that date, indeed, the Duke had intended to give a ball himself on 21 June, the second anniversary of the battle of Vitoria. Operations were not expected to begin before 1 July.

Since those dignified ducal exchanges circumstances had altered with a vengeance, more radically than Wellington even now supposed. That very afternoon there had been a close run thing, though a small one, at Quatre Bras. Prince Bernhard of Saxe-Weimar with 4,000 infantry and eight guns had occupied on his own initiative the empty crossroads at Quatre Bras and had easily driven off 1,700 French skirmishers unsupported by artillery; next moment, however, Marshal Ney himself rode forward to reconnoitre and but for shoulder-high rye which concealed the true weakness of the Prince's position, Ney might have ridden straight through into Brussels. It was a splendid initial triumph for Prince Bernhard and his Dutch–Belgian troops, many of whom were afterwards to behave with the unsteadiness of raw boys called from the plough. Neither Ney nor Wellington knew anything of the crisis which had come and gone. Ney, only just recalled by Napoleon to his post from having been rusticated in the country, was still getting his bearings. All Wellington knew was that the Prince of Orange, who was now dancing at the ball, had reported all quiet on the Nivelles–Namur *chaussée* earlier in the day.

It has often been asked why Wellington did not cancel the ball at 3 P.M. instead of going to hear the fiddlers while Rome burned, or at any rate did not ride out to Quatre Bras at midnight to see for himself what was on the other side of the hill.[6] Apart from Wellington's extreme sensitivity to the chances of a Belgian stab in the back, his

6. In 1837 the Duke regaled young Lady Salisbury with tales of the Waterloo campaign. 'For four days previous to the 16th (the 12th, 13th, 14th and 15th), he never went further than 20 yards from his own house in Brussels, that they might know where to find him' (Carola Oman, p. 260). Though he forgot the cricket match he made his point.

place was in Brussels. Having at last redirected his whole army towards Quatre Bras, nothing more remained for him to do there that
night. He was personally to lead out the reserve in the morning.
Orders had still to be distributed among officers in Brussels and
personal interviews held. Why not under the convenient camouflage
and at the ready-made rendezvous of a ball? This was to be Wellington's explanation to his friends during later post-mortems of Waterloo, and it is confirmed by Lord Fitzroy Somerset's own brief statement: 'As it [the ball] was the place where every British officer of
rank was likely to be found, perhaps for that reason the Duke dressed
& went there.'

Morale-building, duty, convenience—they all played their part in
getting Wellington to the ball. Why not admit also that the Irish devil
in him wanted to go? He would go; and see 'those fellows' damned.

Wellington's decision gave Byron his chance to include Brussels
in Childe Harold's Pilgrimage and Thackeray to make Becky Sharpe
roll her green eyes and flaunt her pink ball dress in a perfect
setting.

> *There was a sound of revelry by night,*
> *And Belgium's Capital had gather'd then*
> *Her Beauty and her Chivalry—and bright*
> *The lamps shone o'er fair women and brave men. . . .*

The ballroom, situated on the ground floor of the Richmonds'
rented house in the rue de la Blanchisserie, had been transformed
into a glittering palace with rose-trellised wallpaper, rich tent-like
draperies and hangings in the royal colours of crimson, gold and
black, and pillars wreathed in ribbons, leaves and flowers. Byron's
'lamps' were the most magnificent chandeliers and the list of chivalry,
if not beauty, was headed by H.R.H. the Prince of Orange, G.C.B.
All the ambassadors, generals and aristocrats were present as well as
dashing young officers like Arthur Shakespear of the Light Dragoons
and Captain Pakenham of the Royal Artillery—Sir Charles Stuart,
General Alava, the Mountnorrises and Wedderburn-Websters, the
Capels, Grevilles and Mrs Pole. Creevey's stepdaughters, the Misses
Ord, got their tickets, for the amusing Radical moved in the best
circles, treasuring the probably correct conviction that he was the
illegitimate son of a former Lord Sefton. The rear was brought up
by the diplomat Mr Chad, Wellington's surgeon Dr John Hume and

his chaplain the Reverend Samuel Briscall whose name as usual was spelt wrong.[7]

Wellington arrived 'rather late' at the entrance, where streams of light poured through the open windows into the warm streets and over the thronged carriages. In the ballroom those officers whose regiments were at any distance were already beginning to slip quietly away. The seventeen-year-old Lady Georgiana Lennox, whose sisters used to enjoy riding across the Phoenix Park with 'the great Sir Arthur' in 1807, was dancing. She immediately broke off and went up to Wellington to ask whether the rumours were true. (Arthur Shakespear wrote in his diary, 'about twelve o'clock it was rumoured that we were to march in the morn!') Wellington replied, as she thought, very gravely,

'Yes, they are true, we are off tomorrow.' As this terrible news (Georgiana's words) rapidly circulated, the ballroom was like a hive that someone had kicked: an excited buzz arose from all the tables and elegantly draped embrasures. The Duke of Brunswick felt a premonition of death and gave such a shudder that he dropped the little Prince de Ligne off his lap. Some officers flew to and fro saying their good-byes and departed, others clung so desperately to the loved one's hand or to the champagne bottle that when the hour struck there was no time to change and, like the heroine of *The Red Shoes*, they had to march in their dancing pumps. The Duke meanwhile appeared to the two youthful Miss Ords to be as composed as ever, while the even younger William Lennox, covered with plaster after a riding accident at Enghien, particularly noticed the serenity that 'beamed' all over his face.

'On with the dance! Let joy be unconfined.'

A rather more perspicacious guest, however, Lady Hamilton-Dalrymple, who sat for some time beside Wellington on a sofa, was struck by his preoccupied and anxious expression beneath the assumed gaiety: 'Frequently in the middle of a sentence he stopped abruptly and called to some officer, giving him directions, in particular to the Duke of Brunswick and Prince of Orange, who both left the ball before supper.' But even the lady on the sofa did not suspect

7. 'Brixall' on the Duchess of Richmond's list. In the Peninsula one officer did him the honour of admiring his Sunday sermon but called him 'Driscoll'.

the degree of drama with which the Prince of Orange's departure was attended.

Shortly before supper, as Wellington stood with Lady Charlotte Greville on his arm, a despatch was brought in by Lieutenant Henry Webster from Quatre Bras for the Prince of Orange. Slender Billy, merry as a marriage bell, handed it unopened to Wellington who quietly slipped it into his pocket for the moment.[8] The message, dated about 10 P.M. that night, announced the repulse of Prussian forces from Fleurus on the road north-east of Charleroi and less than eight miles as the crow flies from Quatre Bras. As soon as Wellington had read this enlightening but grim piece of news he recommended the Prince to miss supper and return straight to his headquarters in the field.

'Webster!' he called to the Prince's aide-de-camp, 'four horses instantly to the Prince of Orange's carriage. . . .' After other instructions now made necessary had been delivered in whispers or scribbles, Wellington proceeded to the supper-room.[9]

Hardly had he sat down before the Prince of Orange reappeared and whispered something to him for several minutes. Wellington looked incredulous but said nothing except to repeat that the Prince should go back to his quarters at Braine-le-Comte and to bed. Wellington kept up an animated and smiling conversation for twenty minutes more, when a lesser man would have fled the moment

8. Byron: *And all went merry as a marriage bell.* The Prince of Orange was soon to become engaged to the Tsar's daughter, Anna Pavlovna.

9. Lieutenant Henry Webster of the 9th Light Dragoons was aide-de-camp to the Prince of Orange. His recollections given verbally to an actor, Julian Young, in London over thirty years later are splendidly dramatic, including an hour's dash from Quatre Bras to Brussels by moonlight, but understandably inaccurate. Webster among other things described the royal party as about to go *upstairs* from the dining-room to the ballroom (both were on the ground floor) and said the Prince of Orange had the Duchess of Richmond on his arm while Wellington had Lady Charlotte Greville. The Prince in fact, as a result of Webster's message, did not go into supper. The present author suggests that Webster gave the Prince his despatch while the four (Wellington, Lady Charlotte, the Duchess and Prince) were coming out of the ballroom before the supper procession was formed, when Georgiana Lennox would have taken Wellington's arm. (For Webster's full account, see Antony Brett-James, *The Hundred Days*, pp. 42–3.) According to Lady Hamilton-Dalrymple (Ropes, p. 89), 'Near Observer', II. 31, and 'Officer', Wellington reached the ball by 10 P.M. and received the Mons despatch there. If so he must have left again unnoticed to inform Müffling, and returned later.

he heard Slender Billy's news. A notable Belgian aristocrat, indeed, the Marquise d'Assche, who sat next to the Duke of Richmond and opposite the Duke of Wellington at supper, did not relish the English nonchalance. Painfully conscious that her brother was somewhere out there where the cannon had been booming at dusk she looked across at the Duke with a jaundiced eye. His own *placement* was agreeable: Georgy Lennox on one side, who received from him a miniature of himself painted by a Belgian artist, and Frances Webster on the other. 'I would willingly have throttled him,' recalled the Marquise d'Assche, 'from the impatience which his phlegm caused me, and the ease of his conversation with Lady Withesburne [*sic*] to whom he paid ardent court.'[10]

At last the necessary interval was up and Wellington turned casually to the Duke of Richmond.

'I think it is time for me to go to bed likewise. . . .' The party rose and moved into the hall. As Wellington was saying good-night to his host he whispered something in Richmond's ear—the last recorded and most celebrated whisper of an evening remarkable for its undertones.

'Have you a good map in the house?' He needed to discover the exact implications of the almost incredible message verbally passed on to him at the supper table by the Prince of Orange. The written message which the Prince had received from his headquarters at Braine-le-Comte was dated 15 June 1815, '10½ P.M.' and signed by Baron Jean de Constant Rebecque, the Prince's chief-of-staff.

The enemy, de Constant Rebecque reported, were said to have pushed up the *chaussée* towards Brussels as far as Quatre Bras. 'It has been my duty,' he continued, 'to take upon myself to instruct General de Perponcher to support his second brigade [Prince Bernhard's] by his first. . . .' De Constant Rebecque added that he had ordered all other units at or near Nivelles to stand by in readiness.

First a threat to Fleurus; now, a few minutes later, to Quatre Bras. Napoleon was forking right and left up the roads like a streak of lightning. No wonder Wellington was incredulous, or so the Prince of Orange imagined. For he wrote later across the original of de

10. *Extracts from the Notebook of the Comtesse d'Assche, née d'Ives.* English names seem to have made her as impatient as the Duke's phlegm. Besides mis-spelling Wedderburn, she writes Lord Oxbright for Lord Uxbridge and Lord Ragston for Lord Raglan (Fitzroy Somerset's later title).

Constant Rebecque's despatch, that he had given the news it contained to the '*Duc de Wellington qui ne voulut pas le croire*'.[11]

De Constant Rebecque's action was in fact a vital sequel to the march on Quatre Bras of Prince Bernhard during the early afternoon, which had temporarily precluded Ney from occupying the crossroads himself. But Ney's vanguard had withdrawn no farther than Frasnes, only two miles south of Quatre Bras. Ney was now in charge of Napoleon's left wing as Grouchy was of his right, and they would almost certainly advance simultaneously up the Frasnes and Fleurus roads at dawn on the 16th. Therefore around 8 P.M. de Constant Rebecque had decided on his own initiative to reinforce Quatre Bras that night. What his despatch did not reveal was that Wellington's earlier order to concentrate at Nivelles had arrived when Perponcher's two brigades were already beyond it. To obey would have meant marching back again, away from the guns. Rebecque showed the order to Perponcher in silence. Perponcher looked at it with the sightless eye which common sense prescribed. The two tacitly agreed to ignore it and to pursue their plan of strengthening Wellington's position at Quatre Bras, the crossroads which were now literally the crux. In de Constant Rebecque, Perponcher and Prince Bernhard, Wellington at last had three subordinates or 'insubordinates' who could take the initiative in a rapidly changing situation without committing a howler, like the less fortunate Stewarts and Dalhousies of Spain. Next morning he was to congratulate warmly the Prince of Orange on the moves of the night before.[12]

*   *   *

Once Wellington knew the full truth he acted with decision. Orderlies again scoured the country; Brussels was awake. He had guessed wrong but not irretrievably. (It would have been irretrievable if he

11. De Constant Rebecque's despatch with the Prince's comment on Wellington's reaction to it is now in the Archives of the Royal House, The Hague.

12. De Constant Rebecque was a charming as well as a brilliant personality, acquainted with Wellington and an intimate friend of the Prince of Orange. He had been his governor at Oxford and tutor in the Peninsula and later wrote him some amusing French–English letters. To be in London in October (1813) without H.R.H. or society was '*affreuse*'—'*Londres est toujours empty*'. He sent love from the Bishop of London and Mrs Howley and '*un petit mot d'amitié de ma part au vieux Brown horse et à chestnut mare*'. Signed, Constant (*Hague Royal Archives*, IV.c.B.19).

had moved towards Blücher and Napoleon had then come up on his outside flank—Wellington's sole responsibility—where there would have been nobody to oppose him.) Like a great fighter he was still on his balance though tipped the wrong way. Now he righted himself.

The Duke of Richmond took him into his study next to the ball-room and spread out a map. Wellington looked at it wryly:

'Napoleon has *humbugged* me, by God! he has gained twenty-four hours' march on me.'

'What do you intend doing?'

'I have ordered the army to concentrate at Quatre Bras; but we shall not stop him there, and if so, I must fight him *here*.' Wellington passed his thumb-nail over the map just south of the Waterloo position. Then he left the scene of his acute discomfort, avoiding for once the hall-door.[13]

The party hardly looked like a ball any longer. Guests were scurrying rather than drifting away. Georgiana Lennox went out to help her brother Lord March, another of the Prince of Orange's aides-de-camp, to pack. When she returned expecting to find the last guest gone there were still a few 'energetic and heartless young ladies' dancing.

Wellington returned to his hotel in the rue Montagne du Parc for under two hours' sleep, between 3 A.M. and 5 A.M. on the morning of 16 June. He was interrupted by the arrival of yet another delayed despatch describing the Prussian position. 'I cannot tell the world,' he said afterwards, 'that Blücher picked the fattest man in his army to ride with an express to me, and that he took thirty hours to go thirty miles.' He also remarked that things like this never kept him awake.

'I don't like lying awake, it does no good. I make a point never to lie awake.'

So he slept soundly through the rising clamour of bugle calls,

13. The Duke of Richmond described this scene to his aide-de-camp, Captain George Bowles, two minutes after it happened. Bowles passed it on in a letter to Lord Malmesbury (Malmesbury, *Letters*, vol. II, pp. 445–6). Lady Shelley recorded that the Duke of Richmond later showed her a pencil mark he had made on his map at the exact place where Wellington put his thumb-nail (*Diaries of Frances Lady Shelley*, vol. I, p. 171). That the Allies were surprised before Waterloo was frankly admitted to Greville by Wellington five years later: 'The Duke says that they were certainly not prepared for this attack, as the French had previously broken up the roads by which their army advanced, but as this was in the summer this did not render them impassable' (*Memoirs*, 10 December 1820). Bowles became a general and K.C.B.

clash of arms and confusion of bagpipes, drum-beats, hammering, shouting, neighing, barking, crying of children suddenly awakened and of wives whose husbands had already marched. In the Park Picton inspected his division at 4 A.M. and soon his green-jacketed riflemen and kilted Highlanders went swinging out of the Namur gate for Quatre Bras, the Highlanders marching so steadily that the black plumes on their bonnets scarcely quivered. It was only an hour or two earlier that some of their sergeants had been dancing reels for the amusement and education of the Duchess of Richmond's Belgian guests. At the same hour Arthur Shakespear left Brussels to join his regiment at Woorde: they reached Nivelles at 6 A.M. and Quatre Bras at 8. Captain Johnny Kincaid, still with his 95th Rifles, spent the early hours either asleep on a Brussels pavement or advising agitated civilians who disturbed him to 'keep themselves perfectly cool'. Sir Augustus Frazer, commanding the Horse Artillery as in the Peninsula, received an early report that Wellington was moving at 6.30 A.M. to *Waterloo*—or so Sir George Wood thought, who commanded the Artillery. Frazer could not find the odd-sounding place on the map and remarked disgustedly that this was 'the old story over again'. He sent to de Lancey, the quartermaster-general, to learn 'the real name'. His letter home, dated 10 P.M. on the 15th, concluded nonchalantly: 'I never suffer myself to be disturbed by these alerts.' Captain Cavalié Mercer, commanding 'G' Troop of Frazer's Horse Artillery, woke up with a jump to find himself abruptly ordered to proceed to Enghien 'with the utmost diligence'. Such was Mercer's diligence that he gave his first order while putting on his stockings, the second as he got one leg into his overalls and the third (for breakfast) as he buttoned them up. The rush and bustle, the sounding of the 'boot and saddle' followed by the 'turn-out' and parade, were in Mercer's words 'animating and soul-stirring'. Twenty-seven-year-old John Haddy James, however, assistant-surgeon to the 1st Life Guards and no veteran, found the trumpets sounding 'to horse' at 2 A.M., the sudden confusion and the troops' sardonic humour somewhat daunting.

'I don't think I shall go to bed now,' shouted a Hussar, rolling up drunk to answer the call to arms.

'Belike you will be put to bed with a shroud this night,' said a Life Guard, who overheard him, 'and know nothing about it.'

Frederick Ponsonby, colonel of the 12th Light Dragoons, met one of his captains, William Hay, and said ruefully,

'You were lucky not to go to the ball, I am quite knocked up. . . .' Wellington was up at 5.30 A.M. and out giving orders.

The de Lanceys leant out of their window together, 'very solemn and melancholy'; he had only a few more dawns to see. By 8 A.M. Brussels was returning to serenity and the quiet clip-clop of donkeys bringing in their loads of cauliflowers and strawberries for the civilian population. Lady Hamilton Dalrymple, who had left the ball at 2.30 A.M. and watched from her window the Highlanders passing at 4, was woken at 8 by her maid.

'Oh my lady, get up quick; there he goes, God bless him, and he will not come back till he is King of France!'

It was Wellington at the head of his staff riding off to Quatre Bras.

22 Quatre Bras:
The Knotted Rope

It was still a fine calm morning, though becoming sultry, when the Duke trotted into Quatre Bras on 16 June 1815 at 10 A.M. The scene at the crossroads, twenty-one miles from Brussels and twelve from Charleroi, was hardly less quiet than the city he had left behind. He was not surprised, for a reassuring despatch from the Prince of Orange was in his pocket.

> *Near Frasnes.* June 16 1815
> 7 A.M.
>
> My dear Duke—I am just arrived. The French are in possession of Frasnes, near *Quatre Bras* . . . but not as yet in force. . . .

In fact Ney's force at Frasnes, only two miles away, already outnumbered the Dutch–Belgians at Quatre Bras by nearly three to one in men and seven to one in guns: 20,000 men in Reille's corps with sixty available guns against the Prince's 7,000 men and eight guns; but the rolling, wooded country concealed the two armies from one another.

The Prince went on to inform Wellington that he had immediately sent for one of his Dutch–Belgian cavalry brigades from Nivelles and at the same time ordered his sharp-shooters to cease fire, which had the desired effect of further tranquillizing the enemy. All Wellington heard when he arrived was what Fitzroy Somerset called 'a little popping Musketry'.

At 10.30 A.M., after having approved the Prince's disposition of his exiguous force, Wellington dictated a memorandum for Blücher: the Anglo-Dutch reinforcements would reach Genappe and Nivelles by noon; he would wait at Quatre Bras until they arrived. An hour or so later he realized that his memorandum had been guilty of wildly optimistic predictions. His reinforcements would reach him nothing like so soon.[1] He therefore decided to ride the six miles over to

---

1. Wellington's own explanation of why the cavalry was late was given to Lady Salisbury, wife of the 2nd Marquess, years later and recorded in her diary for 18 September 1836: 'Lord Anglesey committed a great fault in not

Blücher, concert their joint plans and incidentally put the picture right.

About 1 P.M. Henry Hardinge, Wellington's young attaché with the Prussians and as such Müffling's opposite number, saw a small party approaching Blücher's headquarters on horses with cut tails. Guessing they were English he rode out to meet them. The Prussians were very much intrigued by the equipment strapped to the Duke's horse: a change of clothes behind the saddle and a portfolio of pen, ink and paper in place of the pistol holster. A few minutes later Wellington and Blücher were together climbing the windmill of Bussy on a ridge behind Ligny. At the top they opened their telescopes. The sight revealed to Wellington was alarming.

Napoleon was clearly visible among his staff. He too had his telescope out; indeed, the three generals may at that historic moment

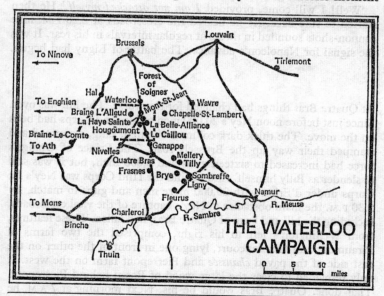

THE WATERLOO CAMPAIGN

bringing up his cavalry at Quatre Bras. The Duke had ordered them to march in an extended column, but Lord Anglesey [Uxbridge], instead of keeping with the head of his column, remained with the tail, four or five miles behind, so when the aide-de-camp arrived where Lord Anglesey ought to have been, he found them all gone to bed and nobody to whom he could communicate his orders' (Carola Oman, p. 213).

have been looking at one another. Napoleon's 68,000 infantry and 12,500 cavalry confronted Blücher across the Ligny brook.[2] Blücher, it is true, commanded 84,000 Prussians; but they were drawn up on forward slopes with no cover from the enemy's imminent cannonade. Wellington muttered to Hardinge,

'If they fight here they will be damnably mauled.' Then he faced Blücher and Gneisenau and said the same thing more tactfully.

'Everybody knows their own army best; but if I were to fight here, I should expect to be beat.'

'My men like to see their enemy', replied Gneisenau with annoyance. A forward position was in fact taken for granted by Continental armies, and the magic of the 'reverse slope' was Wellington's alone. The discussion ended with Wellington giving the suspicious Gneisenau a pledge of support, though a qualified one.

'Well! I will come, provided *I am not attacked myself*.' He then started to ride back. As he neared the crossroads at 2.20 P.M. nine cannon-shots sounded in threes at regular intervals in his rear. It was the signal for Napoleon's advance. The battle of Ligny had begun.

*   *   *

At Quatre Bras things had changed for the worse. The lull was over. Since just before noon Ney's 20,000 men of his IInd Corps had been on the move. The thick dark columns shouted, sang, drummed and stamped their way up the Brussels road. The Prince of Orange's force had increased to sixteen guns and 8,000 men, but it was still as slender as Billy himself. And behind the IInd Corps was Ney's Ist Corps under d'Erlon with 20,000 more men and guns to match. By 2.30 P.M. the main obstacles to Ney's capture of the vital crossroads, including the hill and farm of Quatre Bras, had fallen. These features, from Wellington's left to his right, comprised the two farms of Piraumont and Gemioncourt, lying one in front of the other on the east side of the paved *chaussée* and Pierrepont farm on the west. It only remained to clear the large wood of Bossu behind Pierrepont. That done, Quatre Bras would be his. Next morning at 7 A.M. he would be precisely where Napoleon hoped, insisted and positively foretold—in Brussels.

As Wellington galloped up, the resilient young Prince (he was twenty-three) did his best to break the bad news cheerfully. The deep

2. The numbers given by Chandler, p. 1038, have been used here.

glades of Bossu wood, he emphasized, would hold Ney back for several hours yet. At that instant there was a roar of '*Vive l'Empereur!*' A powerful voice began chanting the famous jingle which had spurred French soldiers all over the world to gain and glory: '*L'Empereur récompensera celui qui s'avancera!*' Wellington did not need to hear it twice.

'That must be Ney going down the line. I know what that means; we shall be attacked in five minutes!'

The time was 3 P.M. Wellington had returned after an absence of several hours to find the battle of Quatre Bras not only begun but in a fair way to being lost. Could even he retrieve a situation so desperate? The only other question worth asking was why Ney, with overwhelming force since morning, had not won hours ago.

* * *

It is true that if Ney had done for Napoleon what Rebecque did for Wellington the Allies might have been swept out of Quatre Bras by noon. By that high standard Ney no doubt deserved some of the epithets which have since been hurled at him—lethargic, apathetic, sunk in a trance, slow-witted, shell-shocked and suffering from battle-fatigue. Napoleon, however, was at least as culpable. His first orders of the day did not reach Ney until 11 A.M., nor did they convey a clear-cut sense of urgency. Ney was not to march forthwith but only to be ready to march as soon as his reserves reached him. (Collecting his army was in any case a protracted business. French soldiers needed to cook before fighting and to requisition their food before cooking.) Further directions would reach him when the Emperor had finally cleared his own mind. General Reille, meanwhile, proved to be no less lethargic than Ney himself. Expatiating to Ney on the 'blind' country around Quatre Bras behind whose tall rye stalks, thickets, hedges and reverse slopes Wellington might be concealing a great army, Reille suggested waiting, as ordered for d'Erlon.

'This is going to be a battle as in Spain,' he hinted darkly, 'where the English only showed themselves at the last moment.' But Ney's blood was up at last. Having been beaten in the Peninsula by Wellington's brains he was not going to be beaten at Quatre Bras by his mere reputation. Without waiting for d'Erlon he ordered the attack.

Nevertheless Reille's healthy respect for Wellington continued to prevent the French attack from turning into an avalanche. While Wellington was hurrying to the battlefield his reputation was there already, fighting for him.

*   *   *

Once on the spot, Wellington met the crisis at the crossroads with an immediate and daring counter-stroke particularly aimed at the captured farm buildings on his left. Despite the heavy odds, it was his only chance. At all costs he must play for time and keep in his hands the *chaussée* linking Quatre Bras to Ligny. The weakness of his line was partially concealed by the standing corn which in those days the farmers grew to a height of five or six feet for the straw. Behind him Picton's 8,000 men had come up from their prolonged 'cooking' at Waterloo, though they still had to be deployed.[3] Behind Picton were the Brunswickers in their black uniforms and black plumes, with a silver death's-head on their caps—all in pious mourning for the Duke of Brunswick's father, killed by Napoleon's soldiers at Jena. To Lady de Lancey they had looked like an immense moving hearse. To Wellington they looked like salvation. Behind them were the Nassauers from Ussingen, the Hanoverians, Halkett's brigade, the Guards. . . . Time was on his side.

The first counter-attack did not succeed in recapturing Piraumont and Gemioncourt; indeed no counter-attack could at present be more than a temporary check, since Wellington was forced to continue for some time his awkward game in which each additional card had to be played the moment it was dealt to him. Nevertheless, by the time Ney was ready to launch his second, far more massive assault, Picton's division was in action and the pattern of Quatre Bras was beginning to emerge. Time and time again Wellington's thin line was destined to receive the furious onrush of cavalry preceded by a cannonade and stinging swarm of sharp-shooters; every time something would give way for lack of ammunition, cavalry support or guns, and there would be imminent risk of a break-through or envelopment of one or other

3. After parading at 4 A.M. Picton's 5th Division were ordered to stop at Waterloo on the way to Quatre Bras and cook. Wellington came up with them about 9 A.M. 'As he passed Picton,' wrote Fitzroy Somerset, 'he ordered the 5th Division, Brunswick & Nassau troops to resume their march which they did between 12 & 1 o'clock' (*Raglan MSS*, no. 24). Why so late? Perhaps because of a rumour that Quatre Bras was already lost (Allan's diary).

of his flanks; always some contingent which had received its marching orders from him the night before would come up in the nick of time—each new arrival a *deus ex machina* to save him from destruction.

Ney also had his share of divine apparitions, but in his case they took the form of confused messages emanating from Napoleon and sailing down on a cloud which formed part of the fog of war. It is this dramatic contrast that still gives Quatre Bras the power to move today—on Wellington's side a steady build-up from the most desperate weakness (7,000 troops) to superiority (26,000) and on to absolute supremacy (36,000); on Ney's, no increase whatever on his original 20,000 men but constant depredations on his temper and judgement. Looked at another way, Ney's *deus ex machina* should have been Count Drouet d'Erlon; thanks to counter-orders from Ligny, d'Erlon was to be the god who never descended. Ney's bitter experiences were the bones of the battle and imposed its shape.

*   *   *

At 4.15 P.M. the voice from Ligny first spoke to Ney; that is, for the first time since the battle of Quatre Bras began. A 'definitive' despatch dictated by Napoleon to Soult at 2 P.M. ordered Ney to destroy immediately any force in his front (i.e. Wellington) and then to swing right and envelop '*un corps de troupes*' which Grouchy was on the point of assaulting at Ligny.

This message, far from conveying to Ney the fact that *un corps de troupes* meant the whole Prussian army and that Grouchy therefore required reinforcements, simply impressed Ney with the burning need for reinforcements of his own. He sent an urgent message to d'Erlon at Frasnes. Let him lose not a moment in bringing up the 1st Corps.

That Quatre Bras would not be captured without d'Erlon became evident when Ney's grand, second attack failed, even though its repulse cost the young Duke of Brunswick his life and put Wellington's in sudden jeopardy.

*   *   *

Wellington had held or driven off Ney's onslaught on his left and centre but a body of young, raw Dutch–Belgian troops in Bossu wood gave way. The Duke of Brunswick, sent to support them, was beaten back and both Netherlanders and Brunswickers broke and fled. Brunswick, with the badge of a death's-head already grinning on his cap, was hit by a ball in the stomach while trying to rally his countrymen. He died that evening. He was the brother of Princess Caroline of Wales, but so bad were her relations by now with the English royal family that her daughter, Princess Charlotte, did not dare condole with her on the hero's death until she had obtained leave from the Prince Regent: 'I could not do so,' she wrote to him, 'without your permission.'

On the battlefield, the defeated Netherlanders continued in headlong flight from Ney's Chasseurs, leaving havoc in their train. First, Wellington and Fitzroy Somerset who were up in front had to gallop for their lives, Wellington skimming a bank and ditch lined with Picton's Gordon Highlanders.

'Ninety-second, lie down!' he shouted as he sailed over the retracted *chevaux de frise* of bayonets. 'On a worse horse,' commented Fitzroy, 'he might not have escaped!' Nor if he had been a less athletic rider.

Next, the fleeing horsemen ran into a mass of camp-followers and carts creaking out from Brussels on the high road. Panic-stricken, the wagoners turned tail and joined the stampede back to the city.

Here, tourists like Charlotte Waldie and her family had been revelling in rumours of a huge French defeat. Now the cry was of a huge French victory. The alarm spread. Magdalen de Lancey, removed by her husband to the safety of Antwerp, heard from her maid Emma that streams of refugees from Brussels (among them the Waldies) were pouring into the town. As the sound of gun-fire grew more insistent she shut her windows and doors, stopped her ears and tried to think of something else. 'I only heard a rolling like the sea at a distance.' But the house shook.

*   *   *

The flight of the young Netherlanders, many of them mere boys, had no permanent effect; indeed it put the veteran 42nd on their mettle. Sergeant James Anton proudly noted how their strange bonnets and kilts suddenly rising out of the tall rye seemed to paralyse the French: 'We were on them, our pieces were loaded, and our bayonets glittered, impatient to drink their blood.'

Wellington's opponent, moreover, was about to be visited again from on high, a visitation far more devastating to Ney and valuable to Wellington than all the volleys of British infantry so far assembled. A message from Count d'Erlon disclosed that he and his 20,000 men had been halted just short of Quatre Bras on the pencilled order of Napoleon's aide-de-camp, La Bédoyère, and marched off to Ligny.

Ney was beside himself. He could not know that Napoleon only needed d'Erlon on the Prussian flank to fell the staggering giant with a blow from which he would never recover. All Ney knew was that one mad stroke had suddenly halved the threat to Wellington. Before he had recovered from the shock he was called on again in an Imperial order dated 3.15 P.M. to look sharp, finish off the business at Quatre Bras and fall on Blücher's rear. This time the divine voice, as interpreted by Soult, added to its instructions a solemn warning and exhortation: 'The fate of France is in your hands.' At the same instant Wellington, as if supernaturally guided, threw the newly arrived Hanoverian division into the attack.

Ney could bear no more. If the fate of France was in his hands, so was the fate of his corps commander, d'Erlon, or soon would be. He ordered d'Erlon to return forthwith. A speeding aide found the Ist Corps about to enter the Ligny battlefield. D'Erlon took the easy way out. He turned round and began, like the noble Duke of York, marching back again.

*   *   *

About this time a young Prussian officer, von Wussow, got through to Wellington with a somewhat grim message from Gneisenau. (A similar emissary from Blücher had been disabled before he could deliver his despatch.) Though none of the villages behind the Ligny stream had as yet fallen, 'the most we can do is to hold the battlefield until dark'. Von Wussow was struck by the characteristic 'serenity and sangfroid' with which Wellington received this unattractive news, especially as cannon-balls were flying around them in all directions. The Duke took no notice of them whatever.

As the savage fighting at Quatre Bras reached its climax Wellington's strokes, always controlled and effective, were countered with a fury that was sometimes crazy, sometimes sublime. At 5 P.M. his infantry were submitted to a sudden, fantastic onslaught of cavalry led by Kellerman, the ugly and brilliant negotiator of Cintra. A frantic

Ney had launched him with the watchword, *The Fate of France is in your hands*, and the staccato commands, 'Crush them. Ride them down.' Kellerman dashed in with his single brigade and before Wellington knew where he was he had a few daredevil French squadrons for the first time in possession of his crossroads.

Then came the reaction. Without immediate support, Kellerman was at the mercy of a raking musket-fire from the 30th and 73rd of Halkett's brigade, and the usual assortment of 'delicacies' (grape and canister) from a hidden battery. Ensign Macready (brother of the famous actor) and some others of the 30th had got left behind by their regiment in the early morning dash for Quatre Bras. As they now panted up, a crowd of wounded from a regiment which had suffered severely, the 44th, cheered and called out faintly:

'Push on old three tens—[they had fought together in Spain] pay 'em for the 44th—you're much wanted, boys—success to you my darlings.' A Gordon Highlander, bleeding to death from a severed arm, gasped out to Morris of the 73rd:

'Go on, 73rd, give them pepper! I've got my Chelsea commission.'

Wellington himself saw to it that the volleys of his Gordon Highlanders were lethal.

'Ninety-second, don't fire till I tell you!' He allowed the huge French Cuirassiers to come pounding up to within thirty yards of his steady square.

'Fire!' Riders and horses dropped or fled. A British ball got Kellerman's charger but the quick-witted general managed to seize two of his troopers' bits and run off the field between them. Still the French cavalry came on. As fast as a column was beaten off another was rallied and reformed for a new attack. At one point it was Picton who intervened to prevent disaster. A torrent of enemy horse was about to descend on the 28th, not in one column but in a triple wave on three sides of their already shaken square. Then Picton's great voice roared out:

'Twenty-eighth, remember Egypt!' Regimental pride and Picton's personality won. The infantry stood fast and the French Lancers and Cuirassiers could only swirl harmlessly round the squares until they were called off. At another point nemesis overtook Halkett's brigade. Somebody forbade the 69th to form a square and consequently they were cut to pieces and lost their Colour; while Wellington's old 33rd, having withstood the fire of a French battery from Bossu wood, succumbed to a cry, 'The cavalry are coming!' and instead of getting into square, melted away. But as ever at a critical juncture reinforcements came up, this time the Guards.[4]

Suddenly a fourth apparition, Soult's staff officer, Major Baudus, appeared to Ney with the news that Napoleon now attached little importance to his doings at Quatre Bras but much to the arrival of d'Erlon. It was the end for Ney. His face turned as red as his hair and speechless with rage he turned his back on Baudus and rushed on foot—his second horse had just been killed under him—to rally his faltering columns.

Wellington's crisis was over, once the Guards and fresh Brunswickers had brought up his ever-growing force to 36,000 men and seventy guns. 'It was now his turn to attack,' writes Houssaye, '—and to attack with certainty of success, as was his wont.' The tone of Houssaye's last phrase, implying that a greater than Wellington would have taken a chance earlier, will be familiar to Wellington's successors.

At 6.30 P.M. the Allied bugles sounded the advance.[5] The French were driven out of Piraumont and Gemioncourt while the Guards had the honour of clearing Bossu wood, over which hung a great cloud of black smoke and wheeling, screaming birds. The Guards succeeded, though with severe losses, 'not perhaps going about it', according to Fitzroy Somerset, 'as a Rifle or Light Corps would have done'. Ensign Batty, who went into Bossu wood with the 1st Foot Guards wrote: 'The trees were so thick, that it was beyond anything difficult to effect a passage. As we approached, we saw the enemy behind them taking aim at us: they contested every bush . . . but could not resist us. . . . The moment we endeavoured to go out of the wood (which had naturally broken us) the French cavalry charged. . . . Our loss was most tremendous. . . .'

The Guards had approached Quatre Bras in the later afternoon, as their assistant surgeon, John Haddy James, recalled. (This young

4. Most British writers say that an over-excited Prince of Orange gave the fatal order to the 69th to receive the cavalry in line. Captain B. Pigot, however, late of the 69th, wrote a different account to Major-General Siborne, on 7 July 1844. It was a Major Lindsay, wrote Pigot, who made two companies of the 69th 'face to right about, in open Column, and commence firing upon the Cuirassiers. But for that we should have got into square. Poor man to the day of his death he regretted having done so, but at the time he did it for the best (Siborne, *Waterloo Letters*, pp. 337–8).
5. Bugles not trumpets were used on the battlefield, since trumpets being several feet long, were too cumbersome to carry.

doctor from the West Country was to become a specialist on in-flammation, and to be known as 'James of Exeter'.) The interesting sight of Germans marching along with outsize packs and sacred music, could not keep James's eyes from a sinister cloud to the south —a solid pyramid with a perfectly flat base. 'It was the canopy which the combatants had formed for themselves.' The marchers of the German Legion, including Edmund Wheatley, arrived just too late. They bivouacked in a field listening to the cannonade at Ligny in dreadful 'suspense and anxiety'. When would they be allowed to fight? The moments 'stretched out'; then it was sunset and all sounds were hushed.

Most of the cavalry missed the battle also. Like Arthur Shakespear and William Hay, they had long distances to cover, Hay fifty-two miles. When he and his colonel, Frederick Ponsonby of the 12th Light Dragoons, at last reached the scene of carnage, Ponsonby im-mediately made for a dead Frenchman's cuirasse, punctured in three places.

'I wanted to find out if these cuirasses were ball proof or not; this plainly shows they are not.'

Shakespear's journal registered the cavalry's deep disappointment:

—moved up immediately to support the Infantry—but it was too late for any thing—lay in a stubble field that night—no baggage *no nothing*! The night before, how very different, all gaiety & champagne! Such are the chances of war!

One thing Shakespear, like Ponsonby and Hay, was in time to see: his first vision of the famous Cuirassiers. Six of them were lying dead close together at the corner of Bossu wood. That was how Welling-ton remembered them when he later gave his opinion that these armourplated champions (partly Saint Denis and partly a tank) were not worth it. At a party in the Admiralty in 1826, someone asked the Duke whether the Cuirassiers 'had not *come up very well at Waterloo*?'

'Yes, and *they went down very well too*,' replied the Duke with his whooping laugh. After the 92nd gave them a couple of volleys at Quatre Bras, he explained, they could not get up but lay sprawling and kicking in their cuirasses and jackboots 'like so many *turned* turtles'.

*   *   *

By 9 P.M. Dr James's solid pyramid had faded, darkness was falling and the battle was over. Sergeant Robertson and his Gordon Highlanders turned to their sombre and respectful task of removing the wounded and burying as many dead as possible—'especially the officers'. In every sense the battle had been a draw. The heavy casualties were almost equal: 4,800 Allied losses (exactly half of them British) and only a few hundred less French. It was perhaps that slight balance in Napoleon's favour which made him claim a victory, for there was no other justification. Both sides were back to start at nightfall, Wellington holding Quatre Bras, Ney in Frasnes. As far as objectives went, each had prevented the other from achieving his aim. Wellington checkmated Ney's advance to envelop Blücher; Ney prohibited Wellington from sending Blücher help.

D'Erlon's imbecile promenade, caused by Soult and Napoleon, contributed to the draw in its own way. He returned to start just after the battle ended. There was nothing for his veterans to do, no muskets even to clean, for it had not rained, nor had they fired a shot on either battlefield all day.

Wellington was not the man to underestimate the help he had received from d'Erlon. Writing to one of the Ponsonbys[6] some time later, he said that Napoleon's greatest disaster during the Hundred Days was his failure to persuade Berthier to rejoin him. If his skilful chief-of-staff had been there to interpret the voice, instead of the bumbling Soult, d'Erlon would have got somewhere, there would have been no Waterloo and Napoleon would have lasted much longer.

Berthier, however, had refused to fight for Napoleon and then fallen out of a window on 1 June 1815. In choosing Soult as a substitute Napoleon picked the wrong man.

Wellington could not help adding on another occasion that if the d'Erlon fiasco had occurred in *his* army he would never have been allowed to forget it.

* * *

Firing in the direction of Ligny ceased about 9 P.M. also. As Wellington and his staff trotted back the three miles to Genappe where supper and beds were awaiting them at the *Roi d'Espagne*, he cheerfully assumed Blücher had repulsed the enemy.

6. Professor Edmund Ford, All Souls College, Oxford, read this and other letters from Wellington belonging to the Ponsonby-Fane family in Somerset. Where these letters are now is not known.

'Blücher is a damned fine old Fellow,' he said to Fitzroy as they rode along side by side.

So he was, even finer than Wellington guessed. At that moment Blücher was lying in a little house crammed with wounded at Mellery, unknown to the rest of his army, battered, bruised and dosed up to the eyes; in fact 'damnably mauled'.

Even without d'Erlon's help, Napoleon had relentlessly burnt and blasted the exposed Prussian columns, until the Ligny stream flowed red like a river in hell. Blücher led a last gallant cavalry charge; its failure was complete. The grey war-horse which the Prince Regent had given him on his visit in 1814 was killed, and he was twice ridden over. Only the presence of mind of his aide-de-camp, Nostiz, who threw a cloak over his medals, saved him from being recognized and taken prisoner. He was attended in the cottage by Nostiz alone; 16,000 of his Prussians were casualties, as against 12,000 French, while 8,000 more of his 'children', as he called them, were streaming over the dark fields towards home. Gneisenau had taken over. Who could tell what he would decide, now that the 'fine old fellow' was removed?

Something of this reached Wellington's ears when he entered the inn at Genappe. He found an agitated young captain there, brother of Henry Hardinge whose left hand had been shot off by a cannon at Ligny. Captain Hardinge was looking for a surgeon; though he could not be sure he thought there had been a Prussian defeat. At any rate, the Prussians had 'suffered severely'.

Wellington, always optimistic, hoped that young Hardinge's gloomy report was due to his anxiety over his brother. Fitzroy went so far as to write to his wife Emily (Wellington's niece) in Brussels: 'The Prussians and we have repulsed the French.' Wellington's actions, however, showed no complacency. He ordered his aide-de-camp, Colonel Alexander Gordon, to reconnoitre. When French vedettes but no Prussians were reported at Sombreffe, he recalled his most advanced posts. He was not in bed until nearly midnight but rose again at 3 A.M., galloped straight back to Quatre Bras and sent Gordon to Ligny to find out the worst.

*   *   *

In Brussels, meanwhile, the rhythmic booming of the guns had brought large crowds on to the ramparts towards the evening of the

16th, among them Thomas Creevey; while Lady Charlotte Greville's house became a centre where news of Quatre Bras from Wellington and others was disseminated. It came as a great relief to Georgy Lennox (despite her mother's partiality for the Gordons) to hear that Scottish regiments had borne the brunt. 'Thank God, my dearest G.,' she wrote to her friend Lady Georgiana Bathurst, 'all our friends are safe. . . . The Guards were not engaged. . . . the Scotch were chiefly engaged, so there are no officers wounded that one knows.'

While Creevey was dining with a friend, another of Wellington's aides, Colonel Canning, walked past the window and was called in to share the feast. It was to be his last dinner but one. At night young Major Hamilton rode in to tell them about the day's two most dramatic events: Brunswick dead and Wellington nearly captured.

It is probable that Wellington was not averse to accounts of his narrow escape being circulated. Despite Vitoria and Orthez there had been persistent, malicious rumours since May 1814 that 'he had not over-exposed himself to danger' in the Peninsula. His many raw troops at Quatre Bras had now seen for themselves what sort of a man this 'Nosey' was.

*   *   *

The crossroads were chilly at 6 A.M. on 17 June 1815 as Wellington waited for Gordon's return from Ligny in a draughty hut made of branches. 'Ninety-second, I will be obliged to you for a little fire.' His Highlanders lit one for him and were much pleased with his enthusiastic thanks. Here he interviewed his senior staff officers, occasionally breaking off to tell his friend Captain George Bowles of the Coldstream Guards how extraordinary it was that he had still heard nothing from old Blücher. All night long his cavalry had been streaming in and he was ready, if Blücher were ready too, to challenge Napoleon again.

It was nearly 7.30 A.M. when Gordon returned, his horse in a lather and his news so grave that he preferred to whisper it to his chief. Wellington appeared totally unmoved. He gave Gordon some quick orders and turned to Bowles.

'Old Blücher has had a damned good licking and gone back to Wavre, eighteen miles. As he has gone back, we must go too.'

For a brief moment he could not help wondering how his retreat would appear to the Opposition.

'I suppose in England they will say we have been licked. I can't help it; as they are gone back, we must go too.'

In five minutes, still standing where he had received the news, he gave his preliminary orders for the retreat. Then he shut himself in the hut to work out details with his staff. General Müffling was sent for. Few of Wellington's staff could at first find Wavre on the map. They imagined it, reported Fitzroy Somerset, to be only a little in the rear of Ligny, never dreaming that Blücher could have fallen back so far. Müffling soon disillusioned them.

'*Ma foi, c'est fort loin!*' he exclaimed. Wellington shot him a look, implying that the Prussians had purposely suppressed the bad news in order to keep his army at Quatre Bras as a cover for Blücher's retreat. When Müffling hastily suggested that the Prussian aide who had been disabled on the 16th must have been carrying Blücher's warning, Wellington instantly returned to his usual friendly manner.[7] Together he and Müffling debated the next move. Was a renewed challenge to Napoleon by the combined Anglo-Dutch and Prussian armies still possible? They agreed that it was. Wavre was only seven miles due east from the nearest point on the Brussels road, not much farther than Ligny from Quatre Bras. Wellington would retire level with Wavre and await a further report from Blücher. For his part, Müffling argued that since Bülow's corps had not been engaged at Ligny and Napoleon had allowed the rest of the defeated army to reach Wavre, the affair 'could not be so bad'.[8]

*　　*　　*

7. Müffling, whose story this is, skates over the fact that a duplicate of the wounded officer's message was safely delivered by von Wussow. What Gneisenau forgot altogether to give the Duke was not a mere warning but the facts of his actual retreat.

8. Fitzroy Somerset's unpublished account of the Wavre episode does not entirely square with that of Bowles, given above. Somerset says that neither the staff nor Wellington himself knew where Wavre was. General Müffling was the person 'who opened the Duke's Eyes, who had sent for Him & upon being told the Prussians had fallen back on Wavre observed, "*Ma foi c'est fort loin!*" The Duke immediately resolved on making a corresponding movement & to fall back on the Road to Brussels' (*Raglan MSS*, no. 24). It is quite possible that Wellington did not at first know the distance of Wavre from Ligny and that Bowles put the words 'eighteen miles' into Wellington's mouth.

Exactly how bad the Prussian affair had been was not known to Wellington until much later, if ever.[9] When Gneisenau stood in the moonlight on the night of the 16th and ordered, 'Retreat on . . . Wavre,' his options were wide open. From Wavre he could indeed keep in touch with Wellington—or strike off obliquely through Louvain to his home bases in the north-east. It is true that by choosing Wavre he ruled out the direct road home, due east through Namur and Liège. Moving obliquely may have had its own appeal for Gneisenau.

Wellington rightly hailed the Wavre decision as crucial. 'It was the decisive moment of the century,' he wrote after Waterloo. But the moment was Blücher's.

The indomitable old man, partially resuscitated, was discovered during the night by Gneisenau at Mellery. In this rough and ready rendezvous, with the wounded Hardinge lying on straw in the ante-room, Blücher and his quartermaster-general demolished Gneisenau's arguments for parting company from Wellington. It was not the least of Blücher's victories.[10]

Next morning, 17 June, Blücher summoned Hardinge and embraced his '*lieber Freund*', despite Hardinge's amputation and his own highly spiced condition. '*Ich stinke etwas,*' he said, apologizing for the results of last night's medicinal debauch on gin and rhubarb flavoured with garlic. Before setting off for Wavre he bathed his bruises in brandy and fortified his stomach with a generous *schnapps*. Then, fit for anything, he rode out with his men, sending ripples of good humour all down the line.

* * *

It was 8 A.M. when Wellington finished his business in the hut. He came out and for an hour paced up and down alone in front of his 'splendid Mansion' (as a Highlander called the hut), his left hand behind his back and in his right a switch which he sometimes gave a ruminative bite. The same observant Highlander calculated that his Grace was travelling at a speed of $3\frac{1}{2}$–4 miles an hour. He and

9. The detailed memoirs of Colonel von Reiche, Olbech and Kircheisen were all published after Wellington's death.

10. Gneisenau did not admit that Wellington's promise of assistance at Ligny had been subject to his not being attacked himself, and therefore regarded him as perfidious.

Müffling had just settled themselves on the grass when at 9 A.M. the first personal message of the day arrived from Blücher.[11] Old Marshal 'Vorwaerts' had gone backwards but was in great heart. What did Wellington intend?

Wellington intended to retreat—to stand—to fight. A year ago he himself had reconnoitred the open ground in front of the Forest of Soignes and the village of Waterloo. His engineers had been surveying the ridges to the south of Waterloo during the past weeks. That was where he had put his thumb on the Duke of Richmond's map. That was where he would defend Brussels—if Blücher could support him 'even with one corps only'.

The retreat began an hour later at 10 A.M., Wellington sending ahead his quartermaster-general, de Lancey, to mark out the army's positions.[12] Not everyone was happy to surrender the ground so heroically fought for the day before. Picton was surly to a degree, and later denounced the 'Waterloo' position as one of the worst ever chosen. Only his servant knew that he had had two ribs broken at Quatre Bras and his body was black and swollen under his uniform. The roads back to Brussels were already choked with wounded. Over-loaded carts broke down. Many soldiers put wounded comrades across their saddles and led their horses through the narrow street of Genappe. The tender-hearted Wheatley bundled beef and brandy out of commissary wagons at the risk of his life and loaded them with wounded. His cap was accidentally knocked off during the operation and out bounced a brown loaf. Lieutenant Jackson of the Staff Corps cleared a passage for the wounded higher up the road with the flat of his sword and swear-words of three languages.

Wellington covered his army's retreat with a strong screen of cavalry and artillery, including a few of the Congreve rockets which had given him so little satisfaction in the Peninsula. He had been at his most characteristic when the question of using these rockets was first mooted. Major Edward Whinyates, to whose troop they belonged, was sharply forbidden to take with him such poor substitutes for

11. Gordon's 7.30 A.M. news was not from Blücher; Houssaye says that Gordon got it from General Zieten's rear-guard, while Fitzroy Somerset says it came from some captured enemy vedettes. The two accounts are not incompatible (Houssaye, p. 194, and *Raglan MSS*, no. 24).

12. '. . . & he despatched Delancy . . . to make out a position in front of the Forest of Soignes, which the Duke proposed to take up with his Army' (*Raglan MSS*, no. 14).

guns. One of Whinyates's superior officers, however, dared to plead his cause with Wellington.

'It will break poor Whinyates's heart to lose his rockets.'

'Damn his heart, sir; let my order be obeyed.' After the big bark the Duke had promptly relented and allowed Whinyates to bring 800 rockets to Quatre Bras. Here they were, ready to prove themselves.

At intervals during the morning, Wellington rode forward and swept the Frasnes and Namur roads with his telescope. The French were so strangely quiet that for a moment an odd thought struck him: perhaps Ney like himself was retreating after all.

*   *   *

At Ligny and Frasnes also there was, if not a retreat, an unaccountable pause. Napoleon, tired and torpid despite seven hours' sleep, had begun the day badly by dictating one of his obscure messages to Ney. The order gained nothing in clarity after Soult had worked on it. Ney received the impression that Saturday 17 June was to be a day of rest and revictualling—apart from the occupation of Quatre Bras.

> *Should this prove impossible*, you must report at once all details and the Emperor will move in your direction. . . .

Ney's men were out requisitioning their breakfasts as usual, and Wellington was still at Quatre Bras, in force; its capture did indeed seem '*impossible*', unless the Emperor should arrive, as promised, with help. The Emperor, however, remained in a curiously detached though unusually agreeable mood until 11 A.M., speculating on war and peace, visiting the battlefield and threatening a Belgian peasant with hell-fire unless he succoured a wounded Prussian officer. Suddenly at 11 A.M. he awoke, as only he could, to the needs of the day. Marshal Grouchy was packed off with 33,000 men to shadow Blücher, having been earlier slapped down with the remark—'I will give you orders when I judge it to be convenient.' Grouchy should have seized the point that he was intended to shield Napoleon as well as shadowing Blücher. Happily for Wellington, Grouchy was not the man to comprehend strategic subtleties.

By noon Napoleon was at length advancing along the east–west *chaussée* to join Ney in the day's long-postponed attack. They were too late. At 1 P.M. a stray camp-follower, formerly attached to Wellington's army, brought astounding news from Quatre Bras. The village was empty. Wellington had flown.

Napoleon turned to d'Erlon and said with acid emphasis in front of Ney:

'*On a perdu la France.*'

*　　　*　　　*

It was Wellington's own cool, even carefree behaviour which had set the tone for the retreat. Anxious officers were cheered to see him sitting on the grass between reconnaissances, laughing over the tittle-tattle in the London newspapers. Once he lay down in his cloak and slept for a few minutes with the gossip columns of the *Sun* shading his face. General Alava joined him from Brussels in an apprehensive state. Was he still the same imperturbable Wellington who had never failed in Spain? The great man's first words to him set his mind at rest:

'*Etiez vous chez Lady Charlotte Greville hier soir?*'

When the Duke added that his defence of the new position at Waterloo would give those fellows the devil of a surprise, Alava knew for certain all was well.

The commander of the Horse Artillery, Augustus Frazer, had been with Wellington all along and did not need reassuring: 'These things will happen,' he wrote, 'and there will be jumblings just at first, but all will be very well.'

Waiting about for one's turn to retreat was an unpleasant experience, thought the Guards' young surgeon, John James. Just then Wellington and his staff trotted past. His smile and 'air of calm put heart into us all'.

When the order was given for the Guards to move off, Wellington felt that the testing operation was almost over.

'Well, there is the last of the infantry gone,' he said briskly, 'and I don't care.'

The time was 2 P.M. He turned abruptly to the commander of his rear-guard, Lord Uxbridge.

'No use waiting. The sooner you get away the better. No time to be lost.' And indeed something bright and shiny was beginning to emerge from the *chaussée*. Wellington thought it was bayonets. Uxbridge said lancers. Sir Hussey Vivian handed Wellington his own spy-glass. It was lancers. In a few moments the vision became vast and awe-inspiring: billows of startlingly white dust rolling through the vivid green trees, and marching columns glittering in the rays of a sickly sun that was fast being swallowed up by the inkiest, most pendulous thunder-cloud which Captain Mercer and his troop of horse-artillery had ever seen. An ominous wind rushed down from the north-west. A deep shadow had already swept over the British rear-guard. To complete the 'ballet of war', as Colonel Taylor of the 10th Hussars called it, a single, dark horseman whom Mercer at once recognized as Napoleon himself, stood silhouetted for an instant against the still brilliant fields to the south.

Suddenly there was a violent detonation and sheet of flame as the British guns opened. A second later the swollen storm-cloud, blasted by the concussion, burst apart with a flash and a roar like a gigantic battery, reducing the man-made cannonade to a whisper. Surgeon James thought this 'unique clap' showed nature was on the side of the French. He had not had the benefit of Peninsular campaigning, where it was well known that British victories were preceded by a deluge. Even Wellington, who knew the rains in India, had never seen such a storm. Others spoke of a tropical drenching, tubs, pitchers and walls of water.

'Captain Mercer, are you loaded?' yelled Uxbridge through the downpour and din.

'Yes, my lord.'

'Then give them a round as they rise the hill, and retire as quickly as possible.' Turning to Colonel Frederick Ponsonby of the 12th—

'Light dragoons, threes right, at a trot, march!' William Hay, who was in the leading squadron, had always been taught to lead on steadily, but it was utterly impossible when the word was constantly piped from behind, 'Faster, faster in front.'

Faster and faster they flew, firing and galloping, until many had safely squeezed through the dangerous bottle-neck of the single Genappe street—for Uxbridge dared not take his cavalry off the paved road into the surrounding fields. They had suddenly become a bubbling, hissing quagmire.

'Make haste!—make haste! for God's sake, gallop, or you will be taken!' shouted Uxbridge more vehemently than ever. Indeed the Lancers were on their heels, thrusting irresistibly at the 7th Hussars and only stopped and driven out of Genappe by the sabres of the Life Guards, led by the dauntless Captain Edward Kelly, who spurred twenty yards ahead of his troop and killed the Lancers' colonel and a private.

After this decided check, however, the waterlogged ground prevented the French from exhibiting their usual cross-country agility, and fighting on 17 June petered out in skirmishes and artillery duels where Major Whinyates's rockets played a picaresque part. The first rocket demolished a French gun and its crew, but all the rest either shot vertically into the air or wriggled sideways, one turning to the right about and chasing Captain Mercer up the Brussels road. Mercer on the whole agreed with Wellington's view of rockets, but Surgeon James, who escaped being chased, was deeply impressed by these wicked weapons: he found their sound alone 'more harsh and horrid than the thunder of the guns'.

Captain (later General) Mercer's rip-roaring story of the retreat—'a confused dream'—'wild'—'all blunder and confusion'—makes such good reading that it may have misled Houssaye into calling the retreat a 'mad flight'.[13] It was no such thing. The total casualty list of ninety-three killed, wounded and missing showed what an extraordinarily skilful operation it had been. After the first rush through Genappe, Uxbridge noted that 'the retreat was conducted at a walk'. Fitzroy Somerset did not disagree. Wellington, he wrote, 'proceeded leisurely towards Waterloo . . .'.

Napoleon had started too late and providence, in the shape of the weather, did not forgive.

*   *   *

On his leisurely progress that afternoon of 17 June, Wellington dined at the *Roi d'Espagne* in Genappe. A waiter overheard one of his aides explaining how the Prussian army would march from Wavre to join the English. This was hot news. A few hours later the waiter passed it on to Prince Jerome Bonaparte, ex-King of Westphalia and the Emperor's youngest brother, who slept that night in the *Roi d'Espagne*. Next morning Jerome informed Napoleon at Le Caillou, a farm farther up the Brussels road where he had spent the night of the 17th—with what results will appear in due course.

By the late afternoon of the 17th Wellington had passed Le Caillou

13. Houssaye, p. 149. Houssaye's book was published in 1895, Mercer's in 1870. Houssaye quotes from Mercer on p. 146. Mercer was a brilliant writer and something of a specialist in painting scenes of confusion.

and was approaching the ridges in front of Waterloo where he meant to do battle next day. On the first of these ridges stood the inn of *La Belle-Alliance*, to the right of the road.

At this point Lord Fitzroy Somerset enters the story with a most interesting but unforeseen disclosure about Wellington's strategy, forming part of his account of the Waterloo campaign apparently written in 1816:[14]

> ... on arriving near to La Belle Alliance He [the Duke] thought it was the position the Qr.M.Genl. would have taken up, being the most commanding ground, but He [de Lancey] had found it too extended to be occupied by our Troops, & so had proceeded further on & had marked out a position.

So much has been written about Wellington's inspired and highly individual choice of the crossroads on the Mont-Saint-Jean ridge for his Waterloo battle-ground, that it is hard to believe his first preference was for something different. Yet Somerset was close to Wellington and had long been renowned for his truthfulness, exact execution of his master's orders and accurate echo of his master's voice. The *Belle-Alliance* site would certainly have meant a much larger battle-field, though one not lacking in essential features such as reverse slopes, a good lateral road to the right (facing south) and tracks off to the left. Moreover, Wellington had made a point of not fortifying *à la* Torres Vedras whatever site he selected, for this would have given the show away to Napoleon. It is possible that his passion for preserving the elasticity and secrecy of his plans kept his colleagues as well as Napoleon in the dark.[15]

The *Belle-Alliance* position having been left to Napoleon (though

14. Somerset's MS has survived in (1) General Allan's diary quoted by Col. J. G. O. Whitehead by courtesy of Lt.-Col. Fitzgerald, 1935 (Allan replaced Somerset as Military Secretary, July 1815); (2) Lord Raglan's copy 3 April 1845, which concludes 'in addition to the above' Somerset wrote a note at 'Badminton—1816'.

15. Colborne relates how Wellington examined the ground fixed for the site of battle himself on 14 June 1815, and when someone asked if they were to throw up entrenchments he rapped out, 'no, of course not; that would show them where we mean to fight' (Moore Smith, p. 218). Sir John Jones says that Wellington selected 'the Waterloo positions' during the preceding spring and turned down entrenchments as they would force Napoleon to bypass them and attack Wellington's vulnerable right flank by Hal (Jones, vol. III, pp. 53–6).

of course in reverse, facing north instead of south) Wellington went on to climb the ridge at Mont-Saint-Jean and quietly enter his head-quarters in the village of Waterloo. He soon found, however, that his opponent was determined not to be kept in the dark any longer. The Emperor ordered some batteries to begin firing and the English incautiously made reply, thus revealing their position. Wellington began the evening in a raging temper.

Another, less successful attempt made soon afterwards by Lord Uxbridge to extract information probably tried the Duke's temper almost as much; this time his practice of giving short answers in order to preserve self-control was successful. Lord Uxbridge, who would be his successor as Commander-in-Chief if the finger of Providence were unexpectedly withdrawn, wished to know before he went to bed something of the great man's strategy. He issued, therefore, from the whitewashed cottage at Waterloo on whose humble door 'The Earl of Uxbridge' was written in chalk, and splashed through the downpour to the door on which was chalked 'His Grace the Duke of Wellington'. In some trepidation Uxbridge said his piece. The Duke listened to him in formidable silence. At the end of the recital he briefly asked:

'Who will attack the first tomorrow, I or Bonaparte?'

'Bonaparte.'

'Well, Bonaparte has not given me any idea of his projects: and as my plans will depend upon his, how can you expect me to tell you what mine are?' Nevertheless he did not want to break Uxbridge's heart any more than Whinyates's. He got up, put his hand on the general's shoulder and said encouragingly:

'There is one thing certain, Uxbridge, that is, that whatever happens, you and I will do our duty.'

Only a leader of moral grandeur could afford to preach such pragmatism.

In later years he used to dwell lovingly on the pragmatic theme, with special reference to his method of defeating the French marshals:

> They planned their campaigns just as you might make a splendid piece of harness. It looks very well; and answers very well; until it gets broken; and then you are done for. Now I made my campaigns of ropes. If anything went wrong, I tied a knot; and went on.

*   *   *

The rope had broken and been knotted several times already since the Waterloo campaign began, and there were still loose ends. He went to bed, according to Fitzroy Somerset, between 11 P.M. and midnight. He was still waiting to hear officially that 'Old Forwards' was going to knot them together. The final Prussian arrangements for support had in fact been made just as his talk with Uxbridge finished.

At 11 P.M. Blücher received confirmation from Müffling that Wellington was actually in position to give battle at Mont-Saint-Jean. Could he now expect at least one Prussian corps? After a last session with Gneisenau, Blücher summoned Hardinge and told him triumphantly,

'Gneisenau has given in! We are going to join the Duke.'

Then he showed Hardinge the draft of his despatch in reply to Wellington.

> Bülow's [IInd] Corps will set off marching to-morrow at day-break in your direction. It will be immediately followed by the [IVth] Corps of Pirch. The Ist and IIIrd Corps will also hold themselves in readiness to proceed towards you.

Next day Blücher repeated these lavish promises—double what Wellington expected—in a despatch written about 9.30 A.M. to Müffling: ill as he was, he had made up his mind to lead his troops himself against Napoleon's right wing. Rather than miss the battle, he added later, he would be tied to his horse. When Gneisenau was shown this glowing testament of faith by Blücher's aide-de-camp, he added a sour corrective in his own hand for Müffling. The Duke, that 'master knave', might still only be using Blücher to cover his army's retreat. Let Müffling 'penetrate Wellington's inmost thoughts and find out whether he really entertains the firm resolution of fighting in his present positions . . .'. By the time this ungracious document arrived, events had already answered Gneisenau's question.

Meanwhile Wellington at Waterloo either did not sleep when he had the chance (an unheard of procedure for him) or someone or something woke him before 3 A.M., for at that hour he was up again, writing letters.

Beginning with Houssaye, it has been universally assumed (though never proved) that the 'something' was Blücher's messenger bringing the despatch of 11 P.M. The distance between Blücher's headquarters, near Wavre, and Waterloo was fourteen miles. Though the roads were poor and the night execrable, a Prussian officer who was not too fat and did not lose his way should have reached Waterloo by 2 A.M.—as all the books say a Prussian officer did. The only evidence of soldiers who were close to Wellington, however, told a different story.

Both Fitzroy Somerset and Müffling stated that Blücher's despatch arrived much later next morning, Somerset at 6 A.M., Müffling at 9 A.M. Somerset wrote:

> About six o'clock the Duke got on Horseback; on the way to the front of the Line, He met a Prussian Officer who came from Blücher, in consequence of the Duke having the night before, sent to Him for one or two Corps of Prussians to support Him. Blücher promised to do so.

Houssaye, on whose account all others rest, brusquely dismisses Müffling's evidence as 'wrong'. Fitzroy Somerset's he had not seen, since it is now published for the first time. These two may yet turn out to have been nearest the truth. If so, this is how things went. Wellington was waiting at Waterloo at least up to 1 or 2 A.M., probably longer, on the 18th for Blücher's despatch—but not in growing anxiety. He relied on Müffling's arguments delivered at 9 A.M. on the 17th and no doubt repeated throughout the day, that Blücher was still strong enough to support him and would not let him down. The confident remarks of his aide at the *Roi d'Espagne* inn suggest he had received further assurances, amounting to unofficial confirmation, before nightfall. In this case, Houssaye's castigation of Wellington for waiting at Waterloo until the small hours instead of writing off Blücher and organizing a further retreat, is unjustified. 'Fortune had favoured him,' wrote Houssaye sternly and not overpleased with the goddess, 'but he had nevertheless remained too long expectant.' If Houssaye could have been convinced (by Somerset's evidence) that Wellington was to remain 'expectant' for yet another four hours, he would no doubt have felt still less warmly about the Child of Fortune. But whether the official confirmation arrived at 2 A.M., 6 A.M. or 9 A.M. on Sunday 18 June, makes little difference to the real point at issue. Was Wellington a lucky gambler? Or a strategist whose security was factually if not formally guaranteed, and who respected his veteran ally enough not to contemplate his being over-ruled at the last minute by a subordinate? Wellington did Blücher, and perhaps Gneisenau also, the honour of ignoring this possibility.

For whatever reason, Wellington rose between 2 A.M. and 3 A.M., according to Somerset. He had been called at the same time the night before. As the rain swished and gurgled round the rambling hostelry in which he was quartered and drummed on the small chapel opposite (soon to be enlarged, given a handsome dome and filled with memorial tablets) he pulled up his arm-chair to the two candles on his table and began to write. It was important to explain to persons in authority how to avoid putting too much strain on the rope and its knots. First, the Ambassador, Sir Charles Stuart, must be firm with the English population of Brussels during the coming crisis. Wellington warned Stuart that Napoleon might turn his right flank at Hal, in which case he would have to retreat and uncover Brussels. (There was no mention of his left flank being turned, showing that he counted on the Prussians here, either because Blücher's despatch had arrived or for the other reasons given above.) He continued to Stuart:

Pray keep the English quiet if you can. Let them all prepare to move [to Antwerp], but neither be in a hurry or a fright, as all will yet turn out well.

Next, the Duke of Berry must also be ready to move the French royal family to Antwerp (whose Governor was simultaneously warned to admit them and various ladies) but not a moment before the enemy had actually entered Brussels.

The instant Wellington's letter was received the Duke of Berry fled.

Then there was a personal letter to Lady Frances Webster.

Waterloo, *Sunday morning, 3 o'clock* June 18th 1815
My dear Lady Frances,
    ... We fought a desperate battle on Friday, in which I was successful, though I had but very few troops. The Prussians were very roughly handled, and retired last night which obliged me to do the same to this place yesterday. The course of the operations may oblige me to uncover Bruxelles for a moment ... for which reason I recommend that you and your family should be prepared to move to Antwerp at a moment's notice.
    I will give you the earliest information of any danger that may come to my knowledge; at present I know of none.

So far the knotted rope held.

23 Waterloo: The Finger of Providence

PROLOGUE

For the third night running the Duke had hardly any sleep. What he had was sound and dry. When he met his landlady next morning she was in tears over her danger. He slapped her cheerfully on the back:

'I answer for everything, no French person shall suffer today except the soldiers.'

To the majority of his army bivouacking in the open, the night of 17 June 1915 had demonstrated all the suffering of war and none of its grandeur. Even a Peninsular veteran like Wheatley of the King's German Legion spoke laconically of their 'miserable state'. The rain poured down ceaselessly, the ground became quaking mud. Coming through the rye was like navigating a waterfall.

Captain William Hay, Sergeant Edward Cotton and Ensign William Leeke, just seventeen years old, were three who believed in prayers before battle. Strength to do his duty was all Hay asked; Leeke, who was to grow up into an argumentative clergyman, thought there should be compulsory prayers for victory; Cotton, who later became a Waterloo guide, began his story with the injunction:

> Kneel, warrior, kneel; to-morrow's sun
> May see thy course of glory run.

If the army had knelt it would have been to pray for the rain to stop.

The redoubtable 52nd 'Light Bobs' whom Leeke had joined five weeks earlier, were encamped in soaking corn to the west of the Brussels road. All night long tethered horses kept breaking loose and galloping down the hill to the château of Hougoumont and then back again, making Leeke dream he was in a cavalry charge.

Below, in the Hougoumont enclosures, Private Matthew Clay and some of his comrades in the 3rd Foot Guards were sleeping on the side of a wet ditch that ran beside the orchard. Back along the ridge thousands upon thousands of bedraggled soldiers lay in their sodden lines, each under his dripping blanket, head on haversack, stomach yearning for the rations which were still on the commissariat wagons, splashing and grinding their way out from Brussels through the ruts and pools of the Forest of Soignes.

Some of the regimental doctors, in view of their likely work next day, felt particularly unhappy at the army's 'disastrous state'. Caked in mud, Assistant-Surgeon James had to settle down without knowing where his equipment had got to, lucky in having a thimbleful of brandy and slice of tongue. Assistant-Surgeon Gibney slept like a top huddled up with a bunch of the 15th Hussars, while another assistant-surgeon, John Smith of the 12th Light Dragoons, bivouacked without food, wine or water but warmed by a row of bonfires placed on the Ohain road behind the crest of the ridge, and fed with furniture and farm implements from the village of Mont-Saint-Jean. The glow was watched with pleasure from across the valley by Napoleon. He had been haunted by the fear that the leopards would elude him after all by fleeing to their ships. Now he knew they were still there.

Surgeon Smith fell asleep in a drain by the roadside, and as the night wore on the water gradually rose through his bundle of straw until he seemed to be lying at the bottom of a leaky boat.

If the Allies were miserable so were the French. Thanks to Napoleon's late start on the 17th, his soldiers were still taking up their positions long after darkness had fallen. Sergeant Dickson of the Scots Greys, who lay near the crossroads of Mont-Saint-Jean, listened all night to a rumbling like the wind in a chimney—the French wagons coming up. Napoleon's famous '*grognards*' grumbled as only they knew how, blaming the weather and their rationless state on treachery. Rather than lie down in seas of mud some of the soldiers slept on their horses' backs. It was not a good preparation for uphill charges next day.

*   *   *

For the civilians, the night before Waterloo was hardly more pleasant. Fanny d'Arblay and an English friend had failed to make their escape from panic-stricken Brussels on Saturday owing to the implacable heroics of Wellington's military commandant, who refused to issue passports.

'It is not for *us*, the English, to spread alarm, or prepare for an overthrow.' He complained also of the Bourbons' tameness.

'We want blood, Madam! What we want is blood!'

Cowed by the dreadful soldier's thunder, Fanny tottered home. At 6 A.M. on Sunday she was awakened by loud thumps and her friend calling:

'Open your door! There is not a moment to lose!'

Fanny's friend had received instructions to rush on foot to the wharf and go by barge to Antwerp. But when the two ladies arrived they heard all was lost: Wellington had commandeered every barge for the wounded and Boney was marching on Brussels.

'The Horrors of that night are not to be forgot,' wrote Caroline Capel from a rustic retreat outside the city: rumours that Wellington was defeated—their courtyard full of 'poor wounded drenched soldiers and horses'—Mr Capel resolved to move again though unable to get a conveyance to Antwerp—Caroline, expecting a baby, in despair—

> This has indeed come upon us like a Thief in the Night—I am afraid our Great Hero must have been deceived for he certainly has been taken by surprise.

At Ghent most members of Louis XVIII's makeshift Court could not bear to think of French armies either beaten or victorious. The King, however, summoned a council and declared:

'Let those who are afraid depart. For myself, I shall not leave here unless forced to do so by the march of events!'

The march of events suddenly gave him back the use of his legs; but now, the more he shuffled to and fro between chair and window, listening and peering, the more his fortitude ebbed. Next morning (the 18th) he was in no better shape than the Duke of Berry whose courier informed the Minister of the Interior, Chateaubriand, that all was lost.

'Bonaparte entered Brussels yesterday. . . .'

Among the wise virgins to reach Antwerp before the 'tumult, terror and misery' of a refugee avalanche, was Miss Charlotte Waldie. She arrived with the first crash of the thunder-storm and had to listen at midnight to a sinister hammering in the hotel room next door. The nails were being driven into the Duke of Brunswick's coffin. At dawn on the 18th she too heard the dismal refrain that all was lost. But instead of preparing to flee once more like the Capels and poor old Louis, she told herself firmly that Wellington had been despaired of once before, in Portugal. She clung to the thought of Torres Vedras.

*   *   *

On Sunday 18 June at 6 A.M. Wellington rode out from Waterloo village on his chestnut horse, Copenhagen, the thoroughbred which had carried him at Vitoria, the battles of the Pyrenees and Toulouse. His appearance was a tonic to the troops. Setting off along the ridge to inspect the positions taken up the night before, he began with Clinton's division on his extreme right and then moved back towards Hougoumont.

'Now Bonaparte will see how a general of sepoys can defend a position,' he said to Müffling. Soon afterwards he ran into the usually exuberant Harry Smith who had sent his Juanita to Brussels and needed cheering. The sight of the Duke so 'animated' on his noble horse, so cool and clear in his orders, so hawk-like in his watch upon the enemy, struck Smith as being 'delightful'. Wellington had extra loopholes made in the orchard wall and further work done on the garden wall and the rampart behind it. A battalion of Nassauers posted on the edge of the Hougoumont fields began to feel uncomfortably close to the gathering French. Finally they made off.

'Do you see those fellows run?' said Wellington to General Vincent, the Austrian attaché on his staff.

'Well, it is with these that I must win the battle, and such as these.' Then he galloped over and rallied them. When a few irreconcilables aimed shots at him as he rode off, he took no notice. It was only afterwards that he remarked how different the history of Europe might have been if one of 'those fellows' had been a better shot.

Some of his orders at Hougoumont were made on General Müffling's advice, who feared that this vital bastion on the army's right flank would prove untenable. Wellington reassured him.

'Ah, you don't know Macdonnell. I've thrown Macdonnell into it.' Colonel James Macdonnell of Glengarry and his Foot Guards were among the pick of Wellington's troops. None the less, Müffling still feared a dangerous movement by Napoleon.

'But how will it be if the enemy advances on the Nivelles road . . . on the English right wing?' His hint was followed, the Duke ordering an *abattis* to be thrown across the Nivelles road and drawing in his right wing at Braine l'Alleud closer to Hougoumont.

Why did he not also bring back the IIIrd Corps under the eighteen-

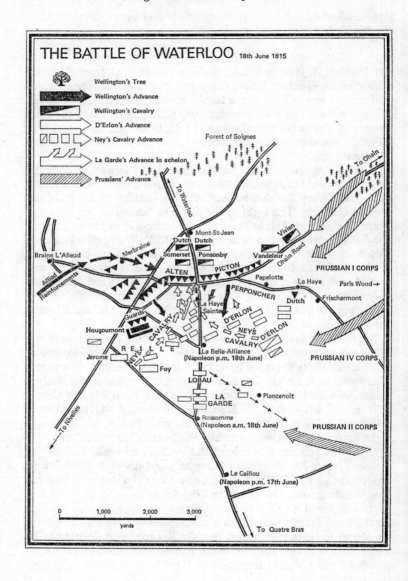

THE BATTLE OF WATERLOO 18th June 1815

Wellington's Tree

Wellington's Advance

Wellington's Cavalry

D'Erlon's Advance

Ney's Cavalry Advance

La Garde's Advance in echelon

Prussians' Advance

Forest of Soignes

To Ohain

To Waterloo

Mont-St-Jean

Vivian

Braine L'Alleud

Merbraine

Dutch Dutch

Somerset   Ponsonby

Vandeleur

Ohain Road

PRUSSIAN I CORPS

ALTEN   PICTON

Papelotte

La Haye

Paris Wood →

Allied
Reinforcements

PERPONCHER

Dutch

Frischermont

La Haye
Sainte

Guards

D'ERLON

Hougoumont

CAVALRY

NEYS

D'ERLON

Jerome

R E I L L E

CAVALRY

NEYS

La Belle-Alliance
(Napoleon p.m. 18th June)

PRUSSIAN IV CORPS

Foy

LOBAU

To Nivelles

LA
GARDE

Plancenoit

PRUSSIAN II CORPS

Rossomme
(Napoleon a.m. 18th June)

Le Caillou
(Napoleon p.m. 17th June)

0   1,000   2,000   3,000

yards

To Quatre Bras

year-old Prince Frederick of the Netherlands ten miles away, at Hal? Daylight showed clearly that the French were massing for a frontal, not a flank, attack.

Müffling said it was because Prince Frederick's corps became 'superfluous' once Wellington knew Blücher was going to support him with more than one corps of Prussians. Wellington himself noted in a memorandum of 1842 that he had sent a 'small detachment' to Hal. As things turned out this 'small detachment' of 17,000 men would have been far from superfluous at Waterloo. Three inter-related ideas were in his mind: he was still harping on the political effect of a turning movement against Brussels and perhaps still fearing a Belgian stab in the back; he needed a large reserve in case he had to retreat from Mont-Saint-Jean, when he would march to the right rather than straight through the Forest of Soignes; he mistakenly credited Boney with a healthy respect for 'that article', the British infantry, which would prevent him risking a head-on clash. Wellington always held that Napoleon ought to have gone for the Allied right.

About a mile to the east of Braine l'Alleud was the village of Merbraine, where Ensign Leeke was now eating his breakfast; at least, he had just received his ration of one biscuit and was putting a mess-tin of soup to his lips when an officer interrupted—

'Master Leeke, I think you have had your share of that.'

Sergeant Tom Morris of the 73rd, who as part of Colin Halkett's brigade was stationed next along the ridge after the rest of the Foot Guards, was too old a soldier to be caught like Leeke. He and his friend Sergeant Burton settled down to their grog ration which had now come up and was pleasantly augmented by the shares of Quatre Bras casualties. Why not keep part of this bonus for after the battle? suggested Burton. Tom was dubious.

'Very few of us will live to see the close of this day.' But Sergeant Burton had a veteran's intuitions.

'Tom, I'll tell you what it is; there is no shot made yet for either you or me.'

*   *   *

The Allied army, formed into squares like a chequer board with spaces between for deployment, seemed to those who like Ensign Gronow gazed along the ridge to form one solid human wall. In

reality the 'wall' was built of remarkably heterogeneous material.
One brigade in particular, Bylandt's Dutch–Belgians, stuck out like
a sore thumb. When the rest of the army were ordered to lie down
behind the crest, Bylandt's men stood forward prominently in front
of the ridge, looking 'very well', as Sergeant Dickson observed, in
their blue coats with orange facings, but an easy target for French
guns. Bylandt, as a Continental soldier, did not understand what
Houssaye calls Wellington's 'very peculiar tactics'. His men were
not trained to await the nerve-racking advance of an invisible enemy
lying down. When Bylandt did understand it was too late. Along the
rest of the front the weak units of the 'infamous army' were intermingled and aligned with the veterans.

*   *   *

Wellington's staff was by now swollen into a jingling, glittering
cavalcade, some forty strong, which included such determined camp-
followers as the elderly Duke of Richmond and his injured, fifteen-
year-old son. Wellington tried in vain to send these two home.
    'William, you ought to be in bed. Duke, you have no business
here.' The two simply moved off towards Picton's division farther
along the ridge. Besides his staff proper there were the foreign commissioners: Pozzo di Borgo, the Tsar's man, a Corsican whose
hatred for Bonaparte was personal; Alava; and Baron Vincent and
Baron Müffling representing Austria and Prussia. There was also a
swarm of aides including Captain Wedderburn-Webster of the 9th
Dragoons attached to Lord Uxbridge. 'They all seemed as gay and
unconcerned,' said Gronow, 'as if they were riding to meet the
hounds in some quiet English county.'
    From every part of the line came the same comments. Surgeon
James, stationed to the east of the crossroads with Lord Edward
Somerset's brigade of Household Cavalry, saw Wellington go by as
smart as if 'riding for pleasure'. Almost the same words as James had
used after Quatre Bras came to him again: 'the very sight of him put
heart into us all . . .'. Sergeant Cotton pitied the blue faces, long wet
beards and filthy clothes of his comrades in the 7th Hussars. Then
the smiling Duke and his staff came by and Cotton was proud to
observe that his leader required no glistening cascade of white
cock's feathers to give him distinction; only the four cockades of
Britain, Spain, Portugal and the Netherlands on a low cocked hat

worn as usual 'fore and aft'. (Bonaparte's hat was no more gaudy than Wellington's but worn square.) The Duke was in his comfortable civilian clothes: white buckskin breeches with tasselled top-boots and short spurs; a white stock, blue coat over the gold knotted sash of a Spanish field-marshal and his blue cape which he put on and off fifty times in the day. 'I never get wet when I can help it.' Though there were gleams of sun in some parts of the field it was still raining in others and it was not Wellington's policy to remain long in the same spot.

When he needed a command-post there was one available—the elm tree which stood at Mont-Saint-Jean in the south-western corner of the crossroads. As he stood by the 'Wellington Tree' his army was spread along the ridge on either hand, in front the infantry supported by artillery, the cavalry behind. Hougoumont, surrounded with fruit trees and woods, lay in the valley below him to his right, but hidden by rolling cornfields. Straight in front of him stood the white-walled farmhouse of La Haye Sainte a quarter of a mile down the Brussels high road which bisected the battlefield. With its garden, barn and dovecot over the gateway into the *chaussée*, it formed a bastion corresponding to Hougoumont, though not so strong. It was garrisoned by a detachment of the King's German Legion and further strengthened by a gravel pit on the opposite side of the road, held by the 95th Rifles.

Not far away Captain Mercer of 'G' Troop Horse Artillery spent a soaking night, though no one disturbed him by complaining. The 'Johnny Newcomes' who might have complained were afraid of being laughed at by the old Peninsular hands. Towards morning Mercer made a fire under a friend's umbrella: 'We lighted cigars and became—comfortable.' Across the road Johnny Kincaid bivou-acked against the wall of a cottage inside which his commander, Sir Andrew Barnard, was asleep. In the morning Kincaid brewed a huge kettle of sweet tea which he shared with the bigwigs as they passed up and down the *chaussée*. A cup went to the Duke. Another old soldier across the road from Mercer who could speak of comfort on this abysmal night was Sergeant Wheeler of the 51st. He and his friends sat on their knapsacks in the mud, 'wet and comfortable' because he had bought quantities of gin in Waterloo with money dropped by a fleeing Belgian the day before. Wheeler was happy to think that the enemy were just as badly off and that it had rained before Fuentes, Salamanca and Vitoria. 'It was always the prelude to a victory.' He might have added that it had rained all night before the battle of Agincourt exactly four hundred years ago.

On Wellington's extreme left, roughly level with La Haye Sainte, stood the bastions of Papelotte farm and La Haye, defended by Prince Bernhard's Nassauers. Here among a group of officers belonging to Sir Hussey Vivian's cavalry, Arthur Shakespear found himself making 'a good stewing' in the middle of the night out of two old hens and a sack of potatoes. He was so far out on the wing that he heard nothing of the rest of the army that night nor of Wellington next morning. His critical mind, however, was greatly occupied with the actual and probable errors of his chief, Lord Uxbridge. Arthur Kennedy, who usually had something to say about Wellington, 'the Great Lord', flattering or otherwise, had been jumped on by a horse while asleep under a hedge the day before and was feeling extremely sorry for himself. Nevertheless, his confidence was unbounded. They would soon be in Malplaquet, he felt sure, and this man who led them was 'our modern Marlborough'.

*   *   *

Wellington's intense activity, deliberately showing himself everywhere and heartening all who saw him by his habitual calm and unusual geniality, contrasted in every way with Napoleon's morning performance.

At 8 A.M. the Emperor, attended by Soult and others of his staff, breakfasted at Le Caillou off crested silver plate, which suggests that he fortified himself with more than the Duke's tea and toast. He had been relieved to see the Allied army still on Mont-Saint-Jean at dawn.

'Aha, now we've got them—those English!' But he postponed the hour for getting them from soon after daybreak, as originally designed, until 9 A.M. and finally until 1 P.m.; officially in order to let the ground dry. This delay was his first blunder of the day, mainly due to contempt for Wellington as an opponent and disbelief in the Prussian powers of recuperation. What was the hurry to get those English?

'We have ninety chances in our favour and not ten against.'

Marshal Soult, who knew a good deal more than Boney about Wellington, felt uneasy. He advised the immediate recall from the eastern flank of Grouchy's 33,000 men, to reinforce Napoleon against Wellington. The Emperor jeered.

'Just because you have been beaten by Wellington, you think he's a good general. I tell you, Wellington is a bad general, the English are bad troops, and this affair'—here Napoleon glanced towards the plates which had just been cleared from the breakfast table and replaced by maps—'this affair is nothing more than eating breakfast.' Soult looked grim.

'I earnestly hope so.'

Somewhat unwisely the Emperor next asked Reille, who had also experienced defeat in the Peninsula, what he thought of Wellington's army.

'Well posted,' replied Reille, 'as Wellington knows how, and attacked from the front, I consider the English infantry to be impregnable'—Napoleon began to look black—'owing to its calm tenacity and its superior aim in firing.' Reille hastily got on to the French advantages: 'If we cannot beat it by a frontal attack, we may do so by manoeuvring.' But the Emperor interrupted with a bark of incredulity and turned his back on Reille. His brother Jerome had just arrived from the *Roi d'Espagne* with the piece of gossip about a junction between Blücher and Wellington.

'Nonsense,' snapped the Emperor. 'The Prussians and English cannot possibly link up for another two days after such a battle,' and he went on to demonstrate how Grouchy would deal with what remained of the Prussians while he himself, after a cannonade and cavalry charge, would march straight at the English with his Old Guard.

'The battle that is coming will save France and will be celebrated in the annals of the world.'

It was now 10 A.M. and he at lasted drafted a reply to a vital despatch from Grouchy which had been lying about since he first read it six hours earlier. Grouchy announced his intention of following the Prussians towards Wavre in order to keep them away from Brussels and Wellington. This was Napoleon's chance urgently to redirect Grouchy away from Wavre and towards Waterloo. Instead, the opening sentence of his reply perfectly illustrated the looseness of his thinking (and of Soult's drafting) when it concerned the Prussian menace.

His Majesty desires you will head for Wavre in order to draw near to us. . . .

in the circumstances a plain contradiction, since Wavre lay north of

Grouchy and Napoleon ('us') to the west. Grouchy was also to 'push before him' the Prussians who were marching in 'this direction'—an operation which, taken literally, would mean Grouchy pushing the Prussians towards Wellington—and reach Waterloo 'as soon as possible'.

In this verbal fog Grouchy was to discover only three luminous words: 'Head for Wavre.' They were to prove fatal.

*   *   *

Not until 9 A.M. when the baggage was ordered to the rear did some of Wellington's soldiers realize that a battle was definitely to be fought that morning. From one end of the ridge to the other men were still cleaning their weapons and drying their scarlet tunics. Humourists in the ranks noticed that their white belts were already dyed blood-red.[1] The quickest method of cleaning weapons was to shoot them off into the air. Such waste of ammunition was to bring its nemesis later, particularly to the brave German riflemen in La Haye Sainte. Now the popping all along the plateau anticipated cheerful hours ahead. Crack riflemen expected to achieve one aimed shot a minute with their Baker rifles, for as long as required. The best musketeers would fire three or even four volleys in the same time (though really accurate only up to a range of 100 yards) with the sturdy 'Brown Bess' which had served the army almost unaltered since 1759; no comparable Continental weapon equalled it. When Wheatley had finished his cleaning at 10.30 A.M. he was allowed to lie down and rest, which he and the King's German Legion thankfully did. As the last regiments took up their positions behind the crest silence fell, broken only by a murmur of conversation like the sea on distant rocks which Cotton had noticed earlier. The popping had died away and there was no music or singing.

The Earl of Albemarle's sixteen-year-old son could not help wishing it would begin. He remembered his father once telling him about a conversation between himself and Henry Pearce, the Game Chicken, on the eve of a prize-fight.

'Well, Pearce, how do you feel?'

1. The same thing happened on 18 June 1965, when the 150th anniversary of Waterloo was celebrated on the battlefield. There was a torrential downpour just as the commemoration service began and in a few minutes all the white belts were red.

'Why, my Lord, I wish it was *fit*.' Young George did not feel much like a Game Chicken except in that one way—he wished the fight was fought.

There were several champion pugilists flexing their muscles along Wellington's ridge: Dakin and Shaw, for instance, the latter a six-footer in the Life Guards. Both had posed for Benjamin Robert Haydon, in their peaceful moments, Dakin sitting for one of the blood-stained grooms in *Macbeth*. His remains were soon to be found by his comrades looking the part only too well.

*   *   *

For those with steady nerves there was plenty to watch on the slopes opposite during the last hours of suspense. Wet ground and absent pillagers may have prevented Napoleon from beginning on time; he well knew how to fill the gap. Fear could maim the enemy almost as effectively as shot. As his regiments arrived they were deployed with a portentous display of power and noise. Their head-gear alone made them shine like gods and showed from what a variety of countries and peoples the conqueror had drawn his might. There were Lancers in red shapkas with a brass plate in front bearing the imperial N and crown and a white plume eighteen inches long, Chasseurs in kolbachs with plumes of green and scarlet, Hussars whose shakos carried plumes kaleidoscopically coloured according to their countless regiments, Dragoons with brass casques over tiger-skin turbans, Cuirassiers in steel helmets with copper crests and horse-hair manes, Carabiniers all in dazzling white with tall helmets of a classically antique design, Grenadiers of the Old Guard in massive, plain bearskins towering above powdered queues and ear-rings of gold. Against the dark, menacing background of the Imperial Guards' long blue coats thousands of pennants fluttered and brilliant uniforms flaunted facings of scarlet, purple and yellow, big bright buttons, trimmings of leather and fur, gold and silver fringes, epaulettes, braid, stripes.

Many a young Dutch–Belgian soldier gazed at the nest of beautiful serpents across the valley wishing his country were still on their side. Wheatley noticed a new English recruit staring as if in a trance, the muscles on his round, chalk-white face quivering. Yet all this display was absorbing, even exhilarating to the British veterans. A thrill of excitement shot through Sergeant Cotton at the thought that two such noble antagonists as Wellington and Napoleon were to meet at last; Sir Hussey Vivian, commander of cavalry, later referred to the tyrant almost affectionately as 'the little hero'. Kincaid listened with interest to the soldiers' shouts of '*Vive l'Empereur!*' as they filed past Napoleon, who had moved forward to a command-post at Rossomme, and to the *rub-a-dub* and *tantarara* of their drums and trumpets. It was lucky, reflected Sergeant Dickson, that a shaft of sunlight had burst through the mist in front of him and allowed him to see the beautiful breastplates of his foes.

At 10 A.M., while his men were watching the French spectacle unfold, Wellington's sharp eyes had detected Prussian advance guards away to the east, on the fringe of Paris Wood. Clearly they had not got far on their march to Waterloo. Yet he still expected them to arrive by early afternoon. He did not know that Bülow's fresh IVth Corps, ordered to set off first, had been posted *behind* the other three, holding them up and themselves obstructed by a fire in Wavre and the difficult country beyond.

Napoleon was about to order the cannonade. He had at last brought into line 71,947 men with 246 guns in support. Opposite him were Wellington's 156 guns and 67,661 men: a total of nearly 140,000 men and over 400 guns, not to mention 30,000 horses, all crammed into under three square miles. Wellington had seen a mass of troops squeezed into a small space at Assaye; never anything like this.

*   *   *

At 11.25 A.M. the French guns opened up with an ear-splitting roar. Within a few minutes the shredding mists were thickened and deepened into a poisonous fog of black smoke, as the Allied gunners replied with their cannon grouped between the regiments along the edge of their hill, many in embrasures cut in the hedges of the Ohain road. The French bombardment was particularly heavy on Wellington's right in the direction of Hougoumont. Violent as it was, however, the attack on Hougoumont was planned only as part of a diversionary operation to weaken Wellington's centre by forcing him to draw away reinforcements. Over on the left wing, Prince Bernhard of Saxe-Weimar and his Nassauers were dealing with a similar though less determined demonstration against Papelotte and La Haye. It was exactly noon by Major Chalmer's watch (probably fast) when the shells began to fall near the 52nd. The innocent young Leeke firmly believed that the first shell of all had been aimed personally at the Duke. It was true that Wellington, with his battlefield intuition, had stationed himself above Hougoumont on the right, beside the Guards, before the action began. He was thus something of a target from the very outset, but also in a key position to direct Hougoumont's defence. He was where he was needed.

Leeke himself soon saw something swishing through the corn. His colour-sergeant was instructive.

'There, Mr Leeke, is a cannon-shot, if you never saw one before, Sir.'

Sergeant Wheeler was surprised by the intensity of the attack: 'grape and shells were dupping [*sic*] about like hail, this was devilish annoying'. Then the bugles sounded to lie down and Wheeler and the 51st gladly did so. Some of Wellington's staff were seen to disperse over the field soon afterwards in response to their chief's remark, as Leeke heard, that 'some of the generals were too thick on the ground'. A gaggle of generals not only attracted cannon-balls but could be hampering in other ways.

While the cannonade boomed and belched at Waterloo its reverberations travelled over the low hills and disturbed Marshal Grouchy, who had just reached the strawberry stage of a late breakfast. He and his staff went into the garden and put their ears to the ground. General Gérard was emphatic:

'We ought to march to the guns.'

Grouchy objected.

'A rear-guard affair.'

Again Gérard listened:

'The ground trembles under us.'

Smoke could now be seen in the west and a tetchy dispute developed in which Grouchy, the more he was pressed to follow the sound of the guns the more he resolved to follow Napoleon's orders— 'head for Wavre'. (Wavre was still some miles away.) In the end Grouchy won the argument—and Napoleon lost. For if Grouchy had turned half left instead of butting on ahead he must have cut the Prussians' line of march. Once again a serious situation, created by Napoleon himself, demanded a Rebecque to reinterpret his orders. Once again the man on the spot failed him.

*   *   *

11.30 A.M.: HOUGOUMONT[2]

There is something so ponderously classical about the battle of Waterloo that it comes as no surprise to find it unrolling in five acts. Prince Jerome Bonaparte took a hand in moulding the drama and transformed Hougoumont into the first act, when it should have been part of the prologue.

The Guards by whom Wellington was standing when the struggle for Hougoumont opened were part of the Prince of Orange's Corps. Wellington began by giving all his orders through the Prince, for transmission to divisional and other commanders. When 'things got on', as Fitzroy Somerset noted, the Duke gave his orders direct. At Hougoumont things got on fast and furiously.

Prince Jerome, Napoleon's youngest brother, who was in command of the attack, saw a unique chance for glory and snatched at it greedily. Four splendid regiments of veterans, protected by swarms of skirmishers, were launched against the château. They fought their way obstinately but bloodily through the woodlands, out into the orchard and up to the château walls. Here a stream of bullets through every loophole brought them down in heaps. From inside the Hougoumont buildings, Nassauers, Hanoverians and Guards under Macdonnell poured their volleys into the besiegers. At the same time Wellington ordered Bull's battery of howitzers which he had himself led into position close to the back of the château, to begin the delicate task of firing shrapnel over the defenders' heads into the besiegers beyond. He knew he could trust the gunners to make no mistakes. He was right. Their fire allowed the Allied infantry in front to counter-attack, recapture the orchard and even some coppices. Hougoumont was once more secure.

Jerome now had a choice of by-passing this stubborn bastion or blowing it to pieces. He did neither, but summoned fresh infantry, against General Reille's advice, to support him in another bull-headed assault. Napoleon did nothing to stop him.

At first there was a savage moment of success. A gigantic subaltern named Legros and reinforced with the nickname of *l'Enfonceur*, the Smasher, stove in a panel of the great north door and followed by a handful of wildly cheering men, dashed into the courtyard. Pandemonium broke out. The defenders slashed and hewed at the invaders in desperate hand-to-hand duels. But the real thing was to

2. The times given for the acts of phases of Waterloo are approximate.

prevent any more of the enemy from entering the yard. Five powerful Coldstreamers—Macdonnell, three other officers and a sergeant—threw themselves bodily against the huge door and slowly, slowly, by main force pushed it back against the pressure outside. This done they turned their attention to the invaders. Soon not a single Frenchman remained alive except for a drummer boy who stood forlorn, having lost all his friends including his drum. Private Clay entered the yard in time to make the drummer comfortable in one of the outbuildings where the wounded of both sides lay in rows, and to see Macdonnell, his face splashed with blood, carrying a massive beam to barricade the doors.

'The success of the battle of Waterloo depended on the closing of the gates of Hougoumont.' So said Wellington afterwards.

Among the heroic five was Henry Wyndham, who had opened the door of King Joseph's coach at Vitoria. Now he shut a door to more purpose. It was said afterwards by his niece when she found herself sitting in a draught, that no Wyndham had ever closed a door since Hougoumont.

Jerome's obsessive reaction to this second repulse was to throw in even more battalions, this time drawing on Foy's fresh division. With extraordinary confidence and economy, Wellington replied by sending down only four extra companies of the Guards.

'There, my lads, in with you, let me see no more of you.'

Though they could not hold the woods, the balance of Hougoumont was restored for the third time. Still Jerome would not let go. The affair, begun as a feint, was destined eventually to suck from Napoleon's main army the best part of two divisions to one brigade of Wellington's. Despite Wellington's advantage, Napoleon should have put a stop to the fighting at Hougoumont, after the first desperate one-and-a-half hours.

It was now 1 P.M., time for Wellington to move from the spot where he had played his masterly hand since 11.30 A.M. Hougoumont could be reasonably regarded as impregnable, though it was never out of his thoughts. Other sectors of the battlefield were far from impregnable. It was towards one of these that the Emperor was about to direct his great push. Wellington put spurs to Copenhagen and the chestnut horse carried him up over the rolling cornfields to his command-post at the crossroads of Mont-Saint-Jean. Before the second act could begin, however, there was an unexpected flurry off-stage.

The Emperor, still on his high bank at Rossomme, surrounded by his staff, decided on a sweep of the distant hills with telescopes before they were blotted out by smoke.

Immediately they all saw it. The black line over by Chapelle-Saint-Lambert on the edge of the wood. A cloud shadow? A row of trees? Napoleon knew at once it was soldiers, and in a few minutes that it was the vanguard of Bülow's IVth Corps. The Emperor had just drafted for Grouchy another instalment of the usual mysterious instructions—'keep manoeuvring in our direction . . . I do not indicate to you any special direction'—now he added a postscript in a different tempo: 'Do not lose a minute to draw nearer to us and to join us and crush Bülow. . . .' At the same time he revised the odds. 'This morning we had ninety odds in our favour.' They had shortened but—'We still have sixty against forty. . . .' And to make sure that they did not shorten any more he sent off in support of Grouchy two cavalry divisions and Lobau's whole VIth Corps. That meant well over 50,000 men (counting those at Hougoumont) tied up and nine hours of daylight used up; for it was already half past one. Napoleon, Grouchy and Jerome had made serious mistakes. Could d'Erlon and Ney redeem them?

*　　*　　*

1.30 P.M.: THE INFANTRY DEFEATED

Ney's great advance had been heralded by a renewed cannonade, beginning at 1 P.M. 'One could almost feel the undulation of the air from the multitude of cannon-shot,' wrote Wheatley. A battery of no less than eighty-four guns, twenty-four of them Napoleon's wicked and beautiful daughters, the twelve-pounders, was ordered to soften up the enemy's left-centre and centre aligned on the high ground to either side of the crossroads. Unfortunately for Napoleon, the ground was already too soft. Many cannon-balls buried themselves instead of ricocheting and sent up nothing but a volcano of mud. Most of Wellington's troops in any case had taken cover on the reverse slopes; only Bylandt's exposed Dutch–Belgians suffered heavy losses.

At 1.30 P.M. Napoleon moved to his most forward post at *La Belle-*

Alliance and ordered the advance. Ney passed on the word to d'Erlon, and d'Erlon's magnificent corps of 16,000 men began their march down into the smoke-filled valley and up again towards the plateau of Mont-Saint-Jean, all burning to revenge themselves for the frustrations of Quatre Bras and Ligny. As Wheatley watched them approach a chill ran along his spine. These 'gloomy bodies' gliding down the slopes opposite, 'disjointing then contracting, like fields of animated clods . . . had a fairy look and border'd on the supernatural in appearance'. A German officer of the King's German Legion brought him back to earth with a cheerful clap on his shoulder.

'That's a battle, my boy! That's something like a preparation!'

The formation of d'Erlon's divisions added to their daunting look: three out of the four drawn up in dense phalanxes, 200 files wide and twenty-four to twenty-seven deep. Yet the men who had fought and conquered at Bussaco could have told them it would not do. There were better ways of using these intrepid men than in unwieldy columns through which Allied cannon-shot could plough to three-quarters of their depth, while their own fire-power was restricted to the first two ranks and the whole so tightly packed that they could not deploy. As they began to mount the slopes, greasy mud and long twists of rye broke their impetus.

Nevertheless their first onslaught was worthy of the *Grande Armée*. The Germans defending La Haye Sainte were driven from the orchard and garden into the farm buildings and there isolated. Wheatley marvelled at the 'gigantic fellows' among the detachment of Cuirassiers operating against the defenders' flanks. It was thanks only to the German Legion's valour that La Haye Sainte was isolated, not overrun.

On swept d'Erlon's infantry, having driven out Prince Bernhard's men from Papelotte and La Haye, and forcing the 95th Rifles from the gravel pit. Then they crashed into Bylandt's light brigade, already badly shaken by the cannonade. A few wild shots were all the Dutch–Belgians managed. With every one of their officers above the rank of major either killed or wounded, they were withdrawn according to some accounts, according to others they broke and fled. Whichever it was, the survivors retired in disorder, booed by the Cameron Highlanders as they passed. (Corporal Dickson of the Scots Greys did not agree with the booing: he considered the fugitives to be more Bonapartists than cowards.) Throughout the rest of the battle they camped in the Forest of Soignes, quietly smoking, cooking and waiting for the result. At least, as Wellington himself conceded, none of his foreign troops deserted to the enemy.[3]

The situation on the crest was critical. But Picton's division of splendid infantry were only waiting to spring up and fight. Picton gave the word. His Peninsular commanders, Pack and Kempt, dashed forward.

'Ninety-second, you must advance!' shouted Sir Denis Pack to the Gordons. 'All in front of you have given way.' His brigade had been reduced to 1,400 by the fighting at Quatre Bras, but the Gordons, Black Watch and 44th flung themselves with bayonets on 8,000 French, while Kempt's brigade poured in volleys at close range. Sir Thomas Picton led Kempt's front line himself.

'Charge!' he roared, waving his sword. 'Hurrah! Hurrah!' Then to Kempt as the Gordons staggered under the weight of d'Erlon's mass,

'Rally the Highlanders!' Those were his last words. A bullet pierced his famous top hat, worn to protect his eyes, and struck him on the temple. He fell off his horse stone dead.[4]

Suddenly the Gordons were aware of huge grey horses thundering down on top of them with wild, exultant greetings.

'Hurrah, Ninety-second! Scotland for ever!' Some of the Gordons were knocked flying, others opened their ranks to let the horsemen through and a few gripped their comrades' stirrups and were carried along in the mad whirlwind to share for a few moments the charge of the Scots Greys, which itself was part of the greatest thunderbolt ever launched by British cavalry.

Wellington had seen from his tree that Picton's counter-attack must be overwhelmed by sheer numbers without immediate support. Indeed to Napoleon, tramping up and down at his post with his hands behind his back or stopping to take a large pinch of snuff, victory

3. The behaviour of Bylandt's light troops is still a matter of controversy. Two distinguished historians, F. de Bas and Count de T'Serclaes de Wommersom (*La Campagne de 1815 aux Pays Bas*, vol. II, pp. 142–6) have put the Dutch–Belgian case: that the brigade was ordered to the rear after appalling casualties. They attribute the story of *lâcheté*—cowardice—to Siborne, and upbraid Houssaye for resurrecting it in his *1815 Waterloo*. Fortescue, however, who greatly admired the Dutch–Belgian historians and re-examined the whole question, came to the sad conclusion that the broken brigade did indeed flee and failed to return.

4. The hat, with a bullet-hole near the junction of crown and brim, is in the National Military Museum, Sandhurst.

seemed in sight. It was then that Lord Uxbridge ordered a double advance of the Union and Household Brigades of heavy cavalry, the one under Sir William Ponsonby on the left, the other under Lord Edward Somerset, Fitzroy's brother, on the right.[5] Wellington personally led forward the Life Guards, with a resonant command to their officers:

'Now, gentlemen, for the honour of the Household troops.' As the sixteen-year-old John Edwards, field-trumpeter to Somerset, raised his bugle ready to sound the Charge—ten compelling blasts climbing in threes to the long, insistent G—the excitement was unbearable. Suddenly a martial-looking civilian, whom some Irish troopers recognized as the Duke of Richmond, popped up from behind the hedge and found himself shouting:

'Go along, my boys! now's your time!' It was enough for the Inniskillings. They took wings. Lord Uxbridge, who should have remained behind to throw in the reserves when necessary, was drawn irresistibly into the first line and led the charge of the Household Cavalry himself. 'To Paris!' shouted Colonel Fuller as the Royals charged.

In they went like a torrent shaking the very earth, or so it seemed to Captain Hay. The Life Guards and King's Dragoons, wearing the classical helmets with horse-hair crests and plumes designed by the Prince Regent, smashed up against Travers' Cuirassiers like a wall, and the sound of British swords on French breastplates reminded Sergeant Robertson of a thousand coppersmiths at work. Lifeguardsman Shaw cleft a skull so violently that the face 'fell off like a bit of apple'. Big men on big horses everywhere bore back the lighter French until they turned and fled, some of them bearing left and tearing madly into their own infantry which the Union Brigade had already sent flying. The French horses were blown. All had galloped uphill; some had carried sleeping troopers on their backs all night. The British were not only fresh but fierce, as Corporal Dickson realized when his Rattler, one of a long line of giant grey horses with flowing manes and heads down, dashed at the sunken Ohain road.

I felt a strange thrill run through me, and I am sure my noble beast felt the same, for, after rearing a moment, she sprang forward,

5. The Union Brigade was so called from its combination of English, Scottish and Irish regiments—Royals, Scots Greys and Inniskillings. In the Household Brigade were the Life Guards, King's Dragoon Guards and Blues.

uttering loud neighings and snorting, and leapt over the holly hedge at a terrific speed.

Wellington's cavalry, like d'Erlon's infantry, had been deeply chagrined at missing the battle of Quatre Bras. Now Dickson's 'strange thrill' swiftly became in all of them an ungovernable frenzy. To swarm over the valley was nothing. Up they thundered on the other side, on and on, deep into the enemy lines. Buglers sounded the Rally—the imperious, staccato call that was meant to halt and gather the men. No one listened. For the few who retired or herded the haul of prisoners to the rear there were thousands who went completely out of control, equally ready to perform deeds of matchless valour or unparalleled folly. Two eagles were captured and fifteen guns in Napoleon's great battery disabled, while the French gunners sat on their limbers and wept. It was the colonel of the Scots Greys himself who shouted that they should take it out of the battery which had done so much harm. Rattler went as mad as her master, biting and tearing at everything in her way, until she dropped down from her many wounds, apparently dead.

'Those terrible grey horses, how they fight,' said Napoleon on his mound. Then he watched with equal interest the moment of retribution.

Dickson saw all at once that the whole valley behind them was flooded with French troops. They were cut off.

'Come on, lads; that's the road home!' Dickson was lucky to acquire a riderless horse and burst through into his own lines—even to find a chastened Rattler waiting for him there. Out of 300 of his comrades, 279 failed to return and sixteen out of twenty-four officers. Their colonel was last seen with both arms shot off and the bridle in his teeth. Dickson recognized Sir William Ponsonby lying in the valley stabbed to death by lances, his open coat showing a locket with his wife's portrait. Frederick Ponsonby who had come to the 'heavies'' rescue with the 12th Light Dragoons was nowhere to be seen and was presumed killed. In losing only his horse and the flap of his collar from a cannon-ball, Edward Somerset was most fortunate. Young John Edwards also survived, together with his bugle, which now hangs among the battle honours in the Household Cavalry Museum at Windsor. Beside the bugle is a bullet extracted from the leg of that Captain Edward Kelly who had led so gallantly at Genappe. Three horses were shot under him in the great Waterloo charge before he himself fell. 'My dearest dear love,' he wrote to his wife next day. He was alive. But there was little joy. 'All my fine Troopers knocked to pieces. . . .'

*   *   *

How did Wellington's account stand? D'Erlon's first great attack had been defeated but at a fearful cost: 4,500 British and Dutch–Belgian infantry dead and 2,500 cavalry, a quarter of the whole. Though Wellington personally welcomed back the Life Guards with a lift of his cocked hat and a warm, 'Guards! I thank you', next day the Household Cavalry were to receive warnings against impetuosity mingled with his renewed thanks. Uxbridge never forgave himself for losing control. 'It was all dash,' wrote Arthur Shakespear bitterly. He had ridden in with Vivian's light cavalry to shepherd back the remnants.[6] Yet Uxbridge's fault was endemic in British cavalry. It cannot have surprised Wellington. Whether or not it crossed his mind that the safe Combermere would not have fallen into the trap, he said nothing.

On the positive side, no cavalry had ever before routed so great a body of infantry in formation. As the village clocks at Mont-Saint-Jean struck three, not a live Frenchman was to be seen on the ridge. Papelotte and the gravel pit had changed hands again and the bastion of La Haye Sainte stood firm. So did Hougoumont.

*   *   *

Hougoumont had received such a terrible visitation at 3 P.M. that the peasants universally believed it was saved by a miracle. Haystack, outbuildings and chateau were all set on fire by howitzers, the wounded of both sides burnt to death in the barn and the horses in the stables. Wellington saw the smoke and flames. Always concerned for his right flank, he sent over a parchment slip of instructions, which still survives.[7] They were to hold on as long as possible but without endangering lives from falling timbers.

6. Whinyates's rockets also helped to cover the heavy cavalry's retreat, thus providing a nice touch of irony: the type of charge of which Wellington always disapproved was succoured by the type of artillery he approved of equally little.

7. Four of these Waterloo slips have survived, written in pencil on asses' or goatskin which could be wiped clean and used again. They are now in the Wellington Museum, Apsley House.

The flames stopped abruptly in the chapel, at the foot of the cross. Here, and in a few other undamaged corners, the defiant garrison clung on.

At the same time (3 P.M.) Napoleon learnt that his own miracle was not to happen. A message from Grouchy showed that if any fresh troops reached the field of Waterloo they would not be his.

Napoleon came forward from Rossomme to *La Belle-Alliance* and sharply ordered Ney to take La Haye Sainte now—before the Prussians arrived.

Wellington had just had his first glimpse of the Prussian vedettes, at about 2.30 P.M. Never had he watched a troop movement with such desperate concentration.

> The time they occupied in approaching seemed interminable; both they and my watch seemed to have stuck fast.

In Brussels the coming of one man only appeared certain. Every rush of stragglers into the city was thought to be Napoleon himself or his vanguard. All the morning Georgiana Lennox had walked up and down, unable to sit still. A great victory dinner, she heard, was being prepared for the Emperor.

*　　　*　　　*

3.45 P.M.– 5 P.M.: THE CAVALRY REPULSED

With possession of La Haye Sainte, Napoleon could hardly fail to break Wellington's centre. It was Ney's duty to take it. Left to decide for himself how it should be done, Ney thought of a positive horde of light cavalry. The preliminary cannonade must match the cavalry in volume and terror.

'We had nothing like this in Spain, Sir,' said a white-faced sergeant-major to his superior officer as the tempest of metal tore into the Allied ranks. Wellington's lighter and fewer artillery blazed away in reply but the infantry had much to endure. Though all could lie down, many could not escape the varieties of death that came whistling out of the smoke. A surgeon with Wellington's artillery found his own retort to what Captain Mercer called 'the heavy answers': he scrambled away on hands and knees under a silk umbrella 'like a great baboon'.

In the rear, some ammunition wagons blew up, but though Mercer could see a great pillar of smoke spreading into a mushroom-head, the event was quite soundless. 'Never had the oldest soldiers,' wrote General Charles Alten of the King's German Legion, 'heard such a cannonade'; indeed it was the mightiest that the world had so far known.

Part of the Allied line was drawn back by Wellington a hundred yards. This partial withdrawal combined with the streams of wounded, prisoners and stragglers going to the rear, looked to Ney like a retreat. It was the moment to send 4,500 horsemen into what he firmly believed would be a pursuit. On his side Wellington realized as the French artillery slackened that the unbelievable was about to happen. Ney was going to attack his still unbroken infantry with light cavalry alone.

The supernatural impression of the French army's earlier advance, felt by Wheatley, was caught independently by Victor Hugo in describing Ney's cavalry attack.[8] He called it 'a prodigy': a prodigy crawling over the battlefield in two columns, 'undulating and swelling like the rings of a polyp'; through rents in the vast veil of black smoke the cuirasses could be seen, 'smooth and shining as the hydra's scales'. To most of the British, however, this mounted host was as beautiful as the sea—and as helpless, when it dashes itself against a wall of rock.

'Prepare to receive cavalry!' The order rang out along the ridge and Wellington's infantry formed into squares. The artillery he instructed to go on firing until the very last moment and then to make a dash for the nearest square, bowling along with them one wheel from each immobilized gun. The squares were ready and resolute when the third act of Waterloo began.

Up through the deep, sucking mud pounded the French horses, forced to hurry their pace in order to keep moving at all. Grape and canister cut hideous swathes, but the living rode on over the wounded and dead, laughing all at once to see abandoned cannon and British gunners running away. Exclamations of delight broke from Napoleon's watching staff:

> The English are done for! . . . Their general is an ignoramus . . . he has lost his head. Hold on—look! They are leaving their guns.

8. *Les Misérables* was first published in 1862, Wheatley's contemporary diary in 1964.

Now the squares were only thirty yards away. Pistols cracked, sabres flashed and with blood-curdling yells the French horsemen gathered themselves together to overwhelm the enemy, who by the laws of Napoleonic warfare should already be paralytic with terror and on the point of dissolution. Next moment volleys of musketry lashed men and horses at close range with a fiery hail; horses crashed on their riders, riders toppled and reeled, riderless horses plunged into the mêlée to increase the disorder, tumult and din.

Wellington's veterans had not fought for five years through the Peninsula for nothing. This 'cold infantry', wrote Hugo as if the Duke had cast his own peculiar spell over his men, 'remained impassive'. The front ranks knelt, the butt ends of their muskets resting on the ground and *chevaux de frise* of bayonets lacerating the French horses with cruel cuts. Charge upon charge swirled round the squares trying, failing to find a way in. Above the sharp knives two deadly lines of muskets fired and reloaded and fired again.

Inside the squares all was horror: stench of powder and burnt cartridge-papers, patches of blood-stained ground reserved for field-hospitals, piles of dead. To the outward eye they were unmoved: wasted, no doubt; but every time a red-coat fell in his death-agony, his comrades dragged him inside the square and closed the ranks.

'Keep your ground, my men!' To Corporal Lawrence it was a mystery how the casualties in the 40th rose and rose and yet they never lost an inch of ground. Whenever Wellington saw an opening he ordered his cavalry to counter-attack.

At last Ney called off his shattered columns to reform. Immediately the Allied artillerymen sprang back to their guns and fired into the enemy's backs. Why were those guns not disabled? The French might have dragged them away, spiked them, tipped them into the hollow road or just destroyed their sponges. They did nothing and all Wellington's 'captured' batteries stood ready to shoot down yet more brave horsemen when they charged again. Altogether Wellington's confidence was greater at the end than at the beginning of the first wave of cavalry attacks. He turned to his aide-de-camp, Colonel James Stanhope, and asked the time.

'Twenty minutes past four.'

'The battle is mine; and if the Prussians arrive soon, there will be an end of the war.'

He had heard the first Prussian guns on the fringe of Paris Wood.

★　　　★　　　★

The idea of another series of charges tried the Emperor hard, indeed he condemned Ney for launching the first wave an hour too soon. But 'the bravest of the brave' must be supported, even though the day's events had injected a dose of frenzy into his admirable courage. A huge addition of 5,000 heavy cavalry was ordered forward under Kellerman, the last of Ney's reserve. As at Quatre Bras, Kellerman expostulated at such recklessness, but while he was still arguing one of his own subordinates without waiting for orders dashed into the fray. Such was the madness generated on both sides at Waterloo.

Wellington, meanwhile, galloped up and down strengthening his line and encouraging his men. Numbers of his 'young gentlemen' had begun to lose hope, though his Peninsular officers like Andrew Barnard never doubted the Duke would win. 'We had a notion,' said Barnard afterwards, 'that while he was there nothing could go wrong.'

*   *   *

When Ney's second wave of attacks was launched, still head-on and now so tightly packed that many horses were lifted bodily from the ground—no manoeuvring, no mobile artillery, no foot-soldiers— then at last the Duke realized Napoleon had never done him the honour of studying his tactics in the Peninsula. His British infantry, the best in the world, were to be pulverized like any Continental militia before 1814.

'Damn the fellow,' he said turning to Barnard, 'he is a mere pounder after all.'

Stylized as a tapestry but violent as a tornado, the poundings repeated themselves endlessly. One square claimed to have received twenty-three attacks, though the average was seven or eight. Bullets drummed on breastplates, sabres clashed with bayonets; ever more squadrons came hissing over the slippery steaming plateau, eddied round and behind the squares and fell back, their force spent, into the valley.

> *On came the whirlwind—steel gleams broke*
> *Like lightning through the rolling smoke.*

That was how Sir Walter Scott imagined it afterwards. At the time the men in the squares simply said, 'Here come these fools again!'

A demented Ney was seen through a rent in the fog beating an abandoned British gun with his sword. His fourth horse had been killed under him. For brief, frozen moments the squares and horsemen seemed to be aimlessly intermingled, incapable of deciding what to do next. One of these moments dragged out into a 'dreadful pause' lasting a quarter of an hour, as George Chad later learnt from the Duke, with neither side willing to move first. At other times a whole blanket of fog would rapidly roll away disclosing some unimagined peril only a few yards off. Horace Seymour, one of Uxbridge's aides, was riding along with Wellington when the fog vanished in this way and the two of them escaped capture only by 'a very sudden run'. Here, there, everywhere the Duke was seen. Wheatley of the King's German Legion saw him waving his hat to 'beckon' the Horse Guards forward, and later riding past 'slowly and coolly' while his aides scurried to and fro with 'inconceivable velocity'; Gronow of the Foot Guards saw him sitting 'perfectly composed' on Copenhagen, though very pale; Morris of the 73rd saw him addressing General Halkett just as the Cuirassiers arrived, when he promptly took refuge in the 73rd's square. Kneeling on Morris's right was a man who could receive cavalry but not pronounce it. 'Tom, Tom,' he would sing out at each new rush, 'here comes the *calvary*,' until at last a cannon-ball put an end to his refrain.

Macready of the 30th saw the Duke constantly moving about among the squares and the shells. Whenever he came up there would be a shout of, 'Silence—stand to your front—here's the Duke,' and all was steady as on a parade. Mercer saw him waiting for 'G' Troop to arrive on the ridge above Hougoumont, where the air was like a furnace and full of an infernal humming, and every face was black as a sweep.

'Ah! that's the way I like to see horse-artillery move,' said the Duke as 'G' Troop galloped up. His warm approval reflected anxiety about the western end of his line, which Mercer had come to support.

'I'll be damned if we shan't lose this ground if we don't take care,' he said to Fitzroy Somerset, who agreed that the troops were 'much thinned'. Some of them were also unsteady, like the young Brunswickers whom Mercer watched being thumped like blocks by their officers into the gaps. Mercer wisely refrained from leaving his guns and running into the Brunswickers' square when the cavalry came, lest these boy-soldiers should catch the idea and run away. However, there was no-one who could restore a shaky battle-line like the Duke. He made the Guards move left towards Halkett's badly mauled brigade, and sent for Adam's and Mitchell's reserves from across the Nivelles road. Adam's brigade he formed four deep—a useful compromise between lines and squares which could hold an extensive area in relative safety.

Hardly had he crowned the crest with these fresh troops when, between 5.30 and 6 P.M., Ney made a new attack with a mixed force, at last, of 6,000 cavalry and infantry—a development which Wellington had foreseen. Ney's sensible postscript to the disastrous cavalry avalanche came too late. The Allied squares, though shrunk, stood firm from above Hougoumont to La Haye Sainte, positively welcoming the renewed charges as a relief from the cannonade. The French columns, unable to make an impression, were mowed down by the Allied artillery and raked with fire from Maitland's Guards and Adam's Light Brigade. General Foy called it *'une grêle de mort'*; he was wounded and carried to the rear. The thirty-one-year-old Frederick Adam, riding at Wellington's side, heard him say half to himself, 'I believe we shall beat them after all.'

Nevertheless the Duke's cavalry, without the sorely missed 'heavies', were not altogether effective at this stage, especially as one Dutch–Belgian regiment refused to charge and the Cumberland Hussars from Hanover left the field. Composed entirely of decorative 'young gentlemen', this body had never contemplated action. As they wheeled to fly, Horace Seymour grabbed their colonel by the collar. With an anguished bleat that he couldn't trust his men, the colonel tore himself away and raced with his regiment to Brussels, shouting that the French were at their heels. The regiment was afterwards disbanded and its colonel cashiered.

*   *   *

Time and the Prussians marched on. By 4 P.M. Bülow was in action against Lobau, by 5 P.M. he had captured Plancenoît; and though it was swiftly retaken by Napoleon's Young Guard, it soon changed hands again. So determined were the Prussians to press on and reach Wellington in time that when General Thielmann begged for reinforcements to deal with Grouchy at Wavre, Gneisenau turned him down as stonily as before he had tried to turn down Wellington: 'It doesn't matter if he's crushed as long as we gain the victory here.'

The sturdy little man at the *Belle-Alliance* command-post knew that his chances were down to ten to one against—his line regiments hammered, his cavalry squandered, one army on his front, another on his flank. He rode to and fro before *La Belle-Alliance* among the shot and shell, sizing up Wellington's position. Then he decided to seize that one chance. *Coûte que coûte*, Ney must take La Haye Sainte.

*   *   *

6 P.M.– 6.30 P.M.: LA HAYE SAINTE LOST

Until now the tenacious garrison of La Haye Sainte had managed by courage and ingenuity to resist all attacks. There were 376 of them, all King's German Legion, under a British officer, Major George Baring. The place had been set on fire more than once but Baring organized chains of camp kettles from the farm pond. Now it was not ingenuity they needed but ammunition. They had begun the day with sixty rounds each; they were down to four or five. Wellington had been able to reinforce them with two light companies but that was all. Why were their desperate demands for ammunition not answered? This is one of the unsolved puzzles of Waterloo. Long afterwards Wellington thought the trouble had been a lack of communication, and that he himself ought to have had a door cut in the north wall to get men and ammunition through—'but one cannot think of everything'. Captain Shaw (afterwards General Sir John Shaw-Kennedy) however, the soldier-historian of the battle, saw with his own eyes that the necessary door did exist. It is probable that the ammunition was non-existent. Light infantry like the companies of the King's German Legion in the farm, using Baker rifles, needed special cartridges. There were rumours that a wagon bringing supplies had overturned. It may have been one of those Mercer saw going up in silent smoke.

La Haye Sainte went up in a storm of fire. Ney, raging with frustration and resolved as never before to do or die, led out a combined force of infantry, cavalry and guns. Bullets from the farm picked them off man by man but those behind climbed the wall on a pile of dead bodies, to shoot down the defenders in the courtyard, while others fired from the barn roof or battered in the yard door. After their last cartridge was spent the King's German Legion defended the farmhouse with bayonets. 'But now they flocked in,' wrote an eighteen-year-old British survivor, Lieutenant George Graeme.

'*C'est ce coquin*,' shouted a French officer catching him by the collar, shaking him and then leaving him to fight it out with four of his men. The four faces, however, were so white that Graeme knew he could escape.

'You shan't keep me——' and he bolted. Forty-one men besides Graeme and Baring were the only survivors from La Haye Sainte. General Charles Alten and the Prince of Orange had made one attempt to relieve the farm. It was little short of disastrous. Alten ordered an attack in line by two battalions of the King's German Legion and when their colonel, Wheatley's friend Christian Ompteda, pointed out the fearful danger from French cavalry, the Prince, in a highly tense state, enforced Alten's order. The colonel said solemnly:

'Then I will. . . . Try to save my two nephews.' The boys, fourteen and fifteen years old, were saved. But Edmund Wheatley went down in Ompteda's catastrophe. He had been standing in his square alternately taking a pinch of snuff and a pinch of Southey—*But 'twas a famous victory*—when he realized it was all set for a famous defeat. Then he was knocked senseless. When he came to, the colonel was lying on his back beside him with a hole in his throat and he himself was a prisoner of the French.

Now that Wellington's bastion had fallen his centre was at Ney's mercy. The marshal did not fail to press home his advantage. He sent a vast cloud of skirmishers all over the terrible slopes—Wellington had not the heavy cavalry to subdue them—and rushed a battery up to within 300 yards of Wellington's line, changing the bastion of La Haye Sainte into a nest of sharp-shooters. Fitzroy Somerset, riding close beside his chief, lost his right arm. His left arm and Wellington's right were actually touching at the time. Nothing between them but the finger of Providence.

The Duke was running short of aides-de-camp. It was said that once or twice he was reduced to using stray civilians, with whom the battle-field was still supplied, to carry his messages—a young Swiss, perhaps a traveller in buttons from Birmingham, as well as a small Londoner on a pony who turned out to be a commercial traveller for a City firm.

'Please, Sir, any orders for Todd and Morrison?'

'No; but will you do me a service? Go to that officer and tell him to refuse a flank.'

These were only incidents in a mounting crisis. His raw, second-line battalions could not be relied on. 'Little specks,' said Hay, were all that remained of the veteran squares under Pack, Kempt and Halkett.

'Well, Halkett, how do you get on?' asked the Duke, white in the face but unmoved as marble.

'My Lord, we are dreadfully cut up; can you not relieve us for a little while?'

'Impossible.'

'Very well, my Lord, we'll stand till the last man falls.'

Denis Pack got the same orders: 'They must hold their ground to the last man.'

One hopeful gunner with a good view of Napoleon suggested a quick way out.

'There's Bonaparte, Sir, I think I can reach him, may I fire?' The Duke was aghast.

'No, no, Generals commanding armies have something else to do than to shoot at one another.'

Mercer's beautiful troop was a wreck: horses heaped up dead on top of smashed guns and gunners, Mercer himself deaf and confused by cannon-fire. Deafness was welcomed by Sergeant Morris for it silenced the cries of the wounded. Cotton and Macready both noticed that the 'gallant frenzy' which an army generates by repeated charges, had completely vanished under the bludgeon-work on the ridge.

It was now to be seen which side had most bottom, and would stand killing longest.

Harry Smith and Kincaid (and no doubt hundreds more) wondered whether this battle would be the exception where everyone was killed. To Wheatley, being hustled by his captors down the road to Charleroi, the little squares seemed to be entirely engulfed by foes.

The hands of Wellington's watch had crawled on to six-thirty. As he looked at it yet again someone said they heard him say:

'Night or the Prussians must come.'

*   *   *

6.30 P.M.–7 P.M.: THE DREADFUL PAUSE

He was not to be saved by night, nor even by the Prussians, beyond a certain point. By the impact of what had already been achieved, and by his inexhaustible personal resorces, he was to save the day himself.

The signs that the Allied centre was crumbling were apparent to Ney. He sent the Emperor an urgent appeal for reinforcements to deliver the *coup de grâce*. Napoleon hesitated. He thought of d'Erlon's infantry and Ney's cavalry, both destroyed. Should he send good money after bad? Fourteen battalions of the Imperial Guard were still untouched. How should he use them? This was Napoleon's crisis. He decided to reinforce the clamouring Lobau, and turned down Ney's call for troops in words of such petulance as to suggest that he already half knew he had made the wrong choice.

'Troops? Where do you expect me to find them? Do you expect me to make them?'

In these words he threw away his chance of victory.

With Ney rebuffed a lull supervened. Only Napoleon's artillery continued to bombard the ridge. No 'dreadful pause' was ever used by Wellington to more purpose.

* * *

Three things had to be done: the gaping hole in his centre plugged and the waverers there steadied, his line to right and left reorganized and every man persuaded not to seek relief in wildly hitting back but to stand and hold fast a little longer.

Chassé's reserve division of Dutch–Belgians was ordered up from the extreme right at Merbraine, and Wellington could rely on Peninsular regiments like the 52nd, to the west of the Brussels *chausée*. Here Master Leeke nearly lost a foot by reaching out to stop a gently rolling cannonball. A tortoiseshell kitten two yards away had stopped something and lay dead in the mud. It made Leeke suddenly think of home.

All the reserves Wellington could lay hands on were brought up to the centre.

'Go you and get all the German troops you can to the spot,' he ordered Captain Shaw, 'and all the guns you can find.'

Five fresh battalions of Brunswickers, in their extreme youth and terror, at once gave way. It was a bad moment and could be overcome only by direct personal effort. Wellington himself rallied both Brunswickers and Nassauers, with the gallant assistance of officers like Canning, Gordon and the Prince of Orange. As a result, Canning fell dead and Gordon mortally wounded; the Prince of Orange was struck on the left shoulder and carried off. He made an honourable exit from a field where he had shown consistently high courage, if not always an equal degree of judgement; neither ignoble nor surprising in a youth of twenty-three.[9] With another crisis surmounted, the second line battalions were back in position and the gap filled. The 'electrifying voice' in which the Duke revived these unhappy children was long remembered.

Sir Hussey Vivian did well in spontaneously supporting the weak centre with his light cavalry from the extreme left: 'we formed line', wrote Shakespear, his aide-de-camp, 'with *intervals closed*'—so that there should be no exit for the raw infantry to Brussels. Wellington immediately ordered up Vandeleur's cavalry also, from the same area, for though La Haye and Papelotte were in French hands he could see the dark masses of the Prussian Ist Corps only two miles away.

But for Müffling, however, the Prussians might have been deflected from the battle-field at the last moment. A Prussian staff officer informed General Zieten that Wellington was withdrawing; like Ney he had mistaken the procession to the rear for a full-scale retreat. Zieten at once prepared to do a d'Erlon. Though on the edge of Wellington's battle-field he turned round and marched back towards Blücher. Müffling dashed after him.

'The battle is lost if the Ist Corps does not go to the Duke's rescue.' Zieten again changed direction and started back.

All along the battered ridge Wellington pursued his charmed course, reining in Copenhagen wherever the tension was greatest to speak a word of caution or encouragement.

'Are we to be massacred here? Let us go at them, let us give them *Brummegum!*' the men shouted at him, brandishing their bayonets.

'Wait a little longer, my lads, you shall have at them presently.' To their officers he said:

9. British historians have tended to treat the Prince of Orange's errors more harshly than those, for instance, of the heavy cavalry. Perhaps one might fairly apply to him in general the words used of his actions in March and early April 1815, by the Netherlands' historians, namely, that he showed '*une certaine témérité dans ses idées*' (De Bas and de T'Serclaes de Wommersom, vol. I, p. 183). That a royal youth of twenty-three should be a corps commander at all was a fault of the system, not of the Prince.

'Hard pounding, this, gentlemen; try who can pound the longest.' Once there was an echo of *Henry V*:

'Standfast . . . we must not be beat—what will they say in England?' When he came up to the Horse Artillery's commander, Sir Alexander Frazer, his words were grave but confident.

'Twice have I saved this day by perseverance,' he said, meaning that nothing should stop him from saving it again. He spoke 'most justly', wrote Frazer afterwards, putting into words what thousands had felt on that awful field:

> Cold and indifferent . . . in the beginning of battles, when the moment of difficulty comes intelligence flashes from the eyes of this wonderful man; and he rises superior to all that can be imagined.

*   *   *

7 P.M.–9 P.M.: THE CRISIS

All that can be imagined. . . . Wellington could easily imagine what would come next. Not a single foot soldier and only a few horsemen of Napoleon's Imperial Guard had as yet been opposed to him. Sooner or later the Guard must come.

The reinforcements which the Emperor denied to Ney and sent to Lobau had stabilized his position against the Prussians in the east. It was time to strike in the west with the Guard. A royalist deserter galloped melodramatically into Wellington's lines with a breathless message. The Guard were coming.

Napoleon himself led out his 'Immortals'—Grenadiers and Chasseurs of the Middle Guard, supported by all d'Erlon's and Reille's remaining contingents: a total force of 15,000 men. Riding on his white charger, he took the Grenadiers as far as La Haye Sainte and there handed them over to Marshal Ney. The excitement was at fever pitch. '*Vive l'Empereur!*' they roared again and again in an ecstasy of pride, joy and gratitude. A damaging rumour that Prussian troops had been seen was promptly transformed for their benefit by the Emperor's magic into wonderful news. He ordered La Bédoyère to announce the arrival of Grouchy. Soon the false, heartening words were winging down the lines: '*Vive l'Empereur! Soldats, voilà Grouchy!*'

*   *   *

And now the fog of war again intervened, as at Quatre Bras, to obscure certain aspects of the final clash. Ney struck out diagonally from the Brussels *chaussée* in echelon, but shortly afterwards the Guard formed two separate columns, whether by Ney's order or accidentally because of the smoke and undulating ground is not clear. Nor has the exact number of the Guard battalions to attack the ridge of Mont-Saint-Jean ever been agreed. It was probably five. Nor precisely where the Grenadiers and Chasseurs respectively struck. But the effect of the Allied fire was clear and unforgettable. As soon as the Guard began to emerge out of the smoke, British and K.G.L. gunners cut their first swathes, with double charges, in the densely packed columns, each presenting a front of up to eighty men. Lieutenant Pringle of the Horse Artillery remembered how the Guard 'waved' at every successive discharge like corn blown by the wind; but not a man retired. They closed ranks and came on steadily towards death the reaper.

Then it was the turn of the Allied infantry to watch mesmerized a race of giants breasting the plateau. The Guard's leading officers waved their swords and Ney, blackened with smoke and without a horse for the fifth time, marched on foot up the reeking slopes. The men in Halkett's brigade marked the ranks of long blue overcoats, broadened by huge epaulettes and packs containing ceremonial dress for the victory march into Brussels. Red plumes on their high, hairy bear-skins seemed to nod menacingly at Macready of the 30th, who muttered to himself, 'Now for a clawing.'

Wellington stood in the right-centre of his position with the 1st Foot Guards of Maitland's brigade, all of whom he had ordered to lie down behind the Ohain road.[10] At least one young soldier in that *élite* corps, Ensign Gronow, couldn't help recalling that his French opposite numbers were 'the heroes of many memorable victories';

10. Houssaye, pp. 227–8; Henry Lachouque, *Anatomy of Glory, Napoleon and his Guard*, p. 488, and others say Maitland's Foot Guards were attacked by the 3rd Chasseurs of the Imperial Guard; Chandler, p. 1088, follows General Maitland himself in saying it was the Grenadiers. The uniforms of the Chasseurs and Grenadiers looked somewhat similar.

they looked to him to be 20,000 strong. Captain Harry Powell, also of the 1st Foot Guards, was nearer the mark in reckoning them at 6,000 (they were 6,500); but he too was painfully conscious as they advanced *au pas de charge* that '*La Garde*' had never yet failed in an attack. Beyond Gronow and Powell, Master Leeke in the 52nd managed to concentrate on the rhythm of the drum-beats in that awful advance: 'the rum dum, the rum dum', they seemed to say, 'the rummadum dummadum, dum dum'.

Wellington still had the Guards lying down when he noticed signs of confusion on his left. The 'clawing' of Halkett's brigade had begun.

'See what's wrong there——' he shouted, unaware that he was continually sliding the tube of his telescope in and out. An assistant quartermaster-general dashed away to question Halkett, who before he could answer was shot in the mouth and carried off; nevertheless his 30th and 73rd were rallied while the Duke himself galloped over and brought back into position two battalions of Brunswickers who were actually in flight. Vandeleur's cavalry backed him up, as Vivian's had done earlier, by refusing to let them get through to the rear. As Harry Smith said, every moment of Waterloo was a crisis.

The Duke wheeled again and returned to Maitland's concealed Guards. The advancing French were only sixty yards from the Ohain road. They could see nothing opposing them but the Allied guns. There was dead silence behind the ridge. Then Wellington alerted Maitland.

'Now, Maitland, now's your time!' The enemy still came on and had covered another twenty yards when the Duke gave his final commands:

'Stand up, Guards!' Up sprang 1,500 men as if out of the ground, bringing the startled French to a momentary halt.

'Make ready! Fire!' The long lines of British muskets, 400 in the first of four ranks and a full half of the total force able to bring their fire to bear, lapped the enemy at twenty yards in a stream of bullets. Down crashed three hundred of the Guard at the first volley. Some of Halkett's men fired into their right flank. Their close formation prevented them from deploying and they began to give way. To the 1st Foot Guards' amazement they suddenly found themselves looking at the backs of long blue overcoats.

'Now's your time, my boys,' called out Colonel Lord Saltoun. Without waiting to fire another volley they charged with their bayonets;

but before they knew where they were their opponents had dispersed and they were down near Hougoumont with a column of Chasseurs on their flank and no inkling of whether to go forward, form square, or retreat. By the time they had reformed and returned to the ridge, another British regiment had stepped in with dramatic suddenness to dispatch the Imperial Guard.

*   *   *

Well aware of Wellington's mind and methods from hard-fought Peninsular actions, Colonel Colborne of the 52nd was one who did not hesitate to strike without orders when he saw the need. Wellington had himself brought up Adam's Light Brigade, of which the 52nd formed a part, to lie in wait for the Chasseurs. Now Colborne sprang forward out of the concealing corn, wheeled his thousand men to the left, brought his right shoulder round until the regiment was standing parallel to the French. General Adam galloped across to find out what the Colonel of the 52nd was up to.

'What do you intend?'

'To make that column feel our fire.'

'Move on.'

At the same moment Wellington sent over one of his few remaining aides-de-camp, Colonel Percy, to order Colborne's advance.

The 52nd were already pouring volley after volley into the French left flank. Unable to deploy, the Chasseurs recoiled under this violent, totally unforeseen attack. In a moment Colborne's bayonets were flashing and his men driving the enemy in a slanting line south-eastwards across the field. Wellington at once followed up with all available bayonets; he had personally ordered the 95th Rifles to charge before Colborne's action began. Captain Budgeon saw him for the first time that day as he rode down their line, and Kincaid remembered how he himself and his fellow-riflemen began cheering when the Duke appeared. As usual he stopped them:

'No cheering, my lads, but forward and complete your victory!'

Both Uxbridge and Colin Campbell, one of the Duke's surviving aides-de-camp, were alarmed by the risks he was running and begged him to move away from such exposed positions. He said much the same thing to each:

'So I will when I see those fellows driven off.'

When Colborne, finding himself far out in front of his supports, prepared to call a temporary halt, he heard the Duke's voice at his side:

'Well done, Colborne! Well done! Go on. Never mind, *go* on, *go* on. Don't give them time to rally. They won't stand.'

It was not mere line regiments but the Imperial Guard itself which would not stand. As the relics of d'Erlon's and Reille's columns, already demoralized by their earlier defeats, realized the appalling truth, a cry of horror went up such as Napoleon's army had never heard before:

'*La Garde recule!*'

Something told Wellington that their splendid harness had snapped, and unlike his own contrivance of much-knotted rope, once broken it could not be mended. The finest army in the world stopped in its tracks, pennons still fluttering, the sun twinkling slyly on lances and breastplates—the setting sun. Down in the valley Hougoumont still flamed and still held out. The apple trees in the orchard hung in shreds like weeping willows but the garden had never changed hands; its stone balustrade was covered with jasmin and honeysuckle.

'You see, Macdonnell has held Hougoumont!' With this triumphant salute to Müffling, the Duke gathered up Copenhagen's reins and galloped with Uxbridge towards the crossroads. The finger of Providence was pointing at his tree. The last crisis of Waterloo had arrived.

$$* \qquad * \qquad *$$

Half an hour or more of daylight remained, for it was not yet 8 P.M. Wellington's army was down to some 35,000 men, but all proven in defence and now only anxious to prove themselves in attack. The French army was shaken but not routed. Napoleon still held some of the Old Guard in reserve; others had driven Bülow's Prussians out of Plancenoît yet again and installed the Young Guard there, where they were to remain till the battle was over. Zieten's Ist Corps, on the other hand, had driven a wedge between Lobau and d'Erlon and cleared Papelotte and La Haye, though thanks to Prince Bernhard this area had never caused Wellington real anxiety.[11]

As Wellington's telescope swept these eastern hills for the

11. One of the tragedies of Waterloo was that the Prussians mistook Prince Bernhard's troops for French and did them great damage.

hundredth time, it showed him something which Sergeant Robertson of the Gordons noticed a few minutes later: 'something extraordinary' going on. The enemy's extreme right was under a cross-fire—was turned—was in flight. Could it be a mutiny in their army? Robertson, using a spy-glass for the first time because of the dearth of officers, was perplexed. At that instant—somewhere about 7.30 P.M.—an aide-de-camp from the Duke himself came spurring down the Highlanders' rear.

'The day is our own! The Prussians have arrived!'

Then the Highlanders and all other regiments who were near fixed their eyes impatiently on the focal point—the Duke of Wellington standing in his stirrups at his command-post by the tree, a sudden ray of the setting sun throwing into relief the unforgettable but indescribable expression on his face. This was the decisive moment. Every soldier knew it. Some, of whom Uxbridge may have been one, advised only limited action. The Duke knew better.

'Oh, damn it!' he exclaimed. 'In for a penny, in for a pound,' and taking off his hat he waved it three times towards the French. In a flash his signal was understood. Three deafening cheers of relief and exultation burst out as the foremost regiments, led by Vivian's and Vandeleur's light cavalry, swooped on to the plain.

*   *   *

The Duke put spurs to Copenhagen and plunging through the mêlée, called on each regiment to charge under whatever officer had survived to lead it.

'Who commands here?' he asked the 40th.

'Captain Brown.' Then Sergeant Lawrence, who as long as he could remember had always found Wellington appearing at the critical moment to 'entice' his army on, heard the order to attack.

Standing amid billows of smoke Wellington caught sight of Harry Smith. Smith had been stupefied by the sudden silence of the guns, knowing that one side must have retreated—but which? A hearty 'British shout' had given him the answer. Then came the Duke's urgent voice:

'Where are your people? . . . Tell them to form companies and move on immediately.'

'In which direction, my lord?' Smith had completely lost his bearings in the fog. Wellington pointed, 'Why, right ahead.'

Hardly a French gun was still firing. One of the last cannon-shots to rake the fields below La Haye Sainte flew over Copenhagen's neck and smashed into Uxbridge's right knee.

'By God! I've lost my leg!'

'Have you, by God?' Wellington lowered his telescope and supported his gallant second-in-command until others came to carry him away. Then he galloped on.[12]

Now Frederick Adam was galloping with him, and they both saw the group of enemy infantry and artillery rallying on a hill opposite. It was one of their shells which had brought down Uxbridge.

'Adam, you must dislodge those fellows,' ordered the Duke in his staccato way. Adam's brigade did their work and the French cannonading ceased for good.

Kennedy and Shakespear were both charging with Vivian's Hussars whom Uxbridge had been about to join before he was struck. Until the guns ceased Shakespear had been unable to make Sir Hussey hear a word he said without leaning right over him. Now Sir Hussey's voice rang out:

'Eighteenth! you will follow me.'

'To hell!' they roared back. All three Hussar regiments, the 18th, 7th and 10th, charged furiously down the hill, the 18th capturing a French battery at *La Belle-Alliance* and the other two breaking a square of the Guard, though with terrible loss. Even the dead inflicted wounds, for the countless swords and bayonets sticking up all over the fields cut the fetlocks of their horses.

Major Luard, who charged with Vandeleur's cavalry, was one of the many to describe Wellington suddenly appearing in their front 'in great spirits', to start them off. Luard pursued the enemy as far as his bivouac huts where they found wagons laden with food and brandy—all of which the good Luard dealt out equally among the men.

The Highlanders above La Haye Sainte rushed down upon the

12. Wellington's brusque retort to the valiant Uxbridge may be apocryphal, though it was told to Greville by Fitzroy Somerset. It is sometimes quoted by his critics as an example of his hard-heartedness. This is to misunderstand war. Indeed one of the critics' particular heroes, John Colborne of the 52nd, behaved in just the same way when the circumstances were similar. Having been told in the heat of battle at Orthez (1814) that the Duke of Richmond's son, Lord March, had been wounded, Colborne simply said, 'Well, I can't help it. Have him carried off,' and dashed on (Moore Smith, p. 202).

farm and gravel pit, 'like a legion of demons', driving the French before them and mingling with the first Prussian soldiers on the Brussels road. A Prussian band began to play *God Save the King* and the English responded with *Nun danket Alle Gott*. Fortunately for the Highlanders their bonnets and kilts distinguished them from the French. Other units in both Wellington's and Blücher's army were cut up in error by their own allies. One British regiment did not join in the advance but remained quietly on the ridge. This was the 27th Foot. They lay dead to a man in their square.

At the heart of the struggle was still the Duke, urging Copenhagen over the blood-soaked cornfields and splintered hedges. Above him the Congreve rockets streaked ever more brightly across the darkening sky.

This time it was Colonel Felton Hervey who tried to make him go back.

'We are getting into enclosed ground, and your life is too valuable to be thrown away.' But again the Duke had a reason, if the opposite one from before, for staying where he was.

'Never mind, let them fire away. The battle's won; my life is of no consequence now.'

The numb horror with which Napoleon's army had first watched the Guard give way was rapidly passing into panic. Which were the fatal words that started the rout? '*Nous sommes trahis*'—the spectre of treason ushering in Blücher instead of Grouchy? Treason has been called the 'heart-cry of the Hundred Days'. Or '*Sauve qui peut*'— the fear that in another moment there would be no more army to serve, and therefore it was already time to say, 'Every man for himself'? The birth of panic cannot be pinned down to a particular moment or cause. It is enough that Wellington sensed its potential presence when he gave the word to advance, and nothing Napoleon and Ney could do availed to arrest it. Ney stood on the battlefield in his tattered, blood-stained uniform, a broken sword in his hand, and screamed at d'Erlon:

'If they catch us, you and I will be hanged.'

Napoleon, pale but resolute, formed the reserve of his Old Guard into squares to stem the torrent. It was impossible. Yet even their failure was magnificent and at least one British soldier watched in awe as a Guard's regiment, amid the bedlam that surrounded them, stalked majestically from the field. Posterity has been no less impressed by the language with which their general, Cambronne, received the Allies' invitation so surrender. Scarcely majestic, it could not be misunderstood.[13]

Napoleon just had time to spring into his *berline* and reached Genappe before he was overtaken by the Prussians. Out he jumped and on to a horse, his escort of Red Lancers keeping off the mass of fugitives until he had forced his way through Quatre Bras and Frasnes and arrived in Charleroi at 5 A.M. next morning. Edmund Wheatley, footsore and still a prisoner but soon to escape and rejoin his regiment, passed by Quatre Bras that same night. Thousands of stripped, unburied corpses covered the fields. With excruciating candour he confessed that his lacerated feet were eased by treading on 'soft jellied lumps of inanimate flesh'.

Among the treasures captured by the Prussians in Napoleon's handsome dark blue and gilt carriage with vermilion wheels and bullet-proof panels, were close on a hundred pieces from a splendidly appointed travelling-case, nearly all in solid gold, two leather bottles, one of rum and the other of fine old Malaga, a million francs-worth of diamonds and a cake of Windsor soap. The carriage was presented to the Prince Regent, but instead of coming to rest royally at Windsor it was exhibited in London and then lost sight of, until picked up for a song by the owner of Madame Tussaud's waxworks. There it was destroyed in the fire of 1925.

*   *   *

It was 9 P.M. on 18 June 1815 and nearly dark when Blücher and Wellington rode forward to greet one another on the Brussels road between *La Belle-Alliance* and Rossomme.

'*Mein lieber Kamerad!*' cried the old hero, leaning forward from his horse to kiss Wellington; '*Quelle affaire!*' That was about all the French he knew, said the Duke long afterwards. But when they were both in Paris a year or two later and the Duke came to visit him, he spoke of the dreadful elephant which had again made an appearance, in French:

'*Je sens un éléphant là,*' he said, pointing to his stomach. This last pregnancy seemed peculiarly ironical since the elephant, he believed, had been fathered on him by a French soldier.

13. ' "*Merde!*" Historians sometimes translate this as "The Guard dies but never surrenders" ' (C. J. Herold and Professor Gordon Wright, *The Battle of Waterloo*, p. 138). Cambronne denied to his son that he had ever used the obscenity.

Also ironically, Wellington and Blücher could communicate only in the language of their common enemy—France. War, like Blücher, was a little mad.

*   *   *

THE END OF THE BEGINNING

The pursuit was given over entirely to the Prussians with Wellington's consent. Though both armies were exhausted his was more so. And in Gneisenau the Allies had the finest man alive to organize what he called a hunt by moonlight. The French were driven before him without respite or quarter until he reached Frasnes. 'It was the best night of my life.'

For Wellington it was the worst, not forgetting Assaye. As he silently walked Copenhagen back to Waterloo, the moonlit fields on either side of the *chaussée* were littered with the dead and dying, with horses, weapons, helmets, caps, belts and feathers. Here and there a wounded man rose to his feet and staggered away or the sinister shadow of a robber bent over a corpse. Grey-hooded orderlies with stretchers had done their best to collect the casualties but 12,000 British and Hanoverians alone made the task hopeless. Wellington's total losses were close to 15,000. The French lost 25,000 in killed and wounded, the Prussians over 7,000. Altogether between forty and fifty thousand dead and wounded men lay on that small stricken field. Here Major Ramsay had been killed, there Whinyates wounded; Shaw and Dakin, the giant pugilists, had gone into the ring for the last time. Dakin's body was found cut to pieces and Shaw, after slaying nine Cuirassiers, had crawled down to La Haye Sainte and bled to death propped against its wall.[14] Generals Cooke, Duplat, Kempt, Pack, Barnes, Alten, Adam and Grant had all in the end joined the melancholy procession of wounded to the rear. De Lancey had been struck down by blast, close to the Duke, and no one knew his whereabouts. It was true that there were lucky ones: Frederick Ponsonby, desperately wounded first by French sabres and then by Polish lances, ridden over and tossed by the Prussians, robbed, used as a musket-rest by a *tirailleur* and as a

14. Sir Walter Scott, having once met and admired Shaw in Haydon's studio, had his body brought home to his native Nottinghamshire. A cast of his skull is in the Household Cavalry Museum, Windsor.

place to die on by a mortally wounded soldier, but later found still alive by a British infantryman who mounted guard over him till morning; and Sergeants Morris and Burton of the 73rd.

'Out with the grog, Tom: didn't I tell you there was no shot made for you or me?' Sergeant Burton had his own ideas about the hand of Providence. He and Tom Morris were two out of the seventy surviving men from their battalion of 550.

There were also dauntless characters who though desperately wounded had not felt the finger of death: Lord Uxbridge, whose pulse never changed when his leg was amputated and who next morning joked with the Marquise d'Assche when he arrived on a stretcher shaded with leaves at her hotel:

'Well, Marquise, you see I shan't be able to dance with you any more except with a wooden leg.' And Fitzroy Somerset who called out to his surgeons:

'Hallo! don't carry away that arm till I've taken off my ring'—the ring given him by Wellington's niece Emily at their marriage.

It was too soon after the terrible events of the day for Wellington to feel even a gleam of comfort. He was in a state of emotional shock. Nevertheless, life must go on. After dismounting at 11 P.M. outside his inn at Waterloo he gave Copenhagen an approving pat on the hind quarters, no doubt thinking that the little horse was as tired as himself. On the contrary, Copenhagen lashed out and nearly inflicted the wound which Wellington had miraculously escaped on the battle-field. Copenhagen had Arab blood from his dam and was a grandson of the famous race-horse Eclipse, whose son, Young Eclipse, was the second horse to win the Derby (1781). The Duke was never sentimental about Copenhagen, but the tribute he paid him after his death expressed, as always, exactly what he felt:

There may have been many faster horses, no doubt many handsomer, but for bottom and endurance I never saw his fellow.

* * *

Supper was a subdued meal. Wellington had just seen his favourite aide-de-camp, Alexander Gordon, whose smashed leg Dr Hume had amputated on the battlefield two or three hours before.

'Thank God you are safe,' whispered Gordon. The Duke told the wounded man about the victory and then said encouragingly, 'I have no doubt, Gordon, you will do well.' But his young friend felt the finger of death and could not answer. Attended by Dr Hume, he was carried on Wellington's instructions to his own bed.

Müffling dropped in about midnight with the news that Blücher was speaking of the 'Battle of *La Belle-Alliance*'. Wellington said nothing for he had already decided to call the battle as usual by the name of his headquarters, Waterloo. Otherwise no one took a seat at his table except Alava, though it was laid for all his personal staff. The Duke looked up anxiously each time the door opened. Could it be one of his missing young men? When hope had vanished he held up both hands and said,

'The hand of Almighty God has been upon me this day.'

He drank one toast only, in a glass of wine with Alava—'To the Memory of the Peninsular War.' Then he got up, quickly lay down on a pallet and was fast asleep.

*   *   *

While the Duke was still sleeping the wounded Prince of Orange wrote at 2 A.M. from Brussels to his parents at The Hague. His letter was as usual in French.

Victoire! Victoire!

Mes très chers Parents

We have had a magnificent affair against Napoleon today . . . it was my corps [the 1st] which principally gave battle and to which we owe the victory, but the affair was entirely decided by the attack which the Prussians made on the enemy's right. I am wounded by a ball in the left shoulder but only slightly. *A vie et à mort tout à vous Guillaume.*

The Prince's bullet-torn jacket, trimmed with black Astrakhan fur and handsomely frogged, was preserved at the Soestdijk Palace (presented by the nation to the 'Hero of Waterloo') together with the ivory-handled sword which had been brandished on the field but not used to lop off any limbs. Wrapped in tissue paper inside a painted box and enclosed in a silver casket are preserved the splintered fragments of bone which, weeks after the battle, were still working their way out of his shoulder.[15]

*   *   *

15. The Prince's Waterloo relics are now in the Royal House at The Hague.

An hour after the Prince had begun his Waterloo letter, the Duke was woken by Dr Hume. For once the Beau had been too tired to wash. He sat up in bed and stretched out his hand to the doctor. Hume took it and held it while he told the Duke that Alexander Gordon had just collapsed and died in his arms. Then he recited the long list of casualties which had come in since midnight. It was even more shocking than Wellington had suspected. Dr Hume felt tears dropping on his hand and looking up from the list he saw them chasing down the Duke's face, making furrows in the sweat and grime. As Wellington brushed them away with his hand he said in a broken voice,

'Well, thank God, I don't know what it is to lose a battle; but certainly nothing can be more painful than to gain one with the loss of so many of one's friends.'

Less than twenty miles away Napoleon, ashen and haggard, was weeping over his lost army.

After Hume had gone Wellington dressed and began his dispatch to Lord Bathurst, the War Minister—the renowned but controversial 'Waterloo despatch'.

It described the four days from 15 to 18 June and when published on the 22nd covered under four columns in *The Times*. The stupendous event, the titanic endurance, the blaze of glory, the oceans of blood deflected him not an inch from his accustomed brevity and restraint.

> It gives me the greatest satisfaction to assure your Lordship that the army never, upon any occasion, conducted itself better. The division of Guards, under Lieut. General Cooke, who is severely wounded, Major General Maitland, and Major General Byng, set an example which was followed by all; and there is no officer nor description of troops that did not behave well.

The Duke's 'description of troops' was reduced to a minimum. The Horse Artillery were not mentioned by name, nor any of the Hussar regiments, nor Colborne and his victorious 52nd. A reference to bravery found its way into the text only once (over the Guards at Hougoumont) as did steadiness (the infantry at Quatre Bras) and glory (when Picton fell) but there were four mentions of distinguished or highly distinguished conduct and five of gallantry or the utmost gallantry (the Brunswickers at Quatre Bras and the Guards at Hougoumont again).

The above exercise in semantics might seem peculiarly profitless today and one would prefer, like Sergeant Cotton, only to admire the despatch's 'noble simplicity, perfect calmness and exemplary modesty'—but for the effect on the Duke's popularity of his sparing hand. Every sentence was scrutinized for praise or neglect of individuals or regiments. Lord Uxbridge's sister, Caroline Capel, called it 'odious', and even Georgiana Lennox thought Gordon's groans must have distracted him, while one Waterloo officer, William Leeke, busied himself for over half a century in trying to convince the world that the 52nd alone and single-handed had repulsed the Imperial Guard and won the battle of Waterloo.[16] The omission of Colborne's name from the despatch was certainly an error on Wellington's part; it was said that when he asked for Colborne's report, that great and good soldier was seeing to his wounded and could not be found. Colborne himself, though hurt, defended Wellington's assessment of regimental merits on the practical ground that regimental officers could not see what was happening outside their own 'small angle' of the battlefield.

This generous argument was only partly relevant. Even the Commander-in-Chief sitting on Copenhagen under the elm could not see everything through the unprecedented smoke of Waterloo. And to Wellington's eternal credit, he was more often in the thick of the fight than raised above it. The solution to his problem could have been a regular chief of staff and a team to collect, check and write out the material for the despatch. This would no doubt have resulted in more lavish descriptions of exploits and might have prevented some of the embittered post-mortems which were to plague him for years afterwards. Wellington himself may have come to regret his reticence. Sir Winston Churchill told Field-Marshal Montgomery that a friend once asked the aged Duke whether, if he had his life over again, there was any way in which he could have done better. The Duke replied, 'Yes, I should have given more praise'.

To posterity, however, the idea of a gracious and group-minded Duke of Wellington mechanically ladling out honours is repugnant.

16. See Leeke's *History of Lord Seaton's (Colborne) Regiment* (the 52nd), and numerous articles. Colborne's champions also included William Crawley Yonge of the 52nd (his brother-in-law and father of Charlotte M. Yonge the novelist) and Leeke's cousin Colonel Gawler. According to Leeke, however, Gawler let down the side by a 'sadly vexatious Statement' in the *Army & Navy Gazette* (1869), admitting that one column of the Imperial Guard *was* driven off by Maitland's Guards.

Better all the subsequent inconveniences to himself and others than to lose the picture of that sad, solitary figure dipping his pen minute by minute into the ink while the sun outside became warm and the body of his friend grew cold.

*   *   *

Who won the battle of Waterloo? Wellington refused to discuss it. When Colonel Gurwood, editor of the *Despatches*, tried to pin him down, he said impatiently,

'Oh, I know nothing of the services of particular regiments; there was glory enough for all.'

This left the field open to claims (besides those already mentioned) ranging from Sir Hussey Vivian[17] to the Prussian army—and of course Napoleon, as some of the monuments erected and literature sold on the battlefield today make clear.[18] In the case of the Prussians nothing could have prevented national rivalries, but the Duke at least paid them an unqualified tribute in his despatch:

> I should not do justice to my own feelings, or to Marshall Blücher and the Prussian army, if I did not attribute the successful result of this arduous day to the cordial and timely assistance I received from them. The operation of General Bülow upon the enemy's flank was a most decisive one. . . .

Those who believe Napoleon's campaign entitled him to the moral victory are usually concerned to prove that his total genius as a man

17. William Tomkinson of the 52nd afterwards heard that the 10th Hussars under Vivian were the true victors. He laughed uproariously.

18. The author visited the field of Waterloo on the 150th anniversary of the battle, 18 June 1965. One British tourist, hitherto somewhat disconcerted by the dearth of national monuments, was overwhelmed with delight at the enormous (Netherlands) Butte de Lion: 'Ah, there's the British lion at last!' Apart from the excellent Museum away in the village of Waterloo, the only recent British addition is a handsome new plaque on the obelisk to Sir Alexander Gordon, erected by the Aberdeen family. The 'Society for Napoleonic Studies' has added to the predominant French aura by affixing a dignified new inscription on the wall of Wellington's great bastion: '*Aux Derniers Combattants de la Grande Armée—A la mémoire des Combattants Français qui sacrificièrent héroiquement devant les murs de la Haie Sainte le 18 Juin 1815. Société d'Etudes Napoliennes. 1965.*'

was greater than Wellington's. This grand question, like other important comparisons, must be left until the end of the Duke's life. At Waterloo, Wellington's fire-power served him better than Napoleon's, his lines better than Napoleon's columns, his generals better than Napoleon's marshals, even though he had not selected or welcomed all of them; indeed it was Napoleon's own fault that the army's idol, Ney, was not at the head of his troops until the eve of Quatre Bras, that a great cavalry commander, Grouchy, was weighed down with the cares of infantry, and that a great manoeuvrer of armies, Soult, was employed to interpret, if not manoeuvre, nothing but the Emperor's thoughts.

Manoeuvres give a battle its cachet. In one sense no one was to blame for the absence of manoeuvres at Waterloo. Napoleon had to strike quickly. There was not time for a typically Napoleonic sweep through the difficult, waterlogged country on his right, and Wellington was prepared for him—over-prepared—on his left. The Duke's 'infamous army', or 'very bad army' as Kincaid called it, was incapable of manoeuvres, certainly of the brilliant strokes delivered at Salamanca, Vitoria and Sorauren. Its glory was to stand firm in dumb, patient agony, some said like blocks, others like heroes.

Nevertheless, without risking lengthy sweeps, Napoleon could have fought a battle, as Reille suggested, of movement. That Waterloo became a pounding-match was his responsibility. Weary and still dispirited, Wellington described it to Beresford on 2 July 1815:

> Never did I see such a pounding match. Both were what the boxers call gluttons. Napoleon did not manoeuvre at all. He just moved forward in the old style, in columns, and was driven off in the old style.

Napoleon's contempt for the 'Sepoy General' had always served him ill and at Waterloo it ruined him. 'He is a bad general. . . .' The Emperor would eat him up.

Wellington did not make the mistake of despising his opponent.

Rather than admit that Wellington routed Napoleon, the matter is sometimes passed over with the remark that neither was at his best. This was true of Napoleon's health which may have affected his tactics, but not of his strategy: here he was triumphant beyond all expectations, and certainly over Wellington. Indeed, Wellington himself told Charles Greville in 1820 that 'Bonaparte's march upon

Belgium was the finest thing ever done—so rapid and so well combined'. Nor was it true of the Duke's tactical and personal achievements on the battlefield, which far outshone Napoleon's and showed his peculiar brilliance at its most superb. Even his reserves—raw, second-line battalions—were made to serve him better at the crisis than Napoleon's reserve of the inimitable Guard. His whole army vibrated under his inspiration. He *was* the battle, as countless eye-witnesses felt.

> He was everywhere ... the eye could turn in no direction that it did not perceive him, either at hand or at a distance; galloping to charge the enemy, or darting across the field to issue orders. Every ball also ... seemed fired, and every gun aimed at him. ... But he suffered nothing to check or engage him ... his entire concentrated attention, exclusive aim, and intense thought were devoted impartially, imperturbably and grandly to the Whole, the All.

*   *   *

Before 5 A.M. on Monday morning the Duke started off with his unfinished despatch for Brussels. It was going to be hot, torturingly hot for those who were to lie where they had fallen for yet another day. His feelings, as he trotted up the *chaussée* through forest glades which were no better than jungles of broken carts and guns, with rusty red pools where the wounded had rumbled by on wagons or dropped off and died—his feelings—the truth was he had none. 'While in the thick of it,' he told Lady Shelley a month later, 'I am too occupied to feel anything; but it is wretched just after. It is impossible to think of glory. Both mind and feelings are exhausted.'

Some twenty years on, in 1836, a new generation in the shape of young Lady Salisbury tried to recapture from the Duke the flavour of victory. If he could not feel triumph on the field itself as he strenuously assured her, not even when the Guards charged, it must have come to him on the way back to Brussels.

'But now!' she urged, 'while you were riding there! Did it never occur to you that you had placed yourself on such a pinnacle of glory?'

The Duke might have replied, with Johnny Kincaid, that it was the most uncomfortable heap of glory he ever had a hand in. He was more matter of fact.

574 Wellington—The Years of the Sword

'No. I was entirely occupied with what was necessary to be done.'

Napoleon had not yet been scotched, the Allied army had to be reorganized, and there was still the despatch to finish. The Duke went up to his hotel room in Brussels and sat down at the open window, pen in hand. There was a crowd round his door among whom he recognized Mr Creevey.

'What news?' called Creevey, for the accounts in Brussels were still confused: the Misses Ord, indeed, had spent the night fully clothed with their shutters barred, though Creevey had slept soundly through all the hubbub. Wellington called back,

'Why, I think we've done for 'em this time.' Creevey looked incredulous.

'Come up here,' said the Duke, 'and I'll tell you all about it.'

Wellington at once began to fire off his views in what Creevey now knew to be his natural way—short and blunt, with a succession of quick monosyllables; but without a spark of joy.

'It has been a damned serious business. Blücher and I have lost 30,000 men. It has been a damned nice thing—the nearest-run thing you ever saw in your life.'[19]

As he walked up and down he kept praising the troops and expressing astonishment at 'our men's courage'. When he again repeated how near, how close run it had been, Creevey asked whether it was because the French had fought better than usual? No, it was not that. They had always fought with the same valour, ever since Vimeiro. Then the Duke let his thoughts play on the battle, on the crises at Hougoumont and above La Haye Sainte, on the endless watching for trouble, galloping towards it, rallying the waverers under shot and shell—and under the finger of Providence. It had all hung on the thread of one life. At last he burst out:

'By God! I don't think it would have done if I had not been there!'

He did not tell Creevey about the finger of Providence at Waterloo, though he did bring it in at the end of a note written that same day to Lady Frances Webster: 'The finger of Providence was upon me, and I escaped unhurt.'

His brother William, who had already heard about the finger at

19. *Creevey*, p. 142. Wellington's rough figures, given less than twenty-four hours after the battle, are too high. They should be between 22,000 and 23,000 for his own and Blücher's combined casualties at Waterloo. Many of those reported to Wellington as missing were afterwards found to have gone back with the wounded but later rejoined their units.

Sorauren, was given an insight into that other force on which Arthur had depended at Waterloo—the British infantry:

> ... It was the most desperate business I ever was in. I never took so much trouble about any Battle, & never was so near being beat. Our loss is immense particularly in that best of all Instruments, British Infantry. I never saw the Infantry behave so well.

Creevey on his side refrained from quoting to his friend Bennet, the Radical M.P., to whom he immediately posted an account of his interview, the Duke's saying that he himself had been indispensable. It might have been misunderstood. But looking back seven years later to that sombre morning after Waterloo, Creevey showed that he himself had understood the Duke very well. There was nothing like vanity, he wrote in his journal, in the way the Duke spoke. Creevey found that in 1822 he held the hero in exactly the same honour as in 1815: honour for his misery at 'the loss of lives', honour for admitting his nearness to defeat, honour for the justice done to the enemy, high honour despite the fact that the Duke had since become a politician—'very foolishly' in Creevey's opinion— and done 'many wrong and foolish things'.[20]

* * *

Did Wellington expect to become a politician? The charms of Party had died on him during the Peninsular War. At the same time he could not stomach the thought of any more battles. Within a few weeks his view that victory was almost as bad as defeat had grown into something like a revulsion from war itself.

'I hope to God that I have fought my last battle,' he told Lady Shelley. 'It is a bad thing to be always fighting.'

His hope was to be fulfilled. But would it be easy, even possible, to set aside for ever the trade in which he had shown his incomparable genius, and yet remain the nation's servant, retained for life? There was no talk of retiring, as after the battle of Vimeiro, to shoot red-legged partridges.

He was a hero for life. That would not make it any easier. It meant

20. Wellington's misery impressed another Radical in exactly the same way. 'In my eyes,' wrote John Cam Hobhouse, 'this does him no less honour than his victory' (*Recollections*, vol. I, p. 310).

beginning again at the top. Personal problems, also, would have to be solved in the limelight. As a soldier he had scolded or promoted his young men in the secluded villages of Portugal or the Pyrenees. Now it would be young women, and his headquarters an opera box. In handling his own boys, Douro and Charles, he would have a second-in-command. Kitty was too much in awe of her hero to learn from him and Arthur had never believed in a second-in-command anyway.

'My die is cast.' He had said it in 1808 when he gave up politics for soldiering. Now the hero of Waterloo was about to reverse the decision. Creevey and others would think it a foolish gamble for a hero to take. But he had never felt a hero, not even on the morning after Waterloo, as young Lady Salisbury, cross-questioning him in 1836, was at last to be convinced.

'I cannot conceive,' she persisted, 'how it was that you did not think how infinitely you had raised your name above every other.'

'That is a feeling of vanity,' he said simply. 'One's first thought is for the public service.'

'But there *must* be a satisfaction, and a lasting one, in that feeling of superiority that you *always* enjoy. It is not in human nature it should be otherwise.'

'That is true . . .' he conceded, perhaps thinking of the brilliant days in France after his spirits had lifted and before they tried to assassinate him. . . . 'But when the war is over, and the troops disbanded, what is this great General more than anybody else?'

'But that does not apply to you, you are equally great in the Cabinet and in the field.' Round and round the woods of his Walmer home they walked. Try as she would she could not get him to tell her what it was like to be a hero. He only kept saying that carpenters and shoemakers and farmers could all beat him on their own ground.

'I feel I am but a man.'

He probably did not remember he had used those very words to a friend twenty-three years earlier, in 1813, after his triumphal entry into Cádiz.

I ought to have somebody behind me to remind me that I am 'but a man'.

They stood for what was almost his hair-shirt, but worn as naturally and comfortably as his civilian clothes on the battlefield.

Select Bibliography

MANUSCRIPT SOURCES

Royal Archives, Windsor Castle. 1813–15.

Royal Archives, the Royal House, The Hague. 1814–15.

Wellington MSS. in the possession of the Duke of Wellington, K.G.

Raglan MSS. in the possession of Lord Raglan. For the correspondence of Wellington and his brother William Wellesley-Pole (1808–15) and Lord Fitzroy Somerset's memoranda.

Confidential Memoranda of Admiral Sir George Seymour, in the possession of Mrs Freda Loch. For 1812.

Letters of Captain Arthur Kennedy, in the possession of Sir Anthony Weldon. 1813–15.

Arthur Shakespear's journal, in the possession of the Countess of Albemarle. 1808–15.

Extracts from the *Notes Journalières* of General Maximilien Foy, in the possession of the Comte Sébastien Foy.

Longford MSS. in the possession of Mr Thomas Pakenham.

Archives of the House of Rothschild, London.

Archives of the Household Cavalry Museum, Windsor.

British Museum Additional Manuscripts. For the Wellesley Papers.

National Library of Ireland. ⎫ For various letters and memoranda
Irish State Papers Office. ⎬ mainly covering Wellington's Chief
⎭ Secretaryship.

Public Record Office of Northern Ireland. For the Drenan MS, 1803.

Pratt Papers, Kent County Archives. For 1795–6.

PUBLISHED SOURCES

Albemarle, George Thomas, Earl of: *Fifty Years of my Life* (London, 1877).

Aldington, Richard: *Wellington* (London, 1946).

Allan, General: Extracts from diary published by Lt.-Col. J. G. O. Whitehead, *Army Quarterly*, October 1965.

Anglesey, Marquess of: *One-Leg, The Life and Letters of Henry William Paget, 1st Marquess of Anglesey* (London, 1961).

Arbuthnot: *The Journal of Mrs Arbuthnot*. Edited by Francis Bamford and the Duke of Wellington (2 vols., London, 1950).

Archer, Mildred: *Tippoo's Tiger* (Victoria and Albert Museum, 1959).

Barnard: *The Barnard Letters*. Edited by Anthony Powell (London, 1928).

Barnes, Thomas: *Parliamentary Portraits* (London, 1815).

Barrington, Daines: *Miscellanies* (London, 1781).

Barrington, Sir Jonah: *Personal Sketches of His Own Times* (2 vols., London, 1869, first published, 1827).

Bartlett, C. J.: *Castlereagh* (London, 1967).

Beatson, Lt.-Col. Alexander: *Views of the Origin and Conduct of the War with Tippoo Sultaun* (London, 1800).

Bennell, A. S.: 'Wellesley's Settlement of Mysore, 1799' (*Journal of the Royal Asiatic Society*, October 1952).

Bennell, A. S.: 'The Anglo-Maratha Confrontation, Factors in the Marquis Wellesley's Failure against Holkar, 1804' (*Bulletin of the School of Oriental and Asian Studies*, vol. xxviii, part 3, 1965).

Berry: *Journal and Correspondence of Miss Berry, 1783–1852*. Edited by Lady Theresa Lewis (London, 1865).

Blakeney, Robert: *A Boy in the Peninsular War* (London, 1899).

Blanch, Lesley: *The Game of Hearts, Harriette Wilson and her Memoirs* (London, 1957).

Bolitho, Hector: *The Galloping Third* (London, 1963).

Bowring: *Autobiography of Sir John Bowring* (London, 1877).

Bragge: *Peninsular Portrait. Letters of Captain William Bragge*. Edited by A. C. Cassels (London, 1963).

Brett-James, Antony: *Wellington at War, 1794–1815. A Selection of his Wartime Letters edited and introduced* (London, 1961).

Brett-James, Antony: *The Hundred Days. Napoleon's Last Campaign from Eye-witness Accounts* (London, 1964).

Brialmont and Gleig: *The Life of the Duke of Wellington* (2 vols., London, amended edition, 1862).

Briggs, Asa: *The Age of Improvement* (London, 1965).

Broughton, Lord (John Cam Hobhouse): *Recollections of a Long Life* (2 vols., London, 1911).

Bryant, Sir Arthur: *The Napoleonic Wars* (3 vols., London, 1942–50).

Buckingham and Chandos, Duke of: *Memoirs of the Court and Cabinets of George III* (4 vols., London, 1853).

Burghersh: *The Correspondence of Lady Burghersh with the Duke of Wellington*. Edited by Lady Rose Weigall (London, 1903).

Byron's Correspondence. Edited by John Murray (2 vols., London, 1912; first published, 1903).

Calvert: *An Irish Beauty of the Regency.* Compiled from the unpublished journals of the Hon. Mrs Calvert, 1789–1822, by Mrs Warrenne Blake (London, 1911).

Camden Miscellany: Some Letters of the Duke of Wellington to his Brother William Wellesley-Pole. Edited by Sir Charles Webster (vol. xviii, Royal Historical Society, 1948).

Capel: *The Capel Letters, 1814–1817.* Edited by the Marquess of Anglesey (London, 1955).

Castlereagh: *Despatches* (12 Vols., London, 1848–1853).

Chad: *The Conversations of the First Duke of Wellington with George William Chad.* Edited by the 7th Duke of Wellington (Cambridge, 1956).

Chandler, David G.: *The Campaigns of Napoleon* (New York, 1966, London, 1967).

Chateaubriand: *The Memoirs of Chateaubriand.* Edited by Robert Baldick (London, 1961).

Chesney, R. E.: *Waterloo Lectures. The Campaign of 1815* (London, 1869).

Christophe, Robert: *Napoleon on Elba* (Paris, 1959; London, 1964).

Clarkson, Thomas: *History of the Abolition of the African Slave Trade by the British Parliament* (London, 1808).

Cloncurry, Lord: *Personal Recollections of the Life and Times of Valentine (Lawless) Lord Cloncurry* (Dublin, 1849).

Cobbett, William: *The Political Register.*

Cobbett, William: *History of the Regency and Reign of King George IV* (London, 1830).

Colborne: *Life of Sir John Colborne, Field-Marshal Lord Seaton* by G. C. Moore Smith (London, 1903).

Cole: *Memoirs of Sir Galbraith Lowry Cole.* Edited by M. Lowry Cole and S. Gwynn (London, 1934).

Coleridge: *Unpublished Letters of Samuel Taylor Coleridge.* Edited by E. L. Griggs (2 vols., London, 1932).

Combermere: *Memoirs and Correspondence of Field-Marshal Viscount Combermere.* Edited by Lady Combermere and W. Knollys (2 vols., London, 1866).

Cooper, Duff: *Talleyrand* (London, 1932).

Cooper, Leonard: *The Age of Wellington* (London, 1964).

Costello, Edward: *Adventures of a Soldier* (London, 1952).

Cotton, Edward: *A Voice from Waterloo* (Brussels, 5th edition 1854).

Creasy, Sir Edward: *Fifteen Decisive Battles of the World* (London, 1867).

Creasy, Sir Edward: *Eminent Etonians* (London, 1876).

Creevey, Thomas: *The Creevey Papers*. Edited by Sir H. Maxwell (London, 1904).

Creevey, Thomas: *The Creevey Papers*. Edited by John Gore (London, 1934).

Croker, John Wilson: *The Croker Papers, 1808–1857* (3 vols., London, 1884).

Croker, John Wilson: *The Croker Papers*. Edited by Bernard Pool (London, 1967).

Dalton, Charles: *The Waterloo Roll Call* (London, 1900).

D'Arblay, (Fanny Burney): *The Diaries of Madame D'Arblay*. Edited by her niece (7 vols., London, 1854).

De Bas, Colonel F., and Le Comte J. de T'Serclaes de Wommerson: *La Campagne de 1815 aux Pays-Bas d'après les rapports officiels néerlandais* (3 vols., Brussels, 1908).

De Lancey: *A Week at Waterloo in 1815. Lady de Lancey's Narrative*. Edited by Major B. R. Ward (London, 1906).

Delany: *The Autobiography and Correspondence of Mary Granville, Mrs Delany* (2 vols., London, 1861).

Demeter, Karl: *The German Officer Corps in Society and State, 1650–1945* (London, 1965).

De Ros: *A Sketch of the Life of Georgiana Lady de Ros* (née Lennox) by the Hon. Mrs J. R. Swinton (London, 1893).

Dixon, Pierson: *Pauline, Napoleon's Favourite Sister* (London, 1964).

Eaton, Charlotte A. (née Waldie): *The Days of Battle, or Quatre Bras and Waterloo* (London, 1853, first published, 1816).

Edgeworth: *The Life and Letters of Maria Edgeworth*. Edited by Augustus Hare (2 vols., London, 1894).

Edgeworth, Maria: *Castle Rackrent* (London, 1800).

Edgeworth, Maria: *The Absentee* (London, 1812).

Edgeworth: *The Memoirs of Richard Lovell Edgeworth* (2 vols., London, 1820).

Egremont, Lord: *Wyndham and Children First* (London, 1968).

Elers: *Memoirs of George Elers, 1777–1842*. Edited by Monson and Leveson Gower (London, 1903).

Ellesmere: *Personal Reminiscences of the Duke of Wellington by Francis, First Earl of Ellesmere.* Edited by Alice, Countess of Strafford (London, 1903).

Ellison, The Rev. C. C.: *Riocht Na Midhe.* Records of Meath Archaeological and Historical Society (vol. iii, no. 4, Dublin, 1966; vol. iv, no. 1, 1967).

Fitzpatrick, W. J.: *Ireland before the Union, with revelations from the unpublished diary of Lord Clonmell* (Dublin, 1887).

Following the Drum: Edited by Sir John Fortescue (London, 1931).

Fortescue, Sir John: *History of the British Army* (vols. iv–x, London, 1906–20).

Fortescue, Sir John: *Wellington* (London, 1925).

Foy: *Vie Militaire du Géneral Foy*, by Maurice Girod de l'Ain (Paris, 1900).

Fraser, Sir William: *Words on Wellington* (London, 1899).

Frazer: *Letters of Colonel Sir Augustus Frazer* (London, 1859).

Fulford, Roger: *The Life of Samuel Whitbread* (London, 1967).

Gibney, Dr: *Eighty Years Ago, or the Recollections of an Old Army Doctor.* Edited by Major R. D. Gibney (London, 1896).

Gleig, G. R.: *Life of Arthur Duke of Wellington* (London, 1889).

Gleig, G. R.: *The Subaltern* (London, 1845), reprinted with an introduction by Ian Robertson (London, 1969).

Glover, Michael: *Wellington's Peninsular Victories* (London, 1963).

Glover, Michael: *Wellington as Military Commander* (London, 1968).

Glover, Richard: *Peninsular Preparation* (Cambridge U.P., 1963).

Granville: *G. Leveson Gower, 1st Lord Granville, Correspondence* (2 vols, London, 1916).

Grassini: *La Chanteuse de l'Empereur par René Jeanne* (Paris, 1949).

Grattan, William: *Adventures with the Connaught Rangers* (2 series of 2 vols. each, 1847; edited by C. Oman and republished, 1902).

Gray, Denis: *Spencer Perceval* (London, 1963).

Greville: *The Greville Memoirs, 1817–60.* Edited by H. Reeve (8 vols., London, 1875–87), by L. Strachey and R. Fulford (8 vols., 1938).

Griffiths, Major Arthur: *The Wellington Memorial, Wellington and His Contemporaries* (London, 1897).

Gronow: *The Reminiscences and Recollections of Captain Gronow.* Edited by John Raymond (London, 1964).

Guedalla, Philip: *The Duke* (London, 1931).

Hamilton, John: *Sixty Years Experience as an Irish Landlord* (London, 1894).

Hamwood Papers of the Ladies of Llangollen. Edited by Mrs G. H. Bell (London, 1930).

Harris: *Recollections of Rifleman Harris* (London, 1829).

Haswell, C. J. D.: *The First Respectable Spy: The Life and Times of Colquhoun Grant, Wellington's Head of Intelligence* (London, 1969).

Hay, Captain William: *Reminiscences, 1808–1815* (London, 1901).

Haydon, B. R.: *Correspondence and Table-Talk* (2 vols., London, 1876).

Haydon, B. R.: *Lectures on Painting and Design* (2 vols., 1846).

Hemlow, Joyce: *The History of Fanny Burney* (Oxford U.P., 1958).

Henderson, E. F.: *Blücher and the Uprising against Napoleon* (London, 1911).

Herold, J. C.: *Mistress to an Age, a life of Madame de Staël* (London, 1959).

Hickey: *Memoirs of William Hickey.* Edited by Alfred Spencer (4 vols., London, 1925).

Hill, Constance: *Juniper Hall* (London, 1905).

Holland: *Lady Holland's Journal.* Edited by the Earl of Ilchester (2 vols., 1908).

Holland, Lord: *Further Memoirs of the Whig Party, 1807–1821.* Edited by Lord Stavordale (London, 1905).

Hook, Theodore: *Life of Sir David Baird* (2 vols., 1833).

Houssaye, Henry: *1815: La Première Restauration—Le Retour de l'île d'Elbe—Les Cent Jours* (Paris, 1893).

Houssaye, Henry: *1815: Waterloo.* Translated by A. E. Mann, edited by A. Euan-Smith (London, 1900).

Houssaye, Henry: *1815: La Seconde Abdication—La Terreur Blanche* (Paris, 1905).

Howarth, David: *A Near Run Thing* (London, 1968).

Hudleston, F. J.: *Warriors in Undress* (London, 1925).

Hussars: *Memoirs of the 10th Hussars* (1891).

Jackson, Lt.-Col. Basil: *Notes and Reminiscences of a Staff Officer.* Edited by R. C. Seaton (London, 1903).

James: *The Journal of Surgeon James.* Edited by Jane Vansittart (London, 1964).

Jeejeebhoy, J. R.: *The Duke of Wellington in Bombay, 1801 and 1804* (Bombay, 1927).

Jenkins, Roy: *Asquith* (London, 1964).

Jones, Lt.-Col. Sir John T.: *Account of the War in Spain, Portugal and the South of France, 1808–1814* (3 vols., London, 2nd edition, 1821).

Jones, Lt.-Col. Sir John T.: *Journals of the Sieges in Spain, 1811–1814, with Notes and Memoranda relevant to the Lines, 1810* (London, 3rd edition, 1846).

Kelly, Christopher: *The Memorable Battle of Waterloo* (London, 1818).

Kincaid, Captain John: *Adventures in the Rifle Brigade* (London, 1830).

Kinsey, Rev. W. M.: *Portugal Illustrated in a Series of Letters* (Lisbon, 1829).

Kurtz, Harold: *The Trial of Marshal Ney* (London, 1957).

Lachouque, Henry: *Anatomy of Glory, Napoleon and his Guard.* Translated by A. S. K. Brown. (London, 1961).

Larpent: *The Private Journal of F. Seymour Larpent, Judge-Advocate General.* Edited by Sir George Larpent (2 vols., 2nd edition, 1853).

Lawrence: *The Autobiography of Sergeant William Lawrence.* Edited by G. N. Bankes (London, 1886).

Leeke, William: *The History of Lord Seaton's Regiment and Autobiography of the Rev. William Leeke* (2 vols., London, 1866, Supplement, 1871, 1st edition, Le Havre, 1850).

Lennox: *Life and Letters of Lady Sarah Lennox* (Napier). Edited by Ilchester and Stavordale (2 vols., London, 1901).

Lennox, Lord William: *Three Years with the Duke, or Wellington in Private Life,* by an ex-aide-de-camp (London, 1853).

L'Eveque, Henry: *Costumes of Portugal* (Paris, 1814).

Liddell Hart, B. H.: *Famous British Generals,* essay in (London, 1951).

Liddell Hart, B. H.: *Strategy, the Indirect Approach* (London, 1954).

Livermore, H. V.: *A New History of Portugal* (Cambridge U.P., 1966).

Londonderry and Gleig: *The Story of the Peninsular War* (London, 1827).

Long: *A Peninsular Cavalry General: The Correspondence of Lt.-Gen. Robert Ballard Long.* Edited by T. H. McGuffie (London, 1951).

Lynch, P. and Vaizey, J.: *Guinness's Brewery in the Irish Economy, 1759–1876* (Cambridge U.P., 1960).

Macaulay, Rose: *They Went to Portugal* (London, 1946).

McGrigor: *The Autobiography of Sir James McGrigor*, late Director-General of the Army Medical Department (London, 1861).

Malcolm: *The Life and Correspondence of Maj.-Gen. Sir John Malcolm.* Edited by J. W. Kaye (2 vols, London, 1856).

Malmesbury: *Letters of the First Earl of Malmesbury, 1745–1820* (2 vols., London, 1870).

Marchand, Leslie A.: *Byron: A Critical Introduction with an annotated Bibliography* (3 vols., London, 1957).

Markham, Felix: *Napoleon* (London, 1962).

Marshall-Cornwall, Sir James: *Marshal Massena* (Oxford U.P., 1965).

Maxwell, Constantia: *County and Town in Ireland under the Georges* (London, 1940).

Maxwell, Constantia: *Dublin under the Georges, 1718–1830* (London, 1956).

Maxwell, Sir Herbert: *The Life of Wellington* (2 vols., London, 1899).

Maxwell, W. H.: *The Life of Wellington* (London, revised edition, 1893).

Mercer, General Cavalié: *Journal of the Waterloo Campaign* (2 vols., London, 1870).

Montgomery, Field-Marshal Viscount: *A History of Warfare* (London, 1968).

Moody, T. W. and Martin, F. X. (editors): *The Course of Irish History* (Cork, 1967).

Moore, Thomas: *A Selection from Tom Moore's Diary.* Edited by J. B. Priestley (London, 1925).

Morgan, Lady (Sidney Owenson): *The Wild Irish Girl* (London, 1818); *The O'Briens and The O'Flaherty's* (London, 1828); *Florence Macarthy* (London, 1839).

Morton, Frederic: *The Rothschilds* (London, 1962).

Mudford, William: *The Campaign in the Netherlands in 1815* (London, 1817).

Müffling, Baron von: *A Sketch of the Battle of Waterloo* (6th edition, London, 1870).

Müffling, Baron von: *Passages from my Life.* Translated and edited by Philip Yorke (London, 2nd edition, 1853).

Napier: *The Life and Opinions of Gen. Sir Charles Napier*, by Lt.-Gen. William Napier (4 vols., London, 1857).

Napier: *Passages in the Early Life of Gen. Sir George Napier*. Edited by his son Gen. William Napier (London, 1884).

Napier, Sir William F. P.: *History of the War in the Peninsula and the South of France, 1807–1814* (6 vols., London, Cavendish edition, 1886).

Napier: *Life and Letters of Sir William Napier*. Edited by H. A. Bruce (2 vols., London, 1864).

Napoleon at Waterloo: Edited by Bruce Low (London, 1911).

Napoleon's Memoirs. Edited by S. de Chair (London, 1948).

Naylor, John: *Waterloo* (London, 1960).

Neale, Dr Adam: *Letters from Portugal and Spain* (London, 1809).

Neumann: *Diary of Philip von Neumann, 1819–1850*. Edited by E. B. Chancellor (2 vols. London, 1928).

Old Soldier: *Life Military and Civil of the Duke of Wellington digested from the materials of W. H. Maxwell and re-written by an Old Soldier* (London, 1852).

Oman, Carola: *The Gascoyne Heiress, The Life and Diaries of Frances Mary Gascoyne-Cecil, 1802–39* (London, 1968).

Oman, Sir Charles: *A History of the Peninsular War* (7 vols., Oxford U.P., 1902–30).

Oman, Sir Charles: *Studies in the Napoleonic Wars* (London, 1929).

Pakenham Letters: Edited by the 5th Earl of Longford (London, privately printed, 1914).

Pakenham, Thomas: *The Year of Liberty: The Great Irish Rebellion of 1798* (London, 1969).

Peninsular Sketches by Actors on the Scene. Edited by W. H. Maxwell (2 vols., London, 1845).

Percival, H. V.: *Wellington* (Victoria and Albert Museum, 1969).

Petrie, Sir Charles: *Wellington, a Reassessment* (London, 1956).

Picton: *Memoirs of Sir Thomas Picton*. By H. B. Robinson (2 vols., 1836).

Pirenne, Jaques-Henri: *La Sainte Alliance* (Brussels, 1961). *Great Britain and the Treaty of Ghent, Herdenking van de 150e Verjaardag van de Vrede van Ghent*, with Sir Charles Petrie and others (Brussels, 1965).

Redding, Cyrus: *Personal Reminiscences of Eminent Men* (3 vols., London, 1867).

Richardson, Ethel M.: *Long Forgotten Days—leading to Waterloo*. From the diary of William Verner (London 1928).

Roberts, P. E.: *India Under Wellesley* (London, 1929).

Rogers: *Recollections of Samuel Rogers.* Edited by W. Sharpe (London, 1859).

Rogers: *Recollections of the Table-Talk of Samuel Rogers.* Edited by A. Dyce (London, 1856 and 1887).

Rolo, P. J. V.: *George Canning* (London, 1965).

Ropes, John Codman: *The Campaign of Waterloo* (New York, 1892).

Rose: *Diaries and Correspondence of the Rt. Hon. George Rose.* Edited by L. V. Harcourt (2 vols., London, 1860).

Rose, John Holland: *A Short Life of William Pitt* (London, 1925).

Rose, John Holland: *William Pitt and the Great War* (London, 1911).

Russell, G. W. B.: *Collections and Recollections* (London, 3rd edition, 1898).

Salisbury: *A Great Man's Friendship. Letters of the Duke of Wellington to Mary, Marchioness of Salisbury, 1850–1852.* Edited by Lady Burghclere (London, 1927).

Schaumann, A. L. F.: *On the Road with Wellington. The Diary of a War Commissary in the Peninsular Campaigns.* Edited and translated by A. Ludovici (London, 1924).

Shaw-Kennedy, Sir James: *Notes on the Battle of Waterloo with a Memoir* (London, 1865).

Shelley: *The Diary of Frances Lady Shelley, 1787–1817.* Edited by her grandson Richard Edgcumbe (2 vols., London, 1912).

Sherer, Moyle: *Recollections of the Peninsula* (London, 4th edition, 1825).

Smith: *Autobiography of Lt.-Gen. Sir Harry Smith.* Edited by G. C. Moore Smith (2 vols., London, 1901).

Smyth, Sir John: *In This Sign Conquer: The Story of the Army Chaplains* (London, 1968).

Spencer-Stanhope: *The Letter-Bag of Lady Elizabeth Spencer-Stanhope* (2 vols., London, 1912).

Stacton, David: *The Bonapartes* (New York, 1966; London, 1967).

Stanhope, Philip Henry, 5th Earl: *Life of Pitt* (vol. 4, London, 1879).

Stanhope, Philip Henry, 5th Earl: *Notes of Conversations with the Duke of Wellington, 1831–1851* (London, 1888).

Tomkinson, Lt.-Col. William: *The Diary of a Cavalry Officer in the Peninsular and Waterloo Campaigns, 1809–1815.* Edited by his son James Tomkinson (London, 1894).

Trench: *The Remains of the late Mrs Richard Trench* (Mrs St George) *being selections from her Journals etc.* (London, 1862).

Trevelyan, Sir G. M.: *British History in the Nineteenth Century and After* (London, 2nd edition, 1937).

Tussaud, John Theodore: *The Romance of Madame Tussaud's* (London, 1925).

Tussaud: *Catalogue of Pictures and Historical Relics* by W. Wheeler (London, 1901).

Tollemache, L. A.: *Old and Odd Memories* (London, 1908).

Twiss, Richard, F.R.S.: *A Tour in Ireland* (London, 1775).

Vivian, Hon. Claud: *Richard Hussey Vivian, First Baron Vivian, A Memoir* (London, 1897).

Waterloo Letters. A Selection from original and hitherto unpublished Letters bearing on the 16th, 17th, and 18th June, by Officers who served in the Campaign. Edited by Maj-Gen. H. T. Siborne (London, 1891).

Ward, S. G. P.: *Wellington's Headquarters, 1809–14* (Oxford U.P., 1957).

Ward, S. G. P.: *Wellington* (London, 1963).

Waterloo. Account by a Staff Officer, Paris, 10 July 1815 (London, 1815).

Waterloo, The Battle of, by 'A Near Observer' (London, 1817).

Waterloo: by 'An Officer' (Pack's brigade), *United Service Magazine,* part II, 1841.

Webster, Sir Charles: *The Congress of Vienna, 1814–15* (London, 1934).

Weller, Jac: *Wellington in the Peninsula, 1808–14* (London, 1962).

Weller, Jac: *Wellington at Waterloo* (London, 1967).

Wellesley: *Diary and Correspondence of Henry Wellesley, 1st Lord Cowley, 1790–1846.* Edited by the Hon. F. A. Wellesley (London, 1930).

Wellesley: *The Indian Despatches of the Marquess Wellesley* (5 vols., London, 1836).

Wellesley, Lord Gerald, and Steegman, J.: *Iconography of the 1st Duke of Wellington* (London, 1935).

Wellesley, Muriel: *The Man Wellington* (London, 1937).

Wellesley, Muriel: *Wellington in Civilian Life* (London, 1939).

Wellesley Papers by the Editor of the *Windham Papers,* (2 vols., London, 1914).

Wellington: *The Dispatches of Field Marshal the Duke of Wellington during his various Campaigns.* Compiled by Lt.-Col. Gurwood (12 vols. London, 1834–8).

Wellington: *Supplementary Despatches, Correspondence, and Memoranda of Field Marshal Arthur Duke of Wellington, K.G.* Edited by his son the Duke of Wellington (Vols. I–XI, London, 1858–64).

Wellington: *A Selection from the Private Correspondence of the First Duke of Wellington.* Edited by the Duke of Wellington (The Roxburghe Club, London, 1952).

Wellington Studies: Essays by five Old Wellingtonians, edited by Michael Howard (1959).

Wellingtoniana: Anecdotes, Maxims and Characteristics of the Duke of Wellington by John Timbs (London, 1852).

Wheatley: *The Diary of Edmund Wheatley.* Edited by Christopher Hibbert (London, 1964).

Wheeler: *The Letters of Private Wheeler, 1809–1828.* Edited and with a Foreword by Captain B. H. Liddell Hart (London, 1951).

Whitehead, Lt.-Col. J. G. O.: 'Wellington at Waterloo', Army Quarterly, October 1965.

Wilkins, W. H.: *Mrs. Fitzherbert and George IV* (2 vols. London, 1905).

Wilson, Harriette: *Harriette Wilson's Memoirs of Herself and Others* (London, 1929).

With Napoleon at Waterloo and other unpublished documents of the Waterloo and Peninsular Campaigns. Edited by Mackenzie Macbride (London, 1911).

Young, Arthur: *A Tour in Ireland* (Dublin, 1780).

Young, Desmond: *Fountain of the Elephants,* Life of de Boigne (London, 1959).

Ziegler, Philip: *The Duchess of Dino* (London, 1962).

Ziegler, Philip: *A Life of Henry Addington, 1st Viscount Sidmouth* (London, 1965).

INDEX

INDEX

Index

In this index W = Duke of Wellington.